Principles of Irish Property L
Second Edition

Principles of Irish Property Law
Second Edition

By
Dr Fiona de Londras

BCL, LL.M, PhD (NUI)

Published by
Clarus Press Ltd,
Griffith Campus,
South Circular Road,
Dublin 8.

Typeset by
Datapage International Limited,
18 Docklands Innovation Park,
East Wall Road,
Dublin 3.

Printed by
MPG Books Ltd, Cornwall

ISBN
978-1-905536-40-5

A CIP catalogue record for this book is available from the British Library.

To Bridget Carroll, my grandmother

PREFACE TO THE SECOND EDITION

Since the first edition of this book was printed in 2007 both the law of property and the context in which it operates have changed immensely. On a doctrinal level property law has been enormously reformed by the introduction of the Land and Conveyancing Law Reform Act 2009 as well as by more discrete, although no less important, developments in particular areas. The context in which the law of property operates has changed from a booming economy as existed in 2007 to a much more difficult economic climate in which the average home and commercial property owner is finding two areas particularly difficult: mortgage repayment and keeping rental costs under control. In this new edition of *Principles of Property Law* I have tried to pay attention to both the doctrinal and contextual changes that have arisen since the first edition. I hope I have done so successfully.

Since the main text of the book was finalised, the High Court has handed down an important decision that identifies a possible difficulty with the enforcement of mortgages under the pre-2009 law. In *Start Mortgages Ltd v Gunn & Ors* [2011] IEHC 275 Dunne J held that s 62(7) of the Registration of Title Act 1964 could no longer be used to enforce mortgages if it was first being used after the commencement of the Land and Conveyancing Law Reform Act 2009, which repeals that provision of the 1964 Act. In other words, if there is a mortgage that is not enforceable under the 2009 Act, but in relation to which the enforcement procedure did not begin until after 1 December 2009, then s 62(7) was of no avail. The reasoning in this case suggests that the same conclusion would be reached in cases relating to enforcement under provisions of the Conveyancing Act 1881, which have been repealed by the 2009 Act and where the enforcement did not begin until after the 2009 Act was commenced. This does not mean that the mortgages in question cannot be enforced, but simply that it must be done by means of a more complex, lengthy and costly mechanism and the case neatly identifies what seems to be an unintended lacuna consequent to the new enforcement mechanisms of the 2009 Act. The enforcement of mortgages is dealt with in Chapter 13 of this book, and that should be read bearing this decision in mind. In all likelihood this lacuna will be filled by a piece of amending legislation, and indeed it is conceivable (although in my view unlikely) that the Supreme Court might reverse the decision.

In revising this book I have taken on board both the generous praise and justified criticisms that people have been kind enough to share with me. I hope I have responded to them appropriately. I have not, however, departed from the primary mission of the book, which is to present property law in a principled, interesting and comprehensible way for a student who is either progressing through undergraduate property law or preparing for professional or graduate examinations in property law. Thus it is not, and does not purport to be, a complete "catalogue" of property law: that is ably done by other titles in the field and my interest here is in the topics and debates with which students are most commonly engaged during their studies. While a number of practitioners have been kind enough to tell me that they found the first edition useful—for which, of course, I am very grateful—this is and ever will be a book written for students and with their needs in mind. I have therefore always tried to involve students in the process of preparing the book. For the first edition Miriam McColgan-Hughes read large chunks of the book and responded to it, and since then Sarah Jenkinson has carried out a thorough "student review" of the first edition, which has aided enormously in the preparation of the second. I remain grateful to both of them. My wonderful students—both undergraduate and graduate—in UCD School of Law have also been extremely forthcoming in their comments on the book, and those comments, as well as the exciting and insightful questions with which they keep me on my toes in our classes, have been borne in mind in the preparation of this edition.

In addtion to continuing gratitude to those who helped and supported me with the first edition of this book, I want to thank the tutors on the property law course in UCD School of Law (Ciarán Lawlor BL, Mary O'Heocha BL, David Jones and previously Garry Wynne) for their excellent insights and conversations on teaching and communicating property law, and Andrew Lyall, Andrew Hayward, John Mee and David Gwynn Morgan for various conversations on particular areas of property and land law. Ronan Lupton BL and Barry Quirke in the High Court office have both also helped me in tracking down some decisions, for which I am very grateful. David McCartney at Clarus Press encouraged me greatly with the first edition and has done the same with this one. As well as that he has committed Clarus Press fully to the production of high quality, student-oriented and affordable books for undergraduates and I am delighted to be part of that enterprise with him.

Finally, I rededicate this to my grandmother and thank, once more, my lovely and supportive family and the incomparable—and indispensible—Aurélie.

Fiona de Londras
September 2011

PREFACE TO THE FIRST EDITION

Anyone who teaches property law cannot help but be aware that most students detest the subject. There are various reasons for this; complexity, out-datedness, linguistic peculiarities and density being primary among them. This can not always have been the case, but Ireland's tardiness in reforming property law has dissociated students from the concepts of property law and resulted in its (undeserved) reputation for tediousness. Since the Law Reform Commission's Land Law Working Group began to consult and publish recommendations, property law has experienced something of a Renaissance. The Commission has even managed to make some students enthusiastic about property again – an achievement beyond the capabilities of most of us. The immense proportions of the draft legislation developed by the Commission and now contained in the Land and Conveyancing Law Reform Bill 2006 are almost overwhelming. This Bill is taken into account and analysed where appropriate throughout the book. Although not enacted at the time of writing, the Bill had been passed by the Seanad and further substantive changes are not expected, although readers are advised to keep track of the progress of the Bill through the Oireachtas in the future. As well as making practitioners' lives easier (at least after the transitional period), the 2006 Bill when enacted ought to reduce the animus that students feel towards the subject.

This book attempts (where appropriate) to take into account relevant jurisprudence and principles from the European Court of Human Rights following the Convention's incorporation in the European Convention on Human Rights Act 2003. Now that the Convention is a central part of Irish law it is essential that text books in the foundational subjects such as property law attempt to consider its potential impact on our disciplines and this is one of my objectives in this book. Human rights law can no longer be conceived of as a stand-alone subject; rather it is interwoven in all areas of law and must be learned in this integrated manner. The book does not purport to be a complete catalogue of Irish property law; rather the areas that I felt are most relevant to the study and understanding of property law have been selected for consideration and it is to be hoped that these selections will prove adequate for property law courses at all but the most specialised levels.

When I decided to write this book I had a particular aim. I wanted to produce something that equipped students with enough knowledge and understanding to 'get' property law as well as introducing them to the principles and controversies surrounding the subject. Thus, while I hope that practitioners will find the book of use it is primarily designed with the student in mind. The creation of an interesting and accessible text on property proved to be a considerable challenge and if I have achieved it at all it is largely down to Miriam McColgan who read most of the book and cast a welcome and critical 'student eye' over it.

A number of friends and advisers have helped along the way with this book. David McCartney and his team at Clarus Press are to be commended for their work in arranging the manuscript for publication and David in particular deserves thanks for the support and faith he afforded the project. I'm grateful to friends and colleagues

Aoife O'Donoghue, Claire McHugh, Ciara Fitzgerald, Cian Murphy and Liz Campbell who read and commented on a number of chapters. Máiréad Enright has always been a source of wit and wisdom in my work on property law and I want to thank her in particular for keeping my spirits up and advising me on contract law as it relates to property at a time when she herself was finalising a book manuscript. A special word of thanks is devoted to Kieran Walsh BL who, if it is not tempting fate to say so, can only be described as a future giant of Irish law. Kieran provided hours of discussion and analysis that informed this book and the finished product is all the better for his critical eye and sharp mind. I am indebted to him as much for his friendship as his assistance. I am also grateful to my family who supported me in their customary way through this project. Aurélie Gilbert was patient and supportive throughout the process, in spite of the sometimes challenging circumstances in which it took place and the ill-humour and insomniac writing schedules that occasionally accompanied it. Finally, I gladly dedicate this book with love to my grandmother, Bridget Carroll, whose influence, ambition, intelligence and affection have been fundamental in my life.

None of these people, of course, bear any responsibility for opinions, errors or omissions that may appear in the book; those I gladly claim for myself. I must note that nothing in this volume is intended to act as or as an alternative to legal advice and that neither I nor Clarus Press can accept any liability of any kind for any omissions, errors or misstatements that might be contained herein.

I have endeavoured to state the law as of 31 July 2007.

Fiona de Londras
Killiney, Co. Dublin
August 2007

CONTENTS

TABLE OF LEGISLATION

Post 1922 Legislation

Secondary Legislation

TABLE OF CASES

H

I

J

P

Q

R

S

Y

Z

CHAPTER 1
Foundational Concepts

As an initial matter, the study of any distinct area of law requires familiarisation with some basic foundational concepts, without which understanding the specific and complex elements of that area of law can be difficult. The purpose of this chapter is to familiarise the reader with some of the foundational concepts of property law that, if understood at this point, ought to ease the path through the remainder of this book and, indeed, through your property or land law course itself. In that respect we deal with questions of what property actually is, the meaning of ownership and possession, and the concept of "land" (the commodity whose ownership we are primarily concerned with in this book). **[1–01]**

I. Property

It is imperative at the outset to replace one's vernacular understanding of property (i.e. a piece of land or a thing) with a more precise legal concept. In legal terms, property is a bundle of rights relating to something, and the extent and nature of these rights dictate the extent and nature of one's property. Thus "owning" a house is, in essence, having certain kinds of rights and privileges in relation to that house: rights that can be exercised in relation to all other people within the boundaries of the general law over a particular period of time. Property, or bundles of rights, can be shared out among numerous people. As we will see in some detail in later chapters, it is possible for there to be both legal and equitable rights over the same piece of land, and for those rights to be held by different people. This may add an additional level of complexity to any transaction in relation to land as the purchaser's solicitor will have to familiarise herself with *all* of the rights relating to the land that her client may want to purchase. The solicitor will, therefore, have to find out whether the vendor (i.e. the seller) has title to the property that permits him to offer it for sale, whether there are any other parties with rights over the land whose rights might have to be discharged prior to the sale (e.g. a mortgage) or indeed whose rights might have to be respected by the purchaser even after the conveyance has been completed (e.g. a neighbour who has a right of way over the land to be sold). Thus, property is a complex notion and one of the primary roles of property law is to help us to identify, categorise and manage those various rights that **[1–02]** can exist over the same parcel of land so that anyone who intends to transact in relation to it knows exactly what kind of property can be acquired and what burdens might exist over it.

[1–03] Our concern in this book is with what we call "real property". This requires us at the outset to explore the term "real property" and come to a clear understanding of its meaning. Real property is the term used to describe the rights held in freehold[1] in relation to land, or things attached to land. This kind of property developed through the historical treatment of rights relating to land. It used to be the case that freeholders could take an action to the king's court in order to vindicate their property rights. If successful, these claimants would be awarded what was known as a "real remedy", or a remedy directed at the restoration of the claimant's rights in relation to the property. All property in relation to which these "real actions" could be taken, and which could result in "real remedies", became known as real property.

[1–04] On the other hand, all those who had rights in relation to things or to leases could take a personal action only and were therefore said to have personal property. In the case of personal actions, a court could award a personal remedy such as compensation, but would not generally award remedies directed at the restoration of one's property. Until the late 1400s rights in relation to leases were said to be contractual, purely personal and therefore subject only to personal actions. Over time the courts changed their view on this matter and began to allow leaseholders to take real actions and to be awarded real remedies. Leasehold rights were never re-classified as real property, however, and therefore became known as "chattels real", i.e. personal property in relation to which a real remedy is possible. For this reason, although this book deals primarily with real property, leasehold rights are included for consideration.[2]

[1–05] In summary, the distinction between real property (with which this book is concerned) and personal property (with which this book is not generally concerned) is as follows:

- Real property
  - Freehold rights in relation to land and things attached to land (defined by application of the maxim *superficies solo credit*, or, "that which is attached to the land becomes part of the land", which is considered below).
- Personal property
  - Rights in relation to things *and* leasehold rights (known as "chattels real") in relation to land and things attached to land (defined by application of *superficies solo credit*).

Property can be further divided into tangible and intangible rights. In general terms, tangible rights will be described as corporeal, or rights with physical substance (such as ownership rights over a house, for example), whereas intangible rights will be described as incorporeal, or rights without physical substance even though they can allow for a

[1] Freehold is considered in full in Chapter 4, but for now might be described as ownership rights that are neither leasehold nor merely permissive (like licences).

[2] See further Chapter 15.

physical exercise over the land of another (such as a right of way over someone else's land, for example).

II. Property as a Right

Not only is property to be defined as a bundle of rights, but the holding of private property is generally conceived of as a human right that is worthy of respect and protection in the law. It is important to note that this generally exists as a negative right (i.e. a right not to have one's property interfered with by the State) and not as a positive right (i.e. a right to hold property and, as a corollary, to have it provided by the State, or for the State to ensure that property retails at a reasonable price). Positive rights relating to property and other social and economic needs are generally resisted heavily at both domestic and international levels because they are seen as creating too onerous a burden on the State.[3] That said, States frequently impose statutory obligations on themselves and on local authorities to provide housing on the basis of need.[4] **[1–06]**

The right to private property is afforded double protection in the Irish Constitution. Article 43 provides: **[1–07]**

> 1. 1° The State acknowledges that man, in virtue of his rational being, has the natural right, antecedent to positive law, to the private ownership of external goods.
> 2° The State accordingly guarantees to pass no law attempting to abolish the right of private ownership or the general right to transfer, bequeath, and inherit property.
>
> 2. 1° The State recognises, however, that the exercise of the rights mentioned in the foregoing provisions of this Article ought, in civil society, to be regulated by the principles of social justice.
> 2° The State, accordingly, may as occasion requires delimit by law the exercise of the said rights with a view to reconciling their exercise with the exigencies of the common good.

In addition, Art 40.3 protects private property by means of a State guarantee:

> . . . by its laws [to] protect as best it may from unjust attack and, in the case of injustice done, [to] vindicate the. . . property rights of every citizen.

The duplication in the Constitution of the guarantees relating to private property has been the subject of much debate, and the Constitution Review Group has recommended that the guarantee be expressed in a singular provision[5]: however, it seems that, after much uncertainty, the courts have come to a conclusion on the appropriate relationship between these two provisions. This jurisprudence suggests that the reference to social justice and the common good in Art 43 is an important **[1–08]**

---

[3] It should be noted that this is a very outmoded and disconnected view of socio-economic rights, which sees them as unusually "expensive" as if civil and political rights (such as the right to vote) were somehow free or inexpensive.

[4] For an excellent treatment of housing law in Ireland, see Kenna, *Housing Law Rights and Policy* (2011, Dublin, Clarus Press).

[5] *Report of the Constitution Review Group* (1996, Dublin, The Stationery Office), p 361.

consideration in the courts' analyses of whether the substantive right to private property has been interfered with in a manner inconsistent with Art 40.3.[6] The constitutional guarantee of private property is well established as covering land and things affixed to land, but its remit is broader than real property.[7] Where measures are challenged on the basis of constitutional property rights, the Irish courts will assess whether they (a) interfere with private property rights, (b) are directed at the achievement of a legitimate aim, and (c) are a proportionate exercise of State powers in pursuance of that legitimate aim.[8]

[1–09] The European Convention on Human Rights (ECHR),[9] which was transposed into Irish law by means of the European Convention on Human Rights Act 2003,[10] protects the right to possessions in Art 1 of Protocol One (to which Ireland is a party). The right to possessions is contained in an Optional Protocol to the Convention—rather than in the main body of the Convention itself—because of the political disagreement within the continent of Europe about possessions and, particularly, about private property. This disagreement was mostly a matter of capitalism verses communism. The inclusion of the right within an Optional Protocol made the main text more inclusive and conciliatory, while at the same time allowing States that wished to do so to bind themselves to an obligation relating to possessions, including private property. Article 1, Protocol One provides:

> Every natural or legal person is entitled to the peaceful enjoyment of his possessions. No one shall be deprived of his possessions except in the public interest and subject to the conditions provided for by law and by the general principles of international law.
>
> The preceding provisions shall not, however, in any way impair the right of a State to enforce such laws as it deems necessary to control the use of property in accordance with the general interest or to secure the payment of taxes or other contributions or penalties.

[1–10] Article 1, Protocol One protects possessions, including private property, from unjustified or arbitrary State interference, but—as the second paragraph shows—it does not absolutely prohibit State interference with property. Rather, it requires that any such interference would be lawful (by reference to both domestic and international law) and would pursue a legitimate aim in a proportionate manner. As should be clear immediately, the standards relating to property applied at constitutional and ECHR level are not hugely disparate. Indeed, the adoption by the Irish courts of a

[6] See generally Hogan & Whyte, *Kelly's Irish Constitution* (4th ed., 2003, Dublin, LexisNexis Butterworths), Chapter 7.7.

[7] For more on this see, for example, *Attorney General v Southern Industrial Trust Ltd* (1960) 94 ILTR 161; *Buckley v Attorney General* [1950] IR 67; *Phonographic Performance (Ireland) Ltd v Cody* [1998] 4 IR 504.

[8] See, for example, *In re Art 26 and Part V of the Planning and Development Bill 1999* [2000] 2 IR 321.

[9] The right to property is also protected in Art 17 of the Universal Declaration of Human Rights.

[10] On the Act see de Londras & Kelly, *The European Convention on Human Rights Act: Operation, Impact and Analysis* (2010, Dublin, Round Hall).

proportionality approach to interferences with property law can arguably be linked back to ECHR jurisprudence.

It should be noted that "possessions", as defined in this Article, are a relatively broad concept and can be taken to include any sufficiently established economic interest, such as movable or immovable property, shares,[11] patents,[12] leases[13] and judgment mortgages.[14] The European Court of Human Rights originally conceived of this provision as laying down three distinct rules: [1–11]

> [T]he first rule, set out in the first sentence of the first paragraph, is of a general nature and enunciates the principle of the peaceful enjoyment of property; the second rule, contained in the second sentence of the first paragraph, covers deprivation of possessions and subjects it to certain conditions; the third rule, stated in the second paragraph, recognises that the Contracting States are entitled... to control the use of property in accordance with the general interest. However, the three rules are not 'distinct' in the sense of being unconnected: the second and third rules are concerned with particular instances of interference with the right to peaceful enjoyment of property and should therefore be construed in the light of the general principle enunciated in the first rule.[15]

In later jurisprudence, however, the Court has tended to conceive of the Article, in general, as laying out a right to the enjoyment of possessions in fair balance to the needs of society by means of the proportionality test considered above. Compliance with the provision requires that any interference with possessions ought to be lawful, i.e. it must be done on the basis of clear, precise and properly promulgated domestic law.[16] Secondly, Art 1, Protocol One requires that any interference with possessions be done in a manner consistent with the requirements of procedural justice.[17]

It should be noted that, to date, Art 1, Protocol One has not shown any great degree of transformative character within the ECHR scheme. This is particularly because the European Court of Human Rights has tended to afford a very wide margin of appreciation (i.e. discretion) to States in decision-making regarding the needs of social justice and the mechanisms for the achievement of legitimate objectives. In one of the areas where it was thought that the Convention might have a significant impact on Irish property law, namely in relation to adverse possession, the Court has now firmly established that Art 1 of Protocol One is not violated.[18] In this light, the Irish constitutional jurisprudence tends to be more proactive. While the Irish courts have generally tended to accept legislative and executive decisions as to the dictates of social [1–12]

---

[11] *Bramelid and Malmström v Sweden* (1986) 8 EHRR 45.

[12] *SmithKline and French Laboratories v the Netherlands* (1990) 66 DR 20.

[13] *Mellacher and Others v Austria* (1989) 12 EHRR 391—see further Chapter 15.

[14] *Stran Greek Refineries and Stratis Andreadis v Greece* (1994) 19 EHRR 931—see further Chapter 13.

[15] *AGOSI v United Kingdom* (1986) 9 EHRR 1 § 48.

[16] *Hentrich v France* (1994) 18 EHRR 440.

[17] *ibid.*

[18] *JA Pye (Oxford) Ltd v United Kingdom* (2007) 46 EHRR 1083 *reversing* (2006) 43 EHRR 43.

justice and the common good, they have been quite proactive in requiring different mechanisms of implementation.[19] In addition, the European Court of Human Rights has not been at all proactive in the formation of any positive duties on the part of states in relation to Art 1, Protocol One. Thus, while there is a negative obligation not to interfere disproportionately with people's possessions, there is no positive obligation to take appropriate action to regulate interpersonal economic activity to ensure that people can acquire possessions even with very limited resources. Not only is this characteristic common to the ECHR and the Constitution, it is also related to the lack of willingness to accept positive obligations relating to social and economic rights generally mentioned above.

III. Ownership and Possession

[1–13] The concepts of ownership and possession are absolutely central to the law of property and are used with some exactitude in the context of this subject. For this reason everyday conceptions of ownership and possession should be put aside and the reader ought to commit to the precise technical meanings of the terms in law.

[1–14] In simple (and somewhat simplified) terms, ownership is control: the owner of something is the person who acquires the right to control the thing that is owned. This control is manifested through two relationships—the first is the owner's relationship with the thing owned; the second is the owner's relationship with the rest of the world in relation to the thing that is owned. This can be well illustrated by means of an example. Imagine that Patrick "owns" a pen and therefore enjoys two relationships of control in relation to it. The first is his control of the pen itself: he can take the pen with him, leave it at home, write with it, chew it, stand on it, throw it away, etc. He can, in essence, do whatever he wants with the pen.[20] The second relationship of control is between Patrick and the rest of the world in relation to this pen: Patrick can decide to allow another person to use the pen, to sell it to someone, to give it away to someone for free, etc.[21] The control Patrick holds over this pen is limited to a certain extent, however, as is the control all owners hold over the thing(s) they own. The general law interacts with property law to restrict one's exercise of control in fairly logical ways and in order to ensure that this control is not exercised in a reckless manner. For example, the criminal law recognises Patrick's control over the pen, but nevertheless does not allow him to hide cocaine inside it and transport the cocaine over national borders; nor does the law allow Patrick to use this pen to vandalise the property of another.

[1–15] We can go beyond the simplified concept of "ownership as control" and break the idea of ownership down further. The classical iteration of what have become known as the "incidents" of ownership is that offered by Honoré.[22] According to Honoré, the "liberal concept of full individual ownership" can be broken down into the following

---

[19] See generally Hogan & White, *Kelly's Irish Constitution* (4th ed., 2003, Dublin, LexisNexis Butterworths), p.1970.

[20] This sentiment is subject to some common-sense limitations that are considered shortly.

[21] *ibid.*

[22] Honoré, "Ownership" in Guest (ed.), *Oxford Essays in Jurisprudence* (1961, Oxford, Oxford University Press) and reprinted in Honoré, *Making Law Bind: Essays Legal and Philosophical* (1987, Oxford, Clarendon Press).

eleven incidents, not all of which need necessarily be present at the same time but all of which, in conjunction, make up this classical liberal ownership idea. The eleven incidents are: (i) the right to possess; (ii) the right to use; (iii) the right to manage; (iv) the right to the income; (v) the right to the capital; (vi) the right to the security; (vii) the incident of transmissibility; (viii) the incident of absence of term; (ix) the duty to prevent harm; (x) liability to execution; and (xi) residuary character. For Honoré the right to possess is the basic and foundational right upon which the concept of ownership rests. This does not mean that ownership and possession cannot be separated; they can, but ownership implies the capacity to transfer possessory rights and capacities and, by corollary, anyone who does not have that capacity cannot be said to have ownership in the full, classical and liberal sense. The remaining incidents are powers, privileges, liabilities and protections that arise from ownership. Honoré's fragmentation of property into these different incidents has had an immense impact on the theory of property law and, indeed, for some who argue that all eleven must be present and, where they are, that this constitutes "full ownership", they offer a powerful argument against necessary evils such as taxation which, it is sometimes claimed, are at odds with ownership.[23] However, even if one prefers to think of ownership in the "unified" sense of control rather than the "fragmented" sense of incidents—as I do in this book—that control conception does not preclude (and, in fact, largely incorporates) all of those incidents classically outlined by Honoré.[24]

[1–16] As noted above, property law does not exist within a vacuum; all owners are restricted, to some extent, by planning law, criminal law, the law of torts and so on in the extent to which their control may be exercised. In addition, of course, we put some limits on *what* can be owned or can be the subject of property law recognising that there are some things (such as living human beings, for example) that ought not to be made the subject of an area of law concerned with recognising, regulating, delineating and vindicating proprietary rights. In addition to the limitations on ownership flowing from the general law, certain categories of owners are subjected to additional limitations for either protective or punitive reasons. Children are an excellent example of such specific limitations.[25] Children can own and deal with land in law; however any land owned by a child is said to exist in trust.[26] Children are not the only category of landowner subjected to limitations—certain convicts,[27] persons of unsound mind,[28] people who have acquired property through criminal activities[29] and limited companies[30] are also subjected to particular limitations on ownership.

---

[23] For an excellent overview of these arguments, and refutation thereof, see Attas, "Fragmenting Property" (2006) 25 *Law and Philosophy* 119.

[24] For an excellent and extremely thorough exposition of this see Harris, *Property and Justice* (1996, Oxford, Clarendon Press).

[25] In this context, a child can be taken as someone under the age of 18 *per* Age of Majority Act 1985, s 2(1).

[26] Land and Conveyancing Law Reform Act 2009, s 18(1)(c). This was previously governed by the Settled Land Acts 1882–1890. See further Chapter 6.

[27] See Forfeiture Act 1870.

[28] See Lunacy Regulation (Ireland) Act 1871.

[29] See Criminal Assets Bureau Act 1996.

[30] The company's internal documents, such as the memorandum of association, will dictate the extent of the company's capacity to transact freely in relation to property that it holds.

[1–17] Possession—which is at the heart of ownership, although separable from it—is the right to use and enjoy the thing being possessed. Ownership and possession very often go together so that, for example, the person who "owns" a house is the same as the person who "possesses" that house. It is important to realise, however, that this need not be the case; rather, ownership and possession can easily be separated. Take, for example, a typical situation where a person purchases a house for the purposes of renting it out. In that case the person who purchases the house "owns" it but, by entering into a landlord and tenant relationship over it, no longer has the right to possess it as that possessory right has gone to the tenant.[31] Possession can have important legal consequences in property law. In the case of adverse possession, for example, possessing land for the appropriate amount of time and with the appropriate intention can have the effect of extinguishing the land owner's title.[32] In other situations the *lack* of possession can be important. Where, for example, a third party acquires rights over land that is held by a tenant, those rights may not be enforceable against the landlord once the lease has come to an end simply because the landlord had no possessory rights over the land during the period of acquisition.[33]

IV. Land

[1–18] The law of real property deals with property rights relating to land. The concept of land is, therefore, important. While "land" appears to be a relatively straightforward concept, the legal extent of land is rather more complex than one might imagine at first. For that reason it is worthy of some consideration. There are two particular questions that must be considered in order to grasp fully the meaning of "land" for the purposes of property law. The first is the extent to which things that are attached to the land can be said to be part of the land. This is important because if an attachment is deemed "land" it is subject to the law of real property and, in the case of a leasehold arrangement, for example, the tenant may not be empowered to remove such "attachments" at the end of the lease. The second question to be considered is the extent to which one has rights over and above the surface of the land itself.

Attachments

[1–19] Whether or not things attached to land become part of the land can be a particularly important consideration when property is being sold or when a lease comes to an end. The purchaser of a house will want to know whether, for example, the beautiful mural in the living room or the centrepiece statue in the landscaped gardens are part of the property and therefore come with it when it is sold. This is also an important consideration for tenants upon termination of a lease because, with relatively few

[31] The tenant also has a kind of ownership of the house: a leasehold ownership. Leasehold is considered in full in Chapter 15. It is a fundamental feature of a lease that the tenant has the right to *exclusive possession* of the property, thereby reinforcing the separation of the landlord's freehold ownership from the possession.

[32] The law of adverse possession is considered in full in Chapter 14.

[33] This is the case where a third party adversely possesses against a tenant or where an easement is acquired by prescription over land that is held by a tenant, both of which are considered in Chapter 14.

exceptions, anything attached to the land by the tenant will become the property of the landlord at the end of the lease provided it is what one might call *sufficiently attached*.[34]

Whether or not something is sufficiently attached to the land for it to be considered part of the land (and therefore treated as real property) is assessed by reference to the maxim *superficies solo credit*, meaning "that which is attached to the land becomes part of the land". The difficulty is that the concept of "attachment" is somewhat ambiguous from a stand-alone perspective and needs to be substantiated by reference to a test of some kind. This test is now well established and can be said to consist of the application of two questions: **[1–20]**

(a) To what extent is the relevant thing attached to the land? *and*
(b) What was the intention of the person who attached this thing to the land?

The application of this two-pronged test will then dictate whether the thing attached has become part of the land, or whether it is still a mere chattel to which the law of real property does not apply. The relative weight to be given to each of these questions is more or less circumstantial, as demonstrated by a pair of cases—*Leigh v Taylor*[35] and *d'Eyncourt v Gregory*.[36]

Leigh v Taylor concerned a house in which a number of valuable tapestries were attached to the walls. The tapestries belonged to a tenant for life (i.e. someone with rights for as long as he was alive), and when he died a dispute arose as to the ownership of the tapestries. The remainderman (i.e. the person entitled to the property when the previous owner died) claimed that these tapestries were attached to the property and, as a result, that he was now entitled to them as part of the land. On the other hand, the heirs of the deceased claimed that the tapestries were merely ornamental and, therefore, were not attached to the property. The Court considered the competing claims by reference to the two prongs of the test outlined above. **[1–21]**

First of all, the tapestries were not affixed to the property with any great permanence. In the law report the means of attachment is described as follows: **[1–22]**

> Strips of wood were placed over the paper which covered the walls, and were fastened by nails to the walls. Canvas was stretched over the strips of wood and nailed to them, and the tapestries were stretched over the canvas and fastened by tacks to it and the pieces of wood. Mouldings, resting on the surface of the wall and fastened to it, were placed round each piece of tapestry.[37]

Reflecting on this, the Earl of Halsbury LC held: "I can hardly imagine how a piece of tapestry of that extent, fourteen feet long, stretched against a wall, could be more slightly attached than this was".[38] The means of attachment was, therefore, particularly

[34] The exceptions to this general rule—known as the law of tenants' fixtures—are considered in Chapter 15.
[35] [1902] AC 157.
[36] [1896] 2 Ch. 497.
[37] [1902] AC 157 at 157.
[38] *ibid.* at 160.

slight and from this the Court could infer that the tapestries were never intended to become part of the land, but rather were attached in this manner in order to better display them. This conclusion was bolstered by the fact that they could be removed without doing any damage whatsoever to the property.

[1–23] This case is easily distinguished from *d'Eyncourt v Gregory*, which concerned a tenant for life over property on which he had erected and furnished a mansion house. The tenant for life—who had rights over the property for his lifetime only—left all of the tapestry, marbles, statues, pictures and frames and glasses to persons in his will. A dispute arose as to whether he was entitled to leave these matters in his will, or whether they were part of the land and, therefore, beyond his power of disposition as soon as he died. In this case, the items at issue were not attached to the land in any substantial way—they were placed on shelves, hung on wall-hooks or, in the case of garden statues, attached merely by the force of gravity of their own weight.

[1–24] The first prong of the test did not, therefore, seem to suggest that these items ought to be considered as part of the land. However, when the Court went on to consider the intention of the person who had attached these items, it became evident that a great many of them were intended to essentially become part of the house and grounds and were essential to the architectural design of the property. Lord Romilly in this case expressed the principle upon which it was decided that at least some of the items were in fact "attachments" thus:

> I think it does not depend on whether any cement is used for fixing these articles, or whether they rest by their own weight, but upon this—whether they are strictly and properly part of the architectural design... and put in there as such, as distinguished from mere ornaments to be afterwards added.[39]

This intention that the items would form part of the architectural structure of the house overrode the slightness of the means by which they had been affixed or attached and they were therefore "attachments" to be governed by the law of real property.

Ownership Rights Above and Below the Surface of the Land

[1–25] Those with rights over land will not merely have rights to the surface of the land but also—to some extent at least—to the materials below and the airspace above the surface area. It was traditionally assumed that the maxim *cujus est solum, ejus est usque ad coelum et usque ad inferos* (i.e. "ownership is up to the heavens and down to hell") was an accurate statement of the extent of one's property rights over land, but it ought not be assumed that this is the case. As one can easily imagine, such a position introduces serious difficulties in practice, particularly in built-up areas where metros or other underground transportation links may be constructed and in the contemporary world of air travel, satellite technology and so on.

[1–26] In general terms, it is right to say that one has rights to the property underneath the surface of the land and the airspace above it, but it would be inaccurate to assume that

[39] [1896] 2 Ch. 497, 500.

this is an absolute principle, or that these rights really do extend in physical terms to the "ends of the earth".[40] It certainly appears to be relatively accurate to say that a property owner is entitled to the property underneath the surface, at least inasmuch as that property does not include minerals or what might be called "treasure trove", both of which properly belong to the State. In relation to airspace, it is clear that one is entitled to enjoyment of a *reasonable* amount of airspace above the surface of one's land,[41] but that this right does not extend to the point at which it interferes with the operation of satellites or obstructs air travel.[42]

One of the most important implications of the fact that one has rights in relation to the airspace above the surface of the land is that it is possible to have property rights in a strip of airspace.[43] A horizontal line of airspace property is known as a "flying freehold" and can be bought, sold, mortgaged, etc. in precisely the same way as any other piece of real property, although for practical reasons such conveyances will require particular care to be taken in both the process of mapping and the formulation of covenants[44] relating to support, maintenance and so on. **[1–27]**

Statutory Definition of "Land"

Reflecting these principles, the Land and Conveyancing Law Reform Act 2009 includes the following, non-exhaustive, definition of "land" for the purposes of the Act in s 3: **[1–28]**

> "land" includes—
> (a) any estate or interest in or over land, whether corporeal or incorporeal,
> (b) mines, minerals and other substances in the substratum below the surface, whether or not owned in horizontal, vertical or other layers apart from the surface of the land,
> (c) land covered by water,
> (d) buildings or structures of any kind on land and any part of them, whether the division is made horizontally, vertically or in any other way,
> (e) the airspace above the surface of land or above any building or structure on land which is capable of being or was previously occupied by a building or structure and any part of such airspace, whether the division is made horizontally, vertically or in any other way,
> (f) any part of land.

[40] *Commissioners for Railways v Valuer-General* [1974] AC 328.

[41] *Lord Bernstein of Leigh v Skyviews and General Ltd* [1978] QB 479.

[42] See, for example, Air Navigation and Transport Act 1936, s 55; the rights do extend to the point of disallowing advertising hoardings to protrude over someone else's property (*Kelsen v Imperial Tobacco Co* [1957] 2 QB 334) and to requiring that cranes operate at a high enough level to not interfere with others' property rights (*Anchor Brewhouse Developments Ltd v Berkley House (Docklands Developments) Ltd* [1988] NLJ 385).

[43] *O'Gorman & Co. Ltd. v Jes Holdings Ltd* [2005] IEHC 168; *Irredale v Loudon* (1908) 40 SCR 313.

[44] Covenants are, simply put, promises made under seal (or in a deed) such as a promise to support the land of another with the structures on one's own land. Covenants can be either leasehold (in leases) or freehold. Leasehold covenants are discussed in Chapter 15 and freehold covenants are considered in Chapter 11.

Furthermore, s 71 of the Act provides that a conveyance of land includes within it all buildings, drains, fences, fixtures, hedges, water, watercourses and other features forming part of the land.[45] If the land has houses or other buildings on it, the conveyance will also convey all cellars, drains, fixtures, gardens, lights, outhouses, passages, sewers, watercourses and other features that form part of the land, houses, or other buildings.[46]

V. Title

[1–29] While ownership can be defined as control over the thing owned, title is an important legal concept by which one assesses the strength of one's right to exercise this control. In essence, title refers to one's legal "entitlement" to property. Title is generally proved by a documentary process, which has now been greatly simplified by the introduction and sophistication in Irish law of systems of land registration.[47] In this way title can be taken to mean the collection of documents used within a conveyancing process to make out the vendor's entitlement to transact in the proposed manner and to show the extent to which any third parties might have rights in relation to the land. In the case of unregistered land, title consists of a number of documents showing the range of interests and entitlements extant over the property. One of the most important aspects of the conveyancing process whereby rights over land are transferred (usually by sale or lease) is the establishment of "good marketable title".[48] What constitutes good marketable title is, in essence, a question determined by whatever the prevailing conveyancing standards are.[49] In general terms, however, we can say that good marketable title is established where a purchaser can be satisfied that, should he want to sell that property again in the future, it could be sold without special conditions designed to deal with defects in title. So the purchaser will want to be satisfied that the vendor has the right to sell the property as proposed and that there are no outstanding questions as to that title (for example, that there are no third parties who might be able to enforce a right against the purchaser or someone intended to enter into a subsequent transaction over the land).

[1–30] The law recognises that there are different strengths of title that exist over property. In other words, a person—Patrick—may have title over a piece of land, but his title might not be the strongest title out there. This may be because, for example, Patrick is an adverse possessor and his title is merely possessory. This does not mean that Patrick can not transact in relation to the land; there may well be a purchaser in the marketplace who would be happy to accept the merely possessory title and acquire it from Patrick. That purchaser would not, however, be acquiring the strongest possible title to the land and must therefore accept that the risk of future claims against the property is higher than it would be if a stronger title (such as a good marketable title) had been acquired. The stronger the title of a vendor, then, the lower the level of risk a purchaser is taking on and, in all likelihood, the higher the market value of the property.

---

45 s 71(1)(a), Land and Conveyancing Law Reform Act 2009.

46 s 71(2)(a), *ibid.*

47 These systems of land registration are considered in full in Chapter 7.

48 *Clarke v Taylor* [1899] 1 IR 449.

49 See also Land and Conveyancing Law Reform Act 2009, Part 9, Chapter 2 (ss 56–61).

VI. Moral Limits to "Property"

It is important to consider whether there are any moral limitations to the concept of property—in other words, whether there are contexts in which one would say that property in the form of ownership rights is impossible. The concept of moral limits to property is probably best demonstrated through a consideration of the evolution of the rule that there is no property in the human body. It was originally the case that the law recognised that "a portion of our fellow creatures may become the subject of property".[50] This viewpoint essentially survived in the law until the abolition of slavery in both international and domestic legal systems, although it should be noted that the courts had begun to show a reluctance to enforce contracts over human property as early as the 1500s.[51] While the origin of the rule that there can be no property in the human body is somewhat contested,[52] by now the veracity of the rule is beyond doubt. This is so not only as a matter of property law, but also as a matter of international law which forbids slavery and servitude (both of which are fundamentally founded on the concept of "ownership" or "control" of a person[53]) in the strongest terms known to international law.[54] [1–31]

That said, there are a limited number of scenarios in which human bodies—usually dead—or parts thereof can be protected by the law against interference from others. In the case of corpses, for example, next-of-kin may be recognised as having enforceable rights to ensure that prior to the burial there is no interference with the corpse by medical or other practitioners. This was defined in *Smith v Tamworth*[55] as a "sort of quasi-property" in the corpse, i.e. a right to control what happens to the corpse. This *quasi*-property right has been interpreted in the United States as allowing for the same enforcement rights as any other property rights. This was confirmed by the 6th Circuit Court of Appeal in *Brotherton v Cleveland*,[56] in which corneas were removed from the deceased without the consent of the next-of-kin. The Court held that the plaintiffs were [1–32]

---

[50] *Gregson v Gilbert* (1783) 99 ER 629.

[51] See *Cartwright's Case* (1569) 2 Rushworth 468 and *Somerset v Stewart* (1772) Lofft 1.

[52] See Atherton, "Claims on the Deceased: The Corpse as Property" (2000) 7 *Journal of Law and Medicine* 361; Magnusson, "The Recognition of Proprietary Rights in Human Tissue in Common Law Jurisdictions" (1992) 18 *Melbourne University Law Review* 601; Matthews, "Whose Body? People as Property" (1983) *Current Legal Problems* 193.

[53] For an exhaustive examination of the foundations of slavery in classical thought see Garnsey, *Ideas of Slavery from Aristotle to Augustine* (1996, New York, Cambridge University Press). For a review of the "ownership" foundation to slavery, including international law on slavery, see generally Allain, *The Slavery Conventions: The Travaux Preparatores of the 1927 League of Nations Convention and the 1956 United Nations Convention* (2008, Leiden, Martinus Nijhoff).

[54] The prohibition of slavery is found not only in the slavery conventions (see Allain, *ibid.*) but also in all general human rights instruments, including Art 4 of the European Convention on Human Rights. It has the status of *jus cogens* in international law, which means that it is a peremptory norm that can never be violated or derogated from in any circumstances and that any treaties that violated this norm can be invalidated. On *jus cogens* see Art 53, Vienna Convention on the Law of Treaties (1969) and, generally, Orakhelashvili, *Peremptory Norms in International Law* (2009, Oxford, Oxford University Press).

[55] Unreported, No. 4196 of 1996, 14 May 1997; cited by Taylor, "Human Property: Threat or Saviour" (2002) 9(4) *Murdoch University Electronic Journal of Law.*

[56] 10 Cent LJ 325 (1880), as cited by JFH, "The Nature of Rights in a Dead Body" (1926) *University of Pennsylvania Law Review* 404 at 404.

entitled to the protections of their property guaranteed by the due process clause in the same way as those rights would be guaranteed to them in relation to any other piece of property. However, in general it is the case that there are no property rights *per se* in a corpse—although it appears that, in the 1800s, a corpse could be arrested by a creditor of the deceased for failure to pay a debt.

[1–33] Perhaps the most contentious—and the most grizzly—exception to the rule that there is no property in human beings is what is sometimes termed "the work and skill" exception. This flows from the decision of the Australian High Court in the case of *Doodleward v Spence.*[57] This case concerned the corpse of a two-headed baby, which had been preserved and had become the subject of a dispute as to who was properly entitled to it. While the Court accepted that, in general, human bodies were not capable of being property, it did not accept that this was an absolute rule. Griffith CJ held that the possession of a corpse for purposes other than burial was not, *per se,* unlawful and proceeded to carve out "the work and skill" exception in the following terms:

> [A] human body, or a portion of a human body, is capable by law of becoming the subject of property. It is not necessary to give an exhaustive enumeration of the circumstances under which such a right may be acquired, but I entertain no doubt that, when a person has by the lawful exercise of work or skill so dealt with a human body or part of a human body in his lawful possession that it has acquired some attributes differentiating it from a mere corpse awaiting burial, he acquires a right to retain possession of it, at least as against any person not entitled to have it delivered to him for the purpose of burial, but subject, of course, to any positive law which forbids its retention under the particular circumstances.[58]

[1–34] This principle was endorsed recently by the Court of Appeal in *R v Kelly.*[59] This case concerned an artist who had limited access to cadavers at the Royal College of Surgeons, London, but who was charged with the theft of "three heads, three torsos, part of a brain, six arms and ten legs and feet", which were removed without authorisation, used by him for the creation of bronze sculptures and never returned to the College. The Court of Appeal upheld his conviction, holding that there is a distinction between corpses and body parts and, furthermore, that body parts could be transformed into property by "virtue of the application of skill".

[1–35] The question of whether there is property in the human body has become all the more urgent with the advancements in medical research and technology that frequently require the harvesting of and experimentation with cells, or other body tissue, and can result in the production of "body parts", such as embryos. In the United States of America there has been some recognition that people can sell blood, or that there can be property in hair, urine, bone marrow, etc.[60] that casts considerably difficult

---

[57] [1908] 6 CLR 406.

[58] *ibid.* at 414.

[59] [1999] QB 621.

[60] For more on these developments, see Griggs, "The Ownership of Excised Body Parts: Does an Individual Have the Right to Sell?" (1994) 1 *Journal of Law and Medicine* 223.

questions on the matter of whether there is property in the human body. At the same time, there is case law that suggests the absolute rule against property in the human body may continue to be applied notwithstanding developments in scientific and medical research. This is suggested by the case of *Moore v Regents of UCLA*.[61]

John Moore was being treated for hairy cell leukaemia in UCLA, where blood, bone marrow and other body substantives were removed for the confirmation of his diagnosis. Approximately one year after he began treatment in UCLA, Moore was advised to have his spleen removed, which he was told was vital to slow down the progress of his disease and to delay or prevent death. Moore consented to the splenectomy on the basis of these advices and his spleen was removed. Moore continued to attend at UCLA for check-ups that, he was told, were necessary to his health and well-being. As part of every visit, blood, blood serum, skin, bone marrow and sperm were sampled. **[1–36]**

It transpired that, throughout his treatment, doctors at UCLA Medical Centre had been engaged in research on hairy cell leukaemia involving the use of his cells and other bodily substances without his knowledge. These substances were available to them only because of the continued doctor–patient relationship with Moore. In 1979 a cell line was developed from Moore's cells, which his doctors patented successfully. This discovery led to large amounts of revenue for the UCLA Medical Centre and, upon discovering what had transpired, Moore sued on the basis that he had property rights in these cells. The Court held that Moore had no property in his cells or the profits made from them, although it did find that his medical staff had an obligation to reveal their research and financial interests in the bodily substances harvested from Moore's body. **[1–37]**

These cases and trends raise profound questions about the nature of the rule that there is no property in the human body. Is it the case that there is no property in the entire human body when it is living or in cells, but that there are *quasi*-proprietary rights in a corpse, property rights in corpses and body parts that have been subjected to work and skill, and property rights in parts of the living body, such as blood and hair, but only if the person decides to sell them? The answers to these questions are not entirely clear, but the continuing evolution of the matter of property in human beings not only alerts us to the complexity of property but also to the difficult moral questions that can arise in our decisions as to the limits of property. **[1–38]**

VII. A Short Note on Property Law and Social Change

In recent years the Irish law of property has undertaken massive reform. The greatest example of this will arise repeatedly throughout this book: the Land and Conveyancing Law Reform Act 2009. Social changes in Ireland were part of that process of reform. Take, for example, the provision in s 9(2) that abolishes any remnants of feudal tenure from Irish property law.[62] We will see in the next chapter that in fact many of our building blocks in property law have a feudal provenance, and we did not abolish all of **[1–39]**

---

61 793 P 2d 479 (Cal 1990).

62 This is considered in more detail in paras [2–58] and [2–59].

those concepts and doctrines in the 2009 Act. Rather we reconstituted them, often in a tidier and more manageable way but always on a new footing. A statutory footing; a *democratic* footing. We did this because, in common with many other States, we do not consider that a feudally based property law system is appropriate in a modern democratic State. Reflecting on this in the context of the United States, Joseph Singer has written that at the birth of the United States of America, the rejection of feudalism was an essential element of that country's commitment to democracy:

> Democracies are premised on the idea that we must show equal concern and respect for every person. For that reason, we reject distinctions of status... The feudal system was premised on distinctions among persons... [it] placed people in ranks and it was a fundamental principle that you were defined by your status. It was also a fundamental principle that some men were not free.
>
> ...
>
> American property law was born at a time when great changes were happening in the world. Prime among them was the American rejection of feudalism as a way of life. Movie stars and sports players aside, we want no lords here.[63]

[1–40] As well changes that reflect socio-political change, such as a shift to democracy or emergence from colonialism, property laws often reflect socio-economic change. Many of the changes that were introduced in the 2009 Act were done with a view to ensuring that our organisation of the law of property does not unduly hamper property-based transactions, the foundation upon which so much of our economic prosperity was built.[64] We have also, rather late in the day, introduced the Multi-Unit Developments Act 2011 to deal with particular questions that arise in multi-unit developments, such as apartment blocks. In the main this reform focuses on the creation of Owners' Management Companies to manage the development, including the common areas and the enforcement of covenants. Again, the growth of multi-unit developments and of the problems associated with them—especially problems of essentially exploitative service charges paid to maintenance companies frequently entirely neglectful of the property—was one that came to prominence because of the "Celtic Tiger" and changes that this brought to how we use land in development terms and to what kinds of properties people bought (or could afford to buy).[65]

[1–41] If our rise to economic superstardom can help to explain some legal changes that have come about in the last few years, then our descent into economic purgatory can also

---

[63] Singer, "Property Law as the Infrastructure of Democracy", The 4th Wolf Family Lecture on the American Law of Real Property, 4 April 2011. Available at SSRN: http://ssrn.com/abstract = 1832829

[64] See, for example, the discussion of the reform of estates in land by the Land and Conveyancing Law Reform Act 2009 in Chapter 4.

[65] For a full outline of the difficulties that MUDs presented see the Law Reform Commission's work on this matter: *Consultation Paper on Multi-Unit Developments* (LRC CP 42-2006) (2006, Dublin, Law Reform Commission) and *Report on Multi-Unit Developments* (LRC 90-2008) (2008, Dublin, Law Reform Commission).

help to explain some other changes that we will consider at various points in the book. Two areas of particular concern are notable at this point. The first relates to mortgages and, in particular, to the process by which mortgagees (usually banks and other financial institutions) can repossess and sell mortgaged property if the repayments are not made in full and on time. As we will see in Chapter 13, the Land and Conveyancing Law Reform Act 2009 reformed the operation of mortgages but it did not insert what we might call substantial "stalling mechanisms" to delay repossessions. That has, however, been seen as an important public policy concern because of: (a) the huge number of people who we know are either in arrears or about to go into arrears on their mortgages, and (b) the significant support given by the State to banks operating in Ireland. In fact, these stalling mechanisms were not introduced by legislation in the end; rather they were introduced by the Financial Regulator through a Code of Conduct. In other words, the Code of Conduct—which, at the time of writing, is the Code of Conduct on Mortgage Arrears as last revised on 6 December 2010—is a regulatory instrument that tries to ameliorate the difficulties people are facing by forcing banks to delay on their use of statutory mechanisms for repossession and sale (or "enforcement") of mortgages that exist over residential properties. We will consider how the Code works in Chapter 13.

Of course, it is not only home owners who are having property-related difficulties in the current climate. Commercial tenants also face particular difficulties, especially where they possess their commercial premises on the basis of leases that pre-date the "crash". It had become common course for these leases to include what are known as "upward only rent review clauses"; conditions that provided that rent would either go up on review or stay the same, but could never go down. These clauses raised relatively few eyebrows during "the boom", but of course are problematic now when market activity is low, property values are declining, but rents can still be increased. Section 132 of the Land and Conveyancing Law Reform Act 2009 resolves this difficulty when it comes to leases executed after it came into effect, but it does not retrospectively abolish such clauses. There are continuing calls for a retrospective abolition of upwards only rent review clauses, which we will consider in Chapter 15, and commercial organisations continue to claim that rent levels are a significant factor in failing businesses. [1–42]

Perhaps one of the most significant property-related developments since the beginning of the economic crisis is the establishment of the National Asset Management Agency, reputed to be one of the largest property holding companies in the world.[66] NAMA, as this agency is known, is established by statute and has the capacity to acquire lands from those who fall within its remit. It has also been suggested that NAMA will establish its own mortgage scheme in the future with the hope of stimulating activity in the property market. Although the establishment of NAMA is significant, it is primarily dealt with in law schools in financial regulation and banking law courses, and is not addressed in this book.[67] [1–43]

[66] National Asset Management Agency Act 2009.

[67] The operation and composition of NAMA is extensively considered in Dodd & Carroll, *NAMA: The Law Relating to the National Asset Management Agency* (2011, Dublin, Round Hall).

[1–44] We should not, however, fall into the trap of thinking that economic collapse is the only "social change" that has an impact on property law. Social change, and its effect on the formulation of public policy, has long has an impact on how property law is designed and implemented. The relationship between the two has usually been one of legal reaction to social change. In other words, property law tends to react to changes in social patterns rather than to induce those changes itself. This is not, of course, always the case: in the United Kingdom, for example, Margaret Thatcher famously brought about massive social change when she created a scheme for people to buy their corporation houses and, by so doing, ushered in what has been termed an "ownership society" there. However, in general the relationship works in the other direction. So, for example, it was increased social pressure for women's liberation and equality that brought about the introduction of the Married Women's Property Act 1882 (allowing married women to own and manage their own land), rather than the other way around. Similarly, it was a social demand for a system of family recognition that aligned more closely to people's lived experiences that brought about the Civil Partnership and Certain Rights and Obligations of Cohabitants Act 2010 and its associated property law changes, rather than a spontaneous legal move designed to bring about greater family diversity in Irish society.

[1–45] This is not to suggest that changes in property law cannot do more than merely reflect a broader social change; they can help us to adapt to that social change as a democracy (for example, by abolishing feudalism), as an economy (for example, by restricting rents), as families (for example, by protecting the homes of married couples and people in civil partnerships), and as individuals (for example, by ensuring that a woman with property can choose to marry without running the risk of losing her capacity to own and manage that property).

CHAPTER 2
Feudalism and Tenure

The concept of tenure, which can be traced back to the feudal system, relates to the basis upon which one person might be said to hold land from—or "under"—another. Although the two concepts are somewhat connected, tenure must be distinguished from the concept of an estate, which is the length of time for which someone will be said to have rights in relation to land (considered in full in Chapter 4). Tenure can be traced back to the basic principles of feudal landholding systems. In feudal systems no individual, apart from the crown, could be said to have absolute ownership of land or allodial ownership, as it was known. Rather, the conquest of a territory vested ownership of all of that territory in the crown, and landholders then held that land under the king, or his subordinates, by means of tenure. The type of tenure that one held determined the types of rights and obligations one had in relation to the land in question. As discussed below, feudalism is a highly contested concept among historians and sociologists. For lawyers, on the other hand, our primary concern is with the **[2–01]** land-related transactions and customs that developed during the feudal period, and with how those transactions, rules and customs influenced the development of modern property law. Although, as considered at the end of this chapter, the Land and Conveyancing Law Reform Act 2009 has radically changed the foundational basis of residual structures from feudalism to a statutory one, the impact of the feudal system of tenure on the development and understanding of modern Irish property law justifies its consideration here.

I. Non-Legal Perspectives on Feudalism

[2–02] Despite the tangential nature of the modern debates around feudalism, they are worth some discussion by means of introduction. Feudalism has traditionally been described as a socio-legal system introduced to England by virtue of the Battle of Hastings in 1066, and subsequently introduced to Ireland in the 1100s.[1] In general, traditional views considered feudalism to be a matrix of military and legal relationships that existed within the nobility of the Middle Ages and were concerned, in particular, with how military and legal obligations were bound up with landowning, landholding and the transfer of land. As lawyers, there is a tendency to be somewhat clinical in the consideration of feudalism, seeing it as a mere developmental step within the history of property law and therefore not dwelling too long on the political and social inequalities that prevailed throughout the system. Other fields of study have engaged in a deeper interrogation of the concept of feudalism, however, and of our assertions or assumptions in relation to it.

[2–03] The term "feudalism", which was coined largely for political and philosophical purposes, was not popularised until the 17th century when the practice of feudalism was generally in decline. The term was developed in order to describe the traditional obligations that existed between members of the aristocracy and that were identified by revolutionaries as being particularly objectionable. Its first major usage was in Montesquieu's classic 1748 work, *De L'Esprit des Lois* (The Spirit of the Laws)[2] and it was quickly seized upon by other Enlightenment thinkers as a pejorative term to describe and denigrate the *Ancien Régime*, i.e. the French monarchy. In a similar vein, Karl Marx used feudalism as a derisory term to describe the situation as it existed prior to the rise of capitalism; it epitomised the class system in which the aristocracy exploited peasants through landholding structures. According to Marx: "The hand-mill gives you the society with the feudal lord; the steam-mill society with the industrial capitalist".[3] In his view, the dominance of the ruling class was common to both systems.

[2–04] While political philosophers have by and large used feudalism as a descriptor of what they perceived to be an undesirable situation, historians have concentrated more on the

---

[1] As we will see later, the integration of the feudal system in Ireland was a somewhat protracted affair and it did not really take hold and displace the pre-existing Brehon system until the Plantations.

[2] Cohler, Miller, and Stone (eds), *Montesquieu, The Spirit of the Laws* (1989, Cambridge, Cambridge University Press).

[3] Marx, *The Poverty of Philosophy* (1847), Chapter 2.

structure and underlying supports of that system. Conventional reports (typified by the work of John Horace Round[4]) claim that feudalism came to England in the 11th century but, according to the renowned historian Frederic William Maitland, the fundamental requirements for feudalism were already in place before the Battle of Hastings. The debate between the two points of view is certainly lively. Round's account paints a far more equitable picture of pre-Norman England than Maitland's. However, it is in the area of the internal structure of feudalism that historians, particularly sociological historians, have engaged in the most interesting and vigorous debate stemming from the contesting views of two French historians: François-Louis Ganshof and Marc Bloch.

Ganshof viewed feudalism as a system of reciprocal personal relations among members of the military elite, which ultimately led to parliament and then Western democracy.[5] **[2–05]** In his model, the peasants are not part of the feudal relationship or structure in any meaningful way. In contrast, Bloch has argued that the peasants did form part of the feudal structure. While the vassals[6] received land-related rights in return for their services and incidents,[7] peasants received protection and the right to engage in subsistence farming in return for their physical labour.[8] According to Bloch, both are

[4] Round's work was somewhat fragmented; he never wrote a long and detailed account of feudalism but rather wrote most of his commentaries in the form of essays concentrated on particular elements of the system. That said, his work was based on slender historical materials, which resulted in him having to accept a number of premises without interrogating them to the full. As FM Stenton wrote: "[Round] rarely entered into the fundamental questions which underlie the history of English feudal organization. In other words, he accepted the existence of a centralized feudal state in England without inquiring into its origins. He gave little of his attention to the internal organization of the individual honours of which that society was composed, and he was always inclined to regard the independent action of a twelfth-century baron as an encroachment upon royal authority. The very success of his early work may have contributed something to this attitude. He had shown that the whole elaborate system of knight-service in England could be traced to the conditions which the Conqueror had imposed on his leading followers, and he was perhaps too ready to assume that King William and his sons had controlled feudal justice and feudal administration as they certainly controlled the military organization which they had created for the defence of the realm. It is also worth remembering that much of Round's work was devoted to the great record in which the authority of the Norman monarchy is most clearly expressed. The shadow of the king falls across every page of Domesday Book. No one knew better than Round how limited was the scope of this record, and how clear in it are the signs of an exceptional effort made upon a great occasion. But the student of Domesday Book will always emphasize the power which called it into being, and of the materials which show the purely feudal aspect of Anglo-Norman society, comparatively few were accessible in print when Round began to write". Stenton, *The First Century of English Feudalism 1066–1166: Being the Ford Lectures Delivered in the University of Oxford in Hilary Term 1929* (1932, Oxford, Clarendon Press), p 3.

[5] See Ganshof, *Feudalism*, trans Grierson (1952, London, Longmans Green).

[6] Vassals were individuals with free tenure who pledged homage and fealty to their lord (see para 2–30 below).

[7] Services and incidents were, in essence, types of payments. They are considered in paras 2–23 to 2–40 below.

[8] See Bloch, *Feudal Society*, trans Manyon (1989, London, Routledge), vol 2.

reciprocal and feudal relationships. In this account feudalism is, in fact, a sociological concept—a type of society that extended beyond the nobility and was characterised by various levels of hierarchical reciprocal relationships.

[2–06] Irish property law accounts of feudalism tend to accord more with Bloch's view. It must be stressed, however, that lawyers have not really engaged in the same level of detailed analysis of feudalism as historians and philosophers. A property lawyer's interest in the system is far narrower than historians' and philosophers' broad theories about its social and political impact. In this, it should be said, lawyers are some way behind other disciplines, which are now beginning to reject the term in its entirety.[9] Property lawyers, however, can engage in a necessary simplification of the term in order to reduce it to consideration of the rules and customs relating to landholding that existed within the socio-legal system known as feudalism. The sociological, political and historical complexities of the contested territory are interesting, but do not touch upon the main property law-related elements of the system, which is where our primary interest lies.

II. The Tenurial Structure

[2–07] Bearing in mind the simplifications required by our limited interest in feudalism, one can conceive of the tenurial structure of feudalism in relatively basic terms. Upon conquering a realm, the king considered himself to be entitled to all of the lands within it. Accordingly, after the Battle of Hastings, William the Conqueror considered himself to have the ultimate entitlement to all of the lands within the English realm. Of course, from a practical perspective, there was no way in which he could control and administer all of these lands himself. Instead, he would use them to reward loyalty, ensure continued loyalty and raise income. This was done by subdividing the realm into parcels of land, some of which the king retained, transferring rights in relation to the rest to his most loyal supporters (the barons and sometimes bishops) who became known as tenants-in-chief. These tenants-in-chief held the land as the vassals, or feudal tenants, of the king, who was their feudal lord.

[2–08] Although the tenants-in-chief had some obligations to their overlord, considered in full below, they also had a number of entitlements, which often included the entitlement to reproduce the subdivision-and-transfer pattern themselves. Thus, tenants-in-chief would divide their lands into further manors and transfer them to their supporters, who in turn would take on certain responsibilities in relation to the land and in relation to their lord. These were known as *mesne* lords (or tenants in *mesne*) and they in turn could carry out the subdivision-and-transfer process to tenants in *demesne*, who actually held the majority of the land.

[9] This movement developed through the work of Elizabeth Brown and, in particular, her seminal essay, "The Tyranny of a Construct: Feudalism and Historians of Medieval Europe" (1974) 79(4) *American Historical Review* 1063*HH*. The argument is based on re-readings of historical texts and a revolt against the uniformity that the concept of a "feudal system" suggests in terms of medieval society. See Reynolds, *Fiefs and Vassals: The Medieval Evidence Reinterpreted* (1994, Oxford, Oxford University Press) for the best development of Brown's thesis.

The feudal structure was, therefore, essentially pyramidal, leading to the concept of the feudal pyramid, which is represented in fairly rudimentary form as follows: [2–09]

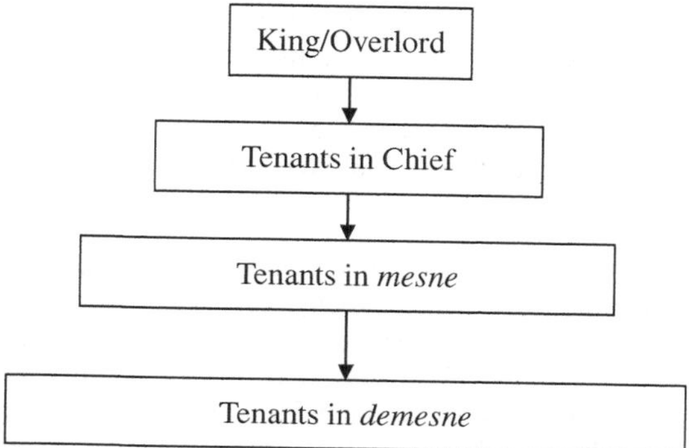

As this structure shows, in landholding terms the feudal system comprised various layers of relationships between parties, which are referred to here as feudal lords and feudal tenants. The use of the word "tenant" here does not mean that there was a "lease" between the parties; rather it reflects the fact that the conditions upon which a feudal tenant held the land were known as "tenure", hence the description "tenurial system".

In the feudal system only one person could be said to "own" the realm, and that was the king. His title was known as radical title, i.e. a title only the crown can hold: the sovereign title to the country. The concept was well described by the Australian High Court in *Mabo & Ors v Queensland (No 2)*[10]: [2–10]

> There is a distinction between the Crown's title to a colony and the Crown's ownership of land in the colony, as Roberts-Wray points out... "If a country is part of Her Majesty's dominions, the sovereignty vested in her is of two kinds. The first is the power of government. The second is title to the country... This ownership of the country is radically different from ownership of the land: the former can belong only to a sovereign, the latter to anyone. Title to land is not, per se, relevant to the constitutional status of a country; land may have become vested in the Queen, equally in a Protectorate or in a Colony, by conveyance or under statute.[11]

Thus the king's radical title was his ownership of the sovereignty over the land, although in later times property lawyers have begun to describe it as ownership of the land itself in a way that is neither entirely desirable nor entirely accurate.[12] Radical title did not necessarily equate to allodial title, however. Allodial title is the full legal and

[10] *Mabo & Ors v Queensland (No 2)* (1992) 175 CLR 1, High Court of Australia.
[11] *ibid.*, para 45 *per* Brennan J.
[12] Writing about the medieval concept of materialism, Simpson observed: "The [medieval] lawyers never adopted the premise that the King owned all the land; such a dogma is of very modern appearance. It was sufficient for them to note that the King was Lord, ultimately, of all the tenants in the realm, and that as lord he had many rights common to other lords... and some peculiar to his position as supreme lord..." *A History of Land Law* (2nd ed, 1986, Oxford, Oxford University Press), p 47.

beneficial ownership of land. Where a sovereign arrived in an unoccupied land he might be said to acquire both radical (sovereign) and allodial (beneficial) title; where the sovereign arrived in occupied land he would acquire radical (sovereign) title but not necessarily allodial (beneficial) title.[13] The fact that only the crown enjoyed radical title and held land free of taxes and other obligations meant that while people lower down the feudal pyramid could be said to own control rights over the land for a certain period of time, as defined by their tenure, they could not really be accurately said to "own" the land itself. Rather they held land subject to certain conditions and obligations, i.e. in tenure.

[2–11] When a feudal lord transferred landholding rights to his feudal tenants, he imposed conditions upon the holding which, as noted already, were known as tenure. As discussed below, these conditions varied with the type of tenure that existed between the parties. For now it is sufficient to note that, in general, the conditions ensured that the income from the land was always moving upwards within the feudal pyramid, i.e. towards the king. The feudal lord's entitlement was known as *seigniory*[14] and, as the diagram shows, every person within the pyramid, with the exception of the king, had a superior lord; thus everyone owed *seigniory* to another. In return for this *seigniory* the feudal tenant received not only landholding rights but also vital protection.

[2–12] In summary: the king had sovereign ownership of all the land. He divided the land among his loyal supporters, who were known as tenants-in-chief. They in turn divided it among their supporters, known as tenants in *mesne*, who in turn divided it among others, known as tenants in *demesne*. The tenants in *demesne* actually held most of the land, although they themselves had tenants (free and unfree) who worked most of the land. The feudal pyramid comprised a series of feudal lord–feudal tenant relationships in which the feudal tenants received landholding rights and protections and the feudal lords received payments of some kind. This continued throughout the different levels of the pyramid, with wealth constantly moving upwards towards the king.

III. The Manor

[2–13] The manor was the base unit of the tenurial system, but although it formed a part of the system it should not be confused with the system itself. There was a separate manorial system within feudalism, which dictated how the manors would be run, the

[13] *Mabo & Ors v Queensland (No 2)* (1992) 175 CLR 1, High Court of Australia. This relates to one of the most important, difficult and controversial questions in contemporary property law disputes in countries where aboriginal and native peoples were dispossessed of their lands by colonial powers. The question of "native title" relates, at a rather basic level, to the distinction between radical and allodial title. Although this has not arisen as a question of concern in this jurisdiction, it is the basis of much scholarship in others, particularly Australia, New Zealand and Canada. There is an extensive literature on native title, but interested readers will find an interesting and engaging account in Ritter, *Contesting Native Title* (2009, NSW, Allen & Unwin).

[14] *Seigniory* encompasses the idea that, in this system, there could be no land without a lord and that even after the lord had transferred the right to hold the land (the tenure) he retained lordship. That retention of lordship, and its service through compliance with tenurial obligations considered further below, made up *seigniory*.

rights of villiens[15] who were bound to the manor, the conduct of the Manor Court, the rules and systems relating to crop rotation and subsistence farming exercised by villiens, and so on. While the workings of the manorial system are interesting, they are something of a distraction within a consideration of the tenurial system. For this book's purpose it is enough to bear in mind that the manor was the basic unit of land, was run by the person with landholding rights, and formed what was tantamount to an autonomous social unit in itself.[16]

IV. Alienation

If entitlement holders on practically every layer of the feudal pyramid could divide up the land and transfer it to others, it is logical (and correct) to assume that there must have been some concept of alienation within the feudal system. Alienation is the technical term used for transfer of rights over land, and the concept of formalised transfer of land rights was highly developed in the feudal system. Feudalism recognised three different types of alienation: subinfeudation, substitution and mortmain. All three are important for a full understanding of the system and how it contributed to the development of property law as we now know it. **[2–14]**

Subinfeudation is best defined as the transfer of rights to a subordinate. In other words, it occurs when an individual transfers landholding rights to someone who enters the feudal pyramid on a lower level than the transferor and becomes the feudal tenant of the transferor. When, for example, a tenant-in-chief transfers some landholding rights to a tenant in *mesne,* a subinfeudation takes place: the tenant in *mesne* is the feudal tenant and subordinate of the tenant-in-chief and, as a result, occupies a lower position on the feudal pyramid than the tenant-in-chief. **[2–15]**

Substitution, on the other hand, involved the tenant surrendering his rights to his lord, who would then transfer those rights to another. Hence the original tenant's rights were extinguished and he was substituted by a third party. The third party, or transferee (person to whom rights were being transferred), became a tenant of the original feudal lord; there was no feudal relationship between the transferee and the original tenant. In the words of Susan Reynolds, "it put the new owner in the same relation to his lord as the previous one had enjoyed".[17] Although one now distinguishes quite sharply between subinfeudation and substitution, it is possible that this distinction is a historical construct and that contemporaries didn't often acknowledge the exactitudes of the distinction. However, as noted shortly, the decline of feudalism came about by means of laws that began to treat both very differently. **[2–16]**

The third means of alienation, mortmain, stands alone to some extent. Mortmain is an anglicised version of the Old French, *amortisement,* and can be broken down into the constituent elements: *mort*, meaning dead, and *main*, meaning hand. In other words, mortmain was the transfer of property rights into "dead hands", i.e. to someone who **[2–17]**

---

[15] See para 2–28.

[16] For more on the manorial system, see Douglass North and Robert Thomas's classic essay, "The Rise and Fall of the Manorial System: A Theoretical Model" (1971) 31(4) *Journal of Economic History* 777.

[17] Reynolds, *Fiefs and Vassals: The Medieval Evidence Reinterpreted* (1994, Oxford, Oxford University Press), p 300.

could not die. This "someone" was a corporation, which was recognised as having legal personality. In the main, this corporation was a religious organisation or a corporation sole, such as a bishop. By means of example, the Catholic Church was recognised in feudal systems as "possessing a legal personality and the capacity to take and acquire property".[18] The Church was seen as *ens æterna eadem perpetuo permanens quasi in ea nemo uniquam moritur*, or an everlasting body continuing perpetually as if no one in it could ever die.[19] Mortmain posed particular political problems for the king. As the amount of land and accompanying power, wealth and influence being accumulated by the religious orders increased, the king's position of power became precarious. As a result of this, and of the fact that property rights transferred in mortmain were effectively removed from the market forever, this form of alienation was effectively abolished by the Statute of Mortmain 1279. This Statute terminated the tenure of anyone who purported to alienate in mortmain, therefore representing a strong disincentive to such action (although the king could grant an exempting licence from the Statute at his will). The laws restricting mortmain presented particular difficulties once limited companies began to proliferate, and found themselves impacted detrimentally by them. The mortmain laws were eventually repealed in Ireland in the Mortmain (Repeal of Enactments) Act 1954.

[2–18] The transfer of landholding rights generally took the form of "feoffment with livery of seisin". The notion of feoffment is that of a gift or something (in this case freehold rights) being given; "livery" signifies the idea of delivery; and "seisin" signifies the idea of possession. Thus, feoffment with livery of seisin was the symbolic ceremony by which possession was transferred to another, as a result of which landholding rights were transferred. The ceremony would take place on, or in view of, the land. The words of transfer would be said (or sometimes read from a written charter, especially if the transfer had some particular political significance[20]), and then the transferor (known as the feoffor) would hand something representing the gift to the transferee (known as the feoffee).[21]

V. Inheritability

[2–19] In the earliest manifestation of the feudal system, when a feudal tenant died the feudal lord had a number of choices available to him: he could allow the deceased tenant's heir to succeed to the tenure, or he could choose to create an entirely new feudal relationship with another person from another family. To do the former was seen as a manifestation of "good lordship"—honourable, fair, not unnecessarily complicated and encouraging to other feudal tenants. To do the latter may still have been attractive to the feudal lord who would wish to avoid having an undesirable tenant. The relevant question, however, is to what extent the feudal lord had that choice. In other words, was there a *right* or an *entitlement* of the heir of a feudal tenant to inherit the deceased tenant's tenure, or was this truly at the discretion of the feudal lord?

[18] *Municipality of Ponce v Roman Catholic Apostolic Church in Porto* (1908) 210 US 296.

[19] Individual members of the Church were seen as civilly dead because of their vows, but were recognised as *viri religiosi*, who lived perpetually through their ownership of property.

[20] The charter did not constitute the transfer itself; it was merely evidence of the transfer.

[21] More often than not that would be a twig or some dirt from the land, which would sometimes be flung at the transferee. Nowadays we use deeds of conveyance to transfer rights over land to one another instead of throwing dirt in each other's eyes!

Maitland and Pollock claim that at the higher levels of the feudal pyramid inheritance was normal, while *mesne* lords' tenures were "indubitably hereditary".[22] While few commentators disagree that the tenures of those higher on the feudal pyramid were normally passed to the tenants' heirs, there is some dispute as to whether this ought to be taken to suggest a system of succession or a system of inheritability. The difference between the two is important and it is expressed clearly by Thorne in the following example: [2–20]

> [I]f I hire my gardener's son after his father's death, and my son hires his son after him, the place as gardener has descended through three generations of the same family. Yet it is obvious that it has come to each by gift, and that the son and grandson of my gardener can in no way be said to have inherited it. What we have is a fief held by successive tenants in return for service, each succeeding by gift.[23]

In other words, if this was a practice of succession, then every heir received the land as a result of a lord's decision to grant it to him; if it was a practice of inheritance, on the other hand, then every heir received the land by entitlement. Although the original position appears to have been that of succession (i.e. a gift or discretion rather than a right), this gradually changed,[24] and in 1176 it was considered settled-law that an heir of a feudal tenant had the right to a fair "relief", or inheritance tax, thus suggesting the right to inherit.

VI. Tenures in Practical Terms

In general terms there were two broad categories of tenure: free tenure and unfree tenure. In Ireland to these were added three particular types of landholding relationship: gavelkind, rundale and commonage. In the main, the difference between free and unfree tenure related to the status of the tenure-holder: the free tenant was a freeman; the unfree tenant was bonded to a particular manor. Unfree tenants had no certainty in terms of what their services would be as these services were, in a way, decided on the basis of the needs of their lord in any particular situation. [2–21]

Free tenants had certain entitlements from their lords. If someone claimed they had the better entitlement to the land than the feudal tenant, the feudal lord could be vouched to warranty, which meant he took over the defence of the tenant. If the defence was unsuccessful, the feudal lord was obliged to give the tenant rights over land of equal value to the land lost. In addition, a feudal lord could not deny the tenure of the feudal tenant and was obliged to guarantee the peaceful possession of the tenant. In return for the landholding rights held by the tenant, he paid services and incidents to the lord. Services were the obligations one had to perform as part of the tenure and as such they were ongoing. Incidents, on the other hand, were obligations imposed by the general law and triggered by particular events. The types of incident payable depended on which type of tenure an individual held and are considered below. [2–22]

---

[22] *The History of English Law before the Time of Edward I* (2nd ed, 1968, Cambridge, Cambridge University Press), vol 1, pp 314–16.

[23] Thorne, "English Feudalism and Estates in Land" (1959) 17 *Cambridge Law Journal* 93.

[24] Hudson, *Land, Law and Lordship in Anglo-Norman England* (1994, Oxford, Clarendon Press), pp 65–7.

[2–23] Each of the various forms of tenure filled very different roles. Unfree tenure, known as "villienage", mainly ensured that menial tasks and labour were completed within the manor, whereas the four types of free tenure ensured that less menial but equally important roles were filled within the feudal pyramid. Military needs were guaranteed by knight's service, spiritual welfare was provided for by frankalmoign and divine service, serjeanty secured personal officials and services for the king, and the land was cultivated through "socage" in combination with villienage. Each type is considered by descending status.

1. Knight's Service

[2–24] Knight's service required the tenant to go to battle for the king and to bring a specified number of knights with him. This was a precarious way of raising an army, for it resulted in various feudal tenants cultivating "mini-armies" that would then be made available to the king, but could just as easily be amalgamated and turned against him. As a result, the king commuted this service to a monetary payment known as scutage, or shield money, which he then used to hire mercenary soldiers. Scutage was a fixed monetary payment, which, with the development of the economic system, became practically worthless in time.

2. Frankalmoign and Divine Services

[2–25] Frankalmoign and divine services were the services paid by religious organisations where manors were subinfeudated to them. In reality, the tenure consisted of the saying of prayers or masses for the feudal lord, therefore the value of the services was not really quantifiable materially and the services were not generally enforceable in the king's courts.

3. Serjeanty

[2–26] Serjeanty, which was the provision of tenure, fell somewhere between knight's service and socage, although it has always been difficult to tell exactly where the distinction between the three lay. In basic terms serjeanty involved the fulfilment of certain tasks, oftentimes quite menial, for the king or feudal lord. There was no real commonality to the kinds of tasks that might be included: they varied from providing a sword per year to holding the lord's arrows while he hunted and tending to his injured animals. Despite involving the performance of tasks that were often quite menial in nature, serjeanty was considered an honour. It was inalienable and indivisible, but it was also inheritable—much like many of the higher aristocratic positions in a number of monarchical systems.

4. Socage

[2–27] Essentially, all free tenures that were neither military nor spiritual in nature were known as socage, the most frequent form of which was "common socage". In general this consisted of the provision of labour on the feudal lord's land. *Petit socage* was also popular and comprised the provision of goods to the feudal lord.

5. Villienage

[2–28] Villienage was the general form of tenure and the social class of unfree tenants. It consisted mostly of the provision of physical labour on the feudal lord's land. Unfree tenants were, as the name suggests, conceived of as bound to the land. In other words, they came with the land, were transferred with the land, and were not free to leave the land at will. Because the villien did not have seisin, there was no remedy available in cases of ejectment or violation: this was part and parcel of one's social status. Over time, however, the king's courts began to recognise villiens as holders of a protectable kind of tenure and to provide real remedies in cases of ejectment. As a result of this, the practice was developed of entering a record of remedies and proceedings relating to villiens in the manor rolls. A copy of this entry would be provided to the villien and could be used as proof of the villien's entitlement to the land. In time this practice resulted in villienage becoming known as "copyhold tenure".

VII. Incidents

As already mentioned, incidents were triggered by certain events, such as death, a celebration in the lord's family, etc. The types of incident one was bound to perform depended on the type of tenure enjoyed. The more important types of incident for this book's purposes are: [2–29]

1. Homage and Fealty

The concept of loyalty to one's lord was central to the feudal system and was manifested, in the first place, in the notion of homage and fealty. The homage ceremony varied to some extent depending on individual circumstances, but in general J Russell Major's description is a good one: [2–30]

> [T]he vassal, without sword, belt or spurs, knelt bareheaded, placed his joined hands between those of his lord, and declared that he was the lord's man in return for a specified [landholding]. The lord then kissed the vassal on the mouth and said that he took him as his man. Fealty consisted of the vassal taking an oath of fidelity, most frequently upon the Gospels.[25]

Although homage and fealty were separate incidents, they were performed at the same time in the case of what is known as "military tenure", but all other tenants performed fealty only.

2. Suit of Court

Freeholders generally owed a suit of court to their lords.[26] On each manor there was a court.[27] Unfree tenants were bound to attend the court whenever it was held: the [2–31]

[25] Major, "Bastard Feudalism and the Kiss: Changing Social Mores in Late Medieval and Early Modern France" (1987) 27(3) *Journal of Interdisciplinary History* 509 at 509–10.

[26] As a matter of interest it ought to be noted that some historians dispute the classification of "suit of court" as an incident of tenure and claim instead that it "had become a burden on specific lands; and that when the number of freeholders was increased by subsequent subinfeudation the number of suitors was not thereby increased". See Maitland, "The Suitors of the County Court" (1888) 3(11) *The English Historical Review* 417.

[27] In fact, there were two courts—one for freeholders and one for unfree tenants—but we are concerned here with the freeholders' court.

Statute of Marlborough 1267[28] provided that in the case of a free tenant, the number of required attendances would have to be specified.

3. Primogeniture

[2–32] In some types of tenure the death of the tenant resulted in the inheritance of the tenure by the eldest male heir or, if there were no male heirs, all of the female heirs together in a type of co-ownership known as coparcenary.

4. Relief

[2–33] When a tenure was being inherited, the heir was required to pay a kind of inheritance tax, known as a relief, to the feudal lord. One's inheritance was therefore conditional on fulfilment of this relief obligation, which was a substantial source of income for feudal lords.

5. Wardship and Marriage

[2–34] Where the tenant's heir was underage (which, at the time, meant under 21 years for men and under 16 years for women), his tenurial rights were suspended until he reached the age of majority. The feudal lord was entitled to enjoy all of the income and profits from the land for as long as the infancy lasted, but was also required to take custody of the infant heir's body and to provide at least some kind of rudimentary maintenance. Thus, "[f]eudal guardianship was two-fold: guardianship of the land and guardianship of the body".[29]

[2–35] With this came the profitable and socially important right of "proposing" a marriage to the ward (i.e. the infant heir). If the ward refused to marry the person proposed, a fine became payable. If the ward consented to the marriage, the lord received a payment from the proposed spouse or her family. Once the ward reached the age of majority, he was entitled to have the lord ousted from the land and take over the tenure himself; this right was known as *ousterlemain*.[30]

[2–36] If, however, the tenant who died was a tenant-in-chief, then an incident known as *primer seisin* was triggered. In this case an inquest would be held to determine who the heir of the deceased tenant actually was and, while this was going on, the king was entitled to the right to the land (*primer seisin*). In essence, this process allowed the king to exercise considerable discretion as to whom he would recognise as the heir and thereby to maintain political control over who acquired the status of tenant-in-chief.[31]

---

[28] 52 Hen 3.

[29] Walker, "Violence and the Exercise of Feudal Guardianship: The Action of *Ejectio Custodia*" (1972) 16(4) *American Journal of Legal History* 320 at 320.

[30] The concept of *ousterlemain* is sometimes referred to as "suing out your livery", which Rushton explains as follows: "When the male heir arrived to the age of twenty-one, or the heir female to that of sixteen, they might *sue out their livery*, or *ousterlemain*, that is the delivery of their hands out of their guardian's hands. For this they were obliged to pay a fine, namely, half-a-year's profits of the land." Rushton, *Shakespeare: A Lawyer* (1858, 1918, New York, Harvard Press), p 27.

[31] On *primer seisin* see further McGlynn, *The Royal Prerogative and the Learning of the Inns of Court* (2003, Cambridge, Cambridge University Press), esp. Chapter 1.

6. Aid

Aid was a system by which a feudal lord could levy an occasional tax on a tenant in order to fund a specific event or serve a particular financial need. The arbitrary nature of aid soon resulted in it being confined to the limited situations of a son becoming a knight, or a daughter being married.[32] [2–37]

7. Escheat

Escheat was the means by which the tenurial relationship between lord and tenant was terminated and the lord thus became entitled to whatever the tenant had previously enjoyed, be it the holding of the land or the seignory from those to whom the tenant had subinfeudated. [2–38]

There were a number of reasons why escheat might be triggered, but most commonly it resulted from a defect in the blood (*escheat propter defectum sanguinis*), or misconduct (*escheat propter delictum tenentis*). Dying without an heir was considered a defect in the blood and resulted in the tenant's entitlements returning to the feudal lord. In this context misconduct meant being convicted of a felony. Felonies were defined as offences against public order, with the public represented by the king who would become entitled to seisin over the land for a year and a day, following which it returned to the feudal lord of the felonious tenant. [2–39]

8. Forfeiture

Forfeiture arose when a feudal tenant committed treason. The result of this was that the king became entitled to the land forever and all feudal relationships between the king and the treasonous tenant were destroyed. [2–40]

VIII. Decline of the Feudal System

Modern Irish property law features some elements that have descended from feudalism, but it could not, by any stretch of the imagination, be described as a feudal system. This is because feudalism declined slowly, through a combination of law and circumstance, to the point where it is no longer in existence in a formal sense. [2–41]

The starting point for the decline of feudalism was the feudal lords' dissatisfaction with the extent to which their feudal tenants were fragmenting their property through alienation in subinfeudation. This was a particular problem in relation to incidents, the value of which was dictated by the size of the landholding of a feudal tenant. If a vassal's landholding reduced in size, then, by logical extension, the value of incidents assessed by the size of the landholding would also decrease. Near the end of the feudal period people also began to recognise land as a valuable commodity in itself. In other words, people began to realise that land was worth more than what it could produce; it had an inherent value. As a result, the concept of selling landholding rights through substitution became particularly common, again resulting in loss of income for feudal lords. The *Magna Carta* 1215 reformed the extent to which feudal tenants could engage in this fragmentation and forbade alienation that was so extensive as to result in the retained land being insufficient to raise the services and incidents owed to the feudal [2–42]

[32] *Magna Carta* 1215.

lord. It was, however, a later and much more radical statute that instigated the substantive decline of feudalism: *Quia Emptores* 1290.

[2–43] The *Quia Emptores* had four main provisions that are important to our consideration of property law:

(a) it prohibited subinfeudation in the fee simple, i.e. it forbade the creation of subordinate feudal relationships that would last forever;
(b) it granted all free tenants the right to substitute without the consent of their lord, i.e. it introduced, in practical terms, the notion that landholders should be as free as possible to deal with their property;
(c) it required people to ensure that where land was divided, by partial substitution for example, the services and incidents on the land were divided proportionately;
(d) it provided that substitution was to be the only mechanism of transferring land, i.e. there were to be no more transfers in mortmain.

The importance of the *Quia Emptores* cannot be overstated. It created a philosophical foundation for property law that remains in place to this day, namely that landholders ought to be as free to deal with their property as is possible in the circumstances of organised society. This concept of not being unduly restrained in one's alienation of property rights is known as the Principle of Alienability and is one of the most important legacies of the feudal period to modern Irish property law.

[2–44] Although the *Quia Emptores* did apply in Ireland, from the beginning exceptions to its operation in this country were recognised, usually for reasons of political expediency. The most used exception resulted from the fact that the Act did not apply to the crown[33]: in other words the crown could subinfeudate in fee simple and create new feudal relationships unrestricted by the *Quia Emptores.* As noted shortly, this was common practice during the Plantations of Ireland.

[2–45] *Quia Emptores* contributed to the decline of the feudal system in two ways. First, it sharply restricted those situations in which perpetual feudal relationships could be created because it prohibited subinfeudation in the fee simple. As subinfeudation was the way in which the subordinate layers of the feudal pyramid were created, restricting subinfeudation necessarily restricted the growth of the feudal pyramid. Combined with incidents such as escheat and forfeiture by which feudal relationships were terminated, this resulted in the eventual shrinkage of the feudal pyramid.

[2–46] Secondly, by giving free tenants the right to substitute their lands freely, i.e. without their lord's consent, the *Quia Emptores* reduced some of the practical control feudal lords had over (a) who their feudal tenants would be and (b) in a more fundamental sense, how the feudal pyramid would develop. In the end, most people became tenants-in-chief and the political power became completely centralised at the top of the pyramid. This resulted in a necessary inconsistency, however: while political power became centralised in the king, economic power became decentralised in all free tenants. It was this tension that ultimately resulted in the end of absolutist monarchy in the United Kingdom and the creation of a parliamentary system. One of the first

[33] See, for example, *Verschoyle v Perkins* (1847) 13 IR Eq R 72.

actions within the parliamentary system was to attempt to abolish feudal principles of property law resulting (after something of a legislative saga[34]) in the Tenures Abolition (Ireland) Act 1662.

The Tenures Abolition (Ireland) Act 1662 did exactly what its title suggests: it abolished most forms of tenure[35] and incidents[36] and provided that any remaining or future tenures be free and common socage.[37] The importance of this provision is immense because it is through this Act, combined with the *Quia Emptores*, that the right to alienate property rights became widespread. The *Quia Emptores*, as noted, gave all free tenants the right to substitute without the consent of their feudal lord: under the Tenures Abolition (Ireland) Act, *all* tenants became free tenants and therefore had the right to substitute freely. **[2–47]**

Remaining incidents gradually became obsolete or were abolished by subsequent legislation. Thus, suit of court was not abolished by the 1662 Act but became obsolete on the ultimate demise of manor courts with the Copyhold Act 1841. Reliefs were preserved by the Act but as, under the Statute of Wills (Ireland) 1634, no relief was payable where land rights were left by will, these reliefs became obsolete in practice. Forfeiture for treason was abolished by the Forfeiture Act 1870. **[2–48]**

The final step in the abolition of feudalism and tenure came with the Land and Conveyancing Law Reform Act 2009, which is separately considered below. Notwithstanding the slow but steady decline of feudalism, culminating in the 2009 Act, we must bear in mind that our modern system of property law retains some principles and features that descend from this system. **[2–49]**

IX. The Residue of Feudalism

It is a remarkable fact that a significant amount of the fundamental principles of modern Irish property law can be traced back to feudal times.[38] The penultimate task of this chapter is to outline some of the more prominent features of the relationship between modern property law and the feudal landholding system. **[2–50]**

1. Estates

As outlined above, the feudal system conceived of only one owner of land in anything close to absolute terms, and that was the king. Although his ownership was really a manifestation of sovereignty, it resulted in the concept that, in relation to land, other people could only be entitled to rights for a period of time. In some cases that period of **[2–51]**

---

34 This process was begun by a resolution of the Irish parliament in 1641, resulting ultimately in the Act for Taking Away the Court of Wards and Liveries 1656, which was re-enacted in Irish terms, for political reasons, in the Tenures Abolition (Ireland) Act 1662.

35 Serjeanty and frankalmoign were not affected by the Act.

36 Homage, fealty, aids and wardship were abolished by this Act.

37 s 3 converted any remaining knight's service to free and common socage; only tenures in free and common socage could be created in the future, including by the crown.

38 In a similar vein, and writing in 2004, the Law Reform Commission remarked that it "is remarkable that much of our current law stems from the introduction of the Normal feudal system of land ownership". *Consultation Paper on the Reform and Modernisation of Land Law and Conveyancing Law* (2004, Dublin, Law Reform Commission), p 9.

time was "forever", or at least "potentially forever", and in some cases it was for life or for as long as a bloodline continued to exist. What is material is that it was through this concept of landholding, as opposed to land "owning" (in an absolutist sense of the word), that the basic building-block of modern property law developed: the estate. Estates are considered in full in Chapter 4 and have been significantly reformed by the Land and Conveyancing Law Reform Act 2009, but for now it is sufficient to have an awareness of their existence and connection to the feudal system.

[2–52] Rather than "owning land", as we might commonly consider ourselves to do, Irish property law conceives of people as having rights over land for a certain period of time. The king, of course, no longer has sovereign entitlement to all land in Ireland. However, the State might be said to have this ultimate entitlement as a result of the provisions of s 73 of the Succession Act 1965, which deems the State the ultimate intestate successor of land. In other words, if someone dies without having distributed landholding rights by means of a valid will and does not have any next-of-kin, the rights over the land transfer to the State.[39]

2. Freehold and Leasehold

[2–53] The concept of freehold emerged through the combined effects of the *Quia Emptores* and the Tenures Abolition (Ireland) Act 1662. As considered above, *Quia Emptores* gave all free tenants the right to substitute without the consent of their lord, whereas the 1662 Act extended the classification of free tenant to all those in possession of tenure. These people became known as freeholders.

[2–54] In contrast, the concept of leasehold also developed. Leaseholds would arise when tenure-holders entered into what was originally a purely personal contractual relationship with another, whereby that other was entitled to hold the land specified in the agreement. This was not a tenurial relationship and therefore the rules of the tenurial system did not apply to it. Instead, the terms of the relationship were those of the agreement between the parties themselves. In the normal course of events the contract resulted in one of the parties having the right to use and occupy defined land in return for rent. These relationships were said to be purely contractual because the "tenant" did not have any estate in the land nor the capacity to bring a real action for infringement. As outlined in Chapter 1, this position gradually changed in the 17th century when the courts began to allow lessees to bring an action for a real remedy in respect of their contracts. Over time these leasehold arrangements have been recognised as giving rise to rights and obligations on the part of both parties and to a kind of estate. The modern leasehold relationship is considered in full in Chapter 15.

3. Principle of Alienability

[2–55] As considered above, the *Quia Emptores*, in conjunction with the Tenures Abolition (Ireland) Act 1662, firmly entrenched the Principle of Alienability in Irish property law. This fundamental principle can be summed up in the notion that landowners ought to be as free to dispose of their property as is reasonably possible. Of course, as considered in Chapter 1, there are restraints on this freedom for punitive, protective and social reasons, but in general terms the principle remains paramount.

[39] See further Chapter 16, "Succession".

The rule applies to freeholders as opposed to leaseholders and is an expression of autonomy and of market values. Freeholders should be able to alienate their property rights freely, not only in recognition of their autonomy in relation to the property rights in question, but also because the market demands it. Land is a valuable commodity. In fact, in the "boom" years we saw that property was one of the main drivers of the Irish economy and, even more recently, has become one of the main difficulties in ensuring economic stability. While there are significant limits to this principle, its fundamentality to the modern property law regime ought not be underestimated and it is preserved in the Land and Conveyancing Law Reform Act 2009.[40] **[2–56]**

4. Feudal Fee Farm Grant

As considered above, the *Quia Emptores* did not prevent the crown from subinfeudating in the fee simple in Ireland. This was particularly common during the Plantations of Ireland when the crown subinfeudated to supporters in Ireland by letters patent. The original recipients were obliged to pay a chief rent, known as a quit rent, to the crown, but they also received the right to subinfeudate *non obstante Quia Emptores* (i.e. notwithstanding the prohibition on subinfeudation in the fee simple contained in *Quia Emptores*). These loyal subjects could therefore subinfeudate and create feudal pyramids in Ireland hundreds of years after they had begun to disappear in England. In some circumstances current landholders can trace their rights back to a feudal grant. These fee farm grants created a feudal relationship of lord and tenant. The feudal tenant is obliged to pay a rent service to the feudal lord and this obligation extends to the successors in title of the feudal tenant. Feudal fee farm grants are considered in Chapter 4. **[2–57]**

X. Impact of the Land and Conveyancing Law Reform Act 2009

One of the reasons why the Law Reform Commission described the basic foundation of modern property law on the feudal system at the beginning of the 21st century as "remarkable" was that such a system—based as it was on the idea of owing honour and service to a feudal lord—is difficult to reconcile with the founding principles of a constitutional democracy such as Ireland. In a constitutional democracy one expects that our social, economic and political systems of ordering (such as the law of property) would recognise and reflect the social contractarian and, in Ireland, republican nature of the State's relationship with the people. It therefore ought to come as no surprise that one of the first tasks of the Land and Conveyancing Law Reform Act 2009 was to abolish the system of feudalism and tenure, inasmuch as it persisted in doctrinal terms. In this respect, s 9(2) of the 2009 Act provides: "In so far as it survives, feudal tenure is abolished". The Act both replaces the feudal foundations of Irish property law with a statutory, democratic foundation (the Act), and leaves landlord and tenant law untouched.[41] Ownership of land is now governed by the law of estates as reformed by the Act,[42] and all feudal incidents have been excised from the law.[43] **[2–58]**

[40] s 9(4), Land and Conveyancing Law Reform Act 2009.
[41] Leasehold is dealt with in Chapter 15.
[42] Estates are dealt with in Chapter 4.
[43] s 10(2), Land and Conveyancing Law Reform Act 2009.

[2–59] The abolition of feudal tenure in the 2009 Act cleared the way for the repeal of a number of pieces of legislation that had long been on the statute books. Among them, and important in the context of this chapter, were the Forfeiture Act (Ireland) 1639, the Tenures Abolition Act (Ireland) 1662, the Copyhold Acts 1843–1887 and the *Quia Emptores* 1290.[44] Given the importance of *Quia Emptores*, emphasised in earlier paragraphs, its repeal may initially strike the reader as being somewhat surprising. However, the repeal of the Act did not constitute the repeal of either the fee simple (which we saw was influenced by the *Quia Emptores*) or the principle of alienability (which emerged from the Act). Both the fee simple[45] and the principle of alienability[46] are retained by the Land and Conveyancing Law Reform Act 2009, but again their retention through modern legislation gives them a sound, democratic footing in theoretical terms. The fee simple, the principle of alienability and the feudal fee farm grant are all considered in Chapter 4.

[2–60] The impact of the Land and Conveyancing Law Reform Act 2009 on feudalism and tenure might be dismissed as being nothing more than an exercise in "cleaning up" and symbolism. Of course, in part it is right to say that the Act was engaged in "cleaning up" by "finishing the job" that had begun many centuries ago in terms of bringing feudalism to an end. Cleaning up, in this sense, is, however, not an unimportant task. Property law—as we will discover while we progress through this book—is sometimes complex and the existence of arcane rules and statutes did not help in cutting through that complexity in either the study or the practice of law. That is not to suggest that simply because a rule or a law is particularly old it ought not to be retained, but in the case of feudalism and tenure we were faced with not only "old" law but law whose foundations were inconsistent with the nature of the Irish constitutional State. Thus, while moving from a feudal system to a system where we retain estates and alienability through statutory provisions might seem superficial at first, its resonance is significant and ought not to go unappreciated.

---

[44] Schedule 2, *ibid.*

[45] s 11, *ibid.*

[46] s 9(4), *ibid.*

CHAPTER 3
Equitable Principles in Land

The concept of acting equitably is a familiar one in everyday life, where "equitable behaviour" is generally perceived of as behaviour that is fair, or just, or conscionable. While the legal meaning of equity is by no means as vague or as broad as this, the law of equity does have a long-standing connection to the concept of acting "fairly" and in accordance with the exigencies of the case before it (as opposed to acting in accordance with the strict application of formal, rigid rules to whatever someone's circumstances might be). As the materials below will make clear, this does not mean that equity is an entirely unpredictable area of law: rules have been developed and are applied, but always with an eye to the equitable (or "just") resolution of the circumstances at hand. **[3–01]**

[3–02] From the perspective of property law, the law of equity has made an immense contribution to the development of three of the most important central features in this field: equitable interests, trusts and notice. Throughout this chapter the focus will be to highlight these legal developments and principles and to become familiar with how equitable interests actually work.

I. Development of Equity as a Body of Law

[3–03] In medieval times the chancellor was an important member of the king's court. Usually an ecclesiastical minister of some kind[1] (most often a cardinal), the chancellor was the king's primary advisor; his "prime minister", in a sense.[2] Although the king's courts had significant judicial functions, they were not equipped to deal with absolutely every case that came before them, did not always provide appropriate remedies, and were not available to villiens. For freeholders, who had access to the king's courts, the fact that they could not hear a case for which there was no appropriate writ or where there was a procedural breach was particularly problematic. All was not lost for people who had a dispute that could not, or would not, be heard by the king's courts, for the king had residual judicial power. In other words, the king had the capacity to hear disputes upon which the courts would not, or could not, adjudicate. In practice, the function of issuing new writs or, if necessary, "doing justice" where the courts did not, would fall to a large extent to the office of the chancellor (instead of being exercised directly by the king). The chancellor would make his decisions based on "the effect produced upon his own individual sense of right and wrong by the merits of the particular case before him".[3] Over time, rules and principles were developed by which the chancellor would carry out this role and these functions expanded to a "Court of Chancery". The law that developed in this way is known as the law of equity.[4]

II. The Use

[3–04] From the perspective of property law, equity's most important contribution may well have been the recognition of the use. The use was a device employed in transfers of land and designed, in the main, to avoid certain incidents (particularly the incidents that arose on death)[5] and to circumvent a number of strict common law rules pertaining to inheritance and transfer of land. The basic concept of the use was that land rights would be transferred to someone who would be instructed to hold the land to the use of (or for the benefit of) another person. The issue for law and for equity was whether or not the person to whose benefit the property was said to be held had any kind of enforceable rights against the person to whom the land was actually transferred.

[3–05] The common law would only recognise the rights of the person to whom the land-ownership rights had been transferred; after all, he was now the "owner" of the land. Equity, on the other hand, was concerned with the importance of fulfilling the intention of the transferor, and the terms of the use made it very clear that the transferor wanted the land to be held for someone else's benefit. Thus, while equity

[1] The office was secularised under Queen Elizabeth I.
[2] Maitland, *Equity* (2nd ed, 1936), p 3.
[3] Martin, *Hanbury and Martin: Modern Equity* (16th ed, 2001, London, Sweet & Maxwell), p 7.
[4] For a more detailed history of the law of equity, see, for example, Martin, *ibid.*, Chapter 1.
[5] See further Chapter 2, paras 2–29 to 2–40.

would recognise that the person to whom the land was given was the "owner" in legal terms, it would also recognise that the person to whose benefit the land was to be held had enforceable rights. In practice this meant that the person to whom the land had been transferred was required to give all of the benefit of that land to the person who was intended to receive that benefit by the terms of the disposition itself. Take the following scenario as an example: "My house Willow Cottage to Patrick to the use of Sally." While both the common law and equity recognised that Patrick was the owner of Willow Cottage, equity also recognised that Sally was entitled to the benefit of Willow Cottage and would compel Patrick to ensure that she received it. The person who received the land was known as the *feoffee to uses* (feoffee), while the person to whose benefit the land was to be held was known as the *cestui que use* (cestui). Thus, in the example above, Patrick is the feoffee and Sally is the cestui.

Over time the chancellor developed a number of important principles relating to uses. **[3–06]** The first was to say that anyone who acquired the land-ownership from the feoffee would have to take his place, in other words, he would be required to respect the beneficial rights of the cestui. In 1483 it was decided that heirs of the feoffee were also to be bound by the use.[6] In 1466 the Chancellor declared that a purchaser from the feoffee would be bound by the use (i.e. have to respect it) where the purchaser had express notice of it.[7] This principle was further developed into the doctrine of notice, which is considered in more detail below. Secondly, equity began to intervene to treat parties as if they held property under a use where the justice of the case demanded it. This was the forerunner of the constructive trust, which is further considered later in this chapter. Thirdly, equity decided that the cestui could not be said to have a greater estate than the feoffee (i.e. the cestui may not have entitlements that lasted for a longer period of time than those of the feoffee).

1. The Statute of Uses (Ireland) 1634

In 1535 Henry VIII promulgated the Statute of Uses. The passage of the Statute was **[3–07]** quite a struggle, as it undermined almost entirely the utility of the use for ordinary people in favour of effective income generation on the part of the king. In the words of Maitland, the Statute was "forced upon an extremely unwilling Parliament by an extremely strong-willed king"[8] and some 100 years later was transposed into Irish law by the Statute of Uses (Ireland) 1634. The effect of the Statute was to "execute" the use, which meant to "take" the legal ownership from the feoffee and "vest" it in the cestui. Thus, as a result of execution, the feoffee would be left with no ownership and the cestui would have legal and equitable ownership. This can be illustrated by the following example:

> "My house *Willow Cottage* to Patrick to the use of Sally."
> Feoffee—Patrick; legal rights
> Cestui—Sally; equitable rights

[6] YB Pasch 22 Edw IV f4 pl 18.
[7] YB Mich 5 Edw IV f7 pl 16.
[8] Maitland, *Equity* (2nd ed, 1936), p 34; for more on the history and political significance of the Statute of Uses, see Ives, "The Genesis of the Statute of Uses" (1967) 82 *English Historical Review* 673.

Use executed by the Statute of Uses
Feoffee—Patrick; no rights
Cestui—Sally; legal and equitable rights

[3–08] The purpose of executing the use in this way was to prevent its successful deployment as a means of avoiding feudal incidents and to ensure that the flow of resources up the pyramid towards the king was restored.[9] It ought to be noted that there were a limited number of situations in which the use could not be executed by the Statute of Uses. These exceptions resulted mostly from the recognition that there were certain commercial advantages to the operation of the use in limited circumstances. Thus, the Statute of Uses would not operate if the use was leasehold (i.e. said to operate for a specified number of years), if the feoffee was seised to his own use (i.e. the feoffee and cestui were the same person), if the feoffee was a corporation, or if the feoffee had active duties to perform (known as an active use). In all other circumstances the use was executed, resulting in the feoffee having no rights over the property and the cestui having rights both in law and in equity.

2. Particular Applications of the Statute of Uses

[3–09] There were two perhaps unanticipated applications of the Statute of Uses recognised by equity. The first related to gratuitous transfers of land, i.e. land transferred in return for no consideration. In such cases, equity would presume that the transferor did not intend to transfer all legal and equitable rights for no consideration and would imply a use in favour of the transferor (i.e. consider the transferee the feoffee and the transferor the cestui). The Statute of Uses would then execute that use, meaning that the parties would be returned to their original positions.

Fionn transfers *Willow Cottage* to Pat for no consideration by the disposition, "To Pat in fee simple."
Equity presumes that Fionn intended to retain some ownership of the property as he did not receive any consideration, therefore reads the disposition as "To Pat in fee simple *to the use of Fionn in fee simple.*"
Feoffee – Pat; legal rights
Cestui – Fionn; equitable rights
Use executed by the Statute of Uses
Feoffee – Pat; no rights
Cestui – Fionn; legal and equitable rights

As this operated on the basis of a presumption, its operation could be rebutted by evidence of a contrary intention, which explains why—for example—one will often see property transferred for no financial consideration but in recognition of one's "natural love and affection" for the transferee, especially where a parent is giving property to a child. In addition, one could merely include words in the disposition that would pre-empt and rebut any such presumption. The presumption of advancement is also an important consideration here, and is dealt with later in this chapter.[10]

[9] See Chapter 2.
[10] paras 3–22 to 3–27.

The second particular application arose where the feoffee was given rights in a greater estate than the cestui (i.e. for a longer period of time than the cestui).[11] In such cases the feoffee would be left with nothing, but the cestui could acquire only a legal enlargement of the estate granted, therefore the grantor would receive the "residual" rights in remainder. **[3–10]**

3. The Double Use

As is usually the case, the people were somewhat aggravated by the king's successful introduction of an Act that prevented them from avoiding their "taxes" in the form of feudal incidents. As a result, people attempted to develop an alternative mechanism of splitting the rights between a legal and equitable holder and, by so doing, to circumvent unpalatable common law rules and feudal duties. The mechanism chosen was the double use (also known as "the use upon a use"). In essence, a double use is merely the conflation of two uses, as follows: "To Bob to the Use of Sam to the Use of Tom." ="To Bob to the Use of Sam; to Sam to the Use of Tom". **[3–11]**

The difficulty for equity was in coming to some kind of decision as to what impact, if any, the Statute of Uses would have on this double use. Prior to the introduction of the Statute of Uses, it had been held that in such a case the second use was void.[12] Thus, in the example above, Sam would have the legal and equitable rights; Bob would have nothing because of the execution of the first use; and Tom would have nothing because the second use was void. Shortly after the promulgation of the English Statute of Uses, this principle was upheld in *Jane Tyrell's Case*.[13] It was not until later[14] that the courts reconsidered their position on the double use. It was then established that the use upon a use would be enforced, so that the feoffee of the second use would be said to have legal rights, and the cestui of the second use would be said to have equitable rights (the first use, remember, would have been executed by the Statute of Uses so that the feoffee of the first use would have nothing). Thus, applying this to our example, Sam would have legal rights, Tom would have equitable rights and Bob would have nothing. This is the genesis of the modern trust, which is often defined as "a use upon a use" or a double use. In more precise terms, one might say that a trust is a double use where the first use has been executed and the second use has been allowed to run unfettered by the Statute of Uses. **[3–12]**

Thus, if someone wished to transfer land to Simon and have him hold it to the Use of Mary (or for her benefit), that person simply had to find someone willing to step into the conveyance, perhaps for a nominal compensation, and create a double use. Imagine that Deirdre is the volunteer and the conveyance takes the form: "16 Butterfield Park to Deirdre in fee simple to the Use of Simon in fee simple, to the Use of Mary in fee simple." Because of the application of the Statute of Uses, Deirdre receives nothing, **[3–13]**

[11] Estates are considered in full in Chapter 4.

[12] *Dillan v Frain* (1595) 1 and 309 at 313; *Corbet's Case* (1600) 2 and 134 at 136.

[13] (1557) Dyer 155a. For an interesting account see Ames, "Tyrell's Case and Modern Trusts" (1892) 4 *Green Bag* 81.

[14] *Sambach v Dalston* (1634) Tothill 188 has long been thought of as the first authority for this, however, there is evidence of earlier enforcement of a similar position. See Baker, "The Use Upon a Use in Equity 1558–1625" (1977) 93 *Law Quarterly Review* 33.

and Simon receives the legal rights but holds the land for the benefit of Mary. Over time the wording was modified to read, "Unto and to the Use of Simon in trust for Mary", with "unto and to the Use of..." indicating an executed use.

4. Repeal of the Statute of Uses

[3–14] Although it may seem that the material so far is primarily of historical interest only, the use and the Statute of Uses were in fact important devices within property law until the passage of the Land and Conveyancing Law Reform Act 2009 when the Statute of Uses (Ireland) 1634 was repealed. Up until that point we continued to employ uses in order to circumvent some inconvenient or difficult rules of property law, such as the traditional prohibition on the transfer of property to oneself.[15] The 2009 Act repeals the Statute of Uses (Ireland) 1634[16] and, indeed, introduces specific provisions to deal with discrete situations where the Statute of Uses might previously have operated.[17]

[3–15] The first implication of the repeal of the Statute of Uses that concerns us here relates to gratuitous transfers. As considered above, where property was transferred for no consideration we previously presumed that, unless a contrary intention was shown, the transferor intended to maintain the benefit for himself and therefore implied a resulting use that was executed by the Statute of Uses. That presumption has not existed in relation to registered land since the introduction of s 123(3), Registration of Title Act 1964 and is now also undone in relation to unregistered land. In this respect, s 62(3) of the Land and Conveyancing Law Reform Act 2009 provides that "a resulting use to a grantor is not implied merely because the land is not expressed to be conveyed for the use or benefit of the grantee". Thus, if one wants to ensure that a resulting trust will arise one must include words to that effect; in other words, legislative change has ensured that where gratuitous transfers are concerned we will now presume that the grantee was to receive *both* the legal and equitable ownership unless a contrary intention is shown.

[3–16] As mentioned above, it was previously the case that one could not transfer legal rights in property to oneself. This caused some frequent and very real difficulties for people in their everyday transactions in relation to land. Take, for example, the rather common scenario where someone who previously purchased a piece of land later decides to transfer the property to herself and her partner in co-ownership. In those scenarios one

---

[15] While it may seem that one would not want to transfer property to oneself, this rule has in fact always been very problematic where people wanted to transfer property to oneself in co-ownership with another such as, for example, where a person who has property decides to transfer it into the co-ownership of herself and her partner.

[16] Schedule 2, Part 1, Land and Conveyancing Law Reform Act 2009.

[17] In this chapter I deal with only two implications of repeal: previously implied resulting trusts and transfers to oneself. The impact of the Act on the reservation of easements is considered in Chapter 12. The repeal is also of importance in relation to the older notion of bargain and sale, covenants to stand seised, and powers—none of which are dealt with in this book as they do not tend to form substantial parts of the average undergraduate syllabus. However, an explanation of the changes introduced in these contexts can be found in Maddox, *Land and Conveyancing Law Reform Act 2009: A Commentary* (2010, Dublin, Round Hall), pp 101–102, considering s 62, relating to bargain and sale (s 62(1)) and covenants to stand seised (s 62.4); and 54–58, considering Part 6 on powers.

previously used a feoffment to uses. This is no longer necessary under the 2009 Act; not only is the Statute of Uses repealed, but s 66(1) provides that "any property may be conveyed by a person to that person jointly with another person in the same way in which it might be conveyed by that person to another person". Furthermore s 66(2)(a) provides that "a person may convey, but not lease, property to that same person in a different capacity".[18]

III. The Trust

The trust is the modern equivalent of the use inasmuch as it is the mechanism by which [3–17] ownership rights are split between two entities, transferring legal rights to one and requiring that individual to hold the land to the benefit of (or on trust for) the other, who in turn is said to have equitable rights. The trust has many important functions within property law, including arranging ownership in a manner that reduces tax liability, doing justice, recognising people's financial contribution to the purchase of property and so on. For the purposes of clarity, it is important to outline the operation of and terminology used within the trust mechanism.

	Use	Trust
Legal Rights	Feoffee	Trustee
Equitable Rights	Cestui	Beneficiary

Detailed consideration of all types of trust is beyond the purview of this book and is, in any case, dealt with exceptionally in other core texts,[19] however, it is worth considering express, constructive, and resulting trusts briefly, together with an important evidentiary principle that applies in this context: the presumption of advancement.

1. Express Trusts

Express trusts are expressly created by the settler. In order to create an express trust [3–18] what are known as the "Three Certainties" must be present. These are the certainty of intention (the intention to create a trust), certainty of subject matter (clarity as to what is be the subject of the trust), and certainty of objects (certainty as to who the beneficiaries of the trust are).

2. Constructive Trusts

The constructive trust is imposed by equity where the justice of the case requires it, [3–19] even though a trust was neither expressly created nor within the intentions of the parties. The typical situation in which a constructive trust will be imposed by equity is where a trustee (who, as already seen, owes fiduciary duties towards the beneficiaries)

[18] The other standard situation in which one used a feoffment to uses in order to transfer property to oneself was where a fee tail was being disentailed. This is considered in detail in Chapter 4 but for now it is sufficient to note that the abolition of the fee tail by s 13 of the 2009 Act puts an end, in practical terms, to the disentailment of the fee tail.

[19] See especially Delany, *Equity and the Law of Trusts in Ireland* (5th ed, 2011, Dublin, Round Hall).

makes a personal profit from the trust fund.[20] While the constructive trust was originally thought to arise only in a limited number of situations, the contemporary view of the constructive trust conceives of it as a remedial concept that can be imposed in cases where the courts find its imposition justified. This newer view is certainly supported by the Irish courts[21] and will be considered in relation to estoppel in Chapter 10.

3. Resulting Trusts

[3–20] Resulting trusts are implied by equity in order to give effect to the implied intentions of the relevant parties. In the main, they are used to ensure that all those who contribute financially to the purchase of property have their contribution recognised as a share of ownership. Therefore, if a person contributes to the purchase of a property but is not recognised as a formal (i.e. legal) owner, then equity may imply the presumed resulting trust in order to ensure that the contributor acquires some ownership rights in equity. This would happen *unless* the transfer itself conveyed a contrary intention by, for example, including words expressing that the property was transferred in law and in equity to the transferee. Resulting trusts will generally arise in cases of gratuitous transfers and of unequal (and unrecognised) contributions to the acquisition of property, although s 62(3) of the Land and Conveyancing Law Reform Act 2009 provides that—for transactions done after the Act came into effect—a resulting trust will not arise "merely because the land is not expressed to be conveyed for the use or benefit of the grantee". In other words, where someone transfers land without expressing that the transferee is to acquire both the legal *and* the equitable rights over it, this will not give rise to a resulting trust on its own. Rather, some other additional evidence would be required to rebut the new presumption that the transferor did not intend to retain any rights over the property.

4. Presumption of Advancement

[3–21] As mentioned above,[22] prior to the introduction of the Land and Conveyancing Law Reform Act 2009 there was a general presumption that, where land was transferred gratuitously, the transferor would retain the equitable interest in the property by means of a resulting trust. This remains the case for voluntary conveyances executed before the 2009 Act came into effect.[23] In these circumstances, that presumption can be rebutted if a relationship existed between the transferor and the transferee of a nature that courts recognise as creating a moral obligation of support or provision between the parties.[24] In such a case what is known as the presumption of advancement operates (i.e. the presumption that the property was advanced gratuitously between the parties). As it operates on the basis of presumed intentions, the presumption of advancement can, of course, be rebutted by evidence that the parties did not intend for

[20] See, for example, *Keech v Sandford* (1726) Sel Cas Ch 61.
[21] See, for example, *NAD v TD* [1985] ILRM 153.
[22] paras 3–09 and 3–21.
[23] s 62(3), Land and Conveyancing Law Reform Act 2009.
[24] See, for example, *Bennet v Bennet* (1879) Ch D 474; *McCabe v Ulster Bank Limited* [1939] IR 1 at 9–15 *per* Murnaghan J; Breslin, "Survivorship Rights and Joint Deposit Accounts: *Lynch v AIB Bank PLC*" (1996) 3(1) *Commercial Law Practitioner* 12.

the equitable rights to be transferred.[25] The question of which relationships attract the presumption of advancement is not at all settled, and whatever conclusions can be drawn from the case law appear to suggest an approach that is at best anachronistic and perhaps more accurately described as sexist. Authority suggests that the presumption operates where a husband or father transfers property to a wife or child,[26] but probably not where a wife or mother transfers property to a husband or child.[27] Interestingly, the presumption will operate in the case of a transfer from a person acting *in loco parentis* to the child, regardless of the gender of the "parent". More recently, however, the Irish courts have indicated a willingness to pay closer attention to relevant factors that may rebut the presumption of advancement[28] or, indeed, may point to an intention of the parties that the presumption would operate within relationships to which it would not normally be attached.[29]

While the idea that someone might want to transfer property gratuitously without a resulting trust arising is not, in itself, terribly difficult to imagine or agree with, the presumption of advancement can be criticised on the basis that it communicates sexist and heterocentric conceptions of the nature of relationships. In this respect, the presumption assumes the masculinity of the "provider" role, as well as assuming that moral obligations arise only in the context of opposite-sex couples. These assumptions are no longer in line with the reality of Irish society, not only in an experiential sense but also, following the introduction of civil partnerships,[30] in the sense of the kinds of intimate, interdependent relationships recognised by the law. Whether or not the introduction of civil partnership will result in a broadening of the scope of the presumption of advancement—by broadening the range of relationships to which the presumption will be said to apply—remains to be seen. Although limiting the presumption of advancement to marriages, as opposed to other forms of intimate adult relationships, might suggest that the introduction of civil partnerships ought not to result in an undermining of the gendered nature of the presumption, the fact that civil partnerships are the only formal legal infrastructure available to same-sex couples (and operate in a manner that is extremely close to, though not the same as, marriage) suggests that there may be an expansion of the presumption of advancement beyond its traditional paradigm of male-to-female. Should there be a recognition that the presumption of advancement can operate as between two men or two women who are in a civil partnership with one another, there would appear to be essentially no reason to maintain a gendered presumption as it relates to opposite-sex couples. Equity certainly has the capacity to amend its doctrines to recognise changing social conditions, and it is quite possible that the gendered nature of the presumption could be essentially undone by recognising the fact that women now have more opportunities for the amassment of independent wealth than was the case when the presumption of advancement was originally developed. That, combined with the equal levels of affection women and men hold for their partners, together with women's equal moral **[3–22]**

---

[25] *Anson v Anson* [1953] 1 QB 636; *Re Gooch* (1890) 62 LT 384.

[26] *Talbot v Cody* IR 10 Eq 138; *In Re Hood* [1923] 1 IR 109.

[27] *Mercier v Mercier* [1903] 2 Ch 98; *Bennet v Bennet* (1879) 10 Ch D 474; *McCabe v Ulster Bank Limited* [1939] IR 1.

[28] *Walsh v Walsh* [1942] IR 403 at 407 *per* Gavin-Duffy J.

[29] *Lynch v Burke & AIB Bank* [1995] 2 IR 159.

[30] Civil Partnership and Certain Rights and Obligations of Cohabitants Act 2010.

obligation to support and provide for their partners, would provide a sound grounding for eroding the presumption's gendered nature as it applies between intimate adult partners.

[3–23] The presumption of advancement is also relevant to gratuitous transfers from parents to their children or to those for whom they are *in loco parentis*. In recent years a number of questions have arisen as to whether or not the presumption should apply only to transfers from fathers to children or also to maternal transfers, and furthermore whether it should apply to transfers from parents to adult children. Both of these questions arose for discussion in the Canadian decision of *Pecore v Pecore*.[31] This case concerned monies that had been deposited by a father in a joint account of himself and one of his children, who was the eldest of his children and had substantially less secure finances than the other children. Although this was a joint account, all deposits were lodged by the father, who managed the account, paid all taxes on it and so on. Upon his death, the father left certain specific bequests to his daughter but no mention was made of the joint account, which the daughter then took under the principle of survivorship (a principle that applies to a certain kind of co-ownership known as joint tenancy). In the course of a subsequent matrimonial dispute between this daughter and her husband a question as to the ownership of these monies arose, with the Court being asked to consider whether that money belonged to the daughter (under the presumption of advancement) or belonged properly to the deceased's estate. In the Supreme Court consideration was given to whether (a) the presumption of advancement still applied, and (b) if so, whether it could apply in relation to an adult child.

[3–24] In respect of the first question the Court held that the presumption of advancement did still operate as an equitable doctrine, acting as an evidentiary tool to assist courts in determining questions of equitable ownership where there had been gratuitous transfers between, *inter alia*, a parent and child. The Court held that the presumption was not limited to advancements between fathers and their children, but also applied to advancements between mothers and their children, especially given the modern reality that mothers may now have significant financial resources and, indeed, have equal levels of obligations to their children as do fathers.[32] However, the Court did not consider that the presumption of advancement should apply to gratuitous transfers to adult children. This conclusion was based on the Court's finding that the presumption of advancement was intended to enable the provision of support to dependent children, and that category certainly does not include *independent* adult children. As for dependent adult children, the Court was reluctant to find the principle presumptively applicable largely because of the difficulties of setting clear parameters for the concept of "dependence" in relation to adults. While evidence could certainly be adduced (to the civil standard of proof) as to the nature of the relationship between a parent and an adult child that might rebut the presumption of a resulting trust, this should not take the form of a *presumption* of advancement. In fact, the Court concluded that because it is now quite standard for aging parents to advance funds to their adult children in

[31] [2007] 1 SCR 795, 2007 SCC 17.

[32] *ibid.*, paras 32–33 *per* Rothstein J. The presumption applies to transfers from mothers to children in other jurisdictions, including Australia: *Nelson v Nelson* (1995) 184 CLR 538.

order to enable the easy management of those funds, we ought to assume that property and funds so transferred would be held in trust for the aging parent unless there was evidence of a contrary intention. The presumption of advancement should, therefore, be limited to "transfers by mothers and fathers to minor children".[33] Although there was a strong dissent from this portion of the decision by Abella J, who felt that the presumption of advancement can be rationalised by reference to parental affection and life-long obligation to one's chid and can therefore apply to transfers to adult children, the majority decision in *Pecore* suggests the severe limitation of the principle based on prevailing social circumstances.

Of course, prevailing social circumstances are not universally the same. An argument can be made that, while the finding that the presumption should apply to maternal as well as paternal advances to children should stand (and may, in fact, be required on equality grounds), its limitation to advances made to adult children is not appropriate in Ireland. This is the argument advanced by Eoin Carolan in his consideration of the implications of *Pecore* in this jurisdiction.[34] Carolan reaches this conclusion by reference to the basis for the presumption in Irish law (parental affection[35]), the recognition in Irish law of a life-long obligation from parent to child regardless of the child's age,[36] and prevailing social practices in Ireland. As to this latter point, Carolan notes that: **[3–25]**

> Anecdotal evidence would suggest that the increase in Irish property prices over the last 15 years has created a situation in which many adult independent children have purchased property with the aid of a parental gift. To amend the presumption in such a way that it assumes that parents retain an equitable interest in these purchased properties could be contrary to the intentions of the parties in many of these instances.

Although property prices in Ireland have fallen rapidly since the decision in *Pecore*, the practice of parents making advances to their children to enable them to acquire property seems—again anecdotally—to both predate and survive the current economic crisis. Whether that practice necessitates the maintenance in law of the presumption of advancement is a somewhat different question, however, especially since (as noted above) deeming the transfer an expression of "natural love and affection" may be a way of clearly demonstrating the intention to transfer gratuitously. Of course, those words will be included in a transfer only where it is done by means of paperwork (such as in the gratuitous transfer of a site to a child in order to enable that child to build a home on it). In the common case where a parent advances some cash to a child to help them, for example, pay the deposit on a house, there is usually no opportunity for the expression in written form of such a sentiment and in those cases it seems the presumption of advancement would sensibly continue to operate, especially since (as a mere presumption) it can be rebutted by evidence of a contrary intention.

---

33 *ibid.*, para 40 *per* Rothstein J.

34 Carolan, "Amending the Presumption of Advancement: The Decision in *Pecore v Pecore*" (2008) 26 ILT 26.

35 *In re James McDonald* [2000] 1 ILRM 382.

36 This is reflected in s 117, Succession Act 1965, considered in Chapter 16.

[3–26] In England and Wales the presumption of advancement has, it appears, had its death warrant signed and duly executed by parliament. Section 199 of the Equality Act 2010 provides as follows:

> (1) The presumption of advancement (by which, for example, a husband is presumed to be making a gift to his wife if he transfers property to her, or purchases property in her name) is abolished.
> (2) The abolition by subsection (1) of the presumption of advancement does not have effect in relation to—
> (a) anything done before the commencement of this section, or
> (b) anything done pursuant to any obligation incurred before the commencement of this section.

This provision thus provides that, while this will not have a retrospective effect, the presumption of advancement will otherwise be abolished. As its inclusion in the Equality Act 2010 should suggest, the proposal for abolition was based on anti-discrimination grounds. Introducing the amendment that resulted in the inclusion of s 199, Lord Lester of Herne Hill noted, "The effect of the presumption of advancement is clearly discriminatory and its abolition will not have any unfair or undesirable effects",[37] although the proposal did not attract any significant attention in the parliamentary debates[38]. As a result of s 62(3) of the Land and Conveyancing Law Reform Act 2009, providing that a resulting trust will not arise *merely* because a transfer made after the commencement of the Act is gratuitous, the extent to which the presumption of advancement will have a significant impact in Irish property law going forward is likely to be minimal.

IV. Bona Fide Purchaser for Value Without Notice

[3–27] As equitable rights are generally dependent on the generosity of the courts for their recognition and enforcement, these rights are more precarious than legal rights. This does not mean, however, that they cannot be protected in any way. As already considered, the court of equity began to develop protections for equitable interests in the late 1400s. Perhaps the most significant situation considered by the courts is that of the purchaser of lands over which a third party holds equitable rights of some kind: would the purchaser be required to honour and allow the exercise of those rights, or are they negated by the sale or inheritance of the property?

[3–28] In the late 1400s equity recognised that it was inherently unfair to undo someone's equitable rights just because the legal owner—at that time, the feoffee—decided to sell the property. It is important to remember that the holder of equitable rights did not have the capacity to prevent the feoffee from dealing with the land; he was, after all, the owner of the land and therefore could act relatively freely in relation to it. Accordingly, equity held that all purchasers would be bound by (or required to

[37] Lord Lester of Herne Hill, House of Lords, 9 February 2010.

[38] This is, perhaps, unsurprising given the enormous and comprehensive nature of the Equality Act 2010 in the context of which the abolition of the presumption of advancement is a minor change. The decision to abolish the presumption has received some attention elsewhere, and indeed has been lamented somewhat. See, for example, Brightwell, "Good Riddance to the Presumption of Advancement?" (2010) 16 *Trusts & Trustees* 627.

honour) the equitable interests of third parties over land they purchased unless they could prove that they were the bona fide purchaser of the property for value without notice. This principle has survived into the era of the modern trust. Again, the trustee is the legal owner of the property and therefore is entitled to deal with the land as freely as the general law of trusts will allow. But the purchaser of the land cannot deny the rights of the beneficiaries of the trust unless he can prove that he is the bona fide purchaser for value without notice of the beneficiaries' rights *or* that there is a legislative provision that "frees" the purchaser from those equitable interests.[39]

The bona fide purchaser for value without notice is free of third-party rights of which he was not aware. So privileged is his position, in fact, that he is known as "equity's darling". This is, of course, the ideal scenario for the purchaser, so it is important that the characteristics of equity's darling are clear. **[3–29]**

1. Bona Fide

To act bona fide simply means to act in good faith, thus no purchaser will enjoy the status of equity's darling unless he can show that, when purchasing the property, he did so in good faith. The trustee of the property, for example, could not be the bona fide purchaser for value, nor could someone who colluded with the trustee in order to acquire the property free of the third-party interests. **[3–30]**

2. Purchaser

The concept of purchaser is quite precise in property law. To be a purchaser one must acquire property rights by means of a legal transaction. A squatter, for example, could not be a purchaser in this context because he acquires his property rights by means of the passage of time and not as a result of engaging in a process culminating in a legal transaction.[40] In addition, someone who acquires property as a result of the operation of the rules of intestacy would not be a purchaser,[41] whereas someone who acquires property by means of a will would be a purchaser. In the context of the Land and Conveyancing Law Reform Act 2009, "purchaser" is defined as "an assignee, chargeant, grantee, lessee, mortgagee or other person who acquires land for valuable consideration",[42] seemingly removing the gratuitous transferee from the category of purchaser. As considered in the next paragraph, equity's darling in any case was required to give value for the property rights acquired. **[3–31]**

3. For Value

In order to be free from the pre-existing equitable interests over property, a person must not only be a purchaser but, importantly, must give value for his interest. **[3–32]**

[39] See, for example, s 21 Land and Conveyancing Law Reform Act 2009 considered at para 3–41 below and in detail in Chapter 5.

[40] The law of "squatting" is properly known as the law of adverse possession and is considered in full in Chapter 14.

[41] For more on intestacy, see Chapter 16.

[42] s 3, Land and Conveyancing Law Reform Act 2009.

4. Without Notice

[3–33] Finally, and very importantly, the purchaser must satisfy the court that he did not have any notice of the third-party interest. Notice can be loosely equated with knowledge or awareness; thus a purchaser can be released from responsibility for third-party equitable interests only if he did not know, or was not aware of, those interests. This does not mean, however, that purchasers can protect themselves by simply limiting their knowledge of the property. The law of notice has been developed to bind purchasers of all third-party equitable interests that they actually knew about, or which they ought to have known about. The doctrine of notice was codified by s 3 of the Conveyancing Act 1882, recognising that there are three kinds of notice: actual, constructive and imputed. Section 3 of the 1882 Act was repealed by the Land and Conveyancing Law Reform Act 2009, s 86 of which maintains the doctrine of notice in the following terms:

> (1) A purchaser is not affected prejudicially by notice of any fact, instrument, matter or thing unless—
>
> (a) it is within the purchaser's own knowledge or would have come to the purchaser's knowledge if such inquiries and inspections had been made as ought reasonably to have been made by the purchaser, or
>
> (b) in the same transaction with respect to which a question of notice to the purchaser arises, it has come to the knowledge of the purchaser's counsel, as such, or solicitor or other agent, as such, or would have come to the knowledge of the solicitor or other agent if such inquiries and inspections had been made as ought reasonably to have been made by the solicitor or agent.

This provision essentially reinstates the terms of s 3 of the Conveyancing Act 1882, and indeed s 86(3) clearly provides that the 2009 Act does not extend the doctrine of notice in any way. Thus, there are still three kinds of notice that apply in Irish property law: actual, constructive and imputed.

(i) Actual Notice

[3–34] Subsection 1 of s 86 makes clear that actual notice arises where the interest in question "is within the purchaser's own knowledge". How the purchaser came about that knowledge is not, generally, a material question.

(ii) Constructive Notice

[3–35] Constructive notice relates to the interests that the purchaser would have known of had he made "such inquiries and inspections... as ought reasonably to [be] made". In other words, constructive notice ensures that one cannot attempt to escape from liability for an interest simply by claiming ignorance of that interest; as prospective purchasers, we are required to make enquiries about the interests that exist over the property that we want to purchase. There is, therefore, an expectation that certain processes will be engaged in and certain questions will be asked in the course of a transaction; if they are not engaged in or asked, then the purchaser is treated as if he were aware of the truthful information he would have received pursuant to such processes and enquiries. The law of conveyancing—the practical side of property law, so to speak—is made up, *inter alia*, of practice directions that dictate the processes and questions expected of the purchaser.

Section 86 expressly provides that what we are referring to here is the enquiries and inspections that "ought reasonably to [be] made" by a prospective purchaser. In other words, the standard of enquiry expected is assessed on an objective scale. This was so before the introduction of s 86 and is well demonstrated by the case of *Northern Bank v Henry*.[43] This case concerned a leasehold property that had been purchased in the name of the husband with money belonging to his wife. When the couple separated, discussions began about the ownership of the property and the wife initiated proceedings in the High Court, claiming that the husband held the property on trust for her by means of a presumed resulting trust. On that same day, the husband acquired a mortgage over the property and in this case the mortgagee bank (Northern Bank) was attempting to enforce the mortgage while the wife (Henry) was claiming that the bank was bound by her equitable interest in the property of which it had constructive notice, for it had failed to carry out reasonable enquiries. The bank had, in fact, made no enquiries as to the property beyond carrying out a Registry of Deeds search in which the equitable interest of the wife would not have appeared. **[3–36]**

At the time that the husband acquired the mortgage with the plaintiff bank he was in some severe financial difficulties, and the bank was convinced that there was an imperative for it to act swiftly in order to secure the transaction. Even though the bank knew that the property was a family home (within the meaning of the Family Home Protection Act 1976[44]), and that the husband no longer used it as his correspondence address with them (suggesting he no longer resided there), they did not proceed to make any substantive enquiries beyond a registry search. So cursory was the process, in fact, that Henchy J in the Supreme Court remarked, "A competent solicitor, acting for a normal purchaser of the property, would not have been content to take the title on such a cursory investigation".[45] Had the bank undertaken more substantive enquiries, they would have discovered both that the wife resided in the property and that she was claiming an equitable interest in it (a claim that was upheld by the High Court); they would then have known that the husband did not have a good title with which to offer them security by means of the mortgage in question. Considering the enquiries that ought to have been made in the context of s 3 of the Conveyancing Act 1882, Henchy J held: **[3–37]**

> . . . the test of what inquiries and inspections ought reasonably to have been made by the plaintiffs is an objective test which depends not on what the particular purchaser thought proper to do in the particular circumstances but on what a purchaser of the particular property ought reasonably to have done in order to acquire title to it . . . In a particular case a purchaser, looking only at his own interests, may justifiably and reasonably consider that in the circumstances some of the normal inquiries and inspections may or should be dispensed with. The special circumstances, thus narrowly viewed, may justify the shortcut taken, or the purchaser may consider that they do so. In either event, such a purchaser is not the purchaser envisaged by s. 3, sub-s. 1, of the Act of 1882. That provision, because it is laying down the circumstances in which a purchaser is not to be prejudicially affected by notice of any instrument, fact or thing, is setting as a standard of conduct that which is to be expected from a reasonable purchaser. Reasonableness in this

43 [1981] 1 IR 1.
44 See Chapter 9.
45 [1981] 1 IR 1, 8.

> context must be judged by reference to what should be done to acquire the estate or interest being purchased, rather than by the motive for or the purpose of the particular purchase.
>
> A purchaser cannot be held to be empowered to set his own standard of reasonableness for the purpose of the sub-section. He must expect to be judged by what an ordinary purchaser, advised by a competent lawyer, would reasonably inquire about or inspect for the purpose of getting a good title. If his personal preference, or the exigencies of the situation, impel him to lower the level of investigation of title below that standard, he is entitled to do so; but, if he does so, he cannot claim the immunity which s. 3, sub-s. 1, reserves for a reasonable purchaser. A reasonable purchaser is one who not only consults his own needs or preferences but also has regard to whether the purchase may affect, prejudicially and unfairly, the rights of third parties in the property. In particular, a reasonable purchaser would be expected to make such inquiries and inspections as would normally disclose whether the purchase will trench, fraudulently or unconscionably, on the rights of such third parties in the property.[46]

Because s 86 of the 2009 Act essentially re-enacts s 3 of the 1882 Act, there is nothing to suggest that the test or standard of reasonableness required by s 86 differs from that laid down in these concise terms by the Supreme Court in *Henry*.

(iii) Imputed Notice

[3–38] To have imputed notice of an equitable interest is to be treated as though one has all of the knowledge—actual and constructive—of one's agents engaged in relation to the transaction. There is no need for one's agent (such as a solicitor) to have actually communicated the relevant knowledge to the purchaser; the purchaser is treated as if he knew it regardless. Agents may, of course, be subject to liability for negligence if they fail to communicate important information of this kind. Section 86(2) of the 2009 Act clearly maintains imputed notice in Irish law, referring as it does to both the knowledge of one's agent *and* the knowledge one's agent ought to have, had a reasonable level of enquiry and inspection been undertaken.

(iv) Working with Notice

[3–39] As a matter of practice, it is sensible for purchasers to try to find out as much as possible about the various interest-holders over the property in order to ensure that (a) if there are third-party interests, the purchaser can make an informed decision as to whether they would rather buy the property and respect those interests *or* try to buy the interests from the third-party interest-holders *or* simply abandon the transaction and (b) if a third-party interest-holder later emerges of whom he was not aware, the purchaser's chances of being deemed "without notice" are higher. This is especially so in relation to unregistered land. Registered land, which we consider in detail in Chapter 7 and is governed by the Registration of Title Act 1964, is impacted to only a limited degree by the doctrine of notice in its classical form. This is because it operates on the basis of a comprehensive record of title, in which (almost) all interests should appear.[47] This is in contrast to unregistered land, where there is no such unitary record and instead one must sift through numerous different records in order to establish the current "state of play" in

[46] *ibid.*, 9.

[47] s 31, Registration of Title Act 1964.

relation to the piece of land in question. In addition, there are some other ways in which the relevance of the doctrine of notice has been minimised recently. Where land is held in a Part 4 trust under the Land and Conveyancing Law Reform Act 2009, and that land is being transferred in accordance with the requirements of the Act, then the conveyance will be said to "overreach" equitable interests.[48] This simply means that the purchaser will not be affected by those interests, although they can still be enforced by their holders against the trustees of the land. If all of the requirements of Part 4 of the Act are complied with, then the equitable interests will be overreached *regardless* of whether the purchaser (who must be a purchaser for value[49]) had notice of them or not, although the Act cannot be used as an instrument of fraud.[50] This is considered in much more detail in Chapter 6.

In situations where the doctrine of notice in its conventional form continues to operate, a purchaser will normally engage in both physical and documentary investigations in relation to property she is interested in acquiring. The extent of the documentary enquiries to be engaged in is defined by conveyancing procedures, which are not of concern here. The physical inspections are important because a third-party interest may be indicated by the conditions "on the ground" where the documents do not in any way suggest that such interests exist over the property. In particular, prospective purchasers must be vigilant in relation to those who reside in the property because the rights of all occupants are binding upon purchasers who fail to enquire of them what the basis of their occupations might be. If the purchaser does ask the occupants the basis of their occupations and is given false answers, then the occupants will be said to have foregone their rights in relation to the property in question. This is known as the rule in *Hunt v Luck*.[51] **[3–40]**

Importantly, even if a purchaser is fixed with notice of a third-party interest over the property, this does not normally invalidate the transaction[52]: rather, the purchaser will still own the property, but will hold it *subject to* the rights of the third party. If the purchaser succeeds in convincing the court that she is equity's darling, then the third-party interest-holder will have no claim against her, although he may have a claim against the vendor. Anyone who acquires the property from the bona fide purchaser for value without notice will equally be free of the third-party interest (even if he knew of this interest), unless he has colluded with the original vendor to attempt to undermine the equitable rights of the third party.[53] **[3–41]**

V. The Nature of Equitable Rights

Equitable rights are more controversial than might at first appear. For this book's purposes, we need engage in only a brief consideration of this controversy in the form of asking whether equitable rights are *in personam* or *in rem*, i.e. are they personal **[3–42]**

[48] s 21, Land and Conveyancing Law Reform Act 2009.
[49] s 3, *ibid.*
[50] s 21(3)(a), *ibid.*
[51] [1902] 1 Ch 428.
[52] However, see in Chapter 9 the effect of notice of lack of valid consent under s 3 of the Family Home Protection Act 1976 as a *quasi*-exception.
[53] *In re Steward's Estate* (1893) 31 LR IR 405.

rights or real rights?[54] As considered in Chapter 1, the traditional position was that real property resulted in real remedies and personal property resulted in personal remedies. In relation to equitable rights in trusts, at least, the rights held by the beneficiary are certainly proprietary interests, albeit in equity only. The difficulty arises when one considers the long-standing equitable maxim that equity acts *in personam*. This is reflected in the development of the law of trusts where, in strict technical terms, the result of the intervention of equity was to recognise that "Equity did not say that the [beneficiary] was the owner of the land, it said that the trustee was the owner of the land, but added that he was bound to hold the land for the benefit of the [beneficiary]".[55]

[3–43] In strict technical terms, then, we conceive of equitable interests as lying *in personam* from the perspective of equitable remedies, although we conceive of the holder of equitable interests within a trust as having some kind of ownership in land. As a result, the equitable interest in a trust has always been treated much like a proprietary interest inasmuch as it can be bought, sold, mortgaged and so forth. This paradox ought not to trouble the student of property law to too great an extent. Jill Hanbury explains it thus:

> Even though, historically, the protection of the beneficiary was based on the Chancellor's willingness to proceed *in personam* against the trustee, that protection has ended up by creating rights in the nature of ownership. To argue that a beneficiary's rights are proprietary is not to say that legal rights are the same as equitable, or that equitable ownership is the same as legal. Rather, it is to accept the basic peculiarity of ownership under the [Irish] law of trusts. The trustee is the owner at law; and the beneficiary is the owner in equity.[56]

The Irish courts appear to be quite willing to set aside the academic difficulties of this paradox and to accept that the equitable rights of a beneficiary of a trust are best described as rights *in rem*, particularly as such rights-holders are entitled to avail of the equitable remedy of tracing.[57] Importantly, equity recognised a range of rights *in rem* in property that lie outside of the trust scenario. It is possible for one to have, for example, a lease in equity, an easement in equity and a mortgage in equity.[58]

VI. Maxims of Equity

[3–44] As already mentioned, the law of equity is a flexible and fairness-based one, but this is not to say that it exists without rules. In fact, the law of equity has developed a clear set of central principles, known as "the maxims", which are, in essence, the guiding principles or rules of this body of law. A relatively good working knowledge of the maxims is fundamental to a complete understanding of the relationship between law and equity its relation to property rights.

---

54 For the distinction between the two, see Chapter 1.

55 Maitland, *Equity* (2nd ed, 1936), p 17.

56 Martin, *Hanbury and Martin: Modern Equity* (16th ed, 2001, London, Sweet & Maxwell), pp 18–19.

57 See, especially, *Re Cuff Knoxi* [1963] IR 263 *per* Kingsmill-Moore J.

58 All of these interests are discussed in full in the relevant chapters of the book, i.e. Chapters 15, 12 and 13 respectively.

1. Equity Will Not Suffer a Wrong To Be Without a Remedy

This is possibly the most basic concept of equity, i.e. that equity will intervene and protect a recognised right where the common law fails to do so. This is the basis upon which, for example, equity can recognise the rights of beneficiaries in a trust, although the trustee is the owner at law and entitled—within the bounds of reasonableness—to do with the land as he wishes in the eyes of the common law. Although the maxim itself appears to suggest a broad and sweeping equitable hand across the face of legal transactions, its exercise has become exceptionally formalised, to the extent that the maxim does not now appear to allow for equitable interventions in all cases that may, on a surface analysis, lend themselves to it. Rather, it seems that equity will now intervene only in cases of well-established equitable interests, which "have an ancestry founded in history and in the practice and precedents"[59] of the courts of equity. Although this maxim is not of purely historical interest (and can be observed in action in every case of equitable remedy, enforcement of beneficial interests in land, and so on), its extreme formalisation does appear to have stymied the development of new forms of equitable remedies. [3–45]

2. Equity Follows the Law

Like so much of the law of equity, this maxim ought not to be taken literally. It does not mean that equity will always reach the same decision as the law; if it did, it would somewhat undermine the whole idea of equity. Instead, it means that equity will follow legal rules unless a modification thereof is required in order to further the requirements of fairness. Property law has a number of useful illustrations of this maxim. On the one hand, equity follows the law inasmuch as equitable interests in land are usually thought of as being more or less correspondent with legal interests. On the other hand, equity will ensure that a statute is not used as an instrument of fraud by creating, for example, the doctrine of part performance to avoid fraudulent application of the Statute of Frauds (Ireland) 1695. [3–46]

3. He Who Seeks Equity Must Do Equity

At its core equity is not a punitive body of law. It seeks to achieve fairness between the parties, taking into account all circumstances, including the behaviour of the plaintiff. In order for equity to come to the aid of a plaintiff, that individual must have acted equitably in the circumstances. In the context of property law, this maxim is of particular importance as it features relatively prominently in decisions regarding equitable remedies. Because all equitable remedies are discretionary, factors such as the behaviour of the litigants can be taken into account. Thus, equity may find that a remedy would be appropriate on the basis of legal analysis, but adjust that remedy as a result of the inequitable behaviour of the plaintiff. For this reason it is important to avoid speaking of equitable remedies in terms of certainties; one should be relatively circumspect when considering equitable remedies, as their breadth in any particular scenario is dependent on a number of such extra-legal considerations. [3–47]

4. He Who Comes to Equity Must Come with Clean Hands

The requirement to come to equity with clean hands very much complements the requirement of a plaintiff to "do equity", although it might be said to be something of [3–48]

[59] *In re Diplock* [1948] Ch 465 at 481–2 *per* Greene MR.

a "last resort defence" in practice.[60] In essence, this maxim requires that plaintiffs would not have engaged in any form of reprehensible behaviour, such as fraud or misrepresentation. Importantly, only behaviour that has "an immediate and necessary relation to the equity sued for"[61] is relevant in "clean hands" considerations: it is not enough that one generally engages in legally reprehensible behaviour; one must have engaged in such behaviour in relation to the matter at issue in order for this behaviour to meet the basic requirement of relevance.

5. Where the Equities Are Equal, the Law Prevails; Where the Equities Are Equal, the First in Time Prevails

[3–49] These two maxims of equity are directly relevant to the assessment of priorities in unregistered land. As is considered in full in Chapter 7, there will sometimes be situations in which there are various different interests over land that cannot all be satisfied. In such circumstances one is required to assess which of these interests has priority, i.e. which interest will be satisfied when resources (time, land, money, etc.) are limited. The answer to this question very much depends on which system of priorities is being applied—is it the equitable system, or is it the rule system introduced by statute? The answer in turn depends on the circumstances and is considered in full in Chapter 7. For now it is sufficient to state that where the two interests are equal (i.e. they are both legal, or both equitable, or both registered, or both unregistered), priority will be given to the interest that was created first—unless an interest created later is (a) legal and (b) held by a bona fide purchaser for value without notice of the earlier equitable interest.

6. Equity Presumes an Intention to Fulfil an Obligation

[3–50] Where a person has undertaken an obligation, equity presumes that he intends to fulfil it. As a result, acts done that might be construed as fulfilment of that intention will be constructed as such. Perhaps the most pertinent example of this maxim in operation from the perspective of property law is satisfaction, which is considered in full in Chapter 16.

7. Equity Sees as Done that which Ought to Have Been Done

[3–51] This maxim is of particular importance in the context of contracts relating to land. It requires that specifically enforceable contracts would in fact be enforced.[62] Thus, as will be considered in full in Chapter 15, the Rule in *Walsh v Lonsdale*[63] provides that where a contract for a lease is entered into and has been partly performed, equity will see as done that which ought to have been done by enforcing that contract and creating a lease in equity.

---

[60] See Delany, *Equity & The Law of Trusts in Ireland* (3rd ed, 2003, Dublin, Round Hall), p 19, no 39.

[61] *Dering v Earl of Winchelsea* (1787) 1 Cox 318 at 319–20 *per* Eyre LCB.

[62] While the English case law suggests that the maxim is limited to specifically enforceable contracts (see, for example, *Davis v Richards & Wallington Ltd* [1990] 1 WLR 1511), the High Court decision *In the Matter of the Trustee Act 1893 & the Succession Act 1965* (*Shanahan v Redmond*), unreported, High Court, 21 June 1994, Carroll J, suggests this may not be the case in Ireland.

[63] (1882) 21 Ch D 9.

8. Equity is Equality

This maxim is of direct relevance to property law because essentially it provides that where multiple people are entitled to land, equity favours an equal division. As will be considered in full in Chapter 8, this is particularly important in the context of co-ownership, where the common law favours the joint tenancy and equity favours the tenancy in common. The difference between the two, expressed in relatively simplistic terms, is that the joint tenancy operates on the basis of the right to survivorship, i.e. the principle that once a joint tenant dies, his entitlements die with him and the other joint tenants absorb his share so that there is nothing that can be left to an heir. The tenancy in common operates on the basis that all co-owners have shares of ownership that can be demised through a will or passed on by means of intestacy on the death of a co-owner (i.e. the right of survivorship does not operate in the tenancy in common).[64] **[3–52]**

9. Equity Looks to Intent Rather than Form

This maxim reflects the essential function of equity discussed above, i.e. to resist the undermining of clear intention by virtue of failure to comply with "unnecessary formalities".[65] This does not mean that equity abandons the need for formalities and certainty in property law. Rather, it means that clear intention will not be cast aside on overly formalistic grounds. **[3–53]**

10. Delay Defeats Equity

The maxim that equity may refuse relief from an application on the basis of undue delay is well established and is most commonly explained by reference to the *dicta* of Lord Camdeb LC in *Smith v Clay*: **[3–54]**

> A court of equity... has always refused its aid to stale demands, where a party has slept upon his right and acquiesced for a great length of time. Nothing can call forth this call into activity but conscience, good faith and reasonable diligence.[66]

It must be noted that the principle of delay has almost no application to cases where the limitation period for the action is already governed by the Statute of Limitations 1957. In such cases, one can rarely be said to have engaged in delay of a kind resulting in the action being struck out where one has acted within the prescribed limitation period.[67] The only exception appears to be where an "inordinate and inexcusable delay" has resulted in an unfair burden being placed on the defendant.[68]

The principle of delay defeating equity usually applies only in cases where the cause of action falls outside of the Statute of Limitations. In order to successfully avail of this maxim, the defendant must establish either (a) laches or (b) acquiescence. Laches comprises the concept of unreasonable delay in taking an action, where that delay has amounted in practice to a waiver of the right to take an action, or has resulted in the **[3–55]**

---

[64] For more on the role of equity in the law of co-ownership, see Chapter 8.
[65] *Sprange v Lee* [1908] 1 Ch 424 at 430 *per* Neville J.
[66] (1767) 3 Bro CC 639 at 640n.
[67] s 5, Statute of Limitations 1957; *Re Pauling's Settlement Trusts* [1964] Ch 303.
[68] *O'Domhnaill v Merrick* [1984] IR 151.

taking of an action being unreasonable to a potential defendant.[69] In other words, there is a two-pronged test for laches: (a) reasonability of delay and (b) effect of delay on the prospective defendant. Acquiescence is quite a similar concept. It arises where the prospective plaintiff expressly or impliedly leads the prospective defendant to believe that he does not intend to pursue an action in a matter.[70] In such cases, the taking of an action subsequent to such a representation is normally considered unjust (although, of course, all of the relevant circumstances are taken into account in the court's consideration).

11. Equity Acts *In Personam*

[3–56] As considered above, the traditional position is that equity acts *in personam*. In essence this means that rights recognised by virtue of equitable adjudication or the application of equitable principles would be said to be purely personal. As considered above, however, this maxim has a limited application in the context of property law. While it is true that equitable rights in land are, strictly speaking, *in personam*, they have conventionally been treated as proprietary rights. In spite of the conceptual difficulties of this position, this is simply an intellectual incongruity that the law has found itself willing to accept.

VII. The "Jointure" of Law and Equity

[3–57] While the parallel systems of equity and the common law complemented one another (inasmuch as the legal system benefited from the certainty resultant from a rule system imposed by the common law and managed to avoid the pitfalls of complete inflexibility as a result of the infusion of equity), the existence of two systems of law administered in separate courts resulted in practical difficulties for litigants. In an effort to ameliorate these difficulties, the decision was taken to "join" law and equity in the same court. This was achieved by means of the Supreme Court of Judicature Act 1877.

[3–58] In essence, this jointure was practical and procedural: instead of having to plead in separate courts, litigants would now be able to make both legal and equitable arguments in the same court and as part of the same litigation. While the initial view was that the jointure of the two bodies of law was solely of this nature (i.e. procedural),[71] ambiguity has since arisen. This is a result of a number of judicial pronouncements that suggest that differentiating between legal and equitable bases of rules is essentially unnecessary now that the two corpora of law have become joined.[72] These comments are mostly *obiter* and therefore of no binding effect, and in fact the sounder (and now resurgent[73]) view appears to be that the jointure was procedural only.

---

[69] *Lindsey Petroleum v Hurd* (1874) LR 5 PC 221 at 239–40 *per* Selbourne LC.

[70] *Archbold v Scully* (1861) 9 HLC 360, 383.

[71] See, for example, *Salt v Cooper* (1880) 16 Ch D 544 at 549 *per* Jessel MR.

[72] See, for example, *AG for the United Kingdom v Wellington Newspapers Ltd* [1988] 1 NZLR 129; *United Scientific Holdings Ltd v Burnley Borough Council* [1978] AC 904; *Federal Commerce & Navigation Co Ltd v Molena Alpha Inc* [1978] QB 927; *Hynes Ltd v Independent Newspapers Ltd* [1980] IR 204.

[73] See especially Millett, "Equity—The Road Ahead" (1995) 9 *Trust Law International* 35.

From the perspective of property law, this is particularly important, especially as litigants are reliant on the discretion of the court for equitable remedies. While equitable principles have influenced the interpretation and application of legal rules since the Judicature Act, it would be inaccurate to suggest that the bodies of law have, in fact, become "fused" or "merged" in this substantive manner. While they continue to move closer to one another, law and equity remain distinctive bodies of law that are administered by and pleaded before the same court. **[3–59]**

CHAPTER 4
Estates in Land

In Chapter 2 we saw that, to a large extent, modern Irish property law can trace its operation back to feudal principles and structures. One of those feudal structures that persisted up until the Land and Conveyancing Law Reform Act 2009 was that individuals do not "own" land *per se*; rather we hold land in estates. An estate, loosely put, is the "time capsule" of ownership rights that one holds in relation to a piece of land and which dictates (a) the duration of that ownership, and (b) the limitations on that ownership that are based on the nature of the ownership itself rather than on any conditions imposed by the contract between the parties or by the general law of torts, planning, crime etc. So an estate is "control over land for a period of time" and in the context of freehold estates the parameters of that control was largely determined by the nature of feudal tenure that attached to the estate. Although s 9(2) of the Land and Conveyancing Law Reform Act 2009 expressly provides that, inasmuch as it survives, feudal tenure is abolished,[1] the Act also retains the concept of the estate.[2] Thus, we have retained the basic principle that we do not absolutely own land *per se*; rather we **[4–01]**

[1] See further Chapter 2, paras 2–58 to 2–60.

[2] s 9(3)(b), Land and Conveyancing Law Reform Act 2009.

enjoy control rights over land for a period of time determined by the nature of the estate that we hold. However, those estates can now be said to only have a feudal provenance and not to be feudal themselves for they are not attached with any incidents or other feudal instruments.

[4–02] This chapter will explain the various estates that exist over land. The estates themselves can be broadly divided into three categories: freehold estates, derived from feudal landholding patterns; leasehold estates, existing between landlord and tenant; and hybrid estates, combining features of both freehold and leasehold. The law of estates has been changed enormously by the Land and Conveyancing Law Reform Act 2009 and those changes—including some potential difficulties with them—are taken into account throughout the chapter.

Part I: Freehold Estates

[4–03] The freehold estates derive from the feudal landholding system. As an initial matter the nomenclature "freehold" deserves some attention. Freehold describes the rights held for life, or in an inheritable form, by those designated "free men" by the *Magna Carta*, i.e. free tenants within the feudal pyramid, as outlined in Chapter 2. In general, freehold estates can be said to have two characteristics: (a) they last for an indefinite period of time, and (b) they exist only in relation to land. During the feudal period the right to hold land in return for services and incidents could be given for someone's lifetime, meaning that it was not inheritable. This idea of rights for life became known as the life estate and was the dominant estate up to the 12th century. The life estate now exists in equity only.[3] In the alternative, landholding rights might be given in a way that made it possible for them to be inherited. These were known as fees: the word "fee" denoting the potential to last forever. If the inheritability of the rights was restricted to lineal blood descendents, it would be said to be entailed and the estate would be described as a fee tail. The notion of an entail arose from the French word *tailler*, meaning to cut or tailor something. The fee tail has now been abolished, although there are very limited situations in which fees tail might continue to operate in the short term.[4] If the inheritability of the rights was not restricted in this way, the fee was described as being simple, meaning "freely alienable". This freely alienable fee therefore became the fee simple. The fee simple is now the only freehold estate in law. It is also the largest estate, i.e. it lasts for the longest time and the holder of a fee simple enjoys (and, before the Land and Conveyancing Law Reform Act 2009, enjoyed) the greatest expanse of controlling rights and capacities of all the freehold owners

1. Fee Simple

[4–04] The fee simple can be defined as control rights that have the potential to last forever and that can be freely alienated. The fee simple largely arose out of the development of a right to inherit. As considered in Chapter 2, it was originally the case that an heir did not have what might properly be described as a "right" to inherit; instead the feudal lord would decide on the desirability of the heir as a feudal tenant and, if he allowed for inheritance, would demand the payment of a relief. Over time, the reliefs demanded

---

[3] s 11(6), Land and Conveyancing Law Reform Act 2009.

[4] s 13, Land and Conveyancing Law Reform Act 2009; see further paras 4–63 to 4–65 below.

became prohibitively expensive, which, combined with a general dissatisfaction with the level of discretionary control exercised by feudal lords, created considerable unrest. In order to try to respond to these grievances, in his Coronation Charter of 1100 Henry I declared a right to pay a reasonable relief. In addition, the Assize of Northampton in 1176 recognised the concept of a right to inherit. This meant that where the holder of a fee simple died, his heir was *entitled* to inherit the land. The fee simple would come to an end when someone died intestate and without an heir. In such cases the rights would escheat back up the feudal pyramid. This, of course, is no longer the case.[5]

We now recognise that heirs of a fee simple holder have a hope, rather than a right, to inherit. This hope of inheriting is known as the *spes successionis*. There is no longer a right to inherit the fee simple because the holder of the estate can alienate it freely, either while he is alive or when he is dead; he is not obliged to pass it on to his heirs. The statutes to which the fee simple has particular attachment are the *Magna Carta* of 1217 and the *Quia Emptores* of 1290. The connection to the *Magna Carta* lies in that statute's confirmation of the absolute maximum charges a lord could levy by means of relief. The connection to *Quia Emptores* arises from that statute's confirmation that all free tenants had the right to substitute without their lord's consent. As land essentially lasts forever, someone holds a fee simple over every single piece of land. [4–05]

Section 11(2) of the Land and Conveyancing Law Reform Act 2009 provides that the "fee simple in possession" is the only freehold estate in law. Section 11(2) provides: [4–06]

> [A] "freehold estate" means a fee simple in possession and includes—
> (a) a determinable fee,
> (b) a fee simple subject to a right of entry or of re-entry,
> (c) a fee simple subject only to—
> (i) a power of revocation,
> (ii) an annuity or other payment of capital or income for the advancement, maintenance or other benefit of any person, or
> (iii) a right of residence which is not an exclusive right over the whole land.

This makes it clear that although the fee simple is now the only freehold estate in law, there are in fact a number of variations of fee simple. Section 11(2)(c) outlines three kinds of provision to which a fee simple can be made subject without losing its character as a fee simple. Thus, in each of these cases the fee simple continues to operate and there is no trust under Part 4. This is really a clarifying clause which does not require much attention here. Rather, our focus is on the absolute fee simple and the two modified fees simple laid down in s 11(2)(a) and s 11(2)(b) of the 2009 Act.

(i) Fee Simple Absolute[6]

If a fee simple is held in possession without any modifications, limitations, or conditions we know it as a "fee simple absolute". This is the closest thing in law to the [4–07]

[5] Escheat was abolished by s 11 of the Succession Act 1965.
[6] s 11(2), Land and Conveyancing Law Reform Act 2009.

absolute ownership of land. The only things that restrict control are the general limitations on land ownership recognised in law, such as planning law, criminal law and so forth. In terms of the two vital indicators of estates—control and time—the fee simple absolute scores well: there is as complete a quota of control as possible and it lasts (potentially) forever.

(ii) A Determinable Fee[7]

[4–08] The fee simple determinable arises when a fee simple is granted subject to the continuation of a state of affairs. A fee simple determinable is identifiable through the use of words that indicate an ongoing state of affairs as opposed to a once-off event. The phrases or words most commonly used in the creation of a fee simple determinable are "until", "while" and "for as long as". The fee simple determinable is subject to come to an end if the state of affairs is not maintained. If the state of affairs should come to an end, the fee simple determinable will *automatically* end, meaning that the grantor of the fee simple determinable (or his successor in title) can retake possession of the property and immediately becomes revested with the fee simple. Upon creation of a determinable fee, the grantor thus retains an alienable[8] future interest, which is known as a possibility of reverter. Simply put, this recognises that the grantor has a proprietary interest in the land inasmuch as the exercisable fee simple rights will revert back to the grantor *if* the prescribed state of affairs comes to an end. It is important to note that if the associated requirement is certain to occur, the estate is not a fee simple determinable. Thus, a disposition "to John until Patrick dies" creates a life estate *pur autre vie* (or until Patrick dies) in John's favour, not a fee simple determinable.

[4–09] Grantors of a fee simple determinable are not permitted to attach any state of affairs that they desire to the fee simple. Rather, as with conditional fees simple to which we will turn next, these determining states of affairs must be valid. There are various bases upon which validity is considered, which are dealt with in full below.

(iii) Fee Simple Subject to a Right of Entry or Re-Entry[9]

[4–10] A fee simple subject to a right of entry or re-entry is a fee simple that has been made subject to a condition subsequent, the right of entry or re-entry being the future interest of the grantor or his successor in title to retake the possession of the property should the condition in question not be fulfilled. Although s 11 only mentions a fee simple subject to a right of entry or re-entry (i.e. subject to a condition subsequent), it remains possible to make a fee simple subject to a condition precedent because—as will be seen below—the fee simple in that case is essentially a fee simple absolute *but* does not get vested until a condition is fulfilled. So, if a fee simple is made subject to a condition and that condition is precedent, the transferee does not receive the fee simple ownership until the condition has been fulfilled. If the condition is subsequent, the transfer of control rights happens immediately and the condition is to be fulfilled

---

[7] s 11(2)(a), *ibid.*
[8] s 11(4)(e), *ibid.*
[9] s 11(2)(b), *ibid.*

subsequently. In other words, the transferee becomes the immediate fee simple holder *subject to* fulfilment of the condition.

Given the operational differences between the two types of conditional fee, it ought to be clear that determining whether a condition is precedent or subsequent is of great significance. In most cases the nature of the condition is easily ascertainable. Take, for example, the following disposition: **[4–11]**

> No. 3, Bayview Road to John Ryan on the condition that he donates €100 to Well Known Charity Inc.

Quite clearly, this is a condition that can be performed immediately as a precedent condition to the receipt of the fee simple and the estate transferred is a fee simple subject to a condition precedent. The process of figuring out the nature of the condition in this example is uncomplicated. This is not always the case, however. Sometimes a condition will be attached that does not reveal its nature clearly. In those cases one reverts to the judgment of Lord Lowry in *In re Porter: Logan v Northern Bank Ltd & Ors.*[10]

This case concerned a will in which the testator had left business premises to his brother subject to the condition that the brother would pay £4,000 to named trustees within six months or make satisfactory arrangements for its payment within that period of time. If this was not done, the will provided, the bequest was to be revoked and was to fall into the residue of the estate. The brother never paid the £4,000 and a dispute arose as to what kind of estate he had been granted in the will. The brother claimed that he had received a fee simple subject to a condition subsequent, and that the condition was void for uncertainty. At this stage we are concerned only with the classification of the estate and not with the arguments relative to the validity of the condition.[11] Lord Lowry held that the estate transferred was a fee simple subject to a condition subsequent, and in the course of his judgment laid down a straightforward schema to be followed when considering the character of conditions attached to fees simple. First, one ought to consider the intention of the grantor. Where the estate is transferred in a will, this is a particularly important consideration as the courts will always try to give effect to the testator's intention.[12] Thus, the court will look at the words used and try to discern intention from them. Secondly, one ought to apply the presumption of early vesting. This is the principle that, where the intention is not immediately clear from the words of the grantor, there is a presumption in favour of the condition being a subsequent one. This presumption arises because it allows for the fee simple to vest at the earliest possible moment and for the condition to be fulfilled subsequently—a position that enhances certainty and alienability of land in line with the market orientation of property law.[13] Thirdly, there are a number of situations that may give rise to this presumption being rebutted and the condition being viewed as a **[4–12]**

---

[10] [1975] NI 157.

[11] The validity of conditions is considered in full below, including the requirement that the condition would be expressed with sufficient certainty.

[12] See "Construction of Wills" in Chapter 16, paras 16–42 to 16–57.

[13] The applicability of this presumption was reaffirmed by Carroll J in *In re Fitzgibbon* [1993] 1 IR 520.

precedent one. In the first place a time limit for the vesting of the estate will normally suggest a precedent condition.[14] Furthermore, if the condition is capable of being performed without delay (or *instanter*), then it is likely to be interpreted as a precedent one. The principles of *Re Porter* can be summarised thus:

(a) the intention of the grantor is the primary indicator of the nature of the condition;
(b) if the grantor's intention is insufficiently clear, the court will lean in favour of constructing it as a condition subsequent;
(c) this presumption in favour of a condition subsequent will normally be rebutted if there is a time limit for fulfilment of the condition, or if the condition is capable of relatively immediate fulfilment.

[4–13] If the condition attached is precedent, it must be fulfilled in order for the fee simple to be transferred. If the condition attached is subsequent, the fee simple estate is transferred and held subject to subsequent fulfilment of the condition. If the condition is found to be precedent, a failure to fulfil that condition will result in the fee simple never vesting. In other words, if the transferee does not fulfil the condition, he does not receive the fee simple. If the condition is found to be subsequent, breach of condition results in the transferor having the right to re-take fee simple ownership. This right is the right of entry or re-entry and it is an alienable future interest[15] retained by the transferor on the grant of the fee simple subject to the condition subsequent. In straightforward terms, it represents the sliver of control, or ownership, retained by the transferor to ensure that the attached condition is fulfilled. If the transferor discovers a breach of condition, he can exercise this right and reassert fee simple rights on his own behalf. Importantly, however, the transferee is in adverse possession against the transferor from the moment of breach and can squat out this right to re-entry.[16] Thus, if the transferor does not re-enter in time (usually 12 years)[17] the right to re-entry is exhausted and the transferee becomes an absolute fee simple holder.

(iv) Validity of Restrictions on the Fee Simple

[4–14] Not every restriction attached to a fee simple will be valid. In general, the validity of restrictions is assessed by reference to their impact on the alienability of the fee simple, the certainty with which they are expressed and their compatibility with public policy. If a restriction is valid, it will stand as a requirement of the transferee. If a restriction is invalid, it will not be performable. In the case of an invalid condition precedent, the fee simple will never vest as a condition cannot be performed if it is invalid. The estate has never vested in the transferee, therefore the disposition has had no effect. In the case of an invalid condition subsequent, the transferee retains the ownership free of the invalid condition. In other words, the invalid condition subsequent is struck out. In the case of

[14] Relying on *In re Doherty* [1950] NI 83. If, however, there is a specified time limit for the performance of the condition but not for the vesting of the estate, the condition will generally be said to be subsequent—relying on *Walker v Walker* (1860) 2 De GF & J 255; 45 ER 619.

[15] s 11(4)(i), Land and Conveyancing Law Reform Act 2009.

[16] Adverse possession is considered in Chapter 14.

[17] The time limit is 30 years in the case of a right of re-entry held by a State agency; see generally Chapter 14 and Statute of Limitations 1957.

a fee simple subject to an invalid determining restriction, the entire estate is invalidated by the invalidity of the associated requirement.

(a) Restrictions that Limit Alienability

As a general principle, the law will not allow conditions that limit the alienability of a fee simple. This resistance arises from the basic nature of the fee simple as an estate that is *freely alienable* and is closely connected to the principle of alienability introduced through *Quia Emptores.* The Land and Conveyancing Law Reform Act 2009 expressly maintains that principle in s 9(4). Given its nature, any condition that attempts to restrict alienation appears to be contrary to the basic concept of the fee simple estate. In addition, there is a general feeling "that restraints and fetters upon the transmission and enjoyment of property are opposed to the policy and spirit of the common law".[18] Nevertheless, it is human nature that people will occasionally try to control the destiny of land through such conditions, even after they have relinquished ownership of it. **[4–15]**

In most cases of restrictions that attempt to limit alienability, the law applies the rule known as the Doctrine of Repugnancy. This rule considers all restrictions that limit alienability to be invalid because they are seen to be repugnant to the fee simple estate. The courts apply this principle to express limitations of alienability, but sometimes fail to recognise the knock-on restriction on alienability imposed by a seemingly innocuous condition.[19] The case of *In re McDonnell*[20] bears out the strict application of the Doctrine of Repugnancy in Irish courts. John McDonnell had left his property in a complex trust system, but, irrespective of the complexity of the trust system concerned, the will contained the following clause: **[4–16]**

> It is my will and I direct that my lands situate at Closutton and Farranafreney shall not be sold but shall remain in my family to this extent that is to say that my said lands shall not be sold or assigned to any person who is not a member or a descendant of a member of my family.

The Court was asked to consider, *inter alia*, whether this restriction on alienation was valid. In delivering the Court's opinion, Budd J outlined the Irish authorities on the question of restrictions on alienation and concluded that this condition was void. He referred, in particular, to the decisions in *Billing v Welsh*[21] and *Byrne v Byrne.*[22] In *Billing* the Court struck out a condition that restricted alienation to a particular class of people, holding that such conditions are repugnant to the nature of the fee simple. In *Byrne* the Court held that a condition preventing alienation by the grantee was to be struck out for invalidity. Relying on these precedents, Budd J in *McDonnell* suggested that there appeared to be a principle against such conditions in Irish law. The only exception to the Irish courts' strict application of the Doctrine of Repugnancy may be

[18] "Restraints Upon Alienation and Enjoyment of Estates" (1852–1891) *American Law Register,* vol 18, no 7, New Series Volume 9 (July 1870) at 393.
[19] See, for example, *Fitzsimons v Fitzsimons* [1993] ILRM 478.
[20] [1965] IR 354.
[21] (1871) IR 6 CL 88.
[22] (1953) 87 ILTR 183.

situations where alienation is allowed to all but one named person, although whether such a minor restriction on alienability would survive the Doctrine remains uncertain.

[4–17] Somewhat inconsistent authorities from England and Wales suggest there is an alternative mechanism for deciding on the validity of conditions that restrict alienability. This might be referred to as a broad, policy-based test. This policy-based approach tends to involve consideration of the extent to which the restriction actually limits alienability; the degree of restriction dictates the validity of the condition. This test is based on the concept that while *Quia Emptores* introduced a freedom to alienate into law, it did not introduce an absolute freedom to alienate—rather limitations were recognised. The test appears to be applied most commonly in cases where alienability is restricted to a certain class of persons. The first case that considered this question in detail was *Doe v Pearson*.[23] Here a fee simple was left to two sisters by a will, and attached was a condition that if either or both of them had no issue, they could only alienate the property to their sisters or the children of those sisters. The fee simple was, therefore, freely alienable if they had issue, but restricted in alienability to a certain class of people if there was no issue. The Court held the condition to be good. *Doe* was thrown into doubt by the decision in *Attwater v Attwater*.[24] Here the fee simple was granted subject to the condition that, if it were to be sold at all, the land could only be sold to one of five brothers. The condition was held to be a void restriction on alienability, but the case suggested that all conditions restricting alienability, to whatever degree, would be resisted by the courts. The suggested absoluteness of the *Attwater* approach (which in essence is, of course, the Doctrine of Repugnancy that we apply in Ireland) was rejected in the later decision of *In re MacLeay*.[25] In this case land was transferred to the grantor's brother on the condition "that he never sell it out of the family". Jessel MR held that the condition was valid, and in so doing attempted to reconcile *Doe* and *Attwater*. In his view the correct test to apply was "whether the condition takes away the whole power of alienation substantially; it is a question of substance, not of mere form".

[4–18] Thus, there are two tests that might be potentially applicable in such cases. The Irish authorities, it must be stressed, are overwhelmingly in favour of the Doctrine of Repugnancy. Despite the general principle that restrictions attached to the fee simple may not limit alienability, there are certain cases in which such restrictions will be upheld. In general, these conditions will be said to accord with public policy. It is allowable, for example, to restrict alienability of a fee simple transferred to a charity. Equally, certain statutes allow for the attachment of these conditions where fees simple are transferred by the state or by local authorities.[26]

(b) Restrictions that are Insufficiently Certain

[4–19] It is a commonsense requirement that any requirement attached to a fee simple ought to be expressed with sufficient certainty to enable a court to assess whether or not it has, in fact, been fulfilled. The certainty requirement is long-standing in this respect. In general, courts are concerned with ensuring that they can both determine what the

---

[23] 6 East 173 (1805).

[24] 18 Beav. 330 (1853).

[25] LR 20 Eq. Cases 186 (1875).

[26] s 2, Land Act 1946; s 26, Housing (Miscellaneous Provisions) Act 1992.

condition requires[27] (what Wylie calls "conceptual certainty") and whether the condition has, in fact, been fulfilled (what Wylie calls "evidentiary certainty").[28] The certainty requirement is applied with particular rigour to conditions subsequent, given the risk of divestment on non-fulfilment of such conditions.

The certainty requirement is long-standing and was clearly articulated in the early case of *Clavering v Ellison*[29] where Lord Cranworth held: [4–20]

> I consider that, from the earliest times, one of the cardinal rules on the subject has been this: that where a vested estate is to be defeated by a condition on a contingency that is to happen afterwards, that condition must be such that the courts can see from the beginning, precisely and distinctly, upon the happening of what event it was that the preceding vested estate was to determine.[30]

This certainty requirement was reiterated in the Irish cases of *In re Coghlan*,[31] *In re Hennessey*,[32] *In re Fitzgibbon*[33] and *McGowan v Kelly*.[34]

(c) Conditions that Offend Against Public Policy

As a matter of principle, there are certain conditions that the law will not allow to stand because of their incompatibility with public policy. In general these might be said to fall into a number of sub-categories: (a) conditions relating to marriage; (b) conditions relating to children; (c) name and arms clauses; (d) conditions relating to religion; and (e) discriminatory conditions. [4–21]

Conditions Relating to Marriage

The Irish Constitution protects the institution of marriage and guarantees an unenumerated right to marry.[35] In addition, the right to marry is recognised by both the European Convention on Human Rights[36] and the EU Charter of Fundamental Rights.[37] Marriage is therefore recognised as a fundamental element of society and as a right of adults, or at least of those within opposite-sex relationships. As a result of the assumed fundamentality of marriage within society, no condition may be attached to a fee simple that absolutely prohibits marriage,[38] although conditions requiring marriage are generally upheld.[39] [4–22]

---

[27] See, for example, *Moffat v McCleary* [1923] 1 IR 16; *Motherway v Coghlan* (1956) 98 ILTR 134; *In re Hennessy Deceased* (1963) 98 ILTR 39; *Sifton v Sifton* [1983] AC 656.
[28] Wylie, *Irish Land Law* (3rd ed, 1997, Dublin, Butterworths Lexis Nexis), para 4.053.
[29] (1859) 7 HLC 707.
[30] *ibid.*, at 725.
[31] [1963] IR 246.
[32] 98 ILTR 39.
[33] [1993] 1 IR 520.
[34] [2007] IEHC 228.
[35] Art 41, *Bunreacht na hÉireann*; *Ryan v Attorney General* [1965] IR 294.
[36] Art 12, European Convention on Human Rights.
[37] Art 9, European Charter of Fundamental Rights.
[38] If the condition is in a fee simple determinable, it will sometimes be upheld as intended to provide for the grantee until they get married.
[39] *Re Coghlan* [1963] IR 246.

[4–23] The situation is somewhat more complex in relation to conditions that partially restrict marriage. Prior to the adoption of the Irish Constitution, it appeared clear that whether such conditions were void or not would depend on both the extent to which they restricted marriage and the requirement of certainty. Thus, a condition that one could only marry someone who enjoyed an exorbitant income standard was struck down because it excluded all but the most exceptional people,[40] whereas a condition that one could not marry someone beneath her social class was upheld as a valid condition[41] (remember that class distinctions were far more defined at the time than they are now). Despite the right to marry being protected by the Irish Constitution, there does appear to some capacity for restricting marriage.[42] The right to marry is not, of course, an absolute right—people within forbidden degrees of relationship may not marry,[43] for example, nor may people of the same birth gender. The non-absolute manner of the right to marry is further borne out by the jurisprudence of the European Court of Human Rights.[44] Therefore, the constitutional protection of marriage does not mean that marriage may never be restricted.

[4–24] It does mean, however, that the State may not restrict marriage in an unjustifiable manner. It also means that private restrictions on marriage may well have to be shown to be only minimally restrictive. In addition, such conditions must fulfil the requirements of certainty. For example, a condition requiring one to marry someone who "practices Buddhism" may be said to be too uncertain: what does it mean to practice a religious philosophy such as Buddhism? Even more troublesome would be conditions requiring someone to marry only someone who is, for example, "a good Catholic". Again, what makes someone a "good" Catholic is an entirely subjective question and probably incapable of being assessed with sufficient certainty for such a condition to stand.

Requirements Relating to Children

[4–25] Children are recognised as an especially vulnerable category of people within both domestic and international law. In relation to conditions attached to fees simple, it is clear that one cannot require action of a child that would infringe upon his constitutional rights. Thus, children cannot be required to live apart from their parents or guardians in order to acquire or retain a fee simple ownership.

[4–26] *In re Boulter*[45] concerned a devise in a will by which the testator's grandchildren were to receive an estate in land "upon the express condition that such children or child are or is at all times during their or his respective minorities (both before and after my decease) maintained in England and do not reside abroad except for periods not exceeding six weeks in each year". This condition was particularly problematic as the children's mother was German. In addition, the children's father—the son of the

[40] *Keily v Monck* (1795) 3 Ridg PC 205.
[41] *Greene v Kirkwood* [1895] 1 IR 130.
[42] This was confirmed by the early case of *In re McKenna* [1947] IR 277, in which a condition that the grantee should not marry a Roman Catholic was upheld by Gavin-Duffy P.
[43] Civil Registration Act 2004.
[44] See especially *Schalk and Kopf v Austria*, application no 30141/04, European Court of Human Rights, 24 June 2010.
[45] [1922] 1 Ch 75.

testator—planned to take up work abroad as a linguist because his normal profession (on the stock exchange) was threatened by the economic depression affecting the economy at the time. Sargant J held that such conditions tended to have a prejudicial effect on children's relationships with their parents, particularly in cases where, as here, the parents' circumstances more or less required them to move abroad in order to earn an income and maintain their family. The condition, were it to be found valid, would require separation of children from parents—a result that would be contrary to public policy. The condition was, therefore, void. *Boulter* was subsequently applied in the Northern Irish decision of *In re Johnson: Morgan v McCaughey.*[46] The condition in this case had the effect of requiring a 15-year-old boy to reside apart from his parents. Carswell J found that "a condition tending to bring about the separation of parent and child [is invalid], whether or not it was designed by the testator to have such an effect".[47] The condition was, therefore, void.

Name and Arms Clauses

Name and arms clauses are sometimes attached to grants of the fee simple to require the grantee to use a particular name and coat of arms in the future. Such a clause may be a condition precedent, a condition subsequent or a determining requirement in a fee simple determinable: its character is ultimately a matter of construction. The law has traditionally found such clauses to be problematic, even beyond ascertaining whether, in any particular case, they are conditions precedent or subsequent. There are clear difficulties relating to certainty: what exactly is required of the grantee? Is he to use the name and coat of arms in all cases, or only in transactions relating to the land? What about a case in which the grantee is not permitted to use the coat of arms because the Chief Herald of Ireland refuses to grant permission? Something similar happened in *Austen v Collins.*[48] Here, the grantee's interest was forfeited because he could not acquire the necessary authority to use the coat of arms. Name and arms clauses thus give rise to various difficulties as to certainty, as well as in relation to the role of the Law of Arms in Ireland. **[4–27]**

For some time the English courts regarded such conditions as contrary to public policy. This position arose from *In re Fry,*[49] in which it was held that a condition requiring a wife to take on a name other than her husband's name may result in familial unrest and was, therefore, contrary to public policy. This position appears to have been overruled by *In re Neeld*[50]: apparently, marriages could now withstand differentiated surnames. The Irish courts have not been kind to name and arms clauses.[51] The main reason appears to be uncertainty. In particular, it is often difficult to tell in which circumstances the name and arms are to be used and how many failures to use the name and arms would result in defeat of the fee simple. Despite the fact that the English Court of Appeal had endorsed the use of a *de minimus* principle in *Re Neeld*, the Irish courts were not convinced. Kenny J, in particular, has criticised the **[4–28]**

[46] [1986] NI 229.
[47] Relying on *In re Boulter* [1922] 1 Ch 75.
[48] [1886] WN 91.
[49] [1945] 1 Ch 348.
[50] [1962] Ch 643.
[51] See, for example, *In re de Vere's Will Trusts* [1961] IR 224.

lack of exactitude within a *de minimus* principle, resulting in the requirement being voided for uncertainty.[52]

Requirements Relating to Religion

[4–29] In the main, requirements that might be described as discriminatory deal mostly with religion. One might require a transferee to never marry or transfer the property to someone who professes a certain religious faith. In the alternative, one may require someone to profess a certain faith. There are numerous public policy difficulties with such requirements.

[4–30] First of all, the Constitution,[53] as well as international law,[54] guarantees a right to freedom of religious belief, which arguably could be said to be violated by requirements to profess, or not profess, a certain religion. It ought to be noted, however, that the Irish courts certainly have not exhibited an over-enthusiasm about assessing the extent to which such conditions might be constitutionally suspect. In *Re Burke's Estate*[55] the High Court had an opportunity to analyse the compatibility of such conditions with the right to freedom of religious conscience. In this case a testatrix left a devise for the maintenance and education in a Roman Catholic school in Ireland of a minor, GQ. The gift stipulated, *inter alia*, that the devise was to be forfeited if GQ should cease to practise the Roman Catholic religion. It appears that the testatrix was particularly concerned with the child's religious faith because GQ was the son of a Catholic mother and a Protestant father. In relation to the provision for forfeiture, should GQ cease to practise Roman Catholicism, Gavin-Duffy P held that such a condition is void for uncertainty. While he felt that extreme cases of express repudiation of faith would be ascertained easily, he also held that there could well be circumstances in which it is practically impossible to decide whether an individual could be said to still practice the Catholic faith. The example offered is useful because it shows, within the context of just one religious faith, the difficulty inherent in adjudicating compliance with conditions on religion:

> Suppose that through human weakness a man who retains his faith neglects or shirks in some measure his duties in respect of the Sacraments, of hearing Mass, or of fasting and abstinence, or vacillates in his fulfilment of his duties of life as a Catholic, and that the material facts are clearly proved, no man will have been able to say in advance with reasonable certainty under what precise circumstances or upon what specific lapse or lapses or after how many lapses from duty the donee would incur a forfeiture under a veto upon "ceasing to practise". The necessary precision is wanting and consequently, in my opinion, the condition is too indefinite to be enforceable as a condition subsequent...

Although this is an undoubtedly commonsense approach to the question at hand, the Court did not consider the extent to which any such requirement might

---

52 *Kearns v Manresa Estates Ltd*, unreported, High Court, Kenny J, 25 July 1975.

53 Art 44, *Bunreacht na hÉireann*.

54 Art 9, European Convention on Human Rights; Art 18, International Covenant on Civil and Political Rights; Art 18, Universal Declaration of Human Rights.

55 [1951] IR 216.

be said to conflict with GQ's right to freedom of religious belief under the Constitution.[56]

Requirements might also be attached to the fee simple that require marriage to someone of a particular religious faith (or, of course, that prohibit marriage to someone of a particular religious faith). There are clearly a number of difficulties with such conditions, including freedom to marry (considered above), freedom of religious belief and whether a person's religious faith can actually be ascertained with certainty. **[4–31]**

Conditions relating to religion can have a broader reach and, as a result of that broadness of reach, bring into question their compatibility with the principles of equality and non-discrimination. If a fee simple were transferred subject to the condition that the transferee may never reside in the property with a member of the Church of Scientology, for example, such questions would understandably arise. The Irish Supreme Court has considered class conditions of this kind in relation to marriage and has concluded that "it is now too late to question their validity". In *Re Knox*[57] the condition required the transferee son to "marry a Protestant wife, the daughter of Protestant parents, and who have always been Protestants". Although the Supreme Court classed this as a marriage limitation that is valid by virtue of precedent, the critique of Andrew Lyall deserves careful consideration: "The test is not concerned with the beliefs or faith of the intended spouse at all but with factors which can only be described as sectarian in nature".[58] Lyall's analysis rings true. Class conditions of this kind, and indeed of the nature of the Scientology example given above, are properly described as sectarian or discriminatory and, as such, they bring into play the guarantee of equality within the Irish Constitution, and the guarantee of non-discrimination within the European Convention on Human Rights. If religious equality, non-sectarianism and freedom of religious belief are truly democratic principles to which we are committed as a State, and thereby reflect public policy, they ought to be subjected to a far stricter degree of scrutiny by the courts than *Knox* suggests. **[4–32]**

Discriminatory Conditions

Public policy militates against allowing conditions that are designed to have, or actually do have, the effect of perpetuating any kind of bad feeling between categories of people. This might, for example, result in the invalidity of a condition that requires the transferee to never transact with someone from another family with whom there is long-standing animosity. This is precisely what happened in the case of *In re Dunne*.[59] In this case property was left in a will in fee simple "subject only to the condition that my dwelling house and lands or any part thereof shall not be sold or otherwise conveyed or transferred by them or either of them, their successors or assigns, to any member of the Meredith families of O'Moore's Forest, Mountmellick". Among other things, the Court was asked to assess whether this condition was void on the basis of **[4–33]**

[56] The requirements as to schooling were struck down on the basis that they infringed parental rights enshrined in Art 42 of the Constitution.

[57] (1889) 23 LR IR 542.

[58] Lyall, *Land Law in Ireland* (2nd ed, 2000, Dublin, Sweet & Maxwell), p 197.

[59] [1988] IR 155.

public policy. Reflecting on the fact that such a condition would serve only to maintain old resentments and antagonisms between the families concerned, O'Hanlon J held that such conditions posed difficulties from a public policy perspective. He thus laid down the principle that "seeking to perpetuate old family divisions and carry them forward into future generations who may occupy the lands after the death of the testator" by means of condition or determining event would be contrary to public policy, resulting in such conditions being struck down.

[4–34] In a contemporary world there are other various types of condition that might be appended to a fee simple and that concern relations between categories of people. If, for example, a xenophobic transferor required a transferee to "never transact with non-nationals" in relation to the land, this would give rise to difficulties of equality, race-relations and integration and may well be found to offend against public policy. Article 40.1 of the Irish Constitution provides:

> All citizens shall, as human persons, be held equal before the law. This shall not be held to mean that the State shall not in its enactments have regards to differences of capacity, physical and moral, and of social function.

While Art 40.1 clearly protects people from unjustifiably differential treatment by the State, the extent to which the equality protection extends to the behaviour of individuals in respect of each other is somewhat more complex. Is the State in any way responsible for others discriminating against someone on the basis of his religion, gender, sexuality, disability, race, and so on? Is someone, as an individual, required to act "constitutionally" in relation to another?

[4–35] The answers to these questions are far from clear. Some constitutional provisions have been held to have (limited) application to private conduct,[60] but there appears to be little or no enthusiasm to regard the equality guarantee as one that so applies.[61] However, whether or not that constitutional provision is horizontally binding between private persons is not relevant to whether it reflects a public policy of equality and non-discrimination, which it appears to do, especially when seen in the context of the Equal Status Act 2000 (which is designed to be applied between private parties) and the European Convention on Human Rights Act 2003. Thus, there is ample evidence to suggest that non-discrimination is a fundamental element of public policy and, as a result and when combined with *Re Dunne*, ought to be capable of invalidating restrictions on fees simple that have a discriminatory intention or effect.

(v) Multi-Part Conditions Subsequent

[4–36] A fee simple can be transferred subject to multiple conditions, which throws up some particular difficulties, especially if one of the conditions is valid under the tests outlined above and one is not. The question that tends then to arise is whether the conditions are in fact to be read separately (in which case the invalidity of one has no impact on the validity of the other) or together as a composite condition (in which case the

---

[60] See *Murtagh Properties v Cleary* [1972] IR 330, in which Art 40.3 was found to apply to a trade union.

[61] For a summary of the current position, see Doyle, *Constitutional Equality Law* (2004, Dublin, Thomson Round Hall), pp 81–2.

invalidity of one will result in the invalidity of all). This becomes important in situations where the valid element of the condition(s) has not been fulfilled in a fee simple subject to conditions subsequent and, as a result, there is the risk that the fee simple will be divested.

Such a case arose for the consideration of the Supreme Court in *In re Coghlan*.[62] In this case a farm was left in trust for the nephew of the deceased, "provided my said nephew shall marry (if he not be married at my death) and come to reside there within one year from the fate of my death, and in the event of my said nephew not marrying and coming to live there as aforesaid, in trust to sell said farm and house and all stock and contents and apply the proceeds of such sale for the celebration of Masses...". The nephew claimed that the residence condition was invalid for uncertainty because it did not specify for how long he was to reside on the farm, and that the condition had to be seen as one composite (as opposed to two severable) condition and therefore struck out in its entirety. The High Court held that the marriage requirement was valid, but agreed with the nephew that the residence requirement was insufficiently certain to be upheld. Contrary to the nephew's argument, however, Dixon J held that the conditions could be seen as two severable conditions to be considered independently. The marriage condition could be upheld and applied despite the invalidity of the residence requirement; however the short High Court decision did not devote much attention to the matter of how a court would decide that the conditions were either severed into two or to be read as one, composite, requirement. Detailed consideration of this question was left to the Supreme Court and, especially, to the judgment of Kingsmill Moore J. **[4–37]**

Kingsmill Moore J reiterated the long-standing principle that conditions subsequent are to be strictly constructed,[63] and as a result held that "if there be doubt as to whether the two conditions are entirely distinct... or are composite... the doubt should be resolved in such a manner as to not invoke divesting".[64] In this case one part of the condition (residence) was invalid for uncertainty, and the other (marriage) was valid. The two were, Kingsmill Moore J noted, capable of severance on the basis of their grammatical construction, however grammatical severability was not determinative. Rather, the Court should also consider the "object and intention of the testator in the will".[65] In doing so the Court took into account what it called "the prevalent desire among Irish countryfolk to preserve a family farm in the hands of the family"[66] and found that it was inevitable that the testator in fact intended for his nephew to live and raise a family on the farm and thereby to maintain the connection between that land and the family. Taking that into account, the marriage condition (which was valid on its own) was in fact subsidiary to and dependent on the residence condition (which was invalid on its own); the two could not, therefore, be severed. They comprised a composite condition: the failure of one meant the failure of the other. Ó Dálaigh J came to a similar conclusion, finding that "the clauses are so interlocked that one **[4–38]**

[62] [1963] IR 246.

[63] *Clavering v Ellison* (1859) 7 HLC 707.

[64] [1963] IR 246, p 252.

[65] *ibid.*, p 253.

[66] *ibid.*, p 253.

clause cannot be condemned without destroying the entire condition"[67] and the entire composite condition failed for the uncertainty of the residence requirement.

2. Life Estate

[4–39] A life estate lasts for the life of a named person, known as the *cestui que vie*. Life estates involve lesser control on the part of the life tenant (i.e. the holder of the estate) than the fee simple, but there are still relatively substantial rights that arise in their favour. Pursuant to s 11(6) of the Land and Conveyancing Law Reform Act 2009, life estates now exist only in equity and become subject to the trusts system laid down in Part 4 of the Act, which is fully considered in Chapter 6. Any life estates that existed as of 1 December 2009, when the Act came into effect, were converted into trusts, meaning that the life estate now exists in equity and the fee simple is held by trustees.[68] Any attempt to create life estates after that date create life estates in equity only, and again a Part 4 trust will operate.

(i) Variations of Life Estate

[4–40] Most life tenants are also the *cestui que vie* of their estates, i.e. in most cases the life of the person who holds the estate dictates the duration of the estate. Thus, if someone has a fee simple and transfers an estate by the following disposition, "To John for life," John is both the life tenant and the *cestui que vie*. However, if someone is a fee simple-holder and transfers an estate by the disposition, "To John for the life of Mary," John is the life tenant and Mary is the *cestui que vie*. In cases like this, where the life tenant and *cestui que vie* are different people, the life estate is said to be *pur autre vie*; for the life of another. The life estate still lasts for the life of the *cestui que vie*, but in this case that person (Mary in our example) is not the same as the person who actually enjoys the life estate (John in our example). Life estates may also be made subject to a further condition. In other words, the potential exists for the creation of conditional life estates. These conditions ought to be certain, consistent with public policy and consistent with the nature of the life estate itself.

(ii) Future Interests

[4–41] As every piece of land has a fee simple over it, i.e. as someone has rights forever over every piece of land, there will always be someone with rights over the land when the life estate comes to an end. That person is called the future interest-holder, being the person who can take possession and enjoy rights in the future. There are two kinds of future interests that can arise, known as remainders and reversions.[69] The remainder arises where someone grants a life estate to another and, usually by the same disposition, grants rights to a third party on the termination of that life estate. For example, "To Patrick for life, remainder to Suzy in fee simple." In this case the transferor has given Patrick rights for his lifetime—a life estate—with rights forever after Patrick's life going to Suzy—a fee simple remainder. Suzy's future interest is in remainder because the remainder of the rights go to a third person—someone other

[67] *ibid.*, p 254.

[68] In fact, in those cases the life tenant also became a trustee of the Part 4 trust as well as the holder of the equitable life estate. This is considered in detail in Chapter 6, paras 6–39 to 6–43.

[69] This is a slight simplification for the sake of clarity. The various forms of future interest and rules relating to these interests are considered in Chapter 5.

than the transferor. In this scenario a Part 4 trust is created, with the land being held in trust for Patrick for life, remainder to Suzy. When the life estate ends (i.e. when Patrick dies) the land is no longer in need of governance through trust of land as defined by the Land and Conveyancing Law Reform Act 2009 as the ownership is now in a fee simple, and as a result the trust ends and Suzy is the fee simple holder in law and in equity.

If, in the alternative, the following disposition were made: "To Patrick for life," Patrick would have received the rights for his lifetime (a life estate) but the transferor would retain the rights for forever after Patrick's life (a fee simple reversion). These rights are retained simply because they were never given away. Thus, the transferor holds what is known as the fee simple reversion, meaning the rights simply revert back to him (or his successors in title) once Patrick dies. Again a Part 4 trust is created which will last for as long as Patrick's life estate. [4–42]

(iii) Rules of Waste

As the life tenant only has a lifetime's worth of rights, he is unlikely to have any vested interest in the long-term welfare of the property. The temptation exists for him to strip it of its worth by, for example, exploiting all the natural resources that it holds. This is a cause of concern to the future interest-holder, of course, who wants to ensure that, on regaining or acquiring control over the property, it holds worth. As a result of this state of affairs, a set of rules was designed to limit the extent of the life tenant's control in favour of the future interest-holder. These rules are known as the rules of waste. Section 18(4) of the Land and Conveyancing Law Reform Act 2009 provides that the life tenant remains liable for waste, even upon conversion of a pre-existing life estate into a life estate in equity only. [4–43]

Waste can be described as anything that has a (usually negative) impact on the land. The basic concept of the rules of waste is that the tenant for life has an obligation to pass the land on to the future interest-holder in the condition in which it was received: no better, no worse. For the purposes of these rules, waste is broken down into four categories: voluntary waste, permissive waste, ameliorating waste and equitable waste. If the future interest-holder detects waste on the land held in life estate, he can attempt to prevent its commission by applying for an injunction. The courts are empowered to grant damages *in lieu* of an injunction in appropriate circumstances.[70] As the interests being protected through the rules are the interests of the future interest-holder, it is the future interest-holder who will make the application for relief. [4–44]

(a) Voluntary Waste

In essence, voluntary waste refers to positive acts that have a negative effect on the land, usually concerning the exploitation of natural resources. All life tenants are [4–45]

---

[70] It used to be the case that injunctions would be granted only if the Court was satisfied that damages were an inadequate remedy—*London and Blackwell Railway Co v Cross* (1886) 31 Ch D 354. Hilary Delaney notes, "This principle still operates today, although arguably in a slightly more modified form and no injunction will be granted where an injury can be properly compensated in monetary terms but will only issue e.g. to restrain a continuing nuisance or the breach of a negative obligation in a contract" (internal footnote omitted). Delaney, *Equity and the Law of Trusts in Ireland* (3rd ed, 2003, Dublin, Thomson Round Hall), p 451.

automatically deemed to be liable for voluntary waste, although it is open to the grantor to relieve a life tenant of this liability. Where this is done, the life tenant is said to be "unimpeachable at waste". In general terms, there are only three circumstances where the natural resources on land held in a life estate can be exploited without incurring liability: where the exploitation is necessary for the repair and/or maintenance of the land; where the property is suited to that purpose only; and where the grantor has given permission for such exploitation.

(b) Permissive Waste

[4–46] Permissive waste comprises the failure to do things necessary for the maintenance of the land. In keeping with the law's general distaste for imposing liability for omissions to act, tenants for life are not generally deemed liable for permissive waste.[71] Rather, the grantor is required to expressly impose such liability in the grant of the estate itself.

(c) Ameliorating Waste

[4–47] Ameliorating waste comprises acts that have a positive effect on the value of land. The original position was that courts would enjoin such action, but courts' willingness to do so was greatly reduced over time. This development resulted mostly from recognition that strict application of the rules of ameliorating waste would have the effect of stymieing development.[72] By 1833 it was firmly established that an injunction could be acquired only if there was actual damage to the future interest.[73] The fact that, in the absence of actual damage to the future interest, the remainderman or reversioner had to accept the land with the improvement was firmly established by the House of Lords in *Doherty v Allman*.[74] Most questions relating to construction and development are now governed by both planning and environmental law. As a result, the rules of ameliorating waste are now of relatively little significance.

(d) Equitable Waste

[4–48] Equitable waste could be described as "malicious waste" and comprises the wanton destruction of land. All tenants for life are automatically liable for equitable waste, even if they have been made unimpeachable at waste by the grantor. The concept of equitable waste was introduced in the case of *Vane v Lord Barnard*.[75] In this case a father had transferred ownership of a castle to his son and retained a life estate for himself. In doing so he expressly made himself unimpeachable at waste and, after some time, proceeded to strip the castle of much of its valuable materials. The son, who held the future interest, attempted to prevent the waste from occurring, but the father held that he had no liability as he was unimpeachable at waste. The Court held that although the father had no liability in law, the law of equity would not allow him to engage in such malicious and wanton destruction of land. Because he had failed to make himself unimpeachable at equity, he remained liable for waste in equity.

---

71 *In re Cartwright* (1889) 41 Ch D 532.
72 See *Meux v Cobley* [1892] 2 Ch 253.
73 *Doe d. Grubb v Burlington* (1833) 5 B & Ad 507.
74 (1878) 3 AC 709.
75 (1716) 2 Vern 728.

(iv) Alienability of the Life Estate

Although the life tenant has rights for life, these rights can be alienated. The life tenant can transfer the rights for his lifetime to another, in which case the other acquires the life estate *pur autre vie*; rather sensibly, the *cestui que vie* will not change. If the life tenant holds a life estate *pur autre vie* and predeceases the *cestui que vie,* the rest of his estate can be transferred in a will or by the rules of intestacy. Land subject to a life estate is now held in a trust under Part 4 of the Land and Conveyancing Law Reform Act 2009 and can be alienated under the rules governing that Act, which are fully considered in Chapter 6. **[4–49]**

(v) Rights and Obligations of Life Tenants

Whether a tenant for life is entitled to the removal of any fixtures will essentially depend on whether those fixtures are sufficiently attached to fall within the maxim of *superficies solo credit*, as considered in Chapter 1.[76] In other words, one must consider (a) the extent of the attachment, and (b) the intention of the person who attached it. If, on application of this two-prong test, the fixture is said to be "part of the land", the tenant for life may not remove it. The status of emblements (i.e. crops grown by some industry of the tenant for life, or *fructus industrialis*) is somewhat more complex. It was traditionally the case that if the crops were sown during the life estate but the life estate was terminated by act of law before they could be reaped, the tenant for life, or his successor-in-title, was entitled to re-enter the property and reap the crops.[77] On the other hand, if the crops were sown during the life estate and the estate was terminated by the act of the tenant for life, then the emblements were lost. This remains the position today. **[4–50]**

3. Fee Tail

Used in past by rich families to keep land in bloodline

The fee tail estate lasted for as long as a bloodline endured: it was an estate that was designed to remain within a particular family. The development of the fee tail is testament to the fact that for quite some time wealth and status were linked almost inextricably to land ownership, and a family relied upon its land for its survival in both economic and social terms. The basic concept of the fee tail was that no individual family member could undertake a course of action that would result in the loss of the wealth and status of landholding for the entire family. Section 13 of the Land and Conveyancing Law Reform Act 2009 abolishes the fee tail, providing that it is no longer possible to create a fee tail[78] and that any fees tail existing on 1 December 2009 were be converted into fees simple.[79] This conversion was subject to some limited exceptions, considered below.[80] **[4–51]**

(i) History and Development

Prior to 1285, families had attempted to retain family property through a gift known as *maritagium*. This was the portion—or landholding—given to the man who was to **[4–52]**

---

[76] paras 1–19 to 1–24.
[77] *Short v Atkinson* (1834) H & J 682.
[78] s 13(1), Land and Conveyancing Law Reform Act 2009.
[79] s 13(3), *ibid.*
[80] paras 4–63 to 4–65.

marry a daughter of the family, and which could revert back to her on his death.[81] The intention was that once both the husband and wife had died, this property would go to their heirs. In the event of there being no heirs, the property would revert back to the wife's father (or his successors). Although this was the intention behind the *maritagium*, the courts systematically interpreted the gift as a conditional fee simple. Under this interpretation the initial grant entitled the husband and wife to a life estate, but once they had produced an heir they were said to have a fee simple absolute. Quite clearly, this was in sharp contrast to the intentions of the grantor, as it meant that heirs could be disinherited by sale and the family could become economically and socially impoverished—precisely the scenario the grant was intended to avoid. As a result of the difficulties with the *maritagium*, the *Statute de Donis Conditionalibus* 1285 was introduced, allowing for the creation of an estate in which the intention of the grantor would be respected so that the grantee "shall have no power to aliene the land so given, but that it shall remain unto the issue of them to whom it was given after their death... or unto the giver or his heirs, if issue fail".[82]

(ii) Types of Fee Tail

[4–53] *De Donis* allowed for the creation of a fee tail general, i.e. a fee tail where the line of succession was determined by the normal rules of heirship. At that time those rules were based on *primogeniture*: the notion that the eldest male heir would inherit, and where there were no male heirs the female heirs would inherit together in a type of co-ownership known as coparcenary.[83] Where there was a fee tail general, therefore, the line of inheritance was determined by these rules. Indeed, the fee tail was the only situation in which primogeniture survived the Succession Act 1965. Subsequent legislation ensured that there was no difference in how marital and non-marital children become entitled under the fee tail.[84] The very essence of the fee tail was that there was nothing the holder of the fee tail, known as the tenant in tail, could do to prevent the property rights proceeding to an heir under this system as long as the fee tail existed; the estate was designed to remove that autonomy. In essence, every tenant in tail had rights for his lifetime only, although those rights were not properly described as life estates.

[4–54] *De Donis* also allowed for alternative forms of fee tail to be created. These fees tail would further limit the category of descendants entitled to take their place within the fee tail and were known as fees tail special. Some examples of these were included in *de Donis* and included fees tail male (where only male descendants can become tenants in tail), fees tail female (where only female descendants can become tenants in tail) and fees tail marital (where only "legitimate" descendants can become tenants in tail). The

---

[81] In reality this was a sort of dowry and only arose in cases where families were reasonably wealthy. In most other cases the "dowry" took the form of money or personal property. See Johns, *Noblewomen, Aristocracy and Power in the Twelfth-Century Anglo-Norman Realm* (2003, Manchester, Manchester University Press).

[82] Statute of Westminster II, 13 Edw 1, c 1.

[83] There are numerous theories on the purpose and development of primogeniture. Possibly the most convincing is that the system "emerged as family heads' optimal policy to minimize their respective lineal extinction probability". Chu, "Primogeniture" (1991) 99(1) JPE 78. In other words, it appears to have been designed in order to prevent families from dying out.

[84] Status of Children Act 1987.

list of fees tail special included in *de Donis* was not exhaustive, as illustrated by *In re Elliot*.[85] In this case the testator left property "to... my son and the heirs of his body (other than... his eldest son)". The Court held that this created a fee tail special inasmuch as it stipulated an additional tailoring, or limitation, of the heirs who could take their place as tenants in tail. Other, more established forms of fee tail allowed for certain descendants to be removed from the fee tail—for example, a fee tail female where the eldest heir is male—therefore, there was nothing in principle to disallow such a scenario here. As *de Donis* was not exhaustive in its list of types of fee tail that could be created, this disposition could take effect as intended. According to O'Connor MR, giving effect to intention was, in fact, the main impetus for *de Donis*.

(iii) Alienability

Every tenant in tail had a lifetime's worth of entitlement that could be alienated, with the transferee receiving a life estate *pur autre vie* (the tenant in tail was the *cestui que vie*). Once a tenant in tail died, however, all entitlements died with him. While they were in force, the Settled Land Acts 1882–1890 gave extensive rights of alienation to tenants in tail, which are considered in Chapter 6. The final and most common method of alienating the fee tail was a process known as barring the entail, the mechanics of which changed somewhat over time and which in fact conveyed a fee simple to the purchaser. **[4–55]**

(iv) Barring the Entail

As sources of economic wealth and status diversified, problems with the fee tail became apparent. Because every tenant in tail had only a lifetime's worth of rights, each individual was limited to alienating a life estate *pur autre vie* to another. This made using land as capital, or as a means to raise capital for alternative investment, exceptionally difficult. The fee tail, which had been designed to retain wealth and status for a family, was now a hindrance to participation in new forms of wealth- and status-generation. As a result of these difficulties, people began to try to find a way of enabling tenants in tail to deal in the fee simple. In other words, people began to try to sell rights forever when their entitlement within the fee tail was merely to rights for life. Despite the fact that this appeared to be illogical the courts allowed for fee simple alienation of the fee tail in the seminal *Taltarum's Case*.[86] As well as arising in the context of the desire to realise the market value of property, this case was significantly influenced by the concerns held by the king about the risk posed to his authority by the fee tail estate. If a tenant in tail committed treason, for example, his estate would still be forfeited, but because it was a fee tail estate, the family would regain their status and wealth on the death of the treasonous tenant in tail. Only his entitlement, i.e. entitlement for life, could be forfeited. The future tenants in tail remained safe. Largely as a result of these concerns, the Court allowed the use of a collusive action (known as a "common recovery") in *Taltarum's Case*, which destroyed rights of the future tenants in tail.[87] Subsequent courts also **[4–56]**

---

[85] [1916] 1 IR 30.

[86] YB 12 Edw 4, fol. 19, Michaelmas Term, pl. 25 (1472).

[87] It should be noted that some commentators believe the common recovery was being practised prior to *Taltarum's Case*, however this is the point at which the practice became somewhat "legitimate" and, subsequently, widespread. See Thomas, "Anglo-American Land Law: Diverging Developments from a Shared History. Part II: How Anglo-American Land Law Diverged after American Colonization and Independence" (1999) 34(2) RPPT 295.

recognised that the common recovery destroyed the interests of the remainderman or reversioner.[88]

[4–57] From that point on, the principle that a fee tail could be converted into a fee simple was established in law, even if there was some lack of clarity around how it really worked.[89] This lack of clarity and need for an efficient mechanism to bar the entail culminated in the Fines and Recoveries Act (Ireland) 1834. This Act introduced a new, straightforward mechanism for converting the fee tail into a fee simple, known as the "disentailing assurance".[90] The word "disentailing" simply meant "removing the entail", or cancelling the limitation, or removing the future interests in the fee tail. The word "assurance" simply meant "deed of conveyance". Thus, the disentailing assurance was the mechanism by which a tenant in tail could convey (or transfer) property rights to another and through the magic of the Fines and Recoveries Act the transferee would receive a fee simple estate. The tenant in tail could also convey the property to another to the use of himself and, provided the requirements of the Fines and Recoveries (Ireland) Act 1834 were complied with, the use would be executed and the tenant in tail would end up with the fee simple in the land.[91] Through the disentailing assurance the tenant in tail could successfully transfer fee simple ownership to someone by using the Fines and Recoveries Act but, naturally, that Act required compliance with a number of conditions in order for its magic to be worked on the conveyance.

(a) A disentailing assurance had to be done inter vivos (i.e. while alive)

[4–58] As the tenant in tail was entitled to rights over the property only for as long as he was alive, he could only transact in relation to that property while he was alive. Any attempt to bar the entail in a will was ineffective.

(b) The tenant in tail after possibility of issue extinct could not issue a disentailing assurance

[4–59] The tenant in tail after possibility of issue extinct was the last person within the line of descent, i.e. nobody qualified to inherit under the fee tail was alive or conceived. Section 15 provided that a tenant in tail after possibility of issue extinct was not entitled to bar the entail. Any attempt to bar the entail contrary to this requirement would be ineffective and the fee tail would continue in operation.

(c) The consent of the protector had to be acquired if the tenant in tail was not in possession

[4–60] The protector of the settlement was either the person who had to give consent to the barring of the entail under the system that existed before the disentailing assurance[92]

---

[88] *Capell's Case* 76 Eng Rep 134 (KB 1581).

[89] Simpson, *A History of the Land Law* (2nd ed, 1986, Oxford, Oxford University Press), p 130.

[90] ss 2 and 12, Fines and Recoveries (Ireland) Act 1834.

[91] The use and the execution of uses are considered in Chapter 3, paras 3–04 to 3–08. The mechanism by which a tenant in tail could convey the fee simple to himself through a disentailing assurance and executed use is considered in more detail in de Londras, *Principles of Irish Property Law* (1st ed, 2007, Dublin, Clarus Press), paras 1–147 to 1–149.

[92] s 28, Fines and Recoveries (Ireland) Act 1834.

or a person expressly named as protector in the settlement.[93] The protector's consent was required for the entail to be successfully barred. The protector would normally give consent when asked for it, although it was quite common for conditions to be attached thereto in the attempt to protect future tenants in tail whose entitlements over the land would be negated by the barring of the entail.

Any attempt to bar the entail without the consent of the protector would only be partially successful: the rights of the future tenants in tail would be barred, but those of the remainderman or reversioner would remain. The estate received by the transferee in such circumstances was the base fee, rather than the fee simple. The base fee comprised rights that would last for as long as the fee tail would have lasted, but which would end when the line of descent stipulated in the fee tail runs out. Although there were a number of ways that the holder of a base fee could convert, or enlarge, it into a fee simple,[94] it was a problematic and somewhat precarious estate. **[4–61]**

(d) The disentailing assurance had to be lodged in the Central Office of the High Court within six months of its execution

The fourth and final requirement under the Fines and Recoveries Act was a procedural one and required that the assurance be lodged with the High Court within six months of its execution.[95] Failure to comply with this requirement resulted in the purchaser receiving only a voidable base fee.[96] This meant that, while the tenant in tail who executed the disentailing assurance had successfully removed himself from the fee tail, any tenant in tail could choose to reconstitute the fee tail in the future. In such a case the transferee's entitlements under the disentailing assurance would be reduced to naught. **[4–62]**

(v) The Fee Tail after the LCLRA 2009

Long before the Land and Conveyancing Law Reform Act 2009 the fee tail had been the subject of sustained criticisms from commentators, which ranged from constitutional difficulties with the potential for gender-based discrimination within the fee tail[97] to simply identifying fees tail as "complex and useless relics of the past".[98] Although the Law Reform Commission had initially refused to recommend the **[4–63]**

---

[93] s 30, *ibid.* allowed for between one and three people to be named as protectors.

[94] The holder of the base fee could acquire the unbarred interests through regular transaction with the remainderman or reversioner (s 37, Fines and Recoveries (Ireland) Act 1934); a fresh disentailing assurance could be executed with the protector's consent or without that consent when the protectorship had ended (*Bank of Ireland v Domvile* [1956] IR 37); and s 19 of the Statute of Limitations allows the holder of a base fee without entitlements under the fee tail to extinguish the interests of the remainderman or reversioner by remaining in possession for 12 years subsequent to the end of the protectorship.

[95] s 39, Fines and Recoveries (Ireland) Act 1834.

[96] *In re St George's Estate* (1879) 3 LR IR 277.

[97] See Lyall, *Land Law in Ireland* (2nd ed, 2000, Dublin, Sweet & Maxwell), pp 224–6.

[98] Pearse and Mee, *Essential Law Texts: Land Law* (2nd ed, 2000, Dublin, Round Hall), p 67.

abolition of the fee tail,[99] this position was reversed in 2004 when the Commission recommended abolition in the strongest terms.[100] This recommendation was given effect in s 13 of the 2009 Act. Section 13(1) prohibits the future creation of a fee tail in law or in equity. Any attempt to create a fee tail after 1 December 2009 vests a legal or equitable fee simple (as appropriate) in the grantee.[101]

[4–64] While this prevented the creation of new fees tail it did not deal with the fees tail that already existed. Thus, s 13(3) provides that where anyone was entitled to a fee tail in law or equity before the commencement of the Act, or becomes entitled to such after the commencement of the Act, that fee tail (whether legal equitable) will be automatically converted into a fee simple, vesting in the person who was entitled under the pre-existing fee tail. Thus, existing fees tail are automatically converted to fees simple. This is subject to two exceptions that are intended to mirror, in effect, the limitations on barring the entail as they existed under the Fines and Recoveries (Ireland) Act 1834 in order to avoid constitutional difficulty. First, where the protectorship has not ended, s 13(3) will not convert the fee tail into a fee simple, although this conversion will happen once the protectorship comes to an end. Second, there is no conversion where the fee tail is held by a tenant in tail after possibility of issue extinct.[102]

[4–65] Section 13(4) of the Land and Conveyancing Law Reform Act 2009 makes it clear that the automatic conversion, subject to the exceptions outlined above, will apply to fees tail, base fees (provided the protectorship has ended) and voidable base fees. Thus, we can expect that within one generation the very limited number of fees tail that might have survived the initial conversion under s 13(3) will have all been converted.

Part II: Words of Limitation

[4–66] Prior to the introduction of the Land and Conveyancing Law Reform Act 2009, there were—as we have seen—three different freehold estates in law: the fee simple, the life estate and the fee tail. Now there is only one freehold estate in law (the fee simple) and two in equity (the fee simple and the life estate). In order to make it clear what kind of freehold estate is being conveyed by any transaction, we have long included what are known as Words of Limitation in conveyances: words that "measure out the quantity of estate".[103] These words must be contrasted with Words of Purchase, which are used to indicate who is to receive the estate transferred, "purchaser" meaning "someone who acquires rights by means of a legal transaction". It was the case that Words of Limitation were different for each of the freehold estates, and also that there were different rules depending on whether the estate was being created *inter vivos* or in a will. The simplification and rationalisation of freehold estates in the 2009 Act has also simplified the rules relating to Words of Limitation, but they continue to require our attention, especially since some attempts at simplification—such as the abolition of the

[99] LRC, *Report on Land Law and Conveyancing Law (1): General Proposals* (1989), p 6.

[100] LRC, *Consultation Paper on Reform and Modernisation of Land Law and Conveyancing Law* (2004), pp 48–9.

[101] s 13(2), Land and Conveyancing Law Reform Act 2009.

[102] s 13(4), *ibid.*

[103] *Goodright v Wright* (1717) 1 P Wms 397 *per* Parker CJ.

Rule in *Shelley's Case*, considered below—seem actually to introduce more complexity than they eradicate.

1. Fee Simple *Inter Vivos*

The common law's original position was that only one formula of words would suffice to transfer a fee simple *inter vivos* and that was "and his heirs". This requirement was applied with a strict hand: any variation on those words would transfer a life estate as the default estate.[104] This situation resulted in an absurdity in the law. As a result of the strict approach that was applied, a disposition that read, "My house to John in fee simple," would have the effect of transferring a life estate to John despite the clear intention evident in the words used. In order to try to ameliorate this absurdity, s 51 of the Conveyancing Act 1881 introduced the alternative, "in fee simple". Thus, from 1881 there were two alternative formulae available: "My house to John and his heirs," or "My house to John in fee simple." **[4–67]**

In addition to the slightly more flexible common law position, whereby people had alternative formulae to choose from, the courts of equity began to intervene and recognise that simple mistakes ought not to result in the loss of the fee simple. Thus, although the common law courts would interpret "to John in fee" as being effective to transfer a life estate only, the courts of equity would read it as transferring a fee simple in equity if they were satisfied that the word "simple" had been mistakenly omitted.[105] On occasion, surplus words might be included in the Words of Limitation. For example, a disposition might read, "To John and his heirs male." In this case the word "male" would be seen as a condition subsequent on the fee simple—"To John and his heirs," created the fee simple and "male" attempted to restrict its alienability to male transferees. This condition would be struck out as void (for restricting alienability) and the fee simple absolute would pass.[106] **[4–68]**

Even the common law recognised the unfairness of transferring only a life estate to someone who had paid consideration for a fee simple. As a result, s 7 of the Conveyancing Act 1881 provided that a transferee of a fee simple for value had an entitlement to have the deed rectified in order to ensure that the appropriate Words of Limitation for transfer of a fee simple were used. **[4–69]**

There was some uncertainty as to whether the same Words of Limitation were required to pass a fee simple in equity (for example, on trust) as were required to pass this estate in law. An initial logical consideration might suggest not. After all, equity is more flexible and intention-based than law. This, in fact, appears likely to be the case. In numerous cases an intention-based analysis has been favoured by the courts. Thus, in *In re Houston*,[107] for example, property rights transferred in equity without **[4–70]**

---

104 *Jack v Reilly* (1829) 2 H & B 301; *Wood v Davis* (1880) 6 LR IR 5; *Lysaght v McGrath* (1881) 8 LR IR 123; *In re Coleman's Estate* [1907] 1 IR 488; *In re Adam's Estate* [1965] IR 57; *In re Houston* [1909] 1 IR 319.

105 *In re Ottley's Estate* [1910] 1 IR 1.

106 *Idle v Cook* (1705) 1 P Wm 70.

107 [1909] 1 IR 319.

any Words of Limitation were held to be a fee simple; the Court was concerned with the intention of the transferor.[108] This stands in sharp contrast to *Meyler v Meyler*,[109] in which it was held that the same Words of Limitation were needed to pass a fee simple in equity as were needed in law. While the weight of modern authority tends to suggest a more flexible approach in equity, the position is therefore not entirely clear.

[4–71] In order to further simplify the transfer of the fee simple in registered land, s 123 of the Registration of Title Act 1964 provided that, in the absence of a contrary intention, a fee simple (or the greatest possible estate in land) would be transferred. Thus, where there were no Words of Limitation, or where the Words of Limitation already laid down as acceptable in common law and statute were used, a fee simple would pass in transactions over registered land. In order to also simplify conveyances of unregistered land, s 67(1) of the Land and Conveyancing Law Reform Act 2009 provides:

> A conveyance of unregistered land with or without words of limitation, or any equivalent expression, passes the fee simple or the other entire estate or interest which the grantor had power to create or convey, unless a contrary intention appears in the conveyance.

Under s 67(1) a fee simple will be passed in a conveyance of unregistered land if there are no Words of Limitation, the common law Words of Limitation, or the statutory Words of Limitation.

[4–72] Section 67(1) has express retrospective effect, i.e. it applies to conveyances executed either after *or before* the commencement of the 2009 Act.[110] This retrospectivity presents an important difficulty that may be best illustrated by an example:

> Patrick conveys his house, which is unregistered land, *inter vivos* "to Ciarán". Under the common law and statutory rules then in operation, Ciarán is entitled only to a life estate because the required Words of Limitation have not been used. Patrick has retained the fee simple reversion. Upon the retrospective application of s 67(1), Ciarán receives a fee simple and Patrick "loses" his fee simple reversion.

If this scenario were allowed to stand without any kind of possibility for Patrick to protect his fee simple reversion, s 67(1) would in fact have operated to deprive him of his property in a manner that is likely to contravene the constitutional protection of private property and the right to possessions under Art 1 of Protocol One of the European Convention on Human Rights.[111] Even if the provision were somehow to escape constitutional invalidity, it is likely that s 67(1) would have been declared incompatible with the European Convention on Human Rights by means of a Declaration of Incompatibility under s 5 of the European Convention on Human

[108] See also *Jameson v McGovern* [1934] IR 758 and *Savage v Nolan*, unreported, High Court, 20 July 1978, where the same result was reached.

[109] (1883) 11 LR IR 522.

[110] s 67(4), Land and Conveyancing Law Reform Act 2009.

[111] See Chapter 1, paras 1–06 to 1–12.

Rights Act 2003.[112] It should, therefore, be clear that some kind of mechanism had to be created for Patrick—or anyone in an analogous position to him—to assert his property rights if they were adversely affected by the retrospective application of s 67(1). An attempt is made to provide such a system in s 68 of the Land and Conveyancing Law Reform Act 2009.

Section 68(1) provides that any interest in land that had been acquired or to which one was entitled because of a lack of Words of Limitation before the commencement of the 2009 Act is extinguished *unless* that individual applies for an order under s 68 within 12 years of 1 December 2009 *and*, if such an order is granted, registers said order.[113] A Court can make an order under s 68(2) that the applicant is entitled to the interest in question or has acquired it. Presumably, in such a case, s 67(1) does not operate on the conveyance by which that interest was acquired. The Court can also order the payment of compensation rather make an order declaring that the applicant is entitled to or has acquired the interest. This is clearly said to be "in lieu of a declaration" and the compensation is to be such as "the court thinks appropriate". In all likelihood, the requirements of proportionality outlined in terms of interference with private property rights in both the Constitution and the European Convention of Human Rights, taken into account in the context of the value of the property in question, will determine the amount of compensation. A Court may also refuse to make an order under s 68 "if it is satisfied that no substantial injustice will be done to any party". [4–73]

In essence, s 68 creates a kind of modified adverse possession system for such interests[114]: the applicant has twelve years to assert his or her title but that must be done by means of a s 68 application. Adverse possession is not, in itself, a disproportionate interference with property rights, but whether the restriction of the avenues for assertion of title to s 68 would "tilt" the balance towards disproportionality is a difficult question to assess. It seems difficult to fully grasp why the 2009 Act did not simply limit the application of s 67(1) to future conveyances and leave past conveyances as they were. It would certainly have been a more straightforward approach to take, especially since all of the conveyances to which s 67(1) might be retrospectively applied were done at a time and in an environment where the required Words of Limitation for a fee simple were well known and well established. To interfere with the interests acquired as a result of a lack of Words of Limitation in conveyances of unregistered land done prior to 1 December 2009 in this way seems, in a sense, to tempt constitutional (or at least Convention) sense. [4–74]

2. Fee Simple in a Will

In the case of a transfer by will, the original position was that rather than insist on particular Words of Limitation, courts would try to ascertain and give effect to the [4–75]

[112] de Londras and Kelly, *European Convention on Human Rights Act 2003: Operation, Impact and Analysis* (2010, Dublin, Round Hall), pp 192–207.

[113] The order is registered in the Land Registry (registered land) or Registry of Deeds (unregistered land) as appropriate—s 68(3), Land and Conveyancing Law Reform Act 2009. On the operation of both registered and unregistered land generally see Chapter 7.

[114] On adverse possession generally see Chapter 14.

intention of the testator. A fee simple could be devised through the use of the words "for ever"[115] or "absolutely",[116] although it appears likely that *some* words would have been seen as necessary; simply saying "to John" would be unlikely to be sufficient to pass the fee simple in the property to John as paucity of words makes intention practically impossible to discern. The Wills Act 1837 changed this to some degree. Section 28 thereof provided that where no Words of Limitation were used, the fee simple or largest possible estate in the circumstances would be transferred unless a contrary intention was shown. One might show a contrary intention through the use of words associated with the transfer of another estate. This position was replicated in s 94 of the Succession Act 1965:

> Where real estate is devised to a person (including a trustee or executor) without any words of limitation, the devise shall be construed to pass the whole estate or interest which the testator had power to dispose of by will in the real estate, unless a contrary intention appears from the will.

[4–76] Thus, where no Words of Limitation are used in a disposition in a will, the fee simple or largest estate possible will be transferred to the beneficiary. But this does not help us to ascertain the repercussions of using incorrect Words of Limitation in wills. In other words, it offers little guidance as to the effect of using words in a will where those words do not accord with the fee simple estate. It would appear that s 95(2) of the Succession Act 1965 guides us in this relation. It provides:

> Words of limitation contained in a will in respect of real estate which have not the effect of creating an estate in fee simple or an estate tail shall have the same effect, as near as may be, as similar words used in a deed in respect of personal property.

Thus, the Court will construct words that are inadequate to pass a fee simple (such as "for ever") as though they were being used in relation to personal property. The estate passed thus becomes a matter of interpretation. If the words are constructed to give an absolute gift of personal property, the beneficiary in the will receives the absolute estate in land, i.e. the fee simple.

3. Fee Simple to a Corporation Sole

[4–77] A corporation sole is a person holding an office that is subject to perpetual succession, such as An Taoiseach or the President of the High Court. In the case of transfers using the official title, a commonsense question arises: are the property rights being transferred to the office, or to the individual holding that office in his private capacity? In order to combat such questions, one began to use the words "and his successors"[117] after the title to show an intention to transfer the fee simple to the office and "and his heirs" to show an intention to transfer the fee simple to the individual incumbent in his private capacity. Section 67(2) of the Land and Conveyancing Law Reform Act 2009 puts this position beyond dispute by providing that a "conveyance of unregistered land to a corporation sole by that person's corporate designation without the word 'successors' passes to the corporation the fee simple or the other entire estate

[115] *Doe d Dacre v Roper* (1809) 11 East 518.
[116] *Hogan d Wallis v Jackson* (1775) 1 Cowp 299.
[117] Ex p *Vicar of Castle Bytham* [1895] 1 Ch 348.

or interest which the grantor had power to create or convey, unless a contrary intention appears in the conveyance".

4. Fee Simple to a Corporation Aggregate

A corporation aggregate is a collection of two or more people in a form that cannot die, such as a limited company. No Words of Limitation are required to pass a fee simple estate to the corporation aggregate—"to Silly Toys Ltd" will successfully result in a fee simple vesting in Silly Toys Ltd.[118] **[4–78]**

5. Fee Simple by the Attempt to Create a Fee Tail

We have already seen that it is no longer possible to create a fee tail in law or in equity and that, according to s 13(2), "Any instrument executed after the commencement of this Part purporting to create a fee tail in favour of any person vests in that person a legal fee simple or, as the case may be, an equitable fee simple and any contract for such a creation entered into before or after such commencement operates as a contract for such vesting". Thus, where the Words of Limitation that were previously used to create a fee tail are used in a conveyance, those words will in fact create a fee simple. The common law originally required a transferor to use one of three alternatives to create a fee tail: "and the heirs of his body", "and the heirs of his flesh" or "and the heirs of his proceedings". Section 51 of the Conveyancing Act 1881 offered the further alternatives "in tail" and "in fee tail". Where those words are used, a fee simple will now be created. **[4–79]**

6. Life Estate

A life estate can now only be created in equity,[119] and is transferred by the use of the words "for life". It used to be the case that where no Words of Limitation were used, the life estate would be transferred as the default estate. However, as we have seen, the fee simple is now created where there are no Words of Limitation in conveyances of registered land (under s 123, Registration of Title Act 1964) or of unregistered land (s 67(1), Land and Conveyancing Law Reform Act 2009). Where Words of Limitation are used but there are not the recognised common law or statutory Words of Limitation for a fee simple or a fee tail (in which case a fee simple would now be created[120]), it appears to be the case that a life estate would be transferred to the transferee. That life estate would, of course, exist in equity only and it would be managed through a Part 4 trust.[121] **[4–80]**

7. The Rule in *Shelley's Case*

The Rule in *Shelley's Case* dates back to the feudal period, despite being named for a decision from the 1500s,[122] and provided that where a freehold estate was transferred to a grantee and, by the same disposition, that estate was limited (with or without an intermediate remainder) to the heirs or heirs of the body of the immediate grantee, then **[4–81]**

---

[118] *In re Woking UDC (Basingstoke Canal) Act 1911* [1914] 1 Ch 300.

[119] s 11(6), Land and Conveyancing Law Reform Act 2009.

[120] s 13(2), *ibid.*

[121] Part 4 trusts are considered in Chapter 6.

[122] *Shelley's Case* (1581) 1 Co Rep 88b.

"heirs" or "heirs of the body" would be Words of Limitation and not Words of Purchase.[123] To put it in somewhat simpler terms, if a grantee acquired a freehold estate and there was a freehold remainder to his heirs or to the heirs of his body, then his estate would be merged with the remainder of his heirs or the heirs of his body and the product of this merger would be vested in him.[124] As it was a rule of law it applied regardless of what the intentions of the grantor were.

[4–82] Although s 67(3) of the Land and Conveyancing Law Reform Act 2009 purports to abolish the Rule in *Shelley's Case*, that abolition is both prospective and retrospective[125] and the retrospective abolition is subject to the right of application under s 68 whereby anyone with an interest in land that is extinguished by the abolition of the Rule in *Shelley's Case* can make an application for protection of that interest or for compensation in lieu.[126] As a result, it would be an overstatement to suggest that the Rule in *Shelley's Case* has been excised from Irish law, for we must be able to ascertain whether someone has an interest in land that predates the commencement of the 2009 Act (1 December 2009) and which arose from the operation of the Rule in *Shelley's Case* and can, as a result, entitle the holder to make an application under s 68.

[4–83] The Rule is best explained by means of examples. Take the following disposition, which we will say was made *inter vivos* in relation to registered land in 1970: "To John for life, remainder to his heirs". At first it appears that John acquires a life estate followed by a fee simple remainder to John's heirs. Because we have, *prima facie*, a freehold estate followed by a freehold remainder to the heirs of the grantee we will apply the Rule. Thus, we merge a life estate with a fee simple remainder: John's life + forever after John's life = forever. The fee simple lasts forever, thus we vest a fee simple in John. Another way of thinking about this is to say that "heirs" are the Words of Limitation for a fee simple. So instead of reading the transaction as written, we read it as follows: "To John and for life, remainder to his heirs".

[4–84] The Rule would work in the same way if there were an intermediate remainder, i.e. if a third party had a remainder in between the estate of the immediate grantee and the estate of his heirs or the heirs of his body. Take the following disposition, which we will say was made *inter vivos* in relation to registered land in 1970: "To John for life, remainder to Sue for life, remainder to his heirs". Once again, the Rule in *Shelley's Case* will apply because, *prima facie*, there is a life estate to John, a life estate to Sue and a fee simple remainder to John's heirs. Thus we have a freehold estate in John followed by a freehold estate in his heirs; the presence of the intermediate remainder to Sue does not prevent the application of the Rule, thus we merge John's life estate and his heirs' fee simple remainder: John's life + forever after John's life = forever. The fee

---

123 The generally accepted definition of the Rule is offered by Megarry and Wade, *Law of Real Property* (5th ed, 1984, London, Sweet & Maxwell), p 1161: "It is a rule of law that when an estate of freehold is given to a person, and by the same disposition an estate is limited either mediately or immediately to his heirs or to the heirs of his body, the words 'heirs' or 'heirs of his body' are words of limitation and not words of purchase".

124 The estates must be freehold, as confirmed by *Harris v Barnes* (1768) 4 Burr 2158.

125 s 67(4), Land and Conveyancing Law Reform Act 2009.

126 The operation of s 68 is considered at paras 4–71 to 4–72 above.

simple lasts forever, thus John is said to be vested with a fee simple. However, Sue's life estate is not negated. Thus, the equation is changed and becomes: (John's life + forever after John's life) – Sue's life = forever – Sue's life = fee simple subject to Sue's life estate.The repercussion of the fee simple being subject to the intermediate estate is that the merger was, in practice, postponed until Sue's death, and the immediate grantee (John) was said to have a fee simple vested in remainder. This simply meant that his fee simple is vested in interest—he holds it, but it does not become possessory until some stage in the future.[127]

If the intermediate remainder were contingent, the same principle could be applied to it. Thus we would apply the same principles if the disposition over registered land made *inter vivos* in 1970 stated: "To John for life, remainder to Sue for life if she becomes a doctor, remainder to his heirs." Here we have a prima facie life estate to John, followed by a contingent life estate (i.e. conditional life estate) to Sue, followed by a fee simple remainder to John's heirs. Thus, we have a freehold estate in John followed by a freehold estate in his heirs; the presence of the intermediate contingent remainder to Sue does not prevent the application of the rule. Thus, we merge John's life estate and his heirs' fee simple remainder: John's life + forever after John's life = forever. The fee simple lasts forever, thus John is said to be vested with a fee simple. However, Sue's life estate is not affected. So the equation is changed and becomes: (John's life + forever after John's life) – Sue's life if she becomes a doctor = forever – Sue's life = fee simple subject to Sue's contingent life estate. In this circumstance the merger is not postponed because Sue is not yet entitled to the life estate. Therefore, the merger takes effect, but if Sue fulfils the contingency and becomes entitled to the life estate, then a "de-merger" will occur. This simply means that the possessory rights will go to Sue for her lifetime as soon as she becomes entitled to the life estate, and will revert back to John on the termination of that life estate. Thus, the fee simple de-merges to allow the life estate in and re-merges on its termination. [4–85]

Anyone who would have been entitled to an estate or interest by the operation of the Rule in *Shelley's Case* to a conveyance that predates the commencement of the 2009 Act (i.e. 1 December 2009) is entitled to make a s 68 application, but the adequacy of s 68 as a means of saving the retrospective application of the abolition of *Shelly* from incompatibility with the Constitution or the European Convention on Human Rights remains open to the same kinds of questions as we considered already with the retrospective application of s 67(1).[128] It once more appears odd that retrospective abolition was favoured over prospective abolition of the Rule. It would certainly have been more straightforward, more certain, and less constitutionally suspect to leave the Rule in *Shelley's Case* in the past rather than creating this questionable situation under s 68. [4–86]

Part III: Leasehold Estates

The law of landlord and tenant is substantively considered in Chapter 15, but for now it is important that we would consider in brief the leasehold estates as they exist in law. Section 11(3) of the Land and Conveyancing Law Reform Act 2009 provides: [4–87]

[127] Future interests are considered in Chapter 5.

[128] paras 4–71 to 4–72 above.

> a "leasehold estate" means... the estate which arises when a tenancy is created for any period of time or any recurring period and irrespective of whether or not the estate—
>
> (a) takes effect in immediate possession or in future, or
>
> (b) is subject to another legal estate or interest, or
>
> (c) is for a term which is uncertain or liable to termination by notice, re-entry or operation of law or by virtue of a provision for cessor on redemption or for any other reason.

Our interest here is in familiarising ourselves with the basic leasehold estates as they exist in Irish property law.

1. Tenancy at Will

[4–88] Before the commencement of the Land and Conveyancing Law Reform Act 2009, we recognised a form of leasehold estate known as the tenancy at will. Tenancies at will lasted for an indefinite period of time, were rarely if ever subject payment of rent, and could be terminated at the will of either party (i.e. without any kind of process of formality). They did not, therefore, conform with our basic conception of a lease and, in fact, the courts had indicated that they were inclined to consider these relationships as licences, as opposed to leases, especially in familial relationships.[129] Tenancies at will are not included in the definition of leasehold estates in s 11(3) of the 2009 Act. As this is an exhaustive provision, the tenancy at will no longer exists as a leasehold estate.

2. Tenancy at Sufferance

[4–89] Before the commencement of the Land and Conveyancing Law Reform Act 2009, we recognised a form of leasehold estate known as the tenancy at sufferance. These arose where a tenant held over, i.e. remained in possession with neither the assent nor the dissent of the landlord, once the lease had come to an end. At this point the tenant was clearly not entitled to be in possession of the property, but their relationship was conventionally described as a leasehold one. Tenancies at sufferance are not included in the definition of leasehold estates in s 11(3) of the 2009 Act. As this is an exhaustive provision, the tenancy at sufferance no longer exists as a leasehold estate.

3. Periodic Tenancy

[4–90] A periodic tenancy will last for a defined period of time. Once that period of time has expired, it will renew itself automatically. Thus, a weekly periodic tenancy will last for an initial week, after which another week will begin to run, after which another week will begin to run, and so on. Periodic tenancies are determined, or brought to an end, by means of notice, i.e. one party informs the other that he wants to bring the landlord and tenant relationship to an end. At common law the amount of notice to be given was generally equivalent to the period of the tenancy—a weekly periodic tenancy required a week's notice, and so on. There were certain, limited exceptions to that, such as allowing for a yearly periodic tenancy to be determined by six months' notice unless it was agricultural or pastoral, in which case a full year's notice had to be given.[130] The notice period must come to an end on the day on which a full period expires. These

[129] *Irish Shell & BP Ltd v Costello Ltd (No. 2)* [1984] IR 511; *Bellew v Bellew* [1982] IR 447.

[130] s 1, Notices to Quit (Ireland) Act 1876.

common law periods of notice have been amended by statute in certain cases. Perhaps the most significant relates to residential tenancies, all of which are now determinable by notice alone. The Residential Tenancies Act 2004 lays down the notice periods to be given by either landlord or tenant. These are considered in full in Chapter 15. Periodic tenancies can arise by the express agreement of the parties, but they can also arise by implication. Normally, if there is a relatively informal landlord–tenant relationship between parties in which rent is paid on a regular, periodic basis, the periodic payment of rent can result in law implying a periodic tenancy between the parties. The periods of the tenancy will be equivalent to the periods of rental payment.

4. Leases for a Term Certain

Leases for a term certain are relatively common and quite straightforward. In these cases the duration of the lease is determined *ab initio,* and once the time has expired the lease is terminated automatically. Despite the automatic termination of leases for a term certain, there is no prohibition on inserting a clause into the lease allowing for its termination through a particular notice period: this does not rid the estate of its "term certain" character. Equally, a renewal clause will not change the estate from a term certain lease to some other genus of leasehold estate. In order to qualify as a lease for a term certain, the duration must be actually certain—duration cannot be said to correspond to some indeterminable or uncertain event, such as the termination of a war or the date at which the landlord decides to sell the property. In essence, the court will examine the terms of the agreement and, from that, determine the nature of the lease in operation.[131] **[4–91]**

5. Reversionary Leases

Almost all leases are followed by a reversion in favour of the landlord. There is no reason why a landlord could not a grant a lease that is to begin once the current lease terminates, and the landlord is entitled to possession again by means of the reversion. A lease that is designed to first become effective in the landlord's reversion is known as a reversionary lease. Section 11(3)(i) of the Land and Conveyancing Law Reform Act 2009 expressly provides for reversionary leases by including leases that take effect in the future in its definition of leasehold estates. **[4–92]**

Part IV: Hybrid Estates

Thus far we have dealt with the relatively comfortable categories of freehold and leasehold estates. There is, however, a third general category of estate that combines both freehold and leasehold characteristics. This is the "hybrid estate". In the main, these estates have freehold features because their duration is indeterminate, and they have leasehold features because they require the payment of rent or compliance with some other requirement normally associated with leasehold estates. As we will see in this section, the general thrust of the Land and Conveyancing Law Reform Act 2009 as it relates to these hybrid estates has been to abolish them in furtherance of the aim of simplifying the law. This is quite sensible as, in the main, these hybrid estates are results of attempts at administrative expediency and historical accident that are no longer very relevant in Irish law. Importantly, however, the 2009 Act does not retrospectively abolish these hybrid estates and, as a result, we must familiarise ourselves with them. **[4–93]**

131 See further Wylie, *Landlord and Tenant Law* (2nd ed, 1998, Dublin, Butterworths), pp 85–86.

1. Leases for Lives Perpetually Renewable

[4–94] It was, at one time, a common practice to give leases that were to last for the lives of (usually) three named people, and to allow the tenant to renew the lease by replacing those named people on the occasion of their deaths. Although a renewal fee, known as a fine, had to be paid for each such renewal, this mechanism resulted in the leases for lives being perpetually renewable and, as a result, potentially lasting forever. While the origins of these kinds of leases are disputed,[132] the effect of their creation is clear: the relationship of landlord and tenant is created between the parties, but the "tenant" holds a freehold estate. Thus, all of the rights and remedies of a landlord were available to the grantor, yet the tenant had a freehold estate *pur autres vies*. Despite being a tenant within a landlord–tenant relationship, the grantee was not necessarily bound by absolutely all of the obligations of a tenant.[133] The law had to be tweaked to some extent to recognise the autonomy of a perpetual interest-holder, which is precisely what the lessee for lives was.

[4–95] There were various reasons why people might create a lease for lives instead of transferring a fee simple estate. As already mentioned, a grantor might see the lease for lives as expedient because it would allow for the enforcement of certain obligations through landlord-and-tenant law. In addition, the grantor would enjoy the considerable rights of landlords in Ireland in the 1800s, when these leases were particularly popular. Perhaps most importantly to some, the grantee would become the freehold estate holder and therefore would have a parliamentary vote, but the grantor would retain some influence over the grantee through his status as landlord and therefore could, more or less, rely on the grantee's vote in elections.

[4–96] Leases for lives were created relatively easily—no particular Words of Limitation were required (despite the granting of a freehold estate). Rather, the court would attempt to ascertain and give effect to the intentions of the grantor.[134] The Irish courts also attempted to give effect to the nature of the tenant's holding, i.e. a perpetual freehold estate. Thus, the Irish courts developed what was known as the "old equity of the country"[135]—a doctrine that held that the landlord was obliged to allow for the renewal of the lease by replacement of lives, even if there was a delay between the time of death and the time of renewal (including in cases where all of the lives were deceased before any were replaced and the lease renewed).[136] While the Irish courts were perfectly satisfied with this position, the House of Lords was beginning to take the view that equity would *never* assist a lessee "where he has lost his right by his own gross *laches* or neglect".[137]

---

[132] See generally Lyne, *Leases for Lives Renewable Forever* (1837, Hodges and Smith).

[133] Lessees for lives perpetually renewable could alienate without the consent of the landlord (s 10, Landlord and Tenant Amendment (Ireland) Act 1860—now repealed) and were unimpeachable at waste in relation to timbers planted by them or their predecessors (s 1, Land Improvement Act (Ireland) 1765).

[134] See *Horan v Horan* [1935] IR 306.

[135] *Sweet v Anderson* (1722) 2 Bro PC 256; *Worsop v Rosse* (1740) 1 Bro PC 281.

[136] See further Delany, "English and Irish Land Law—Some Contrasts" (1956) 5(3) *Am J Comp Law* 471 at 474–5.

[137] *Bateman v Murray* (1785) 1 Ridgw PC 187 *per* Thurlow LJ (action begun in Ireland in 1765)—although reported after its passage, this case (together with *Kane v Hamilton* (1784) 1 Rdigw PC 180) was exceptionally influential in the drafting and enactment of the Tenantry Act (Ireland) 1779—see Wylie, *Irish Land Law* (3rd ed, 1997, Dublin, Butterworths Lexis Nexis), pp 272, n.792.

In order to preserve the old equity of the country, Irish parliamentarians would have to take swift action.

This came in the form of the Tenantry Act 1779, which confirmed that the equitable principles developed by the Irish courts continued to apply. Unfortunately, however, the process for payment of fines by tardy lessees for lives renewable forever was somewhat cumbersome. They could also be taken advantage of, perhaps too easily, by tenants who were now given the right to replace the lives with people of their own choosing. As these new lives were usually outside the terms of reference of the landlord, it became exceptionally difficult to keep track of when one had died and, as a result, of whether your tenant was paying his fines on time or trying to take advantage of the allowance for late payment within the Act itself. In short, the system simply stopped working. **[4–97]**

The solution to this problem was to prevent the creation of any future leases for lives perpetually renewable. This was achieved by means of s 37 of the Renewable Leasehold Conversion Act 1849, which provided that any attempt to create a lease for lives perpetually renewable would, in fact, result in the creation of a fee farm grant. Section 12(2) of the Land and Conveyancing Law Reform Act 2009 now provides that any attempt to create a lease for lives perpetually renewable will in fact create a fee simple in favour of the grantee. Any covenants within the attempted lease for lives perpetually renewable that are compatible with the fee simple will be enforceable as freehold covenants.[138] Furthermore, the Tenantry Act 1779 and Renewable Leasehold Conversion Act 1849 are both repealed by the 2009 Act.[139] **[4–98]**

2. Leases for Lives Combined with a Term of Years

For various reasons, usually connected to elections, leases for lives combined with a term of years were sometimes created in Ireland. These leases involved the creation of a lease for lives through which the lessee would receive a freehold estate *pur autre vie,* but stand in a landlord–tenant relationship to the grantor with a lease for a term of years attached. The lease for lives would not be renewable; it would end when the lives had all died. The landlords here wanted to "have their cake and eat it too": they wanted to secure the votes of the grantees by giving them a freehold estate while, at the same time, granting them a lease that would come to an end after a certain period of time. The only area of any complication here was whether the lease for years attached was to run concurrently with the lease for lives, or was to commence on the termination of the lease for lives. The nature of the lease for a term of years was ultimately a question of construction[140] but, as Wylie noted, "By choosing one's lives carefully, so that they were unlikely to outlast the term of years, and by making the term run concurrently, one ended up with an estate for a certain term but which was freehold for as long as any one of the lives survived".[141] **[4–99]**

---

[138] s 12(3), Land and Conveyancing Law Reform Act 2009; the enforceability of freehold covenants is considered in Chapter 11.

[139] s 8(3) and Schedule 2, Land and Conveyancing Law Reform Act 2009.

[140] See *Duckett v Keane* [1903] 1 IR 409; *Adams v McGoldrick* [1927] NI 127; *Allman & Co v McCabe* [1911] 2 IR 398.

[141] Wylie, *Irish Land Law* (3rd ed, 1997, Dublin, Butterworths Lexis Nexis), p 277.

[4–100] Section 12(2) of the Land and Conveyancing Law Reform Act 2009 now provides that any attempt to create a lease for lives combined with a term of years will in fact create a fee simple in favour of the grantee. Any covenants within the attempted lease for lives perpetually renewable that are compatible with the fee simple will be enforceable as freehold covenants.[142]

3. Fee Farm Grants

[4–101] Broadly speaking, the term "fee farm grant" can be defined as a "fee simple subject to a perpetual rent". In fee farm grants the grantee has the right to hold the land forever, but is required to pay a fee farm rent in relation to it. Failure to comply with the fee farm requirements could lead to the termination of the grant itself. There were a variety of kinds of fee farm grant, each of which needs separate consideration and all of which are now prospectively abolished by s 12 of the Land and Conveyancing Law Reform Act 2009. Section 12(1) provides that the "creation of a fee farm grant at law or in equity is prohibited" and, according to s 12(2), any attempt to create a fee farm grant in the future will in fact create a fee simple. It is, however, important to note that the 2009 Act does not abolish the fee farm grant retrospectively. Therefore, fee farm grants existing on 1 December 2009 retain their validity.

(i) Feudal Fee Farm Grants

[4–102] The *Quia Emptores* did not prevent the crown from subinfeudating in fee simple in Ireland. This was particularly common during the Plantations of Ireland, when the crown would subinfeudate to supporters in Ireland by letters patent. The original recipients were obliged to pay a chief rent, known as a quit rent, to the crown, but they also received the right to subinfeudate *non obstante Quia Emptores* (notwithstanding the prohibition on subinfeudation in the fee simple contained in *Quia Emptores*). These loyal subjects could therefore subinfeudate and create feudal pyramids in Ireland hundreds of years after these structures had begun to disappear in England.

[4–103] The proliferation of these grants, and the creation of sometimes up to 12 layers of "middlemen" between the grantee of the crown and the holder of the land,[143] was a matter of some curiosity for English lawyers. Remember that most of these lawyers were accustomed to a situation in which subinfeudation simply no longer took place, thanks to *Quia Emptores*. For example, in his edition of *Coke upon Littleton*, Hargrave communicated his surprise at the validity of a feudal fee farm grant he came across on this island:

> I have seen a modern grant in fee of a large estate in Ireland, reserving a perpetual rent of great value. But such a rent, considered as a fee-farm rent, I thought clearly void.[144]

---

[142] s 12(3), Land and Conveyancing Law Reform Act 2009; the enforceability of freehold covenants is considered in Chapter 11.

[143] See Delany, "English and Irish Land Law—Some Contrasts" (1956) 5(3) *Am J Comp Law* 471 at 473.

[144] vol 1, 143b n 5.

In some circumstances, present landholders can trace their rights back to such a feudal grant and the abolition of feudal tenure in s 9(2) of the Land and Conveyancing Law Reform Act 2009 does not affect the feudal fee farm grant.[145]

(ii) Conversion Fee Farm Grants

Leases for lives perpetually renewable involved some relatively serious administrative difficulties and expense. Consequently, there was an attempt to simplify their operation while achieving the same result as these estates did. The scheme by which this was achieved was contained in the Renewable Leasehold Conversion Act 1849. The Act provided for two important conversion principles: **[4–104]**

(a) any attempt to create a lease for lives after 1 August 1849 would be ineffective; the grantee would receive a fee farm grant instead (s 37);
(b) any lessees for lives could choose to convert their lease into a fee farm grant under the Act (s 1).

The Act therefore introduced an opt-in conversion mechanism for those who already had a lease for lives perpetually renewable, and it automatically converted any leases for lives perpetually renewable anyone purported to create in the future. The opt-in scheme was surprisingly under-subscribed. This could have been a result of the expense associated with it, as the fee farm rent was to be calculated by reference to the size of any existing rent and the projected price of renewal fines the landlord would forego through this conversion.[146] The Land and Conveyancing Law Reform Act 2009 repeals the Renewable Leasehold Conversion Act 1849,[147] but pre-existing conversion fee farm grants can still operate.

(iii) Grants Subject to a Rentcharge

A rentcharge is a rental obligation attached to a fee simple where there is no landlord–tenant relationship between the parties. In other words, the grantor and grantee are not within a leasehold relationship; the grantee has a fee simple, but the grantor is entitled to a rental payment. The rentcharge is charged on the land and is enforceable against the successors-in-title of the grantee. Thus, the rentcharge is defined as an incorporeal hereditament—an intangible property right. Those entitled to a rentcharge previously had the capacity to enforce that charge through distress (i.e. taking possession and leasing the property to a third party to realise the money owed[148]), but rentcharges can now be enforced as simple contract debts only.[149] Section 41 of the Land and Conveyancing Law Reform Act 2009 prohibits the creation of rentcharges at law or equity after 1 December 2009. **[4–105]**

---

[145] s 9(3)(c), Land and Conveyancing Law Reform Act 2009.
[146] s 2, Renewable Leasehold Conversion Act 1849.
[147] s 8(3) and Schedule 2, Land and Conveyancing Law Reform Act 2009.
[148] s 44, Conveyancing Act 1881.
[149] s 42, Land and Conveyancing Law Reform Act 2009.

CHAPTER 5
Future Interests and Rules against Remoteness

In various circumstances one may have a right over land that does not become effective, either in possession or at all, until some time in the future. These rights or interests are known as "future interests". These future interests can either be "vested in interest" (meaning that they will definitely be enjoyable and possessory in the future) or "contingent" (meaning that they will vest in someone only if a particular contingency is fulfilled). Whether the future interest is vested in interest or contingent, the important point to note is that it is not yet vested in possession, i.e. the holder of that future interest cannot yet enjoy the possession of the land in question. In the main, these future interests now exist in equity only because of the abolition of the fee tail[1] and the continuation of the life estate in equity only.[2] Although future interests were previously governed by a raft of complex and often controversial rules, many of these rules were abolished—sometimes with an attempted retrospective effect—by the Land and Conveyancing Law Reform Act 2009. The purpose of this chapter is to outline future interests as they now operate and to give a flavour of the pre-2009 Act operation of such interests and the rules governing them. **[5–01]**

Part I: Future Interests

In very simple terms, a future interest is one that has not yet vested in possession. In other words, the holder of the interest (grantee) is not yet entitled to possess the land that is the subject of the interest. This means that a future interest might be either (a) contingent or (b) vested in interest (although not yet in possession). **[5–02]**

1 s 13, Land and Conveyancing Law Reform Act 2009.
2 s 11(6), *ibid.*

1. Contingent Interests

[5–03] Contingent interests are those to which the proposed grantee will not be entitled until some contingency or condition has been fulfilled. This condition will normally be related to the conduct of the proposed grantee, for example, a disposition "Woodview House to Simon and Alison on trust for Maia for life if she walks on the moon". Here, the equitable life estate to Maia is clearly contingent: it will vest in her only if she walks on the moon. The fact that the interest is contingent does not, however, mean that Maia has no rights at all before the time that she walks on the moon. She can, in fact, ensure that Simon and Alison—the trustees—would not act in a manner that dissipates the values of Woodview House on the basis that, *if she walks on the moon*, she is entitled to a life estate in that property.[3] That kind of application is, in fact, more likely to arise in a situation where the property in question is personal property in the form of stocks and shares, for example, but the principle (that one can protect one's contingent interest in this manner) stands for real property. Contingencies can be within the control of the holder of the interest vested in interest (such as requiring the holder to complete a particular marathon, for example), outside of the control of the holder of the interest vested in interest (such as making it contingent on a third party completing a particular marathon), unlikely to occur (such as the holder of the interest vested in interest walking on the moon), or certain to occur (such as a named person dying). Although one might find it frustrating to be granted an interest that is subject to a contingency quite outside of one's control, that frustration is not subject to legal censure.

[5–04] Contingent interests are capable of assignment, including by will. This is confirmed by s 11(9) of the Land and Conveyancing Law Reform Act 2009. Thus, a person who holds an interest vested in interest can bequeath that in her will. Take, for example, the following scenario: "No. 18, Elm Road to Andy and Barb in fee simple on trust for Caitriona for life, remainder to Declan in fee simple". In this disposition Declan receives a contingent equitable fee simple remainder, i.e. an equity fee simple that becomes possessory upon the death of Caitriona. Should Declan predecease Caitriona, he is quite entitled to leave his contingent fee simple remainder to anyone he wishes in his will, with the beneficiary of this gift receiving a contingent fee simple remainder and, when Caitriona dies, being vested in possession with the fee simple.

[5–05] Prior to the passage of the Land and Conveyancing Law Reform Act 2009 contingent interests were governed by a much-maligned rule known as the Rule against Perpetuities, which was concerned with limiting the amount of time for which an interest could remain contingent. That rule was abolished by s 16 of the Land and Conveyancing Law Reform Act 2009 and, according to s 17, the abolition is intended to be retrospective. Section 17 provides:

> Section 16 applies to any interest in property whenever created but does not apply if, before the commencement of this Part, in reliance on such an interest being invalid by virtue of the application of any of the rules abolished by that section—
>
> (a) the property has been distributed or otherwise dealt with, or

[3] See, for example, *Jacob v Revenue Commissioners*, unreported, High Court, McWilliam J, 6 July 1983.

(b) any person has done or omitted to do any thing which renders the position of that or any other person materially altered to that person's detriment after the commencement of this Part.

The decision to try to ensure that the abolition of the Rule against Perpetuities has retrospective effect is, in fact, quite problematic. The Rule against Perpetuities is designed to strike out contingent interests in relation to which the contingency is too remote. Although the technical operation of the Rule is outlined later in this chapter, a simple example suffices at this point to illustrate the difficulty with the retrospective abolition of the Rule. Let us consider the following hypothetical disposition that took place in 2007, i.e. prior to the introduction of ss 16 and 17. From Rosemary: "Ivy Cottage to Simon for life, remainder to the first of Tomás' children to become a solicitor". For reasons that become clear below, the contingent remainder here is invalid under the Rule against Perpetuities and that invalidity is considered to take effect *ab initio*. Thus, from the moment at which this disposition becomes effective Rosemary (or her successor in title) was entitled to a contingent fee simple remainder that would vest in possession upon Simon's death. Although that contingent fee simple remainder did not translate to a present right to possession, it was a property right entitled to protection under the Constitution (and, indeed, under applicable international human rights law). Any attempt to abolish the Rule against Perpetuities in a retrospective fashion raises immediate questions, then, of whether Rosemary's property right is being violated. As a result of this concern, savings clauses had to be fashioned and these are contained in s 17. [5–06]

Section 17 provides that the abolition of the Rule against Perpetuities will have retrospective effect *unless* "property has been distributed or otherwise dealt with"[4] or "any person has done or omitted to do any thing which renders the position of that or any other person materially altered to that person's detriment after the commencement"[5] of s 16 "in reliance on"[6] an interest being invalid under the Rule against Perpetuities. Before we consider the various elements of the savings clause, we might note that in fact it would have been considerably easier, and more intellectually coherent, to have simply abolished the Rule against Perpetuities in relation to all dispositions becoming effective after the commencement of s 16 rather than to try to create retrospective abolition in this tortured fashion. Nevertheless, this was not done and so we must tread carefully through the requirements of s 17 as they apply to the Rule against Perpetuities. It is clear that there are in fact two different situations in which a disposition pre-dating the commencement of s 16 will not be effected: [5–07]

(1) Where property has been distributed or otherwise dealt with by someone *in reliance on* an understanding that a contingent interest was invalid under the Rule against Perpetuities;
(2) Where someone has done or not done something in relation to property *in reliance on* an understanding that a contingent interest was invalid under the Rule against Perpetuities *and* that act or omission detrimentally alters the person in question compared to the position that she would have enjoyed had she not acted or failed to act in reliance on such an understanding.

4 s 17(a), Land and Conveyancing Law Reform Act 2009.
5 s 17(b), *ibid.*
6 s 17, *ibid.*

There is an initial difficulty with both of these situations: because of the way in which the Rule against Perpetuities acted (invalidating contingent interests *ab initio*), property rights are implicated by retrospective abolition *whether or not* the person who benefited from the invalidation had dealt with the property, knew of their interest, or had acted in a manner determined by their understanding of the Rule against Perpetuities in a way that now constitutes a detriment to them. The second difficulty here is with the requirement that is common to both scenarios, namely the concept of acting "in reliance on [the] interest [in question] being invalid by virtue of the application of [the Rule against Perpetuities]". It is not at all clear what this means in real terms, particularly when one considers the extremely technical nature of the Rule against Perpetuities, which suggests that a non-lawyer (and perhaps even someone with a law degree) is very unlikely to have acted in reliance of any understanding of the Rule in the absence of expert advice, such as counsel's opinion.

2. Interests Vested in Interest

[5–08] Interests vested in interest arise when the identity of the interest-holder is known; the fact that his interest will become possessory is certain, but he is not entitled to take possession of the land at issue at the moment. This is, perhaps, best illustrated by the classic remainder after a particular estate. If, for example, property is transferred pursuant to the following disposition, "To Alan and Bobby in fee simple on trust for Jack for life, remainder to Siobhán in fee simple," this means Jack has an interest vested in possession (current life estate in equity) and Siobhán has an interest vested in interest but not in possession (fee simple remainder in equity) because she is not entitled to possess the land until Jack's life estate has expired.

[5–09] Vested interests can be further divided into three sub-categories:

(a) Indefeasibly vested interests:
An indefeasibly vested interest will be said to arise where the beneficiary must take possession. In other words, vesting in possession is inevitable and will be limited to the individual(s) identified.

(b) Vested interests subject to open:
A vested interest subject to open will be said to arise where the beneficiary belongs to a class of potential beneficiaries from which more beneficiaries may arise. Gifts of this nature are known as class gifts and are characterised by the uncertainty that surrounds the quantum of someone's interest because the more people who qualify for the class, the smaller each individual beneficiary's share will be.

(c) Vested interests subject to divestment:
A vested interest subject to divestment will be said to arise where a beneficiary acquires an interest but may lose that interest in the future for failure to, for example, comply with a condition. Perhaps the best-known vested interest subject to divestment is the interest of the beneficiary of a fee simple subject to a condition subsequent.

[5–10] Ascertaining whether an interest is vested or contingent is of fundamental importance because contingent interests were subject to rules that do not apply to vested interests. Although, as considered above, the main rule in this relation—the Rule against Perpetuities—has now been abolished, when it comes to pre-2009 Act disposition one must still ascertain whether the interest in question is contingent and, if so, whether it is saved from the retrospective abolition of the Rule by s 17. In essence, one ascertains the status of an interest by application of the following test:

(a) Is the identity of the proposed grantee(s) known and are they born?
(b) Does the proposed grantee become entitled to the land without having to fulfil any condition?

If the answer to both questions is "yes", then the interest is a vested interest and the Rule against Perpetuities could not apply.

3. *Edwards v Hammond*—An Exception to the Test for Vesting

These ordinary rules of ascertaining whether an interest is vested or contingent can be undermined by the application of the Rule in *Edwards v Hammond*.[7] This rule applies only in the case of dispositions in a will and states: [5–11]

> Where property... is given in a will to a person on his or her attaining a certain age and a gift over is given on the event of that person not attaining the age, the primary gift is considered as vested and not contingent, but liable to be divested if the person fails to attain the age.

In more simple terms, the Rule provides that if a will gives a gift to X upon his attainment of 18 years of age, for example, and there is an alternative gift in case X does not reach the specified age, then the gift to X is treated as being vested. If he then fails to reach the age specified, the gift to X will be divested again. In short, this is a rule designed to implement a presumption of vesting in a will in limited situations and can be explained by the benefit that such a principle carries for certainty within the property market. It ought to be added that the Irish courts have shown some reluctance to apply this Rule in recent times. The Rule was designed to avoid the Rule in *Purefoy v Rogers*,[8] and as that rule no longer applies in law,[9] *Edwards* can be abandoned (particularly as it undermines the clear intentions of the testator).[10]

4. Variants of Future Interest

Following the reform of estates contained in the Land and Conveyancing Law Reform Act 2009, the only future interests that now exist in law are the right to re-entry (attached to a fee simple determinable), the possibility of reverter (attached to a fee simple subject to a condition subsequent), the remainder (now in equity only) and the reversion (also in equity only). Each of these requires some attention at this point. [5–12]

(i) The Right to Re-entry

The right to re-entry is the interest retained by the grantor on the creation of a fee simple subject to a condition subsequent. As considered in Chapter 4, the fee simple subject to a condition subsequent is vested automatically in the grantee, but [5–13]

7 (1683) 3 Lev 132.
8 (1671) 2 Wm Saund 380; see further paras 5–39 to 5–41 below.
9 s 16(b), Land and Conveyancing Law Reform Act 2009.
10 See *Re Murphy's Estate* [1964] IR 308 *per* Kenny J.

may be divested if the subsequent condition is not fulfilled. If there is a failure to fulfil the condition subsequent, then the grantor may re-enter the land, thereby divesting the grantee's fee simple. This right is a valuable commodity that may be sold by the grantor and may also be devised in a will.[11]

(ii) The Possibility of Reverter

[5–14] The possibility of reverter is the interest retained by the grantor on the creation of a fee simple determinable. The fee simple determinable is vested automatically in the grantee, but will be divested if the state of affairs (or determining event) is not fulfilled. In this case divestment and re-vesting in the grantor will be automatic. This possibility is known as the possibility of reverter. It is a valuable commodity that may be sold by the grantor and may also be devised in a will.[12]

(iii) The Reversion

[5–15] The reversion is the interest retained by a grantor when he transfers an estate to another that is lesser than the estate held by the grantor himself. For example, a fee simple-holder who transfers a life estate in equity to another will be said to have an equitable fee simple reversion as his rights will once more become exercisable in possession on the expiry of the prior life estate. Reversions therefore arise when the holder of rights over land transfers an estate to another, but retains part of his own estate for himself and does not determine that the remainder of his estate is to be vested in a third party. Reversions are valuable commodities that may be sold by the grantor and may also be devised in a will. As the fee simple in possession is now the only freehold estate that can exist in law,[13] reversions only exist in equity.

(iv) The Remainder

[5–16] The remainder is the interest granted to an individual other than the original grantor (and his successors-in-title) and that is to take effect following the expiry of a prior particular estate. For example, where a fee simple-holder transfers his estate by the disposition "Whiteacre to Aaron and Bobby in fee simple on trust for Sally for life, remainder to Carol in fee simple," he has granted Carol an equitable fee simple remainder that will become effective in possession on the termination of Sally's life estate. Remainders are valuable commodities that may be sold by the grantor and may also be devised in a will. Remainders can now only exist in equity, but prior to the commencement of the Land and Conveyancing Law Reform Act 2009 they could also exist in law and the regulation of these remainders was a complex business, done through the Common Law Remainder Rules. Those rules have now been abolished by s 16 of the 2009 Act and are not considered here.[14] Neither are the rules that applied to executory interests[15] (which were equitable interests not impacted by the Common Law

---

[11] s 11(9), Land and Conveyancing Law Reform Act 2009.

[12] *ibid.*

[13] s 11, Land and Conveyancing Law Reform Act 2009.

[14] A full consideration is available in de Londras, *Principles of Irish Property Law* (1st ed, 2007, Dublin, Clarus Press), paras 5–22 to 5–33. They are also considered in Lyall, *Land Law in Ireland* (3rd ed, 2010, Dublin; Round Hall), pp 300–303.

[15] A full consideration is available in de Londras, *op. cit.*, paras 5–34 to 5–38. They are also considered in Lyall, *op. cit.*, pp 303–304.

Remainder Rules) or the Rule in *Purefoy v Rogers*, both of which are now of historical interest alone.[16]

Part II: Rules against Remoteness

As a result of the uncertainty that they might introduce into the property law system, contingent remainders were previously subjected to a number of rules that have now been abolished by s 16 of the Land and Conveyancing Law Reform Act 2009, namely the Rule in *Whitby v Mitchell*,[17] the Rule against Perpetuities,[18] and the Rule against Accumulations.[19] In spite of the general intention to abolish these rules in a retrospective manner, the "savings clause" in s 17, which is considered above, suggests that there may be some cases in which knowledge of the rules' operations would be useful. As a result, a brief outline of the rules is included here, although a more detailed account can be found in pre-2009 Act publications.[20] In addition, the Rule against Trusts of Undue Duration is not abolished by the 2009 Act and continues to apply. [5–17]

1. The Rule in *Whitby v Mitchell*

The fee tail was introduced by the *Statute de Donis Conditionalibus* and was intended to allow for the creation of an estate by which property rights would transfer automatically through a bloodline. However, the courts began to allow people to bar their entails—or treat them as fees simple—culminating in the creation of a simple mechanism for doing so in the Fines and Recoveries (Ireland) Act 1834. As a result, the fee tail no longer offered people who were so minded the opportunity to create a stable and secure family interest of this nature. In order to try to achieve the objective of keeping land within the family, people began to create what were known as "perpetual freeholds", in which every heir would have a life estate, but no heir would have a fee tail that could be barred. In this way, it was thought, the family's land-related wealth and status was secured. The courts were relatively hostile to this notion, for more or less the same reasons as they were hostile to the notion of the fee tail: it locked wealth into the land, it stripped individual owners of their autonomy and it starved the market of fees simple. It came as no surprise, then, that the courts developed a rule prohibiting such dispositions, which became known as "the Rule in *Whitby v Mitchell*".[21] In relatively bald terms, the Rule in *Whitby v Mitchell* reinforced the pre-existing rule that an estate could not be limited to an unborn person for life followed by any estate to any child of such unborn person. The Court held that this was an absolute rule, which also invalidates all subsequent gifts, whether contingent or not. [5–18]

2. The Rule against Perpetuities

The Rule against Perpetuities forbade future interests that were too remote. In other words, it forbade the creation of a future interest that might not vest within a particular [5–19]

[16] A full consideration is available in de Londras, *op. cit.*, paras 5–39 to 5–41. The Rule is also considered in Lyall, *op. cit.*, pp 304–306.
[17] Abolished by s 16(c), Land and Conveyancing Law Reform Act 2009.
[18] Abolished by s 16(d), *ibid.*
[19] Abolished by s 16(e), *ibid.*
[20] de Londras, *op. cit.*, paras 5–46 to 5–112 and 5–115 to 5–121.
[21] (1890) 44 Ch D 85.

period of time (known as the perpetuity period). The primary reason for the creation and application of the Rule against Perpetuities was to ensure that land remained as alienable as possible, even if bound up in a contingent interest. While future interests do not restrict alienation *per se* (land can still be sold but merely subject to any future interests held by another), future interests that are too remote—or those whose vesting cannot be predicted with any level of certainty—can be said to introduce a risk for a potential purchaser (i.e. the risk of the future interest vesting in favour of a third party) that made land less marketable and, as a result, less valuable. The Rule against Perpetuities attempted to avoid this situation by providing that any contingent interest that was not *certain* to vest within the perpetuity period (relevant period of gestation, *plus* life/lives in being, *plus* 21 years) was void *ab initio*. As the Rule applied only to contingent interests, the first task was to assess whether the interest in question was vested or contingent, which was done by reference to the test for vesting considered above, i.e. "Is the person who is to receive the interest ascertained or ascertainable?" and "Is there a contingency to be fulfilled in order for him to become entitled to that interest?" This was assessed by reference to the information available to the court as of the time that the gift became effective (i.e. at the time of execution for an *inter vivos* gift or the time of death if the gift is contained in a will). The Rule was very strict on this assessment mechanism: the court was not permitted to "wait and see" what happened; indeed, what actually happened was completely immaterial to this assessment.[22] To apply the Rule against Perpetuities, then, a court must ask itself whether the remainder in question was contingent and, if so, and taking into account only the information available at the time that the gift became effective, whether there was any chance whatsoever that the gift might first become vested after the expiration of the perpetuity period. If there was any possibility that this might happen, no matter how remote or improbable, then the interest was void *ab initio*.

[5–20] The perpetuity period began to run the moment the gift became effective. The perpetuity period consisted of any relevant gestation period, the life or lives in being and 21 years. Relevant gestation periods were those related to a foetus in the womb that would be a life in being if it was born (known as children *en ventre sa mère*). Lives in being were people who were either (a) expressly named as lives in being in the disposition, or (b) human beings[23] alive at the time of the disposition[24] and relatively connected to the fulfilment of the condition. Therefore, in "To Mary if she walks on the moon during John's lifetime or within 21 years of his death," it is clear that John is the life in being, for he is expressly named as such. However, in the disposition "To Mary if she walks on the moon," the life in being is Mary. The perpetuity period would then last a further 21 years after the death of the life or lives in being. If there were no lives in being, the perpetuity period would simply be 21 years. The perpetuity period could be crafted to be particularly long by means of the use of "saving clauses", which were the mechanism by which a particularly large line of lives in being could be included in the disposition. The best example of this was the "royal savings clause", in which a remainder might be made contingent on the completion of a condition within

[22] *Exham v Beamish* [1939] IR 336.

[23] *Re Kelly* [1932] IR 255.

[24] This includes connected individuals who are in the womb at the time the gift becomes effective, hence the inclusion of "relevant periods of gestation" in the perpetuity period.

21 years of the death "of the last descendant of Queen Elizabeth II". The "de Valera clause" developed as an Irish alterative to royal savings clauses and, provided they were worded with sufficient care, could be successful.[25] These clauses were acceptable because the lives in being were relatively easily traced, although savings clauses that were too wide, vague or untraceable were not considered legitimate.[26]

The question of concern to the Court was really as to when the remainder would become vested. In this respect, the Rule did not distinguish between remainders vesting in interest or vesting in possession: merely vesting in interest and not yet vesting in possession would be sufficient. If the remainder in question was a "class gift" (i.e. a gift to a number of people, all of whom satisfy a certain qualification), then the gift was first considered vested when the shares of all members of the class were known, i.e. when we could tell how many were actually in the group. This caused class gifts to be particularly susceptible to the Rule against Perpetuities, and class closing rules were developed in the attempt to ameliorate this.[27] **[5–21]**

A cause of much criticism of the Rule against Perpetuities was its exclusive concern with the *possibility* that a gift might not have vested in time; the probability of this actually arising was insignificant. This led to some rather strange, unusual or improbable results that can be illustrated by reference to what became known as the *Magic Gravel Pits Case.*[28] In this case a remainder was to vest when the testator's gravel pits were exhausted. Engineering and other evidence showed that the gravel pits would be exhausted in the relatively near future, if they continued to be exploited at the same rate as at present. The Court held, however, that there was a *possibility* of the gift not vesting in time because there was a *possibility* of the gravel pits not being exhausted. The fact that the gravel pits had, in fact, been exhausted prior to the action being heard was entirely irrelevant. This concentration of possibility rather than probability led to one of the most influential expositions of "unusual" applications of the Rule by Prof. Barton Leech in his well-known article, "Perpetuities: Staying the Slaughter of the Innocents".[29] In this paper, Leech outlined what he called the fertile octogenarian, the precocious toddler and the unborn widow trap, all of which served as illustrations of the ludicrous results that the Rule of Perpetuities could give rise to. **[5–22]**

The fertile octogenarian was based on the premise that, irrespective of age or medical evidence of infertility, it was possible for a woman to have children at any age. This proposition was introduced into English law (for the purposes of the Rule against Perpetuities) by *Jee v Audley*[30] and appeared to be endorsed in *Ward v Van der Loeff.*[31] The Irish courts had demonstrated resistance to the idea of the fertile octogenarian, denouncing it as repugnant to common sense. In *Exham v Beamish*[32] a settlement **[5–23]**

---

[25] For a relatively recent example of a de Valera clause see *Re the estate of ABC* [2003] 2 IR 250.
[26] *Re Villar* [1929] 1 Ch 243; *Re Moore* [1901] 1 Ch 936.
[27] *Andrews v Partington* (1791) 3 Bro CC 401; *Re Poe* [1942] IR 535; *Re Burke* [1945] IR Jur Rep 12; *Williamson v Williamson* [1974] NI 92. See de Londras, *op. cit.*, paras 5–81 to 5–83.
[28] *Re Wood* [1894] 3 Ch 381.
[29] (1952) 68 LQR 35.
[30] (1787) 1 Cox Eq Cas 324, 29 ER 1186.
[31] [1924] AC 653.
[32] [1939] IR 336.

included a contingent gift to grandchildren of the settlers and was worded in a broad enough to manner to include the children of any child who might theoretically have been born to the settlers after the date of the disposition. The court heard arguments based on *Jee* and its progeny and Gavin-Duffy J held that he was entitled to receive evidence of the medical capacity of the settlers to have further children at the time that the disposition became effective. If it was clear that this was then impossible, he held, he was entitled to proceed on that basis. A rule that was clearly absurd would not, he held, have been carried over into Irish law by Art 50 of Bunreacht na hÉireann; instead, Irish law featured a rebuttable presumption of fertility. He concluded:

> Accordingly, where mere improbability of further issue will not do, if it should be satisfactorily proved that modern medical science would regard as an absurdity the supposition that another child might in the ordinary course of nature have been born to Mr. and Mrs. Thompson after the date of the settlement, I should not hold myself bound, as a matter of legal practice in dealing with the rule against perpetuities, to treat the absurdity as being in the eyes of the law a possible event, which must determine my decision, by reason of [pronouncements from another jurisdiction].[33]

Although most people might have considered the proposition of *Jee* and its progeny as being patently absurd, the increasing development of infertility treatments and possibility of adopting children in older age suggested that by the time of the Rule's abolition the "fertile octogenarian" might not have been as ridiculous a proposition as it at one time appeared.[34]

[5–24] The precocious toddler was, in essence, the corollary of the fertile octogenarian and was based on the premise that one was never too young to have children. This arose from the case of *Re Gaite's Will Trusts.*[35] This case concerned a remainder to those grandchildren of Mrs Gaite "as shall be living at my death or born within five years therefrom who shall attain the age of 21 years or, being female, marry under that age". Mrs Gaite was still alive at the time. The remainder was held to be void *ab initio* under the Rules against Perpetuity due to the possibility that Mrs Gaite would have another child, who would then, within five years of the testator's death, have a child of her own. This child, Mrs Gaite's grandchild, could not be a life in being and might qualify under the remainder's conditions outside of the perpetuity period. In addition, at the time the Court was concerned that this grandchild would be "illegitimate" because a child under five could not marry (but could, apparently, beget a child).

[5–25] The unborn widow/er trap was somewhat more logical than the fertile octogenarian and the precocious toddler. It provided that where a gift was left in a disposition of the nature of the following, it might violate the Rule against Perpetuities: "To John for life, remainder to John's widow, if any, for life, remainder to John's children then alive." In this case the remainder to John's children would fail because John may marry someone who was not alive at the time this disposition was made (and would, therefore, not be a

---

[33] *ibid. per* Gavin-Duffy J, p 350.

[34] For a full exposition of the potential relevance of this application, see Mee, "Return of the Fertile Octogenarians" (1992) DULJ 69.

[35] [1949] 1 All ER 459.

life in being for the children's remainder), and who might outlive John by more than 21 years, resulting in the children's remainder first vesting outside of the perpetuity period.

While the Rule against Perpetuity was originally conceived of as a mechanism of ensuring certainty of ownership and thereby reducing the degree of risk involved in transacting in relation to property that was subject to a contingent future interest, it developed into a Rule that had essentially lost credibility because of the artificial and sometimes preposterous way in which it was applied. It was, therefore, quite unsurprising to see the Rule abolished by the Land and Conveyancing Law Reform Act 2009 although, as noted above, the retrospectivity of that abolition is unfortunately problematic. **[5–26]**

3. The Rule against Accumulations

Section 16 of the Land and Conveyancing Law Reform Act 2009 further abolishes the Rule against Accumulations, again with retrospective effect subject to the savings clause contained in s 17. The Rule against Accumulations applied to the income generated by trust property in relation to which the trustees had been directed to accumulate the income from the trust and distribute it on the occurrence of a particular event. The Rule against Accumulations provided that such a direction would be void if the accumulation of the income might persist beyond the perpetuity period.[36] The perpetuity period was any relevant period of gestation, plus life or lives in being, plus 21 years. Given the abolition of the Rule against Perpetuities, it is both unsurprising and intellectually congruent to also abolish the Rule against Accumulations. **[5–27]**

4. The Rule against Inalienability

This Rule remains in force after the commencement of, and is restated in s 9(4) of, the Land and Conveyancing Law Reform Act 2009.[37] The Rule against Inalienability is essentially concerned with ensuring the alienability of property and applied to *vested* interests. It provides that the subject matter of a trust (i.e. the "trust fund") cannot be rendered inalienable for a period of time exceeding the perpetuity period,[38] i.e. any relevant period of gestation, plus life or lives in being, plus 21 years. The rule does not apply to charitable trusts.[39] Because there are no lives in being in relation to purpose trusts or trusts for unincorporated associations, the perpetuity period will be 21 years. If there is a possibility that the trust fund may be alienated outside of that perpetuity period, then the trust will be invalid. **[5–28]**

---

[36] *Thellusson v Woodford* (1805) 11 Ves 112.

[37] It should be noted that, as Irish property law develops further, arguments may be advanced that the Rule is in some ways futile, not least because the exceptions to its operation tend to proliferate as rules relating to trusts, settlements and so forth continue to develop. A body of such scholarship is beginning to emerge in the UK that may be of future relevance in Ireland. For now, however, we appear to remain firmly committed to the Rule's continuance. For an example of this English scholarship, see Dawson, "The Rule against Inalienability—A Rule Without a Purpose?" (2006) 26(3) *Legal Studies* 414.

[38] See, for example, *Re Fossitt's Estate* [1934] IR 504; *Re Nottage* (1895) 2 Ch D 649; *Re Endacott* (1960) Ch D 232.

[39] *Chamberlagne v Brockett* (1872) 8 Ch 206.

CHAPTER 6
Settlements and Trusts of Land

Before land was seen primarily as the subject of transactions that stimulate economic activity, it was seen as a legacy; as an important part of a family's story and heritage. There was understandable anxiety that future generations would sell the land, or worse still gamble or flitter it away, and that the family's legacy and status—both bound up with their ownership of land—might be lost. In addition, people often worried that members of the family who would not inherit the land—widows, daughters and younger sons—might fall on hard times and should be provided for from the land in some way. As a result estates and practices were developed that attempted to keep land within a family, such as the fee tail that we considered in Chapter 4, and mechanisms for providing for non-inheriting family members were imposed that required payments to be made from the land itself. In many cases what are known as "strict settlements" were created, "settling" the ownership of the land for many generations into the future. **[6–01]**

These practices created something of a dilemma for property law, which wanted, on the one hand, to ensure that the market could grow through healthy levels of property transactions and, on the other hand, to respect families' desires to maintain their future generations through the land. Resolving this tension fell to the law of settled land and, ultimately, the Settled Land Acts 1882–1890. While the law of settled land was perhaps a touch old fashioned and contained some uncertainties, it generally worked very well to resolve these tensions. That did not save it from the reforming process, however. Partially for the purposes of simplification, but primarily for the purposes of coherence within property law, the matters dealt with under the Settled Land Acts 1882–1890 are now dealt with by the new law governing trusts of land under Part 4 of the Land and Conveyancing Law Reform Act 2009, whether the settlements were created before or **[6–02]** after the Act's commencement.[1] We consider both the pre- and post-2009 Act law in this chapter.

I. The Original Difficulty with "Strict Settlements"

[6–03] As already mentioned, people were anxious to ensure that the wealth, status and privileges they had built up through the acquisition of land would continue to benefit their family once they were dead. To this end they attempted to create a mechanism of keeping the land within the family without offending against the rules that then applied to limit the extent to which people could control the future ownership of land.[2] The solution to this dilemma was the development of settlements. A settlement—also known as a "strict settlement"—would generally take the form of a disposition of a life estate to an eldest son, with a fee tail remainder to the eldest son's eldest son (remember that, at this time, both life estates and fees tail could exist in law[3]). In this way the land could be tied up for many generations (i.e. for the life of the son and the length of the ensuing bloodline under the fee tail), but the rules against remoteness were satisfied. Furthermore, the land could be made to provide for other members of the family through jointures and portions. A jointure was a payment from the land to the widow of the settlor in order to ensure that she was taken care of. Portions were payments of some kind to the other heirs of the settlor, or to his eldest son who did not acquire land-ownership rights through the settlement but would not, at the same time, be left penniless. These jointures and portions were generally to be raised from the land, but this proved particularly difficult because the heir was only entitled to rights for lifetime, which usually would not give rise to an especially valuable lease and was practically worthless on the open market. As a result, the lands subject to strict settlements often became impoverished because of the many financial drains they were expected to withstand and their lack of marketability stemming from the settlement itself.

[6–04] The family members would occasionally try to come up with solutions to these difficulties. Usually the grandson—who was to receive a fee tail once his father had died—would attempt to bar the entail (i.e. transform it into a fee simple).[4] This required the consent of the Protector, who was normally his father (i.e. the holder of the life estate).[5] The Protector would almost always take into account the needs of the family members into the future and therefore demand a compromise solution, such as the barring of the entail, following which the grandson could take some funds from the property, *provided* he agreed to re-settle the land afterwards. These lands, then, would be settled, de-barred, re-settled, de-barred, re-settled and so on for many generations. The operation of the strict settlement under these systems was clearly problematic and in response a number of means were introduced in an attempt to reach a compromise

---

[1] s 18, Land and Conveyancing Law Reform Act 2009.

[2] These were the rules against remoteness that were considered in Chapter 5, such as the Rule in *Whitby v Mitchell* and the Rule against Perpetuities.

[3] Life estates can now exist in equity only (s 11, Land and Conveyancing Law Reform Act 2009) and fees tail can no longer be created, with most existing fees tail being converted into fees simple under the provisions of s 13, Land and Conveyancing Law Reform Act 2009. The life estate and fee tail are considered in Chapter 4.

[4] Barring the entail is considered in full in Chapter 4.

[5] Failure to acquire the consent of the Protector resulted in the creation of a base fee. This is considered in Chapter 4.

between the desire to keep property within the family and the desire for fees simple on the open market. These attempts were somewhat piecemeal at first, introducing solutions only for specific kinds of property.[6] After some time, however, more general solutions were introduced,[7] culminating in the Settled Estates Acts 1856–1876 and the Settled Estates Act 1877, which replaced all of the previous Acts.

The Settled Estates Acts applied to both Ireland and England and allowed for settled land to be sold in fee simple, provided the vendor acquired the consent of the court to any proposed sale. The need for the court's consent was thought to be particularly inconvenient in this context, which was a major drawback of the scheme. The most acute difficulty, however, was that the settlor could contract out of the legislation altogether, thereby undermining the scheme and leaving the land settled, impoverished and inalienable.[8] In order to try to remedy these difficulties, the Settled Land Acts 1882–1890 were introduced. These Acts did not repeal the Settled Estates Acts but replaced them to a substantial degree; they continue to be the governing laws in relation to settled land in Ireland. **[6–05]**

II. Settled Land Acts 1882–1890

The Settled Land Acts 1882–1890 allowed for land held in a settlement to be alienated with relative freedom, while at the same time requiring that any purchase monies acquired were paid to objective overseers (called trustees of the settlement) so that all those people who had rights over the land under the settlement (future interest holders) would have rights over the monies that represent the land (or whatever those monies are invested in). Thus, the market was served but the desire to ensure security for the family was not frustrated. **[6–06]**

There were three main characters within the Settled Land Acts: the tenant for life, the trustees of the settlement, and the future interest-holders. The tenant for life, who was granted substantial powers of disposition under the Acts, was the person entitled to possession of the property under the settlement at the relevant time.[9] The trustees of the settlement were overseers of the land with particular duties in relation to the exercise of these powers by the tenant for life and the monies raised through disposition of the property. The future interest-holders were the individuals whose rights were protected by the trustees of the settlement and by the imposition of certain duties on the tenant for life in the exercise of his powers under the Acts. **[6–07]**

> *Example*: From John (fee simple holder)—To Patrick for life, remainder to Sally in fee tail. Arthur Arthurs and James Brown are to be the trustees of the settlement for the purposes of the Settled Land Acts 1882–1890.

---

[6] See, for example, Mines Act (Ireland) 1723, as amended by the Mining Leases Act (Ireland) 1749 and Mines (Ireland) Act 1806; Leasing Powers for Religious Worship (Ireland) Acts 1855 and 1875; Leases for Schools (Ireland) Acts 1810 and 1891; Bog Reclamation Act (Ireland) 1771; Leasing Powers for Promoting Linen Manufacture Act (Ireland) 1787; Leases for Cotton Manufacture Act (Ireland) 1800; Landlord and Tenant (Planting of Trees) Act (Ireland) 1788.

[7] Incumbered Estates (Ireland) Act 1849.

[8] s 38, Settled Estates Act 1877.

[9] s 2, Settled Land Act 1882.

Succession of interests—life estate to Patrick, fee tail to Sally, fee simple reversion to John (or his successors-in-title), *therefore* the Settled Land Acts apply
Tenant for life—Patrick
Trustees of the settlement—Arthur Arthurs and James Brown
Future interest-holder—Sally, Sally's blood descendants entitled under the fee tail, John (reversioner)

To sum up, the Settled Land Acts 1882–1890 recognised the two sets of competing desires operating in these situations: the desire to ensure security for a family by means of keeping land within it, and the desire to be able to realise that security by means of putting land on the market and allowing it to operate as a commodity in contemporary economics. The Acts—which Lord Halsbury famously said "intended ... to release the land from the fetters of the settlement—to render it a marketable article notwithstanding the settlement"[10]—would therefore allow for marketability while still trying to achieve security.

1. Definition of Settled Land

[6–08] The Settled Land Acts applied to all settled land,[11] defined as:

(a) Any land held in a succession of estates created by document(s),[12] i.e. land held in something "less than" a fee simple (fee tail, life estate) whether in law or in equity. Here the land was held in a strict settlement or in a holding trust (i.e. a trust without an obligation to sell the land);
(b) the land of minors;[13]
(c) land held in a trust for sale.[14]

The Acts worked somewhat differently for each of the categories, but the same basic principles informed their operation across the board.

2. The Tenant for Life

[6–09] The tenant for life was defined by s 2(5) as the person for the time being entitled to possession of the land by virtue of the settlement. Section 58 elaborated on this by expressly naming as tenants for life, among others, tenants in tail,[15] holders of base fees, holders of perpetually renewable leases[16] and tenants *pur autre vie.*[17] This was designed to rebut any feeling that only holders of a life estate could be said to be tenants for life within the scheme of the Settled Land Acts. Uncertainty as to whether fees simple subject to a condition subsequent and fee farm grants were subject to the Acts continued right up until their repeal by the Land and Conveyancing Law Reform

---

[10] *Bruce v Ailesbury (Marquess)* [1892] AC 356.
[11] s 2(3), Settled Land Acts 1882–1890.
[12] See s 2(1), *ibid.*
[13] s 59, *ibid.*
[14] s 63, *ibid.*
[15] That is, holders of a fee tail.
[16] *Batt v Close* (1848) 12 IR LR 529. For more on perpetually renewable leases, see Chapter 4.
[17] That is, holders of a life estate *pur autre vie* (for the life of another). See further Chapter 4.

Act 2009.[18] Most problematic of all were situations where nobody could be said to be entitled to the benefit of the land. This would arise in cases of a discretionary trust,[19] where no beneficiary of the trust could be said to be "entitled" to the income from the trust and, as a result, there was no tenant for life who could exercise the powers provided for in the Settled Land Acts 1882–1890. The Acts did not cater for such a situation in any way, which was certainly one of their major structural flaws.

(i) Powers of the Tenant for Life

The Settled Land Acts 1882–1890 gave the tenant for life certain powers of sale, mortgage, lease, disposition of the principal mansion house and entry into contracts. These powers were additional to the powers that a tenant for life may possess independently of the Settled Land Acts 1882–1890, i.e. flowing from the nature of the estate held and/or the terms of the settlement. Thus, for example, the holder of a fee tail had the power to bar the entail under the Fines and Recoveries (Ireland) Act 1834 *and* the powers conferred on him by the Settled Land Acts 1882–1890. In essence, the Settled Land Acts 1882–1890 attempted to make land more marketable in fee simple form by providing for a statutory minimum in terms of the rights of the tenant for life. Thus, while the settlor could choose to give the tenant for life greater powers than those allowed for by the Acts,[20] he could not attempt to reduce these powers below the level provided for in the Acts. In fact, s 51 provided that any terms attempting to achieve that end would be invalid. Furthermore, any provisions that attempted to terminate the settlement if the tenant for life exercised his statutory powers were invalid[21] and, in the case of conflict between the terms of the settlement and powers under the Acts, the provisions of the Acts would prevail.[22] Even if the settlement inadvertently undermined the provisions of the Acts by conflicting with the tenant for life's statutory powers, s 51 would invalidate those provisions. **[6–10]**

Not only could the settlement not impose conditions that undermined the Settled Land Act 1882–1890, but a tenant for life was also prohibited from contracting not to exercise his powers under the Acts. A tenant for life could, of course, decide not to exercise those powers, but he could not bind himself to not do so.[23] As a general principle, the tenant for life could assign his powers to any other person[24] and the powers remained exercisable by the tenant for life even where his life interest had been alienated to a third party.[25] With limited exceptions, it was only the tenant for life who could exercise those powers. The exceptions were: first, where the tenant for life was a **[6–11]**

[18] See de Londras, *Principles of Irish Property Law* (1st ed, 2007, Dublin, Clarus Press), para 6–117.

[19] A discretionary trust is one in which the trustees are given the discretion to apply the trust fund for the benefit of the beneficiaries in the manner that they see fit; thus, no beneficiaries can claim actual *entitlements* over the trust fund.

[20] s 57(1), Settled Land Act 1882. In the absence of a contrary intention, any additional powers conferred by the settler were treated as if they were conferred by the Acts (s 57(2), Settled Land Act 1882).

[21] s 52, Settled Land Act 1882.

[22] s 56(2), Settled Land Act 1882; *Atkins & AIB v Atkins & Ors* [1976–7] ILRM 62.

[23] s 50(2), Settled Land Act 1882.

[24] s 50(1), *ibid.*

[25] *Re Earl of Pembroke and Thompson's Contract* [1931] IR 493.

minor, in which case the Acts provided that the powers of the tenant for life were to be exercised by the trustees of the settlement; second, where the tenant for life was of unsound mind, in which case the powers could be exercised on his behalf; third, where a tenant for life assigned his interest to the next tenant for life within the settlement, in which case there was authority to suggest that then the assignee could exercise the powers of tenant for life.[26]

(a) Power of Sale

[6–12] Section 3 of the 1882 Act provided for a power to sell the land[27] or any part of it in fee simple. This very significant power gave tenants for life—who had rights for a lifetime only—the power to sell rights over the property forever. This did not undermine the entitlements of the future interest-holders because the money acquired for the fee simple (known as capital monies) were paid to the trustees of the settlement and the rights over the land became rights over the purchase monies for the land through overreaching, which is further considered below.[28]

[6–13] The tenant for life could choose to exchange the land instead of selling it, provided he received equality of exchange (i.e. something of equal or relatively equal value).[29] The power of sale also included the power to concur in a partition if the land was held in a joint tenancy,[30] and to create sub-grants over the land.[31] Conditions, covenants and reservations could be included in the conveyance in the same way as in any other conveyance,[32] and sales could take place either by private treaty or by means of an auction.[33] In the case of an auction, the trustees of the settlement were entitled to buy the property in the auction provided a reasonable reserve price had been placed on it. The tenant for life had an obligation to get the best price reasonably obtainable for the property in the case of sale[34] and of partition.[35]

(b) Power of Mortgage

[6–14] The Settled Land Acts 1882–1890 introduced a power to mortgage the property in fee simple or by a lease that would extend beyond the lifetime of the tenant for life,[36] thereby binding the future interest-holders, but this extensive mortgage power only applied in very limited situations. Under s 18 of the 1882 Act, the property could be mortgaged in fee simple where the money to be obtained was needed for enfranchisement (the practice of enlarging a leasehold interest into a fee simple interest[37]) or to

[26] *Re Bruen's Estate* [1911] 1 IR 76.

[27] "Land" in this context included easements (Chapter 12), rights and privileges over the land (s 3(i), Settled Land Act 1882); see also *Gilmore v The O'Conor Don* [1947] IR 462.

[28] paras 6–29 to 6–30.

[29] s 3(iii), Settled Land Act 1882.

[30] Partition is a method of physically dividing the land in question between the joint tenants in a manner that brings their co-ownership to an end. See Chapter 8, paras 8–41 to 8–47.

[31] *Re Braithwaite's Settled Estate* [1922] 1 IR 71; *Re Murphy* [1957] NI 156.

[32] ss 5 and 46, Settled Land Act 1882.

[33] s 4(3), *ibid.*

[34] s 4(1), *ibid.*

[35] s 4(2), *ibid.*

[36] The means of creating mortgages are considered in full in Chapter 13.

[37] See *Re Corcoran's Settled Estates* [1919] 1 IR 283.

make up any difference in value where the land was being exchanged or partitioned under s 3. In addition, s 11 of the 1882 Act allowed for the property to be mortgaged in order to raise money for the payment of permanent encumbrances on the property. This extensive mortgage power was, then, more or less limited to situations where the monies raised by the mortgage were to be directed towards the land itself. Thus, if a mortgage was created under s 18 or s 11, the monies raised were regarded as capital monies and paid to the trustees of the settlement. The courts were also quick to restrain mortgages under ss 18 and 11 that unduly prejudiced the future interest-holders.[38]

(c) Power of Lease

Section 6 of the 1882 Act allowed for the creation of a lease for a period of time longer than the estate held by the tenant for life, which would bind the future interest-holders under the settlement. Section 7 allowed that leases made under the Acts had to comply with certain conditions, although it should be noted that the consequences of failure to comply were not entirely clear. The clearest interpretation of its requirements, however, appears to have been that all leases would bind the tenant for life who entered into them, but leases that did not comply with s 7 would likely not bind successors of the original tenant for life lessor. Section 7 required that leases were to be made by deed and counterpart deed, take possession within 12 months of the date of execution, reserve the best rent reasonably obtainable within the circumstances (although a nominal rent could be charged for the first five years of building leases[39]), contain a covenant by the tenant to pay rent and a provision for re-entry and termination if rent was unpaid for a number of days, not to exceed 30 days. Furthermore, the tenant for life was required to give the trustees of the settlement one month's notice of intention to lease the land (except in cases of tenancies of not more than 21 years duration, at the payment of a rent and where the lessee was not made unimpeachable at waste). **[6–15]**

Although the Settled Land Acts allowed for the creation of leases that would bind future interest-holders, it did place some limitations on the duration of these leases. Building leases could not be granted for more than 90 years (or 150 years in relation to land situated in an urban area),[40] although they could be subject to options to purchase under s 6.[41] Building leases could not be granted over residential property following a 1978 enactment.[42] Mining leases could not be granted for more than 60 years[43] and, in the absence of any contrary intention in the settlement itself,[44] any rent received under a mining lease was treated as capital monies and paid to the **[6–16]**

38 See, for example, *Re Richardson* [1900] 2 Ch D 778.
39 s 8(20), Settled Land Act 1882.
40 s 6, Settled Land Act 1882 *as amended by* s 62, Landlord and Tenant Act 1931.
41 *Re Earl of Wilton's Settled Estates* [1907] 1 Ch D 50. s 3 of the Settled Land Act 1889 provided that any such option was to be exercisable within a defined period of time that was less than 10 years and the price had to be the best that could be reasonably obtained. The monies paid under the option to purchase were regarded as capital monies and therefore paid to the trustees of the settlement.
42 s 2, Landlord and Tenant (Ground Rents) Act 1978.
43 s 6, Settled Land Act 1882.
44 See, for example, *Re Rayner* [1913] 2 Ch D 210.

trustees of the settlement.[45] All other leases were limited to a maximum of 35 years in duration.[46] In general, the tenant for life was entitled to enjoy the rents from the property as income.[47] The general law of landlord and tenant would apply to leases created under the Settled Land Acts 1882–1890.[48]

(d) Power to Demand Improvements

[6–17] While everyday improvements, such as repairs, were to be paid for by the tenant for life, more substantial improvements could be met from the capital monies held by the trustees of the settlement or by the court. These improvements included the acquisition of more land, the erection of buildings and so on.[49] To secure the capital monies for this end, the tenant for life had to submit a scheme for works to the trustees or to the court,[50] although the court also had the discretion to order improvements even where such a scheme was not submitted.[51]

(e) Power to Sell the Principal Mansion House

[6–18] At the time of the introduction of the Settled Land Acts, most land that was subject to a settlement would have comprised of a somewhat grand acreage accompanied by a principal mansion house and, very often, ornamental gardens. While the earlier Acts did not introduce any particular rules relating to the tenant for life's exercise of powers in relation to the house and gardens, later legislation introduced particular procedures in relation to them. Section 10(2) of the Settled Land Act 1890 provided that the principal mansion house and "the pleasure grounds and park and lands (if any) usually occupied therewith" could be sold, exchanged or leased by the tenant for life only with the trustees' consent or, if that consent was not forthcoming, pursuant to a court order. "Farmhouses" or houses that, together with their accompanying pleasure grounds, parks and land, are less than 25 acres in size, were exempt from this limitation on the power of sale, exchange and lease.[52] In reality, very few properties in today's Ireland met the definition of "principal mansion house" under the Acts.

(f) Power to Enter into Contracts

[6–19] The Settled Land Acts 1882–1890 allowed a tenant for life to enter into contracts for the sale, exchange, lease or mortgage of the property.[53] These contracts could be enforced against both the tenant for life and his successors-in-title.[54]

(ii) Duties of the Tenant for Life

[6–20] As the preceding pages have shown, the Settled Land Acts 1882–1890 conferred very extensive powers on a tenant for life, the exercise of which could impact not only on the

---

[45] s 11, Settled Land Act 1882.
[46] s 65(10), *ibid.*
[47] *Re Wix* [1916] 1 Ch D 279.
[48] See generally Chapter 15.
[49] See s 25, Settled Land Act 1882, and s 13, Settled Land Act 1890.
[50] s 26, Settled Land Act 1882.
[51] See s 15, Settled Land Act 1890, and *Re Lisnavagh Estate* [1952] IR 296.
[52] s 10(3), Settled Land Act 1890.
[53] s 31, Settled Land Act 1882.
[54] s 31(2), *ibid.*

rights of the individual tenant for life but also on the rights and interests of all those entitled to the property under the settlement in the future. Because of this, it was important that the Acts would introduce mechanisms by which the rights of the future interest-holders could be protected. This was achieved by the imposition of both fiduciary and procedural duties on the tenant for life and by the supervisory role of the trustees of the settlement, which is considered in full in the next section.

Section 53 of the Settled Land Act 1882 deemed the tenant for life a trustee for the future interests in the land. This placed the tenant for life in a position where he had fiduciary duties towards the future interest-holders and, as a result, was required to act in a manner that took account of their interests in the land. This does not mean that the tenant for life was precluded from making a profit from the exercise of his powers; it simply meant that he had to exercise his powers with due regard to the rights of the future interest-holders. Unlike in most "normal" trusts, the tenant for life could acquire the property himself in a lease or sale, but in these cases the trustees of the settlement would exercise the power of sale in order to avoid an irreconcilable conflict of interest on the part of the tenant for life.[55] As with any trustee, the tenant for life had some discretion in relation to his exercise of powers and the courts were quite reluctant to interfere with his activities—even where the trustee appeared to be exercising his powers with dubious motives—provided his actions are not liable to harm the future interest-holders.[56] That said, actions that were clearly detrimental to the future interest-holders were restrained by the courts. This is well demonstrated by the case of *Re Earl Somes*.[57] In this case, the tenant for life proposed to sell a licensed property on the condition that no intoxicating liquor would be sold there. It is clear that a great portion of the value of a licensed premises lies in its capacity to act as a public house in which alcohol is served, and the attachment of a condition of this nature was clearly detrimental to the future interest-holders. As a result, the court prevented the imposition of this condition. **[6–21]**

As well as the fiduciary duty imposed under s 53, tenants for life were required to comply with a number of procedural requirements in the exercise of their powers. Section 45 of the 1882 Act required the tenant for life to serve the trustees of the settlement with a month's notice, in writing and by registered post, of any intended sale, exchange, partition, mortgage or lease of the property.[58] While this notice could usually take the form of a general statement of intention to exercise powers,[59] the trustees were entitled to request such further particulars as might be reasonably required from the tenant for life.[60] Having received notice of the tenant for life's intention to exercise a statutory power, the trustees of the settlement could then consent to the exercise of the power or, in furtherance of their supervisory role, attempt to prevent the proposed transaction by the **[6–22]**

[55] s 12, Settled Land Act 1890.

[56] See, for example, *Cardigan v Curzon-Howe* (1885) 30 Ch D 51.

[57] (1895) 1 TLR 567.

[58] This requirement did not apply to a lease for under 21 years made at the best price reasonably obtainable and in which the lessee had not been made unimpeachable at waste (s 7, Settled Land Act 1882).

[59] s 5(1), Settled Land Act 1884.

[60] s 5(2), *ibid*.

acquisition of an injunction. Problematically, however, the effect of a failure to comply with s 45 was not clear in Ireland.[61]

[6–23] In general, a purchaser was entitled to assume that the applicable notice and consent requirements had been complied with in relation to a particular conveyance, although this was subject to situations where the purchaser knew that there were no trustees of the settlement and that none had been appointed under the s 31 procedure.[62]

3. The Trustees of the Settlement[63]

[6–24] The trustees of the settlement played an essential role in the operation of the Settled Land Acts 1882–1890. They were the primary oversight mechanism built into the Acts and, as a result, the vast majority of transactions could not proceed without some participation on their part. For that reason, it was vital that there would be a clear mechanism for the identification of trustees of the settlement. It became common practice for conveyances or wills creating settlements to expressly identify trustees "for the purposes of the Settled Land Acts 1882–1890" and, where this was done, the named trustees would act as trustees of the settlement.[64] If there was no express identification of trustees, however, any persons (apart from the tenant for life) with a power to sell or a power to consent to a sale of the settled property were considered trustees of the settlement.[65] If trustees of the settlement were still not identifiable, one would assess whether the settlement named someone with power to sell other land within the settlement and, if so, they would be the trustees of the settlement.[66] If trustees of the settlement were still not identifiable, anyone with a future power of sale over the property would be deemed a trustee of the settlement.[67] If no trustees of the settlement could be identified following the application of all of these tests, then one could have recourse to a court to have trustees of the settlement appointed.[68] If the settlement was made by will and trustees could not be identified, the personal representatives of the deceased (if there are two or more) would be the trustees until the court could make the appointment.[69]

[6–25] The ability to go to court to have trustees of the settlement appointed was absolutely vital for the smooth operation of the Acts, which—as already noted—required the involvement of trustees of the settlement for the tenant for life's powers to be effectively exercised. Where trustees of the settlement appointed by the court died, their duties

---

[61] In *Hughes v Fanagan* (1891) 30 LR IR 111 the Court held that failure to provide the required notice would result in the transaction binding the tenant for life only. In contrast, however, Black J later held that a failure to serve these notices ought not to result in the transaction being binding only on the tenant for life (*Gilmore v The O'Conor Don* [1947] IR 462).

[62] s 45(3), Settled Land Act 1882.

[63] It is important to note that in order to be a trustee of the settlement, a person did not have to hold the legal interest in the land; in this way trusteeship within the Settled Land Acts 1882–1890 was a distinct concept from trusteeship generally.

[64] s 2(8), Settled Land Act 1882.

[65] s 2(8), *ibid.*

[66] s 16(1), Settled Land Act 1890.

[67] s 16(2), *ibid.*

[68] s 38, Settled Land Act 1882.

[69] s 50(3), Succession Act 1965.

were taken over by their survivors until, at the death of the last survivor of the court-appointed trustees, the personal representatives would take over these duties. Before appointing people as trustees of the settlement, the court had to be satisfied that the individuals concerned were fit to be trustees and that the application for the appointment of trustees of the settlement was made for purposes that were proper under the Acts and likely to benefit all those who have an entitlement to the property.[70]

The basic function of the trustees was to ensure that the balance between security for the family and marketability of the land was maintained. In general, this was done by means of a supervisory role that revolved around notice and consents and through the central role of the trustee when in relation to capital monies generated by the tenant for life's exercise of statutory powers. Although trustees of the settlement were entitled to receive notice of intended exercises of powers by the tenants for life, s 42 of the 1882 Act provided that the trustees were not to be liable for either consenting to or failing to prevent any such exercise of powers. This immunity from liability somewhat undermined the intention behind the notification requirement because it removed from trustees of the settlement the incentive to act on a notice that indicated an intention to exercise powers in an unwise manner, which seemed to grate against the fact that the main function of the trustees of the settlement was to protect the interests of the future interest-holders.[71] **[6–26]**

The trustees of the settlement had a particularly important role in relation to the capital monies. Capital monies can be defined as monies that represent the land, such as purchase money, mortgage money and rents from mining leases. These monies did not go to the tenant for life; rather, the money was paid to the trustees of the settlement[72] (for which purposes there had to be at least two trustees, unless the settlement provided otherwise[73]) or to the court.[74] The trustees of the settlement would then invest this money under the direction of the tenant for life,[75] who directed this investment while still operating as a trustee of the future interests under s 53 of the Act and, therefore, while still bound by his fiduciary duties towards the future interest-holders. The tenant for life was entitled to the income from the capital monies for his lifetime. Once he died, however, the next tenant for life would take over that role and could authorise a different investment, etc. This is how the doctrine of overreaching, discussed in the next section, operated under the Acts. The payment of capital monies to the trustees of the settlement was the key to the Settled Land Acts 1882–1890, achieving their objective of making land more alienable while protecting the rights of those entitled to the property in the future. **[6–27]**

Trustees of the settlement also had the power to exercise the rights of the tenant for life where the tenant for life wanted to exercise his powers to his own advantage, for example where he would himself intend to purchase the property. This was intended to **[6–28]**

[70] *Burke v Gore* (1884) 13 LR IR 367.

[71] *Hughes v Fanagan* (1891) 30 LR IR 111.

[72] s 22, Settled Land Act 1882.

[73] s 39(1), *ibid.*

[74] s 46(2), *ibid.*

[75] s 22(2), *ibid.* If the tenant for life did not direct investment, then the trustees of the settlement could exercise their discretion to invest the capital monies (s 22, *ibid.*).

avoid a conflict of interests that would make it impossible for the tenant for life to fulfil his fiduciary duties. The trustees of the settlement could be given additional powers (expressly or impliedly) in the settlement and, where the same powers were vested in the trustees and the tenant for life, the trustees could exercise them only with the tenant's consent.[76]

4. Overreaching

[6–29] As already suggested, overreaching was the key to the Settled Land Acts 1882–1890. It ensured that the tenant for life could deal with the property, but that the rights that had applied to the property under the settlement were shifted to that which represented the property, i.e. the capital monies or whatever represented their investment.[77] This meant that whatever estates people were entitled to under the settlement over the land were translated into rights over the capital monies, which had to be held in the same manner and for the same estates and interests as if it were the land.[78] As well as protecting the future interest-holders by ensuring that they could benefit from the land—albeit in the form of capital monies—the doctrine of overreaching benefited the market because it protected purchasers from the potential dangers in dealing with settled land. A purchaser who acquired property under the Settled Land Acts 1882–1890 got the land free of the future interests,[79] which were catered for by means of overreaching of the capital monies. Indeed, even a purchaser who had notice of these future interests would take the property free of them *provided* the conditions for overreaching were fulfilled and the capital monies were paid to the trustees of the settlement. Once the capital monies had been paid to the trustees of the settlement (or the court) a receipt was issued to the purchaser. This receipt formed a vital part of the purchaser's title and protected him from any claims of future interest-holders under the settlement.[80]

[6–30] In order for overreaching to operate, certain conditions had to be fulfilled[81]:

(a) The disposition had to comply with all applicable legal requirements;
(b) The disposition had to be within the powers of the tenant for life;
(c) The capital monies had to have been paid to the trustees of the settlement (or, in their absence, to the court).

If these conditions were not fulfilled, overreaching did not operate, i.e. the rights of the future interest-holders remained in the land. As a result they could be enforced against the purchaser unless he could show that he qualified as the *bona fide* purchaser for value without notice.[82] In such a case the tenant for life would have breached his fiduciary duties and would be liable in actions of the future interest-holders. Those future interest-holders could also avail of the equitable remedy of tracing to try to access the capital monies in appropriate circumstances.

---

[76] s 56(2), *ibid.*
[77] s 22(5), *ibid.*
[78] *Roberts v Kenny*, unreported, High Court, 10 March 1998.
[79] s 20(2), Settled Land Act 1882.
[80] s 40, *ibid.*
[81] s 20, *ibid.*
[82] s 54, *ibid.*

5. Land of Minors

The Settled Land Acts 1882–1890 determined that land held by minors was to be treated as settled land regardless of whether or not it was held in a succession of estates.[83] The purpose of this classification was to protect minors in order to ensure that they did not transact unwisely in relation to their land. Once the minor reached the age of majority (i.e. 18 years[84]) the property was no longer governed by the Settled Land Acts. If the minor's ownership arose as a share in the estate of a deceased individual, the personal representative of the deceased was entitled to appoint a trustee of the settlement for the purposes of the Settled Land Acts 1882–1890.[85] Here the minor was the tenant for life within the meaning of the Settled Land Acts 1882–1890 however, in order to protect his interests, the powers of the tenant for life were be exercisable only by the trustees of the settlement. While the Acts normally required two trustees of the settlement in order for capital monies to be received, the land of minors could be administered by one trustee.[86] **[6–31]**

6. Trusts for Sale

Trusts for sale were defined as settled land by virtue of s 63 of the 1882 Act, provided the beneficial interest was held in a succession of estates. The tenant for life of property held in a trust for sale was defined in s 63 as "the person for the time being beneficially entitled to the income of the land until sale". This caused clear difficulties because as the tenant for life, the beneficiary of the trust had extensive powers (including the power of sale) while, in a trust for sale, the trustees have an obligation to sell under the terms of the trust itself. Some of the difficulties caused by this position were resolved by the Settled Land Act 1884, which allowed the trustees of the settlement to exercise their rights in a trust for sale without the consent of the tenant for life,[87] and required the tenant for life to get the consent of the court before exercising the power of sale.[88] The court would consent to a sale only if the tenant for life could satisfy it of the benefit of the sale to all of the relevant parties.[89] **[6–32]**

III. Trusts of Land under Part 4 of the LCLRA 2009

Although the general framework for the Settled Land Acts 1882–1890 was a clever and well-balanced one, it suffered from a number of flaws and uncertainties and, taking them into account together with the general objective of simplifying and modernising land law in Ireland, the Law Reform Commission recommended their repeal and replacement with a bespoke system to govern trusts of land that would exist within the broader context of the law of trusts.[90] Land formerly governed by the Settled Land Acts 1882–1890 would now be governed by this body of law, together with practically **[6–33]**

---

[83] s 59, *ibid.*

[84] s 2(1), Age of Majority Act 1985.

[85] s 57, Succession Act 1965.

[86] s 58(3), *ibid.*

[87] s 6, Settled Land Act 1884.

[88] s 7, *ibid.*

[89] *Re Tuthill* [1907] 1 IR 305.

[90] LRC, *Consultation Paper on the Reform and Modernisation of Land Law and Conveyancing Law* (2004, Dublin), Chapter 4.

all other land subject to a trust.[91] This change was introduced by Part 4 of the Land and Conveyancing Law Reform Act 2009.

[6–34] There are three different kinds of land that are defined as a "trust of land" within the scheme of Part 4, each of which will be considered presently.[92] Upon such categorisation specific rules relating to the identification of trustees, overreaching and dispute resolution will apply to those trusts but, unlike under the Settled Land Acts 1882–1890, the Act does not specify the range of powers that the trustee can exercise. Rather, as considered below, we can say as a general matter that the trustee has the capacity to exercise the normal powers of trustees subject to the normal obligations of trustees. This reflects the fact that, subject to the matters specifically dealt with in Part 4, trusts of land are governed by the general law of trusts.[93]

1. Scope of Part 4 of the LCLRA 2009

[6–35] Section 18 of the Land and Conveyancing Law Reform Act 2009 outlines the three categories of land to be defined as a "trust of land" for the purposes of Part 4 (which I will now call "Part 4 trusts" for convenience). These are:

(i) Settlements

[6–36] Section 18(1)(a) provides that all settlements of land are to be governed by Part 4. This includes both settlements created after the coming into effect of the Act (i.e. 1 December 2009) *and* all pre-existing settlements (which would previously have been governed by the Settled Land Acts 1882–1890). Section 18(2)(a) makes clear that a "fee simple in possession" is not contained within this definition. As considered in Chapter 4, s 11 of the 2009 Act defines a fee simple in possession as including conditional and determinable fees simple, fees simple subject to rights of residence, annuities and analogous charges, and powers of revocation.[94] By expressly excluding fees simple in possession from the definition of settlement in Part 4, the 2009 Act ensures that uncertainty that persisted as to these kinds of fees' "capture" by the Settled Land Acts 1882–1890[95] would not re-emerge in relation to Part 4.

(ii) Land Held in Trust

[6–37] Section 18(1)(b) provides that land held "on a trust whenever it arises and of whatever kind" is governed by Part 4. This is clearly intended to capture not only trusts created after the commencement of the Land and Conveyancing Law Reform Act 2009 but also those predating its commencement. In order to make express the broad nature of s 18(1)(b), s 18(2)(b) provides that in this context "a trust includes an express, implied, resulting, constructive and bare trust and a trust for sale". In other words, essentially every trust in which land is held "either with or without other property"[96] will be a Part 4 trust.

---

91 s 18(1), Land and Conveyancing Law Reform Act 2009.

92 *ibid.*

93 s 18(3), Land and Conveyancing Law Reform Act 2009.

94 s 11(2), *ibid.*

95 See de Londras, *Principles of Irish Property Law* (1st ed, 2007, Dublin, Clarus Press), para 6–117.

96 s 18(1)(b), Land and Conveyancing Law Reform Act 2009.

(iii) Land of Minors

The third category of land constituting a Part 4 trust is land "vested, whether before or after the commencement of this Part, in a minor".[97] **[6–38]**

2. Trustees in Part 4 Trusts

As with any other kind of trust, it is vital that the trustees of a Part 4 trust can be clearly and relatively easily identified, particularly since s 20(1) provides that they have "the full power of an owner to convey or otherwise deal with" the land the subject of the trust. The powers and liabilities of trustees are considered below,[98] but for now we must consider *who* the trustees are, which varies depending on which of the three categories of Part 4 trusts one is dealing with and, to at least some extent, on whether the settlement, trust or minor ownership predates the commencement of the Land and Conveyancing Law Reform Act 2009. In addition to the specific mechanisms for identifying the trustee under Part 4 that are considered in the following paragraphs, courts retain the right to appoint trustees under s 19(3) of the 2009 Act. **[6–39]**

(i) Settlements Predating the Commencement of Part 4

As of 1 December 2009, settlements previously governed by the Settled Land Acts 1882–1890 would be governed by Part 4 of the 2009 Act, which required some sensitivity to the tenant for life. Remember, as considered above,[99] that the tenant for life had extensive powers of disposition under the Settled Land Acts 1882–1890, which would be lost upon commencement of Part 4 *unless* the tenant for life became a trustee of the Part 4 settlement. Thus, that is precisely what was done and under s 19(1)(a)(i) of the Land and Conveyancing Law Reform Act 2009 the trustees under Part 4 will be those who were trustees of the settlement under the Settled Land Acts *plus* the tenant for life under the Settled Land Acts. **[6–40]**

(ii) Settlements Following the Commencement of Part 4

Where a settlement is purported to be created after 1 December 2009, s 19(1)(a)(ii) of the Land and Conveyancing Law Reform Act 2009 provides that the trustees of the Part 4 trust will be those who would be trustees if what had been created was an express trust. This is governed by s 19(1)(b) of the 2009 Act and considered in the next paragraph. **[6–41]**

(iii) Express Trusts

Section 19(1)(b) of the Land and Conveyancing Law Reform Act 2009 provides for the identification of trustees of a Part 4 trust where what is at issue is an express trust *and* where what is at issue is a purported settlement created after 1 December 2009.[100] If the trust names a trustee, she will be the trustee for the purposes of Part 4.[101] If no trustee is named, s 19(1)(b)(ii) provides that any person with a present or future power of sale *or* with the power to consent to the exercise of a power of sale will be the trustee for the purposes of Part 4. If we still cannot identify a trustee, anyone with the power to **[6–42]**

---

97 s 18(1)(c), *ibid.*
98 paras 6–45 to 6–47.
99 paras 6–12 to 6–19.
100 s 19(1)(a)(ii), Land and Conveyancing Law Reform Act 2009; para 6–41.
101 s 19(1)(b)(i), *ibid.*

appoint a trustee either under the trust instrument itself or under the general law of trusts will be the trustee.[102] In the unlikely event that no trustee has been identified under the preceding three methods, s 19(1)(b)(iv) provides that "the settler or, in the case of a trust created by will, the testator's personal representative or representatives" will act as Part 4 trustees. Furthermore, the court retains the right to appoint trustees and vest in them the legal ownership of land.[103]

(iv) Implied, Resulting, Constructive and Bare Trusts

[6–43] Where the Part 4 trust is an implied, resulting, constructive or bare trust the trustee will be "the person in whom the legal title to the land is vested".[104]

(v) Land of Minors

[6–44] Section 19(1)(c) of the Land and Conveyancing Law Reform Act 2009 provides that in the case of land vested in a minor (whether before or after the commencement of the Act), the Part 4 trustee will be the person who would be trustee under s 19(1)(b), i.e. if what had been created were an express trust.[105]

3. Powers and Liabilities of Trustees

[6–45] Section 20(1) of the Land and Conveyancing Law Reform Act 2009 provides that, subject to some limitations, the trustee of a Part 4 trust "has the full power of an owner to convey or otherwise deal with" the land in question. This is in marked distinction to the situation under the Settled Land Acts 1882–1890 where, as we have seen, the powers exercisable by a tenant for life were extensively prescribed. For the avoidance of any doubt, s 20(2) provides that these powers include the power to allow beneficiaries of the trust to occupy or otherwise use the land,[106] and to sell the land and invest the proceeds of sale in the purchase of other land either within or outside the State.[107] Extensive as these powers are, they are not unlimited.

[6–46] Interestingly, s 20(1)(b) provides that the powers of the trustee are subject to, *inter alia*, "any restrictions imposed... by any instrument... relating to the land". This presumably includes the trust or settlement document itself. Therefore, a person creating a Part 4 trust can set down limitations on what the trustee can do or impose certain processes or conditions on the exercise of the general powers. For example, it would appear possible for the trust to require that the trustee would get the consent of the beneficiaries for any proposed conveyance of the land, notwithstanding the fact that such conveyances are broadly within the powers of the trustee under s 20(1). This again reflects the different orientation of Part 4 when compared to the Settled Land

---

[102] s 19(1)(b)(iii), *ibid.*

[103] s 19(3), *ibid.*

[104] s 19(1)(d), *ibid.*

[105] See para 6–42.

[106] s 20(2)(a), Land and Conveyancing Law Reform Act 2009. In the case of registered land, of course, actual occupation of receipt of rents or income from the land by the beneficiaries would give rise to their interests in the land being further protected against purchasers as "overriding interests" under s 71(1)(j), Registration of Title Act 1964. This is fully considered in Chapter 7, paras 7–35 to 7–40.

[107] s 20(2)(b), Land and Conveyancing Law Reform Act 2009.

Acts 1882–1890. As considered above, the Settled Land Acts were concerned with laying down a statutory minimum of powers, whereas Part 4 is concerned with laying down a broad approach to Part 4 trusts but within which the person creating the trust can organise the exercise of that general power, provided this is done in a manner compliant with the general law of trusts.

The general law of trusts itself acts to limit what trustees can do under s 20. Section 20(1)(a) expressly makes the power to deal with the land subject to "the duties of a trustee". This encompasses the important fiduciary principle that the trustee is required to act for the benefit of the beneficiaries of the trust, rather than for his or her own benefit or enrichment. The powers of a Part 4 trustee are also subject to limitation by statute,[108] by the general law of trusts,[109] and by any court order relating to the land in question.[110] **[6–47]**

4. Overreaching

We have already seen that the doctrine of overreaching operated under the Settled Land Acts 1882–1890 to protect both the purchaser (who would take the land free of future interests provided the requirements of overreaching were complied with) and the future interest holders (whose entitlements over the land would now become entitlements over that which represented the land, i.e. the purchase monies).[111] This basic balancing model of overreaching is maintained and extended by the 2009 Act. The general principle of overreaching is expressed in s 21(1) of the Land and Conveyancing Law Reform Act 2009: **[6–48]**

> Subject to *subsection (3)*, a conveyance to a purchaser of a legal estate or legal interest in land by the person or persons specified in *subsection (2)* overreaches any equitable interest in the land so that it ceases to affect that estate or interest, whether or not the purchaser has notice of the equitable interest.

Although the general principle of overreaching is maintained and, indeed, extended in the 2009 Act, it operates slightly differently depending on whether the Part 4 trust in question is one that would have previously been subject to the Settled Land Acts 1882–1890 or whether it is one that would not have been within the scope of those Acts. As a result, we will consider both categories separately.

(i) Part 4 Trusts that Would Previously Have Been Within the Scope of the SLA 1882–1890

What we are concerned with here is land held in a strict settlement, land held in a trust—including a trust for sale—for successive interests, and the land of minors.[112] In order for overreaching to operate in this case, s 21(2)(a) provides that overreaching will operate where the property is sold by "at least two trustees or a trust corporation". Provided the land is sold by these "persons specified", all equitable interests that exist **[6–49]**

[108] s 20(1)(b), Land and Conveyancing Law Reform Act 2009.
[109] *ibid.*
[110] *ibid.*
[111] paras 6–29 to 6–30.
[112] para 6–08.

over the land will overreach the conveyance, become interests over the proceeds of the sale, and not bind the purchaser whether or not that purchaser had any notice of their existence.[113] That is, in a nutshell, the basic operation of overreaching. There are, however, some exceptions to its operation with which we ought to be familiar.

[6–50] Section 21(3)(a) provides that overreaching will not apply to any conveyance that was made for reasons of fraud, where the purchaser had actual notice of the fraud at the date of the conveyance *or* to which the purchaser was a party. Furthermore, any equitable interests that are expressly protected within the conveyance itself will not be overreached,[114] nor will equitable mortgages by deposit of title deeds.[115]

[6–51] Section 21(6) expressly provides that the operation of the doctrine of overreaching does not affect the operation of the Family Home Protection Act 1976. As a result, the normal consent requirements under s 3 of that Act (which requires that the conveyance of any interest in the ordinary place of residence of a married couple without the prior, written consent of the non-owning spouse will be void) continue to apply.[116] Similar protections were introduced for the ordinary place of residence of civil partners—known as shared homes—by the Civil Partnership and Certain Rights and Obligations of Cohabitants Act 2010[117] but there is no express reference in that Act to overreaching under s 21 of the 2009 Act. Although there is nothing to suggest that the operation of overreaching obviates the requirement to acquire consent under the 1976 and 2010 Acts respectively (quite apart from the inclusion of s 21(6)), the express protection of one such provision (relating to family homes) to the exclusion of the other (relating to shared homes) could be interpreted by a court as purposeful. In other words, should it arise, a court might be justified in holding that if the Oireachtas intended to protect the veto powers of both spouses and civil partners in the context of overreaching they would have done so, especially as one such veto power is expressly protected and the other is not. It would therefore be favourable for s 21(6) to be amended in order to protect the veto power of a civil partner under s 28 of the Civil Partnership and Certain Rights and Obligations of Cohabitants Act 2010 in the same way as spousal veto powers are thereby protected. As an alternative, s 21(6) could simply be deleted by amendment. As the veto power of a spouse or a civil partner does not confer any proprietary interest over that spouse or civil partner, there does not appear to be an equitable interest arising from that veto that can be overreached in any case.

(ii) Part 4 Trusts that Would Not Previously Have Been Within the Scope of the SLA 1882–1890

[6–52] All other trusts can be conveyed, with the equitable interests being overreached, by "a single trustee or owner of the legal estate or interest".[118] In this case the operation of overreaching will be subject to the same restrictions as were considered above for trusts that would previously have been within the scope of the Settled Land Acts 1882–1890

[113] s 21(1), Land and Conveyancing Law Reform Act 2009.
[114] s 21(3)(b)(i), *ibid.*
[115] s 21(3)(b)(ii), *ibid.*
[116] Chapter 9 below, paras 9–19 to 9–34.
[117] s 28, Civil Partnership and Certain Rights and Obligations of Cohabitants Act 2010; *ibid.*
[118] s 12(2)(b), Land and Conveyancing Law Reform Act 2009.

as well as an additional restriction under s 21(3)(b)(iii) of the Land and Conveyancing Law Reform Act 2009. This protects any equitable interest "protected by registration prior to the date of the conveyance or taking effect as a burden coming within section 72(1)(j) of the Act of 1964 (or, in the case of unregistered land, which would take effect as such a burden if the land were registered land)" from overreaching.

Thus, any equitable interest over registered land that is (a) registrable and registered under s 69 of the Registration of Title Act 1964, or (b) overriding and within s 72(1)(j) of the Registration of Title Act 1964, will be protected from overreaching. As will be considered in Chapter 7, s 72(1)(j) interests are those of persons in actual occupation or in receipt of rents or income from the registered land and bind the purchaser of the property, whereas s 69 interests are those that are usually protected against a purchaser of the property if they are registered.[119] Importantly, s 21(3)(b)(iii) of the Land and Conveyancing Law Reform Act 2009 provides that interests that would qualify as s 69 or s 72(1)(j) interests if they existed over registered land, but which actually exist in relation to unregistered land, are also protected against overreaching. **[6–53]**

5. Dispute Resolution

Section 22 of the Land and Conveyancing Law Reform Act 2009 provides for the resolution of disputes relating to Part 4 by application to the court. An application can be made by anyone with an interest in a trust of land (or someone acting on his or her behalf)[120] in relation to the performance by trustees of their functions,[121] the nature and extent of any beneficial or other interest in the land,[122] or—quite broadly—"other operation of the trust".[123] The disputes to be resolved are disputes between the trustees,[124] between the beneficiaries,[125] between trustees and beneficiaries,[126] or between trustees or beneficiaries and "any other persons interested".[127] The court has a very broad discretion as to what orders it may make in response to an application, but in so doing the Act instructs the court to take account of the interests of the beneficiaries "as a whole"[128] together with the purposes that the trust of land is intended to achieve,[129] the interests of any minor or other beneficiary subject to any incapacity,[130] the interests of any secured creditor of any beneficiary,[131] and any other matter the court considers relevant.[132] **[6–54]**

---

119 See Chapter 7 below, paras 7–31 to 7–40.

120 s 22(1), Land and Conveyancing Law Reform Act 2009. This includes mortgagees, secured creditors, judgment mortgagee and trustees (s 22(4), Land and Conveyancing Law Reform Act 2009).

121 s 22(1)(i), Land and Conveyancing Law Reform Act 2009.

122 s 22(1)(ii), *ibid.*

123 s 22(1)(iii), *ibid.*

124 s 22(1)(a), *ibid.*

125 s 22(1)(b), *ibid.*

126 s 22(1)(c), *ibid.*

127 s 22(1)(d), *ibid.*

128 s 22(3), *ibid.*

129 s 22(3)(a), *ibid.*

130 s 22(3)(b), *ibid.*

131 s 22(3)(c), *ibid.*

132 s 22(3)(d), *ibid.*

CHAPTER 7
Systems of Land Registration

In Ireland we have two different systems of land registration, one of which relates to the registration of deeds (unhelpfully known as unregistered land[1]) and the other of which relates to the registration of title (known as registered land[2]). Both systems are now administered by the same entity: the Property Registration Authority.[3] In this chapter we consider the operation of both systems, especially as they relate to purchasers and to establishing the priority of rights or entitlement over the land in question. Land registration is fundamentally concerned with both of these things: with making sure that, as much as possible, prospective purchasers know what they are getting (and what a vendor actually has to sell) in relation to the land in question without having to engage in unduly onerous and expensive investigations *and* with making sure that where there are multiple rights or interests in relation to land that happen to be incompatible in some way (perhaps because there are insufficient funds to pay for both of them, for example) we have a straightforward mechanism of determining which gets satisfied first. Both of these concerns are fundamentally related to the market: to the desire to ensure that property is as freely alienable as possible and that prospective transactors are not disincentivised by uncertainty or prospective liability for third party rights. **[7–01]**

Of course, registration also plays other roles, including an organisational role for the State. Such a role is particularly important where, as in Ireland, large amounts of land are or were distributed by the State after a period of upheaval (e.g. the repatriation of land to the Irish). As our system of property transactions sophisticates and becomes increasingly electronic—through what is known as eConveyancing—we must also ensure that the logistics of land registration are suited to the reality of legal practice. **[7–02]**

---

1 Registration of Deeds (Ireland) Act 1707.

2 Record of Title (Ireland) Act 1865; Local Registration of Title (Ireland) Act 1891; Registration of Title Act 1964.

3 Registration of Deeds and Title Act 2006.

Indeed, it was moving us towards eConveyancing that largely incentivised the establishment of the Property Registration Authority and, as of June 2010, Ireland's entire Land Registry (i.e. information relating to registered land) is now digital, including maps.

I. The Property Registration Authority

[7–03] Established under the Registration of Deeds and Title Act 2006,[4] the Property Registration Authority is largely independent in carrying out its functions[5] and comprises a maximum of eleven members.[6] The Property Registration Authority's responsibilities include[7]:

(1) Managing the Registry of Deeds (unregistered land) and the Land Registry (registered land)[8];
(2) Promoting the registration of land[9];
(3) Undertaking research relevant to the system of land registration[10];
(4) Liaising with the Minister for Justice on the registration of title and on mechanisms for increasing the incidence of registered land[11];
(5) Creating three-year strategic plans on its objectives, aims and resources, which are laid before the Oireachtas by the Minister for Justice.[12] As part of the development of these strategic plans, it is envisaged that the relevant stakeholders in the property-law system will be consulted and that their feedback and needs will be integrated into the continued development of the system. This ought to prevent undue stagnation and help the systems of land registration to cater for the needs of a modern property economy. Although such a responsive system might be said to carry a risk of "knee-jerk" legal developments, the fact that these plans are to be created every three years suggests that the system of generating these reports may be sufficiently reflective to avoid such an outcome;
(6) Producing an annual report for the Minister for Justice on the Authority's progress in fulfilling its functions, which report will also be laid before the Oireachtas.[13]

The Property Registration Authority also makes rules by which the land registration system can be effectively implemented. Much of the system for registered land had been set up by the Land Registration Rules 1972, and in general those rules are retained by the Land Registration Rules 2009.

---

[4] s 9, Registration of Deeds and Title Act 2006.
[5] s 9(5), *ibid.*
[6] s 11(1), *ibid.*
[7] The Authority also has responsibilities relating to ground rents (s 10(1)(c), Registration of Deeds and Title Act 2006), and "miscellaneous" responsibilities (s 10(1)(e), Registration of Deeds and Title Act 2006).
[8] s 10(1)(a), Registration of Deeds and Title Act 2006.
[9] s 10(1)(b), *ibid.*
[10] s 10(1)(d), *ibid.*
[11] s 10(1)(f), *ibid.*
[12] s 18, *ibid.*
[13] s 19, *ibid.*

II. Unregistered Land

"Unregistered land" is the term used to describe property that has been registered under the Registration of Deeds (Ireland) Act 1707, as amended.[14] As has already been mentioned, unregistered land is essentially concerned with the registration of deeds. What we mean by this is that documents relating to interests over unregistered land are lodged—or registered—but, rather than one unified document or record being created for that piece of land upon which all the interests are recorded (as with registered land), these documents together constitute the evidence relating to ownership and interests over the land in question. [7–04]

1. The Meaning of "Deed"

Section 32 of the Registration of Deeds and Title Act 2006 outlines what is meant by deed in this context; it is "a document by which an estate or interest in land is created, transferred, charged or otherwise affected". Section 32 then outlines the following *non-exhaustive* list of what constitutes a deed for these purposes: [7–05]

(a) a conveyance;
(b) a document not attested;
(c) an assent under the Succession Act 1965;
(d) a vesting certificate under the Landlord and Tenant (Ground Rents) (No. 2) Act 1978;
(e) a certificate vesting property in the Official Assignee under the Bankruptcy Act 1988;
(f) a receipt under section 43 of the Industrial and Provident Societies Act 1893, section 53 of the Friendly Societies Act 1896, section 84(1) of the Building Societies Act 1976 or section 18(1) of the Housing Act 1988;
(g) an affidavit or a certificate of satisfaction prescribed by the Judgement Mortgage (Ireland) Act 1850;
(h) a judgment, decree or order of a court or a declaration by a court of title, division or allotment;
(i) a notification or order under the Land Reclamation Act 1949;
(j) a notice under the Family Home Protection Act 1976;
(k) a certified copy of a statement under section 3(8)(*c*) (inserted by section 54(1)(*b*)(ii) of the Family Law Act 1995) of the Family Home Protection Act 1976;
(l) a record of the registration of the ownership of any estate or interest in land as referred to in section 116(2) of the Act of 1964;
(m) information in electronic or other non-legible form which is capable of being converted into any of the preceding documents; and
(n) such other documents as may be prescribed.

Section 32 expressly excludes documents that can be registered under the Registration of Title Act 1964 and leases for a term of less than 21 years in relation to which there is actual occupation in accordance with the lease from the definition of "deed".[15] Any of [7–06]

---

[14] This Act is amended by the Registration of Deeds Acts 1709, 1721 and 1785; Registry of Deeds (Amendment) (Ireland) Acts 1822, 1832 and 1848; Judgment Mortgage (Ireland) Acts 1850 and 1858; Registration of Deeds and Title Act 2006.

[15] s 32(1)(i) and (ii), Registration of Deeds and Title Act 2006.

these deeds can, then, be registered—or lodged—in relation to unregistered land, although it should be noted that, as a general matter, one is not *obliged* to register one's deed. Rather than create a binding obligation for registration of deeds, the unregistered land system creates two important incentives relating to the effectiveness of documents and priorities that sit at the heart of the unregistered land system.

2. Ineffective Deeds

[7–07] To say that an unregistered deed is ineffective is not to say that the interest concerned is invalidated by a failure to register, but rather the interest is valid but cannot be enforced. Prior to the introduction of the Registration of Deeds and Title Act 2006 judgment mortgages, bankruptcy vesting certificates of adjudication and damage and improvement charging orders were ineffective for lack of registration. Judgment mortgages must still be registered,[16] as must bankruptcy vesting certificates of adjudication.[17]

3. Priority

[7–08] There may be times when a number of people hold interests over land, but the land is incapable of satisfying all of these interests at the same time. In such cases the law must assess the order of priority of these interests. The main incentive towards registration contained in the Registration of Deeds Act 1707 was the creation of a straightforward and relatively simple system that determined priority by reference to (a) whether an interest is registered and (b) which interest is registered first. This is quite in contrast with earlier equitable systems of assessing priority, which took into account (a) whether the interest was legal or equitable and (b) when each interest was created. The inclusion of a statutory scheme of priorities in the 1707 Act did not completely rid the earlier equitable principles of their relevance. Rather, the equitable principles operated in situations where, for various reasons, the rules of the 1707 Act could be applied. In order to assess whether the statutory rules or the equitable principles apply, the following test could be applied:

(a) Are all of the interests capable of being registered under the 1707 Act?
   a. If no, then the equitable principles are to be applied.
   b. If yes, then one moves on to the second question.
(b) If yes, are any of the interests actually registered?
   a. If no, then the equitable principles are to be applied.
   b. If yes, then the statutory rules of priority are to be applied.

Having determined whether the statutory or equitable approach would apply, it is appropriate to consider the form and operation of those rules.

(i) Statutory Rules under the 1707 Act

[7–09] In essence, the statutory rules of priority gave registered deeds priority over unregistered deeds and, as between registered deeds, gave priority to the interest that

---

[16] s 116(2), Land and Conveyancing Law Reform Act 2009; 3.3. 6–8 Registration of Deeds (no. 2) Rules 2009, SI no. 457 of 2009.

[17] s 32(1)(e), Registration of Deeds and Title Act 2006; s 46, Bankruptcy Act 1988.

was registered earlier. Thus, where there was a question as to priority between registered interests, priority was assessed by reference to the date at which the interests were registered, with the first registered taking priority.[18] The date of the creation of the interest was entirely irrelevant, as was the question of whether the interest was legal or equitable.[19] In a competition of priority between a registered and unregistered interest, the registered interest took priority over the unregistered interest. Once again, the date of creation and nature of the competing interests were irrelevant considerations.[20] Neither of these situations raised any real difficulties, although situations of competition for priority between registrable but unregistered interests and registered interests.

Under the statutory scheme of priorities, the registered interest took priority notwithstanding the fact that there was an earlier but unregistered registrable interest over the property. However, there were two situations in which the statute's concentration on registration was overridden by other considerations and the earlier registrable but unregistered interest was given priority. First, where the holder of the later registered interest had actual notice of the earlier registrable but unregistered interest *and* registered his interest in order to take advantage of the statutory system of priorities, the law of equity would not allow a statute to be used as an instrument of fraud in this manner and the earlier interest could enjoy priority. In this context, it was important to distinguish between cases where someone registered a deed in a legitimate act of self-protection and cases in which someone registered a deed in order to defraud the holder of the earlier unregistered interest. In the former case the interest-holder would be entitled to use the Act to his advantage; in the latter he would not.[21] Secondly, where the holder of the later registered interest did not give consideration for the interest at issue, the earlier registrable but unregistered interest could enjoy priority. [7–10]

(ii) Equitable Principles of Priority

The equitable principles applied where either (a) at least one of the relevant interests was unregistrable or (b) none of the interests was actually registered. Again, there were various kinds of competitions for priority that might arise. In applying the equitable principles, two things were of particular importance: (a) whether the interest was legal or equitable, and (b) when the interest was created. Where the interests in competition for priority were either both legal or both equity, then the interest that was created first would enjoy priority. In other words, the first in time would prevail. Where there was an earlier legal interest in competition for priority with a later equity interest, the earlier legal interest would enjoy priority as it was first in time. Where there was an earlier equitable interest in competition for priority with a later legal interest then, *in the ordinary course of events*, the earlier equitable interest would take priority because it was first in time. That said, if the holder of the later legal interest was a *bona fide* purchaser for value without notice of the earlier equitable interest, the later legal interest could enjoy priority over the earlier equitable interest. [7–11]

18 s 5, Registration of Deeds (Ireland) Act 1707.

19 *Eyre v Dolphin* (1813) 2 Ball & B 290.

20 s 5, Registration of Deeds (Ireland) Act 1707.

21 *Blades v Blades* (1727) 1 Eq Cas Abr 358; *Reilly v Garnett* (1872) IR 7 Eq 1.

(iii) Priority under the Registration of Deeds and Title Act 2006

[7–12] Section 38 of the Registration of Deeds and Title Act 2006 outlines how priority is to operate in relation to deeds registered under the Act:

> (1) Deeds registered under this Part are deemed and taken as good and effectual both in law and equity according to the priority determined by the serial numbers allocated to... and shall, as regards any right, title, interest or liability arising from their execution, rank in priority among themselves according to the priority determined by the serial numbers so allocated.
>
> (2) A deed which is not so registered is void against a registered deed affecting the land concerned.
>
> (3) This section is without prejudice to the application of any rule of law or equity in cases where a person claiming under a registered deed had knowledge, or is deemed to have had knowledge, of a prior unregistered deed.

As documents are received in relation to unregistered land a serial number is allocated to each of them. These numbers are sequential and allocated annually.[22] Priority is, then, to be determined by reference to the serial number. If documents are received at the same time, a serial number is allocated to each of them randomly so that it is possible to determine priority between them.[23]

III. Registered Land

[7–13] The modern system of registered land can be traced back to the Local Record of Title (Ireland) Act 1865 and the Local Registration of Title (Ireland) Act 1891, as amended.[24] Key to the system of registered land is that what is registered here is ownership—or title—with a view to creating a single, comprehensive and conclusive record of ownership for each parcel of land to which the system applies. In other words, the objective is the creation of a single record that constitutes a "mirror" of the real ownership of the property, so that one need only look at that single record in order to see who has interests in the property in question and what the nature of those interests are.[25] This is known as the "mirror principle" and its achievement has been the objective of the registered land system right since its inception, and was maintained in the Registration of Title Act 1964 and in the Registration of Deeds and Title Act 2006. The beauty of the registered land system is that each piece of registered land in the country is entered onto a central register and identified as a unique folio on which all of the details relating to the property are noted, or at least those that can be noted under the 1964 Act. This central system is now digital, and land certificates (by which the title was documentarily proved) no longer have any legal force,[26] neither are they

[22] r 7(1), Registration of Deeds Rules 2008, SI no 52 of 2008.

[23] r 7(2), *ibid.*

[24] See, particularly, the Registration of Title Act 1942.

[25] s 31, Registration of Title Act 1964.

[26] Land certificates and certificates of charge lost their effect on 1 January 2010 by virtue of the Registration of Deeds and Title Act 2006 (Commencement) (no 2) Order 2006 (SI no 511 of 2006).

routinely issued any more. Rather, the information exists in an electronic register for the purposes of eConveyancing. The register is public.

1. Getting Registered

The reason for registering land is quite simple. If one acquires a piece of unregistered land, then "first registration" (i.e. the registration, for the first time, of the land in question within the registration of title—or "registered land"—system) might be engaged in for the purposes of making subsequent transactions smoother and more attractive from a conveyancing perspective, or because registration is required under the Act. If one acquires a piece of registered land (i.e. land that is already governed by the Registration of Title Act 1964), it is imperative to ensure that title is registered so that the purchaser appears as the owner on the relevant documentation and can protect his interests. While first registration is generally voluntary, one of the aims of the contemporary land registration system is to further compel registration in order to achieve, as far as possible, a situation of universal registration in Ireland in order to aid the successful adoption of quicker and easier conveyancing processes, especially e-Conveyancing. **[7–14]**

Registration of title is only compulsory in limited circumstances, which are laid out in ss 23 and 24 of the Registration of Title Act 1964 as amended. The following transactions are subject to compulsory registration requirements: **[7–15]**

- Land conveyed to or vested in any person under the Land Purchase Acts, the Labourers Acts 1883–1962, or the Irish Church Act 1869[27];
- Land acquired by a statutory authority (Minister, Commissioner of Public Works, local and public authorities, any other entity established by statute[28]) after the commencement of the 1964 Act[29];
- Any property acquired in an area deemed "compulsorily registrable" by the Minister for Justice after consultation with the Property Registration Authority.[30]

If registration of property is compulsory, but does not take place, s 25 of the Registration of Title Act 1964 as amended applies. That provides: **[7–16]**

> A person shall not acquire an estate or interest in land in any case in which registration of ownership of the land is or becomes compulsory under section 23 or 24 unless the person is registered as owner of the estate or interest within 6 months after the purported acquisition or at such later time as the Authority (or, in case of refusal, the court) may sanction in any particular case, but on any such registration the person's title shall relate

[27] s 23(1A), Registration of Title Act 1964 *as inserted by* s 52(c), Registration of Deeds and Title Act 2006.
[28] s 3, Registration of Title Act 1964.
[29] s 23, *ibid.*
[30] s 24(1), Registration of Title Act 1964 *as inserted by* s 53, Registration of Deeds and Title Act 2006.

> back to the date of the purported acquisition, and any dealings with the land before the registration shall have effect accordingly.[31]

This reflects the mirror principle: only the person named as the registered owner will be recognised as the legal owner of registered land.

2. Types of Registrable Interest

[7–17] There are various types of interest that can be registered, as reflected in the different registers in existence[32]: (1) freehold interests, (2) leasehold interests and (3) incorporeal hereditaments held in gross and other rights. For every piece of registered land, the folio—or entry—will include details of each of these types of interest, as appropriate. Where appurtenant rights (i.e. rights attached to two pieces of land such as easements[33]) exist over land, these can be registered as both burdens over the servient land (i.e. the land upon which they are exercised)[34] and as benefits of the dominant land (i.e. the land for whose benefit they are exercised).[35] Any disabilities of the owner—such as age,[36] or being of unsound mind[37]—will be noted on the register in order to alert prospective purchasers that they ought to deal with court-appointed representatives rather than dealing with the registered owner directly.

3. Classes of Ownership

[7–18] Under the Registration of Title Act 1964, one could be registered as either the absolute or limited owner, with the limited owner being someone who had less than a fee simple. However, as considered in Chapter 4, the Land and Conveyancing Law Reform Act 2009 abolished the fee tail,[38] and provided that the fee simple is the only freehold estate in law.[39] Life estates now exist in equity only and are governed by Part 4 of the 2009 Act, i.e. by the law of trusts of land.[40] Thus, in those cases the trustees—the legal holders of the fee simple—will be registered and there is no longer any need for a reference to limited owners in relation to registered land. Thus, the Land and Conveyancing Law Reform Act 2009 removes references to full and limited owners,[41] settled land and the Settled Land Acts 1882–1890.[42] Section 127(a) of the Land and Conveyancing Law Reform Act 2009 inserts a new definition of owner to s 3 of the Registration of Title Act 1964 to reflect this. Co-ownership can also be reflected on the register.[43] In keeping with the common law presumption in favour of a joint tenancy,

---

31 Inserted by s 128, Land and Conveyancing Law Reform Act 2009.

32 s 8, Registration of Title Act 1964.

33 See generally Chapter 12.

34 These will be rights under either s 69 or s 72, both of which are considered in paras 7–31 to 7–40.

35 s 82, Registration of Title Act 1964.

36 s 101, *ibid.*

37 s 102, *ibid.*

38 s 13, Land and Conveyancing Law Reform Act 2009.

39 s 11, *ibid.*

40 See generally Chapter 6.

41 Schedule 1, Land and Conveyancing Law Reform Act 2009.

42 s 127(f), *ibid.*

43 Co-ownership is considered in full in Chapter 8.

co-owners are deemed joint tenants unless there is an entry to the contrary on the register[44] and, in the case of people registered as tenants in common, the shares of ownership will be recorded on the register.[45]

4. Classes of Title

Section 33(1) of the Registration of Title Act 1964 provides for three classes of title in relation to freehold land: absolute title, qualified title and possessory title. In relation to freehold land, one applies for either absolute or possessory title,[46] with qualified title being a class of title said to exist where the requirements for absolute title cannot be met.[47] When it comes to leasehold land, there are four levels of title: absolute, qualified, possessor and good leasehold title.[48] [7–19]

(i) Freehold Land

Absolute title is the most secure form of title that can be recognised and essentially signifies that the registered owner has satisfactorily shown that he is entitled to the title to the property, and that there is no doubt as to the strength of his title in relation to anyone else. The registration of someone with absolute title is an indication that the Property Registration Authority is satisfied that the land is subject only to registered burdens under s 69 and burdens affecting the land without registration under s 72.[49] A trustee can also be registered with absolute title, but will still be subject to the normal duties of a trustee.[50] [7–20]

If the applicant can only show his title for a limited period of time, or subject to certain reservations, then he can be said to have qualified title. In these cases the register will reflect the fact that the registered owner's title is incomplete and is subject to the rights of others either arising before a specified date,[51] arising under a specified instrument[52] or otherwise described in the register.[53] A registered owner with qualified title will be entitled to carry out the same functions in relation to the land as a registered owner with absolute title, but any transactions engaged in will not affect the rights specified within the register as qualifying the title.[54] [7–21]

A registered owner will be deemed to have possessory title where neither absolute nor qualified title is deemed appropriate[55] because the applicant cannot provide any documentary evidence of title. A squatter is, perhaps, the quintessential example of [7–22]

---

44 s 91(2), Registration of Title Act 1964.
45 s 91(1), Registration of Title Act 1964; r 67 of the Land Registration Rules 1972 *as amended by* r 13, Land Registration (no 2) Rules 2009 (SI no 456 of 2009).
46 s 33(3), Registration of Title Act 1964.
47 s 33(5), *ibid.*
48 s 40, Registration of Title Act 1964 *as substituted by* s 57, Registration of Deeds and Title Act 2006.
49 s 37, Registration of Title Act 1964.
50 s 37(3), Registration of Title Act 1964; s 20(1), Land and Conveyancing Law Reform Act 2009.
51 s 33(5)(a), Registration of Title Act 1964.
52 s 33(5)(b), *ibid.*
53 s 33(5)(c), *ibid.*
54 s 39, *ibid.*
55 s 33(7), *ibid.*

someone who would be registered with possessory title. The applicant here will be able to show actual occupation or receipt of rent or profits from the land, rather than documentary entitlement to the land. Unlike the qualified title, a person with possessory title will hold the property subject to any existing rights over it at the time of registration, and these rights need not be specified on the register.[56]

(ii) Leasehold Land

[7–23] Leases with at least 21 years left to run in possession can be registered as stand-alone interests over registered land.[57] The holder of leasehold land can be registered as having either an absolute, qualified, possessory or good leasehold title.[58] In this respect, absolute, qualified and possessory title are essentially the same as in relation to freehold land.[59] Good leasehold title, however, is particular to leasehold and it constitutes a guarantee only of the leasehold owner's rights—it does not purport to represent any claim in relation to the freehold title or, indeed, in relation to any intermediate leasehold title.[60]

(iii) Conversion and Reclassification of Title

[7–24] If someone has been registered with something less than absolute title, she is likely to want—ideally—to be able to "upgrade" to absolute title in time. The Property Registration Authority is empowered to convert title to a better class either on its own initiative or on the application of the registered owner. Usually this would happen either because sufficient time has passed to make doubts as to title irrelevant (perhaps because the Statute of Limitations on claims against the title has expired), or because further documents have been located and presented to clarify any weak or missing links that might have originally caused registration with something less than absolute title.[61]

5. The Conclusiveness of the Register: "The Mirror Principle"

[7–25] As considered briefly above, a primary rationale of registered land as a system is to create a central, unified and conclusive register of interests over land. The success of this is almost entirely dependent on the extent to which we can say that the register is, in fact, a conclusive record of the ownership arrangements in relation to each individual piece of registered land. Section 31 of the Registration of Title Act 1964 is a statutory statement of this rationale and of the general principle of conclusiveness. Section 31(1) provides:

> The register shall be conclusive evidence of the title of the owner to the land as appearing on the register and of any right, privilege, appurtenance or burden as appearing thereon; and such title shall not, in the absence of actual fraud, be in any way affected in

---

[56] s 38, *ibid.*

[57] s 3, *ibid.*

[58] s 40, Registration of Title Act 1964 *as substituted by* s 57, Registration of Deeds and Title Act 2006.

[59] ss 44, 46 and 47, Registration of Title Act 1964.

[60] s 45, *ibid.*

[61] s 50(1), *ibid.*

> consequence of such owner having notice of any deed, document, or matter relating to the land; but nothing in this Act shall interfere with the jurisdiction of any court of competent jurisdiction based on the ground of actual fraud or mistake, and the court may upon such ground make an order directing the register to be rectified in such manner and on such terms as it thinks just.

Section 31 essentially renders the doctrine of notice redundant when it comes to registered land, as a purchaser will be bound only by that which appears on the register *and* that which is expressed by the Registration of Title Act 1964 as binding purchasers without appearance on the register. We will consider the burdens affecting land with or without registration below.[62] Central to the system of registered land is the mirror principle: anyone who suffers loss from official errors in registration or from the registration of an interest by fraud or forgery can apply for compensation from the State compensation fund.[63]

While the idea behind the mirror principle is sound, it would be inaccurate to say that *in fact* the register is conclusive evidence of *every* interest that exists in relation to registered land. Neither is it conclusive evidence of boundaries, for example, of parcels of land. While the mirror principle seems like a silver bullet for conveyancers that makes the process of transacting in relation to registered land as straightforward as could be, what must interest us in the main are the exceptions to this principle; what we might call the "cracks in the mirror". In addition to the exceptions that are built into the registered land system itself, there is of course the potential for mistakes to arise on the register in which case, because of error, the register does not mirror the ownership arrangements. Although the State more or less guarantees the accuracy of the register, and any party who suffers a loss as a result of the rectification of the register may apply for compensation under s 120 of the 1964 Act, the Registration of Title Act 1964 does allow for the rectification of mistakes. Section 32 of the 1964 Act now provides: **[7–26]**

> (1) Where any error originating in the Land Registry (whether of misstatement, misdescription, omission or otherwise, and whether in a register or registry map) occurs in registration—
> (a) the Authority may, with the consent of the registered owner of the land and of such other persons as may appear to be interested, rectify the error upon such terms as may be agreed to in writing by the parties,
> (b) the Authority may, if of opinion that the error can be rectified without loss to any person, rectify the error after giving such notices as may be prescribed,
> (c) the court, if of opinion that the error can be rectified without injustice to any person, may order the error to be rectified upon such terms as to costs or otherwise as it thinks just.[64]

---

[62] paras 7–31 to 7–40.

[63] s 120, Registration of Title Act 1964 *as amended by* s 69, Registration of Deeds and Title Act 2006.

[64] s 32, Registration of Title Act 1964 *as substituted by* s 55, Registration of Deeds and Title Act 2006.

In this—as in other matters—anyone affected by a decision of the Property Registration Authority has a right of appeal to the Circuit or High Court[65] and, should the Authority itself ever have doubts as to fact or law, it can refer such questions to the Court for resolution.[66]

[7–27] As mentioned above, s 31 of the Registration of Title Act 1964 suggests that a purchaser of registered land can now rely on the register itself as conclusive evidence of the ownership arrangements over the land. It should—in theory—be the only thing that one needs to look at to get a full picture of what the vendor has to sell and what other, third party, interests exist over the land. However, because it was considered that entering absolutely every interest on the register would make that register—and the entire system of registered land—too burdensome, there are some interests that can bind without registration. There is also the tricky question of boundaries to be considered, as the register includes maps showing every parcel of registered land in the country.

(i) Boundaries

[7–28] Up until recently, registered land was marked out on the latest available ordinance survey maps, which were kept in the Central Office.[67] Pursuant to the Registration of Deeds and Title Act 2006,[68] and the general move towards eConveyancing, the maps are now in digital form. Although these maps are used to identify the boundary lines and location of various pieces of registered land, they are expressly excluded from the principle of conclusiveness under s 85(2) of the Registration of Title Act 1964.[69] Interestingly, *Boyle v Connaughton*[70] suggests that s 85 is intended to protect the State compensation fund from having to compensate for minor mistakes as to boundaries, which might suggest that s 85 will not necessarily result in courts disregarding claims as to boundaries where the mistake arising is a serious—or "non-minor"—one. This suggests that while boundaries remain "inconclusive" and, therefore, not subject to the mirror principle, they can nevertheless be relied upon by a land-owner to the extent that grievous mistakes in their relation may give rise to a right to compensation.[71]

[7–29] In addition, the Property Registration Authority is empowered to deem boundaries conclusive in a limited manner in certain situations. Thus, owners of adjoining pieces of land (either both registered or one registered and one unregistered) can apply to have the boundaries between their lands registered as "conclusive" as between themselves and their respective successors in title.[72] If a piece of registered land is sub-divided and partially sold, the Property Registration Authority may deem the boundary between the sold and retained lands conclusive under s 88(1) of the 1964

---

65 ss 18 and 19(1), Registration of Title Act 1964.

66 s 19(2), *ibid.*

67 s 84, Registration of Title Act 1964.

68 s 61, Registration of Deeds and Title Act 2006 (substituting a new wording for s 84, Registration of Title Act 1964 to allow for maps to be in "electronic or other non-legible form").

69 s 85, Registration of Title Act 1964 *as amended by* s 62, Registration of Deeds and Title Act 2006.

70 Unreported, High Court, 21 March 2000.

71 *Persian Properties Ltd v Registrar of Titles and Minister for Finance* [2003] 1 IR 450.

72 s 87, Registration of Title Act 1964.

Act. The Authority may also settle questions as to boundaries where any piece of registered land is being transferred[73] although, as mentioned above,[74] this decision can be appealed to the Circuit or High Court[75] and, in situations of uncertainty as to law or fact, the Authority itself can refer to the Court.[76]

(ii) Registrable Interests under s 69

As will become clear throughout the remainder of this book, land is often subject to third-party interests such as easements,[77] mortgages[78] and so on. The holders of these kinds of third-party interests are not considered the owners of the registered land, but they do have an interest that needs—and deserves—protection as against purchasers of that land. Many of these kinds of interests can be protected by registration under the Registration of Title Act 1964. Registrable interests under s 69 of the 1964 Act are ones that, in fact, *must be registered if they are to be protected.* In other words, if you own an interest governed by s 69 over your neighbour's land and that land is sold, you can only enforce that interest (or, in other words, bind the purchaser to it) if you have registered it under s 69 of the 1964 Act. Thus, interests that are registrable under s 69 will be binding on purchasers for value only if they have actually been registered in relation to the property; the purchaser's notice of these interests is essentially irrelevant. Importantly, however, the situation is different for a purchaser of registered land for no consideration, who will be bound by all interests—registered or not—regardless of whether he has notice of them.[79] Section 69 interests can be registered by the owner of the land or by the holder of the interest, provided the owner's consent is obtained; in the absence of consent, a court order for registration will be required.[80] **[7–30]**

The interests covered by s 69 include the following: **[7–31]**

- Any encumbrance on the land existing at the time of the first registration of the land;
    - As considered above,[81] the first registration of property involves the presentation of all of the documents relating to the title and interests over the property. Thus, all interests extant over the property at the time of first registration must be documented at that time and are then noted on the register under s 69.
- Any charge on the land duly created after first registration;
    - Registered charges—which to all intents and purposes are the equivalent of a legal mortgage over registered land[82]—must be registered under s 69.

---

73 s 88(2), *ibid.*
74 para 7–27.
75 ss 18 and 19(1), Registration of Title Act 1964.
76 s 19(2), *ibid.*
77 Chapter 12.
78 Chapter 13.
79 See ss 52(2) and 55(2), Registration of Title Act 1964.
80 s 69(2), *ibid.*
81 para 7–15.
82 These are considered in full in Chapter 13.

- Any lease where the term granted is for a life or lives, or is determinable on a life or lives, or exceeds 21 years, or where the term is for any less estate or interest but the occupation is not in accordance with the lease;
  - Leases of this nature will be both registered on the freehold estate over which they are held *and* registered as its own folio in the leasehold register.[83]
- Any judgment or order of a court, whether existing before or after the first registration of the land;
  - This requirement includes orders—such as property adjustment orders—made under the Family Law Act 1995 (dealing with judicial separation) and the Family Law (Divorce) Act 1996 (dealing with divorce).
- Any judgment mortgage, recognisance, State bond, inquisition or *lis pendens*, whether existing before or after the first registration of the land;
- Any easement, profit *à prendre* or mining right created by express grant or reservation after the first registration of the land;
- Any covenant or condition relating to the use or enjoyment of the land or of any specified portion thereof;
- A right in the nature of a lien for money's worth in or over the property for a limited period not exceeding life, including a right of residence;
- A freehold covenant as defined by s 43, Land and Conveyancing Law Reform Act 2009.[84]

Section 69 interests are, in effect, the prime example of the mirror principle in operation: registration protects the interest *because* the existence of the interest is reflected on the register.

(iii) Overriding Interests under s 72

[7–32] In contrast to s 69, burdens included under s 72 will bind the purchaser of land whether registered or not. For that reason they are known as overriding interests (inasmuch as they override the register), although that term is not itself contained in the Registration of Title Act 1964. Although this clearly constitutes a "crack in the mirror" and has the potential to make conveyances of registered land very burdensome (quite in contrast with the intention behind registered land), we will see that conveyancing practice has adapted to "manage" s 72 interests in a workable way. Reflecting the "overriding" nature of these interests, s 72 provides:

> ... all registered land shall be subject to such of the following burdens as for the time being affect the land, whether those burdens are or are not registered...

[7–33] While it is possible to register notice of the fact that there are,[85] or that there are not,[86] s 72 interests in existence over the land, the fundamental principle of this section is that there is no need to make any such registration: interests governed by s 72 will bind all purchasers whether they are actually aware of them or not. In respect of each

---

[83] s 70, Registration of Title Act 1964 and r 123, Registration of Title Rules 1972.

[84] s 129, Land and Conveyancing Law Reform Act 2009.

[85] s 72(2), Registration of Title Act 1964.

[86] s 72(3), *ibid.*

individual interest, its existence can be registered under s 73 if the registrar is satisfied of its existence *and* if the registered owner of the land consents thereto. Importantly, however, the idea of s 72 is to ensure that *even in the absence of such registration* the interests in question will bind successors in title of the land with or without notice of them. Section 72 governs:

(a) Charges such as estate and succession duties[87] (gift and inheritance taxes[88]), state rents arising under fee farms grants and payments *in lieu* of tithe rentcharges[89]; land improvements and drainage charges[90]; annuities and rentcharges for the repayment of advances made under the Land Purchase Acts (enabling agricultural tenants to buy their farms)[91];
(b) Rights arising under the Land Purchase Acts, i.e. rights of the Minister for Agriculture and Food (and formerly of the Irish Land Commission[92]) or of anyone with a vesting order that was made under the Land Purchase Acts,[93] and rights of the Minister for Agriculture and Food (and formerly of the Irish Land Commission[94]) upon execution of a possession order that was issued under s 37 of the Land Act 1927[95];
(c) Public[96] and customary[97] rights;
(d) Easements and profits *à prendre* not expressly created[98] *or* not in existence at the time of first registration[99];
(e) Tenancies for a term that does exceed 21 years,[100] *or* for "such other period as may be prescribed"[101] where there is occupation under those under tenancies;
(f) Section 72(1)(j) rights, i.e. "the rights of every person in actual occupation of the land or in receipt of the rents and profits thereof, save where, upon enquiry made of such person, the rights are not disclosed";
(g) All rights that are excepted from registration in the case of qualified, possessory or good leasehold title[102];

87 s 72(1)(a), *ibid.*
88 s 68(2), Capital Acquisitions Tax Act 1976.
89 s 72(1)(a), Registration of Title Act 1964.
90 s 72(1)(b), *ibid.*
91 s 72(1)(c), Registration of Title Act 1964.
92 See Irish Land Commission (Dissolution) Act 1992.
93 s 72(1)(d), Registration of Title Act 1964.
94 See Irish Land Commission (Dissolution) Act 1992.
95 s 72(1)(e), Registration of Title Act 1964.
96 s 72(1)(f), *ibid.*
97 s 72(1)(g), *ibid.*
98 As considered in Chapter 12, easements and profits can be acquired by implication, by prescription (or presumption) and through estoppels as well as being expressly created. Therefore, this provision—s 72(1)(h), Registration of Title Act 1964—actually covers a broad spectrum of easements and profits that can exist over land.
99 s 72(1)(h), Registration of Title Act 1964.
100 s 72(1)(i), *ibid.*
101 s 60, *ibid.*
102 s 72(1)(k), *ibid.*; the different levels of title are considered in paras 7–20 to 7–25 above.

(h) Any perpetual yearly rents that are superior to rent registered as a burden[103] and any covenants or conditions that are contained in the document creating this superior rent *apart from* personal covenants or conditions[104];
(i) Obligations and restrictions under the Labourers Act 1936, i.e. purchase annuities that are payable in respect of any cottage vested under that Act[105] *and* restrictions that are imposed by s 21 of the 1936 Act on the creation of mortgages or charges over such cottages[106];
(j) Rights of adverse possessors that are either in the course of being acquired or already acquired under the Statute of Limitations 1957[107];
(k) Burdens that are specifically governed by s 59 of the Registration of Title Act 1964[108] (relating to assignment, subletting, subdivision, mines and minerals) and by s 73 of the Registration of Title Act 1964[109] (relating to covenants that are enforceable when a lease has been enlarged into a fee simple under the Landlord and Tenant (Ground Rents) (No. 2) Act 1978[110]).

It should be clear from this list, that s 72 captures a very broad range of interests and determines that are to be overreaching. It is not necessary for us to consider these interests exhaustively, but the provision in s 72(1)(j)—that the rights and interests of those in actual occupation of land or in receipt of rent and profits from the land are overreaching except in exceptional circumstances—requires some further consideration here.

[7–34] Section 72(1)(j) is clearly intended to create an equivalent of the Rule of *Hunt v Luck* for registered land[111] and is not undermined by the extension of overreaching by s 21 of the Land and Conveyancing Law Reform Act 2009.[112] As we saw in Chapter 3, the Rule in *Hunt v Luck* provides that the rights of all occupants are binding upon purchasers who fail to enquire of them what the basis of their occupations might be.[113] Section 72(1)(j) both displaces the doctrine of notice when it comes to those in occupation of land or in receipt of rents or income from it *and* introduces a standard that appears to be higher, and more burdensome for prospective purchasers, than the Rule in *Hunt v Luck* itself.

[7–35] It is quite clear that a right or interest is binding on a purchaser under s 72(1)(j) because its holder is in occupation/receipt of rents or income and not because the purchaser has notice of it. In this respect, occupation needs to have some element of permanence but does not have to be constant or exclusive, highlighting the danger to

103 s 72(1)(l), *ibid.*
104 s 72(1)(m), *ibid.*
105 s 72(1)(n), *ibid.*
106 s 72(1)(o), *ibid.*
107 s 72(1)(p), *ibid.*; the law of adverse possession is considered in Chapter 14.
108 s 72(1)(q), *ibid.*
109 s 72(1)(q), *ibid.*
110 See Chapter 15.
111 [1902] 1 Ch 428.
112 See Chapter 6.
113 paras 3–41 to 3–42.

which purchasers are exposed.[114] If, for example, A lives in a house over which he has unregistered rights or interests with his partner and goes to New York to study for 10 months, coming home to keep the romance alive for a week every two months, then A may still be said to be "in actual occupation". However, there may not be anything immediately obvious that would alert a purchaser to A's occupation and so a purchaser might acquire the property and be taken unaware of A's rights, by which the purchaser could be bound under s 72(1)(j).

Of course, this does not mean that one can enforce a s 72 interest even after misleading a prospective purchaser who has made some enquiries in relation to same. If someone acts in such a manner that suggests that the purchaser would not be bound under a s 72 burden in relation to his occupation, he will be estopped from enforcing his rights.[115] Compare, for example, the English case of *Williams and Glyn's Bank v Boland*[116] and the Irish case of *Doherty v Doherty*.[117] **[7–36]**

In *Williams*, wives had made actual contributions (by means of lump sum and mortgage payments) towards the purchase of property that was registered in their husbands' sole names. As we will see in Chapter 9, such direct contributions can give rise to a share of ownership in equity in favour of the contributing party, and this was the case here. The wives were also in actual occupation of the properties, which were mortgaged to the plaintiff bank. When the plaintiff bank attempted to repossess the properties, they were found to be bound by the wives' rights under these trusts because they were in actual occupation of the property and had never done anything to suggest that they consented to the mortgages (thereby suggesting the bank would not be bound by their interests).[118] **[7–37]**

In contrast, *Doherty* concerned a couple who were married in 1973. The husband had bought a site in 1974 on which to build the family home. The construction of the house was financed by the wife, but the house was registered in the sole name of the respondent husband and it was their family home. In 1982 the husband acquired a mortgage over the property pursuant to both himself and his wife, acquiring independent legal advice in relation to same. The husband swore a declaration that there were no s 72 interests over the property and a joint statutory declaration was made by both the husband and the wife that the house was in the sole name of the husband. The wife also gave her consent, in writing, to the mortgage under the Family Home Protection Act 1976.[119] The mortgagee (i.e. the lender) sought to enforce the mortgage by means of taking possession in 1989, at which point the wife claimed that **[7–38]**

---

[114] *Kingsnorth v Tizard* [1986] 2 All ER 54.

[115] Estoppel will arise when someone is led to believe that he will acquire an interest and acts to his detriment on the basis of this induced belief. In such circumstances equity will estopp (or prevent) the representor from reneging on his representation.

[116] [1981] AC 487.

[117] [1991] 2 IR 458.

[118] s 70(1)(g), Land Registration Act 1925 then in force identified the "rights of every person in actual occupation of the land or in receipt of the rents and profits thereof, save where enquiry is made of such person and the rights are not disclosed" as an overriding interest.

[119] This is required by s 3 of the Family Home Protection Act 1976, which is considered in Chapter 9.

she had an interest in the property by means of funding the construction and that the bank was bound by this interest as she was a person in actual occupation under s 72(1)(j). In the High Court Blayney J acknowledged that the wife had acquired an equitable interest in the property through financing the construction of the house and that this interest was an overriding interest under s 72 of the Registration of Title Act 1964. This interest did not bind the mortgagee, however, because her conduct amounted to a representation to the mortgagee that she had no beneficial interest in the property. In other words, her conduct—taking advice, signing the consent, swearing the declaration—was such that she led the mortgagees to believe that there were no s 72 interests in her favour over the property. She was therefore estopped from enforcing this interest against the mortgagees at that time.[120]

[7–39] It is now common practice for a registered land-owner to sign a declaration to the effect that there are no s 72 interests over the land; indeed, a person will find it very difficult to sell property without such a declaration. While this resolves the practical difficulties thrown up by s, 72, systematic notion of conclusiveness suffers badly from the existence of s 72 interests.

(iv) Judgment Mortgages

[7–40] The registration of a judgment mortgage against registered land is done under s 116 of the Land and Conveyancing Law Reform Act 2009 and, according to s 117 of the same Act, charges the land in question. The holder of the judgment mortgage can then apply for court orders under s 117 (as a judgment mortgagor) and under s 31 (as a co-owner). Both of these scenarios are considered in full elsewhere in the book,[121] but for our immediate purposes it is important to note that, when deciding on such orders (including an order for the sale of the property), the court will take into account other encumbrances over the land and may determine their priority. Judgment mortgages over registered land are subject to all s 69 and s 72 burdens affecting the land at the time of their creation.[122]

(v) Trusts of Land

[7–41] Where there is an express, implied or constructive trust over registered land,[123] the trustee will simply be registered as the owner and the rights of the beneficiaries will not be expressly mentioned or protected. This has the potential to be somewhat problematic because the trustee, as registered owner, will be free to deal with the land[124] and the purchaser will have no indication of the fact that beneficiaries of the land exist (unless, of course, those beneficiaries are occupying the land or receiving rents or income from it, in which case s 72(1)(j) will apply). Thus, the rights of the beneficiaries are, in the normal course of events, neither s 69 nor s 72 interests; rather they are minor interests (i.e. interests that can be protected only by taking particular

120 See also *Harrison v Harrison*, unreported, High Court, 20 June 1989.

121 See Chapter 8 (on co-ownership) and Chapter 13 (on mortgages including judgment mortgages).

122 s 130, Land and Conveyancing Law Reform Act 2009.

123 s 92(3), Registration of Title Act 1964.

124 The trustee must, of course, act in accordance with his fiduciary duties as trustee and remains personally liable to the beneficiaries under s 37(4), Registration of Title Act 1964.

types of positive action). That does not mean that beneficiaries' interests cannot be protected under the registered land system. In fact, there are two useful options here: cautions and inhibitions.

The first option is for the beneficiaries to enter a caution on the register under s 97(1) of the Registration of Title Act 1964, which provides: **[7–42]**

> (1) Any person entitled to any right in, to, or over registered land or a registered charge, may, on producing an affidavit in the prescribed form of his right, lodge a caution with the Registrar to the effect that no dealing with the land or charge is to be had on the part of the registered owner until notice has been served on the cautioner.

In the alternative, the beneficiaries may wish to take a more extreme form of action to protect their interests. This can be done through the registration of an inhibition on the register under s 98(1) of the Registration of Title Act 1964, *viz:* **[7–43]**

> (1) The court or, subject to an appeal to the court, the Registrar, on the application of any person interested in any registered land or charge, may, after directing such inquiries (if any) to be made and notices to be given and hearing such persons as the court or Registrar thinks expedient, make an order or, in the case of an application to the Registrar, an entry, inhibiting for a time, or until the occurrence of an event to be named in the order or entry, or except with the consent of or after notice to some specified person, or generally until further order or entry, any dealing with any registered land or registered charge.

Part 4 trusts—i.e. trusts governed by Part 4 of the Land and Conveyancing Law Reform Act 2009—fall into a somewhat different category here. As considered in Chapter 6, we are dealing here with three kinds of trust: **[7–44]**

- Trusts arising from a strict settlement;
- Trusts of land held for people by way of succession, including trusts for sale;
- Trusts arising from the vesting of land in a minor.

These kinds of trusts are overreached on sale.[125] In other words, the rights of the beneficiaries over land now shift to the trust fund (i.e. the proceeds of the sale) and never impact on purchasers. Thus, when it comes to trusts governed by Part 4 of the Land and Conveyancing Law Reform Act 2009, there is no mechanism of protecting the interests of beneficiaries through registration. Such protection is simply unnecessary as those interests are already protected by overreaching.

[125] s 21, Land and Conveyancing Law Reform Act 2009.

CHAPTER 8
Co-Ownership

Property is often held and owned by a number of people concurrently. In these cases the rules of co-ownership will dictate the rights and obligations of all co-owners in relation to matters such as alienation and possession of the land. There are four different kinds of co-ownership: joint tenancy, tenancy in common, tenancy by entireties and coparcenary. Of these, only two—the joint tenancy and the tenancy in common—are of any real contemporary importance and therefore will be given sustained consideration in this chapter.[1] In this context the word "tenancy" should not be taken to indicate any kind of leasehold relationship between the parties. Instead, we refer here to "tenancies" because of the feudal roots of co-ownership and the concept of tenure, which was considered in Chapter 2. In fact, co-ownerships can exist in relation to either freehold or leasehold land. **[8–01]**

[1] Tenancy by entireties was effectively abolished by the Married Women's Property Act 1892, which allowed married women to own property independently of their husbands. As a result of the Succession Act 1965, which introduced new rules of intestacy, coparcenary arose only in the case of fees tail, which have now been abolished by s 13 of the Land and Conveyancing Law Reform Act 2009. Both of these types of co-ownership are treated fully in other texts. See Wylie, *Irish Land Law* (4th ed, 2010, Dublin, Bloomsbury Professional), pp 484–488; Lyall, *Land Law in Ireland* (3rd ed, 2010, Dublin, Round Hall), pp 426–427; Coughlan, *Property* Law (2nd ed, 1999, Dublin, Gill and MacMillan), p 141; Pearce & Mee, *Land Law* (2nd ed, 2010, Dublin, Thomson Round Hall), p 117.

I. Joint Tenancy: Primary Characteristics

[8–02] The joint tenancy has two main features: the right of survivorship and the "four unities". No joint tenancy can be said to exist unless both of these features are present. The right of survivorship, also known as *jus accrescendi*, is the concept that once one joint tenant dies there is no interest that he can leave to an heir or that can be passed on by intestacy. This reflects the fact that in a joint tenancy all joint tenants are said to hold 100 per cent of the ownership of (or control over) the property. Thus, if one joint tenant dies 100 per cent of ownership is still held by the other joint tenants and there is simply nothing for the deceased joint tenant to bequeath.[2] In other words, each joint tenant holds the whole jointly and nothing separately.[3] There are two practical repercussions of this position: (a) any attempt by a joint tenant to devise ownership rights over the co-owned property in a will is ineffective[4]; (b) the number of joint tenants is always decreasing until one person remains alive who is then entitled to the sole ownership of the property.[5] The right of survivorship is essentially the defining characteristic of the joint tenancy.[6]

[8–03] In order for a joint tenancy to be in place, the four unities must be present, these being the unity of possession, the unity of time, the unity of title and the unity of interest. The concept of unity of possession is simply that all joint tenants are entitled to possess all of the property. The concept of unity of time requires that the rights of each joint tenant must have vested at the same time (although by means of exception the unity of time is not required where the joint tenancy is created by a disposition in a will or by a conveyance to uses).[7] A necessary implication of the unity of time is that joint tenancies require unity of title, meaning that all co-owners must have acquired their interests from the same document or a set of documents comprising the same transaction. Finally, there must be unity of interest, meaning that the interests of all co-owners must be the same in terms of their nature, extent and duration.

[8–04] Although, as will be considered in full below, the joint tenancy is generally the preferred estate of the common law, it has fallen on somewhat hard times in certain jurisdictions. In the USA, for example, numerous States have abolished the joint tenancy, mostly in protest at the perceived unfairness of the right of survivorship. In fact, it could almost be said that the US courts have shown a "prejudice against survivorship".[8] Importantly, however, the USA was never required to concern itself with the feudal advantages of the joint tenancy (feudal incidents could be managed and enforced in a more straightforward manner because the property would eventually vest in a single owner through survivorship). In the words of Pickering, "The basis for the common-law preference [for the joint tenancy], avoidance of multiplying feudal duties, does not exist here [in the United States]".[9] In countries such as Ireland, where the

---

[2] See also s 4(c), Succession Act 1965.

[3] 39 *Halsbury's Laws of England* (4th ed), para 529, n 5.

[4] *Swift v Roberts* (1764) 3 Burr 1488, 97 ER 941.

[5] *Wright v Gibbons* (1949) 78 CLR 313.

[6] See, for example, *Reilly v Walsh* (1848) 11 IR Eq R 22.

[7] See *O'Hea v Slattery* [1895] 1 IR 7.

[8] Pickering, "Joint Tenancy-Right to Transfer by One Party-Right of Survivorship" (1940) 38(6) Mich L Rev 875 at 879.

[9] *ibid.*

property law system has traditionally been heavily influenced by the concerns of feudalism, the abolition of the joint tenancy (or even a less extreme scenario of the development of a common law dislike for such co-ownership) is difficult to contemplate.

II. Tenancy in Common: Primary Characteristics

The tenancy in common is not subject to the right of survivorship. Nor does it require the four unities to be present. Rather, the tenancy in common is one in which all co-owners are said to be entitled to an (undivided) share of ownership. These ownership rights can then be devised to an heir in a will, or can be passed by intestacy. It is important to note that the property itself is not divided into physical shares; it is the ownership rights (i.e. the control) that are divided. So, we do not carve the co-owned field up into sections that are "owned" by individual co-owners; there is no physical division of the property. There are, however, shares of the ownership of the *entire* property. These shares of ownership will normally be commensurate with the contribution of the owners to the purchase of the property. Thus, if Pat and Anna are tenants in common over a property for which they paid €100,000, Pat contributing €40,000 and Anna contributing €60,000, Pat might be said to have 40 per cent ownership and Anna might be said to have 60 per cent ownership, although the shares in ownership do not necessarily always reflect the proportions of contribution towards the purchase price.[10] In this case both Pat and Anna are owners of, and entitled to use, *all* of the physical land in question. This relates to the fact that, as already mentioned, the four unities need not be present in order for a tenancy in common to exist but the unity of possession *is* required. **[8–05]**

Tenancies in common are quite controversial, particularly because of the potential complexity of transactions to which they can give rise. As the right of survivorship does not operate in relation to tenancies in common, it is quite possible (although, in reality, not that common) for the number of co-owners to increase exponentially until there are many dozens of tenants in common. This would happen where people leave their interest to a number of people on their death, each of which in turn leaves their interest to numerous people. In order to counteract such difficulties, the law of England and Wales prohibits the creation of tenancies in common in law.[11] The Irish Law Reform Commission has twice refused to recommend an analogous provision here.[12] This was primarily because practitioners did not identify a need for such reform—the difficulties of excessive fragmentation of legal ownership simply do not arise on a frequent basis in practice.[13] **[8–06]**

---

[10] *Midland Bank Plc v Cooke* [1995] 4 All ER 562. See further Chapter 9.

[11] They can, however, still exist in equity—ss 1(6), 34(1) and 36(2) of the Law of Property Act 1925 (see Harpum, Megarry and Wade, *The Law of Real Property* (6th ed, 2000, London, Sweet & Maxwell), p 490).

[12] *Report of Land Law and Conveyancing Law: (7) Positive Covenants on Freehold Land and Other Proposals* (2003), p 51; *Consultation Paper on the Reform and Modernisation of Land and Conveyancing Law* (2004), pp 81–83.

[13] *Consultation Paper on the Reform and Modernisation of Land and Conveyancing Law* (2004), pp 81–2.

[8–07] This appears a sensible conclusion. The maintenance of a situation in law in which potential co-owners can choose between quite different forms of co-ownership on the basis of the individual needs of their particular circumstances is the epitome of choice and is necessary in an ever-more diverse property market. If we were to introduce a situation where, as in England and Wales, there is no real alternative to the joint tenancy and its oft-maligned right of survivorship, all co-owners would be tied into a joint tenancy, which would be unlikely to meet their needs. Take, for example, a situation of young professional friends who decide to buy property together: ought people in a relationship of this non-intimate nature be forced by the law to enter into a joint tenancy and be subject to the right of survivorship? Such a situation would appear to counteract both the principle of autonomy in relation to landholding and the basic requirements of logic and fairness. Although the abolition of the tenancy in common in law would not have been accompanied by its abolition in equity and, as a result, individuals such as those used in our example could hold the property as joint tenants in law and tenants in common in equity, this situation would introduce an unnecessary level of complexity. Indeed, it would be tantamount to exchanging one inconvenience for another. While the tenancy in common in law may result in inconvenience from excessive fragmentation in limited situations, its abolition would almost certainly result in inconvenience from differentiated co-ownerships in law and in equity in a great number of cases. The decision not to abolish the tenancy in common in law was, therefore, a sound one and we continue to have both joint tenancies and tenancies in common in both law and equity after the Land and Conveyancing Law Reform Act 2009.

III. Joint Tenancy: Creation

[8–08] The common law has a natural tendency towards the joint tenancy. This was primarily because of the simplicity introduced by the right of survivorship: the property would eventually vest in a sole individual, making the enforcement of feudal incidents more straightforward.[14] As a result of this, the common law presumes that a joint tenancy exists every time there is more than one property owner. If co-owners wish to ensure that the equity in the property will also be held in a joint tenancy, it is advisable for them to expressly state that this is the case. For example: "No 1, Station Road, to John and Victoria in fee simple holding as joint tenants in law and in equity". As the following paragraphs will show, equity can intervene to recognise a tenancy in common in equity where there is a joint tenancy in law: if the parties expressly provide that the equity is to be held in a joint tenancy, then there is no basis for equitable intervention to the contrary.

IV. Tenancy in Common: Creation

[8–09] A tenancy in common will exist where there is something to indicate that the parties intended that the presumption of a joint tenancy would not operate. In order to create a tenancy in common in law, one would either ensure that the four unities were not present or, more commonly, insert certain words into the disposition. These words are known as "words of severance", i.e. words indicating that the ownership rights were to be severed into shares of control between the parties in question. Formulae such as "in

[14] *Morley v Bird* (1798) 3 Ves 628; 30 ER 1192.

equal shares",[15] "share and share alike",[16] "to be divided between [them]",[17] "equally",[18] "between",[19] "amongst",[20] "respectively"[21] and "to be distributed amongst them in joint and equal proportions"[22] have all been held to be sufficient words of severance to create a tenancy in common in law. Importantly, however, even where such words are present, they might be overridden by a clear intention to create a joint tenancy.[23] A tenancy in common may also be created in law where that appears to be the overriding intention of the disposition, notwithstanding the fact that no Words of Severance were used. This was the case in *L'Estrange v L'Estrange*,[24] where a tenancy in common was found to exist in law when an advance of capital was made to a child in a manner compatible only with a tenancy in common.

In some cases, a tenancy in common might be said to exist in equity, even though the legal rights are held in joint tenancy. In the main, this will happen where the law of equity intervenes on the basis of either justice or the presumed intentions of the parties. In such cases, the legal ownership will remain undisturbed but the co-owners, as joint tenants in law, will hold the property on trust for the co-owners as tenants in common in equity. There are a number of typical cases in which a tenancy in common is created in equity. **[8–10]**

1. Unequal Contributions to the Purchase Price

Where parties contribute unequally to the purchase price of the property, equity may find the operation of the right to survivorship to be unfair. In such cases, equity will treat the parties as tenants in common in equity and recognise them as each holding shares of equitable control, usually commensurate with the proportions of their contribution. Consider the following example: **[8–11]**

> Alex and Alicia are unmarried friends who buy a house together for €500,000, with Alex contributing €200,000 and Alicia contributing €300,000. There are no words of severance in the deed and the four unities are present; common law therefore recognises them as joint tenants. Equity, however, regards it as inherently unfair that the right of survivorship could deny Alicia's heirs a share of ownership when she contributed 20 per cent more of the purchase price than Alex did. In addition, equity will presume that Alicia did not intend for the right of survivorship to operate between the parties. As a result, equity will regard them as holding the property as tenants in common in equity. Their joint tenancy at law is not affected by this, however. Thus Alicia and Alex can be said

[15] *Payne v Webb* (1874) LR 19 Eq 26; *Jury v Jury* (1882) 9 LR IR 27.
[16] *Mill v Mill* (1877) IR 11 Eq 158; also "part and part alike"—*James v Collins* (1627) Het 29.
[17] *Peat v Chapman* (1750) 1 Ves Sen 542; *Crozier v Crozier* (1843) 3 Dr & War 373.
[18] *Lewen v Dodd* (1595) Cro Eliz 443.
[19] *Lashbrook v Cock* (1816) 2 Mer 70.
[20] *Richardson v Richardson* (1845) 14 Sim 526.
[21] *Stephens v Hide* (1734) Cat Talb 27.
[22] *Ettricke v Ettricke* (1767) Amb 656.
[23] See, for example, *Cockerill v Gilliland* (1854) 6 IR Jur (os) 357.
[24] [1902] 1 IR 467.

to be joint tenants at law, holding the property for themselves as tenants in common in equity, usually with Alicia holding approximately 60 per cent of the equity and Alex holding approximately 40 per cent of the equity. Thus, if Alicia predeceased Alex, Alex would be the sole owner in law (survivorship) but Alicia's heirs would inherit her 60% equitable ownership so that Alex would hold the land on trust for himself *and Alicia's heirs* as tenants in common in equity.

2. Commercial Arrangements

[8–12] The right of survivorship is inherently unsuited to commercial arrangements, which are, after all, primarily concerned with maximising profit and productivity. As a result of the inconsistency between the right of survivorship and business undertakings, equity will tend to consider co-owners of this nature as tenants in common, even where no formal commercial relationship exists between the parties.[25] This is not to suggest that entities usually created for business purposes are incapable of being joint tenants. Indeed, s 32(1) of the Land and Conveyancing Law Reform Act 2009 expressly provides that "A body corporate may acquire and hold any property in a joint tenancy in the same manner as if it were an individual". Where the body corporate is dissolved, the right of survivorship would operate in favour of the other joint tenants.[26] However, in the absence of an express statement that the equity is also held in a joint tenancy between commercial actors, including bodies corporate, equity will be on the alert in case its intervention is required to recognise a tenancy in common in equity. Importantly, however, equity will be concerned to ensure that the relationship between the parties is described properly as one of a commercial character and would not be more accurately described as a "family relationship" with a business "slant".

[8–13] This is best illustrated by consideration of *Reilly v Walsh*.[27] In this case two brothers had purchased a commercial property together. After some time, one of the brothers developed a mental disability, as a result of which he was incapable of taking any further substantial part in running the business. The other brother, Reilly, then took over the business almost exclusively, but when the former brother died, he purported to leave his share of the property to Reilly by his will. Reilly claimed that, as this was a commercial enterprise, the equitable ownership was held in a tenancy in common: however, the Court held that because of the familial relationship between the brothers, and the fact that the deceased brother had played no material role in the business, this was not a relationship of such a commercialised nature as to require the intervention of equity. Rather, the brothers were joint tenants in equity as well as in law and, as a result, the gift in the will had no effect.

3. Co-Mortgagees[28]

[8–14] As a matter of commercial practicality, multiple mortgagees of a property will be seen as tenants in common in equity, even where they are joint tenants in law. Thus, if two

---

25 *McCarthy v Barry* (1859) 9 IR Ch R 377.

26 s 32(3), Land and Conveyancing Law Reform Act 2009.

27 (1848) 11 IR Eq R 22.

28 The mortgagee is the lender of money in a mortgage relationship; see further Chapter 13.

separate banks had granted mortgages over the same property and, because of some oversight, they were construed as joint tenants in law, equity would intervene and deem them tenants in common in equity.[29]

4. Perceived Intentions of the Parties

In addition to cases of unequal contribution, non-recognition on the title documents and commercial relationships, equity may intervene where the justice of the case requires it. In the main, this will happen in cases when the intention of the parties appears to have been for them to hold as tenants in common. These are not the only situations in which we might encounter such intervention. By its very nature equity is empowered to intervene *whenever* the justice of the case requires it, therefore equity will be likely to intervene where it appears that the intention was that the property was to be held in a tenancy in common. This reflects the very nature of equity itself: guided by maxims and principles, but not unduly restrained by regulation when the circumstances demand intervention.[30] **[8–15]**

The general capacity of equity to intervene and find a tenancy in common in equity where there is a joint tenancy in law is well demonstrated in the decision of the Privy Council in *Malayan Credit Ltd v Jack Chia-MPH Ltd*.[31] The case concerned a lease of premises to two commercial entities for the purposes of them carrying out their respective commercial activities, where the parties were found to be joint tenants in law. As the two business entities were not involved in a commercial partnership with each other—they were, in fact, quite distinct from one another—counsel argued that the court could not intervene to find them tenants in common in equity. According to Lord Brightman: **[8–16]**

> [We] do not accept that the cases in which joint tenants at law will be presumed to hold as tenants in common in equity are... rigidly circumscribed... Such cases are not necessarily limited to purchasers who contribute unequally, to co-mortgagees and to partners. There are other circumstances in which equity may infer that the beneficial interest is intended to be held by the grantees as tenants in common.[32]

V. Joint Tenancy: Severance

In spite of the fact that joint tenants do not have "shares" of ownership, the law allows a joint tenant to behave in a manner that indicates that he conceives of himself as being entitled to a share of ownership. This results from equity's early recognition that all joint tenants have a *potential* share of the ownership of the property equal in size to the potential share of all other joint tenants; the joint tenants should therefore be entitled to sever this potential share during their lifetimes. Severance results in the destruction of at least one of the four unities, without which, as we have already seen, the joint **[8–17]**

---

29 *Pett v Stywaid* (1632) 1 Ch Rep 57; *Morley v Bird* (1798) 3 Ves 628.

30 *Twigg v Twigg* [1933] IR 65; *L'Estrange v L'Estrange* [1902] 1 IR 467; *Malayan Credit Ltd v Jack Chia MPH Ltd* [1986] 1 All ER 711 (Privy Council); see further Chapter 3.

31 [1986] AC 549.

32 *ibid.* at 560.

tenancy simply cannot exist. In other words, severance changes the co-ownership from a joint tenancy to a tenancy in common.

[8–18] Severance is as much of a defining characteristic of the joint tenancy as the right of survivorship that it seeks to escape: in fact, the two concepts go hand in hand. Through severance, the ownership of the property is converted to a tenancy in common as the ownership rights are "severed" into shares. Importantly, the co-ownership itself does not come to an end: it merely changes form. If the action of the joint tenant is formalised, the severance will normally be at law, resulting in the legal ownership being held in a tenancy in common. If, however, the action is not formalised, then it will have no effect on the legal ownership, but it may sever the equitable ownership. In such cases the original co-owners continue to be joint tenants at law, but hold the land on trust for the equitable owners as tenants in common at equity.

[8–19] Before we consider the ways in which severance can be brought about, it is useful to question whether severance ought to be permitted at all. Although it is generally assumed that the possibility for a joint tenant to sever the joint tenancy is simply the corollary to "the grand incident of joint estates"[33] (i.e. survivorship), a more principled approach to the concept of severance is both important and interesting. The majority of commentaries on severance concentrate on *how* severance ought to be brought about but neglect the central question of whether severance ought to be permitted at all. Ought a joint tenant to be capable of severing the joint tenancy, or should he be irreversibly bound by his decision to enter into a co-ownership of this nature? This is, essentially, a question of competing interests. On the one hand, the market requires autonomy on the part of the landowner; indeed, as severance is primarily carried out by an alienation of some kind, the market benefits not only from the creation of an undivided share that can be relatively easily conveyed but also from the transaction that brings about the severance. On the other hand, however, the interests of fairness make a strong showing: if I have entered into a joint tenancy, taking all of the risks that such a co-ownership entails of predeceasing my co-joint-tenant as well as considering the possibility of my benefiting from the right of survivorship, is it fair that I can be deprived of those possibilities by the actions of the other joint tenant? And, if it is not fair, does that matter to the law? Property law is, after all, a discipline concerned more with order, market economics and landowner autonomy than it is with the somewhat nebulous idea of "fairness". While the doyens of property law have tended to assume (as is perhaps reasonable) that severance is a preference of rational actors because it leaves the risks of survivorship in its wake,[34] this view is open to criticism for its latent paternalism. For a variety of reasons people may sometimes wish to enter into a landholding arrangement that holds as much a risk of material loss as it does material gain. The rational choice is not always the one that results in certainty through severance; in some cases it may be the one that best reflects the relationship dynamics of the individuals concerned. All that said, the reality is that we have never seriously contemplated abolishing severance in Irish law, nor are we likely to do so. Severance

[33] Blackstone, *Commentaries on the Laws of England* (Book 2), Chapter 12, pt 3.

[34] *ibid.*: "In general, it is advantageous for the joint-tenants to dissolve the jointure; since thereby the right of survivorship is taken away, and each may transmit his part to his own heirs".

and survivorship are, in effect, two sides to the joint tenancy coin; to have one without the other would in effect be to have no joint tenancies properly so called at all. Thus, in spite of amending *how* some forms of severance operate in order to better and more completely protect the non-severing joint tenants, the Land and Conveyancing Law Reform Act 2009 maintains severance both in law and in equity and it can be done by a number of means.

1. Severance in Law

There are four means by which a joint tenancy might be severed in law, all of which comprise the destruction of either the unity of title or the unity of interest. [8–20]

(i) Alienation to a Third Party

When a joint tenant alienates her ownership to a third party she severs her ownership from the remaining co-owners and the purchaser becomes a tenant in common in relation to the remainder of the joint tenants. This is primarily a result of the destruction of unities of time and title between the purchaser and the remaining joint tenants.[35] The non-acting joint tenants are not impacted upon in relation to one another, however, because the four unities still exist as between them. Take the following scenario as an example: [8–21]

> Ann, Bob and Carl are joint tenants of a field known as Longacre. Ann decides to alienate her ownership to Zack, who receives one-third of the ownership rights over the field. Because the four unities are not present between Zack, Bob and Carl, the three cannot be said to be joint tenants. However, the four unities do continue to exist between Bob and Carl, whose joint tenancy is completely unaffected by Ann's actions. Bob and Carl are therefore joint tenants in relation to one another, but they stand as one in a tenancy in common in relation to Zack.

As we might imagine, situations in which joint tenants act unilaterally in this way have the potential to cause disruption, especially where there are only two co-owners. In such a situation one joint tenant's decision to alienate her share to a third party would bring the joint tenancy to an end and deprive the other co-owner of the potential to become sole owner through survivorship. Indeed, it used to be the case that one could simply alienate the share to another to use of oneself; the use would then be executed pursuant to the Statute of Uses (Ireland) 1634[36] and the one-time joint tenant would be the legal and equitable owner of a share of the ownership. In other words, an act of unilateral dealing would have changed the acting co-owner from joint tenant to tenant in common without the other co-owner being able to prevent this, or even necessarily knowing about it.[37] This caused great concern and the Law Reform Commission considered that its continuance was unjustifiable because of the impact on other co-owners. Although not all commentators agreed [8–22]

---

[35] See, for example, *Gilbourne v Gilbourne*, unreported, High Court, Kenny J, 9 July 1975.
[36] See Chapter 3, paras 3–07 to 3–08.
[37] de Londras, *Principles of Irish Property Law* (1st ed, 2007, Dublin, Clarus Press), para 8–26.

that it was important or necessary to put an end to "secret" severance,[38] s 30 of the Land and Conveyancing Law Reform Act 2009 now requires that a joint tenant would get the prior written consent of all other joint tenants to any proposed alienation of an interest. Section 30 provides:

> (1) From the commencement of this Part, any—
>
> (a) conveyance, or contract for a conveyance, of land held in a joint tenancy, or
> (b) acquisition of another interest in such land,
>
> by a joint tenant without the consent referred to in subsection (2) is void both at law and in equity unless such consent is dispensed with under section 31 (2)(e).
>
> (2) In subsection (1) "consent" means the prior consent in writing of the other joint tenant or, where there are more than one other, all the other joint tenants.
>
> (3) From the commencement of this Part, registration of a judgment mortgage against the estate or interest in land of a joint tenant does not sever the joint tenancy and if the joint tenancy remains unsevered, the judgment mortgage is extinguished upon the death of the judgment debtor.
>
> (4) Nothing in this section affects the jurisdiction of the court to find that all the joint tenants by mutual agreement or by their conduct have severed the joint tenancy in equity.

[8–23] It is clear that the intention behind s 30 is to remove the possibility of unilateral severance from the law by effectively giving all joint tenants a veto over proposed alienation and acquisition of interests in the land. The section is a broad one, covering not only acquisitions that would in fact cause a severance but *all* acquisitions in the land in question: a position that was heavily criticised prior to the passage of the bill.[39] However, it is also true that the design of the section is such that an "escape hatch" is included to prevent unreasonable refusals of consent on behalf of non-transacting joint tenants. Section 31(2)(e) allows for any person holding in an interest in the land to apply for a court order dispensing with consent "where such consent is being unreasonably withheld". Both the requirement of prior, written consent in s 30 and the possibility to acquire a court order dispensing with consent in s 31 highlight the degree to which the "veto" on severance here is modelled on the "veto" on conveyances that we find in s 3 of the Family Home Protection Act 1976, and which was later also created for the shared homes of civil partners by Part 4 of the Civil Partnership and Certain Rights and Obligations of Cohabitants Act 2010.[40] This suggests—although it remains to be seen—that s 30 will work in much the same way as s 3 of the FHPA 1976

---

[38] For a selection of views on this see Mee, "The Land and Conveyancing Law Reform Bill 2006: Observations on the Law Reform Process and a Critique of Selection Provisions—Part I" (2006) 11(4) CPLJ 91; Woods, "Unilateral Severance of Joint Tenancies—The Case for Abolition" (2007) 12(2) CPLJ 47; Conway, "'Leaving Nothing to Chance?': Joint Tenancies, The 'Right' of Survivorship, and Unilateral Severance" (2008) *Oxford University Commonwealth Law Journal* 45; de Londras, *op. cit.*, pp 187–190.

[39] Mee, *art. cit.*

[40] See Chapter 9.

has done, requiring an informed and voluntary consent to any proposed severance or acquisition. Section 30(1) makes it clear that any transaction done without this required consent will be "void both at law and in equity" unless the consent requirement has been dispensed with and, as the consent required is "prior" to the conveyance we can assume that any application to have consent dispensed with would also have to be made and adjudicated upon prior to the completion of any transaction.[41] Mee has argued that requiring consent for *all* acquisitions of an interest in the property is problematic because there are limited situations in which an acquisition might not give rise to a severance.[42] It seems possible that, modelled on areas such as landlord and tenant law,[43] an Irish court would hold that a refusal to consent to an acquisition that does not sever the joint tenancy (and therefore does not impact upon the co-ownership) is presumptively unreasonable and, as a result, consent can be assumed, although to do so would be to replace the clear formal requirements of the Act (either a prior written consent *or* a court order dispensing with consent) with a more practicable, but also a somewhat innovated, system. We must, however, await jurisprudence on the point before we can be entirely clear on how this will operate in practice.

(ii) Acquisition of an Additional Interest

A joint tenancy can also be severed at law by the acquisition of an additional interest. **[8–24]**
In such a case, one joint tenant would acquire an additional estate in the land, thereby destroying the unity of interest between him and the other co-owners. As the four unities continue to operate between the non-acting joint tenants, they continue to stand in a joint tenancy in relation to one another, but stand as one in a tenancy in common in relation to the acting joint tenant. As considered above, the prior written consent of all other joint tenants is now required before *any* additional interest in the co-owned property is acquired.[44]

(iii) An Act of a Third Party Exercising Statutory Powers

Unlike in the previous cases, the severance of a joint tenancy as a result of the act of a **[8–25]**
third party exercising statutory powers is involuntary, i.e. it is done by parties other than the joint tenants themselves. One of the most common cases of involuntary severance used to arise where a creditor obtained a judgment mortgage on the land of a joint tenant. Where the co-owned land is unregistered, the judgment mortgage severed the joint tenancy[45] and, as a result, only the share of ownership held by the debtor was affected by implementation of the judgment mortgage. This was changed by s 30(3) of the Land and Conveyancing Law Reform Act 2009, which provides that a judgment mortgage against one joint tenant of co-owned land *never* severs a joint tenancy, whether the land in question is registered or unregistered. This is balanced by the fact

[41] *Somers v W* [1979] IR 94; see generally Chapter 9.

[42] Mee, *art. cit.*

[43] See, for example, s 66, Landlord and Tenant (Amendment) Act 1980.

[44] s 31, Land and Conveyancing Law Reform Act 2009.

[45] *McIlroy v Edgar* (1881) 7 LR IR 521; *Provincial Bank of Ireland Ltd v Tallon* [1938] IR 361; *Containercare v Wycherly* [1982] IR 143.

that s 31 allows for a judgment mortgagor[46] to apply to the court for a range of orders, including an "order for the sale of the land and distribution of the proceeds of sale as the court directs".[47]

[8–26] It was important for the 2009 Act to be entirely clear on this matter, because when it comes to pre-2009 Act judgment mortgages against joint tenants of registered land, there was a long-standing uncertainty as to whether the joint tenancy was severed or not. Although the Supreme Court has now confirmed that there is no severance of a joint tenancy in such situations,[48] and this accords with the views long expressed by academics in the field,[49] that conclusion followed a lengthy and uncertain course of jurisprudence that is considered in more detail below.[50]

2. Severance in Equity

[8–27] In contrast to a severance in law, a severance in equity will occur where the recognised intention of the parties is for the joint tenancy to be severed, even in the absence of formalities that may be required in order for a severance to be affected in law. There have traditionally been three situations in which a joint tenancy may be severed in equity. These scenarios are evident from the judgment of Page Wood VC in *Williams v Hensman*:

> ... in the first place, an act of any one of the persons operating upon his own share may create a severance as to that share... Secondly, a joint-tenancy may be severed by mutual agreement. And, in the third place, there may be a severance by any course of dealing sufficient to intimate that the interests of all were mutually treated as constituting a tenancy in common.[51]

The three traditional scenarios of severance in equity are therefore: (a) in order to give effect to the mutual intention of the parties; (b) as a result of an act of one party on his own share; (c) as a result of a course of dealing that is sufficient to show that the interests of the parties were conceived of as being held in a tenancy in common. The Land and Conveyancing Law Reform Act 2009 does not appear to change the position relating to either the mutual intention of the parties or a course of dealing, providing in s 30(4) that "Nothing in this section affects the jurisdiction of the court to find that all the joint tenants by mutual agreement or by their conduct have severed the joint tenancy in equity". The requirement of prior, written consent of non-transacting joint tenants for the conveyance of any interest in land, found in s 30(1), does, however, mean that an act of a party on his own share can now sever a joint tenancy in equity *only where* there is either the consent of the other joint tenants *or* an order dispensing with consent has been acquired under s 31(2)(e).

---

[46] s 31(4)(a), Land and Conveyancing Law Reform Act 2009.

[47] s 31(2)(c), *ibid.*

[48] *Irwin v Deasy* [2011] IESC 15.

[49] Conway, *Co-Ownership of Land: Partition Actions and Remedies* (2000, Dublin, Butterworths), pp 198–200; Mee, "Judgment Mortgages, Co-Ownership and Registered Land" (1999) 4(2) CPL 28; Mee, "Partition and Sale of the Family Home" (1993) 15 DULJ 78.

[50] paras 8–45 to 8–47.

[51] (1861) 1 J&H 546 at 557.

(i) Furthering the Mutual Intentions of the Parties

If the court finds that to do so would accord with the mutual intentions of the joint tenants, it may give effect to a severance in equity, even where the parties have not taken any steps to enact their intentions. In order for the court to take this step, however, the intention must actually be mutual and be expressed openly: it cannot be the secretly declared intention of some co-owners. The classical authority for this type of severance in equity is *Burgess v Rawnsley*.[52] **[8–28]**

Burgess concerned the unrequited affections of Mr H for Mrs Rawnsley and the ensuing confusion as to their mutual property interests. Mr H had been offered the opportunity to buy the freehold of the property he was renting from his landlord and, around this time, he became friendly with Mrs Rawnsley, who felt somewhat sorry for him, as he appeared to be experiencing some hard times. Mr H was enamoured with her and intended them to be married, although it does not appear that Mrs Rawnsley held any such "hopes" for their future together. He asked Mrs Rawnsley to join in the purchase of the property with him and she agreed. Her understanding was that she would occupy one floor of the property and he the other; however, Mr H understood that they would marry and use the property as their marital home. Once he had been disabused of this notion and after the sale had been completed (by which they were deemed joint tenants), he refused to allow Mrs Rawnsley to enter the property and offered to buy her share from her. She agreed and offered it to him for £750, but later changed her mind and demanded £1,000 for it. The matter was not resolved, and on Mr H's death, Mrs Rawnsley claimed that she was now the sole owner on the basis of survivorship. Mr H's administrator claimed that there had been a severance in equity by means of their mutual intention for him to purchase Mrs Rawnsley's share from her. Lord Denning agreed that there had been an equitable severance on the basis of the parties' mutual intentions, notwithstanding their failure to formalise those intentions by completing the sale. **[8–29]**

The parties' mutual intentions might also be evident in their decision to enter into a mutual contract for the sale of the co-owned property. The important case of *Byrne v Byrne*[53] confirmed that the mere act of entering into the mutual contract that had not yet been completed would not necessarily result in a severance in equity; rather, the court would have to ascertain whether the joint tenants intended for the contract and sale to result in a severance, or intended for the joint tenancy to continue to exist over the purchase monies. In practical terms it appears that joint tenants sometimes sever their joint tenancy by conveying the property to a third party to the use of the original joint tenants as tenants in common in equal shares. The use is then executed so that the purchaser is left with no interest, and the vendors become tenants in common in law and equity and, as a result, each individual can then proceed to act freely on his or her own share.[54] **[8–30]**

---

[52] [1975] 1 Ch 429.

[53] Unreported, High Court, 18 January 1980.

[54] See Laffoy, *Irish Conveyancing Precedents* (1992, Dublin, Butterworths), Precedent J.1.7.

(ii) Individual Joint Tenant Acting upon his own Share

[8–31] Where an individual joint tenant carries out an act upon his own share, which is not completed, then the contractual rule in *Tempany v Hynes*[55] can intervene to result in a severance in equity. Thus, where a joint tenant enters into an enforceable contract with a third party to alienate their interest to them *and* the third party pays some of the purchaser price *but* the contract is not completed, then *Tempany* dictates that the third party has acquired the interest in equity. In general terms, that interest will be proportionate to the purchase monies paid.[56] As a result, the unity of title is destroyed in equity and an equitable severance occurs. Section 52(1) of the Land and Conveyancing Law Reform Act 2009 reinforces this, providing that "the entire beneficial interest passes to the purchaser on the making, after the commencement of this Chapter, of an enforceable contract for the sale or other disposition of land". Of course, as noted above, s 30 of the 2009 Act now makes the prior, written consent of non-transaction joint tenants or, in the alternative, a court order dispensing with consent under s 31(2)(e), requirements for the conveyance of any interest by a joint tenant. Section 30(1) makes it clear that failure to acquire the consent or the order dispensing with consent will make the conveyance void "in law *and in equity*" (emphasis added) meaning that there would be no severance in equity.

(iii) Course of Dealing

[8–32] There are numerous scenarios in which there may be a severance in equity as a result of a course of dealing. By this phrase we are referring to "not only negotiations that fall short of an agreement but also the way in which the property in question has been dealt with by those concerned".[57] In terms of a course of negotiation, it may give rise to a severance in equity, even if it falls far short of a formal agreement, provided it shows that relations between the co-owners have been altered to the extent that they no longer conceive of themselves as joint tenants, but rather as tenants in common.

3. Commorientes

[8–33] The term "*commorientes*" is used to describe a situation in which two or more people die in circumstances that make it impossible to tell, with any degree of certainty, who died first. Where the deceased are joint tenants, this results in particular difficulties: if we do not know who died first, then we do not know which of the joint tenants is entitled to the benefit of the right of survivorship. Although it was not always the case,[58] the law now provides that in circumstances of *commorientes* the deceased are treated as having died simultaneously.[59] Furthermore, s 5 of the Succession Act 1965, as amended by s 67 of the Civil Law (Miscellaneous Provisions) Act 2008, now provides that where joint tenants die simultaneously, or are deemed to have died simultaneously under *commorientes*, they are deemed to have held the property as tenants in common in equal shares. In other words, their joint tenancy is now severed by statute as a result of their simultaneous death.

---

[55] [1976] IR 101.

[56] On this doctrine generally see Lyall, "The Purchaser's Equity: An Irish Controversy" (1989) 7 ILT 270.

[57] Lyall, *Land Law in Ireland* (2nd ed, 2000, Dublin, Round Hall), p 440.

[58] See, for example, *Re Rowland* [1963] 1 Ch 1.

[59] s 5, Succession Act 1965.

VI. The Rights of Co-Owners

Both joint tenants and tenants in common have a relatively broad range of rights in relation to the co-owned property, however the repercussions of exercising these rights may differ depending on the nature of the co-ownership in question. [8–34]

1. Alienation

All co-owners are entitled to alienate their property rights. Where the parties alienate through a mutual agreement, the purchase monies will most commonly continue to be held in co-ownership between the parties. In other words, the doctrine of overreaching will operate (i.e. the doctrine that interests that previously existed over the land will now exist over whatever represents the land). As considered above,[60] if the parties' intention is that the sale would sever a joint tenancy, then this will be the case. In addition, each individual co-owner has the right to alienate his or her own ownership rights. Such an action by a joint tenant will result in a severance of the joint tenancy *provided* consent of the non-transacting joint tenants has been acquired[61] or, if this consent is being unreasonably withheld, there is a court order dispensing with consent.[62] In contrast, a tenant in common can alienate her share without any need for consent from the other tenants in common and the purchaser simply "slips into" the tenancy in common in place of the vendor. Co-owners are also entitled to rent out the property they hold. In such cases the rental income will be shared between the co-owners. In a joint tenancy the parties will take the rent in equal shares, whereas rent will be split into shares commensurate with the shares of ownership in a tenancy in common. If a co-owner receives more rent than his entitlement, the other joint tenants can apply for a court order "directing that accounting adjustments be made as between the co-owners".[63] Accounting adjustments here include "redistribution of rents and profits received by a co-owner disproportionate to his or her interest in the land".[64] [8–35]

2. Possession

In both the joint tenancy and the tenancy in common, all co-owners are entitled to possess the property as a result of the unity of possession. Possession can be defined as the right to use and enjoy land: in the context of co-ownership, the Irish courts have confirmed that this concept extends to the ability to have a reasonable number of invitees use and enjoy the land as well. This was considered in *Lahiffe v Hecker*.[65] In this case, a father had left all of his property to his four children as joint tenants, including a three-bedroom house over which one named child was to have a right of residence until she married.[66] The children then agreed to sever the joint tenancy and became tenants in common, with each holding an equal share. A dispute later arose as to the nature of the children's right to possess this specific property, particularly given the right of residence enjoyed in relation to it by one sibling. This sibling was particularly worried about the number of keys that existed to the property and wanted [8–36]

[60] paras 8–28 to 8–30.
[61] s 30(1), Land and Conveyancing Law Reform Act 2009.
[62] s 31(2)(e), *ibid.*
[63] s 31(2)(d), *ibid.*
[64] s 31(4)(b)(iv), Land and Conveyancing Law Reform Act 2009.
[65] Unreported, High Court, 28 April 1994, Lynch J.
[66] On rights of residence see Chapter 11.

to ensure that her security would not be compromised by the possessory rights of her siblings. She felt that she was entitled to prescribe when and how her siblings and co-owners could enter, inspect and use the property. In this, the Court held, she "misconceive[d] her rights in and to the property". As the siblings were tenants in common, they were entitled to occupy the property together with "reasonable invitees such as spouses and children", although they could not overcrowd the property in a manner that would make the right of residence "unduly incommodious".

[8–37] Whether or not the right to possess the property extends to a right of all co-owners to possess the title deeds of the property is a question of some controversy. The law of England and Wales certainly appears to suggest that it does. The English Court of Appeal has held that a co-owner may not part with title deeds without the consent of the other co-owners.[67] This has necessary implications for the capacity of a co-owner to create an equitable mortgage by deposit of title deeds without the consent of the other co-owner(s) and appears to be an eminently sensible approach to take. It also appears to have been motivated by a concern that the mortgage, or charge, could have been enforced and thereby could adversely affect the interest of the co-owner, despite it being created without her consent.[68] In contrast, the Irish courts have held that a co-owner could deposit title deeds and, as a result, create an equitable mortgage over the property notwithstanding the other co-owner's objections.[69] The requirements for consent before any interest in land could be alienated, including by means of an equitable mortgage, that is now contained in s 30(1) of the Land and Conveyancing Law Reform Act 2009 make this concern somewhat moot.

[8–38] As every co-owner is entitled to possess all of the land (remember that the land is never divided physically, regardless of which kind of co-ownership exists), any co-owner who attempts to exclude another will be liable for trespass.[70]

(i) Right to Apply for Court Orders

[8–39] As holders of an interest in land, all co-owners—whether joint tenants or tenants in common in law or in equity—can apply to the court for an order relating to the co-ownership. Section 31(1) of the Land and Conveyancing Law Reform Act 2009 reaffirms that right and s 31(2) outlines the orders that can be applied for.[71] In this respect a co-owner can apply for the following orders:

(a) An order for the partition of the land among the co-owners: such an order effectively brings the co-ownership to an end by shattering the unity of possession that is required for both joint tenancies and tenancies in common and is considered in more depth below. Partition constitutes the physical division of the land between the parties and is rare in practice.

---

[67] *Thames Guaranty Ltd v Campbell & Ors* [1985] 1 QB 210.

[68] See, for example, *Harman v Glencross & Anor* [1986] 1 All ER 545.

[69] *O'Keefe v O'Flynn Exhams & Partners*, unreported, High Court, 31 July 1992, Costello J (case affirmed without consideration of this point in *O'Keefe v Russell* [1994] 1 ILRM 137).

[70] *Bull v Bull* [1955] 1 QB 234.

[71] These powers are not generally new; rather they are mostly re-enactments of powers previously found in the Partition Acts 1868 and 1876 (s 31(2)(a), (b) and (c)), the Administration of Justice (Ireland) Act 1707 (s 31(2)(d)).

claims

(b) An order for taking an account of incumbrances on the land and their respective priorities: an order of this nature would generally be sought where an order for sale, under s 31(2)(c) is also sought. It allows for the clear exposition of what imcumbrances exist over the land and the determination of priority so that the order in which they will be satisfied from the proceeds of sale can be clearly outlined.

(c) An order to the sale of the land and distribution of the proceeds of sale as directed by the court: because of the difficulties that exist with partition, which are considered further below, courts are granted a statutory right to order sale of the property and the subsequent division of the proceeds of sale between the (then former) co-owners, once any and all incumbrancershave been satisfied pursuant to an order under s 31(2)(b). In this respect the court has discretion as to the division of the proceeds of sale, although in general they will be divided in a manner that is commensurate with the percentage ownership that the (then former) co-owners had over the property.

(d) An order for accounting adjustments to be made between the co-owners: because co-owners will sometimes actually enjoy the land in question in unequal proportions (so, perhaps, one co-owner will live there on a more or less permanent basis and the others will only visit occasionally), the court is empowered to make order for accounting adjustments that would reflect this unevenness in use and enjoyment. According to s 31(4), the accounting adjustments that can be ordered include, but are not limited to,[72] an order for the payment of an occupation rent by one co-owner to the others,[73] an order for compensation for a co-owner who has incurrent disproportionate expense in respect of the land,[74] an order for contributions by one co-owner to the disproportionate costs incurred by another co-owner,[75] or a redistribution of rents and income between the co-owners in a manner that more accurately reflects their interests in the land.[76]

(e) An order dispensing with the consent required under s 30(1) where such consent is being unreasonably withheld.

(f) "[S]uch other order relating to the land as appears to the court to be just and equitable in the circumstances of the case".[77]

VII. Termination of Co-Ownership

There are only a limited number of ways in which co-ownership can be brought to an end. The termination of a co-ownership must be distinguished from the severance of a joint tenancy which, as considered above, merely moves to change the nature of the co-ownership into a tenancy in common. In order for a co-ownership to be effectively terminated what is required is either the reduction of the number of owners to one (so that, as a matter of logic, the law of co-ownership simply no longer applies) or the shattering of the unity of possession, which is required for both the joint tenancy and the tenancy in common. [8–40]

[72] s 31(4)(v), Land and Conveyancing Law Reform Act 2009.
[73] s 31(4)(i), *ibid.*
[74] s 31(4)(ii), *ibid.*
[75] s 31(4)(iii), *ibid.*
[76] s 31(4)(iv), *ibid.*
[77] s 31(2)(f), *ibid.*

1. Vesting in a Sole Owner

[8–41] As a matter of logic, no co-ownership can be said to exist where there is only one owner. Thus, in a joint tenancy the right of survivorship operates to reduce the number of co-owners until there is only one remaining who then becomes the sole owner of the land; the co-ownership is terminated. A joint tenant may also buy out the other joint tenants. In such circumstances the other joint tenants will transfer their ownership to the purchasing party by means of release.[78] Each release constitutes a severance of that share from the joint tenancy, but once all other joint tenants have released their ownership to the purchasing party, no co-ownership can be said to exist. Of course, prior written consent is now required to such a transfer under s 30 of the Land and Conveyancing Law Reform Act 2009. In a tenancy in common the right of survivorship does not operate, therefore ownership will be vested in a sole owner only when one party buys out or otherwise acquires the shares of the other tenants in common. This in turn will terminate the co-ownership as there will be only one owner.

2. Partition or Sale

[8–42] Partition is the physical division of property between co-owners in a manner that shatters the unity of possession and therefore makes co-ownership impossible. Partition can be done voluntarily by deed[79] or, where no agreement can be found, by court order under s 31(2)(a) of the Land and Conveyancing Law Reform Act 2009. Under the 2009 Act partition can be sought by any "[a]ny person having an estate or interest in land which is co-owned whether at law or in equity", which is expressly said to include "a mortgagee or other secured creditor, a judgment mortgagee or a trustee". Partition can be sought by any "interested party", such as a co-owner, mortgagee,[80] or (in limited situations) judgment mortgagee.[81] Although the Land and Conveyancing Law Reform Act 2009 now outlines a straightforward process by which either an order for partition or an order for sale can be applied for, the law on partition and sale *in lieu* thereof as it operates in relation to pre-2009 proceedings and, in particular, judgment mortgages created prior to the coming into effect of the Land and Conveyancing Law Reform Act 2009 requires some attention here as it continues to be the subject of litigation in Irish courts.

(i) Historical Perspective on Partition

[8–43] Court proceedings for partition were not possible at common law, but were introduced in the Act for Jointenants 1542[82] and became acknowledged as an entitlement of co-owners[83]: they were refined and improved in the Partition Acts 1868 and 1876. These Acts allowed for the property to be partitioned but also for property to be sold and the proceeds of sale divided in *lieu* of physical partition.[84] In reality, sale was often

[78] Challis, *The Law of Real Property* (3rd ed, 1911, London, Butterworths), pp 368–369.

[79] *Clarke v Bodkin* (1851) 13 IR Eq R 492; s 3, Real Property Act 1845.

[80] *Northern Bank v Adams*, unreported, 1 February 1996, Master's Court (NI).

[81] *Farrell v Donnelly* [1913] 1 IR 50.

[82] 33 Hen 8, c 10 (IR) (1542). One of the most problematic areas of this Act was that it allowed for a partition to be acquired regardless of whether this was sensible with regard to the circumstances of the case (see, for example, *Tottenham v Molony* (1856) 2 IR Jur (os) 88).

[83] See the discussion of this in *Ceylon Theatres Ltd v Cinemas Ltd* [1968] AC 792, *per* Wilberforce LJ at pp 802–803.

[84] See, for example, *Re Balfour's Estate* (1887) 19 LR IR 487.

the preferred outcome of a partition action for simple reasons of practicality. It had previously been the case, under the 1542 Act, that courts could not order a sale *in lieu* of partition, which gave rise to some clearly impractical results such as that in the infamous case of *Turner v Morgan.*[85] Here a partition was ordered, but the house in question was partitioned in a way that resulted in one former co-owner having neither a staircase nor a toilet! The introduction of sale *in lieu* of partition in the Partition Acts 1868 and 1876 and now, in the 2009 Act,[86] as an independently achievable order, was therefore welcome. There had been some doubt as to whether or not the Irish courts retain the power of partition or sale following the Statute Law Revision (Pre-Union Irish Statutes) Act 1962, which appeared to have repealed the 1542 Act. However, in real terms the Irish courts appeared satisfied that, at the very least, they retained an equitable jurisdiction to engage in partition or sale, even if the statutory jurisdiction had been revoked.[87] Going forward, there is of course no doubt as to courts' jurisdiction to order partition or sale given the terms of s 31 of the Land and Conveyancing Law Reform Act 2009.

(ii) Is there an "Entitlement" to Partition or Sale in Lieu?

Under the pre-2009 Act law, there was some uncertainty as to whether or not co-owners were *entitled* to either a partition or a sale. Heather Conway has argued that courts did not originally have the discretion to refuse *both* partition and sale[88]: in other words, that courts were originally required to order one or the other when requested and could not refuse both. However, the case of *First National Building Society v Ring*[89] suggested a change in that position and that courts had the discretion to refuse both applications, particularly where third-party interests (such as the rights of the mortgagee) required the exercise of such discretion. This position was closely associated with Murphy J's decision in *O'D v O'D*[90] that partition was traditionally a discretionary remedy (a finding that is quite at odds with precedent), but the matter continued to be hotly disputed. The most firm statement that could have been made was probably that court had the discretion to refuse both partition and sale only where there were extenuating circumstances to justify such a refusal (such as the fact that the property was a family home) and that, in general terms, co-owners might well be said to have been entitled to either a partition or a sale.[91] The Land and Conveyancing Law Reform Act 2009 seems to make clear that courts do enjoy a discretion to refuse either **[8–44]**

[85] (1803) 8 Ves 143.

[86] s 31(2)(c), Land and Conveyancing Law Reform Act 2009.

[87] See, for example, *F v F* [1987] ILRM 1 (*per* Barr J); *O'D v O'D,* unreported, High Court, Murphy J, 18 November 1983; *Irwin v Deasy* [2006] 2 ILRM 226 *per* Laffoy J.

[88] Conway, *Co-Ownership of Land: Partition Actions and Remedies* (2000, Dublin, Butterworths), p 125; see also *Pitt v Jones* (1880) 5 App Cas 651.

[89] [1992] 1 IR 375.

[90] Unreported, High Court, 18 November 1983, Murphy J; for detailed consideration of the case see Conway, *Co-Ownership of Land: Partition Actions and Remedies* (2000, Dublin, Butterworths), pp 143–146.

[91] See, for example, Mee, "Judgment Mortgages, Co-Ownership and Registered Land" (1999) 4(2) CPL 28; Conway, "The Repeal of an Act for Jointenants 1542 and the Jurisdiction to Order Partition or Sale under the Partition Acts 1868 and 1876" (1997) DULJ 1; Pearce, "The Right to Partition and Sale Between Co-Owners" (1987) 5 ILT 36. This aligned with the Northern Ireland position as stated in *Northern Bank v Beattie* [1982] 18 NIJB 1 at 23–4.

or both applications for partition (under s 31(2)(a)) and for sale (under s 31(2)(b)). This flows from s 31(3), which makes it clear that courts considering an application under s 31 may make the order as requested,[92] make the order subject to attached conditions or requirements,[93] combine orders,[94] or "dismiss the application without making any order".[95]

(iii) Partition or Sale of Family and Shared Homes

[8–45] Under the Partition Acts an applicant was entitled to sale *in lieu* of partition in the absence of "good reason to the contrary" as long as the interests of the applicant or the co-owners together comprised at least half of the value of the property.[96] Where the interest of the applicant or co-owners together is less than this, the applicant was required to convince the court that sale *in lieu* of partition was justified and "would be more beneficial for the parties"[97] concerned in the particular circumstances of the case. In recognition of the special role of familial property, the Irish courts have taken particular account of the fact that a property is a family home when an application for partition or sale is made.[98] It is reasonable to assume that, under the processes for orders for sale and for partition under s 31 of the Land and Conveyancing Law Reform Act 2009, the nature of the property in question will remain a factor that is taken into account. In all likelihood, applications of this kind in relation to family homes as defined under the Family Home Protection Act 1976[99] (i.e. ordinary place of residence of a married couple) and shared homes as defined under the Civil Partnership and Rights and Obligations of Cohabitants Act 2010[100] (i.e. ordinary place of residence of a couple with a civil partnership) will continue to receive particularly close attention from the courts.

(iv) Judgment Mortgages over Registered Land Held in a Joint Tenancy

[8–46] Under the pre-2009 Act law, only a co-owner of the property in question could apply for either partition or sale *in lieu* thereof. This raised particular difficulties in the case of judgment mortgages over registered land held in a joint tenancy. As will be fully considered in Chapter 13, the judgment mortgage is a debt-enforcement mechanism by which a creditor is recognised as a mortgagee over property. In the case of unregistered land, it was quite clear that the holder of a judgment mortgage became entitled to a share of ownership of the "mortgaged" property, and there was no doubt as to the right to apply for partition or sale in such situations. However, there was no such clarity in relation to registered land. This is related, in part, to the mirror principle, which underlines all of the law of registered land. Under the Registration of Title

[92] s 31(3)(a), Land and Conveyancing Law Reform Act 2009.
[93] *ibid.*
[94] s 31(3)(c), Land and Conveyancing Law Reform Act 2009.
[95] s 31(3)(b), *ibid.*
[96] s 4, Partition Act 1868.
[97] s 3, *ibid.*
[98] Mee, "Partition and Sale of the Family Home" (1993) DULJ 78.
[99] s 2, Family Home Protection Act 1976.
[100] s 27, Civil Partnership and Certain Rights and Obligations of Cohabitants Act 2010.

Act 1964 judgment mortgagees are chargees rather than co-owners. Section 71 of that Act provides, in relevant part and with added emphasis:

> 71.—(1) The registration of the affidavit required by section 6 of the Judgment Mortgage (Ireland) Act, 1850, for the purpose of registering a judgment as a mortgage shall, in the case of registered land, be made in the prescribed manner and with such entries as may be prescribed.
>
> . . .
>
> (4) Registration of an affidavit which complies with the said sections and this section shall operate to *charge the interest of the judgment debtor* subject to—
>
> (a) the burdens, if any, registered as affecting that interest,
> (b) the burdens to which, though not so registered, that interest is subject by virtue of section 72, and
> (c) all unregistered rights subject to which the judgment debtor held that interest at the time of registration of the affidavit,
>
> and the creditor shall have such rights and remedies for the enforcement of the charge as may be conferred on him by order of the court [emphasis added].

It was quite clear from this provision that the holder of a judgment mortgage did not acquire a share of ownership in the property; rather it created a charge over the interest of the judgment debtor. Notwithstanding this apparent statutory clarity, the Irish courts for many years proceeded upon the somewhat theoretically unsound presumption that judgment mortgagees over registered land could apply for partition or sale because those with judgment mortgages over unregistered land could do so. This approach was at once derivative and dangerous because it made it almost inevitable that a court would finally realise the difficulties inherent in this incongruous "logic" and throw the law into flux. Indeed, that was precisely what happened in a number of judgments in the case of *Irwin v Deasy.*[101]

The litigation relating to this case had resulted in conflicting judgments from the High Court. In 2004, Finlay-Geoghegan J had held that although judgment mortgagees over co-owned registered land did not have a right to partition or sale *per se*, the court could order a partition or sale in such circumstances under s 71(4) of the Registration of Title Act 1964, which "confers on the court a discretion as to the rights and remedies for the enforcement of the charge which may be conferred by order of the court".[102] According to Finlay-Geoghegan J: **[8–47]**

> such discretion should be construed as giving to the court a jurisdiction and discretion to grant orders similar to those which are and have been granted pursuant to the court's pre-existing equitable or common law jurisdiction for the enforcement of judgment mortgages registered against unregistered land.[103]

[101] [2004] 4 IR 1; [2006] 2 ILRM 226; [2006] IEHC 25; [2011] IESC 15.
[102] *Irwin v Deasy* [2004] 4 IR 1, 9.
[103] *ibid.*

In 2006, Laffoy J disagreed, holding that a judgment mortgagee of co-owned registered land had no right to partition or sale of the whole.[104] In contrast to Finlay-Geoghegan J's 2004 approach, in 2006 Laffoy J devoted sustained attention to the matter of whether such judgment mortgagees could apply for partition or sale as a question of co-ownership doctrine. She particularly considered academic commentary that pointed to the absence of the basic prerequisite for such an application in the case of registered land, i.e. ownership rights. As a result, Laffoy J held that the older cases on this matter had proceeded on the basis of an unsustainable assumption of standing and that, in fact, because judgment mortgagees over registered land have no ownership rights, they have no application rights and, therefore, no partition or sale can be acquired. In May 2011 the Supreme Court handed down its judgment in this case, finally bringing some clarity to the matter.[105] The Court was asked to resolve the correct interpretation of s 71(4) of the Registration of Title Act 1964 inasmuch as it related to judgment mortgages against one joint tenant of registered land and the capacity (or lack of capacity) of the judgment mortgagee to make an order for partition or sale. Finnegan J, for the Court, held that judgment mortgagees against one joint tenant of registered land did not acquire an interest in the property and could not, therefore, rely on the Partition Acts themselves. The Court further held that nevertheless it could not allow partition or sale upon the application of a judgment mortgagee against one joint tenant of registered land under the discretion conferred on them by s 71(4) of the 1964 Act, holding that "had it been the intention of the legislature to confer that power upon the court it would have done so in clear terms".

[8–48] The Supreme Court's decision in *Irwin v Deasy* is not merely of historical interest; it is clear that there are many people who find themselves with pre-2009 Act judgment mortgages over registered land and who cannot, now, apply for partition or sale *in lieu* thereof. This creates some concerns around enforceability, particularly since the death of the indebted joint tenant will mean that the judgment mortgage is no longer enforceable against the property because the non-indebted joint tenants will enjoy the right to survivorship and there is no judgment mortgage against them.[106] It also means that, for judgment mortgages registered before 1 December 2009, there is an important distinction between judgment mortgagees over unregistered land and those over registered land. Because judgment mortgages over unregistered land resulted in a transfer of interest to the judgment mortgagee, there is no question whatsoever as to the mortgagee's capacity to apply for partition or sale; the same, as we have seen, is not true of judgement mortgagees over registered land. For judgment mortgages that are registered after the commencement of the Land and Conveyancing Law Reform Act 2009 there is a clear statutory right, under s 31(4)(a), to apply for an order for partition (s 31(2)(a)) or an order for sale (s 31(2)(b)).

(v) Equitable Accounting

[8–49] In cases of partition or sale the courts apply the principle of "equitable accounting" to determine fair shares, payment of costs, etc. Equitable accounting might be described as "the process of taking, and settling, accounts between joint owners in connection

[104] *Irwin v Deasy* [2006] 2 ILRM 226.

[105] *Irwin v Deasy* [2011] IESC 15.

[106] *Judge Mahon v Lawlor* [2008] IEHC 284; *Mahon & Ors v Lawlor & Ors* [2010] IESC 58.

with obligations arising from their joint ownership".[107] This calculus is applied to the proceeds of the sale in the manner classically expressed by Lord Griffiths in *Bernard v Josephs*[108]:

> When the proceeds of sale are realised there will have to be equitable accounting between the parties before the money is distributed. If the woman has left, she is entitled to receive an occupation rent, but if the man has kept up the mortgage payments, he is entitled to credit for her share of the payments; if he has spent money on recent redecoration which results in a much better sale price, he should have credit for that, not as an altered share, but by repayment of the whole or a part of the money he has spent. These are but examples of the way in which the balance is to be struck.

[107] Cooke, "Equitable Accounting—Some Recent Decisions in Northern Ireland" (2001) DULJ 188.
[108] [1982] 1 Ch 391 at 405.

CHAPTER 9
Homes

Although, in general, property law tends to focus much more of its energy on ensuring the alienability and marketability of land than on protecting the welfare of those who reside on that land, the concept of "home" presents something of an exception. In this chapter we consider various ways in which homes are particularly protected, or differently treated, to other kinds of buildings. This trend is also discernible elsewhere in the book. In Chapter 13, for example, we will see that courts tend to be more sympathetic towards and protective of residential mortgagors (borrowers) than of commercial mortgagors: similarly in Chapter 15 we will see that we have developed particular systems for residential tenancies. There is, the law recognises, something special about homes: something that might even be said to "trump" the sheer market [9–01] orientation of efficiency and alienability. What that something special is, however, is difficult to put into words. It is instinctive: we feel that "specialness" when we think about *home* and we don't (usually) feel it when we think about other kinds of property like warehouses and shops or law schools. The special character of the home, which we recognise as both a matter of psychology *and* of law, means that property that is considered a home can be subjected to a different legal regime in some contexts to other kinds of property. This is so even when it comes to activities—such as conveyancing—that are considered "core" to property law.

[9–02] In some ways these regimes are not always easily categorised as "property law" strictly so called, but they are nevertheless relevant to how we deal with homes as pieces of property. For that reason, we consider the principles for the distribution of property on the breakdown of marriages and civil partnerships even though, strictly speaking, this belongs more properly to "family law" than to property law. In a sense, this reflects something that the law relating to the home makes clear for us in property law in a way that other topics, perhaps, do not: life is not arranged in tidy modules marked "contract law", "property law", "human rights law" and so on. It is more complicated than that and, while we can perhaps sideline that complexity in relation to other kinds of property, homes—where messy and complicated human interaction takes places on a constant basis—do not permit of such compartmentalisation.

[9–03] That said, most of the topics considered here are more in the vein of "classic" property law such as restrictions and processes for the conveyance of interests in homes, dispossession of homes, presumed resulting trusts and community of ownership, for example. The law of succession and the ways in which that area of law deals with homes as particular types of property could also be considered within this chapter but is, in fact, considered in Chapter 16 with the remainder of succession. While it was the case that, until 2010, the homes of married couples (with or without children) were generally the only types of homes with special protection of the kind considered in this chapter,[1] the passage and commencement of the Civil Partnership and Certain Rights and Obligations of Cohabitants Act 2010 has extended our interest to other kinds of homes. All are considered below.

I. Defining "Home" as a Matter of Law

[9–04] As alluded to above,[2] the concept of home is an emotive one. In Pádraic Kenna's estimation, "there is hardly a more emotionally loaded word [than "home"], since it epitomises situations of family, affection, love and other human experiences".[3] The home, as we all know, plays a central role in human life; it is the site of a multitude of experiences, both positive and negative, and a basic requirement for the development of

[1] This is considered in de Londras, *Principles of Irish Property Law* (1st ed, 2007, Dublin, Clarus Press), Chapter 9.

[2] para 9–01.

[3] Kenna, *Housing Law and Policy in Ireland* (1st ed, 2006, Dublin, Clarus Press), p 343, referring to Fox, "The Meaning of Home: A Chimereal Concept for or a Legal Challenge" (2002) 29(4) JLS 580.

a family life.[4] In recognition of this, both the Constitution[5] and the European Convention on Human Rights[6] expressly recognise the significance of the home.

In Irish constitutional law the "home" may at first appear to have no more hallowed a position than any other piece of property, but the recognition of the "X factor" inherent in a home (i.e. the "social, psychological, and cultural values that a physical structure acquires through its use as a home"[7]) comes in the constitutional protection of parents' right to educate children in the home[8] and the reference (to which we return later[9]) of the work that women do in the home.[10] In constitutional jurisprudence, however, the concept of home has not been greatly interrogated. Rather, it has been more or less presumed that a place in which a family lives is a home. While this may appear somewhat simplistic at first, there are few who would quibble with the statement that "where a family lives" constitutes a home. The two areas of dispute are, instead, what constitutes a "family" in this context, and whether that definition is an exclusionary one so that *only* the place where a family lives can be defined (and treated) as a home. In respect of the former, it is clear that only a family based on marriage currently enjoys constitutional protection,[11] although other forms of family also have legislative protection, particularly through the Civil Partnership and Certain Rights and Obligations of Cohabitants Act 2010. When it comes to the second issue—the question of a home being the place where people live—the jurisprudence of the European Court of Human Rights suggests a more expansive conception of home.[12] **[9–05]**

The European Convention on Human Rights guarantees respect for the home in Art 8. Homes can also be protected under the auspices of Art 1 of Protocol One to the Convention.[13] Article 8 provides: **[9–06]**

(1) Everyone has the right to respect for his private and family life, his home and his correspondence.

(2) There shall be no interference by a public authority with the exercise of this right except such as is in accordance with the law and is necessary in a democratic society in the

[4] This does not mean that people without a home cannot create a family life, but rather that the lack of a home causes substantial difficulties in the fulfilment of this objective.

[5] Constitutional recognition of the home arises in Art 42.2 (providing that parents can provide education in the home) and in Art 41.2 (providing that the State recognises the support it receives by means of the work of women in the home).

[6] Art 8, European Convention on Human Rights.

[7] Kenna, *Housing Law and Policy in Ireland* (1st ed, 2006, Dublin, Clarus Press), p 344.

[8] Art 42.2, *Bunreacht na hÉireann.*

[9] paras 9–106 to 9–114.

[10] Art 41.2, *Bunreacht na hÉireann.*

[11] *The State (Nicolaou) v An Bord Uachtála* [1966] IR 567.

[12] Although Irish courts are not bound by ECtHR jurisprudence, they do take account of it in interpreting and applying Irish law pursuant to s 5, European Convention on Human Rights Act 2003. See further de Londras and Kelly, *The European Convention on Human Rights Act: Operation, Impact and Analysis* (2010, Dublin, Round Hall), Chapter 6.

[13] See Chapter 1, paras 1–09 to 1–12.

> interests of national security, public safety or the economic well-being of the country, for the prevention of disorder or crime, for the protection of health or morals, or for the protection of the rights and freedoms of others.

The European Court of Human Rights has given the concept of home a relatively broad definition and, rather than focus on the "form" of family (marriage, civil partnership etc) and the question of residence, the jurisprudence of the Court concerns itself more with the connections that people have to one another, the connections the applicants have to the place in question, and the function that the place performs in their lives.

[9–07] In *Gillow v United Kingdom*[14] the European Court of Human Rights had to consider whether a holiday home on the island of Guernsey, which the applicants had leased out for 19 years, could be considered a "home" in the context of Art 8. Taking all of the circumstances into account, the Court held that it did. The applicants had not established a home elsewhere in the UK and had retained a strong connection with the Guernsey property. This reflects the Court's commitment to what has become known as a "factual" test of "home", which was famously expressed in *Buckley v United Kingdom*[15]:

> Whether or not a particular habitation constitutes a "home" which attracts the protection of article 8(1) will depend on the factual circumstances, namely the existence of sufficient and continuous links.

In the context of the European Convention on Human Rights, then, matters such as the lawfulness of one's residence,[16] one's ownership status[17] and one's actual residence[18] in the property are not determinative of whether or not a property enjoys the title and protection of "home"; instead this is determined by the existence of sufficient and continuous links with the property. Under this definition, one might have multiple homes, or a place where one intends to reside may be defined as a home in spite of the lack of actual residence.

[9–08] As mentioned above, the function that a place performs can also be an important consideration in determining if any particular building is a home. This is well illustrated by *Niemietz v Germany*,[19] in which the European Court of Human Rights held that a lawyer's office could be considered a "home" under Art 8. Business functions are often conducted at home and home functions are often conducted in places of business, thus there is no reason under the European Convention on Human Rights why the concept of home cannot extend to business premises in circumstances that require Art 8 levels of protection from State interference in home-related activities carried out in a place of business.

---

[14] (1986) 11 EHRR 335.
[15] (1996) 23 EHRR 101.
[16] *Buckley v United Kingdom* (1996) 23 EHRR 101.
[17] *Khatun v United Kingdom* (1998) 26 EHRR CD 212.
[18] *Gillow v United Kingdom* (1986) 11 EHRR 335.
[19] (1992) 16 EHRR 97.

II. Conveyances of Family and Shared Homes

When it comes to conveyances of property, Irish law has in place some specific requirements for what are known as "family homes" and "shared homes". These arise under the Family Home Protection Act 1976 and the Civil Partnership and Certain Rights and Obligations of Cohabitants Act 2010 respectively. Both acts provide for a veto on conveyances of any interest in the family or shared home, with that veto being exercisable by non-owning spouses and civil partners. Before considering the operation of this "veto on conveyance" it is worth placing the first of these Acts—the Family Home Protection Act 1976—in a little context to explain how the veto came about. [9–09]

In essence, the Family Home Protection Act 1976 was introduced in recognition of the social and personal difficulties associated with families in which one spouse owned the family home and the other had no rights over it whatsoever. In such situations the non-owning spouse (and any children of the family) would be particularly vulnerable; the house could be sold against his/her wishes or mortgaged and then repossessed without his/her knowledge or consent. At the time that the 1976 Act was introduced it was entirely common for family homes to be in the ownership of only one spouse and for that spouse to be the husband. This placed married women in an economically disadvantaged position. These concerns were considered in depth by the Commission on the Status of Women, which recommended that, as one step in reducing discrimination against women, some level of protection regarding the family home would have to be introduced.[20] One of the proposals was to ensure that the primary residence of the family would be protected against secret conveyances, against malicious conduct and against repossession by landlords or mortgagees, wherever possible. All three of these issues came to fruition in the Family Home Protection Act 1976. Although this Act is gender-neutral inasmuch as it protects husbands and wives equally, its broader societal significance was primarily in its impact on married women, who were generally not working in paid employment and usually had no ownership rights in the family home through which they could protect themselves. As Margaret Fine-Davis has noted, the Family Home Protection Act 1976 was one of "a number of significant legislative and administrative changes… which [had] a profound significance for the role and status of women" in Ireland.[21] [9–10]

The limitation of the protections in the 1976 Act to married couples[22] was the subject of some criticism, including from this author,[23] and it was clear that as Irish law began to recognise more diverse family forms either the 1976 Act itself or something very [9–11]

[20] *Report of the Commission on the Status of Women* (1972, Dublin, The Stationery Office). For more on the role that this report, and the legal change introduced in light of it, played in creating a "new gender regime" in Ireland, see, for example, Connolly, "The Role of Ideas in the Construction of Gendered Policy Regimes: The Relationship between the National and the International" (2005), Working Paper in International Studies, Centre for International Studies, DCU.

[21] Fine-Davis, "Attitudes toward the Role of Women as Part of a Larger Belief System" (1989) 10(2) *Political Psychology* 287 at 288.

[22] See para 9–12.

[23] de Londras, *Principles of Irish Property Law* (1st ed, 2007, Dublin, Clarus Press), pp 235–238.

close to it in form would have to be extended to such families. At the time of introducing civil partnership for same-sex couples in 2010,[24] the government elected to create a parallel—and largely identical—system to protect the "shared home" rather than to extend the Family Home Protection Act 1976 to include the homes of civil partners. This parallel system is included in Part 4 of the Civil Partnership and Certain Rights and Obligations of Cohabitants Act 2010.

1. Definition of "Family Home" and "Shared Home"

[9–12] The Family Home Protection Act 1976 applies only to family homes, which are defined as follows in s 2(1) of that Act:

> In this Act "*family home*" means, primarily, a dwelling in which a married couple ordinarily reside. The expression comprises, in addition, a dwelling in which a spouse whose protection is in issue ordinarily resides or, if that spouse has left the other spouse, ordinarily resided before so leaving.

In this context, "married couple" means a couple that is married in a manner recognised by Irish law. We do not require the marriage to be functional or intimate; it merely needs to exist in law. Thus, in ***LB v HB***[25] it was held that the lack of intimate relations between the couple did not have any impact on the applicability of the Act. Similarly, in ***SOB v MOB***[26] the Act was applied to a couple that had acquired a church annulment and where the husband lived in Hong Kong and was now a party to a second church marriage. In this case, the first legal marriage continued to exist as a legal fact (divorce, remember, was not introduced in Ireland until 1996[27]) and the Act therefore applied.

[9–13] The definition of "shared home" is contained in s 27 of the Civil Partnership and Certain Rights and Obligations of Cohabitants Act 2010:

> "shared home" means—
> (a) subject to paragraph (b), a dwelling in which the civil partners ordinarily reside; and
> (b) in relation to a civil partner whose protection is in issue, the dwelling in which that civil partner ordinarily resides or, if he or she has left the other civil partner, in which he or she ordinarily resided before leaving.

Civil partners are those who have entered into a valid civil partnership under Irish law or who have entered into some form of same-sex union in another jurisdiction that is recognised as a civil partnership in Irish law.[28] Thus, a couple that has married in Spain (where same-sex marriage is possible) might be recognised as civil partners in Ireland but are not recognised as married. Therefore their home will be governed by the 2010

[24] Only same-sex couples can enter into a civil partnership and only opposite-sex couples can enter into a marriage. See generally Civil Registration Act 2004 as amended by Civil Partnership and Certain Rights and Obligations of Cohabitants Act 2010.
[25] [1980] ILRM 257.
[26] Unreported, High Court, December 1981.
[27] Family Law (Divorce) Act 1996.
[28] s 5, Civil Partnership and Certain Rights and Obligations of Cohabitants Act 2010.

Act, rather than the 1976 Act. Similar to the situation under the 1976 Act, it is safe to assume that we will not require the civil partnership in question to be functional in order for the Act to apply; as long as it exists as a valid civil partnership in law that ought to be sufficient.

Apart from one scheme governing the homes of married couples and the other governing the homes of civil partners, there is very little difference in definitional terms between family homes and shared homes. In both cases our focus is on the ordinary place of residence. On that basis holiday homes, for example, are certainly omitted from the definition of a shared home under s 27 of the 2010 Act. The wording of s 2(1) of the 1976 Act—referring to "*primarily*, the ordinary place of residence of a married couple" (emphasis added)—suggests that holiday homes might be included in its definition. However, the jurisprudence on this matter confirms that residence is a *sine qua non* of protection under the 1976 Act. It is clear from the case law that an intention to reside in a property will not be enough to bring it within the auspices of the Act. This was the conclusion of the Supreme Court in *National Irish Bank v Graham (No 2)*.[29] Although the Court appreciated that this might result in a serious gap in protection because it meant that a mortgage acquired over property in which the married couple intends to reside, but does not yet actually reside, can be acquired without the prior written consent of the non-owning spouse, it held that it was not the Court's role to "fill in the gaps". The legislation was entirely clear and to interpret it in order to cover properties in which married couples do not actually reside would constitute legislating, which is not the role of the judiciary. The family home must, therefore, be defined within the strict limitations of the Act's precise terms.[30] The same will be true of the concept of "shared home" under the 2010 Act. **[9–14]**

Importantly, both family homes and shared homes are defined by reference to *residence* and not to *ownership*. As a result, a property can be defined as a family or shared home notwithstanding the fact that it is owned by a company, for example.[31] This is particularly important given the fact that, were this not the case, one could easily avoid the Acts' provisions by registering the property in the ownership of a company rather than an individual.[32] **[9–15]**

Both the Family Home Protection Act 1976 and the Civil Partnership and Certain Rights and Obligations of Cohabitants Act 2010 are wide enough in scope to ensure that even if the owning spouse or civil partner has left the home, but the spouse or civil partner in need of protection still resides there, the protections of the relevant Act will be afforded to him/her. It is also wide enough in scope to ensure that a spouse or civil partner who has left the family or shared home for whatever reason (apart from desertion[33]), would still be in a position to acquire protection in relation to that home. **[9–16]**

[29] [1995] 2 IR 244; [1994] 2 ILRM 109.

[30] *CF v JDF* [2005] 4 IR 154 *per* McGuinness J at 166.

[31] *Walpoles (Ireland) Ltd v Jay*, unreported, High Court, 20 November 1980, McWilliam J.

[32] This concern was expressed by Blayney J in *BMC v PJC*, unreported, High Court, 12 May 1983. Of course, it should be noted that, as equity will not allow a statute to be used as a vehicle for fraud, such a registration could be overcome by a court if fraud were proved.

[33] s 4, Family Home Protection Act 1976, see further para 9–45.

This, of course, can be of great utility to a spouse or civil partner who has a left the family or shared home for reasons of abuse or necessity.

[9–17] The concept of "dwelling", which appears in both definitions, is potentially problematic. Under the 1976 Act, dwelling originally included "any building, or any structure, vehicle or vessel (whether mobile or not), or part thereof, occupied as a separate dwelling and includes any garden or portion of ground attached to and usually occupied with the dwelling or otherwise required for the amenity or convenience of the dwelling".[34] This definition was clearly broad enough to recognise that it was not only a house that could be a home; in a particularly important move from the perspective of members of the Travelling Community, it recognised that caravans can be homes. However, the original definition still left some room for uncertainty in relation to property ancillary and subsidiary to the family home. Would property of this nature that is used for commercial purposes, for example, be included in this definition? In order to clarify this matter, s 2 of the 1976 Act was amended by s 54 of the Family Law Act 1995:

> In subsection (1), "dwelling" means any building or part of a building occupied as a separate dwelling and includes any garden or other land usually occupied with the dwelling, being land that is subsidiary and ancillary to it, is required for amenity or convenience and is not being used or developed primarily for commercial purposes, and includes a structure that is not permanently attached to the ground and a vehicle, or vessel, whether mobile or not, occupied as a separate dwelling.

Section 27 of the Civil Partnership and Certain Rights and Obligations of Cohabitants Act 2010 defines "dwelling" in the same terms in the context of shared homes.[35]

[9–18] The family or shared home will sometimes constitute part of a larger landholding, such as a farm or business premises. In these cases, the courts allow for the property that is subject to the transaction to be severed into a part protected by the relevant Act (home) and the unprotected part ("not home"). This, if the land in total has been conveyed without the consent required by either s 3 of the Family Home Protection Act 1976 (for family homes) or s 28 of the Civil Partnership and Certain Rights and Obligations of Cohabitants Act 2010 (for shared homes), the land can be severed into a part subject to the Act and a part immune from the Act. In the absence of consent, the transaction would then be void in relation to the part considered by the court to be the family or shared home, but could stand in relation to the remainder of the property. Such severance will not take place, however, where the nature of the property makes it impracticable. Thus, in ***AIB v O'Neill***[36] the Court held that it could sever the family

---

[34] s 2(2), Family Home Protection Act 1976.

[35] s 27 provides: "'dwelling' means a building or part of a building occupied as a separate dwelling and includes—(*a*) a garden or other land usually occupied with the building that is subsidiary and ancillary to it, is required for amenity or convenience and is not being used or developed primarily for commercial purposes, (*b*) a structure that is not permanently attached to the ground, and (*c*) a vehicle or vessel, whether mobile or not, occupied as a separate dwelling."

[36] [1995] 2 IR 473 esp. at 481.

home from attached farmland property, whereas in *McMahon v O'Loughlin*[37] the Court recognised that it was far more difficult from a practical and planning perspective to sever a family home and adjoining filling station.

2. The Consent Requirement

Rather than absolutely bar the conveyance of any interest in family or shared homes, both the 1976 and 2010 Acts provide that a non-owning spouse or civil partner has a veto over proposed conveyances. This translates into the requirement to get the prior, written consent of the non-owning spouse or civil partner to a proposed conveyance. This is done by s 3 of the Family Home Protection Act 1976 and s 28 of the Civil Partnership and Certain Rights and Obligations of Cohabitants Act 2010. Section 3(1) of the 1976 Act provides: **[9–19]**

> Where a spouse, without the prior consent in writing of the other spouse, purports to convey any interest in the family home to any person except the other spouse... the purported conveyance shall be void.

In practically identical term, s 28(1) of the 2010 Act provides:

> Where a civil partner, without the prior consent in writing of the other civil partner, purports to convey an interest in the shared home to a person except the other civil partner... the purported conveyance is void.

Neither of these provisions confers any ownership on the non-owning spouse or civil partner; rather they confer a veto on proposed conveyances, which is intended to protect the spouse or civil partner. The repercussion of the failure to acquire the required consent is that the conveyance can be declared void by a court in proceedings instituted within six years of the conveyance *or* by a written statement to that effect from the purchasers and executed within six years.[38] This six-year limitation period does not apply in situations where the non-owning spouse has been in actual occupation of the relevant land from immediately before the expiration of the six years to the time of institution of the proceedings.[39] This exception to the limitation period is of particular relevance where the family or shared home has been mortgaged and, as is customary, the mortgaged property has remained in the possession of the mortgagor.[40] Thus, a transaction that does not comply with the consent requirement in s 3 of the 1976 Act or s 28 of the 2010 Act will be void, but can continue to operate until it is declared so.[41] As the voiding of the transaction voids the contract that underlined it, it is logical that the "purchaser" will not be entitled to specific **[9–20]**

[37] [2005] IEHC 196.

[38] s 3(8), Family Home Protection Act 1976; s 28(8), Civil Partnership and Certain Rights and Obligations of Cohabitants Act 2010.

[39] s 3(8), Family Home Protection Act 1976; s 28(9), Civil Partnership and Certain Rights and Obligations of Cohabitants Act 2010.

[40] For more on possession in mortgages, see further Chapter 13.

[41] The authorities suggest, somewhat unusually, that the burden of proof lies on the party claiming validity of the conveyance under the Family Home Protection Act 1976—Family Home Protection Act 1976, s 3(4); *Bank of Ireland v Smith* [1996] 1 IR 241; *McMahon v O'Loughlin* [2005] IEHC 196.

performance of the contract or to an action for damages. However, where monies have, in fact, already been advanced, the "purchaser" is entitled to recover those monies (including deposits) by an action for recovery of a debt or, where necessary, by a lien[42] over the family or shared home.[43]

[9–21] Consent is required from non-owning spouses and civil partners only. If one already owns an interest in the property in question his or her consent is, in any case, already essential to the conveyance. If the civil partners, for example, are joint tenants then one joint tenant cannot convey her interest in the property without the consent of the other civil partner under the rules of co-ownership[44] and, even if the other civil partner gives her consent, the transaction will not sell the consenting civil partner's ownership in the property.[45] If a married couple are tenants in common of their home and the husband wishes to sell, then he can either sell his share freely (which does not convey his wife's share) or they can sell the property jointly. Thus, in cases of co-ownership, there is no need for statutory intervention to protect either spouse or civil partner: his or her property right offers the protection that is needed. It would, therefore, be somewhat absurd for a party who has joined a conveyance to claim that the conveyance is invalid because he/she did not give prior consent in writing.[46]

[9–22] The consent requirement applies to the conveyance of any interest in a family or shared home. For family homes, this "includes a mortgage, lease, assent, transfer, disclaimer, release and any other disposition of property otherwise than by a will or a *donatio mortis causa* [simplistically defined as a "deathbed gift"[47]] and also includes an enforceable agreement (whether conditional or unconditional) to make any such conveyance".[48] For shared homes, conveyance "includes a mortgage, lease, assent, transfer, disclaimer, release, another disposition of property otherwise than by a will or a *donatio mortis causa*, and an enforceable agreement, whether conditional or unconditional, to make one of those conveyances".[49] "Interest" is taken to mean "any estate, right, title or other interest, legal or equitable" in the family or shared home.[50]

[9–23] **3. Consent**

In order to be valid under s 3 of the 1976 Act and s 28 of the 2010 Act, it is important that the consent provided by the non-owning spouse or civil partner would fulfil three conditions. It must be: (a) prior to the conveyance; (b) in writing; and (c) valid. There is

---

[42] A lien is a form of security granted over a piece of property to secure the performance of some obligation—usually the payment of a debt.

[43] *Re Barrett Apartments Ltd* [1985] IR 350.

[44] s 31, Land and Conveyancing Law Reform Act 2009. See further Chapter 8, paras 8–22 to 8–23.

[45] See further Chapter 8, paras 8–22 to 8–23.

[46] Precisely this point was made by Henchy J in the Supreme Court decision of *Nestor v Murphy* [1979] IR 326.

[47] These gifts are further discussed in Chapter 16.

[48] s 1, Family Home Protection Act 1976.

[49] s 28, Civil Partnership and Certain Rights and Obligations of Cohabitants Act 2010.

[50] s 1, Family Home Protection Act 1976; s 27, Civil Partnership and Certain Rights and Obligations of Cohabitants Act 2010.

not yet any jurisprudence on the operation of s 28 of the 2010 Act, but given its mirroring of the 1976 Act the jurisprudence under that Act will almost certainly be applied to s 28 as well.

(a) Be Prior to the Conveyance

Both the 1976 and 2010 Acts expressly require that the consent would be "prior". The question that naturally arises is what constitutes "prior" consent in this context. In essence what we are concerned with is ensuring that consent would be given prior to the completion of the conveyance, i.e. prior to the time when the interest is fully transferred to the purchasing party. Thus, if the shared or family home is registered land, the consent should be given prior to registration of the purchaser's title, and if the home is unregistered land, the consent should be given prior to the delivery of the deed.[51] Both the Family Home Protection Act 1976 and the Civil Partnership and Certain Rights and Obligations of Cohabitants Act 2010 make provision for a non-owning spouse to give a general consent to future conveyances, which constitutes prior consent for the purposes of both Acts.[52] [9–24]

[9–25] Although the 1976 Act clearly requires the consent to be provided prior to the conveyance, the courts appear to have adopted a quite relaxed attitude towards this requirement by the creation of abstract conceptions of time within conveyances. This is evident from the case of *Bank of Ireland v Hanrahan*.[53] In this case, the owning spouse of the family home, who was the husband, went to the Bank of Ireland with the intention of creating an equitable mortgage by deposit of title deeds over this property. Such a mortgage is created by the lodgement of title deeds with the mortgagee *with the intention* of doing so by means of security.[54] The bank informed Hanrahan that his wife's consent was required. He left the deeds with the bank and returned the next day with his wife, who gave her consent to the mortgage. The material question from the perspective of s 3 was whether or not the consent was given in time, i.e. prior to the conveyance. The Court held that it had been so provided because the bank could be said to have held the title deeds for safe-keeping while the husband went and informed his wife of the situation. Thus, the mortgage was not actually created until the wife had given her consent. There are a number of potential objections to this construction. The first is that even if there had been such an abstraction of time in the conveyance, the Court's construction would tend to suggest that the wife's consent was given *at the same time* as the conveyance was completed, even though s 3 clearly requires the consent to be *prior to* the conveyance. The second objection is that the courts' willingness to create such abstractions of time within a conveyance might encourage lackadaisical attitudes towards this element of the s 3 requirement and thereby implicitly sanction non-compliance with the Act. However, it ought to be noted that there is one strong argument in favour of the Court's interpretation of this course of events in *Hanrahan*. The mortgage by deposit of title deeds does not come into effect

[51] *AD v DD and Irish Nationwide Building Society*, unreported, High Court, 8 June 1983, McWilliam J. Registered and unregistered land are considered in Chapter 7.

[52] s 3(9), Family Home Protection Act 1976; s 28(14), Civil Partnership and Certain Rights and Obligations of Cohabitants Act 2010.

[53] Unreported, High Court, 10 February 1987.

[54] For more on mortgages by deposit of title deed see Chapter 13.

until both deposit *and* intention are present. It could be argued that the husband's intention to create the mortgage did not exist until his wife had given her consent and, as a result, that the conveyance was not actually completed until that point in time. This appears to have been the conceptual framework for the decision and, seen in this light, *Hanrahan* may be a less-censurable decision than is sometimes supposed.

[9–26] ***(b) Be in Writing***

Secondly, the consent of the non-owning spouse must be written; it cannot be merely orally provided. This appears to be a perfectly sensible requirement in light of the difficulties of proof that arise in relation to oral representations of any kind. Neither the 1976 Act nor the 2010 Act specifies the kind of writing that is required. We can therefore assume that no particular form is strictly required, although, as a matter of practice, almost all such consents are provided as part of the standard contract of sale issued by the Law Society.

[9–27] ***(c) Be Valid***

Thirdly, the consent must be valid. As an initial matter it should be noted that there had been some doubt as to whether someone who was married but not yet eighteen years old could validly consent under the Family Home Protection Act 1976.[55] This was fully resolved by s 10 of the Family Law Act 1981, which provided that spousal consent under s 3 of the 1976 Act would not be invalid "by reason only that the spouse was underage". This does not arise in relation to consent under the Civil Partnership and Certain Rights and Obligations of Cohabitants Act 2010 as there is no provision for persons under the age of 18 to enter into a civil partnership.[56] In essence, the "validity" requirement can be taken to mean that the consent must be (a) voluntary and (b) fully informed. Involuntary consent can never be said to be consent *per se*. Thus, any sufficiently proved allegation of duress or undue influence, for example, would be particularly relevant to an assessment of compliance with s 3 of the 1976 Act or s 28 of the 2010 Act. The consent should also be fully informed. Given the nature of the concept of "giving consent", this is a perfectly reasonable requirement. If consenting to something means approving something, then knowledge of what one is approving is a logical requirement.

[9–28] In Ireland the concept of informed consent in the context of family property—which is sure to be applied to shared homes under the 2010 Act—can largely be traced back to *Bank of Ireland v Smyth*.[57] In this case, the husband owned a farm and farmhouse that were registered land. Having approached the bank in relation to mortgaging this property, he was informed that his wife's consent would be required. His wife then attended the bank and had a meeting with a bank official, at which the concept of the conveyance and the requirement of consent were explained to her. Following this short meeting, Mrs Smyth signed the consent and the registered charge[58] was subsequently granted. Mrs Smyth later claimed that she had not understood that to which she was

[55] *Lloyd v Sullivan*, unreported, High Court, McWilliam J, 6 March 1981.

[56] s 2A(c), Civil Registration Act 2004 *as inserted by* s 7, Civil Partnership and Certain Rights and Obligations of Cohabitants Act 2010.

[57] [1995] 2 IR 459; [1996] 1 ILRM 241.

[58] On the operation of registered charges, see further Chapter 13.

consenting because she was under the impression that the family home could never be repossessed under this charge.

[9–29] The Court was satisfied that Mrs Smyth did not fully understand that to which she was consenting and that she did not believe that her family home could ever be repossessed as a result of this charge. That lack of understanding was enough to mean that her consent was not valid. For Blayney J, consent under s 3 "must be a fully informed consent. The spouse giving it must know what it is that he or she is consenting to. Since giving one's consent means that one is approving of something, obviously a precondition is that one should have knowledge of what it is that one is approving".[59] The mere fact that Mrs Smyth did not understand what she was consenting to and, as a result, that her consent was not valid under s 3, did not automatically mean that the conveyance would be struck out. Rather, that invalidity would only impact negatively on the purchaser (in this case the bank) if that purchaser had notice of the fact that the consent was invalid. This, of course, is entirely logical for, if notice did not have to be established, any plausible claim of incomprehension might result in mortgages over family and shared homes being struck out and unenforceable. It is to this notice element that we now turn.

4. Notice of Non-Compliance with s 3 of the 1976 Act or s 28 of the 2010 Act

[9–30] The purchaser will be detrimentally affected if it is determined that he had notice of the fact that the consent requirement was not satisfied. In other words, if it is established that either (a) consent was required but not acquired *and* the purchaser had notice of the fact that this was the case; or (b) the consent acquired was not valid *and* the purchaser had notice of this. This reflects the fact that a "purchaser for full value" is exempted from the consent requirement.[60] The meaning of "purchaser for full value" was considered primarily in the case of *Somers v Weir*,[61] where the Supreme Court made clear the role that notice plays here.

[9–31] *Somers v Weir* concerned a property held under a lease in which a married couple had resided until 1973, at which point the wife left the family home with her children. In 1976 the husband contracted to sell the leasehold on this property to Somers and, when asked for the wife's consent, claimed that she had not relied on the property for an appreciable period of time and could not be located. In a later sworn declaration, he stated that the property was not a family home and that, under the terms of a separation agreement between the parties, his wife had given up her statutory rights in relation to it. The separation agreement was never produced and did not include any such surrender of rights, but Somers' solicitor did not ask to see the separation agreement and completed the conveyance. Somers then attempted to sell the property in 1977. The prospective purchaser in the later transaction located Weir and asked for her retrospective consent to the original disposition in order to ensure that there would

[59] [1995] 2 IR 459 at 468.

[60] s 3(3)(a), Family Home Protection Act 1976; s 28(3)(a), Civil Partnership and Certain Rights and Obligations of Cohabitants Act 2010. On the "purchaser for full value" see further paras 9–41 and 9–42.

[61] [1979] IR 94.

be no difficulties in the future. Weir refused, and Somers applied to the High Court to have her consent dispensed with on the basis that the consent was being withheld unreasonably.[62] While the High Court acceded to this application, it was reversed on appeal to the Supreme Court. There were two issues: (1) could consent be dispensed with retrospectively?; and (2) could Somers be negatively impacted by the lack of consent to the original transaction given the vendor's representations? The first of these questions is considered below[63] and our focus, for the moment, is on the second.

[9–32] The Supreme Court held that the 1976 conveyance was invalid because Somers ought to have known that Mrs Weir's consent was required and had not been acquired. In other words, it was held that Somers had constructive notice of the lack of required consent. As Somers knew of the separation agreement that was alleged to remove the need for consent, this document ought to have been demanded and considered by Somers' solicitor. Because these enquiries ought to have been made, Somers was held to have knowledge of the truthful answers to them, including the fact that Mrs Weir's consent was required. The fact that Somers had notice of the fact that the required consent was not acquired resulted in the transaction being void under s 3.

[9–33] Notice also played an important role in *Bank of Ireland v Smyth*, the facts of which have already been considered.[64] As noted above, the Court held that Mrs Smyth's lack of understanding of that to which she was consenting invalidated her consent. The second element of the case was to consider the impact of the invalidity of the consent on the entire transaction. Bank of Ireland argued that it had no responsibility beyond the acquisition of consent itself. On the other hand, Smyth argued that the bank had a duty to ensure that spousal consent was valid and fully informed by, *inter alia*, recommending that she acquire independent legal advice. The Court concluded that the Bank of Ireland did not have any duty to advise Mrs Smyth to acquire independent legal advice, although it ought to have recommended it for the Bank's own sake. However, the mortgage was still invalidated by Mrs Smyth's lack of understanding and by the ensuing invalidity of her consent because the Bank ought to have made enquiries to ensure that her consent was fully informed. The Bank's failure to do so resulted in it being fixed with constructive notice of her lack of valid consent and, as a result, in the transaction being declared void by the Supreme Court.[65] It is important to make it clear that, from the perspective of s 3 of the Family Home Protection Act 1976, *Smyth* does not stand for the proposition that a bank is obliged to advise a non-owning spouse to get independent legal advice. That said, if independent legal advice *is* advised (and acquired) it will be much more difficult for the bank to be fixed with notice of any claimed lack of understanding (as the non-owning spouse will be informed) that would invalidate the transaction.

[62] On s 4, see further paras 9–44 to 9–648.

[63] para 9–44.

[64] paras 9–28 to 9–29.

[65] It should be noted that this is substantially different from a bank's duty of care towards spouses who are co-owners of their property and intend to mortgage it. The bank's duty of care in that relation was considered in full in *Bank of Nova Scotia v Hogan* [1996] 3 IR 239; [1997] 1 ILRM 407. This jurisprudence is of little relevance here because, by necessity, the parties concerned are not co-owners in law when s 3 consent is required (*Nestor v Murphy* [1979] IR 326).

Therefore, s 3(1) of the Family Home Protection Act 1976 requires that the non-owning spouse would give prior written consent to any conveyance of an interest in the family home. The failure to do so will result in the transaction being void, although the transaction will continue to operate until it is declared void. This will happen if the purchaser knew, or ought to have known, that either the required consent was not acquired at all or that the consent acquired was invalid. Given the parallelism between s 3 of the 1976 Act and s 28 of the Civil Partnership and Certain Rights and Obligations of Cohabitants Act 2010, we can relatively safely assume that provision will work in the same for shared homes was as s 3 does for family homes. [9–34]

5. The Usefulness and Effect of Statutory Declarations

It has now become common practice for vendors (i.e. sellers) to make a statutory declaration that the property in question either is or is not a family or shared home. This declaration has the logical purpose of simplifying the conveyancing process in relation to such property in order to ensure that enquiries relating to property's status in this respect are not unduly onerous. The difficulty, of course, is that a vendor could lie and declare the property not to be a family or shared home when, in fact, it is. Thus, the question of the extent to which the purchaser can rely on such declarations becomes germane. Again, jurisprudence on the Family Home Protection Act 1976 can be instructive here. [9–35]

Reynolds v Waters[66] concerned a conveyance in which the vendor had declared the property not to be a family home pursuant to standard enquiries in the course of the conveyancing process. This was accompanied by a statutory declaration stating that the vendor had been separated from his wife, who had deserted him prior to his taking up residence on the premises, and that the wife from whom he was separated had never resided on the premises (which was, therefore, not a family home within the meaning of the Act). The purchaser's solicitors refused to accept the statutory declaration and required either the consent of the vendor's wife to the proposed sale or, alternatively, a joint declaration from the vendor and his wife that the premises was not a family home and setting out the reasons for this. The vendor claimed that the purchaser was not entitled to such consent and ought to accept the declaration. He applied to the High Court for an order to this effect. The Court held that the purchaser ought to have accepted the vendor's declaration as to the status of the property in relation to the Act. In this case, there was nothing to suggest that further enquiries were required or that the vendor's declaration was unreliable. In this way the circumstances of this case could be distinguished from *Somers v Weir*[67] in which a separation agreement was referred to that ought to have been inspected by the purchaser. The effect of *Reynolds* is that purchasers are entitled to rely on statutory declarations that property is or is not a family or shared home within the meaning of the relevant act, but that where there is something to suggest unreliability or a reference to supporting documents further enquiries ought to be made. [9–36]

[66] [1982] ILRM 335.

[67] s 3, Family Home Protection Act 1976; s 27, Civil Partnership and Certain Rights and Obligations of Cohabitants Act 2010.

6. Exceptions to the Consent Requirement

[9–37] Section 3 of the 1976 Act and s 28 of the 2010 Act outline a number of situations in which no consent is required for an interest in the family or shared home to be conveyed.

(i) Conveyance by a Third Party

[9–38] The Family Home Protection Act 1976 and Civil Partnership and Certain Rights and Obligations of Cohabitants Act 2010 expressly require consent only where the conveyance is being carried out by the owning spouse or civil partner.[68] There are various circumstances in which a third party has the power to convey an interest in the family home and, in these cases, spousal consent is not required. This is perhaps most clearly seen in the context of judgment mortgages over the family home. The judgment mortgage is a debt-enforcement mechanism, whereby a debt that is owed is converted into a mortgage on the lands of the debtor in favour of the creditor. In such cases, the property might be sold in order to satisfy this debt. As a judgment mortgage is not a conveyance as defined under the 1976 and 2010 Acts, no consent is required.[69]

(ii) Conveyance Pursuant to a Contract Executed Prior to the Legislation Coming into Effect

[9–39] Contracts executed prior to when the Family Home Protection Act came into effect are not subject to the requirements of the Act. This was confirmed in *Hamilton v Hamilton & Dunne*,[70] in which the Court held that the introduction of the Act substantially changed the substance, not only the procedure, of the law of conveyancing. As a result, the Act could not have retroactive application. Given that the 2010 Act not only introduced a new scheme in relation to shared homes, but an entirely new type of legally recognised interpersonal relationship (the civil partnership) it is logical to assume the same logic would prevent any retrospective application of the 2010 Act (after all, there was no such thing as a "shared home" in legal terms until the commencement of that Act).

(iii) Conveyance Pursuant to a Contract Made Prior to Marriage or Civil Partnership

[9–40] Where a conveyance is carried out pursuant to an enforceable agreement completed before marriage, the Family Home Protection Act does not apply.[71] Equally, where a conveyance is carried out pursuant to an enforceable agreement completed before civil partnership, the Civil Partnership and Certain Rights and Obligations of Cohabitants Act does not apply.[72] This limitation applies because the contract would have been completed at a time when the property in question was not a family or shared home.

---

[68] s 3, Family Home Protection Act 1976; s 28(3)(b), Civil Partnership and Certain Rights and Obligations of Cohabitants Act 2010.

[69] See, for example, *Containercare (Ireland) Ltd v Wycherley* [1982] IR 143; for more on judgment mortgages see also Chapter 13.

[70] [1992] IR 466.

[71] s 3(2), Family Home Protection Act 1976.

[72] s 28(2), Civil Partnership and Certain Rights and Obligations of Cohabitants Act 2010.

(iv) Conveyance to a Purchaser for Full Value

Both the Family Home Protection Act 1976 and the Civil Partnership and Certain Rights and Obligations of Cohabitants Act 2010 provide that the consent requirement does not apply where the conveyance is done to a "purchaser for full value".[73] A purchaser, in this context, is defined as "a grantee, lessee, assignee, mortgagee, chargeant or other person who *in good faith* acquires an estate or interest in property" (emphasis added).[74] The purchaser must give full value for the property in order to avail of this exception to the consent requirement.[75] The material question here is what we mean by a purchaser "in good faith". According to the Supreme Court in *Somers v Weir*,[76] a good faith purchaser is a purchaser without notice of either the lack of consent or the lack of valid consent. As a result, and as considered above, notice of lack of required consent or notice of the invalidity of consent results in a violation of the consent requirement that can void the conveyance. **[9–41]**

In essence, this exception acts as a defence to a claim of invalidity for failure to acquire (valid) consent as required by the Family Home Protection Act 1976 and the Civil Partnership and Certain Rights and Obligations of Cohabitants Act 2010 respectively. When a claim is made that the required consent has not been obtained the burden of proof lies on the party claiming validity of the conveyance.[77] That can be done by showing that the consent was in fact required *or* that the purchaser was a good faith purchaser for full value and therefore exempted from the consent requirement. In the latter case the purchaser accepts that the required consent was not acquired or that the consent acquired was invalid *but* argues that the conveyance ought not to be invalidated on that basis because, as purchaser, he gave full value and did not have notice of the need or failure to satisfy the consent requirement. **[9–42]**

(v) Conveyance in Favour of the Other Spouse or Civil Partner

Both the Family Home Protection Act 1976 and the Civil Partnership and Certain Rights and Obligations of Cohabitants Act 2010 provide that no consent is required for a conveyance to a spouse or civil partner, as appropriate.[78] **[9–43]**

7. Dispensing with Consent

In order to avoid the creation of a situation in which spouses and civil partners can absolutely stymie the use of family and shared homes within a property market, both the Family Home Protection Act 1976 and Civil Partnership and Certain Rights and Obligations of Cohabitants Act 2010 allow for the consent requirement to be dispensed with or for the court to consent on behalf of the spouse or civil partner which, for the sake **[9–44]**

---

[73] s 3(3)(a), Family Home Protection Act 1976; s 28(3)(a), Civil Partnership and Certain Rights and Obligations of Cohabitants Act 2010.

[74] s 3(6), Family Home Protection Act 1976; s 28(6), Civil Partnership and Certain Rights and Obligations of Cohabitants Act 2010.

[75] s 3(3)(a), Family Home Protection Act 1976; s 28(3)(a), Civil Partnership and Certain Rights and Obligations of Cohabitants Act 2010.

[76] [1979] IR 94.

[77] s 3(4), Family Home Protection Act 1976; s 28(4), Civil Partnership and Certain Rights and Obligations of Cohabitants Act 2010.

[78] s 3(1), Family Home Protection Act 1976; s 28(1), Civil Partnership and Certain Rights and Obligations of Cohabitants Act 2010.

of convenience, we will fold into the idea of "dispensing with consent requirement" here.[79] As the consent required under both acts must be prior, an application to have that consent dispensed with must also take place prior to the conveyance.[80] An application to have consent dispensed with may be made by either the proposed purchaser or by the vendor.[81]

[9–45] There are limited situations in which an application for consent to be dispensed with might be granted:

(a) Where the non-owning spouse or civil partner cannot consent by reason of unsoundness of mind[82] *or* where the non-owning spouse cannot be located following reasonable inquiries[83];

(b) Where the non-owning spouse is guilty of desertion, including cases in which, through the unreasonableness of their behaviour, he or she has caused the owning spouse to leave the home and live elsewhere (i.e. constructive desertion).[84] Desertion is not expressly contained in the Civil Partnership and Certain Rights and Obligations of Cohabitants Act 2010 because it is a concept of marriage law, but in analogous situations the court's jurisdiction to dispense with consent where "the court is of the opinion that it would be reasonable to do so" would be invoked[85];

(c) Where the court considers that it would be reasonable to dispense with the consent requirement in the case of shared homes.[86]

[9–46] The concept of unreasonably withheld consent requires some elaboration here. Both the Family Home Protection Act 1976 and the Civil Partnership and Certain Rights and Obligations of Cohabitants Act 2010 indicate that an analysis of reasonableness must take account of (1) needs and resources,[87] and (2) the nature and suitability of alternative accommodation, if offered.[88] The two Acts are not identical in this respect, however. While the Family Home Protection Act 1976 requires the Court to take into account "the respective needs and resources of the spouses *and of the dependent children (if any) of the family*" (emphasis added),[89] the Civil Partnership and Certain Rights and Obligations of Cohabitants Act 2010 refers only to "the respective needs and resources of the civil partners".[90] This distinction is almost certainly a result of the

---

[79] s 4, Family Home Protection Act 1976; s 29, Civil Partnership and Certain Rights and Obligations of Cohabitants Act 2010.

[80] *Somers v Weir* [1979] IR 94.

[81] *Hamilton v Hamilton & Dunne* [1992] IR 466.

[82] s 4(4), Family Home Protection Act 1976; s 29(4), Civil Partnership and Certain Rights and Obligations of Cohabitants Act 2010.

[83] s 4(4), Family Home Protection Act 1976; s 29(3)(a), Civil Partnership and Certain Rights and Obligations of Cohabitants Act 2010.

[84] s 4(3), Family Home Protection Act 1976.

[85] s 29(3)(b), Civil Partnership and Certain Rights and Obligations of Cohabitants Act 2010.

[86] s 29(3)(b), *ibid.*

[87] s 4(2)(a), Family Home Protection Act 1976; s 29(2)(a), Civil Partnership and Certain Rights and Obligations of Cohabitants Act 2010.

[88] s 4(2)(b), Family Home Protection Act 1976; s 29(2)(b), Civil Partnership and Certain Rights and Obligations of Cohabitants Act 2010.

[89] s 4(2)(a), Family Home Protection Act 1976.

[90] s 29(2)(a), Civil Partnership and Certain Rights and Obligations of Cohabitants Act 2010.

fact that, as it stands, we do not have comprehensive provision in law to govern the relationship between children and both of their parents in same-sex families while we do in relation to opposite-sex marital families. In all likelihood, while a court considering an application under s 29 of the Civil Partnership and Certain Rights and Obligations of Cohabitants Act 2010 would in fact take the needs of any children into account (most likely folding them into a consideration of the needs and resources of the civil partner in question), the omission is noteworthy.

In relation to alternative accommodation the acts are in concert with one another, and both provide that where alternative accommodation has been offered the court ought to take into account "the suitability of that accommodation having regard to the respective degrees of security of tenure in the home and the alternative accommodation".[91] **[9–47]**

In addition to the express statutory guidance in this respect, jurisprudence on s 4 of the Family Home Protection Act 1976 makes it clear that the reasonableness of the refusal to consent must be assessed by reference to objective factors and within the context of all the relevant circumstances.[92] In *R v R*[93] a husband and wife who had not lived intimately for some time still cohabited, although the husband was in a relationship with another woman. The husband wished to purchase a property in which his lover could reside, and in order to finance this purchase he proposed to mortgage his family home in which he lived with his wife and children, and to use these mortgage monies to finance the purchase of the second house. When asked for her consent to this mortgage, as required under s 3 of the 1976 Act, his wife refused on the basis that he simply could not afford to run two houses and pay off this new mortgage. The husband claimed that his wife's refusal to give consent was unreasonable and sought an order dispensing with her consent. The Court, however, refused to hold in his favour, finding that his wife's decision was based on objective financial considerations that stood up to serious scrutiny and was, therefore, not unreasonable. In contrast stands the case of *SOB v MOB*.[94] In this case, a husband and wife remained married in law, although they had acquired a church annulment. The husband resided in Hong Kong, where he had entered into a second church marriage. Shortly afterwards he decided to move back to Ireland and proposed to his first wife (who was still his wife in law) that their family home ought to be sold and the proceeds used to purchase two new homes—one for his first wife and children, and one for he and his second wife to live in. His first wife refused her consent, however, and the husband applied to have her consent dispensed with. As her decision to refuse consent was not based on any objective considerations and because she was offered what the Court considered to be adequate alternative accommodation, her consent was dispensed with under s 4 of the 1976 Act. **[9–48]**

[91] s 4(2)(b), Family Home Protection Act 1976; s 29(2)(b), Civil Partnership and Certain Rights and Obligations of Cohabitants Act 2010.

[92] *Hamilton v Hamilton & Dunne* [1992] IR 466.

[93] Unreported, High Court, December 1978.

[94] Unreported, High Court, December 1981.

III. Misconduct by Spouses and Civil Partners

[9–49] Both the Family Home Protection Act 1976 and the Civil Partnership and Certain Rights and Obligations of Cohabitants Act 2010 make provision for spouses and civil partners to protect themselves from spousal/partner misconduct that is intended to result in, or actually has resulted in, the loss of the family or shared home.[95] Here there are two distinct situations governed by both Acts: (a) situations in which conduct may result in the loss of the home or in it being rendered unsuitable for habitation as a family or shared home,[96] and (b) situations in which residence in the family or shared home has been lost or the property has been rendered unsuitable for habitation as a family or shared home.[97] Both situations require consideration.

1. Protection against Future Intended Loss

[9–50] Section 5(1) of the Family Home Protection Act 1976 provides:

> Where it appears to the court, on the application of a spouse, that the other spouse is engaging in such conduct as may lead to the loss of any interest in the family home or may render it unsuitable for habitation as a family home with the intention of depriving the applicant spouse or a dependent child of the family of his residence in the family home, the court may make such order as it considers proper, directed to the other spouse or to any other person, for the protection of the family home in the interest of the applicant spouse or such child.

In a similar, but not identical, way s 30(1) of the Civil Partnership and Certain Rights and Obligations of Cohabitants Act 2010 provides:

> Where it appears to the court, on the application of a civil partner, that the other civil partner is engaging in conduct that might lead to the loss of any interest in the shared home or might render it unsuitable for habitation as a shared home, with the intention of depriving the applicant of his or her residence in the shared home, the court may make any order that it considers proper, directed to the other civil partner or to any other person, for the protection of the shared home in the interest of the applicant.

[9–51] The material difference between the two provisions is the reference to dependent children in s 5(1) of the 1976 Act and the omission of any reference whatsoever to children in s 30(1) of the 2010 Act. Thus, under s 5(1) the court can take into account the possibility of a child losing his or her residence in the family home and make an order in the interest of that child. This means that where one spouse, perhaps, does not live in the family home anymore, an application might still be made by him or her to protect the residence of a child residing there, whereas this is not contemplated at all in relation to civil partners. As in relation to the provisions for dispensing with consent,

[95] s 5, Family Home Protection Act 1976; s 30, Civil Partnership and Certain Rights and Obligations of Cohabitants Act 2010.
[96] s 5(1), Family Home Protection Act 1976; s 30(1), Civil Partnership and Certain Rights and Obligations of Cohabitants Act 2010.
[97] s 5(2), Family Home Protection Act 1976; s 30(2), Civil Partnership and Certain Rights and Obligations of Cohabitants Act 2010.

considered above,[98] the fact that children are not at all referred to in this respect in the Civil Partnership and Certain Rights and Obligations of Cohabitants Act 2010 reflects the lack of a statutory framework to govern the relationships between children and both parents within same-sex led families. The omission of children from this section is lamentable, particularly since there are many cases of same-sex led families with children whose interests ought to be taken into as much account as are the interests of children whose parents are married.

Both s 5(1) of the 1976 Act and s 30(1) of the 2010 Act are concerned with situations of possible future harm. The somewhat speculative nature of protecting against harm that has not yet accrued is counterbalanced in both provisions by the reference to intention. It is quite clear that s 5(1) or s 30(1) order will only be granted where the conduct complained of is done "with the intention of depriving the applicant spouse or a dependent child of the family of his residence in the family home" (under the 1976 Act) or "with the intention of depriving the applicant of his or her residence in the shared home" (under the 2010 Act). **[9–52]**

Based on the jurisprudence of s 5(1), we can conclude that a successful application under either provision will require an applicant to establish a relatively high level of proof that the conduct is not only likely to result in the predicted loss[99] but is actually intended to result in such an eventuality.[100] The intention requirement has been strictly applied, sometimes in a way that causes real difficulties. In *P v P*[101] the owning spouse had substantial debts and had deposited the title deeds of the family home with a bank in order to secure an overdraft. The non-owning spouse claimed that this conduct was such as could lead to the loss of the family home, with the intention of depriving herself and her dependent children of their residence therein. The Court refused the application for a s 5(1) order, holding that the concept of "intention" ought to be construed strictly. This meant that motive could not be said to be determinative of intention, although intention could be imputed to any person as to the natural and probable consequences of his or her conduct *provided* there was an element of deliberate conduct involved. The difficulties of proving this deliberate conduct to the satisfaction of the Court in s 5(1) proceedings is evident in a number of unsuccessful applications under this section.[102] That said, there have been also been some successful cases under this provision, particularly where the court has refused to apply the narrow approach from *P v P* to too great an extent. **[9–53]**

The decision of Barron J in *O'N v O'N*[103] serves as a useful example. In this case, a husband was applying for the transfer to him of his wife's interest in the family home under s 5(1). The application was based on the fact that she had run up debts, which had culminated in a judgment mortgage being placed on her interest in the family home. The husband claimed this was conduct intended to deprive him and their children of the family home. Having considered a number of cases outlining the narrow **[9–54]**

---

98 paras 9–44 to 9–48.
99 On the importance of probability, see *P v P* [1983] ILRM 380 *per* Finlay P at 384.
100 See, for example, *S v S* [1983] ILRM 387.
101 [1983] ILRM 380.
102 See, for example, *DC v AC* [1981] ILRM 357; *S v S* [1983] ILRM 387.
103 Unreported, High Court, 6 October 1989, Barron J.

approach to intention under s 5(1), Barron J noted that it did not seem as if the wife's conduct had the element of deliberate intention that this approach appeared to require for s 5(1) relief to be granted. However, he held that this was not a barrier to relieving the husband under this provision; her financial situation (which was quite dire) was likely to lead her to have to borrow more money in the future, which she would, in all likelihood, be unable to pay back. According to his reasoning, the case came within the auspices of s 5(1). Barron J held:

> I do not think that the claimant spouse must wait until there is a *fait accompli*. If he or she has to, then much of the remedy provided by the subsection would be lost.[104]

[9–55] Although Barron J appears to reject the narrow approach to intention in this case, the jurisprudence on s 5(1) in which applicants have successfully acquired relief under the provision does not tend to support a conclusion that the narrow approach no longer applies. Rather, this case law lays bare a lack of consistency in the courts' approach to such cases. This *ad hoc* approach has the tendency to undermine the potentially significant protective properties of s 5(1) under the 1976 Act and, if it is similarly applied, s 30(1) of the Civil Partnership and Certain Rights and Obligations of Cohabitants Act 2010 for the simple reason that succeeding in such an application must inevitably be perceived as an unlikely eventuality and, as a result, practitioners will be somewhat reluctant to advise their clients to claim under this section alone. Thus, while such applications may form a part of a larger claim, it seems unlikely that the jurisprudence on s 5(1) is stable enough for a practitioner to be able to confidently advise a client as to its potential usefulness in an apposite case and it is likely that the same situation will be found in relation to s 30(1) of the 2010 Act.

2. Remedy for Actual Loss

[9–56] Section 5(2) of the Family Home Protection Act 1976 provides:

> Where it appears to the court, on the application of a spouse, that the other spouse has deprived the applicant spouse or a dependent child of the family of his residence in the family home by conduct that resulted in the loss of any interest therein or rendered it unsuitable for habitation as a family home, the court may order the other spouse or any other person to pay to the applicant spouse such amount as the court considers proper to compensate the applicant spouse and any such child for their loss or make such other order directed to the other spouse or to any other person as may appear to the court to be just and equitable.

In similar, but once more not identical, terms s 30(2) of the Civil Partnership and Certain Rights and Obligations Act 2010 provides:

> Where it appears to the court, on the application of a civil partner, that the other civil partner has deprived the applicant of his or her residence in the shared home by conduct that resulted in the loss of any interest in it or rendered it unsuitable for habitation as a shared home, the court may order the other civil partner or any other person to pay to the applicant the amount that the court considers proper to compensate the applicant for

[104] *ibid.* at 5.

> their loss or make any other order directed to the other civil partner or to any other person that may appear to the court to be just and equitable.

As with protection against future intended loss, considered above,[105] the primary substantive difference between the two provisions is the absence, in the 2010 Act, of any reference to dependent children.

Protection against actual loss does not require any proof that the conduct of the spouse or civil partner was intended to bring this loss about and, in that respect, is clearly distinguishable from s 5(1) of the 1976 Act and s 30(1) of the 2010 Act. Rather, because the residence in the family or shared home has actually been lost or the home has actually been rendered uninhabitable, the loss is actual and it is for this actual loss than compensation is granted. [9–57]

IV. Protection against Dispossession of Family and Shared Homes

Subject to the requirement that the non-owning spouse would first consent to it, a mortgage can be created over both family and shared homes. As will be considered in full in Chapter 13, mortgages result *inter alia* in a right of the mortgagee (the lender) to take possession of the mortgaged property in order to enforce the security (i.e. to satisfy or part satisfy the debt). While mortgagees must now get a court order to take possession of property under s 97 of the Land and Conveyancing Law Reform Act 2009, this was not always the case. Rather, it was traditionally thought that mortgagees had a *right* to take possession, particularly if the mortgage was what we call a "legal mortgage over unregistered land".[106] It is not necessary, at this point, to go through the technicalities of the law of mortgages, but this ought to be sufficient to illustrate the point that—prior to the commencement of the Family Home Protection Act 1976—a mortgagee could take possession of a family home as if it were any other kind of property. Section 7 of the Family Home Protection Act 1976 was introduced to create an extra, primarily procedural, lawyer of protection against possession of the family home on foot of mortgages. The same protection applies also in the cases of landlords who wish to take possession of leasehold property that is a family home. Section 7(1) provides: [9–58]

> Where a mortgagee or lessor of the family home brings an action against a spouse in which he claims possession or sale of the home by virtue of the mortgage or lease in relation to the non-payment by that spouse of sums due thereunder, and it appears to the court—
>
> (a) that the other spouse is capable of paying to the mortgagee or lessor the arrears (other than arrears of principal or interest or rent that do not constitute part of the periodical payments due under the mortgage or lease) of money due under the mortgage or lease within a reasonable time, and future periodical payments falling due under the mortgage or lease, and that the other spouse desires to pay such arrears and periodical payments; and

---

105 para 9–51.

106 The law of mortgages, including the history and current operation of the right to take possession, receives comprehensive consideration in Chapter 13.

> (b) that it would in all the circumstances, having regard to the terms of the mortgage or lease, the interests of the mortgagee or lessor and the respective interests of the spouses, be just and equitable to do so,
>
> the court may adjourn the proceedings for such period and on such terms as appear to the court to be just and equitable.

[9–59] The court also takes account of how long the spouse was aware of the non-payments that were the basis of the desired possession.[107] If the court adjourns possession under s 7 it can do so subject to conditions, which usually include a condition that the spouse would make at least some payments. In the case of a mortgage, those payments would be what we call "direct contributions" to the purchase of the property and entitle the spouse to a share of ownership in equity through a presumed resulting trust, which trusts are considered below.[108]

[9–60] Although, as already noted, a court order is now required for repossession under a mortgage this was not always the case and s 7 proved itself to be a very useful tool for "buying time", because it was interpreted as requiring a court-based process prior to repossession of a family home. This emerged in the judgment of Blayney J in *McCormack v Irish Civil Service Building Society.*[109] In this case, the express terms of the mortgage over the family home allowed for the mortgagee to take possession of the property without consulting with the mortgagor. As a result, the mortgagee took possession of the property following a default on the mortgage payments. The mortgagor and his wife applied for possession to be restored under s 7 of the Family Home Protection Act and, in acceding to their application, Blayney J held that the Act required mortgagees to take proceedings before retaking possession in order to allow for a s 7 analysis to be carried out. This was so even where the express terms of the mortgage allowed for possession without any such proceedings (as was the case here), as to do otherwise would be to undermine the protective objectives of the Family Home Protection Act 1976.

[9–61] Section 32 of the Civil Partnership and Certain Rights and Obligations of Cohabitants Act 2010 introduces the same kind of protective system in relation to attempts to take possession of shared homes under the terms of a mortgage or of a lease. In the case of postponement of possession under both s 7 of the 1976 Act and s 32 of the 2010 Act, a spouse or civil partner can apply for terms in the mortgage or lease that impose charges *other than periodical payments* to be deemed of no effect if, following a postponement, all periodical payments and arrears have been paid and the court is satisfied that all future periodical payments will continue to be paid.[110]

V. Division of Property on Breakdown of a Marriage

[9–62] Irish law no longer considers marriage to be a perpetual state of affairs: rather, marriages can be terminated by divorce under the Family Law (Divorce) Act 1996. When that happens or when, indeed, a separation occurs under the Family Law Act

---

[107] s 7(2), Family Home Protection Act 1976.

[108] 9–93 to 9–114.

[109] *Irish Times Law Reports*, 17 April 1989 (Hearing date: 6 February 1989) *ex tempore.*

[110] s 8, Family Home Protection Act 1976; s 33, Civil Partnership and Certain Rights and Obligations of Cohabitants Act 2010.

1995, the assets of the married couple are distributed between them. From the perspective of property law, the concern is with what orders courts can make in relation to property and what considerations are taken into account in deciding how these assets ought to be distributed. In the case of both separation and divorce, courts can grant a number of property-related orders. Under the Family Law Act 1995, a court may grant a property adjustment order,[111] a right to occupy[112] and an order for sale[113] in the course of a judicial separation. Under the Family Law (Divorce) Act 1996, decrees of divorce can be accompanied by property adjustment orders,[114] rights to occupy[115] and orders for sale of the family home.[116] In addition to these specific orders, s 36(1) of the Family Law Act 1995 provides that "Either spouse may apply to the court in a summary manner to determine any question arising between them as to the title to or possession of any property".

A property adjustment order can take a number of forms. A court may require a spouse to transfer ownership of property to his/her spouse or to a dependent family member. While the term "property" is clearly broader than just the family home, and can include any property in which a spouse has some connection,[117] the home is the asset that is most likely to be made the subject of a property adjustment order. This type of property adjustment order can be particularly useful in cases where a spouse's conduct endangers the family home, but where intention cannot be proved under s 5(1) of the Family Home Protection Act. This is the context in which a property adjustment order was granted as part of separation proceedings in *AS v GS and Allied Irish Bank*.[118] **[9–63]**

Rights to occupy[119] are generally provided on a welfare basis, i.e. where cohabitation is no longer possible between the parties, but the welfare of either spouse or dependent children dictates that a spouse and, where applicable, children ought to remain resident in the family home.[120] Such orders will frequently be expressed to last for as long as the children remain in full-time education, at which stage the property might then be sold and the proceeds divided between the spouses. **[9–64]**

Orders for sale will normally be provided where both spouses have some interest in the property. They allow for the property to be sold and the proceeds of the sale to be divided between the spouses and any other party, or parties, who may have an interest in it. **[9–65]**

---

111 s 9, Family Law Act 1995.

112 s 10, *ibid.*

113 *ibid.*

114 s 14(1), Family Law (Divorce) Act 1996.

115 s 15(1)(a), *ibid.*

116 s 15(1)(a), *ibid.*

117 On the "connection" requirement, see in particular *C(C) v C(J)* [1994] 1 Fam. LJ 22 *per* Barr J.

118 [1994] 1 IR 407.

119 Frank Martin has noted that it is through orders of this nature "that family law responds to marital breakdown in terms of these protective, adjustive and supportive functions", which are carried out by family law in conjunction with its protective function and asset-distribution function. Martin, "Judicial Discretion in Family Law" (1998) 16 ILT 168.

120 See, for example, *CO'R v MO'R*, unreported, High Court, 19 September 2000.

Factors Relevant to the Division of Property

[9–66] The primary objective of a court in providing for the division of property upon the breakdown of a marriage is to ensure "proper provision" between the parties. This concern is rooted in the text of Art 41.3.2 of *Bunreacht na hÉireann*, which allows a court to dissolve a marriage by divorce provided the court is satisfied that "such proper provision as the court considers proper having regard to the circumstances exists or will be made for the spouse, any children of either or both of them and any other persons prescribed by law". This constitutional duty is given statutory expression in s 16 of the Family Law Act 1995 (obliging courts to "endeavour to ensure" proper provision) and in s 20 of the Family Law (Divorce) Act 1996 (obliging courts to ensure that proper provision is made). The duty to ensure proper provision means that the Irish courts are less likely to engage in property provision according to the schema identified by Lord Denning in *Hanlon v Law Society*,[121] and more likely to engage in a more structured and systematic process. In *Hanlon* Lord Denning held:

> The court takes the rights and obligations of the parties all together and puts the pieces into a mixed bag... The court then takes out the pieces and hands them to the two parties—some to one party and some to the other—so that each can provide for the future with the pieces allotted to him or to her... the court hands them out without paying too nice a regard to their legal and equitable rights but simply according to what is the fairest provision for the future, for mother and father and the children.

[9–67] In contrast, the Irish courts take the following factors into account when deciding on the property-related orders to make on the occasion of separation or divorce[122]:

(i) The terms of a separation agreement between the parties are to be taken into account by the court, but are not determinative and can be set aside where this is considered appropriate.[123]

(ii) The income, earning capacity, property and resources available to the spouses now and likely to be available to them in the foreseeable future are also taken into account. In this context the parties' resources include both earned and unearned wealth (such as inheritance) and assets are valued as of the time of the divorce or separation and not as of the time of marriage breakdown.[124] The spouses are required to make a full disclosure of their assets by means of a sworn affidavit before the High Court.

(iii) The financial needs, obligations and responsibilities of the spouses now and likely in the foreseeable future are taken into account. In this relation the court will take into account overheads and capital expenses in addition to everyday cost-of-living considerations. In addition, a court will take into account a second family that the spouse may have because obligations towards a second

[121] [1980] 1 All ER 763 at 770.

[122] These considerations are drawn from s 15 of the Family Law Act 1995 and s 20 of the Family Law (Divorce) Act 1996.

[123] s 14, Family Law (Divorce) Act 1996; *F v F* [1995] 2 IR 354; *PO'D v AO'D* [1998] 2 IR 225.

[124] *T v T* [2003] 1 ILRM 321.

family reduce the resources available for one's first family. Should a person have insufficient resources to fully support both families, however, the needs of the first family will be given priority.

(iv) The standard of living *ante* will be taken into account by the court, which will attempt to achieve some degree of equivalence in standards of living to ensure that the breakdown of the marriage has the least possible detrimental effect on one's everyday life (particularly where there are children of the marriage). The court will attempt to ensure equivalent standards of living between both spouses, where possible.[125]

(v) The age of each spouse and duration of the couple's cohabitation is a relevant consideration in terms of one's earning potential. This is particularly relevant in the case of long-term marriages for the simple reason that the longer people are together, the more likely they are to have sacrificed some or all of their career ambitions or made lifestyle changes for the sake of their relationship and family. Thus, a marriage that lasted 50 years is likely to have had a more profound effect on the careers of one or both spouses than a marriage that lasted six months.[126] This consideration is amplified by the court's further consideration of the impact of the marriage on each spouse's earning potential—particularly where one spouse has been a stay-at-home parent.[127]

(vi) Any physical or mental disabilities of the spouses will be taken into account in an assessment of their financial and other needs.

(vii) Contributions made, or likely to be made, to the welfare of the family are also considered by the court. These contributions are not merely financial, but include the contribution of a spouse who carries out the role of primary caregiver (usually by working only in the home). In this respect, the Irish courts give what McGuinness J has described as "full credit"[128] to a wife's work in the home, parenting duties and support of her husband's career.[129]

(viii) Any social welfare entitlements of each spouse will be taken into account in the course of ensuring that what is arrived at is an accurate picture of each party's resources and financial needs. The court will consider not only the social welfare benefits to which a spouse is entitled but also any social welfare benefits that might be lost as a result of the breakdown of the marriage.

(ix) The court will further consider the conduct of each spouse where that conduct is such that the court considers it would be unfair to disregard it. In general, adulterous behaviour[130] and financial misconduct would be taken into account, although these will not always be seen as relevant to the issues at hand.[131]

(x) The realistic accommodation needs of each spouse are taken into account by the court, particularly given the almost inevitable situation of the need to

[125] *GH v EH*, unreported, High Court, 9 February 1998; *RH v NH* [1986] ILRM 352.
[126] See, for example , *T v T* [2003] 1 ILRM 321.
[127] See, for example, *JD v DD* [1997] 3 IR 64.
[128] *K (M) v P (J) (Orse K (S))* [2001] IESC 87; *Cf. JD v DD* [1997] 3 IR 64.
[129] *T v T* [2003] 1 ILRM 321.
[130] *T v T* [2003] 1 ILRM 321.
[131] *JD v DD* [1997] 3 IR 64.

establish and run two households following the breakdown of marriage. If there are children of the marriage, then the parent who has primary custody will be likely to be provided with more ample accommodations, which are likely to be the "family home"[132] (unless the family home is the only asset and must be sold).[133]

(xi) Finally, the court will take into account the rights of relevant third parties, such as new partners or spouses, children of non-marital relationships and so on. As mentioned above, where there are insufficient resources to fully support both the family and the third parties, then the first family will be given preference.[134]

[9–68] In order to achieve the proper provision, as considered above and required by legislation and the Constitution, the courts will take all of these factors into account and explain their relative weightings in the decision-making process.[135] The basic concept of proper provision, however, appears to be for the court to ensure that a "fair" or a "just" decision is made.[136]

VI. Division of Property on the Dissolution of a Civil Partnership

[9–69] As civil partnership is not constitutionally protected in the way that marriage is, there appears at first glance to be the potential for a less prescribed approach to the division of property on the dissolution of a civil partnership. However, before considering the division of property on dissolution it is appropriate to deal briefly with the matter of nullity and the implications thereof for the property of the parties to a civil partnership that is subsequently nullified.

1. Nullity of Civil Partnerships

[9–70] Civil partnerships can be nullified under s 107 of the Civil Partnership and Certain Rights and Obligations of Cohabitants Act 2010 where a court is satisfied that, at the time the civil partnership was entered to, one or both partners did not have the required capacity,[137] the formalities for civil partnership were not adhered to,[138] one or both partners did not give free and informed consent to the civil partnership,[139] the partners were in prohibited degrees of relationship to one another,[140] or the partners were "not of the same sex".[141] Where a civil partnership is nullified it is deemed to have

[132] See, for example, *Clutton v Clutton* [1991] 1 All ER 340.

[133] *LC v AC* [1994] 1 Fam. LJ 19.

[134] *JCN v RTN*, unreported, High Court, 15 January 1999.

[135] *K (M) v P (J) (Orse K (S))* [2001] IESC 87.

[136] See esp. *T v T* [2003] 1 ILRM 321; Buckley, "'Proper Provision' and 'Property Division': Partnership in Irish Matrimonial Property Law in the Wake of *T v T*" (2004) 7(3) IJFL 8.

[137] s 107(a), Civil Partnership and Certain Rights and Obligations of Cohabitants Act 2010.

[138] s 107(b), *ibid.*

[139] s 107(c), *ibid.*

[140] s 107(d), *ibid.*

[141] s 107(e), *ibid.* The operation of this provision may well be affected by the introduction of gender recognition legislation in the future. Such legislation would follow the finding in *Foy v an t-Ard Chláraitheoir* [2007] IEHC 470 that the inability to have one's documents changed to reflect a reassigned gender is incompatible with the European Convention on Human Rights under s 5 of the European Convention on Human Rights Act 2003.

never existed, and there are no express provisions for property adjustment orders between those whose civil partnership is nullified.[142] That said, s 108(2) provides, "The rights of a person who relied on the existence of a civil partnership which is subsequently the subject of a decree of nullity are not prejudiced by that decree". What that provision means in relation to property is not at all clear.

There is also a further, general, provision that might be relevant in a case of nullity and which is contained in s 106(1) of the Civil Partnership and Certain Rights and Obligations of Cohabitants Act 2010. This provides that "Either civil partner may apply to the court in a summary manner to determine a question arising between them as to the title to or possession of property." The difficulty in the context of nullity is that, pursuant to s 108(1), a decree of nullity means that there never was a civil partnership and, as a result, that the parties never were civil partners. That suggests, at least, that s 106 will not be useful once a decree of nullity has been granted. It may, however, be possible for someone to make a s 106(1) application, get an order as to title or possession, then have their civil partnership nullified under s 105, and *then* rely on s 108(2) to ensure that the rights acquired through the s 106(1) application are not prejudiced by the decree of nullity. **[9–71]**

2. Dissolution of Civil Partnerships

Even though civil partnerships are not touched by Art 41.3.2 of *Bunreacht na hÉireann*, the 2010 Act does refer to "proper provision" in respect of the dissolution of a civil partnership. Section 110 provides that dissolution may be granted where the court is satisfied that, *inter alia*, "provision that the court considers proper having regard to the circumstances exists or will be made for the civil partners".[143] Upon the dissolution of a civil partnership a number of orders can be made, only some of which are relevant to property law: property adjustment orders under s 118, miscellaneous ancillary orders under s 119, and orders for sale under s 128. **[9–72]**

A s 118 property adjustment order can allow for the transfer of property to the other civil partner,[144] the settlement of property in favour of the other civil partner,[145] an order varying a settlement made by and for the civil partners (including a settlement in a will or codicil),[146] and an order extinguishing or reducing the interest of a civil partner in a settlement.[147] A civil partner who marries or enters another civil partnership after dissolution cannot acquire a property adjustment order under s 118[148] and no property adjustment order can be granted in relation to a "a shared or family home in which, following the grant of a decree of dissolution, either of the civil partners resides with a new civil partner or spouse".[149] **[9–73]**

142 s 108(1), Civil Partnership and Certain Rights and Obligations of Cohabitants Act 2010.

143 s 110(b), *ibid.*

144 s 118(1)(a), *ibid.*

145 s 118(1)(b), *ibid.*

146 s 118(1)(c), *ibid.*

147 s 118(1)(d), *ibid.*

148 s 118(3), *ibid.*

149 s 118(9), *ibid.*

[9–74] Miscellaneous ancillary orders under s 119 can be applied for after the dissolution at any point during a former civil partner's life. Available miscellaneous ancillary orders include an order for the exclusive occupation of the shared home for life or for some other specified time,[150] an order for the sale of the shared home and disposition of proceeds of sale,[151] an order to protect the civil partner from future intended loss of the shared home under s 30(1),[152] an order for compensation for the loss of the shared home under s 30(2),[153] an order to postpone repossession of the shared home by a mortgagee or lessor under s 33,[154] an order determining title or possession of property under s 106,[155] and an order for partition of property.[156] If granting an order for exclusive possession or sale under s 119, the court is directed to have regard to the impossibility of cohabitation and the need, where practicable, for proper and secure accommodation to be provided for a civil partner who is wholly or mainly dependent on the other partner.[157]

[9–75] An order for sale under s 128 can made if the property in question is property in which either of both civil partners has a beneficial interest, including an interest in the proceeds of sale thereof *and* a preceding order for secured periodical payments,[158] lump sum payment,[159] or property adjustment[160] has already been made.[161] An order for sale under s 128 cannot interfere with a right to exclusive occupation that has been granted by a miscellaneous ancillary order[162] and can specify the manner of sale and division of proceeds.[163] Anyone apart from the civil partners who has a beneficial interest in the property or proceeds of sale is to be given an opportunity to make representations if a s 128 order is sought[164] and the court must take account of these representations in deciding on whether and, if so, on what terms, to make the order sought.[165] No order for sale under s 128 can be acquired in relation to a "a shared or family home in which, following the grant of a decree of dissolution, either of the civil partners resides with a new civil partner or spouse".[166]

[9–76] As mentioned above, the Civil Partnership and Certain Rights and Obligations of Cohabitants Act 2010 concerns itself to at least some extent with the making of proper provision between the civil partners. To this end, s 129 provides for a range of matters that a court must have regard to when making specified orders, including property

150 s 119(1)(a), *ibid.*
151 s 119(1)(b), *ibid.*
152 s 119(1)(c), *ibid.*
153 *ibid.*
154 *ibid.*
155 *ibid.*
156 s 119(1)(e), Civil Partnership and Certain Rights and Obligations of Cohabitants Act 2010.
157 s 119(2), *ibid.*
158 s 117, *ibid.*
159 *ibid.*
160 s 118, Civil Partnership and Certain Rights and Obligations of Cohabitants Act 2010.
161 s 128(1), *ibid.*
162 s 128(2), *ibid.*
163 s 128(3), *ibid.*
164 s 128(5), *ibid.*
165 s 128(6), *ibid.*
166 s 128(7), *ibid.*

adjustment orders and miscellaneous ancillary orders for exclusive occupation and sale.[167] Thus, when deciding whether to make an order and, if so, what the provisions of the order should be, s 129(2) requires courts to take the following matters into account:

(1) The income, earning capacity, property and other financial resources that each of the civil partners has or is likely to have in the foreseeable future[168];
(2) The financial needs, obligations and responsibilities that each of the civil partners has or is likely to have in the foreseeable future, whether in the case of the registration of a new civil partnership or marriage or otherwise[169];
(3) The standard of living *ante*[170];
(4) The age of the civil partners, the duration of their civil partnership and the length of time during which the civil partners lived with each other after registration of their civil partnership[171];
(5) Any physical or mental disability of either of the civil partners[172];
(6) The contributions that each of the civil partners made or is likely to make in the foreseeable future to the welfare of the civil partners, including but not limited to contributions to the income, earning capacity, property and resources of the other civil partner *and* "looking after the shared home"[173];
(7) The effect on the earning capacity of each of the civil partners of the civil partnership responsibilities assumed by each during the period when they lived with one another after the registration of their civil partnership, and the degree to which the future earning capacity of a civil partner is impaired by reason of that civil partner having relinquished or foregone the opportunity of remunerative activity in order to look after the shared home[174];
(8) Any income or benefits to which either of the civil partners is entitled by or under statute[175];
(9) The conduct of each of the civil partners, if that conduct is such that, in the opinion of the court, it would in all the circumstances be unjust to disregard[176];
(10) The accommodation needs of both of the civil partners[177];
(11) The value to each of the civil partners of any benefit (for example, a benefit under a pension scheme) which, by reason of the decree of dissolution, a civil partner will forfeit the opportunity or possibility of acquiring[178];
(12) The rights of any person other than the civil partners but including a person with whom either civil partner is registered in a new civil partnership or to

---

167 s 129(1), *ibid.*
168 s 129(2)(a), *ibid.*
169 s 129(2)(b), *ibid.*
170 s 129(2)(c), *ibid.*
171 s 129(2)(d), *ibid.*
172 s 129(2)(e), *ibid.*
173 s 129(2)(f), *ibid.*
174 s 129(2)(g), *ibid.*
175 s 129(2)(h), *ibid.*
176 s 129(2)(i), *ibid.*
177 s 129(2)(j), *ibid.*
178 s 129(2)(k), *ibid.*

whom the civil partner is married, or any child to whom either of the civil partners owes an obligation of support[179];

(13) The terms of any separation agreement between the parties that is still in force[180];

(14) The interests of justice.[181]

[9–77] Although these matters largely mirror the matters to be taken into account when ensuring proper provision on the breakdown of a marriage, there are two issues of particular note here. The first is that, once more, children and the welfare or needs of any children are not expressly included as matters to be taken into account here. While, in practical terms, the likelihood is that a court making such an order would "fold in" the needs of children to their consideration of the needs of the civil partners, the omission of children's welfare and needs here is lamentable. While, in all likelihood, the costs associated with schooling and maintaining a child who was parented by both civil partners will *actually* be taken into account, then, there is no express requirement to do so. Secondly, courts are required to take into account the duration of a civil partnership and the length of cohabitation *post* civil partnership in s 129(2)(d) together with the impact of responsibilities assumed by each civil partner during the period when they lived with one another after the registration of their civil partnership on their earning capacity under s 129(2)(g). Limiting an analysis of the impact of the relationship on earning capacity to the time after civil partnership may result in some injustice, at least in the short term. This is quite simply because same-sex couples could not enter into a civil partnership until this Act was commenced; before that there was absolutely no formal recognition of their relationship. Imagine, then, a couple that has been together for 50 years prior to their civil partnership during which time—as is standard in most relationships—one partner made some sacrifices for the professional advancement of the other and those sacrifices had an impact on his or her earning capacity. If that couple enter into a formal civil partnership in 2011 and get a dissolution four years later, s 129 appears to require consideration of impact only during those four years and not to take account of impact for the preceding 50 years. Over time the problematic nature of this will fade out, but there is some need to be sensitive to the reality that prior to 2011 same-sex partners simply could not formalise their relationships but nevertheless made sacrifices for one another's professional lives that it seems unjust to ignore.[182]

VII. Presumed Resulting Trusts

[9–78] We have already seen that a spouse can make an application for questions as to title or possession to be summarily decided under s 36(1) of the Family Law Act 1995 and that a civil partner can make the equivalent application under s 106 of the Civil Partnership and Certain Rights and Obligations of Cohabitants Act 2010. In both cases the

[179] s 129(2)(l), *ibid.*

[180] s 129(3), *ibid.*

[181] s 129(4), *ibid.*

[182] This is qualitatively different to an opposite-sex couple that may have remained unmarried for 50 years prior to their marriage, for the law permitted that couple to marry. That option was not (and, of course, when it comes to marriage, still is not) available to same-sex couples.

question of ownership is frequently at issue and, in particular, disputes as to whether a spouse or civil partner who has made contributions to the home (financial or otherwise) is entitled to any ownership in that home, even if the contributions are not reflected in ownership on the formal legal title, tend to arise. This, then, becomes a question of equity and, in particular, of what is known as the presumed resulting trust (or the purchase money resulting trust). The PRT, as we will call it, arises where equity is satisfied that a contribution has been made towards the purchase of the property that entitles the contributing party to a share of ownership in equity. A trust is then said to exist, with the legal owner(s) holding the property on trust for the contributing parties as tenants in common in equity.

While PRTs are not limited to married couples, civil partners or people in intimate relationships with one another, the reality is that it is *primarily* in situations of trust and intimacy that one is likely to make contributions towards the purchase of a property without insisting on appropriate recognition by means of legal ownership. We do not routinely go around paying other people's mortgages or household bills; normally we do these things in our home lives only. Of course, the intimate nature of home life is such that it is not uncommon for people to make such contributions without formalising the legal implications thereof, or even discussing them. It must, surely, be the exceptional house in which the payment of household bills results in a discussion over dinner as to ownership of the property. Where parties have failed to protect themselves equity can step in and offer that protection, albeit only where it is satisfied that: (a) the contributions were in fact made, (b) the contributions are such as to result in a share of ownership, and (c) the parties had not intended for the payments to be gratuitous. Proving that contributions were actually made can be tricky in intimate relationships, for we do not tend to write receipts for our spouses or partners when they pay the mortgage, for example. However, if the initial barrier of proving the existence of the contribution can be jumped we must then classify the contribution as either direct or indirect and consider whether it results in a share of ownership or not. In this relation there is copious case law for guidance. **[9–79]**

1. Direct Contributions

The proposition that direct contributions to the purchase of property by payment of deposit, lump sum or mortgage give rise to an equitable interest in favour of the contributor is so well established as to be beyond dispute.[183] In *C v C*[184] a husband and wife purchased their family home in their joint names, financed by a mortgage, a gift from the wife's father and a loan from the husband's father. Only two mortgage repayments were made before the building society obtained an order for possession. In addition to their mortgage debt, the couple had a number of outstanding loans, some of which were in their joint names and some of which were in their individual names. After he was violent towards his wife, the husband left the family home and did not maintain his wife and children. The wife sought to have the property transferred into **[9–80]**

[183] This is notwithstanding some technical objections to the Irish courts' approach to the concept of "purchasing" a property by means of a mortgage. This approach is epitomised by the judgment of Finlay P in *W v W* [1981] ILRM 202, and the objections to it are stated definitively in Mee, "Trusts of the Family Home—The Irish Experience" (1993) Conv 351.

[184] [1976] IR 254.

her name under s 5 of the Family Home Protection Act 1976. Although Kenny J did not accede to this application, he did clearly enunciate the principles of direct contributions, holding that the wife's contribution (by means of deposit paid from her father's gift to her) entitled her to a share of ownership, so that the husband held the property on trust for them both as tenants in common.[185]

[9–81] Direct contributions to the purchase of the property can be made expressly through deposit, lump sum or mortgage payments, or can be made by means of contribution to a joint bank account from which the mortgage is paid.[186] In the latter case—of mortgage payments from joint accounts—the actual amount attributable to either party is a question for determination by accountants, more than a question of law *per se*.

2. Indirect Contributions

[9–82] Whether or not indirect contributions give rise to a presumed resulting trust has long been an issue of some controversy in the Irish courts. Indirect contributions here would include paying household bills, for example; payments to the general running of the property but not *direct* payments towards the purchase of the property. The early controversy on indirect contributions related largely to whether indirect contributions ought to give rise to a PRT only where there was an agreement to that effect between the parties, or whether no such agreement would be necessary. If there is an actual (and provable) agreement between the parties then the link between the indirect payment (for example, gas bills) and the direct purchase of the property (for example, mortgage instalments) is made. An agreement to this end acts, therefore, as a kind of evidential shortcut in an area where proof is a difficult thing to achieve. However, reflecting the discussion above about the nature of intimate affairs, one might justifiably argue that it is somewhat unrealistic to expect people in intimate relationships of dependence and interdependence to make such agreements *expressly* between one another.

[9–83] Throughout the 1970s and 1980s there were two distinct viewpoints on this issue. On the one hand, a number of High Court decisions held that indirect contributions would only give rise to a trust if there was an agreement between the parties to this effect.[187] On the other hand, other High Court decisions contended that indirect contributions would result in a trust notwithstanding the lack of such an agreement.[188] These diverse approaches to the issue appear to mirror closely the difference in opinion between Lord Reid and Lords Morris, Dilhorne, Pearson and Diplock in the English case of *Gissing v Gissing*.[189] Lord Reid sensibly held that it was simply unrealistic to expect people in intimate relationships (in that case, a married couple) to give exceptional degrees of consideration to the legal ramifications of their contributions. In his words:

> It must often happen that in coming to and carrying out... an agreement or understanding [whereby a wife makes some contribution to relieve her husband of

---

[185] See also *Heavey v Heavey* (1977) 111 ILTR 1; *W v W* [1981] ILRM 202; *McC v McC* [1986] ILRM 1.

[186] *HD v JD*, unreported, High Court, 31 July 1981.

[187] See, for example, *MG v RD*, unreported, High Court, 28 April 1981; *R v R*, unreported, High Court, 12 January 1979.

[188] See, for example, *FG v PG* [1982] 2 ILRM 155; *Heavey v Heavey* (1977) 111 ILTR 1.

[189] [1971] AC 886.

> house-related financial obligations] neither spouse gives a thought to the legal position or the legal consequences. The law is terra incognita and rather frightening to many people... Spouses... do not discuss the question whether carrying out such an understanding will give the wife a share or beneficial interest in the house. If either of them gives a thought to the matter, he or she may well think that the law will produce a just result without their assistance. Of course many people are more business-like but many are not.[190]

The uncertainty surrounding whether or not an agreement was required between parties in order for indirect contributions to give rise to a trust was finally resolved in the case of *McC v McC*.[191] This case concerned a married couple who were resident in Dublin when they were required to move to Cork for the husband's career. The wife was acknowledged as having a one-third share in the family home in Dublin and when this house was sold and their new home in Cork was purchased, she gave her husband her share of the purchase monies and directed him to use them for the acquisition of the Cork house. However, under an arrangement with his employer, the husband did not need to use this money for the acquisition of the property as the mortgage on the house in Cork was paid directly from his salary. The money his wife had contributed was, in fact, used for the purchase of furniture. When the couple split up, the wife claimed that she was entitled to some ownership on the basis of this contribution. While the Court found that her money was not used for the purchase of the property and, therefore, did not give rise to any trust (although she was entitled to the furniture bought with her money), it did clearly outline the fact that direct and indirect contributions towards the purchase of property will have precisely the same capacity to give rise to a purchase money resulting trust; no agreement is required for either. In the words of Henchy J: **[9–84]**

> Where the matrimonial home has been purchased in the name of the husband, and the wife has, *either directly or indirectly*, made contributions towards the purchase price or towards the discharge of the mortgage instalments, the husband will be held to be a trustee for the wife of a share in the house roughly corresponding with the proportion of the purchase money represented by the wife's total contribution. Such a trust will be inferred when the wife's contribution is of such a size and kind as will justify the conclusion that the acquisition of the house was achieved by the joint efforts of the spouses.
>
> When the wife's contribution has been indirect... the court will, in the absence of any express or implied agreement to the contrary, infer a trust in favour of the wife, on the ground that she has to that extent relieved the husband of the financial burden he incurred in purchasing the house. [*emphasis added*][192]

Thus, while the applicant did not succeed in having her contribution recognised by means of a share of equitable ownership under a resulting trust, the decision in *McC v McC* is of immense importance because it states clearly that direct and indirect contributions are treated in the same manner under the law; neither requires an **[9–85]**

[190] *ibid.* at 896.
[191] [1986] ILRM 1.
[192] *ibid.* at 2.

agreement to give rise to a resulting trust, but both can have this effect only if they are contributions towards the purchase of the property itself. Readers will notice that the words "matrimonial property", "spouses", "wife" and "husband" appear in the above quoted passage from *McC v McC*: does this mean that the case is limited to married couples? Lyall suggests that it does, writing that *McC v McC* "recognises that the social and legal context itself, in this case the institution of marriage, and not any particular conduct by the parties involved, gives rise to an equity unless it can be proved to be unjust in the particular case".[193] I am not sure that I can entirely agree. It is not the mere marriage between the parties that would create the trust, but rather the contribution of one party. Certainly, the "social and legal context" of marriage might influence a court in deciding that it is not sensible to treat direct and indirect contributions differently by requiring an agreement for indirect contributions to give rise to a trust. Marriage is, ideally at least, a partnership in which people routinely pool at least some of their resources in order to provide and maintain the home and, in that context, the payment of household bills is certainly likely to constitute a contribution towards the purchase of property in real terms. However, this is not exclusive to marriage: the same kind of pooling—or interdependence—routinely exists in non-marital relationships between, for example, unmarried couples who cohabit, civil partners, and cohabiting siblings. What *McC v McC* seems to stand for, to me, is the proposition that indirect contributions are to be treated the same as direct contributions unless there is an agreement (express or implied) to the contrary. An agreement not to treat indirect contributions as contributions towards the purchase of the property could, of course, be implied by the nature of the relationship between the parties and the way in which they tend to manage their financial affairs individually and/or jointly.

[9–86] One of the important implications of *McC* has been that the contribution of work to a family business may now be accepted more readily as a contribution resulting in beneficial ownership rights by means of a resulting trust. For quite some time this area of law had been unsettled. While Finlay P recognised work in a family business as giving rise to a resulting trust over the family home (the business was a pub connected thereto) in *HD v JD*,[194] subsequent decisions have tended to suggest that this precedent was not to be followed. Thus, in *L v L*[195] and *CM v TM*[196] Barr J appears to have completely discounted any possibility of such work resulting in an interest in the family home. The importance of *McC* in this relation is that such work, if recognised as an indirect contribution to the acquisition of property, could quite clearly result in a share of beneficial ownership under a trust. This appears to have been the approach adopted in the later case of *N v N*[197] where the wife's management of flats that the couple let out was taken into consideration in the awarding of a beneficial interest in her favour. There are still, however, some kinds of contributions that do not give rise to a PRT, and it is to those that we now turn.

---

193 Lyall, *Land Law in Ireland* (3rd ed, 2010, Dublin, Round Hall), pp 446–447.
194 Unreported, High Court, 31 July 1981.
195 [1992] 2 IR 77.
196 Unreported, High Court, 30 November 1989.
197 [1992] 2 IR 116.

3. Improvements to the Property

It is clear from *McC v McC*[198] that contributions recognised as contributing towards the *purchase* of the property will be said to result in a resulting trust. Contributions to improvements are generally not regarded as giving rise to a trust because the property improved is already owned (i.e. has already been acquired) by one of the parties, who is entitled to enjoy absolutely the benefit of any improvements done to it. **[9–87]**

In the first place, payment for improvements to the property does not give rise to a share in equitable ownership by means of a resulting trust. The parties may have an agreement between themselves, in which case the person who made the improvements might be entitled to financial compensation, but not to ownership rights. Thus, a person who gets a loan to finance improvements and repays that loan gets no ownership, nor does a person who pays for the improvements with cash. However, if the property is mortgaged in order to raise monies for improvements and the person who carried out those improvements pays off the re-mortgage, these mortgage payments are seen as direct contributions, and therefore equitable ownership under a resulting trust can arise. This incongruous position basically means that the mechanism of financing the improvements will determine whether someone achieves ownership rights or not. The fact of the improvements themselves and their impact on the property is essentially irrelevant. This is well demonstrated by a number of superior court decisions both preceding and following *McC v McC*. **[9–88]**

W v W[199] (a pre-*McC* decision) concerned a couple who married in 1966, at which stage a farm was transferred to the husband. Both the husband and wife invested their savings in the farm, including on carrying out improvements to it. The wife, in particular, developed the farm's bloodstock activities and took an active role in the management, development and continuing improvement of the farm. Other improvements, including physical improvements, were financed by a mortgage that had been repaid at the time of this action. The wife claimed that she was entitled to beneficial ownership by means of a resulting trust on the basis of, *inter alia*, her contribution towards financing the improvement of the property. The Court held that the wife's claim for a beneficial interest based on contributions to improvements was not sustainable. This was based on a distinction drawn by Finlay P between the acquisition of property and the improvement of property. In his analysis, contributions towards the acquisition of property would give rise to a trust in the absence of any express or implied agreement. However, contributions towards the improvement of the property would only result in an entitlement on the part of the contributor if "she established by evidence that from the circumstances surrounding the making of [the contribution] she was led to believe (or of course that it was specifically agreed) that she would be recompensed for it". Furthermore, even if the contributor could satisfy a court that there was an implied or express agreement as to the effect of her contributions to improvements, this would result in a right to financial compensation only and not to ownership of any kind. **[9–89]**

198 [1986] ILRM 1.
199 [1981] ILRM 202.

[9–90] Following the decision in *McC v McC*, it might have been thought that *W v W* would no longer stand, particularly since the need for an agreement of any kind now seemed to have been completely abandoned in the Irish law of resulting trusts. This does not appear to be the case, however. In *NAD v TD*[200] Barron J held that the principles of improvements from *W v W* continued to apply. In *CF v JDF*,[201] a Supreme Court decision from 2005, McGuinness J held *obiter* that "Even in the somewhat liberal context of family law the making of improvements to property cannot establish any form of beneficial title".[202] This would suggest that the original position whereby improvements are simply incapable of resulting in a beneficial interest under a resulting trust, is maintained.

4. The Contribution of Work in the Home

[9–91] Whether or not one spouse's work within the home gives rise to a beneficial interest in the property has long been the focus of significant controversy. In the main, the cases in this relation have concerned wives who work in the home to the exclusion of paid work outside of the home. This is substantially related to the fact that Art 41.2 of *Bunreacht na hÉireann* devotes particular recognition to the role women play in the home:

> 1. In particular, the State recognises that by her life within the home, woman gives to the State a support without which the common good cannot be achieved.
>
> 2. The State shall, therefore, endeavour to ensure that mothers shall not be obliged by economic necessity to engage in labour to the neglect of their duties in the home.

This provision has been categorised as "assign[ing] to women a domestic role as wives and mothers" and as a "dated provision".[203] Although the situation in which men were property-owners and "breadwinners" and women were full-time mothers and housewives was a "virtually universal"[204] state of affairs at the time the Constitution was introduced, this provision does not reflect the general position in contemporary Irish society. From the perspective of women who do work in the home, however, it was thought that Art 41.2 might have a protective force against impoverishment as a result of engaging in such work. This was particularly so in

[200] [1985] ILRM 153. See also *N v N* [1992] 2 IR 116; [1992] ILRM 127.

[201] [2005] 4 IR 154.

[202] *ibid.* at 166.

[203] *Report of the Constitution Review Group* (1996, Dublin, The Stationery Office), p 333; for a forceful argument on the effect of Art 41.2 on perpetuating gender stereotypes in Ireland see, for example, Mullally, "Taking Women's Rights Seriously: The Convention on the Elimination of all Forms of Discrimination Against Women" (1992) 10 ILT 6; Mullally, "Feminist Jurisprudence" in Murphy (ed), *Western Jurisprudence* (2004, Dublin, Thomson Round Hall), p 350, and esp. pp 363–365; Connelly, "Women and the Constitution of Ireland" in Galligan, Ward and Wilford (eds), *Contesting Politics: Women in Ireland, North and South* (1999, Boulder, Colorado, and Dublin, Westview Press), p 18. The provision also, of course, undermines a male role as homemaker and primary caregiver: see Flynn, "To Be an Irish Man—Constructions of Masculinity in the Constitution" in Murphy and Twomey (eds), *Ireland's Evolving Constitution 1937–1997: Collected Essays* (1998, Oxford, Hart Publishing).

[204] Forde, *Constitutional Law* (2nd ed, 2004, Dublin, First Law), p 701.

relation to family property and culminated in the presentation, in *L v L*,[205] of an argument that a wife's work within the home ought to be construed as a contribution giving rise to a share of beneficial ownership in the home by means of a resulting trust.

The case concerned a couple that married in 1968 and had two children. The wife—who was the plaintiff in this case—carried out a number of functions in relation to the family home, including being a full-time mother and housewife. The relationship was an abusive one and, in the course of the breakdown of their marriage, she claimed, *inter alia*, a share of beneficial ownership on the basis of her work in the home. This claim was based substantially on Art 41.2 and succeeded before Barr J in the High Court. In a ground-breaking judgment, the Court held that Art 41.2 recognised that women who stay at home to work as mothers and housewives usually remove themselves from the economic market place and, as a result, are generally incapable of making financial contributions to the acquisition of the family home. Their work in the home, however, is of immense value, both financially and socially (as recognised by Art 41.2). As a result, women who work in the home ought to be provided with some financial security. This security cannot be achieved by direct contributions to the purchase of property (for lack of financial means), therefore the work conducted in the home ought to be recognised as giving rise to a resulting trust and a share of ownership in equity. **[9–92]**

This decision was ground-breaking for the simple reason that it was one of the first occasions in which the Irish courts engaged in consideration of Art 41.2 in a manner that recognised it as giving rise to real and substantial socio-economic entitlements, as opposed to being merely an aspirational statement of prevailing values in 1937. Mullally has noted that Barr J's approach "recognised marriage as an equal partnership".[206] By interpreting Art 41.2 in this manner, the High Court showed the potential for this provision to be interpreted in accordance with contemporary values and, through such action, to potentially be a vehicle for the economic liberation of women who work in the home. **[9–93]**

The decision was appealed to the Supreme Court, which reversed without dissent on a number of grounds: **[9–94]**

(a) that the recognition of a presumed resulting trust requires a contribution of money or money's worth;
(b) that the High Court had purported to create a new right in favour of mothers who work in the home that is not supported by precedent;
(c) that Article 41.2 does not create any particular rights within the family nor give any member rights (whether property or otherwise) against other members of the family;
(d) that while women who work in the home are deserving of security and protection, these ought to be provided by means of legislative intervention and not judicial usurpation of the legislative role

[205] [1989] ILRM 528 (High Court); [1992] 2 IR 77 (Supreme Court).

[206] Mullally, "Feminist Jurisprudence" in Murphy (ed), *Western Jurisprudence* (Thomson, Round Hall, Dublin, 2004), at p 363.

The Supreme Court's decision was not hugely surprising, particularly given the highly controversial nature of Barr J's conclusions in the High Court. Prior to that High Court decision, it had been largely assumed that Art 41.2 was a mere statement of aspiration and did not purport to create actionable entitlements on behalf of women. If anything, precedent on this Article had tended to view it as a justification for provisions that discriminated against women (such as the original gender ban against women serving on a jury[207]), as opposed to a provision that valued women.

[9–95] Secondly, Barr J's approach was thought somewhat inappropriate from the perspective of separation of powers. His decision to use Art 41.2 as a launch-pad for the distribution of assets within a marriage was interpreted as a usurpation of the legislative role. Importantly, such redistribution is not inconsistent with the general law of presumed trusts. In most cases contributions are financial, therefore instead of distributing assets, the courts, in recognising resulting trusts, are merely recognising that the asset was acquired through a monetary contribution and are, in a way, rewarding "investors". In the case of domestic work, the contribution is not financial inasmuch as it does not comprise the payment of any monies. This is, of course, a matter of interpretation as the work done by the applicant in this case of cleaning, cooking, child-minding and so on would have to be done in any case and would involve substantial expenditure if an external employee had to be hired to carry it out. However, in general, it was felt that Barr J's decision to distribute ownership rights between the parties on the basis of conceptions of the common good (generally under Art 41.2 and specifically between the parties) was inappropriate. The concept that engagement in what might be called distributive justice is an inappropriate exercise of the judicial function is classically stated by Costello J in *O'Reilly v Limerick Corporation*.[208] Conor O'Mahony succinctly captures Costello J's approach in the following passage:

> Costello J. stated that distributive justice is concerned with the distribution and allocation of common goods and common burdens and that none of the goods held in common (or any of the wealth raised by taxation) belong exclusively to any member of the political community. That distribution can only be made by reference to the common good and by those charged with furthering the common good (the Government)...[209]

[9–96] Later cases on the protection of children, in particular, have shown that the Irish courts do engage in distributive justice in certain cases—where it is felt that such action is required. In other words, whether a court decides to distribute goods (such as ownership rights, bringing with them economic security) or to refuse to do that on the basis of the perceived appropriateness of such action is essentially a matter of choice. To say that courts ought to step in and realise socio-economic rights—such as

207 *De Búrca v Attorney General* [1976] IR 38.
208 [1989] ILRM 181.
209 O'Mahony, "Education, Remedies and the Separation of Powers" (2002) DULJ 57—internal footnotes omitted.

ownership rights for financially disenfranchised stay-at-home mothers and housewives—is not, as Gerry Whyte has noted, "to say that they should be first into the fray. There are good institutional reasons why we should look initially to the legislative and executive branches for protection of such rights... the courts should only be used as a last resort, when it is clear that the political process is incapable of protecting the right in question".[210] Since the introduction of the Constitution in 1937, Art 41.2 had not been used by the other branches of government as a mandate for ensuring that work within the home—primarily carried out by women—would be valued as a common good through the protection and rewarding (by means of security) of those who undertake to perform these functions.

This, then, leads to the third critique of Barr J's approach in the High Court, namely that his action was an inexcusable example of judicial activism. Judicial activism has been classically defined by David Gwynn Morgan in the context of judicial declarations of unconstitutionality thus: **[9–97]**

> ... there is a... category of case in which—in order to resolve the case one way or the other—a judge has to call on some element of policy choice or preference. In this sort of case, if the judge selects the option of not accepting the status quo as it is given in the form of law or government action... then the judge is... performing an act of "judicial activism".[211]

Although Morgan is dealing substantively with declarations of unconstitutionality and the subsequent striking down of law, his basic formulation of judicial activism (that it is judicial recourse to a "policy choice or preference") can be generalised beyond that and applied, in this context, to interpretations of the real-life effects of constitutional provisions. Barr J appeared to call on the concept of equality within marriage and, indeed, in a more implicit manner on societal gender equality in his decision-making process. The Supreme Court's reversal of his decision, on the other hand, appears to have recalibrated the system so that Art 41.2 could continue to be an inert provision, in actionable legal terms, in spite of its potency in terms of the construction of gender roles in society.

Undoubtedly, there were some meritorious arguments in support of the Supreme Court's decision. The most obvious one is quite possibly the strongest: if women are given ownership rights on the basis of their work in the home, then men who work in the home are discriminated against in this relation. There are a number of responses to this claim. First, the privileging of women in such a scenario would be a result of an express constitutional text assigning work of this nature to women and could be resolved through a constitutional amendment changing "mother" to "parent" (or even to the more socially appropriate term, "carer"). In other words, this objection is so easily resolved that it does not appear to be sufficiently strong to justify ignoring this element of the constitutional text. Second, the fact that one class of person is privileged over another as a result of constitutional interpretation does not appear to restrain the **[9–98]**

[210] Whyte, *Social Inclusion and the Legal System: Public Interest Law in Ireland* (2002, Dublin, IPA), p 54.

[211] Morgan, *A Judgment too Far? Judicial Activism and the Constitution* (2001, Cork, Cork University Press), p 7.

application of such interpretations in other contexts. So, for example, families based on marriage are constitutionally privileged over non-marital families; the unfairness of this position is not proposed as a reason not to allow marital families to enjoy and enforce their constitutional rights.

[9–99] Therefore, it appears to be a somewhat unavoidable conclusion that perceptions of gender roles and the appropriate role of a mother may have played a potent but unacknowledged role in the Supreme Court's decision in *L v L*. The Court did not, however, purport that women who work in the home should not have any form of security whatsoever. Rather, the Court, through the judgment of Finlay CJ, expressly left such work to the legislative branches:

> I would have little difficulty in appreciating the very significant social and other values which are attached to what experience would indicate is a very common modern habit, whereby the parties to a marriage and the parents of a family, by agreement between them, become joint owners of the family home. It is difficult to deny the fact that anything that would help to encourage that basis of full sharing in property values as well as in every other way between the partners of a marriage, must directly contribute to the stability of the marriage, the institution of the family, and the common good.
>
> However, the problem which appears to me to arise is a simple question as to whether if this court were to follow the reasoning contained in the judgment of Barr J it would in truth... be developing an existing law within the permissible limits of judicial interpretation, or whether in fact it would be legislating.
>
> After careful consideration and with a reluctance arising from the desirable objective which the principle outlined in the judgment of Barr J would achieve, I conclude that to identify this right in the circumstances set out in this case is not to develop any known principle of the common law, but is rather to identify a brand new right and to secure it to the plaintiff. Unless that is something clearly and unambiguously warranted by the Constitution or made necessary for the protection of either a specified or unspecified right under it, it must constitute legislation and be a usurpation by the courts of the function of the legislature.

Legislative attempts (discussed below) to fulfil this challenge were frustrated in subsequent litigation. It is interesting to note that in 2003 the High Court appears to have decided that a wife acquired some beneficial ownership in the family home by her work within the home as mother and housewife, *per M v M*.[212] The authorities on this point were not considered extensively and no in-depth reasoning was engaged in. It appears, however, that the Court considered work of this nature to be equivalent to the contribution of monies to a joint family fund. This decision therefore appears to be, at most, an aberration that might result in some change in this area of law in the future, but Peart J's willingness to engage in this decision without, it seems, conceiving of it as at all controversial is interesting.

5. Overcoming a Financial Fixation? Common Intention Constructive Trusts

[9–100] By refusing to find that non-financial contributions can give rise to a PRT, the courts have maintained a financial fixation in this context. The same fixation exists in the law

[212] *M(B) v M(A)* [2003] IEHC 170.

of England and Wales, but in that jurisdiction the courts have developed what is known as the Common Intention Constructive Trust that allows for the division of ownership to be influenced by non-financial contributions once the trust has been established. The common intention constructive trust can be traced back to the 1970s. In *Gissing v Gissing*[213] Lord Diplock laid out the concept of a constructive trust arising to give effect to a common intention to share ownership of land, stating that a constructive trust:

> is created by a transaction between the trustee and the [beneficiary] in connection with the acquisition by the trustee of a legal estate in land, whenever the trustee has so conducted himself that it would be inequitable to allow him to deny to the [beneficiary] a beneficial interest in the land acquired.[214]

One might say that this *dictum* is supremely unhelpful from the perspective of clearly outlining the parameters of such a trust, but it does lay down the general principle that a constructive trust can be imposed where to do otherwise would be inequitable *but* the conditions for a PRT do not necessarily exist or cannot be proved. The common intention constructive trust has since developed in a way that is intended, in essence, to deal with the reality of modern domestic relationships where important contributions are made that are not financial but which, in the name of justice and equitability, ought not to be entirely discounted in a dispute as to ownership.

Lord Denning, in characteristically inventive form, claimed to merely be extending the principle laid down in *Gissing* when he developed what became known as the "new model constructive trust".[215] In *Hussey v Palmer* Denning LJ held that this new model constructive trust: **[9–101]**

> ... is a trust imposed by law whenever justice and good conscience require it. It is a liberal process, founded on large principles of equity, to be applied in cases where the defendant cannot conscientiously keep the property for himself alone, but ought to allow another to have the property or a share in it. The trust may arise at the outset when the property is acquired, or later on, as the circumstances may require. It is an equitable remedy...[216]

In fact what Lord Denning was doing here was quite a lot more than Lord Diplock had averted to in *Gissing*, but that is not to say that it does not have something to commend it invoking, as it does, the spirit at least of equity's original functions: deciding things in good conscience.[217] That is not to suggest that it survived the pens of Lord Denning's judicial brothers and sisters, who rejected the new model constructive trust primarily because of the uncertainty that it introduced.[218] In spite of that rejection, the common intention constructive trust has not gone away.

---

[213] [1971] AC 886.

[214] *ibid* at 905. See also *Pettitt v Pettitt* [1970] AC 777.

[215] *Eves v Eves* [1975] 1 WLR 1338.

[216] [1972] 3 All ER 744 at 747.

[217] See generally Chapter 3.

[218] See, for example, *Cowcher v Cowcher* [1972] 1 WLR 425; *Grant v Edwards* [1986] Ch 638; *Springette v Defoe* [1992] 2 FLR 388.

It has, instead, flourished in that jurisdiction and especially in situations where it came to the aid of women.

[9–102] Common intention constructive trusts arise where there is a common intention for the ownership of the land to be shared (whether or not the legal title is in joint ownership). As we have seen in relation to the PRT, establishing that intention can be very difficult (especially in cases where there is only one name on the deed), because of our tendency not to formalise such things in intimate relationships.[219] Of course, where that common intention is clear, this first requirement is easily fulfilled and whether or not there is such an express agreement or understanding between the parties is a question of fact to be determined in each individual case.[220] Thus, if the parties are both named as owners the common intention is clear. In "sole named owner" cases it is somewhat more complex. It had been thought that the common intention could only be inferred from direct financial contributions to the purchase of the property,[221] but in *Stack v Dowden* Baroness Hale expressed the view that this was too high a hurdle to impose on those attempting to infer common intention.[222] In *Abbot v Abbot*[223] the Privy Council held that the whole course of conduct between the parties *as it relates to the property* ought to be taken into account, seemingly bringing indirect financial contributions within the conduct from which a common intention can be inferred. In *Burns v Burns*[224] it was held that work within the home of what we might call a "domestic" nature would not lead to the inference of a common intention, but in *Stack* Lord Walker held that "contributions in kind by way of manual labour, provided that they are significant" could also lead to the inference of a common intention.[225] Here the manual labour contemplated seems to be labour that is, essentially, payment in kind for improvements. One might argue that this is qualitatively different to "housework" and "child-minding" from a property law perspective inasmuch as manual labour for improvements can add to the value of the property, whereas "housework" does not. However, housework, child-minding and so on could be defined as activities that relieve financial pressure, thereby facilitating payment of mortgage instalments, as if they were not done "for free" by one of the partners, someone would have to be paid to do them. That said, however, it would appear that most of these statements are essentially *obiter* and they *probably* do not fully displace the position, land down most decisively in *Lloyds Bank v Rosset*,[226] that non-financial contributions do not give rise to an inference of common intention.

[9–103] This does not mean that non-financial contributions are entirely irrelevant in this context; rather, they play an important role in determining the division of property once the trust has been established. Once the existence of the common intention constructive trust has been established, the court must determine the shares of

---

219 See, for example, *Grant v Edwards* [1986] Ch 638; *Lloyds Bank v Rosset* [1991] 1 AC 107.
220 *Lloyds Bank v Rosset* [1991] 1 AC 107.
221 *Midland Bank v Cooke* [1995] 4 All ER 562; *Lloyds Bank v Rosset* [1991] 1 AC 107.
222 [2007] UKHL 17 at para 63.
223 [2007] UKPC 53.
224 [1984] Ch 317.
225 [2007] UKHL 17 at para 36.
226 [1991] 1 AC 107.

ownership under the common intention constructive trust. Here, factors *beyond* financial contributions are relevant. In *Oxley v Hiscock*[227] the Court of Appeal affirmed that where there is a common intention between the parties that they would hold the property together, but there is no common agreement as to the shares in which the property is to be held, a constructive trust can be imposed with the shares of equity determined by reference to what the court "considers to be fair having regard to the whole course of dealings between them in relation to the property".[228] It is now clear from the important case of *Stack v Dowden*[229] that where there is a common intention constructive trust the court will begin from the assumption of equal ownership, especially (although not exclusively) where both parties are named as legal owners. The person claiming unequal ownership has the burden of proving that this starting assumption ought not to hold. In determining whether it should recognise unequal equitable ownership, the court will look not only to financial contributions but, in a much broader sense, at the relationship between the parties as regards the property in question. At paragraph 69 Baroness Hale outlined this approach thus:

> In law, "context is everything" and the domestic context is very different from the commercial world. Each case will turn on its own facts. Many more factors than financial contributions may be relevant to divining the parties' true intentions. These include: any advice or discussions at the time of the transfer which cast light upon their intentions then; the reasons why the home was acquired in their joint names; the reasons why (if it be the case) the survivor was authorised to give a receipt for the capital moneys; the purpose for which the home was acquired; the nature of the parties' relationship; whether they had children for whom they both had responsibility to provide a home; how the purchase was financed, both initially and subsequently; how the parties arranged their finances, whether separately or together or a bit of both; how they discharged the outgoings on the property and their other household expenses. When a couple are joint owners of the home and jointly liable for the mortgage, the inferences to be drawn from who pays for what may be very different from the inferences to be drawn when only one is owner of the home. The arithmetical calculation of how much was paid by each is also likely to be less important. It will be easier to draw the inference that they intended that each should contribute as much to the household as they reasonably could and that they would share the eventual benefit or burden equally. The parties' individual characters and personalities may also be a factor in deciding where their true intentions lay. In the cohabitation context, mercenary considerations may be more to the fore than they would be in marriage, but it should not be assumed that they always take pride of place over natural love and affection. At the end of the day, having taken all this into account, cases in which the joint legal owners are to be taken to have intended that their beneficial interests should be different from their legal interests will be very unusual.

Thus, the common intention constructive trust does not seem to move the law on from the PRT when it comes to whether non-financial contributions can give rise to a trust in the first place (although this may, of course, change as the law develops). However, it does not entirely disregard those non-financial contributions and instead takes them **[9–104]**

227 [2004] 3 All ER 703.
228 *ibid.*, para 69.
229 [2007] UKHL 17.

into account when determining the division of the equitable ownership under the common intention constructive trust.

VIII. Community of Property between Spouses and Civil Partners

[9–105] As a general matter, the law appears to take the approach that the ownership arrangements over the family home are a matter for the family themselves.[230] This is notwithstanding the Supreme Court's call in *L v L* for the Oireachtas to introduce legislation that would ensure security for both spouses in relation to the family home.[231] This call was answered by the Oireachtas in the form of the Matrimonial Home Bill 1993. Section 4 of the Matrimonial Home Bill 1993 provided that where a spouse was the sole owner of the matrimonial home on the commencement date of the Act or became the sole owner after that date, the equitable ownership in the property would vest in both spouses as joint tenants. The bill therefore proposed to introduce a statutory community of property system on spouses, which was limited to the matrimonial home and the household chattels. This community of property system would apply automatically to married couples, but could be opted out of under s 7, which would allow a spouse (or someone who intended to marry) to waive his/her rights under the bill following receipt of independent legal advice. In addition, the spouse who originally owned the property could apply to the court under s 6 to have the bill's operation over his/her property cancelled. The court would be obliged to accede to a s 6 application if it would be unjust to do otherwise by reference to all of the circumstances of the spouses, including the conduct of the spouse who would benefit by s 4 and, in particular, any failure or refusal by that spouse to contribute or contribute adequately to the mortgage instalments or rent due in relation to the matrimonial home, or to any other necessary expenditure on the home within his/her means.

[9–106] The Supreme Court, in an Art 26 reference, unanimously held that the bill was unconstitutional with reference to Art 41.[232] While the Court once more expressed its support for the objective of achieving co-ownership of the family home between spouses, it expressed concern about the retrospective application of the community of property scheme to couples who had married prior to 1993 and who may have come to an agreement that the property would continue to be held in only one of their names. While such couples could avail of the opt-out clause in s 7, this required the couple to take positive action when they had already done so. As Finlay CJ held:

> In some instances the net effect of these legislative proposals would be automatically to cancel a joint decision freely made by both spouses as part of the authority of the family and substitute there for a wholly different decision unless the spouses can agree to a new joint decision to confirm the earlier agreement or unless the owning spouse can succeed in obtaining a court order pursuant to s 6.[233]

[230] The operation of presumed resulting trusts is an exception to this inasmuch as it involves the court intervening to give effect to what it presumes the parties intended in terms of ownership, even though the parties would have failed to give expression to these presumed intentions.
[231] [1992] 2 IR 77.
[232] *In the Matter of Article 26 of the Constitution and in the Matter of the Matrimonial Home Bill, 1993* [1994] 1 ILRM 241.
[233] *ibid.* at p 254.

Thus, the Court's objection was to a disproportionate interference in the family by the scope of the bill's application, and not to the objective that it sought to ensure. This suggests that a constitutionally compliant bill to achieve community of property could be introduced with relative ease—it seems that it would simply need to have an automatic application from the time of its commencement; couples whose property arrangements predate this could still engage in interpersonal conveyances to achieve co-ownership without stamp duty liability, if they wished to do so.[234]

Notwithstanding this, no government has proposed a community of property scheme since this decision was handed down. This is somewhat surprising as the need for security within a couple subsists and continues to be left unsatisfied by the law. Only spouses who have the financial capacity to contribute towards the purchase of the property and thereby give rise to a resulting trust, or spouses who have the foresight and willingness to engage in express co-ownership relationships, are assured of ownership rights over the property. This becomes all the more surprising when one bears in mind the profound impact that ownership of property has on the achievement of equality between spouses and, more generally, within social campaigns to achieve gender equality.[235] **[9–107]**

IX. The Homes of Qualified Cohabitants

It is not uncommon for people to reside together in intimate and interdependent relationships without either marrying (if opposite sex) or entering into a civil partnership (if same sex). The Civil Partnership and Certain Rights and Obligations of Cohabitants Act 2010 includes some provision for the regulation of property relationships as to cohabitants. Section 172(1) of the Act defines a cohabitant as: **[9–108]**

> one of 2 adults (whether of the same or the opposite sex) who live together as a couple in an intimate and committed relationship and who are not related to each other within the prohibited degrees of relationship or married to each other or civil partners of each other.

While someone who is married or in a civil partnership with a third party can qualify as a cohabitant under s 172, he or she will not be considered a "qualified cohabitant"[236] which, as we will see below, is the first qualification for a number of property-related rights.

While the notion of "an intimate and committed relationship" in s 172(1) might seem like something of a pink elephant—hard to describe but recognisable on sight—the law tends to require somewhat more clarity than that. As a result, s 172(2) provides that the court should take into account the duration of the relationship, the basis for the cohabitation, the degree of financial dependence between the parties, any agreements they might have in relation to financial matters and the nature of their financial **[9–109]**

---

[234] s 14, Family Home Protection Act 1976, exempts married couples from stamp duty on the creation of a joint tenancy between them.

[235] On the important role of female participation in land ownership, see generally Lim and Bottomley, *Feminist Perspectives on Land Law* (2007, London, Routledge-Cavendish).

[236] s 172(5), Civil Partnership and Certain Rights and Obligations of Cohabitants Act 2010.

arrangements including any joint property purchases, the existence of dependent children, whether one adult cares for and supports the children of the other adult, and—somewhat strangely—"the degree to which the adults present themselves to others as a couple" in determining whether there is a cohabitation in fact.

[9–110] All cohabitants—whether "qualifying" or not—can arrange certain elements of their relationship by means of a cohabitation agreement under s 202. Such an agreement can deal with financial matters, and property provision on death or on the breakdown of the relationship. A cohabitation agreement will only be valid if the parties received independent legal advice in relation to it, it is written, it is signed by both cohabitants, and it complies with the law of contract more generally.[237] Cohabitants can waive their right to apply for redress or provision from the estate of the other in the agreement,[238] although courts are empowered to vary or set aside these agreements if it would cause "serious injustice" to enforce it.[239]

[9–111] A qualified cohabitant is defined in s 172(5) as:

> an adult who was in a relationship of cohabitation with another adult and who, immediately before the time that that relationship ended, whether through death or otherwise, was living with the other adult as a couple for a period—
> (a) of 2 years or more, in the case where they are the parents of one or more dependent children, and
> (b) of 5 years or more, in any other case.

This definition is subject to an exception in s 172(6), which disqualifies a situation where one or both adult is "or was, at any time during the relationship concerned, an adult who was married to someone" other than the other cohabitant *and* has not lived apart from his or her spouse for a period of at least four of the previous five years at the time that the relationship ends. Qualifying cohabitants have some limited rights in relation to succession, which are dealt with in Chapter 16.

[9–112] A sub-category of qualified cohabitant—the qualified economically dependent cohabitant—has further rights in relation to property. A qualified economically dependent cohabitant must establish that he or she is financially dependent on the other cohabitant *and* that the financial dependence arises from the relationship or the ending of the relationship. Should one manage to establish that one is a qualified economically dependent cohabitant, one can then apply for a variety of orders, including property adjustment orders,[240] with which we are interested here.

[9–113] A property adjustment order will only be granted upon the application of a qualifying economically dependent cohabitant if the court is satisfied that it is "just and equitable" to do so.[241] This is determined by reference to the factors laid down in s 173(3):

---

237 s 202(2), Land and Conveyancing Law Reform Act 2010.
238 s 202(3), *ibid.*
239 s 202(4), *ibid.*
240 s 174, Civil Partnership and Certain Rights and Obligations of Cohabitants Act 2010.
241 s 173(2), *ibid.*

(1) The financial circumstances, needs and obligations of each qualified cohabitant existing as at the date of the application or which are likely to arise in the future[242];
(2) The rights and entitlements of any spouse or former spouse,[243] bearing in mind that no order will be made that "would affect any right of any person to whom the other cohabitant is or was married"[244];
(3) The rights and entitlements of any civil partner or former civil partner[245];
(4) The rights and entitlements of any dependent child or of any child of a previous relationship of either cohabitant[246];
(5) The duration of the parties' relationship, the basis on which the parties entered into the relationship and the degree of commitment of the parties to one another[247];
(6) The contributions that each of the cohabitants made or is likely to make in the foreseeable future to the welfare of the cohabitants or either of them including any contribution made by each of them to the income, earning capacity or property and financial resources of the other[248];
(7) Any contributions made by either cohabitant in looking after the home[249];
(8) The effect on the earning capacity of each of the cohabitants of the responsibilities assumed by each of them during the period they lived together as a couple and the degree to which the future earning capacity of a qualified cohabitant is impaired by reason of that qualified cohabitant having relinquished or foregone the opportunity of remunerative activity in order to look after the home[250];
(9) Any physical or mental disability of the qualified cohabitant[251];
(10) The conduct of each of the cohabitants, if the conduct is such that, in the opinion of the court, it would be unjust to disregard it.[252]

As should now be clear, these requirements largely mirror the matters taken into account when determining applications for property-related orders on the breakdown of a marriage and of a civil partnership. Like in relation to marriage, but unlike civil partnership, the rights and entitlements of dependent children are taken into account here, regardless of whether the cohabitants are of the same or opposite sex. This further adds to the incongruity of not taking express account of children's needs when dividing property on the breakdown of a civil partnership.

[242] s 173(3)(a), *ibid.*
[243] s 173(3)(b), *ibid.*
[244] s 173(5), *ibid.*
[245] s 173(3)(c), *ibid.*
[246] s 173(3)(d), *ibid.*
[247] s 173(3)(e), *ibid.*
[248] s 173(3)(f), *ibid.*
[249] s 173(3)(g), *ibid.*
[250] s 173(3)(h), *ibid.*
[251] s 173(3)(i), *ibid.*
[252] s 173(3)(j), *ibid.*

Chapter 10
Licences and Analogous Rights

While the majority of the matters considered in this book concern proprietary interests, these are not the only kinds of rights that can be held over land. In some situations landowners might transfer non-proprietary rights to others. The most prominent of these rights for our purposes is the licence, i.e. the permission to use the land of another for either specific or general purposes. As an important starting point, we ought to note that all licences share a number of characteristics: they are non-proprietary; they are revocable (although revocability can be restricted as a result of certain circumstances), and they bind successors in title of the licensor in limited circumstances only. This chapter considers the law of licences and what we will term analogous rights, i.e. rights that operate in a manner similar to licences. In this respect, rights of residence receive the most attention. Rights of residence constitute analogous rights inasmuch as they are (generally) non-proprietary rights over the land of another that entitle the holder to reside in the property for a given period of time. The main bone of contention in relation to rights of residence concerns the nature of the holder's entitlements, and this question will be considered in full. Finally, this chapter briefly considers conacre and agistment agreements: specific types of licence that give a right to till and to graze animals on the land of the licensor, respectively. **[10–01]**

I. Licences

Ownership brings with it a right to possess land.[1] One does not have to own land to be entitled to possess it, however, a licence can be granted to permit a non-owner to possess (i.e. use and enjoy) a piece of land. Licences are permissive rights: the licensee is **[10–02]**

[1] See Chapter 1, paras 1–13 to 1–17.

granted the right to possess and occupy land, even though he has no ownership rights over it.[2] Over time, as we will see below, some equitable principles have been developed that have suggested (to say the least) that a licence can operate in a manner that is analogous to ownership, but the classical common law definition of a licence—handed down by Vaughan J in *Thomas v Sorrell*—remains the appropriate starting point:

> A... licence properly passeth no interest nor alters or transfers property in any thing, but only makes an action lawful, which without it had been unlawful.[3]

While the terms of a licence will be important in assessing how that licence operates in practice, the category of the licence will also be important. To this end there are four main categories of licences with which we are concerned: bare licences; licences coupled with an interest; contractual licences; and estoppel licences. The revocability and transferability of a licence and, in particular, its enforceability against successors in title of the licensor will be determined by the nature of the licence within these categories.

1. Bare Licences

[10–03] Bare licences can be described as "mere permissions": they are permissions given and received without any supporting contract, consideration or legal relationship. Bare licences are, in fact, common in everyday life. For example, if you are reading this in a book shop while considering whether to buy it, you are currently exercising an implied bare licence to be in that book shop for the purposes of engaging in commerce there.[4] Bare licences are generally not transferable, i.e. they cannot generally be enforced by or against successors in title of the original parties. As bare licences are unsupported by consideration, contract or other legal relationship, they can be revoked more or less at will in common law. This does not mean that the licensee will immediately become a trespasser; rather, he will be entitled to reasonable notice of the termination of the licence or, at the least, to a "period of grace" or a "packing-up period".[5] That said, equity can disallow an at-will revocation of a bare licence. If the licensee has acted in reliance on the licence and will incur a detriment on its revocation, the licensor may be estopped from revoking it.[6] A bare licence may become irrevocable if the licensee has acted on it. This can be traced back to the seventeenth century and is well explained by Lord Ellenborough CJ in *Winter v Brockwell,* where he:

> thought it very unreasonable, that after a party had been led to incur expense in consequence of having obtained a licence from another to do an act, and that the licence had been acted upon, that other should be permitted to recall his licence and treat the first as a trespasser for having done that very act.[7]

---

[2] *Ashburn Anstalt v Arnold* [1989] Ch 1 *per* Nourse LJ at 22; *IDC Group Ltd v Clark* [1992] 2 EGLR 184 *per* Nourse LJ at 186; *Street v Mountford* [1985] AC 809 *per* Thompson LJ at 814.

[3] (1674) 124 ER 1098, at p 1109; see also *David Allen & Sons Billposting Ltd v King* [1915] 2 IR 213 *per* Madden J at 244: "a licence... renders lawful as against the licensor an act that would otherwise amount to an actionable act of trespass".

[4] *Davis v Lisle* [1936] 2 KB 434.

[5] *Winter Garden Theatre (London) Ltd v Millennium Productions Ltd* [1948] AC 173 *per* MacDermott LJ at pp 204 and 206.

[6] See, for example, *Pascoe v Turner* [1979] 1 WLR 431; *Sledmore v Dalby* (1996) 72 P & CR 196.

[7] (1807) 8 East 308, at p 310.

This limit on revocation appears to apply only to licences to do particular acts (such as a licence to construct buildings), rather than to licences to engage in repetitious acts, such as fishing, using a pathway, etc.[8]

2. Licences Coupled with an Interest

There will occasionally be situations where someone has an interest (i.e. a proprietary right) of some kind over the land of another that cannot be exercised without a licence. **[10–04]** In those cases a licence will be said to attach automatically to the interest, which must be validly created. Perhaps the best example of the licence coupled with an interest arises when someone is granted a *profit à prendre* on land. In essence, a *profit à prendre* is a right to take the natural resources from the land of another (such as a right to fish, for example) and, as a result, the holder of a *profit à prendre* will need to enter the land of another in order to exercise this right. In such cases the holder of the *profit* will be said to have a licence over the land for the purposes of exercising this right. Licences coupled with an interest are always irrevocable.[9] As Alderson B explained in *Wood v Leadbitter*, "supposing the grant [of the interest]... to be good, then the license would be irrevocable by the party who had given it; he would be estopped from defeating his own grant".[10] The fact that the licence coupled with an interest is irrevocable is entirely bound up with the fact that the interest to which it is attached is irrevocable: as the licence is attached to this interest it is transferred with it[11] and will continue in force until such time as the interest involved has been discharged (if ever).

3. Contractual Licences

Contractual licences are licences that are supported by a contract. In order for the **[10–05]** licence to stand, the contract must, in the first instance, be compliant with the rules of contract law. Contracts can be used as the mechanism for the express granting of licences and in such cases the ensuing licences can be said to be "contractual" without much difficulty. Licences can also arise as the implicit product of a contract, however, and these licences are equally said to be contractual.[12] Thus, if I contract with Simon that he would wash my windows inside and outside once a month and I give him a key to my house for these purposes, he receives a contractual licence over the house for the purpose of washing the windows once a month, even though the contract between us does not expressly grant him a licence. Contracts including a licence element can also be implied from the circumstances of the case, where the court feels that such an implication would be appropriate. This can be demonstrated by reference to the case of *Tanner v Tanner*.[13]

The defendant in *Tanner* gave birth to twins in November 1969. The father of the twins **[10–06]** was the plaintiff, who decided in 1970 that a house ought to be bought for the

[8] *Liggins v Inge* (1831) 7 Bing. 682; *Feltham v Cartwright* (1839) 5 Bing. NC 569; *Hounslow London Borough Council v Twickenham Garden Developments Ltd* [1971] 1 Ch 233.
[9] *James Jones & Sons Ltd v Earl of Tankerville* [1909] 2 Ch. 440.
[10] (1845) 13 M & W 838, at p 845; see also *Wood v Manley* (1839) 11 Ad & E 34.
[11] See, for example, *Muskett v Hill* (1839) 5 Bing NC 694.
[12] On implicit contractual licences of this nature, see, for example, *Tanner v Tanner* [1975] 1 WLR 1346; *Chandler v Kerley* [1978] 1 WLR 693.
[13] [1975] 1 WLR 1346.

defendant and her twin daughters, which he duly did. The defendant left her own property and moved into the house. In 1973 the plaintiff offered her £4,000 to leave the house, but she refused on the grounds that the house was hers and the children's until the twins left school. The plaintiff wrote to the defendant via his solicitor purporting to revoke the licence and, following her refusal to leave the property, brought possession proceedings against her. The defendant claimed that the arrangement between herself and the plaintiff was a contract and included within it a contractual licence by which the defendant had received permission to reside in the property until the children were finished their schooling. The Court inferred from the circumstances that there was such a contract between the parties, by which the defendant had a contractual licence to be accommodated in the house with the children as long as the children were of school-going age and reasonably required the accommodation.

(i) Revocation of Contractual Licences

[10–07] The common law regarded contractual licences as revocable at will because they gave rise to no estate or interest in the land and were therefore purely personal. In relation to contractual licences, this common law position had the potential to cause considerable difficulties because it appeared to allow for the revocation of licences even in contravention of the terms of the contract through which they were created. Over time, however, this common law position was modified to some extent, particularly by the involvement of equity. This modification resulted in the development of principles relating to whether a licensee is entitled to legal or equitable redress for the revocation of the licence.[14] In other words, while it remains the case that contractual licences are revocable in purely doctrinal terms, the way in which the revocation is done can result in the licensee being entitled to protection and compensation. Thus, we say that contractual licences are now to be revoked in compliance with the terms of the contract itself.[15]

[10–08] While this presents a relatively straightforward position where the contract includes terms relating to the revocation of the licence, not all contracts will contain such terms. In such cases the courts will usually imply what it considers to be an appropriate term into the contract.[16] The "appropriate" mechanism for the revocation of a licence will clearly depend on the circumstances of the case, but in most situations the courts will imply a term for revocation on the provision of "reasonable" notice to the licensee.[17] Again, what is "reasonable" will depend on all of the circumstances of the case and will be a matter for the discretion of the courts or the mutual agreement of the parties.[18] Once the licence has been terminated, the licensee must be given a reasonable period of time to vacate the premises before he is regarded as a trespasser.[19] If a licensor ejects a licensee following an attempted revocation that is in breach of either the terms of the contract or the "reasonable notice" requirement, the licensee can avail of a number of

---

[14] *Winter Garden Theatre (London) Ltd v Millennium Productions Ltd* [1946] 1 All ER 678; *Wallshire Ltd v Advertising Sites Ltd* [1988] 2 EGLR 167.

[15] See, for example, *Whipp v Mackey* [1927] IR 372.

[16] *Winter Garden Theatre (London) Ltd v Millennium Productions Ltd* [1946] 1 All ER 678.

[17] *ibid.*

[18] *Australian Blue Metal Ltd v Hughes* [1963] AC 74.

[19] *Winter Garden Theatre (London) Ltd v Millennium Productions Ltd* [1946] 1 All ER 678.

remedies. First, he can sue for breach of contract, although the remedy for breach is likely to be damages and the licensee would be unlikely to recover a right to be on the land itself.[20] Second, the licensee may have recourse to equity and may seek an injunction to prevent his removal from the property if the contract is specifically enforceable.[21] Third, the licensee may sue for assault if he was wrongly ejected and, in particular, if any kind of force was used to remove him.[22]

In the context of contractual licences, it seems perfectly reasonable to allow the law of contract and the terms of the contract itself to dictate the revocability of the licence. This position is certainly preferable to the common law position, which allowed for the revocation of the licence in breach of the contract in certain cases and certainly recognised that licensors had a power (if not a *right*) to remove licensees in contravention of the terms of the contract itself.[23] Contract law is largely governed by the principle that one is free to enter contracts but then is morally and legally bound to abide by their terms, therefore it is sensible for property law to abide by the same principle in the interpretation and enforcement of contractual licences. [10–09]

(ii) Transferability of Contractual Licences

As mentioned above, every licence involves a benefit (held by the licensee) and a burden (suffered by the licensor). One of the most contentious questions in the area of contractual licences relates to the extent to which both the licensee and the licensor can pass on, or transfer, the benefit and the burden of the contractual licence to their successors under the contract (in the case of the licensee), or to their successors in title (in the case of the licensor). Whether the benefit of a contractual licence can be transferred by the licensee will very much depend on the terms of the contract and the nature of the licence. If the licence is intended to be purely personal, it simply cannot be transferred. However, if the licence is not purely personal, there is no reason in law why its benefit cannot be transferred to a third party if the terms of the contract itself allow it.[24] [10–10]

The situation is rather more complex when the law comes to consider whether the burden of a contractual licence can be transferred or, in other words, can bind a successor in title of the original licensor. The law has developed through three stages in relation to this matter, none of which is particularly satisfactory. The first stage—which we will call the "original position"—held that the burden of a contractual licence could never bind successors in title of the licensor because contracts give rise to purely personal, and therefore non-transferable, rights. The second stage—which we will call the "licence-as-equity position"—held that the burden of a contractual licence could bind successors in title of the licensor only if the successor has notice of the licence. The third stage—which we will call the "modern position"—holds that the burden of a contractual licence can bind successors in title of the licensor only if the successor has notice of the licence *and* it would constitute an unconscionable injustice to allow the [10–11]

---

[20] See, for example, *Wood v Leadbitter* (1845) 13 M & W 838.

[21] *Verrall v Great Yarmouth Borough Council* [1980] 1 All ER 839.

[22] *Hurst v Picture Theatres Ltd* [1915] 1 KB 1.

[23] See, for example, *Thompson v Park* [1944] KB 408; reversed by *Winter Garden Theatre (London) Ltd v Millennium Productions Ltd* [1946] 1 All ER 678.

[24] See, for example, *Clapham v Edwards* [1938] 1 All ER 507; *Shayler v Woolf* [1946] Ch 320.

successor in title to operate free of the licence. In those cases the enforceability comes about through a constructive trust.

(a) The Original Position

[10–12] It was originally the case that the common law would not recognise any situation in which the burden of a contractual licence could be binding on a successor in title of the licensor, even if that successor was actually aware of the licence at the time he acquired the property.[25] This meant that where the property was acquired by another, the licensee could no longer exercise his permissions to enjoy it. This situation was clearly absurd from a justice perspective because the licensee could not prevent the licensor from alienating his property rights to another, and would be left with a remedy in damages only against the original licensor.[26] As a result, the contractual licence was exceptionally insecure in real terms.

[10–13] The difficulties with the original position are well illustrated by the case of *Clore v Theatrical Properties Ltd and Westby & Co Ltd*.[27] The case concerned a licence[28] by which the defendant was given exclusive front-of-house rights to serve refreshments and so on in the Prince of Wales Theatre. When the title-holders of the theatre changed, the new owners contended that the defendants had no right to enter the premises and conduct their business *per* the original agreement. The Court of Appeal unanimously held that the contractual licence could not be enforced against the new title-holders of the theatre: rather, the enforcement of this licence required a "contractual nexus"[29] between the parties (i.e. the contractual licence could only be enforced between parties who were in privity of contract to one another). This was not present here and the licensees no longer had any permission to enjoy the property.

(b) The "Licence-as-Equity" Position

[10–14] The difficulties with the original position were relatively clear to all. Indeed, even in the case of *Clore*, Lord Romer expressed his "considerable sympathy with the defendants" in "regretfully arriv[ing] at the... conclusion" that the defendant could not enforce his contractual licence against the new owners. The difficulties with the original position became all the more clear when one considered that even a purchaser with notice of the licence could enjoy the property without having any regard to the contractual licensee because the licence was a purely personal right, giving rise to no proprietary interest whatsoever. In the case of *Errington v Errington*, Lord Denning made the first of his two attempts to introduce what he considered to be a greater degree of fairness to the contractual licensee in such situations.[30]

[25] *King v David Allen & Sons Billposting Ltd* [1916] 2 AC 54.

[26] *Clore v Theatrical Properties Ltd and Westby & Co Ltd* [1936] 3 All ER 483.

[27] *ibid.*

[28] While the agreement itself stated that it was a "lease", the Court concluded that the agreement was properly described as a licence by application of the principles of the "lease v licence distinction". These principles and the distinction in general are considered in full in Chapter 15, below.

[29] *Clore v Theatrical Properties Ltd and Westby & Co Ltd* [1936] 3 All ER 483 *per* Lord Wright MR.

[30] *Errington v Errington* [1952] 1 KB 290. The second attempt came in *Binions v Evans* [1972] 2 WLR 729, which is considered in para 10–18 below.

In this case a father who wanted to provide a home for his recently married son bought a house by means of a deposit and mortgage. He paid all rates and taxes, but allowed his son and daughter-in-law to reside there, promising that if they stayed there and paid the mortgage instalments, he would transfer the property into their names once the mortgage had been redeemed. He handed the Building Society book in which mortgage payments were recorded to his daughter-in-law (of whom he was very fond) and advised her not to part with it. At the time of the father's death, the mortgage had not yet been cleared and the house was left to his widow. At this stage the son left the home to live with his mother, while the daughter-in-law continued to reside in the property and to pay the mortgage instalments. The mother then brought an action for possession against the daughter-in-law who claimed, *inter alia*, that she occupied the property under a contractual licence by which her mother-in-law was bound. Relying on authority stating the original position, the widow claimed that she was not bound by the contractual licence granted by her deceased husband and was entitled to remove her daughter-in-law and retake possession of the property. Quite surprisingly, given the authorities, the Court of Appeal held that a contractual licence could be binding on someone who acquires property through a will, with Lord Denning holding that such a contractual licence created an equitable interest in the property that would be binding on all successors in title of the original licensor, apart from the bona fide purchaser of the property for value without notice of it. As a result, the mother-in-law in this case could not retake possession in breach of the terms of the contractual licence itself; rather, she was bound by it. **[10–15]**

The decision in *Errington* was problematic for a number of reasons,[31] but from the perspective of the law of licences it was exceptionally difficult to reconcile with the definition of licences itself. Licences, as we noted at the start of this chapter, are traditionally seen as creating personal rights and not giving rise to any ownership in the property whatsoever. In direct contradiction of this position, however, Lord Denning suggests in *Errington* that a contractual licence can be analogised to an equity in the property and can therefore be protected by the doctrine of notice. Thus *Errington* represented a potentially massive shift in the law's conceptions of licences and the rights of licensees. **[10–16]**

(c) The Modern Position

Later cases began to move away from the *Errington* position, but the progression was slow. The *Errington* concept of licences giving rise to an equitable interest was reiterated and amplified by Lord Denning in *Binions v Evans*,[32] which might be considered the first step towards the modern position. This doctrine was then very much refined in *Ashburn Anstalt v Arnold*,[33] where the modern position was firmly staked out. Both cases require some attention here. **[10–17]**

[31] It not only contradicted the jurisprudence from the original position, considered above, but the decision also appeared to breach the rule in s 4(1) of the UK's Law of Property Act 1925 forbidding the creation of any new equitable interests.
[32] [1972] Ch 359.
[33] [1989] 1 Ch 1.

[10–18] *Binions v Evans* concerned a woman whose husband had been employed as a labourer on a large country estate and, as a part of his employment, resided in a cottage owned by the estate, for which he was not required to pay rent or rates. When the husband died in 1965, Mrs Evans was 73 years of age and she continued to live in the cottage. In 1968 the estate-owners completed an agreement with her, allowing her to "reside [in] and occupy" the property "free of rent for the remainder of her life". In 1970 the estate was sold to the plaintiffs, who were made fully aware of the agreement with Mrs Evans and who agreed to a clause in the conveyance by which they undertook to allow Mrs Evans to enjoy occupation under the agreement. The plaintiffs received a discount on the purchase price in return for this undertaking, but in February 1971 they attempted to remove the defendant from the cottage. The Court of Appeal, through the judgment of Lord Denning, found that the agreement between the parties was a contractual licence resulting in an equity in favour of Mrs Evans. As the agreement allowed her to reside in the property for her lifetime, her equity was, in effect, an equitable life estate. In order to protect this interest the Court held that the purchasers were bound by a constructive trust in favour of Mrs Evans for her lifetime. Through the use of a constructive trust here, the contractual licence enjoyed by Mrs Evans, which the common law would recognise as a merely personal permissive right, now appeared to have taken on the character of an equitable life estate, with the potential to bind purchasers through a constructive trust and giving rise to the rights of a tenant for life, under the Settled Land Acts, to the licensee.[34]

[10–19] *Binions* thus represented a sea-change in the law of licences and one that was subject to a major difficulty: contractual licences were being characterised as equitable interests pursuant to the decision in *Errington*, but the reasoning behind that decision continued to be dogged by criticism and ambiguity. It was not until the case of *Ashburn Anstalt v Arnold* that the law relating to the enforceability of contractual licences against successors in title of the original licensor began to take on a rational and doctrinally defensible shape. In 1973 the defendant sold its leasehold interest in a shop by means of an agreement that included a clause allowing him to remain in the property until required to vacate it by the purchaser, upon the provision of at least four months' notice to this effect. The plaintiff purchased the property from the original licensor in 1985, with that transaction being made subject to the agreement with Arnold. Ashburn Anstalt attempted to remove the defendant from the property, claiming that it was not bound by the contractual licence of 1973 as it had not been a party to the original agreement. Although the House of Lords held that what actually existed here was a lease by which the plaintiffs were bound, the Law Lords also reflected on what the plaintiff's obligations would be if the agreement constituted a contractual licence. The Court held that even though a mere contractual licence to occupy land was not binding on a purchaser of the land (including a purchaser who has notice of it), appropriate facts may exist that give rise to a constructive trust. A constructive trust would be imposed by the Court only in limited situations, however, and would require the Court

[34] Both Lords Megaw and Stephenson held that Mrs Evans had the powers of a tenant for life under the Settled Land Acts. Although the Settled Land Acts 1882–1890 no longer apply in Ireland, under the Land and Conveyancing Law Reform Act 2009, they are considered in Chapter 6 above.

to be satisfied that it would be unconscionable and inequitable for the successor in title to be relieved from obligations under the licence.

Although these pronouncements in *Ashburn Anstalt* were *obiter*, they can be said to provide a shape for the modern position that has since been adopted by the courts of England and Wales.[35] The modern position, then, has much to commend it: it maintains the traditional position that a contractual licence is a merely personal right and does not, in general, bind purchasers regardless of their state of notice, while at the same time ameliorating some of the harshness of this position by protecting the contractual licensee by means of a constructive trust where the successor in title: (a) has notice of the licence, *and* (b) would be acting unconscionably and engaging in a mischief by ignoring that licence in light of the surrounding circumstances of the case. However, the Irish courts cannot be said to have embraced this position in terms of protecting contractual licensees. Instead, the doctrine of estoppel is more commonly used to prevent licensors from disadvantaging their contractual licensees, and it is to this that we now turn. **[10–20]**

4. Licences and the Doctrine of Estoppel

Although "estoppel has no necessary connection with the law of licences",[36] it is by now well established that where a licensee acts to his detriment on the basis of a representation or belief induced by the licensor, equity may attach to the licence in order to protect the licensee. This can result in the licensor being precluded from revoking the licence or from acting in a manner that would rid the licensee of the capacity to enjoy the licence. In these kinds of situations the contractual licence in question is, effectively, *bolstered* by offering it protection, and sometimes an enhancement, through equity. Licences can also be granted as a remedy to a finding of estoppel. We will consider both of these categories in turn but first we need to familiarise ourselves with the basics of the concept of estoppel.[37] **[10–21]**

(i) Estoppel

Estoppel is an equitable doctrine that prevents someone from reneging on a representation or an induced belief that they will not strictly enforce their legal rights where this representation or induced belief has led another person to act to his detriment. There are two kinds of estoppel in law: promissory estoppel (which is reliant on a pre-existing contractual relationship[38] and can only be used as a shield and never as a sword[39]) and proprietary estoppel (which relates primarily to interests over land). **[10–22]**

---

[35] See, for example, *IDC Group Ltd v Clark* [1992] 1 EGLR 184.

[36] Harpum, *Megarry & Wade: The Law of Real Property* (6th ed, 2000, London, Sweet & Maxwell), p 750.

[37] A full consideration of the ranging and complex law of estoppel is beyond the scope of this book, however it receives its definitive treatment in the Irish canon in Delaney, *Equity and the Law of Trusts in Ireland* (5th ed, 2011, Dublin, Round Hall).

[38] *Hughes v Metropolitan Railway Co.* (1877) 2 AC 439; *Central London Property Trust v High Trees House Ltd* [1947] KB 130.

[39] *Inwards v Baker* [1965] 2 QB 29; *Coombe v Coombe* [1951] 2 KB 130; but *cf Re JR (A Ward of Court)* [1993] ILRM 657 in which the High Court appeared to suggest that promissory estoppel could be used as a sword. This ought to be contrasted with *Association of General Practitioners Ltd v Minister for Health* [1995] 2 ILRM 481.

In both the UK and Australia these two doctrines of estoppel appear to have moved towards a unified doctrine that is concerned primarily with the question of whether it would be unconscionable to allow the representor to renege on his representation.[40] In a number of cases—most notably *McMahon v Kerry County Council*[41] and *Re JR (A Ward of Court)*[42]—the Irish courts appear to have engaged in doctrinally dubious "mixing" of both species of estoppel, but it does not seem sustainable to argue that the Irish jurisprudence suggests any deliberate strategy towards a unified doctrine of estoppel of the kind now to be found in the UK and Australia.[43]

[10–23] In the context of property law we are concerned first and foremost with the operation of proprietary estoppel. Before a court will award a remedy on the basis of a proprietary estoppel, a number of things must be established[44]:

(a) The landowner must have led a third party to believe that they will acquire an interest over property[45] *or* must have acquiesced in a third party's mistaken belief that she held proprietary interests in property that she is developing in some way[46];
(b) The third party must act *in reliance on* this representation or induced belief. In general, this causal connection must be proved,[47] although the UK courts have shown a tendency towards assuming reliance in some cases[48];
(c) The landowner must attempt to renege on his representation or induced belief;
(d) The landowner's reneger must be such as to result in a detriment to the third party. Detriment can be taken to mean "that which would flow from the change of position if the assumption were deserted that led to it".[49] While the UK

---

[40] See, for example, *Walton Stores (Interstate) Ltd v Maher* (1988) 164 CLR 387; *Commonwealth v Verwayen* (1990) 170 CLR 394; *Taylor Fashions v Liverpool Victoria Trustees* (1982) 1 All ER 897; Spence, *Protecting Reliance: The Emerging Doctrine of Equitable Estoppel* (1999, Oxford, Hart Publishing).

[41] [1981] ILRM 419.

[42] [1993] ILRM 657.

[43] In support of this conclusion, see Mee, "Lost in the Big House: Where Stands Irish Law on Equitable *Estoppel*?" (1998) xxxiii IR Jur 187.

[44] These guidelines reflect the so-called Five Probanda, as outlined in *Willmott v Barber* (1880) 15 Ch D 97. In that case Fry LJ famously held: "In the first place the plaintiff must have made a mistake as to his legal rights. Secondly, the plaintiff must have expended some money or must have done some act (not necessarily upon the defendant's land) on the faith of his mistaken belief. Thirdly, the defendant, the possessor of the legal right, must know of the existence of his own right which is inconsistent with the right claimed by the plaintiff... Fourthly, the defendant, the possessor of the legal right, must know of the plaintiff's mistaken belief of his rights. If he does not, there is nothing which calls upon him to assert his own rights. Lastly... the defendant, the possessor of the legal right, must have encouraged the plaintiff in his expenditure of money or in the other acts which he has done, either directly or by abstaining from asserting his legal right." See also *Matharu v Matharu* (1994) 26 HLR 648.

[45] *Dilwyn v Llewelyn* (1862) 4 De GF & J 517.

[46] *Ramsden v Dyson* (1866) LR 1 HL 129.

[47] *McGuinness v McGuinness*, unreported, High Court, 19 March 2002.

[48] *Greasley v Cooke* [1980] 1 WLR 1306.

[49] *Grundt v Great Boulder Proprietary Gold Mines Limited* (1937) 59 CLR 641; see also Ong, "Equitable Estoppel: Defining the Detriment" (1999) 11(1) Bond L R 136.

> courts have shown some willingness to assume detriment,[50] the Irish courts' position is less clear. In *Re JR (A Ward of Court)* the High Court appeared to assume that a detriment arose where the plaintiff left her permanent home on the promise of another, even though there was no evidence that this was the reason for the plaintiff's decision to leave her own property.[51] In contrast, the court refused to assume detriment and required it to be specifically pleaded and proved in *McGuinness v McGuinness*.[52]

Establishing estoppel is the first stage in cases that attempt to either prevent the contractual licensor from acting in a manner that would deprive the licensor of enjoyment of the property (bolstering the licence through equity), or to try to acquire a licence as a remedy to estoppels (estoppel licence as remedy).

(ii) Bolstering Licences through Estoppel

A successful claim of estoppel by a contractual licensee can bolster the licence by making it more secure; perhaps even making it more or less permanent. The Irish case of *Smyth v Halpin*[53] serves as a useful illustration of a case where a licensor was prevented from revoking the licence through a finding of estoppel and, by means of remedy, the previous licensee was granted a fee simple estate in the land. **[10–24]**

In this case Smyth intended to build a house for himself and his wife and, in order to facilitate this, asked his father for a site. In response to this request the father said, "This place is yours after your mother's day—what would you be doing with two places?" and suggested to his son that he build an extension onto the family home. In order to build the extension, Smyth required a loan. In order to secure this loan, his father transferred a site to him, which was then used as security. The extension—which was a self-contained but connected part of the main house—was then built. The father made a number of wills in his lifetime. In 1986—following the agreement with the plaintiff—he made a further will, leaving a life estate in the house to his wife and a fee simple remainder to the plaintiff, subject to certain rights for two of the plaintiff's sisters. The next will was made in 1991 and by it the father left a life estate in the cottage to his wife, with the fee simple remainder to his daughter, Regina. The 1991 will did not make an allowance for the plaintiff in relation to the property. Under the father's last will, made in 1992, he left the farm to his wife for life, with a fee simple remainder to the plaintiff. He also left the cottage to his wife for life, with a fee simple remainder to his daughter, Regina. The plaintiff claimed that he was entitled to the fee simple remainder in the cottage once his mother had died on the basis of the representation of his father and his own subsequent acts relying on that representation. Geoghegan J accepted that the son had made out a case of proprietary estoppel in relation to the property which entitled him to something more than the licence he currently had over the land on which the extension was located. The Court ultimately held that the appropriate mechanism for the satisfaction of the son's equity was the transfer of the fee simple interest in the property to him. The son had a clear **[10–25]**

[50] See *Greasley v Cooke* [1980] 1 WLR 1306.
[51] [1993] ILRM 657.
[52] Unreported, High Court, 19 March 2002.
[53] [1997] 2 ILRM 38.

expectation that he would have a fee simple in the entire cottage, and the most appropriate manner of satisfying that expectation (and the action taken on foot thereof) was to transfer the fee simple to the plaintiff.

[10–26] *Smyth* is what we might describe as a "tidy" case where the estoppel is clear and the remedy does not raise any real doctrinal questions. However, not every case of estoppel and licences is quite as neat. In Ireland there are two cases in particular that illustrate that Irish courts have suggested the use of the doctrine of estoppel to bring about a situation in which someone characterised as a licensee can eventually acquire ownership over the property in question through the application of something akin to adverse possession in cases where the possession in question could not possibly be characterised as "adverse" in real terms. In both cases—*Cullen v Cullen*[54] and *McMahon v Kerry County Council*[55]—the overall outcome of the case might be said to have been the "just" result, but the means by which it is reached (and especially the way in which the laws of estoppel and of licences are applied) can be questioned.

[10–27] *Cullen v Cullen* concerned a businessman and farmer in Co. Wexford whose son had bought his own farm but lived in his parents' house at the insistence of his father. Cullen suffered from paranoia and became convinced that his family would have him committed to an asylum. In order to prevent such an eventuality, he went into hiding in Dublin and, through the intermediary offices of a priest, negotiated with his wife and sons as to what was to happen in relation to his businesses and farm in the future. He represented to his wife that, *inter alia*, he would sign the farm and business over to her. In that same year his wife won a mobile home in a "Spot the Ball" competition in the newspaper and decided to give it to her son, M, to live in. When she asked her husband whether the mobile home could be erected on the farm, he told her that she could put it wherever she wanted as he intended to sign the farm over to her in any case. As a result of this representation M spent a considerable amount of money building foundations and installing plumbing in the mobile home. Shortly afterwards, Cullen wrote to both his wife and his son via a solicitor, instructing them to vacate the premises and cease involvement in his businesses. M challenged this, arguing that he enjoyed a licence over the land that his father was estopped from revoking.

[10–28] The Court found that M had resided in the premises by means of a licence from his father, which he had attempted to revoke by means of the solicitor's letter. However, in this case the Court held that the law of equity restricted the father's capacity to revoke the licence because of the representations he had made in relation to the son's permission to place the mobile home on the land. In other words, Cullen was estopped from revoking the licence because of his representation, the expenditure M had undertaken on the basis of this representation, and the detriment that would arise from a successful revocation. M attempted to acquire a fee simple in the land by means of remedy, but the Court considered that the relevant authority—*Ramsden v Dyson*[56]—did not permit of such a remedy because M was aware that the land upon which he was placing the mobile home was in fact his father's land and was never under any representation that it would be transferred to him.

---

[54] [1962] IR 268.
[55] [1981] ILRM 419.
[56] (1866) LR 1 HL 129.

That said, however, the Court found that Cullen was estopped from asserting his title to the land where the mobile home was erected because he had led his son to believe that he could place the mobile home there and reside in it for as long as he wished, as a result of which the son had expended considerable time and money that he otherwise would not have spent. The means of remedy here was essentially the attachment, by Kenny J, of an equity to the son's licence; in other words, the bolstering of the licence through attaching an equity to it as remedy to estoppel. The attachment of the equity to the licence meant that the licence could be enforced by M against *both* his father (the licensor) *and* any successors in title of his over the land. Furthermore, Kenny J speculated that M might be able to acquire title to the property by means of adverse possession following 12 years' possession under this licence. **[10–29]**

This latter suggestion—that M could acquire the fee simple after 12 years' possession, where that possession is enjoyed by means of a licence—is remarkable. It is difficult to imagine how the possession in question could be classified as "adverse"—a basic requirement of any claim for adverse possession[57]—given its basis in a licence (permission) and one, moreover, that is protected by equity to the extent where it is irrevocable. It is therefore difficult to understand the doctrinal basis for Kenny J's decision relating to adverse possession in this case, *unless* one accepts that the licence under which M resided in the property had been revoked successfully by his father by means of the solicitor's letter.[58] **[10–30]**

It is probably best to see this element of *Cullen v Cullen* as an attempt to reach what the Court likely considered to be the fairest outcome (i.e. to allow the son to acquire title over the property) in a situation where the law did not quite "fit". *Cullen* would certainly not be the first or last case in which, to paraphrase the old saying, "a hard case made bad law" but if it were confined to its own facts it could be considered an aberration that we might tolerate as part of the everyday pragmatism of trying to achieve justice in the messiness of human affairs though the blunt instrument that is the law. *Cullen* cannot, however, be entirely quarantined in this way for its influence was discernible in a different, but nevertheless interesting, case: *McMahon v Kerry County Council.*[59] Although *McMahon* is not properly described as a case about licences it is worth considering here for it suggests the reach of *Cullen* and, indeed, of estoppel as flexible—if somewhat abused—tools to achieve the fairest result in difficult property disputes. **[10–31]**

In 1964 McMahon acquired a plot of land on which he had intended to build a secondary school. By 1965, however, McMahon had decided that the school-building project was not feasible, abandoned the plan and did not visit the site again until 1968. At that stage McMahon discovered employees of Kerry County Council preparing to build on the property and complained, following which the works ceased. McMahon never fenced off the land in any way thereafter, and in 1972 Kerry County Council built two houses on the site in which local authority tenants were housed. When McMahon claimed possession of the property and the houses built thereon, Kerry County Council claimed that he ought not to be permitted to retake possession. **[10–32]**

---

[57] See generally Chapter 14.

[58] *Bellew v Bellew* [1982] IR 447.

[59] [1981] ILRM 419.

[10–33] Finlay P conceded that the circumstances at issue in this case did not fall squarely into *Ramsden v Dyson*,[60] in which Lord Kingsdown explained the doctrine of proprietary estoppel as follows:

> If a man, under a verbal agreement with a landlord for a certain interest in land, or, what amounts to the same thing, under an expectation, created or encouraged by the landlord, that he shall have a certain interest, takes possession of such land, with the consent of the landlord, and upon the face of such promise or expectation, with the knowledge of the landlord, and without objection by him, laid out money on the land, a Court of Equity will compel the landlord to give effect to such promise or expectation.[61]

McMahon had not wilfully acquiesced in a mistaken belief on the part of the Kerry County Council that it owned the property in question; rather he had told the defendants of his interest in 1968 and then complained about the building as soon as it came to his attention in 1973. Nonetheless, Finlay P looked to what he considered the "underlying principle" in *Ramsden*, which he considered to be the requirement for a landowner, on the one hand, to act equitably and in good conscience, and for the Court, on the other hand, to take into consideration "not only conduct on the part of the plaintiff with particular regard to whether it is wrong or wilful but also conduct on the part of the defendant and furthermore the consequences and the justice of the consequences both from the point of view of the plaintiff and of the defendant".[62]

[10–34] Taking into account the circumstances of the case, the Court refused McMahon permission to retake possession of the land. In reaching this conclusion the Court held that:

(a) McMahon had acquired the property for a particular purpose that was never realised, as a result of which the property has no intrinsic value to him;
(b) McMahon had failed to mark out or supervise the property in any way;
(c) Kerry County Council had made an excusable mistake in assuming that it was entitled to build on the property;
(d) Repossession of the property would result in a large and unconscionable windfall on the part of McMahon as a result of the houses constructed on the property;
(e) The houses were now providing accommodation for needy persons.

As a result of the foregoing considerations, the Court held that it would be unconscionable to allow McMahon to retake possession over the property. Instead, McMahon was to be given the market value of the property and a sum in compensation and, citing *Cullen v Cullen*, Kerry County Council was said to be able to acquire title over the property by means of adverse possession on the expiration of 12 years.[63]

---

60 (1866) LR 1 HL 129.
61 *ibid.* at p 170.
62 *ibid.* at p 421.
63 The concept of unconscionability was also highlighted in *Carter v Ross*, unreported, High Court, 8 December 2000.

McMahon is a controversial case, not only because there was clearly no real case of estoppel here in the traditional sense of the doctrine, but also because the Court appeared to take a very charitable view of the County Council's behaviour—not only were the defendants exceptionally well placed to realise that the property they were building on was not theirs but they had been expressly told in 1968 that the property did not belong to them. Finlay P's conclusion that the defendant Council's behaviour was "excusable" is exceptionally difficult to fathom in this light. Nevertheless, there are few who would dispute the fairness of the ultimate conclusion reached by Finlay P, even if, from a doctrinal perspective, his mangling of the law of estoppel is particularly troublesome. The most appropriate approach to the decision in *McMahon* appears to be to take it as a case decided in particular circumstances and to limit it to its own particular facts, rather as we did with *Cullen*. **[10–35]**

(iii) Estoppel Licences as Remedy

Where an estoppel has been made out successfully, the remedy to be awarded by the court will be entirely at the discretion of equity because all equitable remedies are discretionary. In general a court will assess the most appropriate manner to remedy the inequity that has arisen, however, appropriateness is likely to depend on whether the court considers the inequity to result from the unsatisfied expectation of benefit or from the reliance of the actor. Where it is considered appropriate, the remedy awarded can be a licence. It should be noted, however, that a licence will not *inevitably* be the remedy for a case of estoppel; indeed, in appropriate cases the transfer of a fee simple might be the appropriate remedy.[64] In *Pascoe v Turner*,[65] for example, a couple cohabited in the male partner's property, but when he entered into a relationship with another woman and left Turner to cohabit with this woman, he represented to Turner that she could "have the house". As a result, Turner expended significant time and money on the property. When Pascoe later attempted to retake the property, Turner successfully claimed estoppel and was granted a fee simple over the property. She was no longer a mere licensee in the property: she now had an equity that only could satisfied by the transfer of the fee simple. **[10–36]**

(iv) Transferability of Estoppel Licences

Logic suggests that the benefit of an estoppel licence cannot be transferred by the licensee; the estoppel arises because of the unconscionable actions of the landowner in relation to the licensee, therefore the benefit of the equity ought not to be transferable. On the other hand, the burden of an estoppel licence can be enforced against a successor in title of the licensor; as the equity binds the conscience of the licensor, it ought also to bind the conscience of all those who acquire the property through the licensor *apart from* the bona fide purchaser for value without notice of the licence.[66] **[10–37]**

---

[64] *Pascoe v Turner* [1979] 1 WLR 431. As a matter of historical curiosity, readers may be interested to note that Turner was, in fact, the first unmarried cohabiting lover reported to have obtained the absolute ownership over the property of the cohabitants. See also Sufrin, "An Equity Richly Satisfied" (1979) 42(5) MLR 574.

[65] [1979] 1 WLR 431.

[66] See, for example, *Inwards v Baker* [1965] 2 QB 29; *Re Basham* [1986] 1 WLR 1498.

[10–38] The difficulties associated with this position are well illustrated by the case of *Re Sharpe (A Bankrupt)*.[67] Sharpe and his aunt lived together in a maisonette attached to a shop that together formed a leasehold property that Sharpe had purchased in 1975 for the sum of £17,000. The aunt had provided £12,000 of the money for the purchase in 1975, as well as over £2,000 for decoration and fittings, in return for which she was told that she could stay in the maisonette for as long as she would like to do so and that she would be cared for by Sharpe and his wife. The aunt later paid approximately £9,000 to help stave off bankruptcy and, in 1975, acquired a promissory note from Sharpe in the sum of £15,700. The trustee in bankruptcy attempted to ascertain what rights, if any, the aunt claimed as a result of her contribution to the property, but the aunt did not reply to his correspondence. In 1979 the trustee in bankruptcy agreed to sell the property in a vacant state for £17,000, following which the aunt claimed an interest in the property. The Court held that the aunt had a right to reside in the property that could be enforced against a successor in title of the bankrupt until such time as the loan was repaid. Relying on *Binions v Evans*,[68] the Court also held that the aunt's right to occupy conferred an interest in her under a constructive trust that was binding on the successor in title of the bankrupt.

[10–39] The decision in *Sharpe* throws into sharp relief a number of difficulties with such cases. First, the Court did not appear to be capable of deciding whether the aunt occupied the property on the basis of an estoppel licence or a contractual licence. If the right constituted a contractual licence, then, by the principles of constructive trust from *Binions* (and later from *Ashburn Anstalt*), this licence would be binding on successors in title of the bankrupt provided they had notice of the licence *and* the circumstances demanded that the purchaser would be bound to avoid a mischief. If, however, the licence is an estoppel licence, the decision in *Sharpe* appears to suggest that the licence is enforceable against successors in title. Browne-Wilkinson J found that the aunt's rights were certainly binding on the trustee of the bankrupt because the trustee had taken the place of Sharpe, however he suggested that a purchaser from the trustee would be bound only if he could be shown to have actual notice[69] of the aunt's entitlement, although he acknowledged that this area would have to receive consideration in full by the Court of Appeal in order to bring clarity to it.

5. Are Licences Really "Mere" Permissions?

[10–40] In general, as the foregoing paragraphs show, licences operate in a sensible and consistent manner in the law of property. Relatively recent developments in the law of licences have, however, posed a number of questions about the nature of the licence. Is it true to say that licences really are mere permissions and do not result in any proprietary interests in property, or have licences changed in some fundamental way? It is certainly true to say that licences do not create proprietary interests *per se*, however, as we have seen they can operate in a proprietary manner and, through their operation, give rise to proprietary interests.

[67] [1980] 1 WLR 219.

[68] [1972] Ch 359.

[69] On the different types of notice, see further Chapter 3, paras 3–34 to 3–42.

The contractual licence, in particular, has developed in this manner in other jurisdictions. As considered above, contractual licences can now bind on the successor in title of the original licensor if he has notice of the licence *and* the circumstances require the licence to be enforced against him in order to avoid a mischief. The doctrine of notice has traditionally been used for the protection of proprietary third-party interests and therefore seems prima facie to be an inappropriate tool for the protection of a licence; furthermore the licence through this mechanism is enforced by means of a constructive trust and therefore becomes an equitable interest in the property. Although the law resulting in this constructive trust, as laid out in *Ashburn Anstalt*,[70] is clear and arguably doctrinally sound, it nevertheless suggests that the licence is becoming an interest that has at least the capacity to result in proprietary rights, even if it does not constitute a proprietary interest in and of itself. **[10–41]**

This tentative conclusion appears to be reinforced by the development of the estoppel licence. As considered above, in two cases—*Cullen v Cullen*[71] and *McMahon v Kerry County Council*[72]—the Irish courts have developed the concept that a licence (or at least something exceptionally analogous to it) could result in the acquisition of title by means of adverse possession. Although this development seems clearly at odds with the law of adverse possession, it nevertheless causes us to question further the true nature of the licence. It does not appear that these cases suggest that licences, by themselves, have the inherent capacity to result in a proprietary interest; rather it seems clear that these licences result in proprietary interests only because of the equity attached to them as a result of an estoppel. While these cases certainly point towards the need for more clarity and direction in the Irish law of estoppel, they do not appear to place any serious question marks over the nature of the licence itself. **[10–42]**

II. Rights of Residence

A right of residence is a right to reside in the property of another. Rights of residence are not uncommon in Ireland and they are perhaps particularly common in situations where a farm or home is being left to a child but a right of residence is left to the surviving spouse.[73] Rights of residence are often accompanied by rights of maintenance and support. Although these rights are not given detailed consideration here, they do arise in some of the jurisprudence considered and for those purposes we can say that a right of maintenance and support is a right to be "kept" that is akin to a positive covenant,[74] although it is not enforceable by or against successors in title.[75] Rights of residence have a contested character, which is very much dependent on two **[10–43]**

[70] [1989] Ch 1.

[71] [1962] IR 268.

[72] [1981] ILRM 419.

[73] As considered in Chapter 16, surviving spouses can apply for a right to appropriate the family home under s 56 of the Succession Act 1965. A widow or widower who is dissatisfied with a right of residence may well decide to do this, but that is a separate matter to the operation of rights of residence themselves.

[74] *Colreavy v Colreavy* [1940] IR 71.

[75] Rights of maintenance and support are not included in "dominant land" as defined by s 46 of the Land and Conveyancing Law Reform Act 2009 and cannot, therefore, be enforced through s 47 of the same Act. The operation of freehold covenants is considered in full in Chapter 11.

things: (a) whether the right of residence was general or exclusive, and (b) whether the right of residence existed over unregistered or registered land. Although the nature of the right has not been settled, it should be recalled that s 11(2)(c)(iii) of the Land and Conveyancing Law Reform Act 2009 provides that the only freehold estate in law that can be created or transferred is a fee simple in possession, including a fee simple "subject only to a right of residence which is not an exclusive right over the whole land". It is therefore clear that, whatever else might be said of it, a right of residence is not capable of existing as a freehold estate in law. The more precise meaning of s 11(2)(c)(iii) is considered below.[76]

1. Nature of Rights of Residence

[10–44] Rights of residence can be divided into general rights of residence and exclusive rights of residence. A general right of residence is a right to reside in the property of another *in general*, whereas an exclusive right of residence is a right to reside exclusively in the property of another and often in a *particular part* of that (perhaps specifying particular rooms). Whether a right of residence is general or exclusive is an important consideration because it substantially dictates the extent to which the holder of the right of residence can exercise any kind of control over the property. In addition, whether the property over which the right of residence is held is registered (i.e. governed by the registration of title regime) or unregistered (i.e. governed by the registration of deeds regime) can be an important factor in the consideration of rights of residence.[77]

2. Exclusive Rights of Residence over Unregistered Land

[10–45] The holder of an exclusive right of residence over unregistered land is said to have a life estate over the property. Given s 11(2)(c)(iii) of the Land and Conveyancing Law Reform Act 2009, such a life estate can now exist in equity only. Prior to the commencement of the 2009 Act it was the terms of the instrument by which the right of residence was granted that determined whether the life estate was legal or equitable. The principle that an exclusive right of residence over unregistered land is a life estate was laid down in the early case of *National Bank Ltd v Keegan*.[78]

[10–46] In 1915 a landowner agreed to grant his aunt "during her life the exclusive use of the drawing room and bedroom over same". Pursuant to this agreement the aunt went into exclusive possession of the two named rooms and her nephew occupied the remainder of the house. In 1921 the nephew acquired an equitable mortgage over the property by means of the deposit of title deeds,[79] and in 1927 the bank attempted to enforce the mortgage debt. The aunt claimed to be entitled to an equitable life estate in the two named rooms as a result of the agreement of 1915, holding that this interest took priority over the interests of the bank. The Supreme Court agreed that she was entitled to an equitable life interest in the two rooms referred to in the agreement and that this life estate took priority over the bank's claim to the property under the mortgage (as they were both equitable interests, the first in time prevailed). The Court's reasoning in

[76] para 11–48.

[77] On systems of land registration generally, see Chapter 7.

[78] [1931] IR 344.

[79] Mortgages by deposit of title deeds are considered in Chapter 13 below.

reaching this conclusion was that if such a disposition had been made by deed or in a will it would have had the effect of creating a life estate in favour of the grantee, therefore the effect of this agreement would be to create an equitable life estate in the aunt's favour.

The conclusion in *Keegan* was affirmed in the later case of *Atkins v Atkins.*[80] In this case a testator bequeathed his leasehold property for the use of his wife for as long as she remained a widow and wanted to reside there and, upon her death or at the point at which she ceased to reside there, the testator's nephew was to take a life estate with a fee tail remainder to his son. In a codicil to his will the testator provided for a right of residence for the plaintiff. The widow resided in the property until 1956, at which point she moved away and the plaintiff moved in. The widow claimed that the right of residence equated to a life estate in her favour and, as a result, that she had the rights and powers of a tenant for life under the Settled Land Acts 1882–1890. As such, she claimed, her decision to vacate the property could not result in her loss of rights because that would constitute an illegitimate limitation of her powers as a tenant for life under the Settled Land Acts.[81] The Court agreed with the widow's submission and found her right to use the property for as long as she wanted was a general right of residence resulting in a life estate over the property in her favour and, as a result, to the powers of a tenant for life under the Settled Land Acts. The right of residence in question in *Atkins* was a general right of residence rather than an exclusive right of residence, suggesting that the "right of residence as a life estate" position was potentially capable of broader application. The provisions of the Registration of Title Act 1964, considered below,[82] together with subsequent case law on the nature of general rights of residence clearly show that only exclusive rights of residence over unregistered land can now be said to give rise to a life estate. **[10–47]**

Even limited as it is to exclusive rights of residence over unregistered land, the decision in *Keegan* is troublesome on a number of levels. Not only is the Court's reasoning weak but it resulted, at the time, in the holder of the right of residence being defined as a tenant for life within the meaning of the Settled Land Acts 1882–1890 and, as a result, acquiring broad powers of disposition.[83] Although Coughlan has argued that the decision was unproblematic at the level of principle,[84] such an outcome would not appear to accord with the presumed intention of the grantor of a right of residence that the grantee would have a place in which to reside for the entirety of her life. Of course, incompatibility with the intention of the grantor is not and never has been a barrier to particular outcomes in property law, as we have seen with the pre-2009 Act operation of the Rule in *Shelley's Case*[85] and the Rule against Perpetuities,[86] for example, but it is no less disconcerting for its commonness. Furthermore, unlike with the Rule in *Shelly's Case* and the Rule against Perpetuities, the outcome of *Keegan* was such as to create **[10–48]**

[80] [1976] ILRM 62.

[81] s 51, Settled Land Act 1882. See also Chapter 6.

[82] See para 10–52.

[83] The powers of a tenant for life were considered within the general scheme of the Settled Land Acts in Chapter 6.

[84] Coughlan, *Property Law* (2nd ed, 1998, Dublin, Gill & MacMillan), p 300.

[85] *Shelley's Case* (1581) 1 Co Rep 88b; see further Chapter 4.

[86] See further Chapter 5.

significant conveyancing inconvenience rather than to make the land in question more attractive, and less risky, for potential purchasers. *Keegan* remains good law in Ireland although, as we have seen, the Settled Land Acts 1882–1890 no longer apply. Instead, where someone is granted an exclusive right of residence over the whole of a piece unregistered land they hold a life estate in equity under a trust, with the freehold owner as the trustee, and governed by Part 4 of the Land and Conveyancing Law Reform Act 2009.[87] Where someone has any other kind of right of residence—whether it is over the whole land or over a specified part of it—the suggestion from s 11(2)(c)(iii) is that the holder of the right of residence will have no interest in the land: rather, the freehold owner (the fee simple holder) will have the capacity to deal freely with the land, albeit subject to a need to satisfy the right of residence. We will consider the means of satisfaction of such a right below.[88]

3. General Rights of Residence over Unregistered Land

[10–49] The broadly accepted view is that general rights of residence over unregistered land give rise to a charge that can be satisfied in monetary terms. The genesis of this view can be traced back to the early decision of *Ryan v Ryan*.[89] In this case a testator provided that his wife was to have her "lodging in this my house of Owenduff as long as the lease of it will last, provided she will wish to remain in it with my... nephew Patrick Ryan...". The testator's wife resided in the property for some time until Patrick Ryan married, at which point she left for a period of time. On her return, Patrick Ryan refused to provide her with her lodging in accordance with the terms of the testator's will, which resulted in the litigation at issue. The Court held that the widow was entitled to have her right of residence enforced as she had not done anything to suggest to the nephew that she would not enforce her rights following his marriage. The difficulty for the Court lay in how to enforce this right of residence. Brady LC held that "If the Court cannot compel the maintenance bequeathed to be specifically provided, it can compel the payment of a proper sum to provide it".[90] Thus, the Court held that a general right of residence over unregistered land constitutes a licence that can be revoked by the licensor, provided the licensee is given appropriate levels of financial compensation. Although the Lord Chancellor's decision is somewhat problematic because it suggests that he regarded rights of residence and rights of maintenance as being more or less indistinguishable, it can be credited with introducing the notion of general rights of residence as *liens,* or charges over land. This proposition was stated as authoritative fact (on exceptionally dubious authority) by Johnston J in *National Bank v Keegan*[91]:

> It is well settled that a general right of residence and support in a house or upon a farm does not amount to an estate in the land, but is a mere charge in the nature of the annuity upon the premises in respect of which it exists, and when it becomes necessary to sell such

[87] See Chapter 6.
[88] paras 10–53 to 10–58.
[89] (1848) 12 IR Eq Rep 226.
[90] *ibid.* at p 228.
[91] [1931] IR 344.

> property a Court of Equity has power and authority to ascertain the value of such charge, so that the purchaser may get the property discharged from the burden.[92]

This conclusion was substantively based on the decision in *Kelaghan v Daly*[93] and *Re Shanahan*.[94] In *Keleghan* Boyd J held that a general right of residence can be treated in the same manner as a *lien* over land. A *lien* is a form of security interest granted over a property to secure the payment of a debt (or performance of some other obligation) and normally applies only where a specific sum of money is involved. The comparison of a *lien* with a right of residence is doctrinally dubious because by its nature a right of residence cannot easily be said to be equivalent to a debt of a particular amount of money. *Re Shanahan*, on the other hand, did not concern the nature of a right of residence at all, but in fact dealt with an application to have a charge deleted from the Folio. Thus, the Court's reliance in *Keegan* on these precedents as support for its conclusion that a right of general residence is to be considered as a mere charge on property is questionable. **[10–50]**

That said, however, it now appears to be widely accepted that the general right of residence is considered to be a charge over the unregistered property over which it is granted. Section 40 of the Statute of Limitations 1957 provides that a right over land "in the nature of a *lien* for money's worth in or over land for a limited period not exceeding life, such as a... right of residence" can only be enforced within 12 years of an infringement. This is reinforced, as mentioned above, by s 11(2)(c)(iii) of the Land and Conveyancing Law Reform Act 2009. **[10–51]**

4. Exclusive and General Rights of Residence over Registered Land

At the time of the drafting of the Registration of Title Act 1964, the Oireachtas was particularly concerned with minimising the impact of the decision in *National Bank v Keegan*.[95] In order to ensure that a right of residence over registered land would never result in a life estate for the right-holder, s 81 of the Registration of Title Act 1964 provides: **[10–52]**

> A right of residence in or on registered land, whether a general right of residence on the land or an exclusive right of residence in or on part of the land, shall be deemed to be personal to the person beneficially entitled thereto and to be a right in the nature of a lien for money's worth in or over the land and shall not operate to create any equitable estate in the land.

This provision clearly rejects any suggestion that a right of residence over registered land gives rise to a life estate and confirms that both general and exclusive rights of residence over registered land are personal rights "in the nature of a lien for money's worth in or over the land". This provision has resulted in the principle that rights of residence over registered land are to be enforced by "objective valuation"[96] of the right. Rights of residence are expressly said to be s 69 (i.e. registrable) burdens over registered

---

[92] *ibid.* at p 346.
[93] [1913] 2 IR 328.
[94] [1919] IR 131.
[95] [1931] IR 344.
[96] *Johnston v Horace* [1993] ILRM 594 *per* Lavan J at p 600.

land.[97] As a result, purchasers for value of registered land will be bound by rights of residence (and have to satisfy them by means of monetary payment) if the right of residence is registered, although purchasers for no value will be bound by the right of residence regardless of whether it is registered or not.

5. Satisfying Rights of Residence

[10–53] A question of some importance arises when we consider whether a right of residence is what it suggests it is—that is, a right to reside in the land in question—or whether it is a more flexible kind of a right, which permits the landowner *either* to allow the holder the right to reside in the property *or* to pay the holder a sum of money in satisfaction. The first point is that exclusive rights of residence over the whole of the land in question are now governed by Part 4 trusts, under s 11(2)(c)(iii) of the Land and Conveyancing Law Reform Act 2009 and so can be quarantined into that bracket and dealt with under the law of trusts as laid down in Part 4 itself and considered in Chapter 6. All other rights of residence, however, are now more or less considered to exist as a kind of charge or *lien*. This suggests that the freehold owner ought to be able to satisfy those rights through a money payment, but this gives rise to two important questions: (a) Can the freehold owner *compel* the holder of the right of residence to accept monetary satisfaction? and (b) How can a right of residence be valued as a financial matter?

[10–54] Whether or not there is, in effect, a right on behalf of the freehold owner to simply "pay off" the right of residence, rather than allow actual occupation, is a question of some importance, for it goes to the very heart of the utility of the right of residence. Indeed, the nature of the right of residence and the implied intention of the grantor thereof are now central to an analysis of whether or not, in any particular case, a right of residence can be satisfied in financial terms. This is clear from the case of *Johnston v Horace*.[98] The plaintiff in this case had been granted a right of residence over a property in which she had lived for all of her life, which she proceeded to register pursuant to s 69 of the Registration of Title Act 1964. She continued to reside in the property for some time, including after it had been inherited by her nephew. After some time, the relationship between the plaintiff and her nephew disintegrated to the point where their cohabitation was no longer sustainable and she left the property. The plaintiff claimed that her nephew had engaged in a concerted bullying campaign against her, which resulted in her abandoning the premises against her will. In the proceedings that arose the Court was required to consider whether the plaintiff's right of residence could be satisfied by means of a money payment or not.

[10–55] Lavan J held that the plaintiff had not abandoned her right of residence as abandonment is, by its nature, a voluntary act. In this case the aunt had been placed in a position where she had no reasonable choice but to leave the property; she therefore remained entitled to the right of residence. In assessing the satisfaction of a right of residence, Lavan J held that the Court ought to conceive of the right of residence as an ongoing right intended to cater for a fundamental human need (i.e. a roof over one's head for life), and that the mechanism of valuing the right of residence

[97] s 69(1)(q), Registration of Title Act 1964.
[98] [1993] ILRM 594.

ought to reflect this intention behind the grant of a right of residence. In furtherance of this, Lavan J held that the financial satisfaction of a right of residence ought to be considered on a continuous, periodic basis and not as a once-off calculation. This is particularly significant given the changing rental value of properties of similar value and location as the property over which the right of residence is held.

Johnston therefore appears to suggest that the financial satisfaction of the right of residence ought to take into account the actual needs of the right-holder (including her means or lack thereof) in the context of a current market and ought to be sufficient to provide for a roof over the right-holder's head. In *Johnston* the plaintiff's needs could not be met from the nephew's means and, as a result, the right of residence was preserved over the property. *Johnston* clearly established that while a court *may* order a right of residence to be satisfied in monetary terms, it is not obliged to do so and can instead preserve the right of residence where the landowner "has not the means nor the intention to make proper provision for the plaintiff's right of residence".[99] **[10–56]**

The decision in *Johnston* attracted a great deal of academic commentary,[100] but the principles of the case could have been clearer, especially given the murky nature of the law relating to rights of residence generally. For that reason the decision in *Bracken v Byrne & Anor*,[101] in which *Johnston* was explained, is especially helpful. The plaintiff and first defendant were sisters whose father had executed a deed by which certain properties were transferred to the first defendant and her then-fiancé, subject to certain rights in favour of the plaintiff. Under this settlement the plaintiff held, *inter alia*, a right of residence over property held by the first defendant. Following a falling out in the family, the plaintiff initiated proceedings seeking the payment of a sum of money to represent her right of residence. The Court centred on a dispute as to the calculation of financial compensation for a right of residence over registered land under s 81 of the Registration of Title Act 1964. **[10–57]**

According to Clarke J, *Johnston* does not mean that a right of residence can never be satisfied in monetary terms; rather it stands for the proposition that the holder of the right of residence is not *entitled to* financial satisfaction of the right. The primary entitlement of the holder of the right of residence is to have the right enforced and, where required, to injunctive relief against breach. In the absence of an agreement between the parties to extinguish the right of residence, the Court is empowered to satisfy the right of residence in consideration of the means of the landowner and the culpability of the respective parties for the breakdown of the relationship to the point at which the parties cannot be reasonably expected to cohabit. Clarke J laid down the test to be applied in *Bracken* thus: **[10–58]**

> Having regard to the fact that the primary entitlement of the beneficiary of the right is to exercise of the right conferred upon them, it seems to me that the appropriate test must be that in addition to satisfying the court that it has become

[99] *ibid.*

[100] See, for example, Coughlan, "Enforcing Rights of Residence" (1993) 11 ILT 168; Power, *Intangible Property Rights in Ireland* (1st ed, 2003, Dublin, Butterworths), pp 399–402; Coughlan, *Property* Law (2nd ed, 1999, Dublin, Gill and MacMillan), pp 302–303.

[101] [2005] IEHC 80.

unreasonable in all the circumstances of the case to require the beneficiary to be content with the exercise of the right, it is also necessary for the beneficiary to satisfy the court that the balance of the responsibility for that situation lies upon the owner of the right. It is not, however, necessary for the beneficiary to establish that they are entirely free from responsibility.

III. Conacre

[10–59] Conacre agreements create licences to till land. As the landowner does not part with possession of the property, the agreement does not create a lease of any kind[102]: it does "not [create] any estate or interest in the land... It is a licence to... conacre the lands only for the prescribed period".[103] The licensee under a conacre licence gives a licensee a right to till the land only; it does not give the licensee any auxiliary rights of any kind.[104]

IV. Agistment

[10–60] Agistment agreements create licences to graze animals on the licensor's land. The landowner does not part with possession over the land and, as a result, there is no landlord–tenant relationship between the landowner and the person whose animals are grazed under the agreement,[105] even where the agreement extends for longer than the customary 11-month period.[106] Although the parties have a licence agreement, only the licensee is entitled to a reasonable period of notice of the termination of the agreement, in order to give him sufficient opportunity to remove the animals.[107]

[10–61] The licensee has the right to graze his animals; he has no auxiliary rights. This can have particular implications for the landowner because, for example, the licensee has no right to fence off an area of the land. Any damage that may arise from the animals wandering out of the prescribed area will result in liability on the part of the landowner as he has the obligation to specify the area on which animals are to be grazed and to take any necessary measures to ensure that they do not stray from that area.[108]

---

[102] *Dease v O'Reilly* (1845) 8 IR LR 52; *Lord Westmeath v Hogg* (1840) 3 LR IR 27; *Close v Brady* (1838–1839) Jon & Car 187; *Booth v McManus* (1861) 12 ICLR 418; *McKeowne v Bradford* (1862) 7 IR Jur 169.

[103] *Carson v Jeffers* [1961] IR 44 *per* Budd J at p 47.

[104] *Evans v Monagher* (1872) IR 6 CL 526.

[105] *O'Flaherty v Kelly* [1909] 1 IR 223.

[106] In *re Moore's Estate: Fitzpatrick v Behan* [1944] IR 295, for example, an agistment licence was said to exist where the agreement extended to 50 years.

[107] *Plunkett v Heeney* (1904) 4 NIJR 136.

[108] *Hickey v Cosgrave* (1861) 6 IR Jur 251.

CHAPTER 11
Freehold Covenants

In almost all circumstances the ownership of property is transferred by means of a formal documentary process. It is not at all unusual in the course of this process for the parties to enter into promises to one another in relation to the land. A purchaser might promise, for example, to contribute financially to the maintenance of a road that serves a number of properties, including his own. These promises, i.e. promises made under a deed, are known as covenants.[1] Covenants are commonly found in leases, but the law relating to leasehold covenants is considered in Chapter 15, while this chapter focuses on freehold covenants. In general, freehold covenants are particularly convenient where someone is selling only part of his land. In such circumstances, there will be a physical connection between the land being sold and the land being retained, and as a result the vendor will have some interest in how the land being sold will be used in the future. The imposition of a covenant may help in ensuring some element of control over such matters for the benefit of the land being retained. While this is not the only scenario in which a freehold covenant might be created, it is certainly one of the most common. The imposition of covenants—particularly covenants restricting how land is used—can also be used as a means of maintaining "acceptable" property prices in an area and can, therefore, be a useful economic tool.[2] Covenants were also historically **[11–01]**

[1] The deed must, of course, comply with all the requirements for valid deeds. See, for example, Wylie & Woods, *Irish Conveyancing Law* (3rd ed, 2004, West Sussex; Tottel); ss 62–85, Land and Conveyancing Law Reform Act 2009.

[2] This has been very heavily theorised in the USA. A good summary of various theories about the economic purpose of restrictive covenants in particular is available in Hughes and Turnbull, "Restrictive Land Covenants" (1996) 12(2) JR Estate Finance Econ 9.

used as a kind of proxy-planning law, to try to regulate—through private means—the ways in which property was developed.[3]

[11–02] All covenants necessarily involve two parties. One of the parties will be required to either do something (positive covenant) or refrain from doing something (restrictive covenant). The actions of the acting party will affect the other party's enjoyment of his or her land. The acting party is henceforth known as the covenantor (i.e. promisor) and the benefiting party as the covenantee (promisee). The covenantee enjoys the benefit of the covenant, while the covenantor undertakes the burden. In some cases, property subject to a covenant may be held by a trustee on behalf of beneficiaries. Where this happens, the covenant could be enforced by or against the trustee *or* the beneficiaries under s 5 of the Real Property Act 1845, provided it is not purely personal.[4]

[11–03] Freehold covenants over unregistered land will normally be contained within deeds of conveyance that have been lodged, by means of a memorial, in the Registry of Deeds. As a result, the details of covenants contained within these deeds are normally memorialised and lodged as part of the overall covenant and, therefore, are protected within the system of unregistered land. In any case in which a covenant is created independently by a separate deed, that deed will be registrable in the Registry of Deeds.[5] Restrictive covenants affecting registered land are registrable as burdens under s 69 of the Registration of Title Act 1964. Such registration is essential if they are to bind subsequent purchasers.[6]

[11–04] As a starting point, it is important that we would distinguish between positive and restrictive (or negative) covenants, mostly because the pre-Land and Conveyancing Law Reform Act 2009 law applies differently to both. Positive covenants are ones that require someone to do or pay for something, whereas restrictive covenants are ones that require someone to refrain from doing something. It has traditionally been the case that positive covenants were far more difficult to enforce than negative covenants, although as we will see later in this chapter the 2009 Act largely removes the importance of this distinction when it comes to covenants governed by those new provisions. The reform of the law of covenants in the 2009 Act is extensive and has a clear focus on the simplification of the law of covenants, a development that—in principle—is surely welcome. This is because of the frankly turgid nature of the law relating to freehold covenants as it applied before the 2009 Act and continues to apply

---

[3] There is disagreement as to whether "public planning" (through planning legislation) or "private planning" (through instruments such as easements and covenants) is preferable from a theoretical and efficiency perspective. See, for example, Foldvary, "Planning by Freehold" (2005) 25(4) Economic Affairs 11. For a perspective on how planning law's development was influenced by the use of instruments such as freehold covenants see, for example, Booth, "From Property Rights to Public Control: The Quest for Public Interest in the Control of Urban Development" (2002) 73(2) Town Planning Review 153. In Ireland we have a well-developed system of planning law: Scannell, *Environmental and Land Use Law* (2006, Dublin, Round Hall) and Simons, *Planning and Development Law* (2nd ed, 2007, Dublin, Round Hall).

[4] *Lloyd v Byrne* (1888) 22 LR IR 269; *Grant v Edmondson* [1931] 1 Ch D 1. See also *Walsh v Walsh* (1900) 1 NIJR 53, which was decided without reference to s 5 of the Real Property Act 1845.

[5] On the operation of unregistered land, see generally Chapter 7.

[6] *ibid.*

to covenants that were executed before 1 December 2009 *and* covenants that do not fall within the definition of freehold covenants contained in s 48 of the Act. Because of the continuing relevance of the old law to these categories of freehold covenant, this chapter concerns itself with both bodies of law. The main controversy, and the bulk of this chapter, relates to the ways in which covenants can be enforced by and against successors in title to the original parties to a covenant.

I. The Enforcement of Covenants Between Original Parties

Original parties to a covenant can enforce that covenant (provided, of course, it is valid) as against one another. This is not a problematic proposition; they have, after all, freely contracted to the covenant in question. Cases where the covenant is said to benefit someone who is not a direct party to the deed in question can cause some difficulties, because from the perspective of common law there is no privity of contract between the covenantor and the person said to benefit: the deed in question is not *inter partes* from that perspective.[7] The Real Property Act 1845 dealt with such situations in s 5, which ensured that the covenant could be enforced against those named in the original instrument, even if they were not parties thereto. The Land and Conveyancing Law Reform Act 2009 ensures that its new provisions relating to the enforceability of covenants do not disturb the operation of privity of contract in this context.[8] It also maintains the thrust of s 5 of the Real Property Act 1845 by providing, in s 70(1) of the 2009 Act, that: **[11–05]**

> Where a deed is expressed to confer an estate or interest in land, or the benefit of a covenant or right relating to land, on a person, that person may enforce the deed whether or not named a party to it.

II. The Enforcement of Covenants Between Successors in Title: The Pre-LCLRA 2009 Law

It has always been more difficult to enforce covenants between successors in title of the parties to the original covenant. So, for example, if Alice sells a house to Pádraig in fee simple subject to a covenant and Pádraig subsequently sells the house on to Arnie, can Alice enforce that covenant against Arnie? And, if not, is there any way that she can ensure that the covenant is fulfilled? Prior to the introduction of the Land and Conveyancing Law Reform Act 2009, which substantially reforms this area of the law,[9] complex and sometimes unsatisfactorily burdensome rules had developed in both law and equity to govern the question of the "running of covenants", or their enforceability by and against successors in title to the original covenant. The rules as developed, and which will be considered in full presently, deal with the question of whether the benefit and the burden of covenants can run with the land as separate issues. In other words, the rules are different depending on whether we are interested in the running—or enforceability—of the benefit or the burden. Furthermore, different rules developed for these questions in law and in equity with equity, in particular, focusing largely on the ways in which restrictive covenants might be made to run with the land. We need, therefore, to consider the rules relating to the common law and equity separately and, in each case, to think about the rules as to the running of the benefit and of the burden. **[11–06]**

---

[7] *Lord Southampton v Brown* (1827) 6 B & C 718.

[8] s 70(2), Land and Conveyancing Law Reform Act 2009.

[9] See paras 11–39 to 11–48.

1. The Common Law Approach

[11–07] The common law rules relating to the running of covenants are not concerned with whether the covenant is restrictive or positive; the rules as they apply are uniform to all freehold covenants. However, as mentioned above, the common law takes a different approach to the running of the benefit and the running of the burden.

(i) The Running of the Benefit at Common Law

[11–08] For the benefit of a freehold covenant to run with the land at common law four conditions must be fulfilled: the covenant must "touch and concern" the land, the enforcing party or her predecessor in title must have a proprietary interest in the land, the enforcing party must have the same estate in the land as her predecessor in title had, and the covenant must be intended to benefit successors in title. We will consider each of these in turn.

(a) The Covenant must "Touch and Concern" the Land

[11–09] In order for the benefit of a covenant to run with the land, it must be shown to touch and concern the land, which means that it must substantially impact on the land in its capacity as land and not in a merely incidental manner.[10] This is well demonstrated by the dictum of Tucker LJ in *Smith and Snipes Hall Farm Ltd v River Douglas Catchment Board*[11]:

> . . . [the covenant] must either affect the land as regards mode of occupation, or it must be such as *per se*, and not merely from collateral circumstances, affects the value of the land, and it must then be shown that it was the intention of the parties that the benefit thereof should run with the land.[12]

(b) The Enforcing Party Must Have a Proprietary Interest in the Land and her Predecessor in Title Must also Have Had a Proprietary Interest in the Land

[11–10] This requirement, which is largely historical, provides that a covenant will benefit a successor in title of the original party only if it enhances his enjoyment of some property right.

(c) The Enforcing Party Must Have the same Estate in Law as the Original Party Had

[11–11] The third requirement—that the original and enforcing parties have the same legal estate in the land[13]—is construed strictly by the courts. There was some speculation that s 58(1) of the Conveyancing Act 1881 would lead to an assumption that the

[10] *Austerberry v Corporation of Oldham* (1885) 29 Ch D 750; *GAW v CIÉ* [1953] IR 232. In this context it is important to note that the "land" to be benefited can be interpreted widely as including incorporeal hereditaments, such as easements and profits—*GAW v CIÉ* [1953] IR 232 (where a right-of-way was found capable of benefiting from a covenant to repair it and keep it clear).

[11] [1949] 2 KB 500.

[12] *ibid.* at p 506.

[13] *Spencer's Case* (1583) 5 Co Rep 16a; *Westhoughton UDC v Wigan Coal & Iron Co Ltd* [1919] 1 Ch 159.

covenant's benefit was binding on all heirs and assigns of the original party, regardless of the estate they held. This section provides that a freehold covenant "shall be deemed to be made with the covenantee, his heirs and assigns". However, it now appears to be well established that in this respect, s 58 is nothing more than a measure designed to simplify and streamline the conveyancing process (by introducing a presumption that all covenants were intended to run with the land) and does not have the effect of alleviating this third common law requirement.[14]

(d) The Covenant must Be Intended to Benefit Successors in Title

Once the preceding three conditions have been fulfilled, the court must be satisfied that the covenant was intended to benefit the successor in title of the property. In the main, this will be a question of construction based on the court's assessment of all of the relevant circumstances. This is well demonstrated by the decision in *Shayler v Woolf*.[15] In this case, W sold a piece of land to the plaintiff's predecessor in title for the erection of a bungalow. As part of the original transaction, W covenanted to supply water to the bungalow by means of an existing pump on adjoining land retained by him. He also covenanted to keep the pump in a good state of repair. While the covenant was expressly said to bind the defendant's successors in title, no such express statement was made in relation to the purchaser's successors in title. Following the transfer of the property to S, the pump fell into a state of disrepair. S demanded that the covenant to supply water and to keep the pump in repair would be complied with, but W claimed that the covenant did not run with the property to the benefit of S. In the estimation of Lord Greene MR, the benefit of the covenant did run with the property because: (a) the initial three conditions were fulfilled, and (b) a reasonable reading of the contract in all the relevant circumstances showed that the covenant was intended to benefit successors in title of the purchaser, as any contrary intention would result in the cottage being left without a water supply. Whether this is deemed an absolute requirement or not is somewhat irrelevant because s 58 of the Conveyancing Act 1881 introduced a presumption that all covenants were intended to run with the land. **[11–12]**

(ii) The Running of the Burden at Common Law

As a result of the fact that only parties to a contract can be bound by contractual obligations under common law, only those who are in privity of contract (i.e. the original parties) can be bound by the burden of a covenant at common law.[16] This means that a covenantor will remain liable for the covenant following the transfer of property unless he or she expressly contracts out of this liability. As a matter of logic, most people will try to contract out of their liability because it makes little sense to remain liable for a condition over which one no longer has control. Take the following scenario as an example: **[11–13]**

> Patrick bought *Willow Cottage* from Maria in 2000 and entered into a covenant to maintain surrounding walls and contribute towards the maintenance costs of a road

---

[14] *Westhoughton UDC v Wigan Coal & Iron Co Ltd* [1919] 1 Ch 159.

[15] [1946] Ch D 320.

[16] *Belmont Securities Limited v Crean*, unreported, High Court, 17 June 1988; *Austerbury v Corporation of Oldham* [1885] 29 Ch D 750.

> shared between them. Patrick has now decided to sell *Willow Cottage* to Michael. Under the principles of the common law, Patrick will remain bound by those covenants following this sale. Therefore, if Michael were to fail to fulfil these covenants, then Patrick could be sued for a remedy. As a result, Patrick wishes to find a way to pass this liability on to Michael by contracting out of the liability for the covenant.

In the example above, there are a number of options open to Patrick. He can (a) create a chain of indemnity covenants, (b) rely on the principle of benefit and burden, (c) transfer the property by means of a long lease, or (d) transfer the property by means of a fee simple subject to a condition subsequent not to breach the covenant. Each of these possibilities should be considered in turn.

(a) A Chain of Indemnity Covenants

[11–14] The first way in which the burden of the covenant might be passed is by a chain of indemnity covenants. This is the idea that when the original party transfers the property, he includes a covenant requiring the purchaser to indemnify him against any liability for breach of covenants. Therefore, although the original party would be liable if the purchaser breached the covenant, he would also be indemnified by the purchaser in the event of being sued for breach. If the purchaser were to transfer the property to a third party, he would insert a similar indemnity clause against the subsequent purchaser and so on, so that a chain of covenants can be traced between the original party and the current holder of the land. This can be illustrated by means of a variation and extension of the example begun above:

> Patrick bought *Willow Cottage* from Maria in 2000 and entered into a covenant to maintain surrounding walls and contribute towards the maintenance costs of a road shared between them. Patrick sold the cottage to Michael in 2006 and included an indemnity covenant in the transfer. Michael sold the property on to Ciarán in the spring of 2007 and, in order to avoid liability under his indemnity covenant to Patrick, included an indemnity covenant in the transaction. In June 2007 Ciarán breached these covenants, resulting in Maria suing Patrick for breach. As a result, Patrick could enforce his indemnity covenant against Michael, who enforced his indemnity covenant against Ciarán. Thus, although Patrick remains liable for the covenants, it is ultimately Ciarán—who engaged in the breach—who compensates Maria for the breach of the covenants.

The danger in this mechanism is that the chain is easily broken by a failure to include an indemnity covenant somewhere along the line, or by the death or disappearance of any of the parties.

(b) The Principle of Benefit and Burden

[11–15] The second mechanism is to have recourse to the principle of benefit and burden, i.e. the principle that if someone enjoys the benefit of a covenant, he is also compelled (both morally and legally) to take on the burden. This concept was used to enforce the burden of a freehold covenant against a successor in title in the case of *Halsall v Brizell*.[17] In this case, the original purchasers of property in a housing estate had the benefit of the use of private roads and sewers, but had also covenanted to contribute

---

[17] [1957] Ch 169.

towards their maintenance. Upon purchase from the original party, Brizell began to use the roads and sewers, but refused to contribute towards their maintenance, claiming that the burden of the covenant had not run to him. The Court held that the ancient principle of benefit and burden should be applied and that, therefore, the defendant "cannot benefit under a deed without subscribing to the obligations thereunder".[18] Thus, the burden was said to run to the purchaser.

It is important to bear in mind that this does not create a general principle that the burden of a covenant can be enforced against someone just because a deed also creates some kind of benefit in his favour.[19] Rather, the rule in *Halsall v Brizell* relies on reciprocity, as acknowledged by Upjohn J: if the purchaser forewent the benefit or did not enjoy it, he would not be bound by the burden. **[11–16]**

(c) The Conveyance of a Long Lease

The third mechanism that can be employed is to convey a long lease instead of completing a freehold conveyance. The covenant could be entered into the lease as a leasehold covenant, and the long lease could later be converted into a fee simple under a variety of statutory provisions.[20] In such situations the fee simple is made subject to the covenants of the lease. This has the effect of annexing—or attaching—the covenant to the freehold estate and, as a result, the covenant will bind successors in title. **[11–17]**

(d) The Conveyance of a Fee Simple Subject to a Condition Subsequent

The final possibility is for the vendor to transfer a fee simple subject to a condition subsequent to comply with this covenant. Then, even if the covenant were breached by the purchaser, the breach would give rise to the transferor's right of re-entry, which he could exercise to terminate the purchaser's fee simple. Although the original party would remain bound by the covenant, he would also have the potential to retake the fee simple should his liability be engaged in this way.[21] **[11–18]**

2. The Approach of Equity

The law of equity found these common law rules to be particularly problematic in relation to restrictive covenants.[22] Restrictive covenants are different to positive covenants in their ability to severely impact on the value of property on the open market; one is likely to pay more for an acre of land on which there are no obligations than for an acre of land on which an owner is prohibited from carrying out certain kinds of development as a result of a restrictive freehold covenant, for example. Equity considered that the common law rules, as they apply to restrictive covenants, were particularly troublesome because the successor in title to an original party would be said to enjoy the covenant or to be bound by it merely by reference to formulaic common law tests and with total disregard for the successor in title's knowledge (or **[11–19]**

[18] *ibid.* at 182 *per* Upjohn J.

[19] See also *Rhone v Stephens* [1994] 2 WLR 429 at 437 *per* Templeman LJ.

[20] Renewable Leasehold Conversion Act 1849; s 5, Conveyancing Act 1881; ss 9, 10, 28, Landlord and Tenant (Ground Rents) (No 2) Act 1978; s 3, Landlord and Tenant Amendment (Ireland) Act 1860.

[21] For the operation of the conditional fee simple see Chapter 4.

[22] See, for example, Garner, "Restrictive Covenants Restated" (1962) 26 Conv 298.

lack thereof) in relation to the covenant. Equity therefore developed specific rules relating to the restrictive covenants, based to a degree on the doctrine of notice. As with common law, these rules are firstly dependent on whether we are concerned with the benefit or the burden of the covenant in question.

(i) The Running of the Benefit at Equity

[11–20] Equity has developed a mechanism by which the benefit of restrictive covenants might run with the land, which shares only one characteristic with the common law position, i.e. the covenant must touch and concern the land. In equity, the person seeking to benefit from the covenant must show an entitlement to that benefit through one of three means, which are considered in full below. In other words, there are two requirements for the benefit of a restrictive covenant to run in equity:

- the covenant must touch and concern the land;
- the party claiming the benefit must be entitled to the benefit of that covenant by means of
  - assignment, *or*
  - annexation, *or*
  - a local scheme of development.

(a) The Covenant Must "Touch and Concern" the Land

[11–21] As with the common law, equity will enforce the benefit of a restrictive covenant in favour of a successor in title only if it is not merely personal. In addition to the common law, however, equity appears to be particularly concerned with some sub-requirements within this category: the land said to be touched and concerned by the covenant ought to be (a) the claimant's, (b) identifiable or ascertainable and (c) said in the deed to benefit from the covenant. These sub-requirements make the phraseology used in the conveyance very important, particularly in ascertaining whether the land actually said to benefit from the covenant is, in fact, touched and concerned by it. The importance of the language used is well demonstrated by consideration of the cases of *Re Ballard's Conveyance*[23] and *Zetland v Driver*.[24]

[11–22] In *Ballard* the land said to benefit from the covenant in the deed was some 17,000 acres in size, but the attempt to enforce the covenant was made in relation to only a small portion of that land. Because of this, Clauson J held that even though some of that land would benefit from the covenant, or be touched and concerned by it, the vast majority would not, therefore the land as a whole could not be said to be touched and concerned by the covenant, which, as a result, could not be said to run. Although the piece of land that was touched and concerned by the covenant could, the Court held, be severed and considered in isolation, the case still shows that conveyancers must be particularly cautious in relation to their wording of covenants within general transactions. In contrast, *Zetland* also concerned a claim relating to a small portion of a larger area of land said in the deed to benefit from the covenant. Despite this, however, the Court held that the covenant did touch and concern the land. The difference between the two cases was this: in *Ballard* the covenant was said to be for the

[23] [1937] Ch 473.
[24] [1939] Ch 1.

benefit of "the land"; in *Zetland* the covenant was said to be for the benefit of "the whole or any part or parts" of the land. The wording of the deed was, therefore, of vital importance.

(b) The Party Must Be Entitled to the Benefit of the Covenant

Once the claimant has convinced the court that the covenant touches and concerns the land, he must secondly show that he is entitled to the benefit of it. As mentioned above, there are three ways in which this can be proved: (a) assignment of the covenant contemporaneously with assignment of the land; *or* (b) annexation of the covenant to the land, resulting in automatic transfer of the covenant with the land; *or* (c) inclusion of the covenant in a local scheme. **[11–23]**

i. Assignment

The first of these three possible ways of showing entitlement—assignment—requires the covenant at issue to have been transferred with the land as a separate but connected right. A claimant must therefore satisfy the court not only that he owns land that is touched and concerned by the covenant but that he acquired the covenant when he acquired the land. It is essential that the covenant would be shown to have been acquired at precisely the same time as the land. This is because equity allows restrictive covenants to be enjoyed and enforced only when it can be shown that they were said to be for the benefit of land and not for the benefit of any individual. Therefore, any temporal separation of the land and the covenant severs the link that is required for equitable intervention, and the covenant is treated as having been spent. This means that the covenant will need to be assigned every time there is a new transfer of the relevant land.[25] **[11–24]**

The assignment itself can be express, or implied from words used to show a clear intention to assign the covenant, or carried out by act or operation of law. Express assignment will be done through the terms of the conveyance itself (bearing in mind the need to take care with phrasing that we encountered in *Zetland*[26] and *Ballard*[27]). Assignment can be implied from words within the conveyance that show an appropriate intention for the covenant to be for the benefit of the land and whomever holds it. In this sense the implication of assignment from the words of the conveyance is a classical exercise of equitable jurisdiction, to give effect to the intentions of the parties. **[11–25]**

ii. Annexation

If a covenant is annexed to land, it can be said that it has been attached to the land so that it passes automatically with it on every subsequent transfer.[28] In such cases a successor in title cannot avoid the enforcement of the covenant by claiming that he did not have notice of its existence.[29] In order for annexation to take place, it is imperative that a deed of conveyance would show an intention that future owners **[11–26]**

---

[25] *Stilwell v Blackman* [1968] Ch 508.
[26] [1939] Ch 1.
[27] [1937] Ch 473.
[28] *Federated Homes Ltd v Mill Lodge Properties Ltd* [1980] 1 WLR 594.
[29] *Reid v Bickerstaff* [1909] 2 Ch 305.

would enjoy the benefit of the covenant. This intention can be demonstrated by (a) identifying the land with sufficient certainty, *or* (b) indicating that the covenant has been made for the benefit of the land or for the benefit of the covenantee *in his capacity* as the owner of the land (i.e. not in a personal capacity). It is advisable to ensure that the covenant is expressed to be for the benefit of the land *and any part or parts thereof*. This ensures that the benefit of the covenant can pass to a successor in title part of part of (rather than the whole of) the land.[30] Importantly, it does not appear that s 58 of the Conveyancing Act 1881 is interpreted as introducing a presumption of annexation in this context. This conclusion flows particularly from the case of *Renals v Cowlishaw*.[31]

[11–27] In *Renals* the former owners in fee simple of a residential property and adjoining lands sold part of the lands to the predecessors in title of the defendant. That transaction was done subject to numerous restrictive covenants restricting the right to build on and use the land acquired. These same vendors subsequently sold the residential property they had retained to Renals' predecessors in title without any reference to the restrictive covenants. Renals claimed an entitlement to the covenant on the basis of presumed annexation under s 58. Although he was held to be an assign of the original party for a different reason, the Court held that s 58 did not operate to say that where a covenant is for the benefit of "the covenantee, his heirs and assigns", this resulted in its annexation to the property. This conclusion was bolstered by the finding in *Sainsbury v Enfield London Borough Council*[32] that an interpretation of s 58 introducing a presumption of annexation would be profoundly illogical.

iii. Local Scheme of Development

[11–28] The third alternative is to show that the covenant was created within a local scheme of development. This category covers situations where covenants are intended to be mutually enforceable by and against the owners of land within a local (or development) scheme. In such circumstances, and provided certain conditions are fulfilled, the covenant will be said to run to all successors in title of the original parties and to be enforceable by and against everyone within the scheme. The law relating to local schemes of development is a particularly important example of the capacity of equity to develop in response to new or emerging land patterns when the common law is somewhat stymied by strict and restrictive rules that cannot adapt in this manner.

[11–29] The local scheme is based on the concept that when the purchaser of a property within a scheme buys from the vendor, there is an understanding that the covenants attached are to be common to all lots within the scheme and to be enforceable by the vendor and all of his successors in title. When the next lot within the development is sold, that purchaser covenants with the vendor in relation to the rest of the property still held by him and, at the same time, acquires the capacity to enforce the covenant with the first purchaser. This continues throughout the sale of the various lots within the development until all owners are subject to these mutual covenants, which they can all enforce against one another and to which they are all subject in relation to one

[30] *Federated Homes Ltd v Mill Lodge Property Ltd* [1980] 1 WLR 594.
[31] (1879) 11 Ch D 866.
[32] [1989] 1 WLR 594.

another. Every subsequent successor in title is then also entitled to enjoy the benefit of these covenants (as well as being bound by them). In order for the law of local schemes to apply, the purchasers of the lots from the original developer must have knowledge of the terms of the local scheme of covenants, i.e. they must know that they are entering into covenants that can be enforced by and against the other purchasers.[33]

The case of *Elliston v Reacher*[34] is generally considered to be the *locus classicus* in the area of local schemes of development and the requirements to be fulfilled before a covenant can be said to operate within such a scheme. The case concerned a scheme of development of a property acquired by a Building Society in 1860. Having acquired title to this property, the Building Society divided the land out into a number of plots, all of which were shown on a map used in the sale of the properties. This plan also contained details of conditions upon which the properties were to be sold. Importantly, these conditions did not clearly show who the other parties to the conditions—which included restrictive covenants—were to be. These lots were then sold off subject to covenants not to, *inter alia*, allow the construction of any hotel, tavern, public house or beer-house, or the use of any house for such a function without the vendors' consent thereto. The case at issue concerned the enforceability of these covenants as between successors in title to the original conveyance. It was held that these covenants could be enforced as part of a local scheme of development upon the fulfilment of four conditions: **[11–30]**

(1) The parties to the dispute are able to trace their title to a common vendor.
(2) The property originally sold by this common vendor was separated into lots, which were to be sold subject to restrictions common to all lots and consistent only with a general scheme of development.
(3) The common restrictions were intended by the original common vendor to be for the benefit of all the lots, including those already sold (as opposed to merely being for the benefit of property retained by him). The common restrictions must not only be intended to benefit all of the lots conveyed but must also *in fact* benefit all of these lots.
(4) The parties to the dispute and/or their predecessors in title acquired their properties on the understanding that the restrictive covenants were for the benefit of the other lots within the scheme.

In *Elliston,* the fourth of these conditions was held to be capable of being inferred from satisfaction of the previous three, which in turn were said to be derived from principles laid down in the earlier embryonic jurisprudence on these schemes of development.[35] The later case of *Reid v Bickerstaff*[36] added another condition to the *Elliston* schema, i.e. that the scheme would exist within a defined area of property. **[11–31]**

Of course, while all of these elements of local schemes of development ought to be proved by a claimant, this area of law is equitable and therefore discretionary. As a **[11–32]**

---

33 *Reid v Bickerstaff* [1909] 2 Ch 305.
34 [1908] 2 Ch 374.
35 See *Renals v Cowlishaw* (1878) 9 Ch D 125; (1879) 11 Ch D 866; and *Spicer v Martin* (1888) 14 App Cas 12.
36 [1909] 2 Ch 305.

result, the courts have generally shown themselves to be conducive to relatively flexible interpretations of the conditions in limited circumstances. Thus, in *Baxter v Four Oaks Properties Ltd*[37] the vendor's failure to conceive of the property as divided into individual lots prior to its sale was not fatal to a claim where there was sufficient evidence to show that the vendor did, in fact, intend a scheme to be developed.

[11–33] The difficulty in contemporary Irish property law is that it does not appear clear that commercial schemes can be included in the concept of a scheme of development as traditionally construed. This is suggested by the decision of O'Hanlon J in *Belmont Securities Ltd v Crean*.[38] In this case the developer had built three shops that he intended to operate as a grocery, a pharmacy and a newsagent. The conveyance to each party included a restrictive covenant as to user, i.e. a covenant requiring the property to be used for the particular purpose alone. After some time the lessees of the person who had bought the newsagent began to trade in groceries, and the vendor and owner of the grocer's applied for an injunction to prevent this. The basis of their claim was that the restrictive covenant was binding on the tenant of the newsagent shop-owner. O'Hanlon J refused the application. In his judgment, O'Hanlon J referred to the following passage from *Reid v Bickerstaff*:

> What are some of the essentials of a building scheme? In my opinion there must be a defined area within which the scheme is operative. Reciprocity is the foundation of the idea of a scheme. A purchaser of one parcel cannot be subject to an implied obligation to purchasers of an undefined and unknown area. He must know both the extent of his burden and the extent of his benefit. Not only must the area be defined, but the obligations to be imposed within that area must be defined. Those obligations need not be identical. For example, there may be houses of a certain value in one part and houses of a different value in another part. A building scheme is not created by the mere fact that the owner of an estate sells it in lots and takes varying covenants from various purchasers. There must be notice to the various purchasers of what I may venture to call the local law imposed by the vendors upon a definite area... If on a sale of part of an estate the purchaser covenants with the vendor, his heirs and assigns, not to deal with the purchased property in a particular way, a subsequent purchaser of part of the estate does not take the benefit of the covenant unless (a) he is an express assignee of the covenant, as distinct from an assignee of the land or (b) the restrictive covenant is expressed to be for the benefit of and protection of the particular parcel purchased by the subsequent purchaser... Unless either (a) or (b) can be established, it remains for the vendor to enforce or abstain from enforcing the restrictive covenant.[39]

This approach does not seem to contemplate commercial developments that are now common, although it should be noted that s 48 of the Land and Conveyancing Law Reform Act 2009, which is fully considered below, does make sure that commercial

[37] [1965] Ch 816.

[38] Unreported, High Court, 17 June 1988. It is interesting to note that while the law relating to local schemes was becoming more complex in Ireland, it was being further simplified in England and Wales by the introduction of a flexible approach to *Elliston,* based on inferred intention of the parties. The case law relating to this development is considered in some depth in Power, *Intangible Property Rights in Ireland* (2nd ed, 2008, West Sussex, Tottel), pp 331–333.

[39] *Reid v Bickerstaff* [1909] 2 Ch 305 at 319–320.

developments can now be included in "schemes of development" for the purposes of the running of the benefit of covenants in equity.

(ii) The Running of the Burden at Equity

The principal authority in considering this question is *Tulk v Moxhay.*[40] In this case, a plot of land on Leicester Square had been sold subject to the covenant to keep the Garden Square "uncovered by buildings". The land had changed hands a number of times and when the defendant in this case acquired the land, he had notice of the covenant. Notwithstanding that notice, he claimed that the covenant was not enforceable against him as he was not a party to the original contract. The vendor successfully applied for an injunction to restrain development on the basis that the purchaser had notice of that covenant and was, therefore, bound by it. To be more precise, the Court held that a person may not use land in a manner inconsistent with an agreement in the original contract between the original parties where he has notice of that agreement at the time of purchase. **[11–34]**

This principle—that a restrictive covenant will bind a successor in title of the original covenantor in equity provided he had notice of it—became known as the Rule in *Tulk v Moxhay* and was accepted in Irish law.[41] The rule comprised three important elements: it applied only to restrictive covenants, it applied to covenants intended to benefit land and not purely personal covenants, and it applied only to covenants that were capable of binding third parties. Each element requires a little elaboration. **[11–35]**

(a) The Rule Applies to Restrictive Covenants Only

This principle can be traced back directly to the difficulties with mandatory injunctions: ordering someone not to do something is relatively straightforward and easy to supervise, whereas ordering someone to do something (particularly on his own land) introduces a range of practical and conceptual difficulties that equity was reluctant to embrace. As considered above, whether or not a covenant is to be defined as positive or restrictive is essentially a matter of construction and is dependent on all relevant circumstances. In the context of the Rule in *Tulk v Moxhay*, however, requiring someone to spend money will normally lead to classification as a positive covenant[42] that is not enforceable through the Rule. The best approach is to ask whether the covenant requires the taking of affirmative action, in which case it is likely to be positive and, therefore, unaffected by *Tulk v Moxhay.*[43] **[11–36]**

(b) The Covenant Concerned Must Be Intended to Benefit the Land and not the Individual

Equity intervenes in the area of restrictive covenants on the basis of a view of covenants as rights intended to benefit land as opposed to rights intended to benefit individuals. **[11–37]**

---

[40] (1848) 41 ER 1143; (1848) 2 Ph 774.

[41] See, for example, *Williams & Co Ltd v LSD Ltd*, unreported, High Court, 19 June 1970; and *Whelan v Cork Corporation* [1991] ILRM 19, confirmed by Supreme Court [1994] 3 IR 367.

[42] *Haywood v Brunswick Permanent Benefit Building Society* (1881) 8 QBD 403.

[43] *Zetland v Driver* [1939] Ch 1.

Only those rights deemed to be for the benefit of land itself will be enforced against a successor in title.[44]

(c) The Covenant Concerned Must Be Capable of Binding a Third Party

[11–38] In order for the Rule to apply, the covenant must be capable of binding third parties. This requires the terms of the covenant to be subjected to scrutiny: does the covenant restrict its enforceability to a particular person or otherwise exclude some parties from its terms? If so, is the party currently at issue excluded from the terms? If yes, then the Rule will not operate. If no, then the Rule will operate. In Ireland, this principle has been subjected to various levels of strictness in terms of its enforcement. In *Williams & Co Ltd v LSD & Quinnsworth Ltd*,[45] the terms of the covenant made it enforceable against the purchaser "and tenant or lessee of the premises", thus the rule was not applied in relation to a sub-tenant of another area because they were excluded by the terms of the covenant itself. In contrast, the Rule was applied in *Whelan v Cork Corporation*.[46] In this case, the terms of the covenant, strictly constructed, would have excluded sub-sub-lessees from enforcement, however Murphy J took a broad interpretation of the covenant and of the term "assign" to mean that the covenant was enforceable against anyone who derived title from the lessor. Thus, the Rule could be applied.

III. The Enforcement of Covenants Between Successors in Title under the LCLRA 2009

[11–39] As might be expected, given the complex nature of the enforcement of covenants under both common law and equity, the Land and Conveyancing Law Reform Act 2009 introduces radical reform in this area, abolishing the pre-existing rules for freehold covenants governed by the Act.[47] Before we consider the ways in which covenants covered by these provisions will be enforced from now on, it is important to clearly outline the scope of Chapter 4 of the Act.

1. Definition of "Freehold Covenant" for the Purposes of LCLRA 2009

[11–40] Section 48 provides that, for the purposes of the Act, a "freehold covenant" is to be understood as "a covenant attaching to dominant land and servient land which has been entered into after the commencement of this Chapter". This definition excludes: (a) any covenants entered into prior to 1 December 2009; and (b) any covenants that cannot be construed as attaching to dominant and servient land. These continue to be governed by the old law.[48] The concepts of dominant land and servient land are clearly borrowed here from the law of easements, which is considered in detail in Chapter 12. Both concepts are given express definition in s 48. According to this provision:

> "dominant land" means freehold land with the benefit of a covenant to which other freehold land is subject; and "dominant owner" shall be read accordingly and includes persons deriving title from or under that owner;

[44] See, for example, *Northern Ireland Carriers Ltd v Larne Harbour Ltd* [1981] NI 171 at 178 *per* Murray J.

[45] Unreported, High Court, 19 June 1970.

[46] [1991] ILRM 19; confirmed by Supreme Court [1994] 3 IR 367.

[47] s 49(1), Land and Conveyancing Law Reform Act 2009.

[48] See para 11–48 below.

> ...
>
> "servient land" means freehold land which is subject to a covenant benefiting other freehold land; and "servient owner" shall be read accordingly...

Thus, dominant land is land that benefits from the covenant in question and servient land is land that suffers the exercise of the covenant.

As well as excluding any covenants that are not appurtenant (i.e. not attaching to two pieces of land in this benefit/burden or dominant/servient manner), s 48's definition of freehold covenant clearly (and unsurprisingly) excludes personal covenants. Two other matters of note also flow from s 48. The first is that the 2009 Act is not concerned with whether the covenant in question is positive or restrictive; both types are treated in the same way. Secondly, once the 2009 Act applies there is no need to consider any differences between common law and equity: rather the question of enforceability of the covenant is one of statute law alone. [11–41]

2. Enforcement of Freehold Covenants: General Principle in LCLRA 2009

Section 49(2) of the Land and Conveyancing Law Reform Act 2009 lays down the general principle of enforceability thus: [11–42]

> ... any freehold covenant which imposes in respect of servient land an obligation to do or to refrain from doing any act or thing is enforceable—
>
> (a) by—
>
> (i) the dominant owner for the time being, or
>
> (ii) a person who has ceased to be that owner but only in respect of any breach of covenant occurring during the period when that person was such owner,
>
> (b) against—
>
> (i) the servient owner for the time being in respect of any breach of covenant by that owner or which occurred before and continued unremedied after that person became the servient owner, or
>
> (ii) a person who has ceased to be that owner, but only in respect of a breach of covenant which occurred during the period when that person was such owner.

According to this, the dominant owner can enforce the covenant against the current servient owner where the covenant has been breached by the current servient owner, or by a previous servient owner and that previous breach has continued without remedy since the current owner took over. In addition, the dominant owner can enforce the covenant against a former servient owner in respect of a breach of the covenant that took place during the former servient owner's period of ownership. A former dominant owner can also enforce the covenant in question against both current and former servient owners, but only in respect of breaches of the covenant that took place while he was the dominant owner. These claims are subject to the Statute of Limitations 1957.[49] Where the covenant in question is restrictive, the definition of "servient owner" includes "a licensee or other person in occupation of the land with or without the [11–43]

[49] s 49(6)(a)(2), Land and Conveyancing Law Reform Act 2009.

consent of"[50] the owner. The servient owner generally includes all "persons deriving title from or under that owner, but not a tenant for a period less than 5 years".[51] This makes it clear that the dominant owner can enforce the covenant against successors in title of the original servient owner, with the exception of tenancies for less than five years' duration.

3. "Scheme of Development" under the LCLRA 2009

[11–44] The 2009 Act does not abandon the concept of having a particular approach to freehold covenants that exist within a scheme of development. Section 49(3) provides:

> Where there is a scheme of development subsection (2) [the general scheme] applies so as to render covenants which are capable of reciprocally benefiting and burdening the parts of land within the scheme enforceable by and against the owners for the time being of such parts or persons referred to in subsection (2)(a)(ii) and (2)(b)(ii).

Thus, reciprocal covenants within schemes of development are enforceable by and against successors in title of the dominant and servient owners. This is limited to covenants that "are capable of reciprocally benefiting and burdening the parts of land within the scheme", but apart from that there is no restriction on the kinds of covenants contemplated here (beyond the general definition of freehold covenants under the 2009 Act[52]) and it applies to both positive and restrictive covenants.

[11–45] For the purposes of the 2009 Act, s 48 defines a scheme of development thus:

> [A] development of land under which—
> (a) the land is, or is intended to be, subdivided into 2 or more parts for conveyance in fee simple to each owner of a part;
> (b) there is an intention as between the developer and the owners of parts to create reciprocity of covenants in accordance with section 49 (3);
> (c) that intention is expressed in each conveyance to the owners of parts or implied from the covenants in question as they relate to the parts and the proximity of the relationship between their owners;

This definition seems to include both residential and commercial developments.

4. Sub-Divided Servient Land

[11–46] It will sometimes be the case that a piece of servient land would subsequently be sub-divided by, for example, selling it in three different lots to three separate people. The question that then arises from the perspective of someone interested in the enforcement of a freehold covenant (i.e. the dominant owner) is which of these new owners has responsibility for the covenant. This is dealt with by s 49(4) of the Land and Conveyancing Law Reform Act 2009, which provides that where the servient land is sub-divided, any freehold covenants enforceable against the servient owner will be appropriately apportioned between the sub-divided parts of the land[53] and can then be

---

[50] s 48, *ibid.*
[51] *ibid.*
[52] paras 11–40 to 11–41; s 49, Land and Conveyancing Law Reform Act 2009.
[53] s 49(4)(a), Land and Conveyancing Law Reform Act 2009.

enforced against the owners of each of these parts,[54] "as if those obligations had originally been entered into separately in respect only of each such part".[55] Section 48(5) provides that disputes as to apportionment can be determined by a court.

5. Contracting out of LCLRA 2009 Enforcement

Section 49(6)(b) of the Land and Conveyancing Law Reform Act 2009 provides that s 49 (the new enforcement mechanism) "takes effect subject to the terms of the covenant or the instrument containing it". As a result, it is clear that people creating freehold covenants on or after 1 December 2009 are entitled to provide for an alternative enforcement mechanism in their original agreement by which the covenant is created. In other words, they can contract out of the s 49 scheme. **[11–47]**

6. Status of Pre-2009 Act Rules of Common Law and Equity

Section 49(1) makes it clear that the general intention behind Chapter 4 is to displace the vast majority of the pre-existing rules on the enforceability of covenants: **[11–48]**

> Subject to *subsection (6)*, the rules of common law and equity (including the rule known as the rule in *Tulk v. Moxhay*) are abolished to the extent that they relate to the enforceability of a freehold covenant.

The 2009 Act does not entirely displace the common law and equity rules relating to the enforceability of freehold covenants. Firstly, privity of contract—through which the covenants are enforced through original parties—is undisturbed.[56] Secondly, and as mentioned above,[57] covenants created before 1 December 2009 will still be governed by the pre-2009 Act rules of common law and equity, as will any covenants that do not fit within the definition of freehold covenant laid down in s 48 and considered above.

IV. Discharge of Freehold Covenants

One of the long-standing difficulties with freehold covenants relates to discharge, especially of freehold covenants over unregistered land. It is imperative that there would be a straightforward mechanism for the discharge (and, indeed, the modification) of freehold covenants to reflect the changing nature and use of particular pieces of land over time. Once more, the 2009 Act has introduced a straightforward mechanism for discharge or modification, and expressly provides that it applies to all freehold covenants "whether created before or after the commencement" of the Act.[58] **[11–49]**

Section 50 of the Land and Conveyancing Law Reform Act 2009 provides for a servient owner to apply for a court order for the discharge ("in whole or in part") or modification of a freehold covenant "on the ground that continued compliance with it would constitute an unreasonable interference with the use and enjoyment of the servient land".[59] This raises the immediate and obvious question as to reasonableness: **[11–50]**

[54] s 49(4)(b), *ibid.*
[55] s 49(4), *ibid.*
[56] s 49(6)(a)(i), *ibid.*
[57] paras 11–40 and 11–41.
[58] s 50(1), Land and Conveyancing Law Reform Act 2009.
[59] *ibid.*

what constitutes an "unreasonable interference" in the context of freehold covenants? The Act itself provides some guidance as to that question in s 50(2), in which courts are directed to "have regard as appropriate" to the following factors:

- The circumstances in which the covenant was originally entered into, the purposes of which it was originally created, and the time that has elapsed since its creation[60];
- Any changes in the character of the dominant land, the servient land, and the neighbourhood in which they are located since the covenant was created[61];
- The provisions of the development plan for the area in which the land is location.[62] In this respect the reference is to development plans created under the Planning and Development Act 2000;
- Grants or refusals of planning permission in respect of land in the victinity of the dominant and servient land[63];
- Whether or not the covenant secures any practical benefit to the dominant land and, if so, the nature and extent of that benefit[64];
- Whether compliance with any covenants requiring the servient owner to execute works, "do anything", or pay for or contribute to the cost of any such works or things has become unduly onerous when considered in the light of the benefit that is derived from compliance[65];
- Whether the dominant owner has agreed to the discharge or modification of the covenant. Here the agreement can be either express or implied[66];
- Any representations that may have been made by "any person interested in the performance of the covenant"[67];
- "any other matter which the court considers relevant".[68]

[11–51] Having had regard to the factors outlined in s 50(2), the court can decide to discharge, modify, or leave undisturbed the freehold covenant in question. Where the covenant is discharged or modified, and this is likely to cause a "quantifiable loss to the dominant owner or other person adversely affected", the court can order that compensation would be paid as a condition of the discharge/modification order.

---

60 s 50(2)(a), Land and Conveyancing Law Reform Act 2009.
61 s 50(2)(b), *ibid.*
62 s 50(2)(c), *ibid.*
63 s 50(2)(d), *ibid.*
64 s 50(2)(e), *ibid.*
65 s 50(2)(f), *ibid.*
66 s 50(2)(g), *ibid.*
67 s 50(2)(h), *ibid.*
68 s 50(2)(i), *ibid.*

CHAPTER 12
Easements

Easements are a common feature of property transactions and can be simply described as proprietary rights to do something over the land of another for the benefit of one's own land. As these rights are proprietary, they are materially different from licences, which constitute mere permissions to use the land of another.[1] The law of easements therefore governs a certain class of third-party proprietary interest. It is important to note that although these rights are proprietary, they do not constitute ownership in the sense of having the right to possession of the land. Rather, the holder of an easement or analogous rights has the ownership of the right to do the prescribed action over the land of the other for the benefit of his own land. For this reason easements are known as intangible rights. **[12–01]**

[1] See further Chapter 10.

[12–02] Easements can generally be categorised as either positive or negative. Positive easements are those that allow a third party to act on the land of another for the benefit of their own land, while negative easements are those that prevent a landowner from acting on his own property in the manner proscribed. Negative easements are generally disliked by the law, which leans in favour of enabling landowners to develop and deal with their land as freely as public policy and the general law can tolerate. As with other property rights, easements can exist in either law or in equity[2] and they can also exist in any of the freehold estates (i.e. as a fee simple in law or as a fee simple or life estate in equity[3]).

I. Defining Easements

[12–03] The case of *In re Ellenborough Park*[4] outlines specific defining elements of an easement, each of which is considered below. This definition aligns well with how Irish law saw, and continues to see, easements. Indeed, some 80 years before *Ellenborough Park* was decided, Monaghan CJ had handed down a definition of easements in *Hamilton v Musgrove*[5] that is very similar in its terms to the *Ellenborough Park* definition. He held:

> For the exercise of an easement, properly speaking, there must be two tenements, a dominant and a servient tenement. An easement is an incorporeal right which may be defined to be a privilege, not conferring any right to participation in the profits of the land over which it is exercised, which the owner of one tenement has over the neighbouring tenement, by which the owner of the servient tenement is obliged to suffer something to be done, or to refrain from doing something, on his own land for the advantage of the dominant tenement. It must be imposed for the benefit of corporeal property, and imposed upon corporeal property.[6]

The elements of an easement as defined in *Ellenborough Park* and subsequent jurisprudence comprise positive and negative requirements. In positive terms an easement requires: (a) two pieces of land, known as the dominant and the servient tenements; (b) the capacity to accommodate or benefit the dominant land; (c) the lands to be in the ownership or beneficial occupation of different persons; and (d) the ability to lie in grant. In negative terms easements must not be: (a) of a nature that they constitute an undue infringement on the proprietary rights of the servient owner; (b) rights of mere recreation without utility or benefit; or (c) contrary to public policy.[7] If a right fails to fulfil these requirements, it might still be enforceable as a licence[8] or as a restrictive covenant.[9]

---

[2] See Chapter 3.

[3] See Chapter 4.

[4] [1956] Ch 131.

[5] (1870) IR 6 CL 129.

[6] *ibid.* at p 137.

[7] It is sometimes said that there is a further negative requirement that the easement not be too wide or too vague, but this requirement is considered under the positive requirement that the easement ought to be capable of lying in grant.

[8] The enforceability of licences is considered in full in Chapter 10.

[9] The enforceability of restrictive covenants is considered in full in Chapter 11.

1. There Must Be a Dominant and Servient Tenement

Easements are appurtenant rights, meaning that they exist between two pieces of land to which they are appurtenant (or attached). As a result, easements cannot exist *in gross* (i.e. without being linked to land).[10] In the language of easements we refer to these properties as being the dominant and the servient tenements. The dominant tenement is the piece of land that benefits from the exercise of the easement (or that is accommodated by it), whereas the servient tenement is the piece of land over which the easement is exercised.[11] As appurtenant rights, easements remain attached to these pieces of land and are transferred with them[12]: they are not personal rights and do not attach to the landowner. **[12–04]**

The dominant and servient tenements do not need to be attached to one another or to be directly beside one another; they simply need to be sufficiently proximate to allow the exercise of a right over one that accommodates the other. This is well demonstrated by the case of *Latimer v Official Co-operative Society.*[13] This concerned a terrace of three houses, in which one of the end houses had been demolished. The demolition of this house caused the middle house to detach itself from the third house in the terrace, which suffered structural damage as a result. Even though the two end houses had not been attached to one another, the Court of Common Pleas found that the first house (which was demolished) owed a duty of support to the third house in the terrace. Thus an easement of support existed between the properties, even though they were not physically attached to one another. **[12–05]**

In order for anything to accommodate the dominant tenement, both the dominant and the servient tenement must be identified clearly. This is because we cannot describe as an easement something that accommodates or benefits an undefined or indefinite area of land; it must accommodate a particular and identifiable piece of land that we can call the dominant tenement. Equally it must be exercised over a particular and identifiable area of land that we can call the servient tenement. This is well demonstrated by *Woodman v Pwllbach Colliery Co. Ltd,*[14] in which it was held that the right to scatter coal dust over an indefinite area could not be an easement; the servient tenement was not defined. **[12–06]**

2. The Easement Must Accommodate the Dominant Tenement

In order for a right to do something to be defined as an easement and, as a result, to acquire proprietary and appurtenant characteristics, it must accommodate the alleged dominant tenement in its amenity, utility or convenience.[15] In this context **[12–07]**

---

[10] See, for example, *Whipp v Mackey* [1927] IR 372; *Frank Towey Ltd and Ors v South Dublin County Council* [2005] IEHC 93.

[11] We have seen in Chapter 11 that this language of dominant and servient land has now been extended to how we govern the enforceability of freehold covenants under ss 48–49, Land and Conveyancing Law Reform Act 2009.

[12] *Timmons v Hewitt* (1887) 22 LR 627; see also s 71, Land and Conveyancing Law Reform Act 2009, considered in paras 12–49 to 12–50 below.

[13] (1885) 16 LR IR 305.

[14] [1915] AC 634.

[15] *Scott v Goulding Properties Ltd* [1972] IR 200—it will not be sufficient for the alleged easement to benefit the dominant owner in his personal capacity.

accommodation can be taken to mean "making the use of the land more convenient in a relatively substantial manner"; conveying a personal benefit to the landowner will not suffice.[16] Whether or not an alleged easement accommodates the dominant tenement is a matter of construction based on the particular circumstances of the case, as demonstrated by the facts in *Re Ellenborough Park*.[17] In 1855 the owners of Ellenborough Park sold surrounding properties for the purposes of development. By these conveyances each purchaser received

> the full enjoyment... at all times hereafter in common with the other persons to whom such easements may be granted of the pleasure ground [Ellenborough Park]... subject to the payment of a fair and just proportion of the costs charges and expenses of keeping in good order and condition the said pleasure ground.

After some time a dispute arose as to whether the purchasers of the plots around Ellenborough Park in fact had an easement over it. The Court held that the right to use the pleasure ground was analogous to a right appurtenant to houses to use a garden for normal domestic purposes. Such a right would be beneficial to the houses to which the right was annexed and, as a result, would be an easement, even though it was directed towards recreation and amusement. Although the use of a pleasure ground did not have any *necessary* connection to the enjoyment of the premises sold surrounding the park, it was capable of accommodating those premises and, as a result, of being defined as an easement. Thus Lord Evershed MR described it as a right to use the park as a garden.[18]

[12–08] Leaving to one side the fact that *Ellenborough Park* is a controversial decision because the Court might be said to have recognised "a right to walk around" as an easement,[19] the case demonstrates the principle that accommodation of the dominant tenement will depend on both the nature of the alleged easement and the nature of the dominant tenement. It is difficult to see, for example, how the right claimed in *Ellenborough Park* could have been defined as an easement if the properties claiming the status of dominant tenement had been factories or warehouses, rather than residential premises. In essence, an easement will accommodate the dominant tenement if it confers on it a benefit that is connected with its ordinary use and enjoyment, bearing in mind the nature of the dominant tenement itself.

3. The Ownership and/or Possession of Both Tenements Must Be Held by Different People

[12–09] As a matter of logic, the owner of the dominant and servient tenements must normally be different people; one simply does not need rights in the nature of easements over

---

[16] *Hill v Tupper* (1863) 2 H & C 121.

[17] *In re Ellenborough Park* [1956] Ch 131.

[18] *ibid.* at 179.

[19] The controversy surrounding what is known as the *jus spatiendi* is considered in de Londras, *Principles of Irish Property Law* (1st ed, 2007, Dublin, Clarus Press), paras 12–32 to 12–35. See also Valentine, "The Right to Wander and to Picnic" (1955) 18(6) MLR 599 at 602, in which the author noted that the decision in *Ellenborough* "will of necessity, it is felt, cause a flutter among the footnotes and a reappraisal of accepted notions".

one's own land.[20] In some cases, however, one may have an easement over land that one owns: where the land has been leased to another person who enjoys exclusive possession as a result of the lease,[21] a landlord may reserve an easement over that property for the benefit of other properties retained by him.

4. The Right Must Be Capable of Lying in Grant

It is a fundamental principle of the law of easements that all easements must be capable of being expressly granted (even if, in fact, they have not actually been expressly granted but have arisen by implication,[22] presumption[23] or estoppel[24]). Thus, all easements must be capable of being expressed in written form: they cannot be so vague that it is impossible to tell whether they have been interfered with illegitimately.[25] [12–10]

5. The Right Must Not Overly Infringe on the Servient Owner's Proprietary Rights

While a dominant owner receives a proprietary interest in the servient property, that interest only goes as far as the easement itself and cannot constitute an excessive infringement on the proprietary rights of the servient owner. In other words, the easement cannot go so far as to essentially make the servient owner's rights illusory. As a result it is a general principle that, for example, easements ought not to require expenditure on the part of the servient owner.[26] The case of *Copeland v Greenhalf*[27] illustrates the principle that the alleged easement cannot overly infringe on the servient owner's proprietary rights. [12–11]

Copeland owned an orchard and adjoining house, which was accessed by a strip of land that varied between 15ft and 35ft in width. Greenhalf was a mechanic whose premises were opposite Copeland's land. Greenhalf was in the habit of parking vehicles on this strip of land and, when Copeland litigated to prevent such activity, Greenhalf claimed that he had an easement to do so. The Court, however, held that the right claimed was too extensive to be defined as an easement; in effect, it was a claim to the whole beneficial user of the strip of land and no easement of that nature was, or could be, known to law. This was simply because it would constitute an unacceptable infringement on the servient owner's proprietary rights. According to Upjohn LJ: [12–12]

> I think the right claimed goes wholly outside any normal idea of an easement, that is the right of the owner or the occupier over a servient tenement. This claim (to which no closely related authority has been referred to me) really amounts to a claim to a joint user

[20] See *Roe v Siddons* (1888) 22 QBD 224.
[21] As considered in Chapter 15, exclusive possession by the tenant is an essential element of a lease.
[22] See paras 12–34 to 12–50 below.
[23] See paras 12–53 to 12–80 below.
[24] See paras 12–51 to 12–52 below.
[25] *Bland v Moseley* (1587) 9 Co Rep 58a; *Browne v Flower* [1911] 1 Ch 219; *Dalton v Angus & Co* (1881) 6 App Cas 740; *Cochrane v Verner* (1895) 29 ILT 571.
[26] *Regis Property v Redman* [1956] 2 QB 612; the only exception to this appears to be the ancient easement to fence land (*Crow v Wood* [1971] 1 QB 77).
[27] [1952] Ch 488.

> of the land by the defendant. Practically, the defendant is claiming the whole beneficial use of the strip of land on the south-east side of the track there; he can even leave as many or as few lorries on it as he likes for as long as he likes; he may enter on it by himself, his servants or agents to do repair work thereon. In my judgment, that is not a claim which can be established as an easement. It is virtually a claim to possession of the servient tenement, if necessary to the exclusion of the owner, or at any rate, to a joint user, and no authority has been cited to me which would justify that a right of this wide and undefined nature can be the proper subject-matter of an easement.[28]

[12–13] This negative requirement does not mean that a right that causes some inconvenience for the servient owner can never be defined as an easement. In fact, the Irish courts have shown a willingness to recognise easements where the exercise of the right causes considerable inconvenience for the servient owner. Thus in *Middleton v Clarence*[29] the Court held that "the right of throwing the spoil, arising from the working of the quarry, on the adjoining lands" was an easement. So too was a right to dump lime and manure on the lands of another in *Redmond v Hayes.*[30] The principle here is simply that the inconvenience caused cannot be so extensive as to make the servient owner's proprietary enjoyment of his land more or less illusory.

6. The Right Cannot Be One of Mere Recreation Without Utility

[12–14] It is a general principle of the law of easements that an easement cannot be one of "mere" recreation, although it ought to be noted that there appear to be exceptions to this principle. For example, although the *jus spatiendi*—the right to "walk around" or "to stray"—is generally said to be incapable of definition as an easement, one could certainly argue that it was recognised as an easement in *Re Ellenborough Park.*[31] Thus there is some uncertainty as to the extent to which this definitional element of an easement is actually enforced by the courts.

7. The Right Cannot Contravene Public Policy

[12–15] No right that contravenes public policy will be recognised as an easement in law. In the main, this requirement seems to exclude easements that would have a negative environmental impact. Thus in *Goldsmid v Tunbridge Wells Improvement Commissioners,*[32] the Court held that the defendants could not claim an easement to discharge the town sewage through the plaintiff's stream because the sewage would pollute the stream and its adjoining lake.[33]

II. Common Easements

[12–16] The law recognises an exceptionally broad range of easements, many of which are relatively idiosyncratic and unlikely to arise very commonly (such as the right to use eel tanks on a riverbed in order to benefit an eel weir, which was recognised as an

---

[28] *ibid.* at 498.

[29] (1877) IR 11 CL 499.

[30] Unreported, High Court, 7 October 1974.

[31] [1956] Ch 131.

[32] (1865) LR 1 Eq 161.

[33] See *Blackburne v Somers* (1879) 5 LR IR 1; *Attorney General v Richmond* (1866) LR 2 Eq 306.

easement in *Ingram v Mackey*[34]). Some easements are, however, quite common and deserve individual treatment in this section. In addition, some rights are not recognised as easements in spite of how frequently they are encountered in everyday activity, and there are arguments that their recognition as easements, or at the very least their codification and regulation through legislation as something *other than* easements ought to be considered. A selection of these is also considered in this section.[35]

1. Right of Way

A right of way is a right to cross and re-cross property between two clearly defined points (known as points of ingress and aggress)[36]; it is not a right to wander randomly across the property of another. Whether or not a right of way is limited to crossing and re-crossing by foot or can extend to vehicular access is entirely dependent on the terms of the easement.[37] If a right of way does include a right to vehicular access, it includes the right to stop, or "park", for the time required to load and unload vehicles, but not for an indefinite period of time.[38] Once a right of way has been established for a particular purpose (e.g. crossing and re-crossing the land on foot) it cannot normally be expanded into a different and broader purpose (e.g. rolling trolleys across the property),[39] although a right of way for the broader purpose could be newly acquired by prescription.[40] The holder of a right of way is entitled to enter the land of the servient owner in order to adapt the right of way to the purpose for which it was granted,[41] although he cannot cause any injury to the servient owner's land in the course of doing so.[42] **[12–17]**

The servient owner is obliged to refrain from changing his land in such a manner as to make the right of way unusable,[43] although he may alter the line of the right of way.[44] This does not mean, however, that the servient owner is not entitled to place a gate or other obstruction on the right of way; in fact, it may be necessary for the servient owner to do so in order to maintain the usefulness of his own land for agricultural or **[12–18]**

---

34 [1898] 1 IR 272.

35 This section comprises a mere selection of some easements or purported easements that cause controversy and expose some of the policy and principle debates around the law of easements. Comprehensive consideration of easements generally can be found in Bland, *Easements* (2nd ed, 2009, Dublin, Round Hall); Gaunt & Morgan, *Gale on the Law of Easements* (18th ed, 2008, London, Sweet & Maxwell).

36 *Donnelly v Adams* [1905] 1 IR 154; *Tallon v Ennis* [1937] IR 549.

37 *Gogarty v Hoskins* [1906] 1 IR 173; *Doolan v Murray & Dun Laoghaire Corporation*, unreported, High Court, 21 December 1993; *Orwell Park Management Ltd v Henihan & Anor* [2004] IEHC 87.

38 *Bulstrode v Lambert* [1953] 2 All ER 728.

39 *Austin v Scottish Widows' Assurance Society* (1881) 8 LR IR 197.

40 See, for example, *Orwell Park Management Ltd. v Henihan & Anor* [2004] IEHC 87, in which a vehicular right of way was acquired by the claimants by means of prescription.

41 *Caldwell v Kilkelly* [1905] 1 IR 434; *Newcomen v Coulson* (1877) 5 Ch D 143; *Rudd v Rea* [1921] 1 IR 223.

42 *Ingram v Morecroft* (1863) 33 Beav 49.

43 *Griffin v Keane* (1927) 61 ILTR 177.

44 See, for example, *Crowley v Dowling*, unreported, High Court, 20 March 2002.

other purposes. The erection of a gate or other obstruction on the right of way does not constitute an illegitimate limitation on the easement *provided* the holder of the right of way is given the means to pass through on condition that he closes the gate or reconstructs the obstruction having done so.[45]

2. Right to Light

[12–19] A right to light entitles someone to have lateral sunlight pass unobstructed over the servient tenement and through an aperture in the dominant tenement.[46] Such an easement therefore obliges the servient owner to ensure that the light is not obstructed in passing over his land.[47] Rights to light are rarely expressly granted; instead they usually arise through long user, becoming known as "ancient rights to light" or "ancient lights".[48] The amount of light to which one is entitled under such an easement is, in essence, dependent on the circumstances and the character of the premises (although city premises will normally be entitled to a lesser level of light than rural premises).[49]

3. Right to Support

[12–20] The easement of support generally concerns the support of one building by another, while the common law recognises a natural right of support of one piece of land as against an adjoining piece of land.[50] Rights to support are of particular significance in cases of houses that are attached to one another in a semi-detached or terraced manner. Although properties that support one another will normally be directly attached to one another, the decision in *Latimer*[51] shows that this is not required; all that is required is that the properties would be sufficiently proximate to allow one to accommodate the other by providing it with support. The right to support results not only in the structural support of the property but can also be an important incident in maintaining the value of a property in terms of its appearance and the likelihood that the property could be used as security for the purposes of a mortgage. This is well demonstrated by the case of *Todd v Cinelli*.[52]

[12–21] *Todd* concerned adjoining properties in Howth, Co. Dublin, which were owned by Todd and Cinelli respectively. The defendants' property, *Woodview*, was unoccupied for a substantial period of time, during which it became run down and was vandalised. While the Cinellis had planning permission to carry out some renovations over the property, they did not have permission to demolish it; a fact they acknowledged to the plaintiffs on occasion. Notwithstanding that, the house was demolished in full in

---

[45] *Tubridy v Walsh* (1901) 35 ILT 321; *Flynn v Harte* [1913] 2 IR 322; *Geoghegan v Henry* [1922] 2 IR 1; *Barrett v Linnane* [2002] IEHC 20; *Crowley v Dowling*, unreported, High Court, 20 March 2002.

[46] An aperture is a small opening or hole through which light passes, such as on a camera.

[47] *National Provincial Plate Glass Insurance Co. v Prudential Assurance Co.* (1877) 6 Ch D 757; *Scott v Pape* (1886) 31 Ch D 554; *Andrews v Waite* [1907] 2 Ch 500.

[48] *Higgins v Betts* [195] 2 Ch 210.

[49] *Mackey v Scottish Widows' Assurance Society* (1877) IR 11 Eq 541.

[50] *Blackhouse v Bonomi* (1861) 9 HL Cas 503.

[51] (1885) 16 LR IR 305.

[52] Unreported, High Court, 5 March 1999.

November 1995. Not only did the demolition proceed without the appropriate planning permission, but it was also conducted in what Kelly J deemed "an entirely sub-standard manner". This substandard demolition resulted in substantial damage to the property of the plaintiffs, including damage from wind and weather. The defendants accepted that they had breached the right of support owed to the plaintiffs' property and the main area of contention in the case related to the factors that the Court was entitled to take into account in assessing the quantum of damages. Notwithstanding Kelly J's acceptance of Lord Denning's *dictum* in *Phipps v Pears*[53] that negative easements ought to be limited because of their potential to undermine the development of property, the Court held that it could take into account both the changed appearance of the plaintiffs' house and the likely difficulties they would have in the future in using the property for security. Kelly J concluded that, as *Phipps* was designed to ensure that the legitimate development of property was not unduly hampered, demolition work done without appropriate planning permission did not count as legitimate development and these factors could be taken into account in assessing damages for breach of an easement of support.

Easements of support are frequently important for the protection of property from wind and weather damage, as in many cases the removal or amendment of an attached property can leave the dominant tenement exposed to weather damage. Where the support provided by one property to another also incorporates an element of protection from the weather, a servient owner may be required to ensure that this protection is secured along with support into the future, and exposure to wind and weather may be taken into account in the assessment of damages for breach of the easement of support.[54] This is so even though there is no easement of protection from wind and weather *per se*.[55] **[12–22]**

4. Right to Park Cars

It was originally thought that an easement to park was not recognised in Irish law.[56] **[12–23]** This position appears to have been at least partially reversed in *Redfont Ltd v Custom House Dock Management Ltd*.[57] The plaintiffs in this case operated a pub and bistro in the International Financial Services Centre (IFSC) in Dublin. They had been granted express rights of way (with or without vehicles) to pass over the public areas of the IFSC and their customers were in the habit of parking in these public areas. This resulted in other occupants of the IFSC complaining about congestion. The management company subsequently circulated a memorandum containing details of new parking restrictions in the public areas. Following that memorandum customers of the pub and bistro were denied parking in those public areas. The plaintiffs claimed that the rights of way were expressed in a broad enough manner to include an entitlement for their customers to park in the public areas of the IFSC and that, even if that was not the case, an easement of parking arose by implication. Shanley J held that a right of way could be accompanied by "ancillary" rights that were required to ensure its full

[53] [1965] 1 QB 76.
[54] See *Treacy v Dublin Corporation* [1993] 1 IR 305.
[55] *Phipps v Pears* [1965] 1 QB 76. See paras 12–26 to 12–29 below.
[56] See, for example, Bland, "The Easement of Parking" (1997) 2(2) CPLJ 26.
[57] Unreported, High Court, 31 March 1998.

enjoyment; indeed, the right to park for the purposes of loading and unloading is a recognised ancillary right to a right of way.[58] Shanley J then considered whether the right to park cars by people eating and drinking in the dominant tenement was also an ancillary right and concluded that it could be. Taking into account the terms of the grant itself, the fact that the dominant tenement was leasehold property demised for the purposes of eating and drinking by the public, the nature of the servient tenement and its use, and the physical dimension of the right of way to assess whether it could sustain the parking of vehicles, Shanley J held that a right to park existed in favour of the plaintiffs. He also held that an easement to park could be implied by common intention.[59]

[12–24] *Redfont* suggests that an easement to park can exist either in its own right or as an ancillary right to a right of way, but that in either case the terms of the grant, the nature of the dominant and servient tenements, and the physical capacity of the relevant land to sustain a right to park will be taken into account.[60] The Supreme Court decision in *AGS (ROI) Pension Nominees Ltd & Ors v Madison Estates Ltd*[61] may also be significant here. Even though the claimants did not succeed in establishing a right to park cars by means of prescription, the Supreme Court at no stage suggested that the right to park was incapable of being defined as an easement. In fact, Keane CJ simply assessed whether an easement to park had been acquired by prescription and never averted to the controversy about the existence or otherwise of such an easement.

5. Right of Access to a Dwelling

[12–25] The emergence of a great deal of high-rise and other multi-unit accommodation has given rise to a particularly important question in the area of easements: Do inhabitants of accommodation units within these developments have a right of access to a dwelling? In *Liverpool City Council v Irwin*[62] the House of Lords held that tenants of accommodation units in a high-rise development enjoy implied easements to the use of lifts and stairs to access their accommodation. In *Heeney v Dublin Corporation*,[63] residents of a high-rise development in Ballymun applied for an interlocutory injunction to force Dublin Corporation to take steps to ensure, as far as practicable, that the lifts would be in working order. While the Court did not hold that there was any *easement* of access to a dwelling by means of these lifts, it did hold that the constitutional right to the inviolability of the dwelling resulted in a responsibility on the part of the Corporation to ensure that the lifts were in good working order.

---

[58] *Bulstrode v Lambert* [1953] 2 All ER 728.

[59] The acquisition of easements by common intention is considered in full in paras 12–35 to 12–37.

[60] See also Bland, "Easements of Elevator and of Parking: From Ballymun to the IFSC" (1998) 3(4) CPLJ 80. It ought to be noted that the approach of the Court in *Redfont* is (to a degree, at least) similar to the approach adopted in *London & Blenheim Estates v Ladbroke Retail Parks Ltd*, in which the Chancery Division held that the right to park can exist as an easement where it is a general right within a designated area—[1993] 1 All ER 307 (upheld in the Court of Appeal without substantive consideration of the right to park, [1993] 4 All ER 157).

[61] Unreported, Supreme Court, 23 October 2003 (judgment *ex tempore*).

[62] [1976] 2 All ER 39.

[63] Unreported, Supreme Court, 17 August 1998.

> It is beyond debate that there is a hierarchy of constitutional rights and at the top of the list is the right to life, followed by the right to health and with that the right to the integrity of one's dwellinghouse. The Constitution expressly provides that the dwelling of every citizen is inviolable and cannot be forcibly entered save in accordance with law. In my judgment, the corollary of that guarantee must be that a person should be entitled to the freedom to come and go from his dwelling provided he keeps to the law.

6. Right to Protection from Wind and Weather

The law does not recognise any easement to protection of a property from wind or weather damage, largely because of the general reluctance to impose additional negative easements on landowners in a manner that might inhibit development. This position is usually traced back to the decision of Denning LJ in *Phipps v Pears*.[64] In or around 1930 the owner of two adjoining old houses—No 14 and No 16, Market Street—pulled down No 16. Following this a new house was erected on the site of No 16, with its flank wall flat up against (although not connected to) the old wall of No 14. The owner then sold the newly erected house to the plaintiff in 1951, and No 14 was conveyed to the defendant in 1957. The defendant demolished No 14 pursuant to a demolition order from the local authority in 1962, which resulted in the flank wall of the newly erected building being exposed to the weather. As that wall had never been rendered or plastered, rain got in, which froze, causing cracks and damage. The plaintiff sued for damages, claiming that his property enjoyed an easement of protection from the weather from No 14. Lord Denning held that there was no such easement known to the law and that every property-owner is entitled to pull down his house, if he wishes. If such action exposes another property to wind and weather, then, while that is unfortunate, it is not a matter for legal regulation by means of easements. Any other conclusion, he held, "would unduly restrict your neighbour in his enjoyment of his own land".[65] This position was reiterated in *Giltrap v Busby*,[66] but that case was later distinguished in *Tapson v Northern Ireland Housing Executive*.[67] [12–26]

In *Tapson* the plaintiffs owned a property in Armagh that adjoined another (vacant) premises owned by the defendant. The plaintiffs claimed that, since 1980, the defendant had failed to repair bomb damage on the premises and had allowed the premises to remain in a defective and damp condition, which had resulted in damp seeping in through a party wall between the premises and causing damage and deterioration to the plaintiff's premises. While the Court did not hold that there was an easement to protection from wind and weather, it did find that negligent acts or omissions by the defendants could give rise to liability if such harm were reasonably foreseeable by the landowner. The Court therefore recognised that a landowner may have tortious liability for the failure to protect neighbouring premises from weather damage notwithstanding the lack of an easement to this effect. [12–27]

The Irish courts have similarly not recognised any easement of protection from wind and weather, but have developed mechanisms by which a property might be otherwise [12–28]

64 [1965] 1 QB 76.
65 *ibid.* at 83.
66 [1970] 5 NIJB 1.
67 [1992] NI 264.

protected from damage arising from weather. This conclusion is gleaned from the decision in *Treacy v Dublin Corporation*.[68] Treacy owned a property in Dublin City. This property was adjoined to one that had been deemed "a dangerous structure" under the Local Government (Sanitary Services) Act 1964. Following this, notices of intended demolition were served on the relevant persons, including the plaintiff, who was given the opportunity to take any steps he thought fit for the protection and safety of his premises if they should happen to be "in any manner dependent upon any support" from the premises to be demolished. The plaintiff claimed a violation of his easement to support from the adjoining property and secondarily claimed that the defendant was obliged to protect the plaintiff's property from weather damage. The Supreme Court held that the defendant authority was entitled—if not obliged—to carry out the demolition under the 1964 Act and, relying on *Phipps*, that there is no easement of a right to protection from wind and weather. However, where work was being carried out, the consequence of which would be to remove a support that previously consisted of a wall between two terraced houses and which, by reason of the existence of the rooms on the other side of it, was immune from exposure to weather, it was unreal to limit the requirement of giving back support to carrying out works which would be likely, in a very short time, to become unstable due to wind and weather and to cease to be a source of support. In other words, if a protection from wind and weather happens to be provided in the course of providing support, then the easement of support may require the continued protection of the neighbouring property from wind and weather damage.

[12–29] Thus, while the Court in *Treacy* did not revert from the position in *Phipps,* which holds that there is no easement in law to protection from wind and weather, it does attempt to use the order of the Court to obtusely protect the property of the plaintiffs from any damage that wind or weather might cause. *Treacy* might be developed in the future to recognise a right to protection from wind and weather as an ancillary right to a right to support where the properties are adjoined and the support also protects from wind and weather, however this seems somewhat unlikely given the potential for the law of torts to impose sufficient liability on property owners to prevent foreseeable wind and weather damage.[69] The development of an easement of this nature therefore appears to be somewhat unnecessary and, as far as possible, public policy supports the limitation of new easements to situations of necessity in order to ensure that property-owners have as much autonomy in relation to their property as is reasonably practicable.

III. Acquisition of Easements

[12–30] Easements must be acquired on behalf of the dominant tenement; they do not automatically exist in relation to it. As considered above, the "grant" of an easement is an exceptionally important concept in law. In fact, even where there has not been an express grant of an easement, the law treats almost all easements as having been

[68] [1993] 1 IR 305.

[69] See Bland, "The Easement of Parking" (1997) 2(2) CPLJ 26: "the easement of support may include a right to wind or weather protection in circumstances where without such protection the support becomes unreal".

created by means of a grant that arises either expressly or through implication or presumption (easements granted as a remedy to estoppel are a potential exception to this[70]). Easements can be acquired in a number of different ways, all of which require individual consideration and in relation to all of which, of course, one must first establish that the right being claimed as an easement is in fact capable of being recognised as an easement by reference to the requirements of *Re Ellenborough Park*[71] as considered above.[72]

1. Easement by Express Grant

Easements can be (and commonly are) created by simply granting them expressly through a standard conveyance and this is normally (although not inevitably) done at the same time as the grant of the land intended to be the dominant tenement. Easements must be granted by means of a deed of conveyance for unregistered land[73] and can be granted over registered land by means of a transfer.[74] The actual grant or transfer of an easement must be drafted with considerable care to ensure that the extent of (and, by necessary implication, limitations on) the easement is clear, as is the identity and extent of the servient and dominant tenements. Clarity in drafting is particularly important as the doctrine of *contra proferentem* applies to express grants of easements.[75] This doctrine of contract law provides that where a contractual term is ambiguous, it is to be constructed as against the party who drafted the agreement. In the context of the grant of easements, this is ordinarily the grantor. In some cases a contract between the parties will be interpreted as including the grant of an easement, even though the terms itself do not appear to expressly grant an easement.[76] Prior to the Land and Conveyancing Law Reform Act 2009, words of limitation were required to clearly communicate the duration of an easement, however s 67(1) of the 2009 Act now makes it clear that freehold transfers of land, which includes transfers of easements, will convey the fee simple (or other estate or interest that the grantor has the power to create) in the absence of Words of Limitation.[77] **[12–31]**

2. Easement by Reservation

A vendor may reserve an easement to himself for the benefit of land retained and to be exercised over land that is being transferred. This process previously presented a difficulty at common law because the "easement" did not exist at the time that it was reserved (one cannot have an easement over one's own land[78]) and, as a result, express reservations had to be done by one of two somewhat convoluted means. The first was "grant and re-grant", by which the property was transferred to the purchaser by means **[12–32]**

[70] These easements are granted as a remedy to a proven case of estoppel, but as a result of a constructive grant of the easement by the alleged servient owner. See paras 12–51 to 12–52.
[71] *In re Ellenborough Park* [1956] Ch 131.
[72] See paras 12–06 to 12–15.
[73] s 62, Land and Conveyancing Law Reform Act 2009.
[74] s 3, Registration of Title Act 1964.
[75] *Broomfield v Williams* [1897] 1 Ch 602; *Redfont Limited v Custom House Dock Management Limited*, unreported, High Court, 31 March 1998.
[76] See, for example, *Bayley v Great Western Railway Co.* (1883) 26 Ch D 534.
[77] Words of Limitation are considered in Chapter 4.
[78] para 12–09.

of a Deed that was executed by both vendor and purchaser, and by which the purchaser immediately granted an easement to the vendor. The second was by means of a use executed by the Statute of Uses 1634.[79] The Land and Conveyancing Law Reform Act 2009 has made both of these convoluted mechanisms of reserving an easement redundant in the case of reservations made after the commencement of Part 9 of the Act[80] and instead allows for the straightforward reservation of an easement in either the grantor or any other person for whose benefit the reservation is made, and the reservation need only be executed by the grantor *even if* the transferee of the easement is the grantor himself.[81] Thus, s 69(1) provides that the reservation of an easement in a conveyance will annex that easement to the land for the benefit of which the reservation is made.[82] Pursuant to s 69(2) where the conveyance of land is made subject to any interest that does not exist immediately before the date of the conveyance, that operates as a reservation that is then governed by s 69(1).

[12–33] Easements by implied reservation will very rarely be recognised by the courts. It appears that implied reservation will arise only in cases of common intention (i.e. where the implied reservation of an easement is required to give effect to the common intentions of the parties), and in cases of strict necessity. *Dwyer Nolan Developments v Kingscroft Developments Ltd*[83] is a rare example of the Irish courts recognising an easement as having arisen by virtue of implied reservation. Both the plaintiff and defendant in this case were engaged in the construction business. The plaintiff owned land in Co. Wicklow, part of which he sold to the defendant in 1995. At the time that the contract for the sale of land was entered into, in 1994, there were no roads on the land being transferred, but planning applications submitted by the defendant for the development of the purchased property showed that there were plans to construct roads that could result in access to the property retained by the plaintiff. Amended versions of the planning application showed an intention to construct houses in such a way as to block access to the land retained by the purchaser by means of these intended roads. Following the grant of planning permission, the defendant constructed 164 houses on the purchased property in a manner that the plaintiff claimed left its property landlocked, in contravention of an implied right of way in its favour. Kinlen J held that the plaintiff was entitled to a right of way to access the property it retained, notwithstanding the fact that no such easement had been reserved by it in the conveyance. In the circumstances, Kinlen J held that the common intention of the parties was that the retained property was to be developed. In assessing this common intention Kinlen J held that all of the circumstances were to be taken into account, including the fact that both parties were building developers and acquired properties for the purposes of development. Taking these considerations into account, the Court found that a right of way was strictly required by the vendor and implied the reservation of the easement in favour of the property retained by the vendor on this basis.

---

[79] s 62(1), Conveyancing Act 1881. For how this operated see de Londras, *Principles of Property Law* (1st ed, 2007, Dublin, Clarus Press), para 12–49; Power, *Intangible Property Rights in Ireland* (2nd ed, 2008, West Sussex, Tottel), p 23.

[80] s 69(4), Land and Conveyancing Law Reform Act 2009.

[81] s 69, *ibid.*

[82] s 69(1)(b), *ibid.*

[83] [1999] 1 ILRM 141.

3. Easement by Implied Grant

Where the circumstances allow (or demand) it, the law will imply that an easement has been granted to the alleged dominant owner. Such implication arises from either the common intentions of the parties as perceived by the court, or from statutory intervention. The statutory mechanisms for the implied grant of an easement were revised by the Land and Conveyancing Law Reform Act 2009, which also replaced some common law rules and mechanisms of acquiring an easement by implied grant with codified and more clearly delineated statutory formulae. [12–34]

(a) Easements of Common Intention

Easements of common intention are relatively straightforward and are, to all intents and purposes, easements that the law recognises as having been granted by the servient owner for the benefit of the dominant land on the basis of the presumed common intentions of the parties.[84] It must be noted that the implication of an easement on the basis of common intention is materially different from the implication of a contractual term on that basis; contractual terms are essentially personal, whereas easements are proprietary rights that are appurtenant to two pieces of land. The creation (or recognition) of an easement by means of common intention therefore has very significant implications for the properties concerned. [12–35]

An important question arises as to how a court will discern what the common intention of the parties is. Intention is, after all, a subjective element and as a result courts will tend to seek out some materials on the basis of which to discern the common intention, which is then given effect by recognising the easement as having been granted. In the context of the acquisition of easements—as in many other contexts—the law will look to the words and conduct of the parties in its attempts to identify a common intention to which to give effect. Thus, where there is evidence that something qualifying as an easement has been actually exercised by the alleged dominant owner (i.e. where there is evidence of user) this may evidence a common intention, which then results in the implication of an easement.[85] There certainly appears to be a prima facie overlap here between implied easements on the basis of a common intention that is derived from evidence of user, on the one hand, and prescription (at least as it existed prior to the Land and Conveyancing Law Reform Act 2009) on the other. Indeed, this overlap has been commented on in critical terms both in judicial pronouncements[86] and in academic work.[87] While these arguments have some merit, Power's conclusion that "the concept of an easement based on implied grant has been soundly established in Irish jurisprudence" and thus should be considered "on that account rather than be dismissed on the speculative basis of alleged absence of foundation"[88] seems compelling. As a result, I proceed here without consideration of whether it is appropriate to grant easements by implication on the basis of a common intention derived from evidence of user. [12–36]

---

[84] *Pwllbach Colliery Co. Limited v Woodman* [1919] AC 634; *Redfont Limited v Custom House Dock Management Limited*, unreported, High Court, 31 March 1998.

[85] See, for example, *Conlon v Gavin* (1875) 9 ILTR 198; *Tallon v Ennis* [1937] IR 549.

[86] *Flynn v Harte* [1913] 2 IR 322 *per* Dodd J.

[87] Bland, *The Law of Easements and Profits à Prendre* (1997, Dublin, Sweet & Maxwell), p 261.

[88] Power, *Intangible Property Rights in Ireland* (2nd ed, 2008, Dublin, Tottel), p 25, fn. 9.

[12–37] Where there is a written grant, the court will also look to the words of the grant itself in order to decide whether it identifies any common intention from which the grant of an easement can be implied. This has sometimes been done even where the document between the parties was never actually executed but there was in operative terms a transfer of rights in relation to the property.[89] Where the document in question grants not only the land but also all "appurtenances", this general term can be interpreted as indicating a common intention for a particular easement now claimed to have been granted.[90] Where a grant uses more specific words but does not do so in a manner that expressly qualifies the usage permitted as an easement, those more specific words can also be taken to indicate a common intention for the grant of an easement between the parties.[91] So, for example, the grant of land that also granted the right to use the grantor's land for the purposes of accessing a car parking area might not be expressed as an easement, or even placed within the operative part of the deed, but could be taken up by a court as an indication of a common intention for the grant of a right of way over that land.

(b) Easement by Application of the Principle of Non-Derogation from the Grant

[12–38] It is a well-established principle of law that a party may not derogate from his grant or, in other words, that a party may not deny from a co-contractor that to which he is entitled under the contract or agreement between them. Although this principle is derived from contract, it is capable of binding successors in title of a contractor where it relates to contracts for the sale of land. This will happen where an easement is recognised as part of the subject-matter of the grant, and therefore becomes appurtenant to the property sold (the dominant tenement) and to the property retained (the servient tenement).[92] The doctrine of non-derogation from a grant does not apply solely to voluntary grants of property; rather it seems that it can also be applied to grants of property that result from a court order[93] and, presumably, other forms of involuntary grants of property.[94] In essence, the principle of non-derogation from a grant requires that where land is sold for a certain purpose, the vendor may not use the land retained in a manner that would render the property transferred "materially less fit for the particular purpose for which the grant" was made.[95] The principle therefore prevents a grantor from giving with one hand and taking away with another.[96] It does not, however, prevent the landowner from acting on his property in a manner that reduces the amenities of the purchaser's land in *any* way. Rather the principle, based as it is on the common intentions of the parties and the requirements

[89] *Kavanagh v Coal Mining Company of Ireland* (1861) 14 ICLR 82.

[90] *ibid.*; *Geoghegan v Fegan* (1872) IR 6 CL 139; *Head v Meara* [1912] 1 IR 262.

[91] *Renwick v Daly* (1877) IR 11 CL 126.

[92] *Conneran & Anor v Corbett & Sons Ltd & Anor* [2004] IEHC 389. See also Lyall, "Non-Derogation from a Grant" (1988) 6 ILT 143; Elliot, "Non-Derogation from Grant" (1964) 80 LQR 244.

[93] *Connell v O'Malley*, unreported, High Court, 28 July 1983.

[94] See Lyall, "Non-Derogation from a Grant" (1988) 6 ILT 143.

[95] *Browne v Flower* [1911] 1 Ch 219 *per* Parker J.

[96] *Birmingham, Dudley and District Banking Co. v Ross* (1888) 38 Ch D 295; *Harmer v Jumbil (Nigeria) Tin Area Ltd* [1921] 1 Ch 200.

of conscience, only restrains activity that would reduce amenity for the purchaser in relation to an anticipated situation.[97]

In order to successfully claim an easement by means of the application of the principle that one may not derogate from one's grant, the claimant must satisfy a two-prong test: **[12–39]**

(a) The land acquired was rendered materially less fit for the purpose for which it was acquired; *and*
(b) Given his actual or imputed knowledge of the situation, the grantor ought to have anticipated such a result from his actions.

The concept of land being "materially less fit" appears to require not that the land is entirely unfit for the purpose for which it was acquired, but rather that it is substantially less fit for that purpose than it was when it was originally acquired, and that this change in suitability results from the grantor's activity.[98] The grantor's anticipation that his activity would make the transferred property materially less fit for its original purpose will be based on the knowledge that the grantor actually has about the proposed use of the property *or* the knowledge that can be reasonably imputed to him. While a grantor will not be treated as though he has knowledge of all of the details and requirements of a proposed course of action, he will be treated as if he had the knowledge arising out of the prevailing circumstances. This is well demonstrated by reference to the decision in *Harmer v Jumbil (Nigeria) Tin Area Ltd.*[99]

In 1911 the plaintiff was granted a 21-year lease over property in Cornwall for the express purpose of housing an explosives magazine. The landlord was aware that the letting of property of this nature would subject him to some restrictions, and the tenant was aware that under the Explosives Act 1875 it was a condition of their explosives licence that no buildings be erected within a certain distance of the magazine. In 1919 the landlord leased adjoining land to the tenant for the purposes of working minerals that were known to be to be found extensively in the land. This lease was subject to a condition not to interfere with the explosives magazine or the rights of others. The defendants were entitled to erect buildings for the working of the minerals, provided they complied with these conditions. The defendant proceeded to erect three buildings within a prohibited distance of the explosives magazine, thereby putting the plaintiff's explosives licence at risk. The plaintiff claimed that the erection of these buildings constituted a derogation of the landlord's grant and was granted an injunction by the Court of Appeal. Eves J held that, under the circumstances of the 1911 lease, a condition was implied not to do anything that would violate the conditions of the explosives licence. Although the defendant was not expected to know the exact requirements of the Explosives Act 1875, knowledge of the prohibition of buildings within a certain distance of the magazine could be imputed upon him from the circumstances. If these actions had been done by the landlord, they would have constituted a derogation from his grant and, because the defendants were in the same **[12–40]**

[97] *Browne v Flower* [1911] 1 Ch 219; *Connell v O'Malley*, unreported, High Court, 28 July 1983.
[98] See *Browne v Flower* [1911] 1 Ch 219.
[99] [1921] 1 Ch 200.

position as the landlord *vis-à-vis* this particular scenario, they too were constrained from acting in this manner.

[12–41] The principle of non-derogation from a grant received detailed consideration in the Irish case of *Connell v O'Malley*.[100] Connell was engaged in the building industry and in 1973 learned that O'Malley had a site for sale on which there was outline planning permission for the erection of five houses. The site, which formed part of O'Malley's farm, was accessed by a laneway through the farm. The parties reached an agreement by which Connell was to buy the site, subject to planning permission. Once the planning permission was acquired, O'Malley refused to go through with the sale, but the plaintiff acquired a court order against O'Malley for specific performance and sale of the property to him. O'Malley then placed gates across the laneway and refused to allow the plaintiff to bring a water-main to the site via his property. Following more litigation O'Malley placed a concrete wall across the laneway and continued to behave in an aggressive manner towards the plaintiff and to obstruct his attempts to develop the property in line with the planning permission. Connell applied for an injunction to require O'Malley to remove the concrete wall, claiming that he was entitled to a right of way over the laneway by virtue of the doctrine that one may not derogate from one's grant. The Court held in favour of the plaintiff and granted the injunction, finding that the doctrine of non-derogation from the grant applied in this case because the defendant's actions had made the site purchased by Connell materially less fit for the purpose for which it had been acquired (i.e. development of five houses), and that O'Malley ought to have anticipated this as a result of his actions.

[12–42] Before the introduction of the Land and Conveyancing Law Reform Act 2009, the implication of an easement by application of the doctrine of non-derogation from a grant appeared to have been substantially limited from its parameters in *Connell v O'Malley* by the Supreme Court decision in *William Bennett Construction Ltd v John Greene and Kathleen Greene*.[101] In this case the Court suggested that the doctrine of non-derogation from a grant was to be applied in the context of easements by means of the Rule in *Wheeldon v Burrows*,[102] as it then operated.[103] Since then the Rule in *Wheeldon v Burrows* has been abolished[104] and replaced with a statutory mechanism under s 40 of the Land and Conveyancing Law Reform Act 2009.[105] This reflects the view of the Law Reform Commission that the general doctrine of non-derogation from a grant could be the primary mechanism for the implication of easements.[106] As a result, the principle of non-derogation from the grant now stands on its own as a mechanism for the implied acquisition of easements.

---

100 Unreported, High Court, 28 July 1983.

101 [2004] 2 ILRM 96; [2004] IESC 15; see further paras 12–69 to 12–71, below.

102 (1879) 12 Ch D 31.

103 de Londras, *Principles of Irish Property Law* (1st ed, 2007, Dublin, Clarus Press), paras 12–65 to 12–73.

104 s 40 (1), Land and Conveyancing Law Reform Act 2009.

105 Considered in paras 12–43 to 12–45.

106 LRC, *Consultation Paper on the Reform and Modernisation of Land Law and Conveyancing Law* (2004), p 102.

(c) Easement by Application of s 40, Land and Conveyancing Law Reform Act 2009

Prior to the Land and Conveyancing Law Reform Act 2009, the Rule in *Wheeldon v Burrows*[107] operated as an application of the doctrine that one cannot derogate from one's grant.[108] Its specific sphere of operation was situations in which a landowner disposed of part of his land but retained the remainder.[109] In these cases any quasi-easements that existed over one tract of land for the benefit of the other tract of land would be elevated to the status of an easement. Quasi-easements could be taken to mean exercises of user that would be easements were it not for the fact that the land benefited and the land over which the user was exercised were owned by the same person.[110] The Rule itself is derived from two important statements of Thesinger LJ in *Wheeldon*. First was the statement that: **[12–43]**

> ... on the grant by the owner of a tenement of part of that tenement as it is then used and enjoyed, there will pass to the grantee all those continuous and apparent easements (by which, of course, I mean *quasi* easements), or, in other words, all those easements which are necessary to the reasonable enjoyment of the property granted, and which have been and are at the time of the grant used by the owners of the entirety for the benefit of the part granted.[111]

While it was clear that the Rule required the division of a single tract of land, it was not clear whether the quasi-easement to be elevated to the status of easement had to be *either* "continuous or apparent" (meaning a passively enjoyed right that is reasonably discoverable on inspection of the property) *or* "necessary to the reasonable enjoyment of the property conveyed",[112] or whether *both* of these requirements had to be fulfilled.[113] While many cases concerned quasi-easements that did, in fact, fulfil both of these requirements, case law from the UK suggested the difficulties that arise where this was not the case.[114] The leading Irish case on the Rule—*William Bennett* **[12–44]**

[107] (1879) 12 Ch D 31.

[108] *Head v Meara* [1912] 1 IR 262.

[109] *MRA Engineering v Trimster* (1988) 56 P & CR 1.

[110] The requirements of a valid easement, as laid down in *Re Ellenborough Park* [1956] Ch 131, clearly forbid a person from having an easement over his own land (or land over which he is entitled to the beneficial occupation). See also Sparkes, "Establishing Easements against Leaseholders" (1992) Conv 167.

[111] (1879) 12 Ch D 31, 49.

[112] See *McDonagh v Mulholland* [1931] IR 110.

[113] See Ferris, "Problems Postponed: The Rule in *Wheeldon v Burrows* and *Wheeler v Saunders*" [1996] 3 Web JCLI; Mee, "The Land and Conveyancing Law Reform Bill 2006: Observations on the Law Reform Process and a Critique of Selected Provisions—Part 1" (2006) 11(3) CPLJ 67.

[114] See *Wheeler and Another v J J Saunders Ltd. and Ors* [1995] 2 All ER 697; *Ward v Kirkland* [1967] 1 Ch 194; *Browne v Flower* [1911] 1 Ch 219; *Harmer v Jumbil (Nigeria) Tin Areas Ltd* [1921] 1 Ch 200; *Pwllbach Colliery Co. Ltd v Woodman* [1915] AC 634; *Hansford v Jago* [1921] 1 Ch 322; *Borman v Griffith* [1930] 1 Ch 493; *Squarey v Harris-Smith* P&CR (1981) 42 118. See also Ferris, "Problems Postponed: The Rule in *Wheeldon v Burrows* and *Wheeler v Saunders*" [1996] 3 Web JCLI.

Construction Limited v John Greene and Kathleen Greene[115]—did not engage in the resolution of this question to any substantial degree. Instead, the Court adopted the statement of Bland that "the [quasi-easement] must be capable of existing as an easement and it must have been used at the time of the grant by the grantor for the benefit of the property granted over the property retained."[116] This approach appeared to endorse a reading of the tests in *Wheeldon v Burrows* as synonymous (i.e. essentially requiring the same thing), but the absence of a detailed consideration of this question left some uncertainty in Irish law. The somewhat troubling nature of that uncertainty was exacerbated by the fact that the Supreme Court appeared in that case to regard the Rule in *Wheeldon v Burrows* as the primary (if not the sole) mechanism by which the broader principle of non-derogation from a grant was to be applied in Ireland.[117]

[12–45] The Law Reform Commission recognised the difficulties with the Rule and, as a result, recommended that it be abolished in favour of the more general principle that one cannot derogate from one's grant.[118] Section 40 of the Land and Conveyancing Law Reform Act 2009 now expressly abolishes the Rule in *Wheeldon v Burrows*[119] and replaces it with a test laid down in s 40(2) as follows:

> Where the owner of land disposes of part of it or all of it in parts, the disposition creates by way of implication for the benefit of such part or parts any easement over the part retained, or other part or parts simultaneously disposed of, which—
> (a) is necessary to the reasonable enjoyment of the part disposed of, and
> (b) was reasonable for the parties, or would have been if they had adverted to the matter, to assume at the date the disposition took effect as being included in it.

The new system under s 40 applies as of 1 December 2009, meaning that in situations where a tract of land is being divided and either some is sold or retained ("disposes of part of it") or it is all being sold in smaller tracts ("or all of it in parts"), s 40(2) is to govern situations where previously *Wheeldon v Burrows* might have been used. In order to establish an easement under s 40(2) an applicant will, of course, have to establish that the right claimed qualifies as an easement and then that both s 40(2)(a) and s 40(2)(b) are satisfied. Section 40(2)(a) retains a feature of *Wheeldon v Burrows* inasmuch as it requires only that the easement claimed would be necessary for the *reasonable* enjoyment of the land; not for the enjoyment of the land *per se* (a situation that is dealt with by easements of necessity, considered below[120]). Section 40(2)(b) then introduces an objective requirement whereby a court must determine

115 [2004] 2 ILRM 96; [2004] IESC 15.

116 Bland, *The Law of Easements and Profits à Prendre* (1997, Dublin, Sweet & Maxwell), at para 12–06.

117 See Mee, "The Land and Conveyancing Law Reform Bill 2006: Observations on the Law Reform Process and a Critique of Selected Provisions—Part 1" (2006) 11(3) CPLJ 67.

118 LRC, *Consultation Paper on the Reform and Modernisation of Land Law and Conveyancing Law* (2004), p 102.

119 s 40(1), Land and Conveyancing Law Reform Act 2009.

120 para 12–50.

whether it was reasonable for the parties to have assumed that the easement was in fact included by implication in the disposition at the time that it took effect. Two points arise for note from this objective test. The first is that the parties need not establish that they actually gave express consideration to whether the easement was included by implication or not; they need merely establish that *had they adverted to the matter* it would have been reasonable for them to assume that the easement was included by implication. The second is the use of the words "by implication" in the introductory phrase of s 40(2) when read in conjunction with s 40(2)(b), a reading that makes it clear that words indicating that the easement claimed *was not included* in the grant will prevent the acquisition of the easement by implication under the s 40(2) test.

(d) Easement by Application of s 6, Conveyancing Act 1881 and s 71, Land and Conveyancing Law Reform Act 2009

In order to avoid having to detail every single easement that might be appurtenant to a piece of land in a conveyance, we have long recognised the desirability of some kind of shortcut in the conveyancing process by which all existing easements could be transferred with the land, whether listed in the conveyance or not. This was achieved by s 6 of the Conveyancing Act 1881, which has now been repealed and replaced by s 71, Land and Conveyancing Law Reform Act 2009. Section 6 will, however, continue to apply to conveyances done between 1881 and 1 December 2009[121] and therefore deserves consideration before we focus on the operation of s 71 itself. **[12–46]**

(a) Section 6, Conveyancing Act 1881

Section 6(1) provided: **[12–47]**

> A conveyance of land shall be deemed to include and shall by virtue of this Act operate to convey, with the land, all... easements, rights, and advantages whatsoever, appertaining or reputed to appertain to the land, or any part thereof, or at the time of the conveyance demised, occupied, or enjoyed with, or reputed or known as part or parcel of or appurtenant to the land or any part thereof.

The wording of s 6(1) makes its operation relatively clear: where there was a pre-existing easement over the land at the time that it was conveyed (in leasehold or freehold), the easement would be conveyed with the land *by the power of* the statute and *without the need for* any express words to that effect. A conveyance, in this context, was an "assignation, appointment, lease, settlement, and other assurance, and covenant to surrender, made by deed, on a sale, mortgage, demise, or settlement of any property, or any other dealing with or for any property...",[122] although the effect of s 6 could be excluded by a contrary intention.[123] Section 6 could, then, be clearly distinguished from the Rule in *Wheeldon v Burrows* in two ways. First, a diversity of ownership was

[121] s 6(6), Land and Conveyancing Law Reform Act 2009.

[122] Conveyancing Act 1881, s 2(v).

[123] *Steele v Morrow* (1923) 57 ILTR 89.

required for s 6(1) to apply;[124] second, the primary function of s 6(1) was to convey pre-existing easements (as opposed to "*quasi*-easements", conveyed by *Wheeldon*) with the land.

[12–48] As well as ensuring this kind of ease of conveyancing in s 6(1), s 6(2) of the Conveyancing Act 1881 operated to elevate rights that had the capacity to be easements but were not actually easements to the status of an easement upon subsequent conveyance of the property. Section 6(2) provided:

> A conveyance of land, having houses or other buildings thereon, shall be deemed to include and shall by virtue of this Act operate to convey, with the land, houses, or other buildings, all... liberties, privileges, easements, rights and advantages whatsoever, appertaining or reputed to appertain to the land, houses, or other buildings conveyed, or any part of them, or any part thereof, or at the time of conveyance, demised, occupied, or enjoyed with, or reputed or known as part or parcel of or appurtenant to, the land, houses, or other buildings conveyed, or any part of them or any part thereof.

Section 6(2) could, then, essentially elevate a licence or privilege to the status of an easement, and in fact would commonly do so, especially in landlord-and-tenant contexts upon the renewal of a lease or upon the tenant buying the freehold from the landlord. If a vendor did not want s 6(2) to operate in this way, he had to include an express[125] contrary intention[126] in the grant.

(b) Section 71, Land and Conveyancing Law Reform Act 2009

[12–49] For conveyances after 1 December 2009, s 71 of the Land and Conveyancing Law Reform Act 2009 now applies. Section 71(1)(b) provides that "A conveyance of land includes, and conveys with the land, all... advantages, easements, liberties, privileges, *profits à prendre* and rights appertaining or annexed to the land". This makes it quite clear that *where there is a diversity of ownership* the conveyance of land automatically transfers also the easements that *already exist* in relation to that land without the need for them to be listed on the conveyance itself. Thus, s 71(1)(b) performs the function of a "shortcut" in conveyancing practice, while also retaining the distinction between it

---

[124] It was not always clear that this was the case and, in fact, the controversy relating to this issue raged through the decisions of *Broomfield v William* [1897] 1 Ch 662 and *Long v Gowlett* [1923] 2 Ch 177, until being resolved by the Court of Appeals in *Sovmots Investments Ltd v Secretary of State for the Environment* [1977] 2 WLR 95. This case law is usefully surveyed by Power, *Intangible Property Rights in Ireland* (1st ed, 2003, West Sussex, Tottel), pp 40-44, and has been the subject of extensive academic commentary, also referenced by Power, notably: Jackson, "Easements and General Words" (1966) 30 Conv 340; Harpum, "Easements and Centre Point: Old Problems Resolved in a Novel Setting" (1977) Conv 415; Smith, "Centre Point: Faulty Towers with Shaky Foundations" (1978) Conv 449; Harpum, "*Long v Gowlett*: A Strong Fortress" (1979) Conv 113. In Ireland the need for a diversity of ownership was clearly established in the High Court decision of *Redfont Ltd v Custom House Dock Management Ltd* (unreported, High Court, 31 March 1998) and the Supreme Court decision of *William Bennett Construction v Greene* [2004] 2 ILRM 96; [2004] IESC 15.

[125] See, for example, *Broomfield v Williams* [1897] 1 Ch 602.

[126] s 6(4), Conveyancing Act 1881.

and s 40 (dealing with the subdivision of property, or situations where there is no diversity of ownership). Unlike s 6 of the Conveyancing Act 1881, however, s 71 expressly provides that it will not function in a manner that elevates any licence or privilege to the status of easement. In this respect s 71(3)(a) provides:

> This section—
> (a) does not on a conveyance of land (whether or not it has houses or other buildings on it)—
> (i) create any new interest or right or convert any quasi-interest or right existing prior to the conveyance into a full interest or right, or
> (ii) extend the scope of, or convert into a new interest or right, any licence, privilege or other interest or right existing before the conveyance

Section 71's operation is subject to the express terms of the contract.[127]

(e) Easement by Necessity

Where property is transferred that would be incapable of use (or at least of fruitful use) without an easement, the law may imply an easement in favour of the grantee's land on the basis that the easement is necessary. In limited situations the law has also implied an easement in favour of the land of the grantor,[128] although in practice this is an infrequent occurrence.[129] Easements of necessity are usually rights of way that are necessary to prevent property from becoming landlocked, although the doctrine of easements of necessity does not appear to be limited to rights of way.[130] Easements of necessity do not arise because the easement would make the use of the alleged dominant tenement easier or more in accord with the dominant owner's desired use of the property; the easement must in fact be necessary to the effectual use of the property.[131] Necessity is measured at the time of the conveyance in which the easement was granted or reserved, and not at the time of the claim.[132] In spite of some early confusion on the matter,[133] it is now clear that easements of necessity are granted on the basis of the presumed intentions of the parties.[134] **[12–50]**

4. Easement by Estoppel

Estoppel is a doctrine that prevents someone from reneging on a representation or induced belief that they will not strictly enforce their legal rights, when this representation or induced belief has led another person to act and a detriment would arise from such actions should the representor renege on the original representation. **[12–51]**

---

[127] s 71(3)(c), Land an Conveyancing Law Reform Act 2009.
[128] *Maude v Thornton* [1929] IR 454.
[129] For an example of an implied reservation by necessity, see *Dwyer Nolan Developments Ltd v Kingscroft Developments Ltd* [1999] 1 ILRM 141.
[130] See, for example, *Wong v Beaumont Properties Ltd* [1965] 1 QB 173.
[131] See, for example, *Donnelly v Adams* [1905] 1 IR 154 *per* Barton J at 161.
[132] *Maguire v Brown* [1921] 1 IR 148; [1922] 1 IR 23.
[133] See, for example, *Nickerson v Baraclough* [1981] 2 WLR 773 (judgment of Megarry VC) and the Court of Appeal reassertion of the intention basis for the implication of easements by necessity in the same case at [1981] 2 All ER 269.
[134] *Magiore v Browne* [1921] 1 IR 148; *Dwyer Nolan Developments Ltd v Kingscroft Developments Ltd* [1999] 1 ILRM 141.

An easement might be recognised in equity as a remedy to a proven case of estoppel where that easement would be the appropriate mechanism for the satisfaction of the equity that has arisen in favour of the actor.[135] This is, in essence, how an easement can be acquired by estoppel. In order for the easement to be granted the normal requirements of estoppel (i.e. representation, act in reliance and detriment) must be shown to the satisfaction of the court[136] and, as always, equitable remedies are discretionary. Therefore whether the easement is awarded will be a matter for the discretion of the court.

[12–52] Precisely such a situation arose in the well-known case of *Crabb v Arun District Council.*[137] Crabb agreed to sell some land to the defendants, but required access through that land to some property he was retaining. He sought a right of way from the defendants prior to the sale and, at a meeting between the plaintiff, his architect and a representative of Arun District Council in 1967, the defendants agreed to allow him access. No right of way was formally retained by Crabb in the conveyance and, following the sale, the defendants blocked off the access to his land. Crabb applied for an injunction to prevent this, claiming that the defendants were estopped from denying him a right of way. The Court held in Crabb's favour, finding that the defendants had led him to believe that he would be granted a right of way to his land and had encouraged him to act to his detriment by selling the property without reserving a right of way in his own favour. The equity that had arisen, the Court held, ought to be satisfied by granting Crabb a right of way for the purposes of access to his property. The Irish courts have also held that estoppel can be used as a basis for the acquisition of an easement. In *Annally Hotel v Bergin*[138] the Court held that an agreement, however informal, that land could enjoy light and that resulted in an action by the landowner to his detriment could result in an easement of light. In this case the claimant had, in fact, erected and modified a building on the strength of the representation and was, therefore, recognised as having acquired a right to light through estoppel. In *Smyths (Harcourt Street) v Hardwicke Ltd*[139] the High Court held that where a negotiation for the purchase of the fee simple had proceeded on the basis or understanding that an easement was included in the conveyance and the purchaser acquired the property on that basis, the vendor would be estopped from denying the purchaser that easement.[140]

5. Easement by Presumed Grant, i.e. Prescription

[12–53] It is a long-standing principle of the common law that continuous user, capable of being described as an easement under the definition in *Re Ellenborough Park*, for a

[135] The remedy to estoppel will be that which best remedies the equity that has arisen. See also Delany, "Satisfying the Equity in Cases of Proprietary Estoppel" (2003) 10 DULJ 217.

[136] See, for example, *Frank Towey Ltd & Ors v South Dublin County Council* [2005] IEHC 93; *Dunne v Molloy* [1976–7] ILRM 266.

[137] [1976] Ch 179. The case has been subject to much debate within contract law—see, for example, Atiyah, "When is an Enforceable Agreement not a Contract? Answer: When it is an Equity" (1976) 92 LQR 1974 and the response of Millett—"*Crabb v Arun District Council*—A Riposte!" (1976) 92 LQR 342.

[138] (1970) 104 ILTR 65.

[139] Unreported, High Court, 30 July 1971.

[140] See *Callan v McAvinue*, unreported, High Court, 11 May 1973.

specified period of time can result in the acquisition of an easement. This method of acquiring an easement by long user is known as prescription and arises where the law presumes that an easement was granted as a result of the continuous long user by the prescriptive user.[141] Prescription, therefore, operates on the basis that if someone has engaged in user over the land of another that is capable of being defined as an easement without force, secrecy or permission for a specified period of time, the law can presume he was granted that right as an easement at some stage and, as a result, can recognise the right as an easement enjoyed by the dominant tenement.

Under the pre-2009 law, prescription was rightly described as an "intolerably complex"[142] area of property law in desperate need of either reform or abolition. [12–54] Holdsworth had noted that "There is no branch of English law which is in a more unsatisfactory state"[143] and that was certainly also the case in relation to prescription in Irish law. Not only was the law of prescription complex and muddled in its detail but the maintenance in law of prescription required some moral justification as one could justifiably ask *why* long user ought to result in the acquisition of a proprietary right in the land of another. Was prescription not merely the *ex post facto* legitimisation of trespass by means of treating an especially persevering trespasser as if he had a right to be on the land of another all along? In addition, prescription gave rise to difficulties for purchasers of registered land as they could find themselves bound by an easement that had been acquired by prescription, even though they had no way of knowing that this easement existed over the land (easements acquired by prescription after the date of first registration are s 72 interests under the Registration of Title Act 1964[144]).

The Law Reform Commission devoted an entire *Report* to the acquisition of easements [12–55] and profits by prescription in 2002, in which many of these matters were considered.[145] In choosing to recommend the reform of prescription rather than its abolition, the Commission reflected on the moral justifications for it. In large part these justifications were similar to those commonly advanced for adverse possession (which is not entirely surprising given the historical connections between the two bodies of law) and the Commission recommended the reform of prescription to bring it closer to the law of adverse possession in its operation. The Commission noted that an objective of prescription is to adjust rights in favour of those who have made use of the land for a long time.[146] Although there is certainly an important and worthy *general* argument to be made in favour of rewarding people who actually use land rather than those who do not make use of their land, one might argue that this does not necessarily arise to the same degree in a case of prescription as it does in a case of adverse possession. Although landowners against whom someone successfully claims adverse possession will frequently (if not almost always) have severely neglected the use of their land, this is not at all required or even likely in the case of the acquisition of an easement.

[141] The similarities to adverse possession are not at all coincidental; rather, the two concepts originally developed closely. For more on adverse possession, see further Chapter 14.
[142] Bland, "Clothing Fact with Right: Proposed Changes to Prescription and Adverse Possession" (2003) 8(4) CPLJ 86.
[143] Holdsworth, *History of the English Law* (1903–1972, London), vol 17, p 352.
[144] s 72(1)(h), Registration of Title Act 1964. See Chapter 7 on registered land.
[145] LRC, *Report on the Acquisition of Easements and Profits à Prendre by Prescription* (2002).
[146] *ibid.*, p 19.

Whether the moral argument in favour of the person who makes use of land can be fruitfully applied to the context of prescription is, therefore, questionable. In addition to this, the Commission took the position that "some easements are so crucial to the dominant tenement... that they may be said to be as essential to the utility and value of the plot as a solid title"[147] and, as a result, that prescription has an additional moral basis. The obvious difficulty with this perspective is that easements that are of such a vital and necessary nature can, in fact, already be implied by the law or acquired by the owner of the "dominant" tenement through an ordinary transaction on the open market. Thus, this element of the Commission's reasoning does not appear to offer any defensible justification for the maintenance of prescription within Irish law.[148] Ultimately, however, the Commission's conclusion that "there is no less moral justification for the acquisition of easements by prescription than there is for obtaining a title to land by adverse possession" most likely sums up the approach to prescription most succinctly: if we facilitate one, then we will facilitate the other.

[12–56] Having decided to retain a system of prescription in Irish law, a new system of prescription was introduced in ss 34-37 of the Land and Conveyancing Law Reform Act 2009, which is considered in full below.[149] This does not rid the pre-2009 Act system of prescription of its relevance, however, as it will continue to apply during the transitional period as outlined in s 38:

> In relation to any claim to an easement or *profit à prendre* made after the commencement of this Chapter, sections 34 to 37 —
>
> (a) apply to any claim based on a relevant user period notwithstanding that it is alleged that an additional user period occurred before that commencement,
>
> (b) do not apply to any claim based on a user period under the law applicable prior to the commencement of this Chapter and alleged to have commenced prior to such commencement where the action in which the claim is made is brought within 3 years of such commencement.

This section makes it clear that where the required user period under the old law of prescription (which varied from 20 to 60 years, depending on circumstances) had expired or was extremely close to expiring at the commencement of the Act, claims under the old law of prescription can be brought within the first three years of the Act's operation, i.e. up to 1 December 2012. The Civil Law (Miscellaneous Provisions) Bill 2011 proposes to extend the time limit in s 38(b) to 12 years.[150] The practical implication of this, for our purposes, is that—at least in the short term—familiarity with the both the pre- and post-2009 Act law of prescription is required. As a result, both bodies of law are considered below. First, however, there is a need to consider the general requirements of prescription whether one is applying the pre- or post-2009 law.

---

[147] *ibid.*, p 21.

[148] See Bland, "Clothing Fact with Right: Proposed Changes to Prescription and Adverse Possession" (2003) 8(4) CPLJ 86: "if there was no prescription, one wonders as to why there would be uncertainty as to whether the right exists in the vast majority of cases".

[149] paras 12–71 to 12–80.

[150] s 36, Civil Law (Miscellaneous Provisions) Bill 2011 as passed by the Seanad.

(i) General Requirements of Prescription

Any claim for prescription will require the claimant to establish not only that the particular requirements of the *type* of prescription being claimed are satisfied, but also two general requirements: (1) that the user is capable of existing as an easement, and (2) that there has been open and continuous user "as of right". In order to prove that the user is capable of existing as an easement, one must show that it satisfies the *Re Ellenborough Park* tests, i.e. there is a dominant and servient tenement in the ownership or beneficial occupation of different people, the dominant tenement is accommodated by the user, the user is capable of existing in grant and is not excessively wide or vague. **[12–57]**

The Roman law of praedial servitudes allowed the acquisition of easements by prescription provided the user was done for a required period of time *quod nec vi nec clam nec precario*. This ancient formula allowed for the acquisition of easements by prescription "provided the user did not take place by force, nor by stealth nor as a licensee of the owner" and it encapsulates the common law concept of open and continuous user as of right, which is essential to prescription today.[151] We continue to insist that the claimant's user would comply with this requirement[152] by requiring user "as of right" which is taken to mean user *nec vi, nec clam, nec precario* (i.e. without force, without secrecy, without permission). User should be *nec vi* (without force) because the idea of presuming that a grant of an easement was made is that we can imply or presume this from, *inter alia*, the fact that the "servient owner" has not intervened to prevent the user. The acquiescence of the "servient owner" is therefore required for a successful claim of prescription and anyone who forces their user cannot be said to be enjoying the acquiescence of the "servient owner". By necessary implication the user must also be *nec clam* (without secrecy) for one cannot acquiesce to something of which one is unaware or in relation to which one could not be aware. The *nec clam* requirement marks prescription out from adverse possession in the ordinary course of things, as in the case of adverse possession there is no "openness" requirement[153] (with the exception of a requirement not to fraudulently conceal one's adverse possession).[154] These two previous requirements then feed logically into the third—*nec precario* (without mere permission or grace of the servient owner[155])—inasmuch as the open and notorious continuous use of the servient property is said to be done "as of right", i.e. as if someone were entitled to do it pursuant to a grant of an easement. If a landowner gives mere permission for a particular user, then the user, even if *nec vi* and *nec clam*, can be said to be a result of that permission and a grant cannot be presumed. It should be noted, however, that the user does not necessarily need to be *nec precario* from its inception. While the ordinary and general rule requires a lack of permission *ab initio*, it is now relatively well established that continued user **[12–58]**

---

[151] See Radin, "Fundamental Concepts of the Roman Law" (1925) 13(3) Cal L R 207 at 217.

[152] *Agnew v Barry*, unreported, High Court, 29 November 2005; s 33, Land and Conveyancing Law Reform Act 2009.

[153] See further Chapter 14.

[154] s 71, Statute of Limitations 1957.

[155] See *Burrows v Lang* [1901] 2 Ch 502; *Sturges v Bridgman* (1879) 11 Ch D 852; *R (Beresford) v Sunderland City Council* [2004] 1 AC 889.

following the express or implied revocation of permission can be deemed to be user *nec precario*.[156] The fact that a prescriptive user may be operating under a misapprehension as to his right to use the "servient" tenement is of no relevance in an assessment of a prescription claim.[157]

[12–59] The user must also be continuous, although the meaning of "continuous" here will be dependent on the circumstances. The acquisition of a right of way by prescription, for example, does not require the claimant to walk over and back across the land of another without pause for the required number of years; rather, it requires the consistent use of the land to pass between two determined points over a prescribed period of time. The "continuous user" requirement was considered in *Orwell Park Management Ltd. v Henihan & Anor*[158] in which Herbert J held:

> To establish an easement of way by prescription, the party claiming that right... must provide evidence of continuous use of the way for the prescription period. Continuous use is not, however, to be equated with incessant use: what the law requires is that the use be such as would clearly indicate to a servient owner that a continuous right to do what would otherwise amount to a trespass was being asserted. A right of way is a non-continuous easement: a right to pass and repass over the property of another whenever the person claiming that right has occasion so to do. In my judgment, where the evidence establishes that there has been an open, uninterrupted and continuous use of land as a right of way... the court should presume that the owner of the land was aware of this use and acquiesced in it. The important question is whether the use... would suggest to a reasonably careful and prudent owner of the lane that a casual use only of the lane was being made dependant for its continuance upon the tolerance and good nature of such servient owner, or would put such servient owner on notice that an actual right to do these things was being asserted.

Once a claimant has established user that is capable of being defined as an easement in a continuous manner *nec vi, nec clam, nec precario*, she will be in a position to claim prescription. This claim will be made under the pre-2009 Act law where it falls into the narrow transitional period identified in s 38 or otherwise under the post-2009 Act law.

(ii) Prescription before the LCLRA 2009

[12–60] Most of the discomfort with and criticism of the law of prescription prior to the Land and Conveyancing Law Reform Act 2009 resulted from the extremely convoluted nature of the law's operation. In particular, the fact that there were (and, for the transitional period, continue to be) three different kinds of prescription all operating in parallel to one another was the cause of considerable confusion. All three require our attention here.

---

[156] *Healey v Hawkins* [1968] 3 All ER 836; *Gaved v Martyn* (1865) 19 CB 732; Jackson, "Easements and Prescription" (1969) 32(4) MLR 444; *Sallan Jewelry Co. v Bird* (Mich 1927) 215 NW 349.

[157] *Earl de la Warr v Myles* [1881] 17 Ch D 535; *Agnew v Barry*, unreported, High Court, 29 November 2005.

[158] [2004] IEHC 87.

(a) Common Law Prescription

At common law the courts would recognise an easement by prescription where one satisfied the general requirements considered above and could show user from time immemorial or from the time from which legal memory ran[159]—which was deemed to be 1189.[160] Over the years it became understandably difficult to show that user could be traced back to 1189, therefore the courts began to presume that user could be traced back to 1189 on the basis of the memory of a living witness[161] and, later, on the basis of 20 years of continuous user.[162] Thus, if one could satisfy the general requirements and prove 20 years' user, then the courts would assume that user since 1189 and recognise an easement on that basis. This was nothing more than a mere presumption, however, and could be rebutted by evidence that user since 1189 was impossible because, for example, the building that is alleged to be the dominant tenement did not exist in 1189. **[12–61]**

(b) Lost Modern Grant Prescription

As a result of the difficulties of proof associated with common law prescription, the courts developed the fiction of the lost modern grant as the second mechanism of acquiring an easement through prescription.[163] Legal fictions can be defined as false statements not intended to deceive[164] and arise where the common law "treated as true a factual assertion that plainly was false, generally as a means to avoid changing a legal rule that required a particular factual predicate for its application".[165] In the context of prescription by lost modern grant, the courts will consider that 20 years' user in compliance with the general conditions of prescription, considered above,[166] could be taken to mean that the prescriptive user had been granted an easement, but that the grant itself had been lost and could not therefore be produced before the court. Twenty years' user therefore gives rise not to a presumption but rather to a *fiction* that an easement was granted.[167] As a result, proof that no such grant has actually been made will be of no consequence,[168] although an easement will not be found where it can be **[12–62]**

---

[159] *Knox v Earl of Mayo* (1858) 7 IR Ch R 563; Co Litt 114b, 170.

[160] *Coke on Littleton* (19th ed, 1832), p 170, reporting how the courts adopted this year from the Statute of Westminster I, 1275. See also Nash, "1189 and the Limit of Legal Memory" (1989) New LJ 1763.

[161] *Angus v Dalton* (1877) 3 QBD 85.

[162] See *Daly v Cullen* (1958) 92 ILTR 127; *DPP (Long) v McDonald* [1983] ILRM 223; *Carroll v Sheridan & Sheehan* [1984] ILRM 451.

[163] *Price v Lewis* (1761) 2 Wms Saunders 175.

[164] See esp. Fuller, *Legal Fictions* (1967, Stanford, Stanford University Press), p 9.

[165] Smith, "New Legal Fictions" (2007) 95 Geo L J 1435.

[166] See paras 12–58 to 12–59.

[167] In some cases the status of a lost grant as a legal fiction within the technical meaning of the term appears to be lost on commentators. For an example of how an under-theorisation of the grant as a legal fiction can result in acute practical difficulties relating to the protection of prescribed easements against purchasers, see, for example, Dowling, "The Doctrine of the Lost Modern Grant" (2003) xxxviii IR Jur 225.

[168] *Hanna v Pollock* [1900] 2 IR 664; *Tehidy Minerals Ltd v Norman* [1971] 2 QB 528.

shown that there was nobody with the legal capacity to make such a grant[169] *or* that any such grant would have contravened statutory provisions.[170]

[12–63] Lest we should be tempted to think that lost modern grant prescription was simply a historical curiosity, the case *Orwell Park Management Ltd. v Henihan & Anor*[171] demonstrates the recent operation of lost modern grant prescription in Ireland. The case concerned an alleged right of way for vehicles along a laneway over the defendants' property. While the defendants accepted that there was a pedestrian right of way there, they denied that it was also vehicular. The plaintiff, however, adduced evidence of deliveries by horse and cart and, later, by lorry between 1937 and 1972. The defendants blocked off the laneway to vehicles by planting shrubs and having that part of their property landscaped, however, the plaintiffs claimed a vehicular right of way by prescription. The right of way had not been in "continuous" use between 1978 and 1996. Because there was no user "next before some suit or action", the Prescription Act 1832 could not be used to assert an easement, but the Court found that the right of way had been used for vehicular access for a period of at least 20 years between 1937 and 1972, resulting in the fiction of a lost modern grant arising. Therefore the plaintiffs were found to have a vehicular right of way.

(c) Statutory Prescription

[12–64] The Prescription Act 1832 was transposed into Irish law by means of the Prescription (Ireland) Act 1858 and provided an alternative (*not* a replacement[172]) to both common law and lost grant prescription. Under the Prescription Act easements can be acquired by either a shorter or longer period of user, although easements of light are treated distinctly within the Act and are subject to different prescriptive requirements. Although the Prescription Act has been described as "a spectacular failure"[173] that is "a mystery to many a practising lawyer",[174] it remained operative in Irish law until the Land and Conveyancing Law Reform Act 2009 and, of course, continues to apply in the context of the transitional period.

[12–65] The *shorter period* required: (a) continuous and uninterrupted *nec vi, nec clam, nec precario* user of (b) something capable of being described as an easement for (c) 20 years (d) without consent of the alleged servient owner (e) next before some suit or action.[175] If someone can satisfy this requirement, then it will be presumed that an easement was

169 *Bakewell Management Ltd v Brandwood* [2004] 2 AC 519; *McEvoy v Great Northern Railway Co.* [1900] 2 IR 325.

170 *McEvoy v Great Northern Railway Co.* [1900] 2 IR 325; *Neaverson v Peterborough* [1902] 1 Ch 557.

171 [2004] IEHC 87.

172 *Healy v Hawkins* [1968] 3 All ER 836. See Mee, "Reform of the Law on the Acquisition of Easements and *Profits à Prendre*" (2005) DULJ 86: "The Prescription Act 1832 left the situation even more confused than before, since it did not succeed in replacing the two existing forms of prescription." It should be noted that it seems the legislation was intended to replace common law and lost grant prescription, but did not achieve this aim: see also Simpson, *A History of Land Law* (2nd ed, 1986, Oxford, Clarendon Press), p 267.

173 Bland, *The Law of Easements and Profits à Prendre* (1997, Dublin, Sweet & Maxwell), p 233.

174 Ontario Law Commission, *Report on the Limitation of Actions* (1969), p 149.

175 ss 1 and 2, Prescription Act 1832.

granted. The "counting" of time is subject to the rules laid down as to deductions from the period of user, and of course evidence of permission, satisfaction of the *Re Ellenborough Park* test, or successful interruptions will undo the prescription claim. The shorter period is subject to automatic deductions under s 7. This section provides that times during which the alleged servient owner was a minor, suffered from mental incapacity or was a tenant for life *and* periods of time during which an action was pending and being pursued conscientiously will be deducted automatically from the amount of user. Oral or written consent will defeat a claim under the shorter period.

The *longer period* required: (a) continuous and uninterrupted *nec vi, nec clam, nec precario* user of (b) something capable of being described as an easement for (c) 40 years (d) without written consent (e) next before some suit or action. Satisfaction of these requirements will make title to an easement "absolute and indefeasible", except by evidence of written consent or permission. Deductions from the longer period arise under s 8 of the Act, which allows for the time during which the servient owner was a tenant under a lease to be deducted from the user *provided* the reversioner or remainderman takes an action for deduction within three years of the termination of the lesser freehold or leasehold estates. Written consent will defeat any claim to statutory prescription under the longer period. **[12–66]**

Both the shorter and longer periods of statutory prescription required that the user would be "next before some suit or action".[176] This merely provides that the user must continue right up to the time that a claim is made.[177] The "next before some suit or action" requirement plays a particularly important role in the protection of purchasers who have a better chance of discovering that there is an easement over the land they propose to purchase (or that an easement is in the process of being acquired by means of prescription) when there is a "next before some suit or action" requirement. There is no such requirement in the context of either common law or lost grant prescription. **[12–67]**

The Act also requires that this user would be *uninterrupted* and gives a particular meaning to the notion of "interruption". In this context, an interruption sufficient to stop the time running in favour of the claimant is defined as a factual interruption in which the claimant has acquiesced for one year or more from the date of discovering the interruption and who authorised its placement there.[178] The claimant can show that he is not acquiescing in the interruption by either physically removing the interruption *or* protesting clearly, including by a solicitor's letter[179] *or* taking an action against the "dominant owner".[180] The system of interruptions makes it quite difficult in practice for a landowner to interrupt a period of prescription and is one of the reasons why prescription is thought to be very much weighted in favour of prescriptive users. **[12–68]**

The Prescription Act included seemingly unsettled rules relating to prescription in leasehold property. First, it is likely that a tenant can acquire an easement by **[12–69]**

---

[176] s 4, Prescription Act 1832.

[177] *Reilly v Orange* [1955] 2 QB 112.

[178] s 4, Prescription Act 1832.

[179] See also *Orwell Park Management Ltd. v Henihan & Anor* [2004] IEHC 87.

[180] *Claxton v Claxton* (1873) IR 7 CL 23; *Coleman v Glover* (1874) 10 CP 108.

prescription over land of the landlord by statutory prescription under the longer period, but not under the shorter period.[181] In addition, it appears that tenants can prescribe against another tenant of the same landlord by means of the longer statutory period,[182] lost grant prescription[183] and possible common law prescription.[184] It also appears to be possible for a tenant to prescribe against the landlord under common law prescription, but this is particularly rare.[185] A tenant can prescribe against a stranger, in which case, of course, the easement acquired benefits the land and goes with it to the landlord on the termination of the lease. If another is prescribing against land held by a tenant, then the form of prescription will depend on the circumstances:

- If the prescription began against the freehold owner, then all forms of prescription will be possible;
- If the prescription began against the leasehold owner, only shorter period prescription and lost modern grant prescription are possible[186];
- In addition, if prescription begins against a leasehold owner, all of the time during which the "servient" land was held in lease can be deducted by application from the landlord.[187]

[12–70] Finally, for our purposes, the Prescription Act treated rights of light as distinctive easements subject to different rules of acquisition from most easements. Once light has actually been enjoyed for a period of 20 years in a dwelling house, greenhouse or workshop, then an easement of light will be acquired by prescription and will be said to be "absolute and defeasible". There are no deductions under either ss 7 or 8 of the Prescription Act in the context of easements of light, although written consent to the enjoyment of light will defeat a claim for statutory prescription. Irish authorities suggest that easements of light can still be acquired by lost grant prescription,[188] although that does not appear to be the case in England and Wales.[189]

(iii) Prescription under the LCLRA 2009

[12–71] The introduction, in the Land and Conveyancing Law Reform Act 2009, of a new statutory system of prescription serves as a cause of significant relief for practitioners (and law students) going forward, especially once the transitional period has been completed. The new scheme, which is contained in ss 35–37, significantly simplifies the law as it relates to prescription while maintaining the basic, or general, requirements that we considered above.[190] The first requirement, of course, is that the right claimed to have been acquired by prescription is capable of existing as an easement, after which

---

181 *Beggan v McDonald* (1878) 2 LR IR 560.
182 *Fahey v Dwyer* (1879) 4 LR IR 271.
183 *Tisdall v McArthur & Co (Steel and Metal) Ltd* [1951] IR 228.
184 *Beggan v McDonald* (1878) 2 LR IR 560.
185 See, for example, *Timmons v Hewitt* (1887) 22 LR IR 627.
186 *Beggan v McDonald* (1878) 2 LR IR 560.
187 s 8, Prescription Act 1832.
188 *Hanna v Pollock* [1900] 2 IR 664; *Tisdall v McArthur & Co. (Steel and Metal) Ltd* [1951] IR 228.
189 *Tapling v Jones* (1865) 11 HLC 290.
190 paras 12–57 to 12–59.

the precise statutory requirements can be considered. Section 35 is the primary provision here:

> (1) An easement or *profit à prendre* shall be acquired at law by prescription only on registration of a court order under this section.
> (2) Subject to *subsection (3)*, in an action to establish or dispute the acquisition by prescription of an easement or *profit à prendre*, the court shall make an order declaring the existence of the easement or *profit à prendre* if it is satisfied that there was a relevant user period immediately before the commencement of the action.
> (3) The court may make an order under *subsection (2)* where the relevant user period was not immediately before the commencement of the action if it is satisfied that it is just and equitable to do so in all the circumstances of the case.
> (4) An order under *subsection (2)* shall be registered in the Registry of Deeds or Land Registry, as appropriate.

In order to succeed in a claim for prescription the claimant must show that "there was a relevant user period immediately before the commencement of the action".[191] This implicates two separate requirements: "relevant user period" and "immediately before the commencement of the action". Relevant user period is defined by s 33 as follows: **[12–72]**

> [A] period of user as of right without interruption by the person claiming to be the dominant owner or owner of *profit à prendre* in gross—
> (a) where the servient owner is not a State authority, for a minimum period of 12 years, or
> (b) where the servient owner is a State authority, for—
> (1) a minimum period of 30 years, or
> (2) where the servient land is foreshore, a minimum period of 60 years

The "relevant user period" therefore contains three requirements: (a) user as of right, (b) user without interruption, and (c) user for the required period of time. We can consider each separately.

User as of right simply requires user "without force, without secrecy and without the oral or written consent of the servient owner".[192] It therefore contains the common law requirement of *nec vi, nec clam, nec precario* but makes it express that either oral or written consent will defeat a prescription claim. **[12–73]**

For the purposes of the 2009 Act an interruption is defined as "interference with, or cessation of, the use or enjoyment of an easement… for a continuous period of at least one year".[193] Interruptions should be direct actions, by either the owner of the servient land or a stranger, that *actually* prevent user. The interruption must continue for a year or more, which is a somewhat onerous task for servient owners. Should an interruption be established, this would stop the prescriptive period. So, imagine that Francis has been **[12–74]**

191 s 35(3), Land and Conveyancing Law Reform Act 2009.
192 s 33, *ibid.*
193 *ibid.*

exercising user over a neighbour's land in the fashion of a right of way for six years, and then suffers an interruption for 18 months, following which he recommences user. The six years that predate that interruption are lost for the purposes of prescription; the period of interruption is not merely deducted from the overall prescriptive period but rather *defeats* the user that predates it. Francis could, in this example, protest or even attempt to take proceedings to prevent the interruption, but unless he does so he will acquiesce in that interruption and nullify the user that predated it.

[12–75] If the user has been as of right, and has not been defeated by an interruption, one must then "count" the duration of user. Section 33 makes it clear that in order to succeed in prescription the user must last for 12 years against private owners, 30 years against a State authority, and 60 years in respect of foreshore. These periods of time are the same as the time periods required for a successful claim of adverse possession, which we will consider in full in Chapter 14. State authorities, in respect of which a longer period of user will be required, are defined as "a Minister of the Government or the Commissioners of Public Works in Ireland"[194] and *do not* include local authorities.

[12–76] Once the required user period has been established prima facie, the court will determine whether or not there are any deductions that ought to be made. Deductions are governed by s 37 and are intended to protect particularly vulnerable owners of land from prescriptive claims against them. Section 37 provides:

> (1) Subject to *subsection (2)*, where the servient owner is incapable, whether at the commencement of or during the relevant user period, of managing his or her affairs because of a mental incapacity, the running of that period is suspended until the incapacity ceases.
>
> (2) *Subsection (1)* does not apply where—
>
> (a) the court considers that it is reasonable, in the circumstances of the case, to have expected some other person, whether as trustee, committee of a ward of court, an attorney under an enduring power of attorney or otherwise, to have acted on behalf of the servient owner during the relevant user period, or
>
> (b) at least 30 years have elapsed since the commencement of the relevant user period.

Section 37 is clearly concerned with ensuring that it balances out the vulnerabilities of land owners who are "incapable... of managing [their] affairs because of a mental incapacity" with the integrity of a system of prescription. It does this by, first of all, allowing for a suspension (meaning that the period of mental incapacity will be deducted—or subtracted—from the overall user period claimed by the prescriptive user) *but* protecting prescriptive users by saying that no such deduction will take place where it is reasonable to have expected that someone else, like a trustee, would have acted on behalf of the servient owner during the period of his or her mental incapacity. Furthermore, someone who has been engaged in prescriptive user for thirty years can make a claim for prescription, notwithstanding any period of mental incapacity by the servient owner.

---

[194] *ibid.*

The question of relevant user period is not, then, quite as straightforward as it looks. However, when considering a claim of prescription, we can boil the requirement down to the following questions: [12–77]

(a) How long has the claimant been engaged in this user as of right?
(b) Has there been an interruption? If yes, how long has the claimant been engaged in user *after* the interruption ceased?
(c) Disregarding any time that might precede an interruption, are there any periods of time that must be deducted under s 37?
(d) Taking into account any and all deductions, how long has the claimant been engaged in user as of right?
(e) Does this period of user satisfy the requirements taking into account the nature of the servient owner (12 years, 30 years, or 60 years as appropriate)?

If the required period of time has been fulfilled, the next element to be considered in the context of "relevant user period" is whether or not that user is "immediately before the commencement of the action"[195]; in other words, did it continue right up until the time that the claim for prescription was made? This clearly mirrors the old requirement of user "next before some suit or action", but importantly s 35(3) allows courts some flexibility here. A court that considers that the user did not continue up until the point of the claim can still allow the prescription "if it is satisfied that it is just and equitable to do so in all the circumstances of the case".[196] [12–78]

If the court is satisfied that all the requirements of prescription have been satisfied it will grant an order to that effect, which must be registered under s 35(1). The easement is then formally acquired. Section 35 as originally enacted requires a court order in every case, even if there is no dispute. This raises some clear concerns about efficiency, but also seems unnecessary in relation to registered land, in particular where burdens are frequently registered by consent, i.e. where there is no dispute. At time of writing, the Civil Law (Miscellaneous Provisions) Bill 2011 was under debate, and it includes an amendment to s 35 designed to deal with precisely this matter. The proposed amendment, contained in s 35 of the bill as passed by the Seanad, provides that an easement can be acquired by prescription either by registration of a court order *or* through engagement with the proposed new s 49A of the Registration of Title Act 1964. This proposed new provision in the 1964 Act, which is contained in s 39 of the bill as passed by the Seanad, provides that the Property Registration Authority can enter an easement acquired by prescription onto the register where it is satisfied that the requirements of ss 33–38 of the Land and Conveyancing Law Reform Act 2009 have been met.[197] Where there is any doubt, of course, the Authority would not register the easement and a court proceeding would have to be undertaken. That proposed new "streamlined" process relates only to registered land or to land in relation to which a first registration is being sought.[198] [12–79]

[195] s 35(2), Land and Conveyancing Law Reform Act 2009.
[196] s 35(3), *ibid.*
[197] Proposed s 49A(1), Registration of Title Act 1964 as contained in s 39 Civil Law (Miscellaneous Provisions) Bill 2011 as passed by the Seanad.
[198] Proposed s 49A(2), *ibid.*

[12–80] The 2009 Act lays down some particular provisions relating to leasehold land in s 36. There are, clearly, two different matters to consider here: situations where the dominant tenement is held in leasehold by the prescriptive user, and situations where the servient tenement is held in leasehold. Section 36(1) provides that an easement acquired by prescription by a tenant attaches to the dominant tenement (i.e. the property held by the tenant under a lease) and continues after the termination of the lease. Section 36(2) provides that *as a general matter* where the servient owner is a tenant an easement acquired against that land will end when the servient owner's lease is terminated. This is subject to two exceptions. First, s 36(2)(a) provides that if the servient owner then acquires a "superior interest" in the land, the easement will attach to that superior interest. So, for example, if the servient owner buys the fee simple from the landlord, any easements acquired against the land by prescription while it was held under a lease will now apply against the land in fee simple. Second, s 36(2)(b) provides that if the servient owner extends or renews his tenancy, any easements acquired against the land by prescription while it was held under a lease will continue to apply for the extended or renewed period of the lease. If the easement does lapse, because of the termination of the lease, under s 36(2) the owner of the dominant tenement can then proceed to prescribe against the landlord and must, once more, satisfy the requirements of s 35 in respect of his prescriptive user against the landlord.

IV. Extent of Easements

[12–81] The extent of an easement or profit depends on the mode of its creation. An expressly granted or reserved easement will extend to the degree allowed for in the grant or reservation itself.[199] An easement of necessity will extend to the degree required to meet the necessity at the time of the grant,[200] although Irish law allows for an easement of necessity to extend beyond that to the level suitable to the business the dominant owner might require to be carried out on the premises, particularly when the proposed use of the property is known to (or can be implied from the surrounding circumstances by) the servient owner.[201] An easement of common intention will extend to the degree required to fulfil the common intention.[202] An easement of light will extend to the degree required for the ordinary use and enjoyment of the property.[203] An easement of prescription will extend to the same extent as the user during the period of prescription. One particular question that arises is whether an implied easement can be said to extend to the changed nature of circumstances of the dominant tenement and, if the easement does not extend that much, whether the unilateral change to the use of the easement will result in the easement being discharged.

[12–82] The first of these questions was considered recently in *McAdams Homes Limited v Robinson & Another.*[204] In this case a bakery had been erected on a site adjoining

---

199 *St Edmundsbury and Ipswitch Diocesan Board of Finance v Clark (No. 2)* [1975] WLR 468.

200 *Browne v Maguire* [1922] 1 IR 23.

201 *Dwyer Nolan Developments Ltd v Kingscroft Developments Ltd* [1999] 1 ILRM 141; *Maguire v Browne* [1921] 1 IR 148.

202 *Pwillbach Colliery v Woodman* [1915] AC 634.

203 *Smyth v Dublin Theatre Co.* [1936] IR 692. Of course, what is ordinary will depend on the nature of the building and the purposes for which it is adapted.

204 [2004] 3 EGLR 93; [2004] EWCA Civ 214.

Whyte Cottage in West Sussex, in 1949. The bakery was erected on foot of planning permission and the foul and surface drainage left the site through a drain connected to the pipe serving the cottage, which ran from the cottage into the public sewer. The property changed hands in 1982 and the right to dispose of the foul and surface water passed as an easement under the Rule in *Wheeldon v Burrows.* The building ceased to operate as a bakery in 1986. In 2000, planning permission was granted for demolition of the bakery and the erection of two detached houses on the site. McAdams (the developer) intended to use the same system to discharge foul and surface water. During the development the neighbours, the Robinsons, blocked the pipe. McAdams claimed that this was an unjustified interference with their easement over the pipe, while the Robinsons claimed that the easement ceased when the nature of the dominant tenement changed so radically from bakery to housing development.

The question under consideration was what effect, if any, a radical change of user of the dominant tenement had on the validity and extent of an implied easement. Neuberger LJ held that there were a number of principles applicable to this question. In general, a substantial change in the use of the dominant land resulting in a substantial change in the extent to which the easement is used cannot be objected to by the servient owner. That said, *excessive* use of the easement will render the dominant owner liable for nuisance. According to Neuberger LJ, where there is a change in the use of, or the erection of new buildings on, the dominant land without having any effect on the nature and extent of the use of the easement, the change, however radical, will not affect the right of the dominant owner to use the easement.[205] **[12–83]**

The question appears to turn on the notion of *excessive* user resulting from *radical* change *having an effect* on the nature and extent of the use of the easement. The Court therefore laid down a two-prong test in order to assess whether an easement could be said to extend to the changed user resulting from changes to the dominant land: **[12–84]**

(a) Does the development of the dominant land represent a "radical change in the character" or a "change in the identity" of the site as opposed to a mere change or intensification in the use of the site?[206]
(b) Would the use of the site as redeveloped result in a substantial increase or alteration in the burden on the servient land?[207]

If the answer to both of these questions is affirmative, then the easement does not extend to the extent contemplated by the development or change in use of the dominant tenement. While it was formerly supposed that easements would be discharged should they be found not to extend to the changed character and identity of the dominant tenement,[208] it now appears that the result of such a finding is simply that excessive exercise of the easement will be restrained.[209] The easement can,

[205] See also *Lutrell's Case* (1601) 4 Co Rep 86a.
[206] See also *Wimbledon and Putney Commons Conservators v Dixon* (1875) 1 Ch D 362; *Milner's Safe Company Ltd v Great Northern & City Railway Co.* [1907] 1 Ch 208; *RPC Holdings Ltd v Rogers* [1953] 1 All ER 1029.
[207] See also *Harvey v Walton* (1873) LR 8 CP 162.
[208] See, for example, *Garritt v Sharp* (1835) 3 A & E 325.
[209] See, for example, *Graham v Philcox* [1984] QB 747.

however, continue to be exercised within its extent and is not discharged or extinguished.[210]

V. Discharge of Easements

[12–85] Easements can be discharged by statute, by operation of law, or by release by the dominant owner. They can also be extinguished under s 39 of the Land and Conveyancing Law Reform Act 2009. Statutory discharge normally comes about as a result of powers given to a local or state authority to acquire privately owned land for public purposes: once the land is acquired, any easements existing over it will normally be discharged. Where the dominant and servient tenements come into the ownership and beneficial occupation of the same person, the easement will be discharged by operation of law because easements require the dominant and servient tenements to be in the ownership and/or beneficial occupation of diverse persons.

[12–86] A release can be either express or implied. While express releases, by their very nature, present very little difficulty for the law, implied releases are more complex. An implied release will arise where there is a substantial period of non-user by the dominant tenant accompanied by an intention to release the easement. A long period of non-user may give rise to a presumption of an intention to release, however there is little certainty about how long the non-user must persist (although 20 years will normally suffice[211]), and the presumed intention can be rebutted with relative ease. The courts' reluctance to find that an easement has been extinguished through non-user results from the fact that easements are valuable property rights that the court ought not to be quick to dismiss.[212] This principle was restated recently by the High Court in *Orwell Park Management Ltd v Henihan & Anor*,[213] in which an easement of right of way that had been acquired by lost modern grant prescription had not been used for some 18 years. Herbert J held that non-user on its own is not sufficient to result in the discharge of an easement; a clear intention to release by means of non-user is required.[214]

[12–87] Section 39 of the Land and Conveyancing Law Reform Act 2009 provides that easements acquired by prescription, implied grant or reservation can be extinguished by "a 12 year continuous period of non-user",[215] whether those easements were acquired under the 2009 Act or under the older system (although, if the easement predates the 2009 Act, it can only be extinguished if at least three years of the 12-year period of non-user occurred after 1 December 2009).[216] Easements that are "protected by registration in the Registry of Deeds or the Land Registry" will not be extinguished under s 39(1), although the Civil Law (Miscellaneous Provisions) Bill 2011 as passed by

210 *McAdams Homes Ltd v Robinson & Another* [2004] 3 EGLR 93; [2004] EWCA Civ 214.

211 But see *Benn v Hardinge* (1992) NLJ 1534, in which the Court rejected the argument that 20 years' non-user resulted in a presumption of abandonment.

212 *Orwell Park Management Ltd v Henihan & Anor* [2004] IEHC 87.

213 *ibid.*

214 Relying on *Tehidy Minerals v Norman* [1971] 2 QB 528 and *Carroll v Sheridan* [1984] ILRM 451.

215 s 39(1), Land and Conveyancing Law Reform Act 2009.

216 s 39(2), *ibid.*

the Seanad includes a provision to clarify that this does not undo the capacity of the Property Registration Authority to modify or cancel s 69 burdens.[217] What constitutes a "period of non-user" in this context? Its meaning is, in fact, extremely straightforward, although it may be difficult to prove in real terms. Section 33 of the 2009 Act defines the period of non-user as "a period during which the dominant owner ceases to use or enjoy the easement". The extinguishment provision in s 39 is intended to add to the capacity of courts to determine that an easement has been abandoned or extinguished, so that courts retain that jurisdiction.[218]

VI. Profits à Prendre

A *profit à prendre* is a right to take something from the land of another. In general, *profits à prendre* will be appurtenant to two pieces of land in much the same way as an easement. In order to be defined as a profit appurtenant, the alleged right must, in general terms, comply with the same requirements as those demanded of an easement. *Profits à prendre* can also exist *in gross*—or independently of the land—but in such cases the profits continue to operate as interests in land. Profits can be exclusive (i.e. exercisable by the holder only) or common (i.e. exercisable by people generally). In general, profits can be acquired in the same way as easements; there are some differences, however, in the area of statutory prescription. Appurtenant profits can be acquired by statutory prescription in the same way as easements under the Land and Conveyancing Law Reform Act 2009.[219] **[12–88]**

[217] Proposed s 39(1A), Land and Conveyancing Law Reform Act 2009 as contained in s 36, Civil Law (Miscellaneous Provisions) Bill 2011 as passed by the Seanad.
[218] s 39(3), Land and Conveyancing Law Reform Act 2009.
[219] ss 33–38, *ibid.*

CHAPTER 13
Mortgages

Real property has always been a source of wealth in society, not only as a commodity for sale but also in its capacity to secure large loans from moneylenders. In the contemporary world, real property is frequently used as security for a very particular kind of financial transaction: the mortgage. Mortgages are complex property mechanisms as well as financial instruments, and it is in that context that they are considered here. Within a mortgage the lender is known as the mortgagee and the borrower is known as the mortgagor. Nowadays, the mortgagor is entitled to retain the possession of the property and, in most cases, can carry on as though he were the owner of it, but if he fails to comply with the conditions of the mortgage, the mortgagee will be entitled to take action to secure the debt. **[13–01]**

Mortgages are a complex and interesting part of property law, particularly as they have undergone monumental change since the time of their inception, largely as a result of equity's insistence on fairness for the mortgagor (borrower). The result of equity's intervention was to create a situation in which a mortgage on paper and a mortgage in practice are almost entirely different things: on paper it seems that the mortgagee (lender) now owns the mortgaged property, whereas in practice the mortgagor continues (in almost all contexts) to be treated as the owner. It is from this situation that the complexity of mortgages primarily arises in relation to those mortgages created prior to the commencement of the Land and Conveyancing Law Reform Act 2009. As we will see throughout this chapter, the 2009 Act has greatly revised the law of mortgages, bringing them more in line with our common conception of them and providing a more workable enforcement mechanism. We will also consider the ways in which the economic crisis in Ireland has catalysed a change in the regulatory **[13–02]** environment in which mortgages are enforced, with mortgagors being more protected than the statutory provisions strictly require. Here, as in other areas in the law of mortgages, we will see once again the distinctions drawn in the law of property between residential premises (of which we are quite protective) and commercial premises (of which we are far less protective).

[13–03] In addition to the "standard" mortgage, this chapter considers the judgment mortgage. Judgment mortgages are debt-enforcement mechanisms. Where a debt is owed, the creditor can acquire a judgment of a court showing that it is so owed and, where the debtor has real property, can use an affidavit to create a mortgage over that property so that the property can be used to secure and realise the debt owed, where necessary. The judgment mortgage has been the focus of much controversy in recent years in Ireland. This controversy arises chiefly from the uncertain status of what can be termed the "technical defence" to a judgment mortgage: the position that suggests that any mistake or omission—no matter how insignificant—in the grounding affidavit would result in the invalidity of the judgment mortgage in its entirety. Recent case law casts some doubt on this defence in Irish law and is considered in detail in this chapter.

I. Mortgages

[13–04] The original form of mortgage is very different from what we are familiar with today: a lender would go into possession of the borrower's land and keep the income from that land. If the income from the land was used to pay off the principal sum and interest, the mortgage was known as *vivum vadium* (living pledge), but if the income was not directed towards the payment of capital and simply retained by the mortgagee, it was known as *mortuum vadium* (dead pledge). A redemption date would be set for the mortgage (this is the date on which the mortgage was to be paid off and the property returned to the mortgagor's ownership) and, in most cases, if this redemption date passed without the loan and any associated interest being repaid, the mortgagee could keep whatever had already been repaid *and* the property that was mortgaged. In addition, the debt would continue to be owed and have to be paid off. In the eyes of the common law, the mortgagee was the property-owner. Equity found this situation unpalatable because, rather than being a straightforward and conventional "sale of land", a mortgage involved the use of land as security. In other words, equity recognised that the property was being transferred to the mortgagee, but that the mutual intention of the parties was that ownership would be returned to the mortgagor once the monies and associated interest had been repaid. Equity therefore intervened to construct the mortgage as a transaction in which the mortgagee acquired security only: the mortgagor continued to be the owner of the property.[1] This ownership and all of the rights associated with it became known as the *equity of redemption*.

[13–05] The equity of redemption can be said to represent the mortgagor's ownership of the property and, as a result, is a valuable interest that can be sold, leased and even mortgaged in accordance with the terms of the original mortgage.[2] The equity of redemption is, in essence, the font from which the mortgagor's rights and defences flow. As we will see below, the courts have traditionally been quick to intervene in mortgage

1 *Thornborough v Baker* (1675) 3 Swans 628.
2 *Casborne v Scarfe* (1738) 1 Atk 603.

relationships where the essence of the arrangement *qua* "mortgage" is being impeded by conditions that hamper, or otherwise make vulnerable, the equity of redemption. The equity of redemption must be distinguished from the "right to redeem". The right to redeem is the right of the mortgagor to have the property re-conveyed in his favour once the mortgage and any associated interest have been paid. At common law the redemption date specified in the mortgage was an absolute date. In other words, the mortgage had to be repaid on that date: otherwise the mortgagee could keep the property. In keeping with equity's adherence to the maxim "once a mortgage always a mortgage", this is no longer the case: instead the date of redemption is now no more than the earliest date on which the mortgage can be redeemed. This means that the mortgagor can redeem at any point thereafter within the life of the mortgage *and* that the majority of the mortgagee's powers (particularly those designed to enforce the loan) do not become exercisable until the redemption date has passed.

The Land and Conveyancing Law Reform Act 2009 has radically changed the ways in which mortgages are created after the commencement of the Act (i.e. 1 December 2009), introducing a system of charge over both unregistered and registered land in which there is no transfer of ownership between the mortgagor and the mortgagee.[3] We will consider this throughout the chapter, but for now it is important to note this structural difference between mortgages created before 1 December 2009 (which continue to be governed by the "old" law) and mortgages created after 1 December 2009 (which are governed by the provisions of the 2009 Act). **[13–06]**

1. Creation of Mortgages

Prior to 1 December 2009, the means of creating a mortgage very much depended on whether the mortgage was being created over registered or unregistered land, and whether it was to be a legal or equitable mortgage. The 2009 Act treats registered and unregistered land the same in terms of the creation of a legal "mortgage" (or, rather, a charge[4]) but, as the mortgages created before 1 December 2009 continue to be governed by the old law, it is important to consider both the old and new mortgage-creation mechanisms in law and in equity. **[13–07]**

(i) Legal Mortgages of Unregistered Land Pre-LCLRA 2009

(a) Mortgage by Conveyance of the Fee Simple

The classic mechanism for the creation of a mortgage is for the owner of the land to transfer the fee simple in it to the mortgagee in return for the advance of monies, and for this transfer to be done subject to a proviso for redemption. This proviso for redemption entitles the mortgagor to reacquire the proprietary interest once the principal mortgage monies, interest and any applicable charges have been paid off. The mortgage therefore features a formal transfer of ownership, but differs from an out-and-out transfer because of the equity of redemption that the mortgagor retains, which includes his right to redeem. It is, therefore, the equity of redemption that really gives such a transaction its character as a mortgage. For that reason the equity of redemption is protected jealously by the courts, which are exceptionally sceptical of **[13–08]**

---

[3] s 89, Land and Conveyancing Law Reform Act 2009.

[4] *ibid.*

any terms that tend to undermine the mortgagor's equity of redemption. Thus, prior to the commencement of the Land and Conveyancing Law Reform Act 2009, a fee simple-holder of unregistered land can transfer the fee simple to a lender and retain an equity of redemption, thereby creating a "mortgage by conveyance of the fee simple".

(b) Mortgage by Demise

[13–09] In the alternative, a fee simple-holder (or holder of a lesser freehold estate) could transfer a leasehold interest to the lender and retain the freehold reversion. This demise (or creation of a lease) would be done subject to a proviso for cessar on redemption, i.e. subject to a proviso that the lease will end at the point at which the principal monies, interest and any applicable charges have been paid off. This is known as a "mortgage by demise". The mortgage by demise carries a particular risk for a mortgagee, i.e. that the lease demised to them may not be sufficient to pay off the debt if it were sold in order to enforce the mortgage. For that reason, mortgagees by demise frequently obliged the mortgagor to name them as an attorney. This power of attorney granted the mortgagee the right to sell the fee simple over the property in order to satisfy the debt subject to the rules governing the sale of property by the mortgagee, which are considered below.[5]

(c) Mortgage by Assignment or *Sub-Demise*

[13–10] Leasehold owners can also mortgage their leasehold rights, which are proprietary rights. Leasehold owners have two options for the creation of a legal mortgage over unregistered land. First, they can assign their lease to the mortgagee. An assignment is the out-and-out transfer of the leasehold interest so that the mortgagee would take the place of the mortgagor in the lease. All assignments must be done by deed or in writing.[6] A "mortgage by assignment of a leasehold interest" is made subject to a proviso for redemption, which requires that the assignment comes to an end and the leasehold is reconveyed at the point at which the principal monies, interest and any applicable charges have been paid off. The second option for the leasehold owner is to create a sub-lease in favour of the mortgagee. This is done subject to a proviso for cessar on redemption, i.e. subject to a proviso that the sub-lease will end at the point at which the principal monies, interest and any applicable charges have been paid off, which is known as a "mortgage by sub-demise".

(d) Statutory Mortgages

[13–11] Section 26 of the Conveyancing Act 1881 allowed freehold and leasehold owners to create mortgages over their property by means of a shortened deed. In practice, the "statutory mortgage" is created very rarely.

Legal Mortgages of Unregistered Land post-LCLRA 2009

[13–12] Section 89(1) of the Land and Conveyancing Law Reform Act 2009 provides:

> A legal mortgage of land may only be created by a charge by deed and such a charge, unless the context requires otherwise, is referred to in this Part as a "mortgage"; and "mortgagor" and "mortgagee" shall be read accordingly.

---

[5] paras 13–32 to 13–38 and 13–52 to 13–56.

[6] s 9, Landlord and Tenant Amendment Act (Ireland) 1860.

As a result, the older mechanisms for creating a mortgage by conveyance of fee simple, by demise, by assignment and by sub-demise are no longer available. Although, as s 89(1) provides, we will still use the word "mortgage" to describe the arrangement, one can now only create a "mortgage" by means of a charge over unregistered land. Thus, no ownership rights (leasehold or freehold) are transferred to the mortgagee.

(ii) Equitable Mortgages of Unregistered Land

As mentioned above, mortgages can exist in equity as well as in law. This will normally happen where either the mortgagor mortgages an equitable interest in the property only, *or* where the formalities for creation of a legal mortgage have not been completed but equity enforces the original agreement as a mortgage in equity. Although s 89 of the Land and Conveyancing Law Reform Act 2009 radically changes the means of creating a legal mortgage over unregistered land, it does not change the creation of equitable mortgages at all.[7] **[13–13]**

(a) Mortgage of the Equitable Interest

An individual who holds only an equitable interest in the property can transfer that equitable interest in return for a sum of money and subject to a proviso for redemption and, thereby, create a mortgage. While the mortgage of an equitable interest is frequently done by means of a deed, this is not required, although if the equitable interest in question exists within a trust of land as defined in Part 4 of the Land and Conveyancing Law Reform Act 2009, the rules relating to those trusts will have to be complied with.[8] **[13–14]**

(b) Mortgage on Foot of an Agreement for a Mortgage

Where parties have formed a specifically enforceable agreement for the creation of a mortgage or charge, but the mortgage itself has not been formally created, the law of equity may enforce that agreement as a mortgage in equity by application of the maxim that "equity sees as done what ought to have been done".[9] Contracts for the creation of a mortgage are normally deemed specifically enforceable because of the insufficiency of damages as a remedy.[10] As mortgages comprise conveyances of land, contracts for the creation of a mortgage are governed by s 51 of the Land and Conveyancing Law Reform Act 2009 (and, previously, the Statute of Frauds (Ireland) 1695). Section 51(1) provides: **[13–15]**

> [N]o action shall be brought to enforce any contract for the sale or other disposition of land unless the agreement on which such action is brought, or some memorandum or note of it, is in writing and signed by the person against whom the action is brought or that person's authorised agent.

In some cases the contract for the creation of a mortgage will not have been evidenced by a note or memorandum in writing, but will have been acted upon by one of the parties. In cases of part-performance of the alleged oral contract, the court can accept **[13–16]**

---

[7] s 89(6), Land and Conveyancing Law Reform Act 2009.

[8] See Chapter 6.

[9] *Re Hurley's Estate* [1894] 1 IR 488.

[10] *Swiss Bank Corporation v Lloyds Bank Ltd* [1982] AC 584.

the part-performance as evidence of the existence and contents of that original oral contract and enforce that contract as a mortgage in equity.[11] The acts that are alleged to comprise the part-performance must be explicable by reference to the alleged contract,[12] and must be such that non-enforcement of the contract would result in a fraud on the actor.[13] Section 51(2) of the Land and Conveyancing Law Reform Act 2009 provides that the law relating to part performance continues to operate.

[13–17] Thus, where there is a contract for a mortgage that has not been formally created, but where the contract is evidenced in compliance with s 51 of the Land and Conveyancing Law Reform Act 2009 or an act of part-performance by either party, the law of equity may exercise its discretionary jurisdiction to enforce the mortgage in equity on the basis that "equity sees as done that which ought to have been done".

(c) Mortgage Implied from the Deposit of Title Deeds

[13–18] Where a landholder deposits the title deeds to the property with someone who has advanced money to him and does so with the intention that the property is to act as security for the advanced monies, equity will imply that a mortgage exists between the parties.[14] The mortgagor need not deposit all of the title deeds to the property: he must simply deposit as many as make the general intention to create a mortgage clear.[15] While the nature of this mortgage is disputed—particularly as it appears to arise from an overzealous application of equity's desire to give effect to the intention of an actor—this form of mortgage is now well-established in Irish law.[16] The deposit of title deeds was seen as both a contract to create a mortgage and part-performance of that mortgage[17]:

> An equitable mortgage... may arise in many ways. It arises where without any writing there is a deposit of title deeds by a debtor with his creditor, for the law then presumes that there was an intention to create a security.[18]

[13–19] Although this may appear at first to be a somewhat unreasonably casual mechanism by which to create a serious legal relationship such as a mortgage, it is important to bear in mind that the owner of unregistered land finds it exceptionally difficult to transact in relation to the land without the title deeds: the ability of a landowner to make out good title to the land (which is the responsibility of a vendor) depends on his ability to provide an unbroken chain of title deeds. Of course, to some extent the reach of this rationale is dependent on how many title deeds have been deposited, which is, in itself, dependent on how many title deeds the court deems were required to show the

---

11 *Hope v Lord Cloncurry* (1874) IR 8 Eq 555.

12 *Lowry v Reid* [1927] NI 142; *Steadman v Steadman* [1973] 3 WLR 56.

13 *Clinan v Cooke* (1802) I Sch & Lef. 22.

14 *Russel v Russel* (1783) 18 Eng Rul Cas 26.

15 *Re Lamberts Estate* [1884] 13 LR Ir 234; *Lacon v Allen* [1856] 3 Drew 579.

16 See Hardiman, "Deposit of Title Deeds" (1991) 6(1) CPLJ 3; s 21(3)(b)(ii), Land and Conveyancing Law Reform Act 2009.

17 *McKay v McNally* (1879) 4 LR Ir 438; *Simmons v Montague* [1909] 1 IR 87; *Re Wallis & Simmonds (Builders) Ltd* [1974] 1 WLR 391.

18 *Fullerton v Provincial Bank of Ireland* [1903] AC 309; [1903] 1 IR 483 *per* Walker LJ.

intention to create a mortgage in the particular circumstances of the case.[19] The terms of a mortgage implied from the deposit of title deeds will be implied by the courts from the general law.

The mortgage implied from the deposit of title deeds seems attractive to the mortgagor because the lack of documentation means that no stamp duty is payable on the transaction. As Hardiman has noted, the concept of the mortgage by deposit of deeds [13–20]

> . . . presents the image of a smiling landowner handing a bundle of title documents that he has never read across the lender's mahogany desk, a few home-spun words of legal commitment and a handshake before he leaves, garlanded with borrowed money, whilst the lender locks away the documents confident that his lending is rooted in property. The transaction could not be easier. There are no legal fees, no delays while requisitions are bartered throughout four or six weeks, and no lengthy forms to be completed.[20]

This image of the mortgage by deposit of title deeds is misleading: the transaction is not without its risks and complications for the mortgagor. That said, the lack of documentation carries very clear risks for the mortgagee, too, as the mortgagor may deny the existence of a mortgage and claim that the deeds were lodged for safekeeping or some other innocuous reason. As the courts are unwilling to find a mortgage by deposit of title deeds where there is ambiguity about the reason for the deposit of title deeds, the mortgagee may easily find himself in the unenviable position of being an unsecured creditor.[21] Because of this, the mortgagee may create some document in an attempt to evidence the mortgage by deposit of title deeds, but this is not without risk either. The court may see that document as laying down terms for the mortgage against the wishes of the mortgagee,[22] or the court may find that the document constitutes a deed that was not registered under the Registration of Deeds (Ireland) Act 1707 and, as a result, lost priority as against incompatible registered interests.[23]

(iii) Registered Charges of Registered Land Pre-LCLRA 2009

Section 62 of the Registration of Title Act 1964[24] provided that, rather than legal mortgages over registered land, what would instead be created is legal charges. Rather than transfer ownership over the property that is used as security, the registered charge creates a right for the chargeant (who is the equivalent of a mortgagee) to have the charge satisfied from the land in the event of the landowner's failure to make good on the debt. Due to the operation of the mirror principle over registered land,[25] the existence of a classical mortgage by which the ownership of the land is transferred and [13–21]

[19] *Re Lamberts Estate* [1884] 13 LR Ir 234; *Lacon v Allen* [1856] 3 Drew 579.
[20] Hardiman, "Deposit of Title Deeds" (1991) 6(1) CPLJ 3.
[21] *National Bank Ltd v McGovern* [1931] IR 368.
[22] *Shaw v Foster* (1872) LR 5 HL 321.
[23] *Fullerton v Provincial Bank of Ireland* [1903] AC 309; [1903] 1 IR 483.
[24] See s 62(3), Registration of Title Act 1964, expressly precluding the creation of mortgages by conveyancing of the fee simple, by demise, by assignment and by sub-demise in relation to registered land.
[25] See Chapter 7.

the register would have to be amended would simply be too complex. The registered charge is, therefore, a more straightforward and market-friendly mechanism for the use of registered land as security. Once the registered charge has been registered under s 69(1)(b) of the Registration of Title Act 1964, the registered chargeant receives a Certificate of Charge, which evidences the entitlement to have the charge satisfied from the land.[26] The charge can then be transferred by the chargeant through an instrument of transfer, and the transferee can be registered as the owner of the charge.[27] Although registered charges are different from a mortgage in conceptual terms, s 62(6) of the Registration of Title Act 1964 provides that registered charges that secure a principal sum (with or without interest) operate as mortgages. As a result, the chargeant has largely the same rights and powers as a mortgagee.

(iv) Registered Charges over Registered Land post-LCLRA 2009

[13–22] The provision in s 89 of the Land and Conveyancing Law Reform Act 2009 for the creation of charges, rather than mortgages by conveyance of an interest, represented a radical change in relation to unregistered land but not so in relation to registered land. As we have seen, charges have been used to create "mortgages" in the context of registered land since the coming into force of the Registration of Title Act 1964,[28] and are therefore a well-known and common form of instrument. Section 89 does not distinguish between registered and unregistered land and, as a result, "legal mortgages" over registered land are now created by a charge under s 89. These charges operate as full mortgages over the registered land and are registrable interests under s 69 of the Registration of Title Act 1964.[29] These charges must be done by means of a standard form.[30]

(v) Equitable Mortgages of Registered Land

[13–23] Section 89(6) of the Land and Conveyancing Law Reform Act 2009 does not affect the creation of equitable mortgages over either registered or unregistered land. It used to be the case that equitable mortgages of registered land could be created by the deposit of the land certificate with the intention of doing so by means of security,[31] however the land certificate no longer has legal force and, as a result, this is no longer possible.[32] Equitable mortgages previously created by deposit of the land certificate were neither registrable under s 72 of the Registration of Title Act 1964 nor overriding under s 72 of the same Act.[33] Rather, the mortgagee was protected by his custody of the title documents. The other forms of creating a mortgage by equity (i.e. estoppel and mortgage pursuant to a specifically enforceable agreement for (in this context) a

---

[26] s 62(6), Registration of Title Act 1964.

[27] s 64, *ibid.*

[28] para 13–21.

[29] See paras 7–31 to 7–32.

[30] Schedule 1, Land and Conveyancing Law Reform Act 2009.

[31] Registration of Title Act 1964, s 105(5).

[32] Land certificates and certificates of charge lost their effect on 1 January 2010 by virtue of the Registration of Deeds and Title Act 2006 (Commencement) (No 2) Order 2006 (SI No 511 of 2006).

[33] See paras 7–31 to 7–40.

registered charge) will operate in relation to registered land and the mortgagees are normally protected by means of placing a caution on the land.[34]

2. Enforcement Powers of Mortgagee in Pre-LCLRA 2009 Mortgages

It is a matter of common sense to ensure that the mortgagee of secured property would have powers that could be exercised to protect his investment in the property and to minimise the risk involved. A prospective mortgagee who has no capacity to enforce that mortgage or to ensure that his investment is protected against vindictive or unwise mortgagors would be unlikely to take the risk of advancing monies. The powers and rights of the mortgagee are therefore essential to ensuring that the market in mortgages remains open and attractive to both borrowers and lenders. The operation of the powers and rights of a mortgagee is dependent, first of all, on whether the mortgage in question is governed by the Land and Conveyancing Law Reform Act 2009 (i.e. mortgages created on or after 1 December 2009) or by the earlier law relating to mortgages. For that reason, we consider the two systems separately here in spite of the fact that, in their broad parameters at least, they are quite similar. **[13–24]**

In respect of mortgages created prior to the commencement of the Land and Conveyancing Law Reform Act 2009, the powers and rights of a mortgagee will depend to some extent on whether the mortgage is created by deed or not as well as on the kind of mortgage it is. If there is a mortgage deed, the mortgagee's powers and rights will be dictated by the terms of the deed and by the Conveyancing Act 1881. If there is no deed, the powers and rights of the mortgagee are implied from the general law. **[13–25]**

(i) Power to Insure the Property

In most cases mortgages created by deed contain an express provision requiring the mortgagor to insure the property against fire damage. The Consumer Credit Act 1995 expressly provides that any insurance a mortgagee requires the mortgagor to take out on the property can be taken out with any insurer,[35] and the mortgagee is obliged to inform the mortgagor of the right to choose the insurance provider freely.[36] The mortgagee may not require borrowers to obtain special cover available only from an insurer tied to the lender.[37] Where there is no express insurance term in the mortgage deed, but the mortgage was made by deed after 1881, s 19 of the Conveyancing Act 1881 allows for the mortgagee to require the property to be insured against loss or damage by fire with the premium being paid by the mortgagor. **[13–26]**

(ii) Power to Take Possession

Although it is normal practice for the mortgagor to retain possession of the mortgaged property, there will be cases in which the mortgagee will need to take possession in order to ensure that the monies advanced are sufficiently secured against the property. **[13–27]**

---

[34] Cautions are created under s 97, Registration of Title Act 1964, and ensure that the person who created the caution is provided with notice of the intention to transact in relation to the land. See para 7–43.

[35] s 124(1), Consumer Protection Act 1995.

[36] s 124(2), *ibid.*

[37] ss 124(3) and 124(4), *ibid.*

This will commonly arise in cases where the property is being mismanaged to the extent that its value may fall below the amount secured on the property, or where the mortgagee is exercising his power of sale over the property and requires vacant possession in order to get a sufficient price for the property.[38] Common sense dictates that it is easier to sell a property at a high price when it is empty than when a disgruntled mortgagor continues in possession. While all mortgagees have some capacity to acquire possession of mortgaged property, the mechanism by which possession is secured in mortgages that predate the commencement of the Land and Conveyancing Law Reform Act 2009 will very much depend on the nature of the mortgage.

(a) Legal Mortgage of Unregistered Land

[13–28] Where there is a legal mortgage over unregistered land that was created before 1 December 2009, the mortgagee has an *entitlement* to possession as a result of his ownership—either freehold or leasehold—of the mortgaged property. In essence, the legal mortgagee of unregistered land simply allows the mortgagor to remain in possession unless or until the mortgagee decides to take possession himself. As a result, it is generally accepted that the legal mortgagee of an unregistered property cannot be restrained in taking possession, subject to the potential for repossession to be adjourned under s 7(1) of the Family Home Protection Act 1976 or s 32 of the Civil Partnership and Certain Rights and Obligations of Cohabitants Act 2010, respectively.[39]

[13–29] In all other circumstances it is arguable that courts have an equitable jurisdiction to restrain possession, notwithstanding the "right" or "entitlement" to possession of the mortgagee. Since the Supreme Court of Judicature (Ireland) Act 1877, all superior courts have an inherent equitable jurisdiction.[40] According to Lord Denning in *Quennell v Maltby*,[41] this equitable jurisdiction includes a jurisdiction to restrain possession where the circumstances suggest that this would be the fair or equitable thing to do. While Lord Denning's judgment in *Quennell* has not met with general acceptance in subsequent cases,[42] the *obiter* of Templeman LJ, treating of the requirement that taking possession ought to be bona fide for the enforcement of the mortgage has found some favour.[43]

(b) Equitable Mortgagees

[13–30] Equitable mortgagees in mortgages created before 1 December 2009 do not appear to have any inherent right to take possession of the mortgaged property,[44] however they are entitled to apply for an order for possession, which can be granted if the court is

[38] See *Irish Permanent Building Society v Ryan* [1950] IR 12.

[39] See paras 9–73 to 9–76.

[40] See Chapter 3. See also Art 34.3.1, *Bunreacht na hÉireann*, recognising the inherent jurisdiction of the High Court.

[41] [1979] 1 WLR 318.

[42] *Midland Bank Plc v McGrath* [1996] EGCS 61.

[43] *Britannia Building Society v Earl* [1990] 1 WLR 422; *Barclays Bank Plc v Zaroovabli* [1997] 2 WLR 729.

[44] But see the *dicta* of FitzGilbbon and Holmes LJJ in *Antrim County Land, Building and Investment Company Ltd v Stewart* [1904] 2 IR 357.

satisfied that the money is owed on the land and that possession by the mortgagee would be appropriate in the circumstances.

(c) Legal Mortgagees of Registered Land

As they have no ownership of the property, legal mortgagees of registered land (whose mortgages are, in fact, charges) have no right or entitlement to possession of the property. However, s 62(7) of the Registration of Title Act 1964 provides that the mortgagee may apply for possession once the mortgage money has become due (i.e. once a payment has been missed). The court may then grant possession "if it so thinks proper".[45] This standard will involve the court in applying equitable principles to ensure that the application for possession is intended to secure the debt and is not being made for any inequitable purposes.[46] **[13–31]**

(iii) Power of Sale

The power to sell the mortgaged property in mortgages created before 1 December 2009 can arise in one of three ways: (1) it is expressly provided for in the mortgage deed itself; (2) by means of the statutory power of sale under s 19 of the Conveyancing Act 1881; or (c) by means of an order of the court. Each of these scenarios requires individual consideration. **[13–32]**

(a) Express Power of Sale

The parties were free to negotiate terms by which the mortgagee can sell the mortgaged property. Those terms could not, however, interfere unduly with the mortgagor's equity of redemption. Where the express power of sale does not violate the equitable principles of mortgages, it will be enforced and govern the mortgagee's power of sale. If these terms are struck out, the power of sale will either be governed by statute (where the mortgage was made in a deed after 1881), or achieved by a court order. **[13–33]**

(b) Statutory Power of Sale

If a mortgage is created by deed after 1881, the provisions of s 19 of the Conveyancing Act 1881 will apply in the absence of a contrary intention. Section 19(1) provides for a statutory power of sale of the mortgaged property and gives the mortgagee a particularly broad level of discretion as to how the sale is to be conducted (i.e. by private treaty or by auction; as a single unit or in individual lots, etc.). When a mortgagee enters into a contract for sale of the land with a third party pursuant to the statutory power of sale, this will result in the mortgage becoming irredeemable unless it can be shown that the mortgagee breached his equitable duty and acted in bad faith in the creation of the contract for sale.[47] The statutory power of sale under s 19 is said to arise when the mortgage monies become due, i.e. (in general terms) when the date of redemption has passed.[48] **[13–34]**

---

[45] s 62(7), Registration of Title Act 1964.

[46] *Bank of Ireland v Smyth* [1995] 2 IR 459.

[47] *Waring v London and Manchester Assurance Company Ltd* [1935] Ch 310.

[48] In the case of mortgages by instalments, the monies will be said to fall due if a mortgagor fails to meet an instalment payment: *Payne v Cardiff RDC* [1932] 1 KB 241.

[13–35] Once the power of sale has arisen under s 19, it cannot actually be exercised until it has become "properly exercisable" under s 20 of the 1881 Act. Section 20 provides that the power of sale will be properly exercisable when one of three things has occurred:

- a notice requiring payment of the mortgage money has been served on the mortgagor and three months have passed without payment of the mortgage monies or part thereof; *or*
- some of the interest due under the mortgage is in arrears and has remained unpaid for two months; *or*
- the mortgagor is in breach of a covenant of the mortgage *other than* the covenant to pay the mortgage debt and/or interest thereon.

[13–36] If the sale of the mortgaged property has taken place in compliance with ss 19 and 20, the purchaser takes it free of the mortgagor's equity of redemption. If, however, ss 19 and 20 have not been fulfilled, the sale of the property will have a wholly different impact. Where the property has been sold without the power of sale arising under s 19, the purchaser will acquire nothing more than the mortgagee's interest and will be bound by the mortgagor's equity of redemption. If, however, the power of sale has arisen under s 19 but not become exercisable under s 20, the purchaser will receive the property free of the equity of redemption[49] unless he has actual notice of the lack of compliance with s 20.[50] Thus, although the purchaser is not required "to see or inquire whether a case has arisen to authorise the sale... or the power is... properly and regularly exercised",[51] the courts will not allow a purchaser to proceed unbound by the equity of redemption in the actual knowledge that s 20 has not been complied with. When exercising the statutory power of sale, the mortgagee has the power to convey the estate that was mortgaged free from all estates and interests over which the mortgage has priority. Any estates or interests having priority over the mortgage will be binding on the purchaser, however.

[13–37] Section 21(3) of the Conveyancing Act 1881 outlines how the proceeds of sale under the Act are to be distributed. This requires that prior incumbrances would first be paid off, following which the mortgagee will be a trustee for the balance purchase monies for the payment of all costs, charges and expenses associated with the sale of the property. Once these costs have been cleared, the mortgage is paid with the balance, and is then paid to whoever is next entitled. This person can be (and often is) the mortgagor herself.

(c) Sale by Order of the Court

[13–38] Where the mortgage created before 1 December 2009 is equitable or has been created by deed prior to 1881 and does not include a provision for sale of the property, the mortgagee can apply to the court for sale of the property. In such cases the mortgagee will ask the court to find that the property is "well charged" for the amount of money advanced and, as a result of this order, will have the property sold. It is common practice for the court to delay the sale for a period of time in order to give the

[49] s 21(2), Conveyancing Act 1881.
[50] *Waring v London and Manchester Assurance Company Ltd* [1935] Ch 310.
[51] s 5, Conveyancing Act 1881.

mortgagor an opportunity to make good on the debt, but in the absence of repayment the property can then be sold by way of auction. The court will require the existence of any interests with priority over the mortgage to be ascertained and the purchase monies will be distributed in accordance with this priority. The person who acquired the court order for sale is treated as the vendor,[52] even though the court appoints the auctioneer, decides on the reserve price for the property and receives the purchase monies. It should be noted that a sale by order of the court is a particularly laborious and time-consuming process, resulting in most mortgages including express provisions for the power of sale to avoid the inconveniences involved in the court-ordered process.

(iv) Power to Appoint a Receiver

In some cases the mortgagee might decide to appoint a receiver instead of selling the mortgaged property. This normally occurs in relation to commercial property and results in a receiver being appointed who will manage this property and ensure that the monies raised from it go towards the payment of the mortgage debt. Just as with the power of sale, the power to appoint a receiver in a mortgage predating the Land and Conveyancing Law Reform Act 2009 can arise in three ways: (1) by the express terms of the mortgage; (2) under s 19 of the Conveyancing Act 1881; and (3) by order of the court. **[13–39]**

(a) Express Power to Appoint a Receiver

The parties are free to negotiate terms by which the mortgagee can appoint a receiver to manage the mortgaged property, although they cannot interfere unduly with the mortgagor's equity of redemption. Where the express power to appoint a receiver does not violate the equitable principles of mortgages, it will be enforced. If these terms are struck out, the power to appoint a receiver will either be governed by statute (where the mortgage was made in a deed after 1881) or achieved by a court order. The mortgage deed will almost always provide that any receiver appointed is the agent of the mortgagor in order to minimise the liability of mortgagees for acts and omissions of the receiver. This notwithstanding, courts may find that the mortgagee and the receiver are properly described as principal and agent and apply the law of agency, resulting in the mortgagee having responsibility for the actions of the receiver.[53] **[13–40]**

(b) Statutory Power to Appoint a Receiver

In the absence of a contrary intention, mortgages created by deed before 1 December 2009 include within them a statutory power to appoint a receiver under s 19(1)(iii) of the Conveyancing Act 1881. This power arises when the money becomes due under s 19(1) and becomes properly exercisable only when one of the three conditions stipulated in s 20, considered above,[54] has been satisfied.[55] Persons paying money to the receiver are not under any obligation to ask whether he has authority to act. The mortgagee has the freedom to appoint whomever he wishes as a receiver and does not appear to be under any obligation to appoint someone with any particular area of **[13–41]**

[52] *Bank of Ireland v Waldron* [1944] IR 303.
[53] *Standard Chartered Bank Ltd v Walker* [1982] 1 WLR 1410. The level of care to be taken by the receiver when managing the property is considered in paras 13–62 to 13–70.
[54] See para 13–35.
[55] s 24(1), Conveyancing Act 1881.

expertise in the type or property or business that he will be managing.[56] The mortgagee may also remove or change the receiver in writing.[57] A receiver is deemed to be an agent of the mortgagor[58] and, as a result, the mortgagee will not generally be liable for any loss or damage arising from the receiver's activities.

[13–42] In managing the property the receiver will have the power to direct all income from the property, although he is obliged to apply that income in the manner laid down in s 24 of the Conveyancing Act 1881:

- remuneration and refund of costs, charges and expenses together with a maximum of 5 per cent commission[59];
- discharge of rents, taxes, rates and other outgoings affecting the mortgaged property[60];
- keeping down all annual sums and all other payments and the interest on any principal sums arising under mortgages having priority over the mortgage being enforced[61];
- payment of receiver's commission and insurance premiums and repairs[62];
- payment of any interest due on the mortgage[63];
- payment of the surplus to the next person entitled to the property.[64]

(c) Appointment of a Receiver by Order of the Court

[13–43] If a mortgage is not created by deed and does not contain an express power to appoint a receiver, a mortgagee can apply to the court for such an appointment.[65] The court will make this appointment where it finds it just and convenient to do so, and the receiver will be an officer of the court.

Foreclosure

[13–44] Foreclosure has fallen into disuse in Ireland,[66] but was still technically available to mortgagees[67] until the Land and Conveyancing Law Reform Act 2009 abolished it in s 96(2). Foreclosure was the cancellation of the mortgagor's equity of redemption, resulting in absolute ownership being vested in the mortgagee.[68]

---

[56] See *Bula Limited (In Receivership) et. al. v Crowley et. al.*, unreported, High Court, 10 June 2005.

[57] s 24(5), Conveyancing Act 1881.

[58] s 24(2), *ibid.*

[59] s 24(6), *ibid.*

[60] s 24(8)(i), *ibid.*

[61] s 24(8)(ii), *ibid.*

[62] s 24(8)(iii), *ibid.*

[63] s 24(8)(iv), *ibid.*

[64] s 24(8)(iv), *ibid.*

[65] s 28(8), Supreme Court of Judicature (Ireland) Act 1877.

[66] *Antrim County Land, Building and Investment Company Ltd v Stewart* [1904] 2 IR 357.

[67] *Bruce v Brophy* [1906] 1 IR 611.

[68] *In re Lloyd's Estate* [1911] 1 IR 153.

([illegible]) *Consolidation*

Consolidation may arise where mortgages over separate properties are vested in the same mortgagee and the equity of redemption in each property is vested in the same mortgagor. If such a mortgagor attempts to redeem the mortgage *after the legal date of redemption*, the mortgagee is entitled to require that all of the mortgages are redeemed, if this is provided for in the terms of the mortgage.[69] Consolidation may be advantageous to the mortgagee where the mortgage that is not to be redeemed constitutes the securing of a debt against a property that is no longer worth enough to cover the monies advanced. As already mentioned, consolidation will only be available where the mortgage allows for it and, even then, when the mortgagor is attempting to redeem after the legal date of redemption. Because "late" redemption is an equitable advantage enjoyed by the mortgagor, equity can require that he who seeks equity would do equity, and allow the mortgagee to force the redemption of both mortgages through consolidation.[70] [13–45]

3. Enforcement Powers of Mortgagee in Post-LCLRA 2009 Mortgages

The Land and Conveyancing Law Reform Act 2009 revises the powers and rights of mortgagees. These powers are vested in the mortgagee as soon as the mortgage is created,[71] but their exercise is determined by specific processes and rules contained within the Act and considered below. The revised powers apply only to mortgages created after the commencement of the 2009 Act[72] and are exercisable only "for the purpose of protecting the mortgaged property or realising the mortgagee's security".[73] As will become clear throughout this portion of the chapter, the 2009 Act makes distinctions between what the Act calls a "housing loan mortgage" and other mortgages. Housing loan mortgages are secured loans provided through a mortgage of freehold or leasehold land for the purposes of enabling the construction of a house that would be the principal residence of the mortgagor or her dependents, *or* to improve a house that is already used as the principal residence of the mortgagor or her dependents, *or* to enable someone to buy a house for use as her principal residence or that of her dependents, *or* to refinance a credit for any of the foregoing purposes.[74] In this respect, s 96(3) of the 2009 Act provides that housing loan mortgages are subject to the rights and powers laid out in Chapter 3 of Part 10 of the Act and cannot be contracted out of. In contrast, other mortgages are governed by these provisions but "subject to the terms of the mortgage".[75] In other words, the statutory system cannot be contracted out of in housing loan mortgages but can be contracted out of in other mortgages. [13–46]

---

69 s 17, Conveyancing Act 1881.

70 *Cummins v Fletcher* (1880) 14 Ch D 699.

71 s 96(1)(b), Land and Conveyancing Law Reform Act 2009.

72 s 96(1)(a), *ibid.*

73 s 96(1)(c), *ibid.*

74 s 2(1), Consumer Credit Act 1995 *as substituted by* s 33 and Part 12, Schedule 3 of the Central Bank and Financial Services Authority of Ireland Act 2004. s 3 of the Land and Conveyancing Law Reform Act 2009 defines housing loan mortgages by reference to this section.

75 s 96(3), Land and Conveyancing Law Reform Act 2009.

(i) Power to Insure the Property

[13–47] Section 110 of the Land and Conveyancing Law Reform Act 2009 provides that mortgaged property can be insured by the mortgagee[76] for "the full reinstatement cost of repairing any loss or damage arising from fire, flood, storm, tempest or other perils commonly covered by a policy of comprehensive insurance".[77]

(ii) Power to Possess the Property

[13–48] Under the Land and Conveyancing Law Reform Act 2009, a court order is generally required for a mortgagee to take possession of the mortgaged property. This general statement is subject to a number of exceptions. No court order is required if the mortgage is a non-housing-loan-mortgage and contains terms setting out a separate possession mechanism,[78] *or* if the mortgagor consents in writing to the taking of possession seven days in advance of the taking of possession.[79] It seems clear that, upon an application for possession, the court has a broad discretion as to whether or not to grant the order for possession. Section 97(2) of the 2009 Act provides that the court will make the order "if it thinks [it] fit" and that such orders can be made subject to whatever terms or conditions the court thinks appropriate.

[13–49] In the case of abandoned property, a somewhat different system operates. Section 98 of the 2009 Act provides that where the mortgagee has reasonable grounds for believing that the mortgagor has abandoned the property *and* that action is urgently needed to prevent the deterioration of or damage to the property, or the entry onto the property of trespassers or unauthorised persons, an application can be made for possession to the District Court or to any court seised of proceedings relating to the mortgage. Such an order can be made on whatever terms the court thinks fit, even if the mortgagor does not appear.[80]

[13–50] Where an application for possession is made under s 97 (but *not* in relation to abandoned property under s 98), s 101(1) of the Land and Conveyancing Law Reform Act 2009 provides that the court may adjourn proceedings, or make the order but stay its implementation, postpone the date of delivery, or suspend the order "where it appears to the court that the mortgagor is likely to be able within a reasonable period to pay any arrears, including interest, due under the mortgage or to remedy any other breach of obligation arising" under the mortgage. Section 101 (7) of the 2009 Act provides that this does not affect the jurisdiction of the court to postpone possession of a family home under s 7 of the Family Home Protection Act 1976. No reference is made (by necessary amendment) to the protection of shared homes under 32 of the Civil Partnership and Certain Rights and Obligations of Cohabitants Act 2010. Although there is nothing to suggest that postponement of possession under s 32 of the

---

[76] s 110(1), *ibid.*
[77] s 110(2), *ibid.*
[78] s 96(3), *ibid.*
[79] s 97(1), *ibid.*
[80] s 98(2), *ibid.*

2010 Act would be impeded by s 101, it seems incongruent to expressly (and, incidentally, seemingly unnecessarily) preserve the capacity to postpone the possession of the family home, but not of the shared home.[81]

Applications for possession of mortgaged property under s 97 (although not of abandoned mortgaged property under s 98) are generally to be brought in the High Court,[82] but where what is at issue is a housing loan mortgage, the Circuit Court has exclusive jurisdiction to deal with such applications.[83] Where an order has been granted for possession of mortgaged property, including abandoned mortgaged property, the mortgagee is obliged to take steps to sell or lease the property, subject to the terms (if any) imposed on the possession order by the court.[84] **[13–51]**

(iii) Power to Sell the Property

A mortgagee or "any other person for the time being entitled to receive, and give a discharge for, the mortgage debt"[85] can sell the mortgaged property provided conditions laid down in s 100 are complied with. Section 100 provides that the power of sale becomes exercisable only where one of the following three scenarios have arisen *and* 28 days' notice warning of the possibility of sale has been served in the prescribed form *and* a court order has been granted[86] *or* the mortgagor consents in writing to the sale no more than seven days prior to it.[87] The three possible scenarios are: **[13–52]**

(a) following service of notice on the mortgagor requiring payment of the mortgage debt, default has been made in payment of that debt, or part of it, for 3 months after such service, or
(b) some interest under the mortgage or, in the case of a mortgage debt payable by instalments, some instalment representing interest or part interest and part capital is in arrears and unpaid for 2 months after becoming due, or
(c) there has been a breach by the mortgagor, or some person concurring in the mortgage, of some other provision contained in the mortgage or any statutory provision, including this Act, other than a covenant for payment of the mortgage debt or interest[88]

An application for an order permitting sale can be made any time after the 28 days' notice has expired[89] and can be made in conjunction with an application for an order for possession.[90] Where an application for an order for sale is made, the court has **[13–53]**

---

[81] In general, the family and shared home are treated in essentially the same manner under the Family Home Protection Act 1976 and the Civil Partnership and Certain Rights and Obligations of Cohabitants Act 2010, as considered in Chapter 9.
[82] s 101(4), Land and Conveyancing Law Reform Act 2009.
[83] s 101(5), *ibid.*
[84] s 99(1), *ibid.*
[85] s 100(1), *ibid.*
[86] s 100(2), *ibid.*
[87] s 100(2), *ibid.*
[88] s 100(1), *ibid.*
[89] s 100(3), *ibid.*
[90] s 100(4), *ibid.*

discretion in relation to whether it will grant such an order ("if it thinks fit"[91]) and, if an order is granted, what, if any, terms and conditions will be attached to it.[92] Once the order for sale has been granted the power of sale is exercisable, and the mortgagee is entitled to demand and recover deeds and documents relating to title that a purchaser could expect from all parties, apart from those holding an estate or interest with priority over the mortgage,[93] which enables the conveyance.

[13–54] When exercising the power of sale, the mortgagee enjoys quite significant discretion as to whether to sell the property subject to prior charges or not, in lots or together, by auction, tender or contract, and subject to whatever conditions as to title or other matters he thinks fit.[94] The mortgagee can also rescind any contracts for sale,[95] impose covenants,[96] and sell the land with or without easements and conditions relating to building, mines, and minerals.[97]

[13–55] With the exception of building societies and receivers,[98] the mortgagee is obliged by the Act to take all reasonably practicable steps to sell the property at the best price reasonably obtainable, notwithstanding any condition to the contrary within the mortgage itself.[99] When selling a mortgaged property, the mortgagee has a duty to acquire the best price reasonably obtainable. This obligation, which has statutory force, can be traced back to the equitable duty to act in good faith and is long standing in relation to the sale of mortgaged property. Importantly, the obligation does not place unrealistic obstacles in front of a mortgagee who wishes to sell the mortgaged property in order to secure the debt; the fact that s 103(1) makes reference to "reasonably practicable" efforts reinforces this. Thus a mortgagee is not obliged to delay the sale until such time as a better purchase price might be achieved.[100] The Supreme Court considered whether the pre-2009 Act requirement to get the best price reasonably obtainable goes beyond the equitable obligation to act in good faith in *Holohan v Friends Provident and Century Life Office*.[101] This case concerned an insurance company that was exercising its power of sale over property mortgaged to it by the plaintiff. The defendant company negotiated the sale and price for the property on an investment basis and never attempted to terminate the lease of the then tenants and secure vacant possession, even though both the mortgagor and numerous estate agents had advised that this would result in a higher purchase price for the property. The plaintiff mortgagors took an action for an order to prevent the sale on the basis that the mortgagee was not fulfilling its duty to the mortgagor. The Supreme Court held

[91] s 100(3), *ibid.*
[92] s 100(3), *ibid.*
[93] s 100(6), *ibid.*
[94] s 102(a), *ibid.*
[95] s 102(b), *ibid.*
[96] ss 102(c) and 102(d)(iii), *ibid.*
[97] s 102(d), *ibid.*
[98] s 103(5), *ibid.*
[99] s 103(1), *ibid.*
[100] *Farrar v Farrars Ltd* (1888) 40 Ch D 395; *McHugh v Union Bank of Canada* [1913] Ac 299.
[101] [1966] IR 1.

that when exercising a power of sale, the mortgagee is not entitled to deal with the property as if it were his own: rather, mortgagees ought to act as a reasonable man would in selling the mortgagor's property. On application of this standard the Court prevented the proposed sale. *Holohan* therefore applied a reasonable man test to the mortgagee in the sale of mortgaged premises, meaning that mortgagees must act in good faith, taking all reasonable steps to ensure that the best price reasonably obtainable is secured for the mortgaged property. The reasonable care standard espoused in *Holohan* applies not only to mortgagees but also to agents acting on their behalf.[102]

The mortgagee must serve a notice containing information as to the sale on the mortgagor within 28 days of completion[103] and the failure to do so without reasonable cause is a criminal offence.[104] Where property is being sold by a building society pursuant to a mortgage, s 26 of the Building Societies Act 1989 requires the building society to "ensure as far as is reasonably practicable that the property is sold at the best price reasonably obtainable". The position of receivers is considered below.[105] The sale of the property extinguishes the mortgage (although the mortgagee remains liable for any part of the mortgage debt that is not satisfied from the sale).[106] The purchaser receives the property free of all interests and estates over which the mortgage has priority but subject to the estates, interests and rights enjoying priority over the mortgage.[107] Section 104 of the 2009 Act provides that the purchaser receives whatever estate or interest that was mortgaged[108] and any fixtures or personal property included in the mortgage and sale.[109] The purchaser is extensively protected by the 2009 Act. Section 105(1) provides as follows: **[13–56]**

> Where a conveyance is made in professed exercise of the power of sale conferred by this Chapter, the title of the purchaser is not impeachable on the ground that—
>
> (a) no case had arisen to authorise the sale, or
>
> (b) due notice had not been given, or
>
> (c) the power was otherwise improperly exercised,
>
> and a purchaser is not, either before or on conveyance, required to see or inquire whether the power is properly exercised.

Although this is an extensive protection, it should be noted that the equitable maxim that equity will not allow a statute to be used as an instrument of fraud is likely to be applied to limit protection of any purchaser who had actual knowledge that the power of sale was not being properly exercised under the provisions and structures of the Act.

---

[102] See *In re Edenfell Holdings Limited* [1999] 1 IR 443.
[103] s 103(2), Land and Conveyancing Law Reform Act 2009.
[104] s 103(3), *ibid.*
[105] See paras 13–62 to 13–70.
[106] s 104(2)(b), Land and Conveyancing Law Reform Act 2009.
[107] s 104(1), *ibid.*
[108] s 104(2)(a), *ibid.*
[109] s 104(2)(c), *ibid.*

(iv) Power to Appoint a Receiver

[13–57] A morgagee is entitled to appoint a receiver in writing in three circumstances, all of which are outlined in s 108(1) of the Land and Conveyancing Law Reform Act 2009. This power to appoint a receiver can be exercised where:

> (a) following service of notice on the mortgagor requiring payment of the mortgage debt, default has been made in payment of that debt, or part of it, for 3 months after such service, or
> (b) some interest under the mortgage or, in the case of a mortgage debt payable by instalments, some instalment representing interest or part interest and part capital is in arrears and unpaid for 2 months after becoming due, or
> (c) there has been a breach by the mortgagor, or some person concurring in the mortgage, of some other provision contained in the mortgage or any statutory provision, including this Act, other than a covenant for payment of the mortgage debt or interest.

[13–58] The receiver, who is deemed an agent of the mortgagor in absence of a contrary provision in the mortgage,[110] essentially manages the property. This boils down to demanding and receiving the income in relation to which he is appointed,[111] giving effectual receipts for incomes received,[112] exercising powers delegated to the receiver,[113] and applying the monies received in the manner laid down in s 109. Persons who are paying money to the receiver are not under any obligation to inquire as to the receiver's authorisations.[114] Receivers can be removed or replaced in writing,[115] can insure the property as directed,[116] and can retain remuneration and commission from the money received.[117]

[13–59] Section 109 of the Land and Conveyancing Law Reform Act 2009 provides that the income received is to be applied in the following order:

> (a) in discharge of all rates, rents, taxes and other outgoings affecting the mortgaged property,
> (b) in discharge of all annual sums or other payments, and the interest on all principal sums, which have priority to the mortgage under which the receiver is appointed,
> (c) in payment of the receiver's commission,
> (d) in payment of premiums on insurance, if any, payable under this Chapter or the mortgage,
> (e) in defraying the cost of repairs as directed in writing by the mortgagee,
> (f) in payment of interest accruing due in respect of any principal sum due under the mortgage,
> (g) in or towards discharge of the principal sum, if so directed in writing by the mortgagee.

---

110 s 108(2), *ibid.*
111 s 108(3)(a), *ibid.*
112 s 108(3)(b), *ibid.*
113 s 108(3)(c), *ibid.*; s 108(4) provides that any delegated powers are to be exercised in accordance with the provisions of the 2009 Act.
114 s 108(5), *ibid.*
115 s 108(6), *ibid.*
116 s 108(8), *ibid.*
117 s 108(7), *ibid.*

Should there be any remaining monies these are paid to the person who would have been entitled to receive that money or the mortgaged property if there was no receiver in place.[118]

(v) Foreclosure

Section 96(2) of the Land and Conveyancing Law Reform Act 2009 absolutely abolishes the right of foreclosure. [13–60]

(vi) Consolidation

Section 92 of the Land and Conveyancing Law Reform Act 2009 does not permit consolidation of housing loan mortgages. [13–61]

4. Duties of an Appointed Receiver

Section 108(2) of the Land and Conveyancing Law Reform Act 2009 provides that the receiver is an agent of the mortgagor, unless there is a contrary provision in the mortgage itself. Indeed, prior to the commencement of the 2009 Act, the receiver was also deemed an agent of the mortgagor.[119] Although this fairly plainly suggests that a mortgagee would not be liable for the actions of a receiver (in the absence of fraud), it does not make clear whether the receiver owes any duties to the mortgagor. It is clear from jurisprudence existing prior to the commencement of the Land and Conveyancing Law Reform Act 2009 that courts can find, on the basis of prevailing circumstances, that there is a principal–agent relationship between the receiver and the mortgagee. [13–62]

The question at the heart of this issue is whether or not the receiver is under a duty to act in the same way as the landowner would have acted. It was originally thought that the receiver had no further duty towards the mortgagor than an equitable duty to act in good faith. This position was classically stated by Templeman LJ in the Privy Council decision in *Downside Nominees Ltd v First City Corporation Ltd.*[120] In this case the Privy Council held that the imposition of tortious duties of care into a relationship that had been historically governed by equity would be unnecessary, contrary to principle and undesirable from a policy perspective. Mortgagees (and, by implication, their appointed receivers) were already under equitable duties towards mortgagors to act in good faith and for proper purposes and to acquire the best price reasonably obtainable in the sale of the property—no further duties were necessary.[121] [13–63]

The Court of Appeal's decision in *Medforth v Blake*,[122] however, threw the position outlined in *Downside* into a state of some uncertainty. The defendants in *Medforth* had been appointed as receivers over the plaintiff's pig-farming business in 1984. Once the receivership ended in 1988, the plaintiffs brought an action in negligence against [13–64]

---

[118] s 109(2), *ibid.*

[119] para 13–41 above.

[120] [1993] AC 295.

[121] *Kennedy v De Trafford* [1897] AC 180 *ex tempore*; *Cuckmere Brick & Mutual Finance Ltd* [1971] Ch 949.

[122] [2000] Ch 86; [1999] 3 All ER 97.

the defendants in respect of their conduct of the business. Their claim was based on the argument that the defendants owed a duty of care to the plaintiffs, which had been breached by their failure to request and obtain discounts in the purchasing of pig-feed. The Court of Appeal held that the receiver who is appointed to manage mortgaged property owes duties to the mortgagor (and others with an interest in the equity of redemption). Although these duties were not tortious, they could be extended in scope as required by the circumstances of the case. In the case of receivers appointed to manage mortgaged property, this good faith duty extends to a duty to manage the property with due care and diligence, which required the receiver to take reasonable steps to try to conduct the business in a profitable manner.

[13–65] This conclusion was based on the Court's decision to resurrect the doctrine of wilful default, which used to apply to cases where a mortgagee would be in possession of the mortgaged property.[123] Scott VC, who delivered the judgment of the Court, found that receivers appointed by a mortgagee were in the same conceptual position as the mortgagee in possession and, as a result, could be said to have the same duties:

> . . . a mortgagee in possession would be accountable to the mortgage on the footing of wilful default—that is to say that mortgagee must be treated as having received sums that he would have received if he managed the property with due diligence. The facts pleaded regarding the Receivers' failure to obtain discounts on the price of pig feed disclose, I would think, a failure to manage the business with due diligence. So, if the failure had been that of a mortgagee in possession, the mortgage would be accountable for the lost discounts.

[13–66] This decision was quite clearly based on the Court's disagreement with the judgment in *Downside*, which suggested that a receiver had no duty to the mortgagor other than to act in good faith. As Scott VC asked: If the receiver "does decide to carry on the business why should he not be expected to do so with reasonable competence"? The Court did not overturn *Downside*, in which the Court merely found that the receiver owed no duty of care to the mortgagor *in tort*. Instead, it continued to maintain that the receiver owes no tortious duty of care to the mortgagor,[124] but expanded the meaning of the equitable duty outlined in *Downside* to what the Court of Appeal clearly felt was a more realistic and appropriate level. Scott VC concluded that the duties of a receiver could be summarised thus:

> (1) A receiver managing mortgaged property owes duties to the mortgagor and anyone else with an interest in the equity of redemption. (2) The duties include, but are not necessarily confined to, a duty of good faith. (3) The extent and scope of any duty additional to that of good faith will depend on the facts and circumstances of the particular case. (4) In exercising his powers of management the primary duty of the receiver is to try and bring about a situation in which interest on the secured debt can be paid and the debt itself repaid. (5) Subject to that primary duty, the receiver owes a duty to manage the property with due diligence. (6) Due diligence does not oblige the receiver to continue to carry on a business on the mortgaged premises previously carried on by the

[123] See, for example, *Maddocks v Wren* (1680) 2 Rep Ch 209; *Chapman v Tanner* (1684) 1 Vern 267; *Duke of Bucks v Gayer* (1684) 1 Vern 258; *Coppring v Cooke* (1684) 1 Vern 270.

[124] This approach has been reiterated in *Raja v Austin Gray* [2003] 1 EGLR 91; *Silven Properties Ltd & Anor v Royal Bank of Scotland Plc & Ors* [2004] 1 WLR 997, [2003] EWCA 1409.

> mortgagor. (7) If the receiver does carry on a business on the mortgaged premises, due diligence requires reasonable steps to be taken in order to try to do so profitably.[125]

While Scott VC's approach demonstrated what Quinsby has described as "inexorable logic",[126] it is also subject to criticism on the basis that the *equitable* duty the Court imposed under the "wilful default" standard is practically indistinguishable from the *tortious* duty of care rejected in both *Downside* and *Medforth*. The doctrine of wilful default would apply where a court of equity was considering redemption of a mortgage and what the cost of redemption would be. By application of the doctrine, the court would take into account not only what the mortgagee actually received from the property but also what the mortgagee might have received but for his wilful default. What the mortgagee would have received would, therefore, be taken into account in calculating the redemption.[127] The doctrine was in the manner of "almost penal liabilities"[128] for the failure to administer the property in a manner that did not maximise its capacity to produce income, although the exact standard (whether deliberate conduct or recklessness) was never fully settled.[129] The closest to a clear picture of the standard involved in "wilful neglect" appears to have been the exposition of the duty of due diligence in *Sherwin v Shakspeare*,[130] which was then applied in *Medforth*. In *Medforth*, however, Scott VC had this to say about the kind of conduct that would constitute a breach of the equitable duty to act in good faith: **[13–67]**

> I do not think that the concept of good faith should be diluted by treating it as capable of being breached by conduct that is not dishonest or otherwise tainted by bad faith. It is sometimes said that recklessness is equivalent to intent. Shutting one's eyes deliberately to the consequences of what one is doing may make it impossible to deny an intention to bring about those consequences. Thereapart, however, the concepts of negligence on the one hand and fraud or bad faith on the other ought, in my view, to be kept strictly apart... In my judgment, the breach of a duty of good faith should, in this area as in all others, require some dishonesty or improper motive, some element of bad faith, to be established.[131]

Considering the meaning of this pronouncement in *Niru Battery Manufactury Co v Milestone Trading Ltd*,[132] Sedley LJ held that *Medforth* "does not assimilate bad faith to dishonesty. On the contrary, it explains bad faith as including both dishonesty and improper motive, without—it should be noted—limiting it to these".[133] This meaning of bad faith certainty has a broader reach than the precise situation considered in *Medforth* and can also be taken to suggest a meaning for "bad faith" in relation to the **[13–68]**

---

125 At p 102.

126 Quinsby, "Making a Silk Purse out of a Pig's Ear—*Medforth v Blake & Ors*" (2000) 63(3) MLR 413 at 415.

127 See, for example, *Harnard v Webster* (1725) Cas Temp King 53; *Shepard v Jones* (1882) 21 Ch D 469.

128 *Gaskell v Gosling* [1896] 1 QB 669 *per* Rigby LJ at p 692.

129 See Quinsby, *art. cit.* at 417.

130 (1854) 5 De G M & G 517.

131 At p 103; endorsed in *Starling v Lloyds TSB Bank Plc*, Court of Appeals, *The Times*, 12 November 1999.

132 [2004] 1 WLR 1415.

133 *ibid.*, pp 1436–7.

mortgagee's duty to act in good faith.[134] Scott VC did not appear to be at all troubled in *Medforth* that his interpretation of a receiver's equitable duties was practically indistinguishable from a tortious liability. Indeed, he expressly held that he did not "think it matters one jot whether [the receiver's] duty is expressed as a common law duty or as a duty in equity. The result is the same". He therefore rejected the principled arguments advanced in *Downside* against the imposition of tortious liability. Whereas the Privy Council in *Downside* felt that imposing a common law liability within a traditionally equitable relationship would be intellectually and doctrinally inconsistent, Scott VC rejected a tortious liability for the pragmatic reason that the "origin of the receiver's duty, like the mortgagee's duty, lies... in equity and we might as well continue to refer to it as a duty in equity".

[13–69] It appears unlikely that the "wilful default" standard is applicable to the operation of receivers under a mortgage in Irish law. Prior to the decision in *Medford* the Irish High Court had expressed its approval of an equitable duty to act in good faith that did not extend beyond using the property for proper purposes. In *Kinsella v Somers*,[135] in particular, the High Court appeared to approve of Jenkins LJ's *dictum* in *Re B Johnson & Co (Builders) Ltd*[136]:

> ... in the absence of fraud or *mala fides*... the [mortgagor] cannot complain of any act or omission of the receiver and manager, provided that he does nothing that he is not empowered to do, and omits nothing that he is enjoined to do by the terms of his appointment. If the company conceives that it has a claim against the receiver and manager for breach of some duty owed by him to the company, the issue is not whether the receiver and manager has done or omitted to do anything which it would be wrongful in a manager of a company to do or omit, but whether he has exercised or abused or wrongfully omitted to use the special powers and discretions vested in him pursuant to the contract of loan constituted by the debenture for the special purpose of enabling the assets comprised in the [mortgagee's] security to be preserved and realised.[137]

[13–70] The Irish law on receivers' duties appears to have maintained the equitable level of duty of care and not to have expanded upon it to the extent done in *Medforth*.[138] Where a receiver has the capacity to sell a mortgaged property, he is under an obligation to take all reasonable care to obtain the best price reasonably obtainable for the property at the time of the sale.[139] While a receiver is obliged to fairly expose the mortgaged property to the market, he is entitled to choose the time at which the property would be sold and need not postpone sale for market reasons.[140]

---

[134] *ibid.*
[135] Unreported, High Court, 22 November 1999.
[136] [1955] 1 Ch 634.
[137] *ibid.* at p 663.
[138] For a critical note on *Medforth* from a company law perspective, see Courtney, *The Law of Private Companies* (2nd ed, 2002, Dublin, LexisNexis Butterworths), pp 1297–1299.
[139] *In the matter of Bula Ltd (in Receivership)* [2002] 2 ILRM 513; in company law terms, see also s 316A, Companies Act 1963, as inserted by s 172, Companies Act 1990.
[140] *ibid.*

5. Position of the Mortgagor

Equity's intervention in the law of mortgages through the recognition of the equity of redemption has resulted in the courts being particularly protective of the mortgagor and showing a healthy degree of scepticism about any terms or arrangements within the mortgage that in any way tend to undermine the equity of redemption. This position is connected to two related principles. The first is "once a mortgage always a mortgage", by which equity will ensure that mortgage agreements do not include any terms that would render illusory the equity of redemption and the accompanying right to redeem by an action of the mortgagee. The requirements that the equity of redemption would not be "fettered" or "clogged" flow from this maxim. The second principle is that "Necessitous men are not, truly speaking, free men but, to answer a present exigency, will submit to any terms that the craft may impose upon them".[141] In other words, the law does not treat mortgages in the same way as other contracts: it ignores terms and undermines them and varies them on the basis that the law presumes that there was no equality of bargaining power between the mortgagor (who was "necessitous" of finances) and the mortgagee (who had economic power over the mortgagor). We will see in the following paragraphs how this principle has been somewhat relaxed in relation to commercial mortgages, but continues to underlie and justify judicial paternalism in relation to non-commercial (or "consumer") mortgages, and particularly mortgages acquired for the purchase of one's home. **[13–71]**

In essence, the rule that justifies court intervention on behalf of the mortgagor is that the equity that arises on the failure to exercise the contractual right to redeem (i.e. the equitable right to redeem after the contractual or legal redemption date) cannot be fettered or clogged by any condition or stipulation contained in the mortgage nor entered into as part of the mortgage transaction.[142] In order to ensure that the court's protection was extended to mortgagors in all situations where there was an agreement that was *in substance* a mortgage, even if not so in name, the courts adopted a policy of enquiring into the nature of agreements between parties and treating as mortgages those that had the character of proprietary security. This is evident from the case of *Salt v Marquess of Northampton*.[143] **[13–72]**

In this case, trustees of an insurance society advanced £10,000 to a lender. The lender provided security by means of a contingent life interest that would vest in him if he survived his father. As part of the agreement the trustees insured the lender's life against his father's; the premium was paid by the trustees, but the loan agreement contained special clauses providing, *inter alia*, that the insurance policy was to be assigned to the lender if he paid off the whole sum due before the death of his father. A question arose as to whether this agreement was a mortgage when the parties had never described it in these terms. The Court held that on a true construction of this agreement it was a mortgage, and therefore struck down various terms that were **[13–73]**

---

[141] *Vernon v Bethell* (1762) 2 Eden 710 *per* Lord Nottingham LC.

[142] See *Krelinger v New Patagonia Meat and Cold Storage Company Ltd* [1914] AC 25.

[143] [1892] AC 1; *Williams v Owen* (1840) 5 My & Cr 303.

deemed to clog the equity of redemption. Although Lord Hannen dissented from the Court's interpretation of the agreement, he endorsed an approach that focused on the true construction of an agreement, rather than an approach that simply accepted the "label" that parties to the agreement placed upon it. *Salt*, then, is strong and well-established[144] authority for the proposition that courts will not accept parties' description of an agreement and rather will look to the substance and true nature of the agreement, treating as mortgages those agreements that have the character of mortgages. "In all of these cases the question is what was the real intention of the parties?"[145]

(i) Excluding or Postponing Redemption

[13–74] Redemption is at the very heart of our concept of a mortgage: it is what distinguishes the mortgage from a sale of property and that is even more true, of course, of legal mortgages over unregistered land that were created before the coming into effect of the Land and Conveyancing Law Reform Act 2009.[146] There can be no mortgage without the equity of redemption, and even if redemption is not expressly mentioned in the terms of the agreement it will be said to exist if the agreement is found to be a mortgage in real terms.[147] Any attempts to limit the equity of redemption within the terms of the mortgage itself will be void. Thus, the courts have struck down mortgage terms that attempted to limit the equity of redemption to only part of the mortgaged property,[148] that purported to confine redemption to the lives of named persons[149] and that purported to allow only limited persons to redeem the mortgage.[150] As a matter of logic any terms that purport to exclude redemption altogether are also void.[151]

(ii) Collateral Advantages

[13–75] A collateral advantage can be defined as a term independent to the mortgage itself by which the mortgagee acquires the right to something more than repayment of the capital, interest and any associated charges. While collateral advantages were initially thought to be void *ab initio*, it is clear that this is no longer the case; rather, collateral advantages will stand provided they do not fall into one of the three categories identified in *Bradley v Carritt*[152] and stated authoritatively by Lord Parker in *Krelinger v New Patagonia Meat and Cold Storage Company Ltd.*[153]

---

144 *Lewis v Frank Love Ltd* [1961] 1 WLR 261; *Multiservice Bookbinding v Marden* [1979] Ch 84.

145 *Manchester, Sheffield and Lincolnshire Railway Company v North Central Wagon Company* (1888) 13 AC 554 *per* Lord Macnaghten at p 568.

146 "Redemption is of the very nature and essence of a mortgage, as mortgages are regarded in equity" (*Noakes & Company Ltd v Rice* [1902] AC 24 *per* Lord Macnaghten at p 30).

147 *National Westminster Bank Plc v Powney* (1989) 60 P & CR 420.

148 *Salt v Marquess of Northampton* [1892] AC 1.

149 *Spurgeon v Collier* (1758) 1 Eden 55; *Newcomb v Bonham* (1681) 1 Vern 7; *Salt v Marquess of Northampton* [1892] AC 1.

150 *Howard v Harris* (1683) 1 Vern 190.

151 *Toomes v Conset* (1745) 3 Atk 261.

152 [1903] AC 253.

153 [1914] AC 25.

First, any collateral advantage that is unfair and unconscionable to the mortgagor will be struck down by the courts. This was the basis for Goff J's celebrated decision to strike down a clause in the mortgage in *Cityland and Property (Holdings) Ltd v Dabrah.*[154] In this case, the owner of a dwelling-house sold it to the tenant of the house for £3,500. The tenant paid £600 in cash, but raised the remainder of the money through a mortgage granted by the owners. Under the terms of the agreement the £2,900 loan would cost the tenant £4,553 to pay back. The agreement also included a clause providing that if the tenant should pay in less than six years, then a pro rata discount would be granted to him. While the tenant made repayments from May 1965 to May 1966, the repayment sums became impossibly expensive for him and he fell into arrears. In July 1966 the owner issued a summons claiming, *inter alia*, payment of all monies due under the covenant in the charge, with interest at 5 per cent on the amount due, possession of the property and an order that the charge be enforced by sale. The tenant claimed that the terms of the loan were unreasonable and oppressive and that the large premium, bringing the loan of £2,900 up to £4,553, was harsh and unconscionable and as such provided an unacceptable collateral advantage to the lender. **[13–76]**

The Court referred to *Krelinger* in holding that there is no rule in equity precluding a lender from stipulating for a collateral advantage, provided it is fair and reasonable. This was not the case here. The cost of paying off the premium was held to be entirely out of proportion to investment rates prevailing at the time, indeed the premium was so large that it had the effect of destroying the whole equity of redemption, thus rendering the security offered deficient. In those circumstances the collateral advantage was unreasonable and justified court intervention. Goff J adjusted the arrangement to find that the lender could only demand payment of the principal advanced. **[13–77]**

Lord Parker's second ground for interference with collateral advantages was where those advantages could be construed as penalties that clogged the equity of redemption. He advanced the example of a mortgage clause conferring a right on the mortgagee to take over the property in order to satisfy the debt. This right would arise on default by the mortgagor and could therefore be described as a penalty. In addition, it operated to totally clog the equity of redemption and to make the mortgage irredeemable and it was, therefore, void. A second clause in *Dabrah,* which provided that the full premium of the loan was to be paid on default by the mortgagor, is likely to fall into this category. **[13–78]**

The third category outlined by Lord Parker relates to mortgage provisions that are inconsistent with, or repugnant to, the equitable right to redeem, such as options to purchase. "Once a mortgage, always a mortgage" has been a maxim in the law of mortgages since *Seton v Slade*[155] and is of particular relevance to mortgages in which there is an attempt, including by means of a collateral and connected transaction, to prevent the mortgagor from getting all of the mortgaged property back on repayment **[13–79]**

[154] [1968] 1 Ch 166.
[155] (1802) 7 Ves 265 at p 273.

of the capital, interest and any associated charges. These clauses usually take the form of options to purchase on the part of the mortgagee, and it is clear that express options to purchase will be struck down by the courts.[156] Whether the mortgagee actually intends to exercise the option to purchase is irrelevant.[157] An option to purchase is not always expressly stated in the agreement, however. In fact, such a clause might well be disguised, as happened in *Samuel v Jarrah Timber and Wood Paving Corporation*.[158] In that case a limited company borrowed money using its stock as security and granted the lender an option, exercisable within 12 months, to purchase the stock. The mortgagee purported to exercise this option before the mortgagor had given notice of its intention to redeem the mortgage, and the House of Lords held that the option was void because its exercise would have the effect of preventing the mortgagor from getting the mortgaged property back on repayment of the principal sum with interest.

[13–80] In *Lisle v Reeve*,[159] on the other hand, Buckley J held that where a mortgage is already in operation and, by a separate and distinct transaction entered into after the mortgage, gives the mortgagee an option to purchase the mortgaged property, this option will be valid. The case of *Lisle* makes it abundantly clear that a subsequent dealing with the mortgaged property in favour of the mortgagee will be valid provided it was not part of the original transaction and was not required by the terms of the original transaction. The question of whether an option in favour of the mortgagee to purchase the mortgaged property—which is granted as a result of a term in the mortgage itself requiring the grant of such an option—would be struck down as a clog on the equity of redemption arose in the case of *Lewis v Frank Love Ltd*.[160] In this case the defendant created a legal charge against some of his property for the sum of £6,000. Following the death of the mortgagee, an arrangement was negotiated between the parties for the payment of the remaining debt, which included within it an option for the mortgagee to purchase the property against which the charge had been created. Both parties had the benefit of independent legal advice in agreeing to this arrangement and were aware of the risk that it might be struck down. The plaintiff subsequently sought an order that this option was void as a clog on the equity of redemption. While an option to purchase the mortgaged property is prima facie a clog on the equity of redemption, the fact that the parties had received legal advice and that the plaintiffs were aware that such an option might give rise to the court adopting a *pacta sunt servanda* approach to this agreement, notwithstanding the prima facie clog on the equity. Plowman J held that "the doctrine of a clog on the equity is a technical doctrine which is not affected by the question of whether in fact there has been an oppression, and which applies just as much where parties are represented, as they were here, by solicitors". Mere legal representation was not, therefore, sufficient to prevent the courts from applying the "once a mortgage, always a mortgage" approach to the matter of options to purchase, even in commercial mortgages where—as will be

[156] *Vernon v Bethell* (1762) 2 Eden 110; *Lewis v Frank Love Ltd* [1961] 1 WLR 261.

[157] *Beckett v Tower Assets Co* [1891] 1 QB 1.

[158] [1904] AC 323.

[159] [1902] 1 Ch 53.

[160] [1961] 1 All ER 446.

considered below—the courts are frequently less willing to intervene on behalf of a mortgagor who has bound himself to ill-advised terms in the mortgage.

(iii) Other Unfair Terms

Any terms within a mortgage that might be said to be unduly unfair, unconscionable or oppressive can be struck out by the court, as is clear from *Cityland and Property Holdings Company v Dabrah*,[161] considered above.[162] In Ireland this jurisdiction has been applied to invalidate or to vary mortgage terms imposing, for example, excessive interest rates,[163] unfair commission requirements[164] and terms imposed on a mortgagor who was thought to be of a less sophisticated intellect than most.[165] In addition to this equitable jurisdiction, both contract law and consumer protection law protect the mortgagor from unfair terms. **[13–81]**

Although contract law generally adheres closely to the construct of "freedom to contract", it has slowly recognised that unequal power relationships between individual consumers and large corporations, such as banks and building societies, from which most people acquire their mortgages, may demand judicial interference in these terms. Although McDermott notes: "Judges are bound by precedent and, therefore, there is a limit to what they can do to protect consumers from being held to unfair bargains. In addition, within the classical model of contract law, the relative bargaining strengths of the parties is not of concern to the Courts,"[166] the trend in relation to mortgage terms has always been interventionist. In general, large financial institutions use standard contracts, the terms of which are not negotiated individually between the mortgagor and mortgagee.[167] In commercial leases in particular it is relatively common practice for mortgages to include terms restraining the mortgagor's freedom to trade freely. These terms are subject to a contractual doctrine of "restraint of trade". **[13–82]**

The general principle of restraint of trade was outlined in *Nordenfelt v Maxim Nordenfelt Guns & Ammunition Company*[168]: **[13–83]**

> All interference with individual liberty of action in trading, and all restraints of trade themselves, if there is nothing more, are contrary to public policy and therefore void. That is the general rule. But there are exceptions: restraints of trade... may be justified by the special circumstances of a special case. It is a sufficient justification, and indeed it is the only justification, if the restriction is reasonable—reasonable, that is, in reference to the interests of the parties concerned and reasonable in reference to the interests of the public, so framed and so guarded as to afford adequate protection to the party in whose favour it is imposed, while at the same time it is in no way injurious to the public.

---

161 [1968] 1 Ch 166.
162 See para 13–68.
163 *Kevans v Joyce* [1896] 1 IR 442.
164 *Chapple v Mahon* (1870) IR 5 Eq 225.
165 *Wells v Joyce* [195] 2 IR 134.
166 McDermott, *Contract Law* (2001, Dublin, Butterworths), p 435.
167 The general form of a security document (including a mortgage) is considered in Prentice, "The Anatomy of a Security Document" (2000) 7(4) CLP 83.
168 [1894] AC 535.

Restraint of trade clauses are allowable provided they are *reasonable*. This contractual doctrine is equally applicable to restraint of trade clauses in mortgages, as demonstrated by *Irish Shell & BP Ltd v Ryan*.[169]

[13–84] In addition, consumer protection law affords protection to mortgagors. The Consumer Credit Act 1995 requires mortgagees to provide warnings to prospective mortgagors about the repercussions of failing to comply with the terms of the mortgage, including the risk that one's home may be taken into possession and sold where it constitutes the security for the mortgage.[170] The Unfair Terms in Consumer Contract Regulations 1996 (UTCCR)[171] may also apply to consumer mortgages. The UTCCR apply to contractual terms that are not negotiated individually in consumer contracts and, as a result, will apply to a great number of mortgage terms. A consumer is defined as "a natural person who is acting for purposes which are outside his business"; commercial mortgages and juristic persons are therefore clearly excluded.[172] The UTCCR provide that an unfair term in a consumer contract that has not been negotiated individually is not binding on the consumer.[173] According to the Regulations, a term is unfair if:

> contrary to the requirement of good faith, it causes a significant imbalance in the parties' rights and obligations under the contract to the detriment of the consumer, taking into account the nature of the goods or services for which the contract was concluded and all circumstances attending the conclusion of the contract and all other terms of the contract or of another contract on which it is dependent.

Good faith is assessed by reference to the relative bargaining power of the parties, any inducement given to the consumer to agree to the term, whether the mortgage was tailored to the special order of the mortgagor, and the extent to which the mortgagee has dealt fairly and equitably with the mortgagor, whose legitimate interests must be taken into account.[174]

[13–85] The Consumer Protection Code (2006) introduced a number of new protections for mortgagors and prospective mortgagors. Where a mortgagor intends to acquire a consolidating mortgage (i.e. mortgages in which a borrower consolidates a number of

---

[169] [1966] IR 75.

[170] ss 128 and 133, Consumer Credit Act 1995; for an exhaustive and practitioner-focused perspective on the 1995 Act see also Elliot, "Housing Loans under the Consumer Credit Act 1995" (1996) 3(8) CLP 195.

[171] SI 1995/27 introduced on foot of the Unfair Contract Terms Directive (1993) OJ L095/29. For a critique of the incorporation mechanism, see Murphy, "The Unfair Contract Terms Regulations 1995: A Red Card for the State" (1995) 13 ILT 156; Carney, "The Unfair Terms in Consumer Contracts Regulations: A Standard Form Constitutional Crisis" (1995) 2(5) CLP 118.

[172] For an excellent historicisation of "consumer protection" in the financial services field and the needs of contemporary consumers, see Donnelly & White, "Regulation and Consumer Protection: A Study in the Online Market" (2006) DULJ 27.

[173] Regulations 3 and 6.

[174] Regulation 2; for a full and detailed treatment of the UTCCR, see, for example, Enright, *Principles of Irish Contract Law* (Clarus Press, Dublin, 2007), esp. Chapter 14.

debts), he must be provided with a written comparison of the total cost of continuing with his pre-existing payment plans and the cost of the consolidation mortgage on offer.[175] Lifetime mortgages (i.e. mortgages where interest payments are added to the capital and the loan is repaid in full from the proceeds of selling the property) cannot be created validly unless the prospective mortgagee makes the prospective mortgagor aware of the importance of independent legal advice in relation to such a loan.[176] In addition to the warnings required by the Consumer Protection Code, it also provides that a mortgagor must be informed as soon as possible once the mortgage account goes into arrears of the date at which the arrears accrued, the number and total of payments that have been missed, the amount of arrears interest charged to date and how the arrears interest has been calculated.[177]

In the wake of the economic crisis and the capitalisation of Irish banks, a new Code of Conduct on Mortgage Arrears has been introduced by the Financial Regulator.[178] Central to this is the *general* (although not absolute) principle that there is a 12-month moratorium on house repossessions. The Code of Conduct applies to the mortgage-lending activities of all entitles (apart from credit unions[179]) that are regulated by the Central Bank.[180] It applies only to mortgages where the secured property is the borrower's "primary residence",[181] and where the mortgage is in arrears (arising either before or after 1 January 2011) or "pre-arrears" (i.e. where a borrower contacts the mortgagee to inform that she is in danger of going into arrears). Under the Code of Conduct every lender must have one dedicated person in every branch to deal with people in pre/arrears,[182] and must draw up policies for arrears and pre-arrears that are aimed at assisting borrowers taking their circumstances into account, allow a flexible approach in handling the case, set out how cases will be handled—including how regulations will be implemented and the types of alternative repayment measures or other reliefs that will be offered by the lender to borrowers who are in pre/arrears.[183] This includes being required to prepare a Mortgage Arrears Resolution Process (MARP) laying out the mortgagee's general approach to arrears.[184] In addition, if a borrower requests information that is required to benefit from any state support in relation to mortgages, then the lender is obliged to provide all such information within ten business days of the request.[185] If the borrower requests it then the mortgagee **[13–86]**

[175] para 4–10.

[176] As Mary Donnelly rightly points out, "the Code is not clear regarding whether a simple written statement will suffice or whether more active steps are required on the part of the regulated entity. More clarity here would help regulated entities: for example, it would be useful for regulated entities to know whether there should be a face-to-face meeting with the consumer to convey the need for independent legal advice": Donnelly, "The Consumer Protection Code: A New Departure in the Regulation of Irish Financial Service Providers" (2006) 13(11) CLP 271.

[177] para 4–11.

[178] Code of Conduct on Mortgage Arrears (2010) *came into effect* 1 January 2011.

[179] *ibid.*, Chapter 1, p 2.

[180] *ibid.*, Chapter 1, p 2.

[181] *ibid.*, Chapter 2, p 3.

[182] *ibid.*, Chapter 3, No 1.

[183] *ibid.*, No 2.

[184] *ibid.*, No 15.

[185] *ibid.*, No 5.

must liaise with a nominated third party such as the Money Advice and Budgeting Service (MABS).[186]

[13–87] Once a mortgagor goes into arrears the mortgagee is required to "communicate promptly and clearly" in order to establish why the arrears have arisen.[187] This connects with the general obligation to communicate with mortgagors in consumer-friendly language, making it clear that the lender is willing to work with borrowers in order to address the situation and try to resolve arrears difficulties. More generally, lenders are obliged to "pro-actively encourage" borrowers to engage with them in sharing information relating to financial difficulties that might lead them to going into arrears.[188] If a mortgagor goes into arrears and is co-operating "reasonably and honestly" with the mortgagee, no charges or surcharge interest can be imposed on the arrears.[189]

[13–88] Whenever a mortgage payment is missed (i.e. the mortgage goes into arrears) the mortgagee must communicate with the mortgagor in a clear and jargon-free manner.[190] The mortgagee is obliged to make the mortgagor aware of the consequences of continued non-payment and of non-cooperation with the mortgagee and the options available for an alternative payment schedule to be put in place. In the case of arrears, the mortgagee is obliged to explore all options for alternative repayment arrangements and, if such an arrangement is offered, the mortgagor must be provided with full information as to that alternative, including details of how the amounts to be paid are to be calculated.[191] That alternative repayment arrangement is then to be reviewed every six months.[192]

[13–89] There may be cases in which it is determined that the mortgage is unsustainable, even if an alternative payment schedule were to be put in place. In those cases the mortgagee must outline the mortgagor's options to him or her,[193] and inform the mortgagor of the right to appeal[194] to the mortgagee's Appeals Board about the decision itself *or* his treatment within the process *or* the mortgagee's failure to comply with the Code of Conduct.[195] If the borrower decides not to appeal the decision, the 12-month moratorium on repossessions does not apply and proceedings can be undertaken where appropriate.[196]

[13–90] Where the decision to repossess a property is taken the Code of Conduct puts in place an additional regulatory framework to complement the statutory framework relating to repossessions:

---

186 *ibid.*, No 6.
187 *ibid.*, No 7.
188 *ibid.*, No 8.
189 *ibid.*, No 9.
190 *ibid.*, No 10.
191 *ibid.*, No 37.
192 *ibid.*, No 38.
193 *ibid.*, No 39. Alternatives must also be brought to the mortgagor's attention if an alternative repayment arrangement is offered but not accepted by the borrower—No 40.
194 *ibid.*, No 39.
195 *ibid.*, No 42.
196 *ibid.*, Nos 46–47.

(a) No action for repossession of the primary residence can be taken until "every reasonable effort" has been made to put in place an alternative repayment arrangement[197];

(b) If the mortgagor cooperates with the mortgagee then there is a 12-month moratorium on commencing repossession proceedings.[198] The 12 months run from the time at which the case was classified as a MARP case (i.e. the 31st day after the mortgage went into arrears).[199] Some time periods are excluded from the 12-month calculation:
   a. Periods of time during which mortgagor is complying with the terms of an alternative repayment arrangement;
   b. Periods of time during which an appeal to the Appeals Board is ongoing;
   c. Reflections periods during which the mortgagor is considering whether to make such an appeal;
   d. Periods of time during which a complaint by the mortgagor to the Financial Services Ombudsman relating to any element of the CoC are being processed;
   e. The time between a first contact between a pre-arrears mortgagor and the mortgagee relating to the pre-arrears situation and the putting in place of an alternative repayment arrangement.[200]

(c) The 12-month moratorium does not apply where
   a. The mortgagor does not co-operate;
   b. There has been a fraud on the mortgagee by the mortgagor;
   c. There is a breach of mortgage terms *other than* those relating to repayment.[201]

(d) The mortgagor must be given written notification of the intention to commence repossession proceedings.[202]

(e) Where proceedings are ongoing the mortgagee must endeavour to maintain effective conduct with the mortgagor and/or legal representative.[203]

(f) If an alternative payment arrangement is agreed between commencement of proceedings and full hearing then the proceedings must be put on hold for as long as the alternative payment scheme is complied with.[204]

(g) If a possession order is granted, then the mortgagee must inform mortgagor of the balance outstanding on the mortgage, details and amount of any costs arising from proceedings, and the interest to be charged on outstanding balance.[205]

The clear objective in Code of Conduct is to prevent people from having their properties repossessed to the extent that is possible. Debate about whether or not some form of "debt relief" for the mortgagors ought to be introduced continues, but at the time of writing no such formal debt relief had been introduced, although there were

---

197 *ibid.*, No 46.
198 *ibid.*, No 47.
199 *ibid.*
200 *ibid.*
201 *ibid.*, No 48.
202 *ibid.*, No 49.
203 *ibid.*, No 50.
204 *ibid.*
205 *ibid.*, No 51.

reports of banks coming to individual debt-relief agreements with mortgagors in appropriate circumstances.

[13–91] One question that has not yet been determined entirely is whether or not, when engaging in processes of enforcing mortgages, and particularly repossessing mortgaged properties, banks and other financial institutions are bound by the European Convention on Human Rights Act 2003. Section 3 of that Act provides that

> Subject to any statutory provision (other than this Act) or rule of law, every organ of the State shall perform its functions in a manner compatible with the State's obligations under the Convention provisions.

The first question that arises is whether or not banks are organs of the State. At first glance one might say that such a designation could not be assigned to them, but the definition of "organ of the State" contained in s 1 of the 2003 Act defines same as including "any... body... which is established by law or through which any of the legislative, executive or judicial powers of the State are exercised".[206] An argument might be made that Irish banks that are now effectively within Irish state ownership and are directed in their mortgage enforcement activities by the Irish State (through the office of the Financial Regulator) and are exercising executive functions, but in reality this seems much too far a stretch. However, the Financial Regulator and Central Bank certainly are organs of the State as they are established by legislation.[207] As a result, they are obliged to take into account Ireland's obligations under the European Convention on Human Rights and, to the extent possible within their statutory structures, to act in a manner compliant therewith.[208] In this context—where repossession of houses can result in the loss of homes—Art 8 of the Convention (protecting the right to respect for one's home from illegitimate interference) is clearly apposite. Article 8 does not disallow the repossession of one's home; rather it recognises that the capacity to repossess property is often necessary in a democratic society for, among other things, the enforcement of debts. However, it would require that repossession to be done in accordance with law and to be no more than proportionate interference. As we have seen, the regulatory structure put in place by the Code of Conduct in fact protects mortgagors' homes in a more extensive manner than is strictly required by the statutory system relating to possession and sale, considered earlier, and is therefore highly unlikely to fail an Art 8 assessment. Although the regular banks in Ireland are unlikely to be designated as organs of the State with s 3 obligations under the European Convention on Human Rights Act 2003, it should be noted that NAMA—which is established by legislation[209]—certainly falls within that designation. If NAMA were to begin its own mortgage-lending facility to encourage people into the property market, ECHR Act 2003 obligations would have to be borne carefully in mind in enforcement proceedings.

---

206 For consideration of the meaning of State organs in the context of the Act see de Londras & Kelly, *European Convention on Human Rights Act 2003: Operation, Impact and Analysis* (2010, Dublin, Round Hall), pp 104–111.

207 Central Bank Act 1942; Central Bank and Financial Services Authority of Ireland Act 2003.

208 On the nature of the s 3 obligation generally see de Londras & Kelly, *op. cit.*, Chapter 5.

209 National Asset Management Agency Act 2009.

(iv) Commercial Mortgages

As the preceding paragraphs have shown, in the law there is a traditional [13–92]

> bias in favour of the mortgagor, springing from an antipathy to usurious extortion from the needy borrower [which] is, however, out of place when the Court is considering a transaction between parties who are competent business men, acting on skilled advice, and well able to judge of their own interests.[210]

The position holding that such judicial interference with commercial mortgages is inappropriate is rooted firmly in the realities of commercial life, where corporations advised by highly skilled lawyers negotiate with other corporations, who are also advised by highly skilled lawyers to acquire funds, on the one hand, and to make a sound investment of capital, on the other. Commercial entities are held to a higher standard than non-commercial entities in relation to mortgages because they are viewed as having relatively equal bargaining power and business acumen to negotiate an advantageous mortgage package *and* are accustomed to negotiating and enforcing business agreements as part of their everyday activities. Individual persons, the law feels, are not imbued with the same characteristics. The law therefore takes a *pacta sunt servanda* approach to most commercial mortgages, by which mortgagors are strictly bound by their mortgage terms (even where they seem oppressive *prima facie*): in the words of Tucker LJ, the courts ought to be "less enthusiastic about… intrusion into contracts between commercial parties of equal bargaining strength, who should generally be considered capable of being able to make contracts of their choosing and expect to be bound by their terms".[211]

The case law to be considered in the following paragraphs shows this approach quite clearly, and it is submitted that this position is to be endorsed. The words of Bishop & Hindley appear apt in this context: [13–93]

> In truth, the principle ["once a mortgage, always a mortgage"] is only a slogan and one that is quite out of date, at least in commercial transactions. Courts and textbooks should stop paying lip-service to the phrase when the reality of business mortgages is obviously different. There may still be some role for the principle in consumer mortgages where it can serve as a peg on which to save [consumer mortgagors] from entering into bizarre arrangements with unscrupulous moneylenders.[212]

Wilmott and Duncan express much the same sentiment, although perhaps in less censorious terms. For these commentators, court intervention is simply unnecessary in commercial mortgages because the possibility of unconscionable dealing—which underlines the majority of court interventions in mortgages—simply does not tend to arise:

---

210 Wyndham White, "Mortgages: Postponement of the Contractual Right to Redeem" (1939) 3(1) MLR 72 at p 72.

211 *Granville Oil & Chemicals Ltd v Davies Turner & Co Ltd* [2003] 1 All ER 819.

212 Bishop and Hindley, "*Multiservice Bookbinding v Marden*: Mortgages, Contracts and Indexation" (1979) 42(3) MLR 338 at 342.

> Unconscionable dealing looks to the conduct of the stronger party in attempting to enforce, or obtain the benefit of, a dealing with a person under a special disability in circumstances where it is not consistent with equity or good conscience that he should do so... Whilst it is clear that the relationship of borrower and lender does not give rise, of itself, to any presumption of special disability, there are certainly circumstances where a necessitous borrower may be overborne by a more powerful lender in circumstances giving rise to unconscionability on the part of the lender. However, in ordinary, arm's length, commercial transactions between corporations, this situation is unlikely to arise.[213]

[13–94] The shift away from protectionism in relation to collateral advantages in the context of commercial mortgages is evident in *Krelinger v New Patagonia Meat and Cold Storage Company Ltd.*[214] In 1910 the plaintiff, *Krelinger* (a firm of wool-brokers), agreed to lend the defendant, *New Patagonia Meat and Cold Storage Company Ltd* (a meat-preservation company), £10,000 by means of a mortgage. The agreement was for five years, but the loan could be paid off before the five years had expired. The agreement also provided that for five years after its execution, the company should not sell sheepskins to anyone else other than the lenders, so long as they were willing to buy at the best price offered by any other person, and that the company should pay to the lenders a commission on all sheepskins sold by the company to anyone else. The defendant actually paid off the mortgage in 1913 and protested when the plaintiff attempted to exercise its right of pre-emption over the sheepskins after that time. The Court held that the pre-emption option was not a part of the mortgage itself, but rather was a collateral contract entered into as a condition for the acquisition of the loan and that as a result it would be assessed on the basis of the principles of collateral advantage. The Court endorsed the position outlined by Lindley LJ in *Bradley v Carritt*[215] and held that collateral advantages enduring beyond redemption were valid *provided* they were not unfair or unconscionable, did not clog the equity of redemption and were not inconsistent with, or repugnant to, the contractual and equitable right to redeem. Although the collateral advantage in this case was quite a harsh bargain, the Court had regard to the commercial nature of both parties and of the agreement and held that it was not in violation of any principles laid down in *Bradley* and could therefore stand.

[13–95] The courts have also shown a tendency towards allowing terms that postpone the redemption date to stand in commercial mortgages. The plaintiff in *Knightsbridge Trust Company v Byrne*[216] had borrowed £310,000 from an insurance company by means of a mortgage over a number of properties. The terms of the mortgage provided for repayment of the principal sum plus 5.5 per cent interest through half-yearly payments over a period of 40 years. The terms also provided that the mortgagees could enforce the mortgage if the equity of redemption were sold without its consent, and the mortgagors were prohibited from selling the mortgaged property or granting a lease on it for more than three years without the consent of the mortgagee. The mortgagors

[213] Wilmott and Duncan, "Clogging the Equity of Redemption: An Outmoded Concept?" (2002) QUTLJJ 2.
[214] [1914] AC 25.
[215] [1903] AC 253.
[216] (1939) 55 TLR 196.

claimed that they were entitled to redeem the mortgage, notwithstanding the 40-year redemption date within the agreement itself, on the basis that the right to redeem cannot be postponed for an unreasonable period of time and that 40 years was unreasonable. The Court of Appeal held that the postponement of the right to redeem is not *per se* oppressive, but that a court may provide relief against it on the basis that the postponement is oppressive or unconscionable, or that it renders illusory the equity of redemption. Importantly, the Court stressed that the postponement of redemption is not *necessarily* oppressive or unconscionable and does not necessarily result in the equity of redemption becoming illusory: it will depend to a great deal on the circumstances of the case and on "business realities".[217] In this case the circumstances did not require a finding of oppression or unconscionability on the basis of the postponement of redemption; rather, both parties to this transaction were commercial entities who simply exercised their freedom to contract to certain terms and would be required by the Court to comply with those terms. Wyndham White has noted that "Quite apart from the technicalities of the law of mortgages the judgment... is a striking assertion of the claims of freedom of contract".[218]

The same pattern is present in relation to fairness of terms in mortgage agreements: **[13–96]** courts are reluctant to intervene where the "business realities" of the case are such that the repayment terms are not oppressive or unconscionable, even though they are unusually harsh. This is well demonstrated by *Multiservice Bookbinding v Marden*.[219] In this case the mortgage included a revalorisation clause by which the price of the mortgage in sterling was to be recalculated every four months and re-valued based on an index link between the sterling pound and the Swiss franc. The mortgage also included a term postponing redemption for ten years and provided that the payable interest rate was to be two per cent above the bank rate on the date of the re-valuation. These terms were insisted upon by the defendant mortgagee. The mortgagor attempted to evade the revalorisation and attached mechanism for assessing the interest rate, claiming that it was oppressive and unconscionable.[220] Browne-Wilkinson J agreed that this was a hard bargain, but did not find it to be oppressive and unconscionable. First of all, the mechanism for calculating interest was not unreasonable, taking into account the objectives of interest attaching to the repayment of the principal in a mortgage (i.e. safeguarding against inflation and a return on the mortgagee's investment). In addition, the mortgage market at the time was unlikely to offer to him any better interest rate and, even if a better package had been available elsewhere in the mortgage market, the plaintiff had freely chosen this mortgage package with this valorisation and interest calculation mechanism and, as a business person engaged in a business transaction, would not be offered relief from these terms. When one compares

[217] *ibid., per* Greene MR at p 198.

[218] "Mortgages: Postponement of the Contractual Right to Redeem" (1939) 3(1) MLR 72 at 74.

[219] [1978] 2 WLR 535.

[220] The plaintiff further claimed that index-linked revalorisation was contrary to public policy because it involved an "unpatriotic" valuation of sterling by reference to a foreign currency, however the Court rejected absolutely any such public policy argument. See also Bishop and Hindley, "*Multiservice Bookbinding v Marden*: Mortgages, Contracts and Indexation" (1979) 42(3) MLR 338 at 338–9.

the outcome in *Multiservice Bookbinding* with *Cityland and Property Holdings Company v Dabrah*, considered above, the courts' sympathetic approach to non-business mortgagors becomes quite clear.

6. Lease of Mortgaged Property

[13–97] Section 18 of the Conveyancing Act 1881 provided that mortgagors and mortgagees could both enter into binding leases over the property, depending on which of them was in possession thereof at the material time. Those leases could then bind the other party and their successors in title, provided they were validly created. This continues to be the case for mortgages created prior to 1 December 2009. Mortgages created after that date are subject to s 112 of the Land and Conveyancing Law Reform Act 2009, which provides that a mortgagor in possession can lease out mortgaged property in a manner binding on the mortgagee but only with the consent of the mortgagee, which consent cannot be unreasonably withheld.[221] The lack of consent will only result in the lease being void, however, if the mortgagee can establish that the lessee had actual knowledge of the mortgage when the lease was created[222] *and* that the lease "prejudiced" the mortgagee.[223] A mortgagee in possession, or an appointed receiver, is also entitled to lease the mortgaged property in a manner that binds the mortgagor if the lease is for the purpose of preserving the land's value,[224] or to protect the mortgagee's security,[225] or to raise income for the payment of interest due or otherwise to reduce the debt.[226] The mortgagee can also enter into such a lease where the lease is an appropriate use of the land pending sale,[227] the mortgagor consents to the lease in writing,[228] or a court makes an order permitting lease of the land.[229]

7. Priorities

[13–98] There may be times when a number of people hold interests over land, but the land is incapable of satisfying all of these interests at the same time. In such cases the law must assess the order of priority of these interests: which one is to be satisfied first? This is particularly important in the context of mortgages, where the mortgagee will normally have made a significant investment in the property and will want to have that investment returned.

[13–99] Where the mortgage is of unregistered land, priorities will be decided by reference either to the equitable principles of priority or to the statutory rules of priority under the Registration of Deeds (Ireland) Act 1707. Priorities will then be decided by the normal application of the appropriate rules.[230] Where the mortgage is of registered land, priorities will be decided primarily by reference to whether the mortgage, or other

---

221 s 112(1), Land and Conveyancing Law Reform Act 2009.
222 s 112(2)(a), *ibid.*
223 s 112(2)(b), *ibid.*
224 s 112(3)(a)(i), *ibid.*
225 s 112(3)(a)(ii), *ibid.*
226 s 112(3)(a)(iii), *ibid.*
227 s 112(3)(b), *ibid.*
228 s 112(3)(c), *ibid.*
229 s 112(3)(d), *ibid.*
230 See paras 7–09 to 7–13.

competing interest, has been registered and the order in which it was registered.[231] Registered interests are subject to overriding interests provided for in s 72 of the Registration of Title Act 1964.[232]

In relation to mortgages of unregistered land, only a mortgage can acquire priority by means of tacking. Tacking applies where land is subject to multiple mortgages and allows a mortgagee to acquire priority for his mortgage by tacking (or attaching) it to another mortgage. This could previously take one of two forms: *tabula in naufragio* or tacking further advances. *Tabula in naufragio* is abolished by s 111(3) of the Land and Conveyancing Law Reform Act 2009. Tacking further advances applies where either the equitable or the statutory scheme of priorities apply[233] and arises where a legal mortgagee advances further monies on the same security as the original mortgage, without any knowledge that an equitable mortgage has been made in the intervening period.[234] The later advance in that case will be seen as an equitable mortgage that can be tacked onto the earlier legal mortgage where the equities are equal (i.e. the original legal mortgagee has no notice of the intervening equitable mortgage).[235] Section 75 of the Registration of Title Act 1964 allows for future advances to be secured on an earlier charge, with the exception of situations where the further advance of monies if made after the later charge was created and with express written notice of that charge. **[13–100]**

8. Redemption

A mortgage can be redeemed by any person with an interest in the equity of redemption,[236] including the mortgagor, successors-in-title of the mortgagor[237] and (in limited situations where the lease is not binding on the mortgagee) lessees of the mortgagor.[238] In theory, and in the majority of cases, redemption is a very straightforward process: the mortgagor redeems either on the day of redemption (which is rare) or at a later date, following the provision of a reasonable and fair amount of notice (or the payment of six months' interest in lieu[239]). The remaining capital, applicable interest and any applicable fees are then paid by the mortgagor and the mortgage is redeemed by re-conveyance, surrender or discharge, as appropriate to the type of mortgage being redeemed. **[13–101]**

Where the mortgage is of unregistered land and has been created by conveyance of the fee simple, the deed of re-conveyance to the mortgagor should contain a receipt for the mortgage redemption money. A simple form of special statutory receipt is now available in relation to all mortgages under s 27 of the Building Societies Act 1989 and s 18 of the Housing Act 1988. Where a mortgage of unregistered land is created by **[13–102]**

---

231 s 74, Registration of Title Act 1964.

232 See Chapter 7, paras 7–33 to 7–40.

233 *Re O'Byrne's Estate* (1885) 15 LR Ir 373.

234 *Morret v Paske* (1740) 2 Atk 52.

235 *Brown v Lynch* (1838) 2 Jo 76; *Re Keogh's Estate* [1895] 1 IR 201.

236 *Tarn v Turner* [1888] 39 Ch D 456.

237 *Ocean Accident Corporation v Collum* [1913] 1 IR 328.

238 *Tarn v Turner* [1888] 39 Ch D 456—holding that the lessee of the mortgagor may redeem where the lease is not binding on the mortgagee.

239 *Re Kennedy's Estate* [1889] 32 ILTR 115.

demise or sub-demise the receipt will discharge those also.[240] A mortgage by deposit of title deeds or other documents is discharged simply by the return of those deeds or documents, while an endorsed receipt is probably sufficient for a mortgage by assignment of an equitable interest.[241] A registered charge is discharged by the registration of a note of satisfaction on the register[242] and an ordinary receipt can discharge an equitable mortgage over registered land.[243]

II. Judgment Mortgages

[13–103] The judgment mortgage is a means by which a creditor can enforce a judgment against a landowner. Under the pre-2009 Act system, which comprised the Judgment Mortgage (Ireland) Acts 1850–1858, where the debtor was a property-owner and the creditor had successfully received an order from the court that a particular sum of money is owed, the creditor could swear an affidavit setting out particular matters relating to the debt, judgment, debtor and property. Once filed in the court in which the judgment was granted and with the Land Registry or Registry of Deeds as appropriate, this affidavit converted the judgment into a mortgage over the debtor's property. This system applied to judgments of the High Court and Supreme Court, including decrees, orders or rules, provided they require the payment of a sum of money, charges or expenses to the judgment creditor.[244] They also applied in certain cases to judgments of the Circuit Court. The judgment had to state the sum payable to the judgment creditor,[245] however it need not require immediate payment as it appears that a judgment with a stay of execution may still be executed.[246] The Land and Conveyancing Law Reform Act 2009 now lays down somewhat different processes for the creation of a judgment mortgage, but there are many—probably thousands—of judgment mortgages in existence that were created and are governed by the pre-2009 Act system. Thus, we will deal with the "older system" and the "2009 Act system" separately.

[13–104] As a general matter, a judgment mortgage is a mechanism by which a creditor can obtain rights as against any land owned by the debtor and which will entitle him to have that land sold and the proceeds used to discharge the debt if payment on foot of the judgment is not forthcoming. The creditor can invoke this entitlement unilaterally and without concurrence of the debtor. Equally, no consent is required of a spouse (over a family home[247]) or a civil partner (over a shared home[248]). Once the debt has been paid, the judgment mortgage can be vacated (i.e. discharged).

---

[240] s 106, Land and Conveyancing Law Reform Act 2009.

[241] *Firth & Sons Ltd v IRC* (1904) 2 KB 205.

[242] s 65, Registration of Title Act 1964.

[243] *Firth & Sons Ltd v IRC* (1904) 2 KB 205.

[244] ss 27 and 28, Debtors (IR) Act 1840; s 6, Judgment Mortgage (IR) Act 1850.

[245] *Feeney v Dillon* (1841) 3 IR LR 503.

[246] *Barnett v Bardley* (1890) 26 LR Ir 209.

[247] s 7, Family Home Protection Act 1976. See paras 9–73 to 9–76; also see *Containercare v Wycherly* [1982] IR 143.

[248] s 32, Civil Partnership and Certain Rights and Obligations of Cohabitants Act 2010. See paras 9–73 to 9–76.

1. Judgment Mortgages under the Pre-LCLRA 2009 System

The judgment mortgage is created through a number of stages. First, there is an antecedent debt. Second, the creditor obtains a court judgment that this debt is owed. Third, the creditor swears an affidavit containing the relevant information (considered in detail below), and fourth the affidavit is filed. Once these four steps have been completed a judgment mortgage exists over the land and serves to secure the debt that the Court, in its judgment, found was well owed by the landowner to the creditor. Once created, the judgment mortgage operates in the same way as a mortgage *simpliciter*. [13–105]

Under s 6 of the 1850 Act and s 71 of the Registration of Title Act 1964, a creditor was required to swear and file an affidavit pursuant to the judgment of the court in order for a judgment mortgage to come into effect. Where the judgment creditor was a company, the affidavit could be sworn by the company secretary or law agent.[249] The requirements of the judgment mortgage affidavit were laid down in s 6 of the 1850 Act and can be fairly described as complex, outmoded and "perplexing".[250] This was largely a result of the antiquity of the 1850 Act and presented a serious difficulty for judgment mortgagors in more recent times because of the application of what is known as the "technical defence" to judgment mortgages by which a judgment mortgage could be struck out for any failure—no matter how minor—to comply with s 6 to the letter. Section 6 provided that the affidavit should include: [13–106]

> ... the name and title of the cause or matter, and the Court in which such judgment... has been entered up... and the date of such judgment... and the usual or last known place of abode and the title, trade or profession of the plaintiff (if there be such) and of the defendant or person whose estate is intended to be effected by the registration... of the affidavit... and the amount of the debt...

Where the property in question was registered land, its identification within the s 6 affidavit was fairly straightforward as it was simply done by means of county and folio number.[251] In the case of unregistered land, however, the property had to be identified by reference to county, barony, parish and street (as applicable). Given the "technical defence" to judgment mortgages, considered below, this caused particular difficulties in practice. [13–107]

(i) Effect of a Judgment Mortgage on the Property

In order for a judgment mortgage to be effective the debtor had to be beneficially entitled to the land. Section 6 of the Judgment Mortgage (Ireland) Act 1850 provided that a judgment could be registered as a mortgage against a judgment debtor who: [13–108]

> ... is seised or possessed at law or in equity of any lands, tenements or heridaments, of any nature or tenure, or has any disposing power over any such lands, tenements, or hereditaments which he may without the assent of any other person exercise for their benefit...

---

249 s 3, Judgment Mortgage (IR) Act 1850.

250 *Re Flannery* [1971] IR 10 *per* Kenny J at p 12.

251 s 71, Registration of Title Act 1964.

The judgment mortgage had an impact only on those properties to which the judgment mortgagee was entitled at the time of the mortgage; future interests could not be affected by judgment mortgages.[252] The creation of the judgment mortgage over unregistered land had the effect of vesting the estate or interest prescribed in the judgment mortgage in the judgment mortgagee, subject to redemption. This meant that if the debt was paid off the judgment mortgage was discharged, but if the debt was not paid the property could be sold and the debt be paid off from the purchase monies.[253] The creation of a judgment mortgage over registered land had the effect of charging the property in favour of the judgment mortgagor. This charge could then be enforced by whatever means the court may order.[254]

[13–109] Although the judgment mortgage would operate as a mortgage by deed once it was created,[255] the lodgement of a judgment mortgage had no immediate effect on the property; rather it enabled the judgment creditor to enforce the debt as against that property. Thus, a judgment mortgage over the property empowers the judgment creditor to force a sale of the property and to claim repayment of the debt from the proceeds of sale. The judgment mortgagee will also have other powers provided for by s 19 of the Conveyancing Act 1881, such as the power to appoint a receiver. A judgment mortgage over unregistered land was to be subject to all prior interests, whether registered or not.[256] This is an exception to the ordinary principle that interests in unregistered land gain priority by means of registration under the Registration of Deeds (Ireland) Act 1707.[257] Judgment mortgages over registered land were subject to registered and unregistered rights that bind the mortgagor.[258]

(ii) The "Technical Defence" to Judgment Mortgage[259]

[13–110] The technical defence to the judgment mortgage holds that minor departures from the requirements of s 6 invalidate the affidavit. Thus, a failure to accurately describe the debtor's profession would result in the invalidation of the affidavit and judgment mortgage even if the debtor was, in fact, identifiable with certainty from the information actually included. The technical defence has primarily been applied in cases of either a misdescription or an omission in relation to the identity of the parties or the identity of the land, and a brief survey of a selection of case law on these matters quickly reveals the absurdity that can result from the application of this technical defence.

[13–111] In *Re Flannery*[260] the affidavit erroneously described the lands as being situated in the parish of New Ross. Although the parish was known locally as New Ross, its correct

[252] s 6, Judgment Mortgage (Ireland) Act 1850; *Re Rea's Estate* (1877) 1 LR Ir 174.
[253] s 7, Judgment Mortgage (Ireland) Act 1850.
[254] s 71(4), Registration of Title Act 1964; *Holohan v Aughey* [2004] IEHC 244.
[255] s 7, Judgment Mortgage (Ireland) Act 1850.
[256] *Eyre v McDowell* (1861) 9 HLC 619.
[257] See Chapter 7.
[258] s 71(4), Registration of Title Act 1964.
[259] This section is based on de Londras, "The Technical Defence to the Judgment Mortgage: Time to Say Goodbye?" (2008) 13(1) CPLJ 5.
[260] [1971] IR 10.

name was St Mary's Parish and, as a result, Kenny J held that the affidavit was defective and the judgment mortgage was invalidated. If the purpose of s 6 is to ensure the provision of sufficient information to identify the land with certainty and if it was common and customary to identify that parish by the name "New Ross", invalidating the judgment mortgage in this case appears to frustrate the purpose of s 6. This is equally so in relation to *Re Murphy and McCormack*.[261] In this case the Supreme Court held that the omission of the barony in a judgment mortgage affidavit relating to lands registered under the Local Registration of Title (Ireland) Act 1891 made the judgment mortgage invalid. The fact that the land was clearly and certainly identifiable notwithstanding the omission of the barony was, once again, entirely irrelevant to the court's decision as a result of the application of the technical defence. The technical defence is evoked with equal vigour in the older jurisprudence on the identification of the parties. In *Crosbie v Murphy*[262] it was held that the judgment mortgage had not been effectively created because the judgment debtor, who was a hotel-owner and shopkeeper, was described in the affidavit merely as "Bridget Curran, of Killooghan, in the county of Kerry, widow". Equally, in *Murphy v Lacey*[263] the judgment debtor was said to be a farmer, whereas in fact he was a farm labourer (the difference being, it appears, between a person who owns and works a farm and a person who merely works on the farm of another). The misdescription resulted in the invalidity of the judgment mortgage even though it would not cause prejudice to either party.

While the Irish courts remained quite faithful to a generally applicable technical defence to the judgment mortgage, the English courts had rejected such a strict approach relatively early on. In *Thorp v Brown*[264] the House of Lords held that in assessing whether sufficient information has been provided under the headings of s 6 a court must "look to what the object and intention of the Legislature [was] in requiring that there should be these particulars describing the judgment debtor, with his place of abode".[265] Having decided such information was required "for the purpose of distinguishing [the debtor] from all other persons, and leaving no doubt whatever as to the identity of the person against whom the judgment which was to be a charge upon the lands had been obtained",[266] Lord Chelmsford held that fulfilment of this purpose was to be the test of a s 6 affidavit. In other words, the House of Lords in this case rejected a technical approach to s 6 and preferred instead a common-sense or purposive approach: provided the information in the affidavit did not mislead and was sufficient to identify the debtor without any doubt whatsoever, the s 6 affidavit would not fail. **[13–112]**

The technical and common-sense approaches to s 6 are thus clearly disparate: where the technical approach is applied, the actual sufficiency of the information provided to meet its purpose is of no consequence, but where the common-sense approach is applied, the sufficiency of the information provided is of the essence. **[13–113]**

261 [1930] IR 322.
262 (1858) IR 8 CL 301.
263 (1897) 31 ILTR 42.
264 (1867) LR 2 HL 220.
265 *ibid.*, p 282, *per* Chelmsford LC.
266 *ibid.*

The common-sense approach endorsed in *Thorp* thus requires sufficient information to ensure certainty in the execution of a judgment mortgage but does not hamtie this important debt enforcement mechanism with excessive attention to detail. The technical approach, on the other hand, is obstructionist and pernickety, constituting a "get-out clause" for debtors and a technical quagmire for creditors. While there are some suggestions in earlier Irish case law that the technical defence might not have been uniformly applied,[267] its status as a recognised defence to the judgment mortgage does not appear to have been substantially unsettled until the 1990s, and even then the Irish courts' inconsistent and sometimes timid approach to the matter leaves practitioners in some doubt as the repercussions of technical failure to comply fully with s 6.

[13–114] The technical defence's death rattle seemed audible in the High Court judgment of Costello J in *Irish Bank of Commerce Ltd v O'Hara*.[268] The plaintiff in this case registered a judgment mortgage against the defendant over lands described in the affidavit as "Ashurst, Military Road, Killiney, Borough of Dun Laoghaire, Barony of Rathdown and County of Dublin". The defendant applied to have the judgment mortgage invalidated on the basis that, *inter alia*, the parish was not included. In the High Court, however, Costello J referred to the purpose of s 6 and found that a minor departure from that section's requirements would not necessarily result in the invalidation of the judgment mortgage provided the information actually included was sufficient to identify the land without doubt. According to Costello J:

> To see whether non compliance with the section will result in invalidity, I think the court should firstly consider the purpose of the statutory requirement. If the judgment mortgage affidavit actually filed achieves the purpose which the legislature sought to achieve then there is no reason why the court should construe the section as requiring strict compliance with its provisions... if non compliance with the section arises from a misdescription then it is very likely that this would be fatal to the judgment mortgage. But if non compliance arises from the mere omission of a statutory requirement this will not automatically invalidate the judgment mortgage. *The purpose of the requirement relating to the location of the lands is to identify with precision the location of the lands affected by the judgment mortgage and to enable persons subsequently dealing with the judgment debtor and his lands to be warned of its existence.* The whole affidavit should be looked at including any additional information which it may contain which is not prescribed by the Section. If the particulars actually given achieve this purpose then there is nothing in the statute which would require the Court to invalidate the transaction [emphasis added].

It appears from this judgment that a common-sense approach was to be applied in relation to omissions in the identification of the land, although the technical defence seems to still have been endorsed in relation to misdescriptions of land. There is nothing in the judgment to suggest a rejection of the technical defence in relation to the identification of the parties.

---

[267] For a thorough survey of earlier Irish jurisprudence see Doyle, "Merits versus Technicalities: The Judgment Mortgage (Ireland) Acts" (1993) 11 ILT 52. See in particular the decision of the Supreme Court in *Credit Finance v Grace*, unreported, Supreme Court, 9 June 1972.
[268] Unreported, High Court, 10 May 1989.

This limited reading of *O'Hara* was later applied by Denham J in *Allied Irish Bank v Griffin*.[269] In this case the judgment mortgage affidavit stated that the "title, trade or profession of the said defendant is now a widow and at the time when the said judgment was obtained and entered up was a married woman". In fact, the judgment mortgagor had, at all material times, been a farmer. She claimed that the description of her as a "widow" and formerly a "married woman" in the judgment affidavit was not sufficient for the purposes of s 6 and that, as a result, the judgment mortgage ought to be invalidated. Denham J in the High Court endorsed the technical approach to s 6 requirements, holding that any misdescription of the debtor's title, trade or profession would result in invalidity of the judgment mortgage, whether or not it deceived or misled. Section 6, she held, clearly required the description of a judgment mortgagor by title *and* trade or profession, if she had one; a judgment mortgagee could not choose one and omit the other. She distinguished *O'Hara* on the basis that she felt the decision was limited to omissions in relation to the identity of the land and therefore had no relevance to cases, such as this one, where misdescription of the mortgagor was at issue. **[13–115]**

Some four months later the Supreme Court decided the appeal of the High Court decision in *O'Hara*.[270] Finlay CJ appeared to expand the common-sense approach from its limited endorsement in the High Court and to approve of its application on a more general level: **[13–116]**

> I am satisfied that Costello J was correct in applying to the interpretation of section 6 of the Act of 1850 the principles laid down in *Thorp v Browne*... Though relating to the question of requirement for identification of the judgment debtor and his place of abode, the statement [of Chelmsford LJ in *Thorp v Browne*] would appear to be of, at least, potential general application.

A similar sentiment was expressed by McGrath J, who held:

> In determining the nature of the provision there is no rule of general application save to seek to identify the purpose of the legislation. What is the purpose here? Is it other than to secure the judgment creditor's position both as to the date and amount of his charge if the property is clearly and adequately identified... is the legitimate charge to be defeated by the omission of a detail which few may know and with which even fewer may be concerned? I think not.

These judgments certainly appear to endorse a general common-sense approach, and indeed this was the reading granted them by Laffoy J in the later High Court decision in *Ulster Bank v Crawford*.[271] This case concerned the misdescription of the judgment mortgagor and the claim that this minor misdescription ought to invalidate the judgment mortgage. Refusing the relief sought, Laffoy J extrapolated from *O'Hara* that the appropriate test for compliance with s 6 was "whether the affidavit... leaves any doubt whatever as to the identity of the persons against whom the judgment which was to be a charge... had been obtained".

---

[269] [1992] 2 IR 70.

[270] Unreported, Supreme Court, 7 April 1992.

[271] Unreported, High Court, 20 December 1999.

[13–117] The case of *Dovebid Netherlands BV v Phelan*[272] also suggests a more general application of a common-sense approach to the requirements of s 6. The defendant in this case sought to have a judgment mortgage struck out on the basis that the affidavit failed, *inter alia*, to specify the "County and Barony or County of a City and Parish or the Town and Parish" in which the property was located. Although the plaintiff accepted that this information was not included in the affidavit, it was argued that a technical fault of this nature ought not to result in invalidity where the property could be properly identified from the information included. Giving judgment in the High Court, Dunne J held that it is "necessary to consider what was the purpose of the requirement in the legislation as to the [descriptive contents of the affidavit]... In each case it is for the purpose of adequately and clearly identifying the individual concerned and the property concerned." In this case, the information included in the affidavit was sufficient to ensure the clear and adequate identification of the property and the judgment mortgage could stand. Dunne J was careful to stress, however, "The position might be otherwise if there was reason for confusion as to the identity of either the individual concerned or of the property described." *Dovebid* then follows *Crawford* in applying the common-sense approach in a general sense to both the identity of the land and of the parties.

[13–118] The lack of certainty relating to the exact scope of the common-sense approach, arising from the conflicting High Court decisions in *Griffin*, *Crawford* and *Dovebid* together with the *obiter* status of the Supreme Court's endorsement of the general common-sense approach in *O'Hara* seems to leave practitioners vulnerable to a technical defence, at least in relation to the title, trade or profession of the debtor. This is a matter of more than merely historical curiosity, for those with judgment mortgages created prior to 1 December 2009 are still at risk of the application of a technical defence to invalidate their judgment mortgage.

2. Judgment Mortgages under the LCLRA 2009

[13–119] Judgment mortgages under the 2009 Act can only be created where there is an antecedent debt and the creditor in question has obtained a judgment to that effect in "any court of record".[273] Upon obtaining such a judgment, a creditor can apply for a judgment mortgage against the debtor's estate or interest in land in the Registry of Deeds or the Land Registry as appropriate.[274] Rather than create an affidavit, as was required in the old system, the creditor now simply fills out the appropriate form in order to create a judgment mortgage. On the face of it, this ought to relieve the creditor of any risks associated with the "technical defence", which we considered at length above. However, a closer look at the forms themselves does not make it immediately clear that this has, in fact, been achieved.

[13–120] In the case of registered land this is, as it has long been, rather uncomplicated. Form 112 is used to register the judgment mortgage and that form identifies the land by reference to its unique folio number and the debtor is identified simply by name as well as by the reference to the action in which the judgment is obtained. If the folio number

272 [2007] IEHC 131.

273 ss 115(1) and (2), Land and Conveyancing Law Reform Act 2009.

274 s 116, *ibid.*

or the name are incorrect, it is likely that the form would not be accepted as the basis for a registration and the judgment mortgage will simply be unregistered until a new, correctly completed, form is submitted.

Things are slightly less clear-cut in relation to unregistered land. Form 16 is used to register a judgment mortgage over unregistered land, and this form requires the property to be described by postal address *and* by town, townland, parish, barony, city and county. One is also obliged to include the area of the land, map co-ordinates and geo-directory address if they are known. It is not at all clear what the result of a mistake or misdescription as to the town, townland, parish, barony, city or county would be. One supposes—and hopes—that the other pieces of information required (including address and map co-ordinates, if included) would be capable of identifying the land with sufficient certainty to satisfy a court even in the case of misdescription or mistake, and that would be in keeping with the apparent trend towards a common-sense approach that we identified above, but it is not clear that this will be the case. Thus, solicitors must continue to take extreme care in the creation of judgment mortgages through Form 16 in order to ensure that, at the point of enforcement, the judgment mortgage does not run the risk of being struck out for an innocuous enough mistake or misdescription. It would perhaps have been preferable for the 2009 Act to state expressly that inconsequential and purely technical omissions or misdescriptions in these forms will not be fatal to the judgment mortgage itself. **[13–121]**

Upon registration, a judgment mortgage serves to charge the estate or interest with the debt.[275] It does not transfer any ownership to the judgment mortgagor, regardless of whether the land in question is registered or unregistered. Furthermore, the judgment mortgage is "subject to any right or incumbrance affecting the judgment debtor's land, whether registered or not, at the time of its registration".[276] Judgment mortgagors can then apply for a court order for the priority of interests to be established, for the sale of the land and the distribution of purchase monies, or for enforcement of the judgment mortgage by the means the court sees fit.[277] **[13–122]**

3. Judgment Mortgages over Family and Shared Homes

While the owning spouse of a family home must normally acquire the consent of a non-owning spouse to the creation of a mortgage,[278] this is not required in relation to a judgment mortgage. In *Containercare v Wycherly*[279] Carroll J noted that a judgment mortgage is not a conveyance in the sense that the term is used in the Family Home Protection Act 1976 (because it is a conveyance by a third party, i.e. the court) and, as a result, that the consent requirements of s 3 of the 1976 Act did not apply. In addition, the provisions of s 7(1) of the Family Home Protection Act 1976 (which allow a court to postpone a mortgagee's possession of the property if the non-owning spouse is willing and able to make good the repayments and it would be fair in the circumstances to allow them to do so) do not apply because s 7(1) is designed primarily for mortgages **[13–123]**

[275] s 117(1), Land and Conveyancing Law Reform Act 2009.
[276] s 117(3), *ibid.*
[277] s 117(2), *ibid.*
[278] s 3(1), Family Home Protection Act 1976; see paras 9–19 to 9–48.
[279] [1982] IR 143.

payable by instalments, which is not the nature of a judgment mortgage.[280] This does not mean, of course, that there is no opportunity for a non-owning spouse to acquire some kind of relief in relation to judgment mortgages. The spouse could make a s 5 application based on conduct that is intended to result, or actually has resulted, in the loss of the family home. However, as considered previously, the likelihood of success with an application for relief under s 5(1) (protection from future loss of the property) is slim.[281] Where the non-owning spouse has an equitable interest in the family home, then the judgment mortgage is created subject to that interest on the basis of the rules of priorities as they apply to judgment mortgages.[282] The same situation exists in relation to the shared homes of civil partners as governed by the Civil Partnership and Certain Rights and Obligations of Cohabitants Act 2010: s 28 consent is not required for a judgment mortgage because it is not a conveyance by the owning civil partner, no relief can be acquired from possession under s 32, and an attempt to prevent a judgment mortgage is possible under s 30 of the 2010 Act.[283]

[13–124] The complete omission of judgment mortgages from the Family Home Protection Act 1976 and the Civil Partnership and Certain Rights and Obligations of Cohabitants Act 2010 causes some particular problems. Imagine a scenario in which a spouse acquires a mortgage over the family home, which is subsequently struck down under s 3 for lack of spousal consent. In that case the 1976 Act has done its job well: it has protected the non-owning spouse from a mortgage to which he never gave a fully informed and valid consent. The monies advanced on that mortgage by the mortgagee are still owed to the mortgagee, however—there is still a debt and, if a judgment is acquired, a judgment mortgage could be created under which the family home could be sold to satisfy the debt, in which case the good work of s 3 of the Family Home Protection Act 1976 would come undone. The same would be true in an analogous situation relating to civil partners. What, then, is the solution?

[13–125] It does not appear to be practically possible to require the consent of non-owning spouses or civil partners to proposed judgment mortgages for the simple reason that it is exceptionally unlikely that a spouse or civil partner would give consent and that the refusal to consent would be an unreasonable one given the legitimate risk to one's home that a judgment mortgage poses. What seems to be needed, then, is a protection measure for the spouse or civil partner at the point of the proposed enforcement of the judgment mortgage, as opposed to at the point of its creation. To this end the Law Reform Commission proposed that sale of a family home pursuant to a judgment mortgage ought not to take place without a court proceeding in which all interested parties (in particular, the spouse and minor children[284]) would be heard.[285] As we have seen, s 117 now provides that the judgment debtor can make an application for sale and distribution of the proceeds thereof for any property that is subject to the judgment mortgage and it is to be expected that (as has, in fact, long been the practice)

[280] See also *Murray v Diamond* [1982] ILRM 113.
[281] See paras 9–19 to 9–48.
[282] s 7, Judgment Mortgage (Ireland) Act 1850; s 74(4)(c), Registration of Title Act 1964.
[283] See Chapter 9.
[284] LRC, *Consultation Paper on Judgment Mortgages* (2004), p 54.
[285] *ibid.*, p 50.

the court would take into account the fact that the property is a family or shared home when deciding whether and, if so, on what conditions to make any such order.

The enforcement of a judgment mortgage over a home within the meaning of Art 8 of the European Convention on Human Rights may also result in some difficulties in the future in Ireland, although it seems unlikely that the courts would allow for the rights of the family, which have been jeopardised by a member of the family, to constitute the basis for the denial of debt satisfaction to a debtor. The enforcement of the judgment mortgage might be postponed on the basis of the rights of the family, but it is unlikely that a judgment mortgage would in itself be found to violate Art 8 rights under either the Constitution or the European Convention on Human Rights. This is reflected in the Northern Irish decision in *Re A Solicitor*[286] in which the Court held that, although the enforcement of a judgment mortgage over a family home might result in some inconvenience and disruption in the life of the family, it was nevertheless necessary and proportionate and therefore not a violation of Art 8. **[13–126]**

4. Judgment Mortgages over Co-Owned Properties

Although it was previously the case that a judgment mortgage created against unregistered land held in a joint tenancy resulted in the severance of the joint tenancy, so that only the ownership of the debtor is, in fact, affected by the judgment mortgage,[287] s 30(3) of the Land and Conveyancing Law Reform Act 2009 provides that a judgment mortgage against one joint tenant of co-owned land *never* severs a joint tenancy, whether the land in question is registered or unregistered. This does not appear to be the case in relation to registered land, although the law as it stands is far from clear on the issue. The recent Supreme Court decision in *Irwin v Deasy* has now clarified that even in the case of judgment mortgages created prior to the commencement of the 2009 Act, joint tenancies over registered land would not be severed by the registration of a judgment mortgage.[288] While that is undoubtedly the correct decision in law, it does call into question the value of a pre-2009 Act judgment mortgage over registered land as a debt enforcement mechanism. **[13–127]**

In the first instance, the decision in *Irwin v Deasy* makes it clear that the holder of a pre-2009 Act judgment mortgage over registered land held in a joint tenancy is not in any position to apply for partition or sale of the property and, as a result, will find it extremely difficult to enforce the debt through the judgment mortgage.[289] Furthermore, the lack of severance raises especial problems where the judgment mortgage is against only one of the joint tenants of registered land. If that joint tenant predeceases the other, his interest in the land no longer exists (because of the right of survivorship) and the surviving joint tenant is the sole owner, but the judgment mortgage cannot be enforced against her.[290] In other words, there is no longer any estate or interest held by the judgment debtor in the land, and therefore there is nothing against which a judgment mortgage can exist. **[13–128]**

---

[286] See *Re A Solicitor* [2004] NI Ch 2.

[287] *McIlroy v Edgar* (1881) 7 LR Ir 521; *Provincial Bank v Tallon* [1938] IR 361.

[288] *Irwin v Deasy* [2011] IESC 15.

[289] This is discussed in detail at paras 8–45 to 8–47.

[290] *Judge Mahon v Lawlor* [2008] IEHC 284; *Mahon & Ors v Lawlor & Ors* [2010] IESC 58.

[13–129] Where a judgment mortgage is created after the commencement of the Land and Conveyancing Law Reform Act 2009 these difficulties are somewhat less acute. It is true that the judgment mortgage will not sever the joint tenancy so that survivorship might operate to defeat the judgment mortgage, but this is ameliorated by the fact that judgment mortgagors now have a number of options for the enforcement of the debt. The first, as we have already seen, is that the judgment mortgagor over co-owned land can make an application for an enforcement order under s 117 in the ordinary way. The second is that the judgment mortgagor of co-owned land can also make an application under s 31 of the 2009 Act, including applying for partition and applying for sale.[291]

[291] See further paras 8–38 and 8–47.

CHAPTER 14
Adverse Possession

In the normal course of events the law requires some kind of formality in order for the legal ownership in a piece of land to be transferred.[1] Indeed, as we saw in Chapter 2, the formalism of land transfers can be traced back to the feudal period (and, indeed, to Roman law[2]). In spite of this general principle, however, there are some situations in which ownership can be acquired in land without a formal transaction, one of which is the subject of this chapter: adverse possession. In vernacular terms "adverse possession" can be described as "squatting" and is a means of acquiring rights over land by means of possession, with the intention to exclude all others *including* the **[14–01]**

[1] On the process for transfer of property rights, see generally Wylie and Woods, *Conveyancing Law* (3rd ed, 2005, West Sussex, Tottel).
[2] See Radin, "Fundamental Concepts of the Roman Law" (1925) 13(3) *California Law Review* 207.

landowner for a required period of time. Adverse possession has historical antecedents in numerous legal systems, including Roman law[3] and Brehon law.[4]

[14–02] The law of adverse possession is governed in Ireland by the Statute of Limitations 1957. This reflects the fact that what we are essentially concerned with here is whether or not the formal owner of the land in question—the paper or documentary owner—has taken action to assert her title against an adverse possessor in time, or within the limitation period for an action for recovery of land. Limitation periods are a regular feature of various different areas of civil law and, in essence, they outline the amount of time someone has to initiate an action in relation to any particular dispute. In the context of property law, the failure to initiate an action within the prescribed limitation period has the effect of extinguishing the landowner's title to the property *as well as* barring the owner's capacity to make a claim in relation to it.[5] The adverse possessor will then be recognised as having rights in relation to the land and any attempt by the dispossessed owner to enter and possess the land will constitute a trespass.[6]

[14–03] Throughout the limitation period the "squatter" is treated as someone who is building up entitlements to the property by means of his possession and is dealt with primarily through the civil (as opposed to criminal) law. During the limitation period the "squatter" has a title that is enforceable against all but the holder of a superior title (i.e. anyone whose title has not been extinguished by the adverse possession). Indeed, where the land in question is registered land, the rights being acquired under the Statute of Limitations 1957 constitute overriding interests under s 72(1)(p) of the Registration of Title Act 1964. What differentiates a "squatter" acquiring rights under the Statute of Limitations 1957 and someone who is simply trespassing on another's land is the satisfaction by the squatter of different elements of adverse possession that we will consider in detail below: (a) factual possession, (b) that is adverse to the possessory rights of the paper owner, (c) involving acts that demonstrate *animus possidendi*, and (d) over land where the paper owner has discontinued his use or enjoyment of it. Once those requirements have been fulfilled, the time starts to run in favour of the adverse possessor, who then begins to accrue rights under the Statute of Limitations. Once those conditions have persisted for the required period of time (i.e. once the limitation period has expired) the paper owner's title is extinguished and the adverse possessor has ownership rights over the property.

I. Justifications for Adverse Possession

[14–04] In recent times the language surrounding adverse possession has become increasingly hostile to "squatters", who are generally represented as unscrupulous "land thieves"

[3] The concepts of *usucapio* and *longi temporis praescriptio* operated in Roman law to allow the acquisition of title by long periods of possession, although bona fides and *justa causa* were also frequently required.

[4] Brehon law recognised "usucaption" of land. See Kelly, *A Guide to Early Irish Law* (1988, Dublin, Dublin Institute for Advanced Studies), pp 109–11.

[5] s 24, Statute of Limitations 1957.

[6] *Incorporated Society for Protestant Schools v Richards* (1841) 1 Dr & War 258.

wandering around exploiting landowners' failure to supervise their property effectively.[7] These feelings of discontent are exacerbated by cases in which a person's title to land is extinguished in circumstances in which their good nature seems exploited. This famously happened in the case of *Hayward v Chaloner*.[8] That case concerned a seven-acre piece of land that was leaded out to the rector of a parish on an oral tenancy. The rent had been paid by successive rectors until 1942, after which no rent was paid and the rectors became tenants at sufferance. The landlords, who were all particularly strong supporters of the Church, did not demand the payment of the rent. This situation persisted for more than 20 years, after which it was claimed that the landowners' title had been extinguished by means of adverse possession. Holding somewhat reluctantly against the landowners and finding that adverse possession had been established, Lord Denning famously held that "if the law does penalise good nature in this way, the sooner it is changed the better".[9] In its review of the law of adverse possession, the Law Reform Commission dismissed suggestions that adverse possession is immoral on the basis, primarily, that a great many adverse possessors are not "land thieves", although the Commission did not delve any further into its *moral* justification.[10]

This feeling that there is something "immoral" about a system of law that permits a person to extinguish the proprietary rights of a documentary owner of land has persisted for some time and, in the last decade or thereabouts, had added to it an argument that the law of adverse possession violates the human rights of land owners. As we saw in Chapter 1, Irish law includes constitutional protections for private property and Art 1, Protocol One of the European Convention on Human Rights protects the right to possessions including real property.[11] Neither of these rights are absolute, however, they are subject to limitations provided those limitations are lawful (i.e. regulated by law) and proportionate[12] (including, in the language of the Convention, being "necessary in a democratic society"[13]). The question that has therefore arisen in relation to adverse possession within the European Convention on Human Rights is whether the law of adverse possession is a permissible limitation on the right to possessions including property. We will see later in this chapter that the **[14–05]**

[7] Arguably this is even more so the case with the new system of adverse possession introduced in the UK by the Land Registration Act 2002. The moral implications of the new system are considered in detail in Fox-O'Mahony and Cobb, "Living Outside the System? The (Im)morality of Urban Squatting After the Land Registration Act 2002" (2007) 7 LS 236.

[8] [1968] 1 QB 107 (Court of Appeals).

[9] *ibid.*, at pp 119–20. But see Michael Goodman's criticism of this view, claiming that the case really demonstrates the need to clearly define the concept of "adverse" within adverse possession rather than to use exceptional cases of this nature as the basis for an argument to abolish adverse possession in its entirety—Goodman, "Adverse Possession of Land: Morality and Motive" (1970) 33(3) MLR 281. See also Goodman, "The Morality of Adverse Possession of Land" (1968) 31(1) MLR 82.

[10] LRC, *Report on the Reform and Modernisation of Land Law and Conveyancing Law* (2004), p 8.

[11] paras 1–06 to 1–12.

[12] Proportionality in Irish constitutional law is particularly well demonstrated in the cases of *Cox v Ireland* [1992] 2 IR 503; *Tuohy v Courtney* [1994] 3 IR 1; *Meadows v Minister for Justice, Equality and Law Reform* [2010] IESC 3.

[13] Whether or not something is "necessary in a democratic society" is conceived of, within the Convention jurisprudence, as the way in which proportionality is analysed taking into account the margin of appreciation: *Olsson v Sweden* (1988) 11 EHRR 259.

Grand Chamber has concluded that there is no violation of the Convention,[14] but the rights-based argument continues to have some instinctive attraction even if—as a matter of law—there is no violation. For many people it is an affront to suggest that just because a landowner does not do anything with her land, or survey its use by others and assert her title within the limitation period, she should run the risk of her title being extinguished. Leaving one's land unused and unattended is, this argument goes, an ownership right in itself. In contrast to that is the argument that land is a limited and valuable resource, and that the law ought not to protect landowners who fail to be vigilant about their own rights when others are making use of that limited land resource: *vigilantibus et non dormientibus, jura subveniunt* ("the law protects the vigilant and not those who rest on their rights"). In addition, there is the utilitarian argument for adverse possession: that a system of this kind, which allows the "regularisation" of the rights of those in long term and active possession, ensures certainty about ownership rights over land once an appropriate period of time has passed (and we will tolerate the uncertainty for that limitation period), and that this certainty ensures that prospective purchasers or mortgagees of land will be willing to transact in relation to the land in question. This economic and market-centric justification for adverse possession is largely focused on the doctrine's role in "quieting titles", which the Law Reform Commission recognised as a primary function of this area of law[15] and the European Court of Human Rights recognised as a justifiable objective.[16] Not only is the quieting of titles important in the interests of market stability and fairness to purchasers, but also for people who have long been in possession of property but where documentary title to the property has been lost or destroyed. Similarly, it is of great benefit to people who remain in possession of the land of a deceased individual but no representation has been taken out on the estate. These are the kinds of situations in which the real social benefit of the doctrine of adverse possession is arguably most evident and, contrary to popular opinion, adverse possession is in fact seldom resorted to by political activists attempting to further a Marxist or otherwise anti-capitalist agenda.

[14–06] In addition, there are some strong theoretical justifications for the continued operation of adverse possession in property law. John Locke's "labour-desert theory", for example, claims that natural entitlements to land arise through productive use of that land; that the mixing of one's labour with possession of land is enough to base a solid claim on.[17] Although Locke's theory was concerned with the assertion of first ownership rights in "unowned" property, it might be applied to adverse possession where property, although owned, is not being used by the landowner.[18] This results from Locke's assertion that property rights ought to be awarded to "the useful labourer

---

[14] *JA Pye (Oxford) Ltd v United Kingdom* (2007) 46 EHRR 1083; see paras 14–60 to 14–61.

[15] *Report on the Reform and Modernisation of Land Law and Conveyancing Law* (2004). See also *Dundee Harbour Trustees v Dougall* (1852) 1 Macq 317 *per* St Leonards LJ at p 321.

[16] *JA Pye (Oxford) Ltd v United Kingdom* (2007) 46 EHRR 1083.

[17] Locke, *Second Treatise on Government* (1996, Oxford, Blackwell).

[18] See Krueckeberg, "The Lessons of John Locke or Hernando de Soto: What if your Dreams Come True?" (2004) 15(1) Housing Policy Debate 1, at p 10.

rather than the sluggard".[19] The requirement in adverse possession of *animus possidendi* inferred from positive action on the possessed land arguably provides the "labour" required by the Lockean perspective. In addition, Margaret Radin's theory of "property as personhood" might be deployed to justify adverse possession, at least where the property is being used as a "home" by the squatter.[20] Radin's theory is derived from Hegel's consequentialist theory of private property, which holds that proper self-development "as a *person*" relies to a great extent on one's interactions with their external environment.[21] According to Hegel, people cannot hope to achieve self-development in this way *unless* private property is possible: unless they can assert their control (through ownership) over parcels of the material world. Building on this, Radin claims that a personhood perspective can provide a mechanism for adjudicating property disputes which, Fox and Cobb claim, might result in the claims of adverse possessors being morally superior to those of the landowners who leave their property empty, unused and unsupervised.[22]

These moral arguments were not considered by the Law Reform Commission in its examination of the continued existence of adverse possession in Irish law. Instead, the Commission concentrated on the practical benefits of the doctrine for a modern conveyancing system. This approach—while understandable—is to some extent to be lamented, especially as adverse possession continues to be a contested and hotly debated area of Irish law. The presentation of these moral perspectives must not, however, be taken to suggest that there are *never* situations in which adverse possession operates in a manner that produces what many people would consider to be an unjust result. Take, for example, *Ewing v Barnett*,[23] an American case in which a wealthy neighbour successfully adversely possessed the property of a much less well-off man; or the practice common for a long time in Hawaii of large landowners using adverse possession to dispossess traditional, small, native Hawaiian landholders through the exploitation of their distrust of courts and of the newly imposed legal system.[24] Cases of this kind notwithstanding, the possibility that adverse possession might result in seemingly unjust results is not a sufficient justification for complete abandonment of the doctrine without sustained consideration of the continuing relevance of the moral justifications for this long-established element of property law. **[14–07]**

II. Limitation Periods

The relevant limitation periods—or periods of time during which the paper owner of the land can reassert title and prevent the squatter from accruing rights—are provided by s 13 of the Statute of Limitations 1957 and differ to some extent depending on the **[14–08]**

[19] Locke, *Second Treatise on Government* (1996, Oxford, Blackwell), p 336.

[20] Radin, "Property as Personhood" (1982) 34 *Stanford Law Review* 957 and Radin, *Reinterpreting Property* (1993, Chicago, University of Chicago Press).

[21] Hegel, *Elements of the Philosophy of Right* (1991, Cambridge, Cambridge University Press), pp 73–102.

[22] Fox-O'Mahony and Cobb, "Living Outside the System? The (Im)morality of Urban Squatting After the Land Registration Act 2002" (2007) 7 LS 236 at 250–252.

[23] 36 US (11 Pet) 41 (1837).

[24] See further Parker, *Native American Estate: The Struggle over Indian and Hawaiian Lands* (1989, Honolulu, University of Hawaii Press); Harding, "Justifying Repatriation of Native American Cultural Property" (1997) 72 *Indiana Law Review* 723.

-NAMA Limitation Period 12 years standard

owner of the land being adversely possessed and on the circumstances of the adverse possession. State authorities must take an action to recover land within 30 years[25] unless that land is foreshore, in which case the limitation period is 60 years[26] (or 40 years from the time the land ceased to be foreshore but was still in the ownership of the State[27]). The Act defines "State authority" in limited terms in s 2 of the Statute of Limitations 1957, which provides:

> "State authority" means any authority being—
> (a) a Minister of State, or
> (b) the Commissioners of Public Works in Ireland, or
> (c) the Irish Land Commission, or
> (d) the Revenue Commissioners, or
> (e) the Attorney General.

This limited definition of "State authority" is important inasmuch as it expressly excludes local government, including county councils, urban district councils and so on. These local government authorities must take an action in relation to land within the same limitation period as private property-owners. In the normal course of events, this limitation period is 12 years.[28] There are a number of variations to the 12-year limitation period. Rent and rent charges in arrears must be recovered within a six-year period,[29] for example; although failure to recover rent within this period of time merely bars a landlord's right to the rent: it has no effect on his title.[30]

[14–09] There are some limited cases in which the commencement of the limitation period is postponed. Section 72(1) of the Statute of Limitations provides that:

> Where, in the case of any action for which a period of limitation is fixed by this Act, the action is for relief from the consequences of mistake, the period of limitation shall not begin to run until the plaintiff has discovered the mistake or could with reasonable diligence have discovered it.

This provision is directed towards mistake in title, in particular. This does not seem to mean that the limitation period is postponed where the landowner was not aware of her rights over the property in question. This is well demonstrated by the case of *Murphy v Murphy*,[31] which concerned farmland that had been bequeathed on trust to the testator's widow and two sons for 10 years, and thereafter between the three of them in defined parts. The defendant, who was one of the testator's sons, managed the land during the 10 years of the trust, which lasted until 1946. In 1949 the plaintiff, who was the defendant's brother, left the land and he later sold his portion to the defendant in 1954. The land on the northern part of the farm belonged to the parties' mother under the terms of the testator's will, but the defendant had farmed it as his own since 1946,

---

25 s 13(1)(a), Statute of Limitations 1957.
26 s 13(1)(b), *ibid.*
27 s 13(1)(c), *ibid.*
28 s 13(2)(a), *ibid.*
29 ss 27–28, *ibid.*
30 s 28, *ibid.*
31 [1980] IR 183.

grazing cattle on it, paying the rates in relation to it and making improvements to it. When the defendant's mother died, she left all of her property to her other son—the plaintiff. The plaintiff claimed that he was entitled to the northern portion of the farm, which, as mentioned above, the defendant had farmed as his own land for an appreciable period of time. The defendant claimed that the mother's title to the northern portion of the farm had been extinguished by his adverse possession of it and that, as a result, she could not have bequeathed it to the plaintiff in her will. The plaintiff's claim was that the defendant could not have been in adverse possession of the land when the owner of it (i.e. the mother) was not aware of her rights in relation to that part of the farm. The Supreme Court held in favour of the defendant and found that he had successfully extinguished his mother's title to the northern part of the farm by means of adverse possession. The fact that the mother did not appear to have been aware of her entitlements to that part of the property was irrelevant: the law will not save one from ignorance of one's entitlement.

The decision in *Murphy* clearly built on earlier precedent supporting the proposition that a mistake by either the landowner or the adverse possessor as to the nature of their rights over the property will be no barrier to a successful claim of adverse possession.[32] Indeed, in his Supreme Court judgment in *Murphy*, Kenny J refers expressly to a quotation from Wylie's *Land Law* to the effect that "adverse possession may take place without either party being aware of it".[33] Furthermore s 14(1) of the Statute of Limitations 1957 clearly provides that knowledge of the landowner of his dispossession is not required; what matters is whether the squatter has successfully completed the requirements of adverse possession. However, where the fact of adverse possession has been concealed *fraudulently* from the landowner the limitation period will not begin to run in favour of the squatter until such time as the landowner discovered the fraud, or could with reasonable diligence have discovered it.[34] This is equally the case where the claim of adverse possession is based on a fraud by the alleged squatter or his agent.[35] **[14–10]**

In spite of the suggestion in *Murphy* that ignorance of either the landowner *or* the adverse possessor would not prevent a successful claim of adverse possession, a recent decision of the High Court casts some doubt on the effect on a claim of adverse possession of the individual in question not knowing that he was squatting. In *Kelleher v Botany Weaving Mills Ltd*,[36] Clark J held—among other things—that a person who believed he was the owner of a piece of land could never be in adverse possession of it. I have written before[37]—as, indeed, have others[38]—that this decision seems to be inconsistent with the Supreme Court's holding in *Murphy* where, as already noted, the Court seemed to treat mistakes by both the paper owner and the adverse possessor as **[14–11]**

---

[32] See, for example, *Palfrey v Palfrey* (1974) 229 EG 1593.

[33] [1980] IR 183, at 202 *citing* Wylie, *Irish Land Law* (1st ed, 1975), p 857.

[34] s 71, Statute of Limitations 1957.

[35] *ibid.*

[36] [2008] IEHC 417.

[37] de Londras, "Land Law, Landlord and Tenant and Conveyancing" in Binchy and Byrne (eds), *Annual Review of Irish Law 2008* (2009, Dublin, Round Hall).

[38] See esp. Woods, "Adverse Possession of Boundary Land—Lessons from Abroad", Paper delivered at COBRA 2010. Available at http://www.rics.org/site/download_feed.aspx?fileID=8055&fileExtension=PDF (last accessed 10 July 2011).

being equally inconsequential. In *Kelleher* the Court also seemed to suggest that if one engaged in particularly strong acts of *animus possidendi* (for example, enclosing and locking the land in question) this might "weigh out" the negative impact of a mistaken belief that one was already the owner of the land. In this respect I find it impossible to disagree with the conclusion drawn by Úna Woods that "Either a belief in ownership is fatal to *animus possidendi* or it is not; it is not logical to say that it can be ignored if the squatter is engaged in very strong acts of possession".[39] Although it is not yet certain, the apparent failure in *Kelleher* to take *Murphy* fully into account at the very least suggests that the *Murphy* position ought to be preferred over that suggested in *Kelleher.*

[14–12] The running of the limitation period will be postponed in cases of disability on the part of the landowner. In this context disability can be said to encompass infancy,[40] persons of unsound mind, and convicts subject to the Forfeiture Act 1870 in relation to whom no administrator has been appointed.[41] The rationale behind the postponement of the limitation period against such landowners is that they are seen not to be in a position to take an action in relation to their land. Where the landowner is under a disability, an action against an adverse possessor can be taken within six years of the end of the disability or the death of the landowner (whichever is first), regardless of whether or not the 12-year period has accrued.[42]

III. Requirements of Adverse Possession

[14–13] Section 14(1) of the Statute of Limitations 1957 provides that a right of action will be said to accrue (and the time will start to run in favour of the adverse possessor) once the requirements for adverse possession are present—discontinuance and dispossession:

> Where the person bringing an action to recover land, or some person through whom he claims, has been in possession thereof and has while entitled thereto been dispossessed or discontinued his possession, the right of action shall be deemed to have accrued on the date of the dispossession or discontinuance.

This requires a number of things on the part of the alleged adverse possessor: first, he must be in possession of the land; secondly, the possession must be adverse inasmuch as it may not be permissive; and thirdly, there must be a discontinuance of the landowner's use and enjoyment of the land *or* a dispossession of the landowner. First, however, the paper owner needs to have discontinued his use and enjoyment of the land. In every case, the analysis will be heavily dependent on the surrounding circumstances—adverse possession is perhaps one of the areas of property law in which surrounding circumstances, such as the nature of the land in question, has the heaviest impact on how the legal principles are applied to a scenario and the outcome of that

[39] *ibid.*, p 7.

[40] In this context an infant can be taken to mean someone under the age of 18 within the meaning of the Age of Majority Act 1985.

[41] s 48, Statute of Limitations 1957.

[42] s 49, *ibid.*

application. This is well illustrated by the case of *Lord Advocate v Lord Lovat* in which Lord O'Hagan held:

> The question whether a defendant who relies on the Statute of Limitations was and is in adverse possession must be considered in every case with reference to the particular circumstances..., the character and value of the property, the suitable and natural mode of using it, the course of conduct which the proprietor might reasonably be expected to follow with due regard for his own interest... all these things greatly bearing as they must under various conditions, are to be taken into account in determining the sufficiency of a possession.[43]

1. Discontinuance

Although s 14(1) of the Statute of Limitations 1957 expressly refers to discontinuance, or that the paper owner must not also possess the land in question with the alleged adverse possessor, this element of the Act has received relatively little attention in the Irish jurisprudence.[44] In addition, the use of the words "dispossessed *or* discontinuance" (emphasis added) arguably suggests that discontinuance on its own would be sufficient to start the limitation period running. Notwithstanding that, it is clear that although any situation of concurrent possession by the landowner and the alleged adverse possessor will prevent an action accruing and the time running in favour of the squatter,[45] there are very few cases in which the matter of discontinuance has been determinative of a claim[46] and discontinuance alone is insufficient to start time running here. **[14–14]**

In practice, in the very rare cases where it has been given attention as a stand-alone element of establishing adverse possession, the requirement of discontinuance has been more or less equated with abandonment of the property by the landowner. Recognising that ownership in legal terms is a complex and powerful concept that includes the capacity to not use land, we have tended in this jurisdiction to hold fast to the notion that even very slight activities by a landowner would be sufficient to refute any suggestion that there has been a discontinuance.[47] So, for example, in *Mulhern v Brady*[48] Carroll J held that there had been no abandonment by the landowner because he had occasionally visited the site, had placed a planning permission notice relating to it in a local newspaper, had engaged an auctioneer to erect a "For Sale" sign on it, and had told the plaintiff that he was trespassing on the only occasion when he saw cattle on the land. However, in that case—as is standard[49]—the focus was on the actions of the alleged adverse possessor rather than on those of the paper owner. Indeed, as Úna Woods has noted, "Although the Irish courts have occasionally identified actions by **[14–15]**

[43] (1880) 5 App Cas 273, 288.

[44] Woods, "The Position of the Owner under the Irish Law on Adverse Possession" (2008) DULJ 298.

[45] *Buckinghamshire County Council v Moran* [1990] Ch 623.

[46] Woods, *art. cit.*

[47] *Buckinghamshire County Council v Moran* [1990] Ch 623.

[48] [2001] IEHC 23.

[49] See, for example, *Doyle v O'Neill & Another*, unreported, High Court, 13 January 1995. Neutral Citation: [1995] IEHC 4; *Browne v. Fahy*, unreported, High Court, Kenny J, 25 October 1975.

the owner which demonstrate that he was not dispossessed, in the majority of cases the owner's actions are viewed more holistically, as one of a number of issues relevant to determining the sufficiency of the squatter's acts of possession".[50] Where the question of the paper owner's actions becomes far more relevant in practice is when we are considering whether or not—once the right of action has accrued (i.e. once adverse possession has begun—the owner has done anything to reassert his possession and title in a manner that stops the time from running in favour of the alleged adverse possessor, and this is a matter upon which we will focus later. It also appears clear from *Feehan v Leamy*[51] that the paper owner of the property would only have to exercise "the rights of ownership which he wished to exercise in respect of the lands" in order to establish that he remained in possession and therefore disestablish any alleged exclusive possession by the adverse possessor. In this case the extent to which the paper owner wanted to exercise rights was to come and lean over the gate of the land in question and survey it; he did not graze cattle on it or anything similar:

> The only use to which he put the land was to visit it on a number of occasions each year when he would park his car and standing on the road or in the gateway look over the hedge or the gate into the same. He was never prevented from doing this by the Second named Defendant. Insofar as the Plaintiff's title is concerned the presumption is that it extends to the centre of the road and so when standing at the gate looking into the lands the Plaintiff was in fact standing on his own lands. This he did from the evidence several times a year throughout the period in which the Second named Defendant [was] claiming to have been in adverse possession. As I understand his evidence, the Plaintiff was exercising all the rights of ownership which he wished to exercise in respect of the lands pending the determination of litigators. I find as a matter of fact that he was not dispossessed.

[14–16] The decision in *Feehan* has been criticised for allowing paper owners to prevent adverse possession on very slender materials[52] (in essence by looking over the hedge), and in some ways those critiques are well founded. Section 20 of the Statute of Limitations 1957 provides *inter alia* that "no person shall be deemed to have been in possession of any land by reason only of having made a formal entry thereon". However, there are, I think, three reasons why we should not be overly concerned about *Feehan*. First of all, as is so often the case, the Court also found that the alleged adverse possessor did not have the *animus possidendi* (or intention) required to establish adverse possession and, as a result, it is somewhat difficult to tell how great a role the finding that the landowner remained in possession played in the case as a whole. Secondly, as Úna Woods has noted,[53] if the squatter is in adverse possession then formal possessory acts (such as entering onto the land) will be insufficient: rather there must be a physical act of repossession (or other action sufficient to reassert one's title). And here lies the crux of the issue in *Feehan*, and one that Woods herself also stresses: the Court finds that there was no adverse possession on the part of the alleged squatter; that he did not have the required *animus possidendi*. If that is so, then this was not a case of the landowner having to exercise possession once the adverse possession has commenced; rather it is a

---

[50] Woods, *art. cit*.

[51] [2000] IEHC 118, para 12 *per* Finnegan J.

[52] Buckley, "Adverse Possession at the Crossroads" (2006) 11(3) CPLJ 59.

[53] Woods, *art. cit*.

case of the landowner continuing to exercise possession and, as a result, of the alleged squatter not being in exclusive possession and the time never starting to run in his favour in the first place. This seems to me the only sensible way to read this element of the *Feehan* decision, but it is true that the broader impact of that element of the decision is not engaged with by Finnegan J in what is really a very short decision (the entire judgment is a mere 15 paragraphs long). Thirdly, and as will be considered below, if *Feehan* does stand for the proposition that, where an adverse possession has commenced, the paper owner can retake possession and stop the limitation period from running against him by a mere formal entry, then it would appear that *Dunne v Iarnród Éireann*[54] returns the law to a position where a more robust action would be needed.

The concept of discontinuance can be particularly difficult in cases where the land itself is of a nature that is of no intrinsic use or enjoyment to the landowner. This is demonstrated by reference to *Dundalk UDC v Conway*.[55] This case concerned a small plot of "wasteland" that was acquired by the Dundalk Urban District Council (UDC), but never put to use by it. The defendant claimed an entitlement to that land by means of adverse possession by her predecessor-in-title. The Court, however, found the nature of the disputed land to be of particular importance and echoed the words of Cotton LJ in *Leigh v Jack*,[56] to the effect that "there can be no discontinuance by absence of use and enjoyment where the land is not capable of use and enjoyment".[57] Blayney J found that the land at issue in Dundalk UDC was not capable of use and enjoyment and could not, therefore, be adversely possessed by means of discontinuance: [14–17]

> I consider that the disputed plot, over the years during which it is alleged that the Plaintiff lost its title, was not capable of use and enjoyment. It was in effect a small plot of wasteland dropping fairly sharply to the river. The value of the plot to the Plaintiff is that it adjoins the bridge which carries the road over the river and it may be required in the event of repairs to the bridge becoming necessary. But as for actual use and enjoyment on a regular basis, I am satisfied that it was not capable of any.

2. Factual Possession

As considered in Chapter 1, possession is the use and enjoyment of land.[58] In order to qualify as an adverse possessor, someone must be in actual physical and continuous possession of the land in question. There were originally a number of cases in which someone would be assumed not to possess land within the meaning of the law of adverse possession because of their relationship to the landowner. In other words, one would be said to possess the land for the landowner (and therefore not as an adverse possessor) merely because of one's relationship to the landowner.[59] Since the Real [14–18]

[54] [2007] IEHC 314.

[55] Unreported, High Court, 15 December 1987.

[56] (1879) 5 Ex D 264.

[57] *ibid.*, at p 274.

[58] paras 1–13 to 1–17.

[59] This arose in particular in cases of possession by a younger brother as against an older brother, between co-owners, and in the case of tenants at sufferance. See also Lyall, *Land Law in Ireland* (2nd ed, 2000, Dublin, Sweet & Maxwell), pp 886–887.

Property Limitation Act 1833, however, presumptions of possession no longer operate to any significant extent and factual possession must be demonstrated. This position was reiterated in s 18(1) of the Statute of Limitations 1957. Demonstrating factual possession will, to a great extent, depend on the nature of the land and the circumstances of the case itself, but the need to do so and the meaning of factual possession as a general matter can be gleaned from the judgment of Slade J in *Powell v McFarlane*:

> Factual possession signifies an appropriate degree of physical control. It must be a single and [exclusive] possession... Thus an owner of land and a person intruding on that land without his consent cannot both be in possession of the land at the same time. The question what acts constitute a sufficient degree of exclusive physical control must depend on the circumstances, in particular the nature of the land and the manner in which land of that nature is commonly used or enjoyed.[60]

3. Adverse to the Paper Owner

[14–19] As a matter of logic, possession alone will not be sufficient to result in the extinguishment of the landowner's title; rather, the possession must be *adverse* to the landowner: it cannot be possession as a result of permission or agency.[61] Whether or not someone's possession is adverse will be entirely dependent on the particular circumstances of the case,[62] but there are a number of general principles that can be laid down. A person who uses the land of another in a manner that suggests he acknowledges the title of the landowner (for example, by means of asking permission to use the land or offering to buy the land from the landowner) cannot be said to be in adverse possession.[63] In addition, a receiver or other agent of the landowner cannot be said to be in adverse possession of the property because they possess it on behalf of the principal (i.e. the landowner).[64] As Slade LJ explained in *Buckinghamshire County Council v Moran*:

> Possession is never "adverse" within the meaning of the 1980 Act if it is enjoyed under a lawful title. If, therefore, a person occupies or uses land by licence of the owner with the paper title and his licence has not been duly determined, he cannot be treated as having been in'adverse possession' as against the owner of the paper title.[65]

But what of a situation where one asks another whether they own the land, and that other expresses ambivalence about whether they are the paper owner or not even though—as a matter of fact—he is the paper owner? Can one, in those cases, then enjoy a possession that is adverse to the rights of the owner?

---

[60] (1970) 38 P & CR 452, 470–471.

[61] *Hughes v Griffin* [1969] 1 WLR 23; *Moses v Lovegrove* [1952] 2 QB 533; *Buckinghamshire County Council v Moran* [1990] Ch 623.

[62] *Murphy v Murphy* [1980] IR 183; *Treloar v Nute* [1976] 1 WLR 1295; *The Lord Advocate v Lord Lovat* (1880) 5 App Cas 273; *Bula Ltd v Crowley* [2003] 2 ILRM 401.

[63] *Doyle, Administratrix ad Litem of James Doyle deceased v O'Neill* [1995] IEHC 4.

[64] *Bula Ltd v Crowley* [2003] 2 ILRM 401.

[65] [1990] Ch 623, 636.

This point arises for consideration in *Battelle v Pinemeadow Ltd.*[66] In this case, Battelle bought land in August 1978 that was adjoined at the rear boundary by a piece of land running down to a river. This piece of land was overrun with rats and weeds and Battelle contacted the defendant's predecessors-in-title to ascertain who owned it. The predecessors-in-title were, in fact, the registered owners of the plot of land, but they told the plaintiff that they were unsure about whether it was theirs and were not interested in it in any case because it was of no commercial use to them. On hearing this, Battelle set about clearing the land, incorporating it into his garden, constructing a fence around it, installing water features in it, constructing three walkways within the area and planting hundreds of shrubs and flowers there. When Pinemeadow Ltd became the owners of the land in August 1999, they entered it with machinery and demolished it. Battelle claimed an entitlement to the land as a result of adverse possession, but Pinemeadow Ltd claimed that the plaintiff had used the land with the permission of their predecessors-in-title and his possession was not adverse. Finnegan J held that Battelle had successfully adversely possessed the land and that an occupier cannot be said to be on property with the permission of the owner where the owner is unaware of his right to that property and consequently tells the occupier that he does not care who occupies it. **[14–20]**

4. With Animus Possidendi

The development of the case law interpreting the statutory provisions for adverse possession has been particularly interesting inasmuch as it appears that the courts have made it progressively more difficult for adverse possessors to succeed against landowners. This is particularly evident in the development of the requirement of *animus possidendi* (or intention to possess the land to the exclusion of all others), which appears to have emerged as a requirement in the early 1900s and has caused particular difficulties in cases where the landowner has no immediate use for the land, but intends to use it in a particular way in the future. In every case where someone is attempting to establish adverse possession they *must* establish that they had the required *animus possidendi* and this is done by means of looking at the acts of possession and asking whether, taking all the circumstances into account, those acts are sufficient for us to infer from them that the squatter had the required intention. **[14–21]**

The development of the concept of *animus possidendi* means that it is now well-established that mere possession is not sufficient to establish adverse possession: acts showing *animus possidendi* are required. In the words of Kenny J in *Murphy v Murphy*: **[14–22]**

> Adverse possession means possession of the land which is inconsistent with the title of the true owner: this inconsistency necessarily involves an intention to exclude the true owner, and all other persons, from enjoyment of the estate or interest which is being acquired.[67]

[66] [2002] IEHC 120.

[67] *Murphy v Murphy* [1980] IR 183.

Similarly, in *JA Pye (Oxford) Ltd v Graham* Lord Browne-Wilkinson held that:

> there are two elements necessary for legal possession: (1) a sufficient degree of physical custody and control ("factual possession"); (2) an intention to exercise such custody and control on one's own behalf and for one's own benefit ("intention to possess"). What is crucial is to understand that, without the requisite intention, in law there can be no possession.[68]

[14–23] This, then, is the mental element required for any claim of adverse possession to succeed and it must be shown *in addition to* factual possession, which is adverse for the required period of time. It is not until there is an exclusive factual, adverse possession with *animus possidendi* that the time will start to run in favour of the alleged adverse possessor. *Animus possidendi* can be said to be an intention to adversely possess the land or, to put it in clearer terms, an intention to possess the land to the exclusion of all others, including its paper owner.[69] This concept was given a more elaborate definition by Slade J in *Powell v McFarlane*[70]:

> What is really meant, in my judgment, is that the *animus possidendi* involves the intention, in one's own name and on one's own behalf, to exclude the world at large, including the owner with the paper title if he be not himself the possessor, so far as is reasonably practicable and so far as the processes of the law will allow.

[14–24] *Animus possidendi* is assumed where someone actually owns the land in question or acts for the owner (such as an agent, as considered above). However, where an adverse possessor is claiming an entitlement to the land, "the courts will... require clear and affirmative evidence that the trespasser, claiming that he has acquired possession, not only had the requisite intention to possess, but made such intention clear to the world".[71] Whether or not any particular actions will be sufficient to infer an *animus possidendi* will depend on the circumstances of the case and on the nature of the land in question.[72] In *Murphy v Murphy*,[73] for example, farming the northern part of the land was sufficient to show *animus possidendi*, whereas raising pheasants for the purposes of hunting on the land of another was said to be insufficient in the case of *Hickson v Boylan*.[74] Whether or not a claimant has factual possession with the accompanying

Contrast & Compare

[68] [2003] 1 AC 419, 435.

[69] *Littledale v Liverpool College* [1900] 1 Ch 19 *per* Lindley MR at p 23. There is no evidence of *animus possidendi* having been required in English law before that case and, according to Radley-Gardner, this concept was imported from German law in order to better protect the rights of landowners against adverse possession—Radley-Gardner, "Civilised Squatting" (2005) 25 OJLS 727. The requirement of *animus possidendi* is widely regarded as a judge-made doctrine designed to make it more difficult for possessors of land to make successful adverse possession claims. See also Rhys, "Adverse Possession, Human Rights and Judicial Heresy" (2002) 66 Conv 470; O'Leary, "Adverse Possession at the Dawn of the Twenty-First Century" (2004) 12 ISLR.

[70] (1977) 38 P&CR 452.

[71] *ibid.*

[72] *Wallis' Cayton Bay Holiday Camp Ltd v Shell-Mex and BP Ltd* [1974] 3 All ER 575.

[73] [1980] IR 183.

[74] [1993] IEHC 1.

animus possidendi will be considered by reference to factors such as "the character and value of the property, the suitable and natural mode of using it [and] the course of conduct which the proprietor might reasonably be expected to follow with a due regard to his own interests".[75] The intensity of an alleged adverse possessor's use of the disputed land might also be relevant to a court's consideration of factual possession. Thus in *Egan v Greene*,[76] for example, it was held that the occasional grazing of cattle on the land without objection by the landowner was not sufficient to establish adverse possession, but the cutting of turf was. Although it was held in *Murphy v Murphy* that one can be found to have *animus possidendi* even when one is not aware that the land one is using belongs to another,[77] we have already seen how *Kelleher v Botany Weaving Mills*[78] casts some doubt on that proposition of law, albeit *Murphy* is still the stronger authority.

The general test for *animus possidendi* is essentially to ask whether the alleged adverse possessor's "possession [was] inconsistent with and in denial of the [owner's] rights as legal owner of the land".[79] In spite of this general test, the sufficiency of acts to show *animus possidendi* has been particularly controversial in the context of land for which the owner has no present purpose, but which was acquired for a particular purpose in the future (i.e. where the paper owner has a future intended use for the property). If, for example, John bought an acre of land for the purpose of building a factory on it in the future, would an alleged adverse possessor need to do something inconsistent with the intended use of the land in the future (i.e. inconsistent with building a factory there) in order to demonstrate the required *animus possidendi*? This question has long been a controversial one and remains so, to some extent, today. [14–25]

The original position was laid down in *Leigh v Jack*.[80] In 1854 Leigh sold a plot of land to Jack, on which Jack built a factory. This land was located to the south of a piece of land retained by Leigh, on which he intended to build a road. Since 1854 Jack stored materials on Leigh's land in a manner that made it impassable, except by foot. In 1865 Jack fenced off some of Leigh's land and, in 1872, he fenced in the ends of the intended street. When Leigh attempted to retake possession of the land Jack claimed that he had acquired that property by means of adverse possession. The Court held, however, that Jack had failed to show the relevant and required *animus possidendi*. According to this decision, acts of user that are committed on land but which *do not interfere with and are consistent with* the owner's future intended use of the property do not amount to "dispossession" for lack of *animus possidendi*. So Branwell LJ held: [14–26]

> I do not think that there was any dispossession of the plaintiff by the acts of the defendant: acts of user are not enough to take the soil out of the plaintiff and her

[75] *The Lord Advocate v Lord Lovat* (1880) 5 App Cas 273 *per* O'Hagan LJ.

[76] Unreported, High Court, 12 November 1999.

[77] See *Murphy v Murphy* [1980] IR 183.

[78] [2008] IEHC 417.

[79] *Murphy v Murphy* [1980] IR 183, *per* Kenny J; cited with approval in *Keelgrove Property Ltd v Shelbourne Development Ltd* [2005] IEHC 238.

[80] (1879) 5 Ex D 264.

> predecessors in title and to vest it in the defendant; in order to defeat a title by dispossessing the former owner, acts must be done which are inconsistent with his enjoyment of the soil for the purposes for which he intended to use it...[81]

[14–27] This was and remains a hotly contested proposition, for one might imagine that if adverse possession requires both a physical element (the exclusive, factual and adverse possession of the land) and a mental element (the intention to possess that land to the exclusion of all others, including the paper owner) on the part of the alleged adverse possessor, then the mere existence of a future intended use for the land on the part of the paper owner should be essentially irrelevant to the requirements of establishing adverse possession. Of course, when one looks at the facts of the case in *Leigh* the outcome (that there was no adverse possession) would have been possible and, indeed, justifiable on the basis that, regardless of future intended use, storing scrap metal on another's land would not usually be sufficient to establish *animus possidendi* but, that notwithstanding, *Leigh* has become synonymous with this confounding proposition about one having to do something "more" to establish *animus possidendi* in cases of this nature. Not alone did *Leigh* insert this proposition into the law of adverse possession with which we in Ireland continue to grapple, but it also led to a notion in English law that people who possessed land for which the paper owner had a future intended use without doing something inconsistent therewith would be treated as though they had the implied consent of the paper owner. In other words, as if they were holding an implied licence to possess the land.[82] That "implied licence" idea was, however, abolished by statute in s 8(4) of the Limitation Act 1980.

[14–28] The Court of Appeal considered *Leigh* and its progeny in the later case of *Buckinghamshire County Council v Moran*.[83] In 1955 Buckinghamshire County Council acquired a plot of land that it intended to use for the purposes of a road diversion in the future, but which it did not put to any immediate use. Moran's predecessor-in-title began to maintain the land in 1967 by means of mowing the grass, trimming the hedges, storing a horse-box on it, giving permission for an electricity cable to be laid across it and using the land for his own purposes. In 1971 Moran bought a lock and chain to fasten the gate into the Council's land, resulting in the only unimpeded access to the land being through his garden. Following some correspondence between the parties, the Council brought an action to recover possession in 1985, claiming that *Leigh v Jack* precluded a successful action for adverse possession by the defendant. According to the Council, Moran's actions had not interfered with nor been inconsistent with its intended use of the property for the purposes of the road diversion and, as a result, he could not be said to have the required *animus possidendi*. The Court of Appeal held that the requirement of *animus possidendi* could be fulfilled by acts that show an intention to possess to the exclusion of all others and that the fact that the owner had plans for the future use of the land was irrelevant. It was clear in this case that Moran had acquired full and exclusive physical control of the land because he had secured its complete enclosure (by means of the chain and lock) and annexation to his

---

[81] *ibid.*, at 273.
[82] *Wallis's Cayton Bay Holiday Camp Ltd v Shell-Mex and BP Ltd* [1975] QB 94.
[83] [1990] Ch 623.

property by forcing access through his garden. These actions amounted to an unequivocal demonstration of Moran's intention to possess the land to the exclusion of all others and, having continued for more than 12 years, were sufficient to establish a successful claim of adverse possession. In that case Slade LJ expressed discomfort not only with *Leigh* itself but also with the "implied licence" proposition that had grown out of it.

That discomfort came to a head in the House of Lords decision in *JA Pye (Oxford) Ltd v Graham* where Browne-Wilkinson LJ was scathing in his analysis of Leigh, describing its proposition—and the implied consent idea that grew from it—in strongly condemnatory terms. He held: [14–29]

> The suggestion that the sufficiency of the possession can depend on the intention not of the squatter but of the true owner is heretical and wrong... Bramwell LJ's heresy led directly to the heresy in the *Wallis's Cayton Bay* line of cases to which I have referred, which heresy was abolished by statute. It has been suggested that the heresy of Bramwell LJ survived this statutory reversal but in the *Moran* case the Court of Appeal rightly held that however one formulated the proposition of Bramwell LJ as a proposition of law it was wrong. The highest it can be put is that, if the squatter is aware of a special purpose for which the paper owner uses or intends to use the land and the use made by the squatter does not conflict with that use, that may provide some support for a finding as a question of fact that the squatter had no intention to possess the land in the ordinary sense but only an intention to occupy it until needed by the paper owner. For myself I think there will be few occasions in which such inference could be properly drawn in cases where the true owner has been physically excluded from the land. But it remains a possible, if improbable, inference in some cases.[84]

The Irish position on *Leigh* is arguably still not clear. It was applied in the case of *Cork Corporation v Lynch*.[85] Cork Corporation acquired a plot of land in 1965 that it intended to incorporate into the road as part of a road-widening scheme. This plot of land was adjoined by Lynch's garage business and Lynch had been in the habit of using that land to dump crashed cars there. In or around 1960—before the Corporation had acquired it—Lynch began to use the rest of that plot of land for parking cars and, after some time, he laid chippings on the plot and had tarmacadam laid on the remainder. In 1973 or 1974 Lynch placed a chain-link fence around the plot and a wire between the plot and his garage. When it came time to carry out the road-widening, Lynch claimed that he was entitled to the plot of land by means of adverse possession. The High Court held in favour of Cork Corporation, finding that no right of action had accrued to the plaintiffs as they had not been dispossessed. Cork Corporation had acquired that land for a specific purpose and the actions of the defendants were not inconsistent with the purpose for which the land had been purchased. As a result, the defendant had failed to satisfy the test laid down in *Leigh v Jack* and had not shown the required *animus possidendi*. [14–30]

[84] [2003] 1 AC 419, 438.

[85] [1995] 2 ILRM 598 *decided* 26 July 1985.

[14–31] Although decided on 26 July 1985, *Lynch* was not reported in the Irish Law Reports Monthly until 1995. This resulted in some relatively recent confusion as to its providence, particularly in light of the fact that it had arguably not survived Barron J's convincing and well-constructed judgment in *Durack (Séamus) Manufacturing Ltd v Considine.*[86] Considine was a farmer whose land adjoined other piece land on which there were two sheds. The land and sheds were originally owned by his sister, who had leased them to him for the purposes of grazing cattle and bottling milk for sale. Considine's sister sold that land to the plaintiffs, who intended to use it for the purposes of building a factory thereon. The sister reserved the right to use the sheds to her brother, Considine, but following the sale Considine continued to use all of the land as before, including for the grazing of cattle. He also erected a post-and-wire fence over a portion of the boundary of the land to prevent his cattle from straying onto the plaintiff's adjoining premises. From the time the defendant put up this fence (which amounted to more than 12 years from the proceedings in this case), he had exclusive access to that property. When the sister died, the plaintiff took an action to recover the land and the defendant claimed that he was entitled to the property by means of adverse possession. According to Durak Manufacturing, however, the principle in *Leigh v Jack* ought to apply and, because Considine had not done acts inconsistent with building a factory on the land, he should be found to be lacking the required *animus possidendi*.

[14–32] Barron J in the High Court held that anyone claiming adverse possession must establish *animus possidendi* on his part: the future intended use of the land by the owner does not affect the extent of this obligation. Rather, any acts that sufficiently show *animus possidendi* in the circumstances of the case would be adequate. In this sense Barron J appears to have greatly minimised the impact of the principle in *Leigh v Jack* in Irish law. This does not mean that the intention of the landowner is entirely irrelevant however, rather, Barron J found that it might have an impact on the state of mind of the adverse possessor (which is the only state of mind with which the Statute of Limitations is concerned). In this context Barron J held that where the claimant is aware that the owner is not using the land at the time but that he has an intended purpose for it in the future, this is a factor to be taken into account in assessing *animus possidendi*. This holding is perfectly sensible (and is, indeed, quite similar to Brown-Wilkinson LJ's conclusion in *JA Pye*)[87]: where someone knows that the landowner intends to do something with the property in the future, this may result in an intention to hold the land only in the interim period and such an intention is clearly not equivalent to *animus possidendi*. The value in Barron J's judgment in this case is that it dismisses any misconception that a future intended use of the land by the landowner automatically requires a certain action by the alleged adverse possessor, rather, it may impact on his state of mind and is therefore a factor to be taken into account, particularly where the adverse possessor was aware of this future intended use.

[14–33] Following *Durack* the Irish law was in a state of semi-disarray, with two seemingly conflicting High Court decisions and *Lynch* having been reported some 10 years after being decided, resulting in occasional confusion as to whether *Durack* or *Lynch* ought

[86] [1987] IR 677.

[87] *JA Pye (Oxford) Ltd v Graham* [2003] 1 AC 419.

to be relied on in argument. This sense of confusion was merely compounded by *Dundalk Urban District Council v John Conway*,[88] in which *Leigh* seemed to be applied. Then came the decision in *Feehan v Leamy*.[89] The defendants in this case claimed that they went into occupation of the disputed lands in Co. Tipperary in 1981 and remained in exclusive possession thereof for a period in excess of 12 years. The defendant claimed that he had kept between 20 and 30 cattle on the lands between 1981 and 1982, and again on an intermittent basis between 1982 and 1985. From 1985 he spread manure on the lands and kept sheep and cattle there on a continuous and exclusive basis. He also installed a water system and an electric fence on the land and, to all intents and purposes, treated those lands as his own, including declaring himself the owner of those lands in an application for area aid to the Department of Agriculture in the late 1980s or early 1990s. This state of affairs continued until objections were raised on behalf of the plaintiff in 1997 and 1998. At that stage a contractor had gone to fence the lands on behalf of the plaintiff and, on being refused the opportunity to so by the defendant, had contacted the gardaí. On their arrival the defendant had stated that the lands belonged to "someone in America", thereby showing a clear acknowledgment that the lands were not rightfully his. The plaintiff claimed that he had acquired the lands in 1978 and had visited them six times per year until the mid 1990s, when he had had an accident. According to the plaintiff, he was threatened by the defendant on every occasion that he visited and on every visit he observed the lands to be neglected, unused and devoid of any animals.

The core questions that arose in the case were whether or not the alleged adverse possessor had done enough to demonstrate *animus possidendi*, and whether or not the paper owner had done enough to assert his title and exercise possession over the course of the time period in question. We have already dealt with the second of these questions, and so we focus here on the first. The Court held that Feehan had not established the necessary *animus possidendi*, citing *Leigh v Jack*. The Court did not, however, claim that *Leigh v Jack* is authority for the general proposition that where the paper owner has a future intended use for the land one is required to do something inconsistent therewith in order to establish *animus possidendi*: in that respect, Finnegan J held, "the comments in *Leigh v Jack* have been misunderstood" (internal reference omitted).[90] Rather Finnegan J held that based on the circumstances of the case, including the pending litigation between the parties, there was no intention to possess the land to the exclusion of all others including the paper owner. In other words, Finnegan J undid the perception that an adverse possessor of land for which the owner has a future intended use must do something inconsistent with that intended use in order to establish *animus possidendi*. Rather, the adverse possessor must carry out acts from which an intention to exclude all others, including the owner, can be inferred with reference to the character of the property, its natural and suitable usage, and the course of conduct that an owner might reasonably be expected to follow in due regard for his own interest. In this case the defendant had failed to show *animus possidendi* because, in particular, of his response to questions from the gardaí, at which stage he said that the land belonged to someone who lived in America. This was notwithstanding the fact [14–34]

[88] Unreported, High Court, 15 December 1987.
[89] [2000] IEHC 118.
[90] [2000] IEHC 118, para 12.

that the "only use to which [the plaintiff] put the land was to visit it on a number of occasions each year when he would park his car and, standing on the roadway or in the gateway, look over the hedge or gate into the same".[91]

[14–35] Even after the decision in *Feehan*, confusion reigns as to status of *Leigh* in this jurisdiction. In *Keelgrove Property Ltd v Shelbourne Development Ltd*,[92] Gilligan J refers to *Leigh v Jack* without questioning the proposition for which it stands or referring to its interpretation in *Feehan v Leamy*. In contrast, in *Dunne v Iarnród Éireann*[93] Clarke J held that he preferred "the reasoning of Barron J in *Durack Manufacturing* in which he accepted that factors such as the future intended use of the property by the party with paper title might be a factor in determining whether the necessary intention was present in the party claiming adverse possession but was not otherwise a matter properly taken into account",[94] again without referring to *Feehan*. In spite of this, the most recent Practice Direction on adverse possession from the Property Registration Authority suggests that *Leigh v Jack* continues to apply in its original understanding in this jurisdiction.[95] In the PRA's Practice Direction—which is merely guidance to how the PRA applies the law to claims for adverse possession and not a definitive statement of the law itself—it is said that *Leigh* was applied in *Feehan*. This is certainly true, but as I argued above there appears to have been an attempt by Finnegan J in that case to rehabilitate *Leigh* in some senses; in other words to suggest that what it should really be taken to mean is that where the alleged adverse possessor knows of the future intended use of the land and intends only to use it in the interim period (i.e. does not have *animus possidendi*) there is no adverse possession and that it was in *this* sense that *Leigh* was being applied. This seems to me, at least, to line up well with what Browne-Wilkinson LJ held in *JA Pye* and which we considered above. By means of reminder, his Lordship held:

> The highest it can be put is that, if the squatter is aware of a special purpose for which the paper owner uses or intends to use the land and the use made by the squatter does not conflict with that use, that may provide some support for a finding as a question of fact that the squatter had no intention to possess the land in the ordinary sense but only an intention to occupy it until needed by the paper owner.[96]

Proceeding in the cautious manner that we ought, perhaps, to expect from an agency that is tasked with applying the law rather than interpreting it in the classical sense, the Property Registration Authority's practice direction says:

> Despite the view expressed in *Durack v Considine*, May 1987, IR 677, that it may be too broadly stated, the principle outlined in *Leigh v Jack* still applies in this jurisdiction.

---

91 *Per* Finnegan J.
92 [2005] IEHC 238; [2007] 3 IR 1.
93 [2007] IEHC 314.
94 *ibid.*, para 4.7.
95 *Adverse Possession—Title by Adverse Possession to Registered Land* (7 December 2009), para 2.5.
96 [2003] 1 AC 419, 438.

> Accordingly in circumstances where it has been established that the owner, while having no present use for the land, has a specific purpose in mind for its use in the future and if the ousted owner demonstrates that the use by the squatter or claimant is not inconsistent with their ultimate intention in respect of the property, registration is to be refused. Such issue is properly a matter for the court and not the Land Registry.[97]

That this is properly a matter for determination by the court is beyond question, and it is to be hoped that such determination comes swiftly and rejects the traditional understanding of *Leigh v Jack* for the heresy that Lord Browne-Wilkinson so rightly said it is.[98] Of course, this clarification could also be provided by statute, which course of action has been advised by the Law Reform Commission.[99]

5. For the Required Period of Time

The final requirement of any successful claim for adverse possession is to establish that one has adversely possessed the property for the required period of time *from the point at which a cause of action arose*, i.e. from the point at which there was a confluence of discontinuance, factual exclusive possession, that is adverse to the paper owner and accompanied by *animus possidendi*. It is only then that the limitation period begins to run against the paper owner. That limitation period is generally 12 years,[100] or 30 years[101] where the land is owned by a State authority as defined by s 2 of the Statute of Limitations 1957. [14–36]

IV. Stopping Adverse Possession

A landowner who discovers adverse possession will usually want to stop it: in other words, to stop the time from running in favour of the adverse possessor. This raises the important question of how one is to stop the time running. In general we say that the landowner must either commence proceedings or retake possession. Commencing proceedings within the limitation period clearly stops the time from accruing in favour of the adverse possessor: that is, after all, the purpose of limitation periods. Retaking possession is rather more complex a notion for it causes us to consider what kinds of acts of possession will be sufficient to undo the adverse possession of a squatter: i.e. How strong an assertion of possession must it be? [14–37]

We have already seen that for some at least the case of *Feehan v Leamy*[102] suggests that retaking possession can be done by very slight actions indeed; in this case, you will recall, much focus was placed on the paper owner's habit of leaning over the fence and observing his land. I argued above that this element of *Feehan* might be better [14–38]

---

[97] *Adverse Possession—Title by Adverse Possession to Registered Land* (7 December 2009), para 2.5.

[98] *JA Pye (Oxford) Ltd v Graham* [2003] 1 AC 419, 438.

[99] *Report on Land Law and Conveyancing Law (1): General Proposals* (1989), pp 26–7; LRC, *Consultation Paper on the Reform and Modernisation of Land Law and Conveyancing Law* (2004), p 165.

[100] s 13(2)(a), Statute of Limitations 1957.

[101] s 13(1)(a), *ibid.*

[102] [2000] IEHC 118, para 12 *per* Finnegan J; see paras 14–15 to 14–17 above.

understood within the context that the alleged squatter had never actually had the required *animus possidendi* to start the time running in his favour, but even if I am wrong in that assessment other decisions of the High Court strongly reinforce the long-standing proposition that factual repossession is required to stop the adverse possession. In *Mulhern v Brady*,[103] for example, the alleged adverse possessor failed in his claim on the basis that the landowner had not only visited the land on a regular basis but had also asked the claimant to remove his cattle and had his auctioneer visit the site on a more regular basis than he himself did. These actions together could constitute repossession. In *Dunne v Iarnród Éireann*[104] a dispute arose as to the ownership of a triangular piece of land near Clondalkin Station House, upon which Dunne had originally grazed some horses and later erected some structures. Considering the extent to which a paper owner has to deal with land in order to show there is no dispossession or there has been a repossession, Clarke J held that "minimal acts of possession by the owner of the paper title will be sufficient to establish that he was not, at least at the relevant time of those acts, dispossessed... Provided that there are any acts of possession by the owner, then adverse possession cannot run at the relevant time".[105] This does not mean, however, that any action at all by the owner in relation to a piece of land—no matter how slight—would be enough to stop time running. So, in *Dunne* a caretaker for the defendant entering the land a few times a year was not sufficient, but using some of the land to carry out modernisations to the Clondalkin Train Station in the early 1990s and repairing boundary fences in 2001 were.

[14–39] A question arises as to whether a paper owner must take physical action to retake possession: would a letter asserting title be sufficient to stop the time from running in favour of the adverse possessor? This question was briefly considered in *Mahon v O'Reilly*.[106] In that case the paper owner had written letters asserting title over the land in question; in other words, the letters did not demand that the squatters would remove themselves from the property but rather stated the paper owner's title. In considering very briefly whether this would stop the time running in favour of the adverse possessor (who denied receipt of said letters), Dunne J held "Even if those letters had been received by the occupiers for the time being of the premises, those letters are not of themselves sufficient to prevent the statute of limitations from running against the O'Reillys". In addition to this, the decision in *Mt Carmel Ltd v Peter Thurlow Ltd* provides that even a letter demanding possession would not be sufficient to stop the clock from running in favour of the squatter and against the paper owner.[107] Laura Farrell has correctly identified the only remaining area of uncertainty when it comes to letters: the impact (if any) of letters that acknowledge the squatter.[108] Do these letters comprise consent to the possession, which makes that possession no longer adverse or undoes *animus possidendi*? This has been considered to some extent in the UK, where

[103] [2001] IEHC 23.
[104] [2007] IEHC 314
[105] *ibid.*, para 4.9.
[106] [2010] IEHC 103.
[107] [1988] 1 WLR 1078
[108] Farrell, "Adverse Possession: Will Letters Stop the Time Running?" (2010) 15 CPLJ 88.

there is clear authority for the proposition that the taking[109] "or continuation"[110] of possession with the actual consent of the paper owner can not constitute adverse possession. This does not, in my view, undermine the idea that the intention of the paper owner ought not to impact on whether or not the squatter has the required *animus possidendi*; rather it seems to me that written consent to possess the land is relevant to the physical element of having *adverse* possession.[111] This is not to suggest that there would be some risk to letters consenting to possession: anything done over and beyond the consent given could constitute acts of adverse possession and surveillance would be required.[112]

Acknowledgment of the landowner's title will also stop the limitation period from running, provided it is signed and done in writing.[113] The Statute of Limitations 1957 does not specify what form of writing is required, therefore it has been held that this can be inferred from the actions of the adverse possessor in the context of the prevailing circumstances.[114] A payment or part-payment to the landowner during the limitation period will also result in the adverse possessor having to "start again" because such payment or part-payment is interpreted as an acknowledgment of the landowner's superior title.[115] In both of these cases the limitation period will be "refreshed", although if the required period of adverse possession has already been fulfilled then an acknowledgment of title or offer of payment will not undo the adverse possession; at that point the paper owner's title will already have been extinguished, for that is the effect of a successful period of adverse possession. [14–40]

V. The Effect of Adverse Possession of Freehold Land

If someone does successfully establish adverse possession for the required period of time, what happens to the paper owner's entitlement and what kind of entitlement does the squatter then have? Prior to the introduction of the Real Property Limitation Act 1833, a landowner who failed to take action against a squatter within the limitation period continued to hold title over the land, even though his right to take a legal action against the squatter had expired; in other words, he had title without the capacity to take an action to enforce that title. This meant that the squatter who had fulfilled the requirements of adverse possession had only a precarious (and therefore unattractive) title to alienate on the open market. Section 2 of the Real Property Limitation Act 1833 provided that the title of the landowner was extinguished by the successful adverse possession of the squatter and, as a result, the landowner could no longer enter the property once the limitation period has expired.[116] This concept of "extinguishment of title" is reiterated in s 24 of the Statute of Limitations 1957. While it is now clear that [14–41]

[109] *Ramnarace v Lutchman* [2001] 1 WLR 1651.

[110] *JA Pye (Oxford) Ltd v Graham* [2002] 3 WLR 221, 233.

[111] Farrell (*art. cit.*) suggests that a letter of this kind would undo *animus possidendi* and, while this may be the case, my view is that undoing the adverse nature of the possession as a matter of fact is the more significant impact of such letters.

[112] *JA Pye (Oxford) Ltd v Graham* [2002] 3 WLR 221.

[113] ss 50–60, Statute of Limitations 1957.

[114] *Hobson v Burns* (1850) 13 IR LR 286; *Re Mitchell's Estate* [1943] IR 74.

[115] ss 61–70, Statute of Limitations 1957.

[116] *Incorporated Society for Protestant Schools v Richards* (1841) 1 Dru & War 258.

successful adverse possession extinguishes the landowner's title, the character of the rights acquired by the squatter as a result of this remains the subject of some controversy.

[14–42] The original position was to hold that the squatter received an interest in the land by means of the adverse possession, and that the interest received was that to which the dispossessed landowner was originally entitled, i.e. that the parliamentary conveyance operated, or that the paper owner's title had been conveyed to the squatter by the operation of the statute.[117] Although this was a tidy approach, inasmuch as one could easily quantify the estate held by the successful adverse possessor, it of course did not really sit well with the basic principle that the paper owner's title had been extinguished: How could an extinguished (or, in essence, destroyed) title ever be conveyed to another? Indeed, it was this logical inconsistency that really signalled the end of the "parliamentary conveyance" in English law, when Lord Esher MR held in *Tichborne v Weir* that "The effect of the statute is not that the right of one person is conveyed to another, but that the right is extinguished and destroyed".[118] In the context of freehold land it now seems clear that the successful adverse possessor acquires a fee simple subject to all superior interests and subject to all third-party interests as he can never qualify as the bona fide purchaser for value without notice.[119] In the words of the Law Reform Commission, "there is no doubt that, whatever may be the effect of the Limitation Acts, the squatter acquires a title which is as good as a conveyance of the freehold".[120]

[14–43] The Law Reform Commission has recommended that the parliamentary conveyance ought to be reinstated and placed on a statutory footing for freehold land. In essence this proposal flows very much from their recommendation—considered below—that the parliamentary conveyance would be reinstated in relation to leasehold land and a concern that (as much as possible) adverse possession of both freehold and leasehold land should operate in the same way.[121] This proposal appears to be perfectly sensible given the protections in place for the holders of superior title over freehold land (because adverse possessors are subject to all superior interests) and because s 49 of the Registration of Title Act 1964 applies the Statute of Limitations 1957 to registered land in a manner that does not suggest that its operation ought to differ in any way from its operation in relation to unregistered land. These proposed changes were not, however, implemented in the Land and Conveyancing Law Reform Act 2009, although were contained in the proposed draft bill prepared by the Law Reform Commission itself.[122]

---

[117] See, for example, *Doe d Jukes v Summer* (184) 14 M & W 39; *Rankin v McMurty* (1889) 24 L IR 290; *Kennedy v Woods* (1868) IR 2 CL.

[118] (1892) 67 LT 735, 737.

[119] *Griffin v Bleithin* [1999] 2 ILRM 182.

[120] LRC, *Report on the Acquisition of Title by Adverse Possession* (2002), p 4.

[121] *ibid.*, p 11.

[122] This is appended to the LRC, *Report on the Reform and Modernisation of Land Law and Conveyancing Law* (2005); see pp 322–339 for the originally proposed changes to adverse possession.

VI. Successive Squatters

There is no requirement that the same person must be in adverse possession for the entirety of the limitation period; s 18 of the Statute of Limitations 1957 merely requires that the land would be adversely possessed for the prescribed period of time. The matter of "successive squatters" was considered in *Mount Carmel Investments Ltd v Peter Thurlow Ltd.*[123] The plaintiff in this case was the registered owner of a garage and residential accommodation above it. The plaintiff stopped taking any active interest in the property in 1970, by which stage it had been unoccupied for a number of years. At that time R took possession of the property; in 1971 he proceeded to forge a lease and an assignment of a lease to a company of which he was a director. In 1974 he allowed the defendants in this case to take possession of the property and he fled to the United States to avoid proceedings for forgery. Following a series of communications and a transaction between the plaintiffs and the initial adverse possessor, the Court of Appeal was called upon to determine whether the defendants in this case had successfully adversely possessed the property. The Court held that the mere assertion of entitlement to possession in the plaintiff's letter of January 1981 was not sufficient to stop the limitation period from running. In relation to the succession of squatters the Court held that where a squatter dispossesses another squatter and the first squatter abandons his claim to possession, the second squatter can obtain title to the land by 12 years' adverse possession *by both squatters.* When the initial squatter fled in 1974, he had abandoned his adverse possession and, as a result, the defendants were entitled to depend on his accumulated period of four years' adverse possession. **[14–44]**

VII. Adverse Possession of Leasehold Land

A tenant might go into adverse possession of the land of a third party and, if successful and no contrary intention is evident, any property acquired would in all likelihood take the form of an annexation on the land subject to the lease; therefore the landlord would be entitled to the property on the expiration or termination of the leasehold relationship.[124] The concept of rights acquired through adverse possession by a tenant vesting in the landlord at the termination of the lease is known as the presumption of accretion.[125] The presumption is described in *Halsbury's Laws of England* as follows: **[14–45]**

> Where, during the currency of his tenancy, a tenant encroaches upon, or without title to do so takes possession of, other land, there is a presumption that the land so taken becomes annexed to the demised premises, whether or not it is immediately adjacent to the demised premises, and whether or not it belongs to the landlord or to a third person, and on the determination of the tenancy the land must be given up to the landlord together with the demised premises.[126]

---

[123] [1988] 3 All ER 129.

[124] Although there is no Irish authority on this point, it appears to be generally accepted that the presumption of accretion forms part of Irish law. See also *Meares v Collis and Hayes* [1927] IR 397.

[125] See, for example, *Whitmore v Humphries* (1871) LR 7 CP 1; *Attorney General v Tomline* (1880) 5 Ch D 750; *Kingsmill v Millard* (1855) 11 Exch 313.

[126] *Halsbury's Laws of England* (4th ed, 1998), para 165.

Although this has not been the subject of particular attention in Irish jurisprudence, there is no reason to believe that the principle would not operate thus here in Ireland given the similarities in history and structure between the law of adverse possession in Ireland and the UK.[127] It was previously the case that a tenant could not be said to be in adverse possession against his own landlord[128] unless he became a tenant at sufferance. Importantly, however, the tenancy at sufferance is no longer considered a tenancy as a result of the Land and Conveyancing Law Reform Act 2009.[129] That notwithstanding, we can say that a person who was previously a tenant would go into adverse possession at the point at which they remain on the land without the consent of the landlord. A third party can adversely possess against the landlord while the landlord is not entitled to possess the land (because there is a leasehold relationship in place) by receiving rent from the tenant for a period of 12 years or more, where the rent is in excess of £1 (i.e. €1.37) per annum and the third party is not an agent of the landlord.[130]

[14–46] These situations are relatively straightforward. More complex is the case where a third party adversely possesses against a person who holds only a leasehold title on the property in question. The difficulty can be expressed thus: when someone leases out land, they contract out of their right to possess that land, which right is, instead, held by the tenant for as long as the lease remains in place and is being complied with. Therefore, when a third party squats against leasehold land, they cannot be said to possess the land in a manner that is adverse to the landlord's possession. This is recognised by s 15(1) of the Statute of Limitations 1957, which makes it clear that no limitation period runs against the landlord until the lease has come to an end. That landlord, remember, does not have a possessory right over the land in question while the lease endures. If we say that the title of the dispossessed tenant is extinguished, then there is the risk that the entitlement of the landlord to compliance with the terms of the lease—and the right to terminate that lease for non-compliance—might be endangered, even though the landlord did not have any possessory right or capacity to prevent the successful establishment of adverse possession. We must therefore be concerned with finding some way to do three seemingly contrasting things: (a) recognise the adverse possession of the successful squatter and ensure security of some kind for him in the land; (b) extinguish the tenant's title inasmuch as that title might permit the tenant to exercise possession over the land; and (c) protect the landlord in a way that recognises his right to have the provisions of the lease complied with in return for his not having possessory rights. We originally attempted to do this by means of the "parliamentary conveyance", i.e. the notion that the tenant's title would be transferred to the adverse possessor by the power of the statute on satisfaction of the requirements for adverse possession.[131] This position was later rejected by the courts in the leasehold context,[132]

[127] This was the conclusion of the Law Reform Commission in its *Report on Title by Adverse Possession* (2002), pp 28–32.

[128] *Ellis v Crawford* (1842) Long & Town 664; *Moore v Doherty* (1842) 5 IR LR 449; *Musgrave v McAvey* (1907) 41 ILTR 230.

[129] s 3, Land and Conveyancing Law Reform Act 2009.

[130] s 17(3), Statute of Limitations 1957.

[131] See, esp., *Rankin v McMurty* (1889) 24 LR Ir 290.

[132] *Tichborne v Weir* (1892) 67 LT 735; *St. Marylebone Property Company Ltd v Fairweather* [1963] AC 510.

heralding a great deal of uncertainty and insecurity as to the entitlements of the adverse possessor of a tenant.

1. Unregistered Leasehold Land

The English courts had approved a particularly controversial position in which a dispossessed tenant was said to be in a position to surrender his lease to a landlord, thereby bringing the lease to an end and resulting in a right of possession on the part of the landlord, which could be enforced against the adverse possessor.[133] This was because the title would be considered as extinguished as against the squatter but not as against the freeholder; a somewhat clumsy interpretation.[134] These same authorities had also established that a landlord was entitled to compliance with the covenants of the lease, regardless of whether the tenant had been dispossessed or not, and could therefore forfeit the lease in the absence of compliance and enforce a right to possession against the adverse possessor.[135] This left those who successfully adversely possessed against a tenant in a particularly vulnerable position because the landlord and dispossessed tenant could collude and terminate the lease, resulting in an action by the landlord against the adverse possessor in very early course notwithstanding the adverse possessor's 12 years of possession. In addition to this, there is a clear intellectual incongruity in allowing a dispossessed tenant to surrender his lease: if the adverse possession extinguishes the tenant's title, how can that same dispossessed tenant have leasehold rights to surrender to his landlord? **[14–47]**

By the time the Irish Supreme Court came to consider this matter, it came as little surprise that the Court would remove itself from the English position to at least some extent. *Perry v Woodfarm Homes*[136] concerned an encroachment on leasehold land by a third party. The defendant in *Perry* had been assigned the leasehold by the dispossessed tenant of the relevant lands following in excess of 12 years' adverse possession against him. The defendants then also bought the fee simple estate of the land and claimed that this fee simple reversion had merged with their leasehold entitlements to give rise to a freehold interest, and that they were entitled to take possession of the property notwithstanding the rights of the adverse possessor. The Supreme Court rejected the suggestion that a landlord of a dispossessed tenant could accept a surrender from a dispossessed tenant as the tenant's leasehold entitlements to the land were extinguished by the adverse possession. The Supreme Court did hold, however, that the lease continues to exist as a negative encumbrance on the landlord's title. In other words, although the original tenant no longer had an entitlement to the land, the landlord equally did not have an entitlement to possess the land as he had transferred that entitlement by means of the lease. As a result, the landlord remained entitled to the enjoyment of compliance with the leasehold covenants of the lease, such as the payment of rent. Thus, even though the dispossessed tenant had no title to surrender, he remained bound by the covenants of the lease and his failure to comply with these covenants could result in the landlord terminating the lease. Once the landlord terminates the lease he becomes entitled to possession and, as a result, an action **[14–48]**

---

133 *Tichborne v Weir* (1892) 67 LT 735.

134 *St. Marylebone Property Company Ltd v Fairweather* [1963] AC 510 *per* Denning LJ.

135 *St. Marylebone Property Company Ltd v Fairweather* [1963] AC 510.

136 [1975] IR 104.

accrues in his favour against the adverse possessor and the landlord can bring the possession to an end. The Supreme Court also rejected the concept of a parliamentary conveyance over unregistered land, although as we will see, before the Court thought the notion might still have some relevance for registered land. *Perry* is not an unproblematic decision,[137] but it is at least marginally less problematic than the English position and it seems to make some kind of sense: why should the landlord not be entitled to the benefits of the lease when he is not entitled to possess the land or to take an action to dispossess the squatter while the lease remains in operation? Why should a dispossessed tenant be able to surrender the lease, thereby placing the position of a successful adverse possessor in jeopardy, as the landlord now has a right of action?

2. Registered Leasehold Land

[14–49] The position has long been somewhat more straightforward in relation to registered land. In *Perry* the Court accepted that the concept of a parliamentary conveyance may have some more relevance to registered land than is the case in relation to unregistered land. This is because someone who successfully establishes adverse possession over registered land had their situation governed by s 49(2) of the Registration of Title Act 1964, which provides:

> Where any person claims to have acquired a title by possession to registered land, he may apply to the Registrar to be registered as owner of the land and the Registrar, if satisfied that the applicant has acquired the title, may cause the applicant to be registered as owner of the land with an absolute, good leasehold, possessory or qualified title, as the case may require, but without prejudice to any right not extinguished by such possession.

Section 49(3) provided that "Upon such registration, the title of the person whose right of action to recover the land has expired shall be extinguished": so the title of the tenant would be extinguished and something essentially the same as a parliamentary conveyance would operate in favour of the squatter. However, as s 49(1) provides that, subject to the remainder of s 49, the Statute of Limitations 1957 "shall apply to registered land as it applies to unregistered land" this suggested that as a matter of doctrine the parliamentary conveyance would not be said to apply to the adverse possession of leasehold registered land. So in practice the adverse possessor was registered as owner in the same folio as the dispossessed tenant, but we would not call this a parliamentary conveyance. This is even more confounding in the wake of s 50 of the Registration of Deeds and Title Act 2006 which provides, *inter alia*, that the term "leasehold interest" as used in the Registration of Title Act 1964 is to include "the right or interest of a person who has barred, under the Statute of Limitations 1957, the right of action of a person entitled to such leasehold interest".[138] This is an even stronger suggestion that, in registered land at least, the adverse possessor of a tenant is to be treated in essentially the same way as that tenant himself, notwithstanding the operation of a parliamentary conveyance in formal terms.

---

[137] For an excellent critique see Woods, "Adverse Possession of Unregistered Leasehold Land" (2001) xxxviii IR Jur 304.

[138] This is done by amendment to s 3 of the Registration of Title Act 1964.

3. Securing the Position of an Adverse Possessor of Leasehold Land

While the position of those who adversely possess against leasehold tenants of unregistered land is more secure in Ireland than in England (because the dispossessed tenant cannot surrender the lease), it remains quite precarious. There is no incentive for the dispossessed tenant to comply with the covenants of the lease when he has no entitlement to possess the property. The only way the adverse possessor can ensure secure possession is to ensure that he himself complies with those covenants, but because there is no parliamentary conveyance of the lease, he has no statutory entitlement to knowledge of what the covenants of the lease are. In addition, a landlord is under no obligation to accept rent or compliance with covenants from the successful adverse possessor. Indeed, there is a suggestion in *Tickner v Buzzacott*[139] that the adverse possessor cannot secure relief against forfeiture by the landlord by offering to take over the lease. As a result, an adverse possessor of leasehold land holds a very precarious entitlement to the property to hold the lands for the residue of the terms of the lease. The adverse possessor is not a tenant, however, and therefore does not benefit from landlord and tenant legislation.[140] In fact, the only relief available to the adverse possessor is a claim in estoppel, where the circumstances allow for such a claim to be made out.[141] **[14–50]**

The position of the adverse possessor of a tenant is subject to criticism on a number of bases. The first is the fact that the law, as it stands, results in a great deal of uncertainty, particularly in relation to long leases of unregistered land. If, for example, an adverse possessor were to successfully "squat" against a tenant under a 999-year lease[142] after only 20 years of the lease had expired, then the title to that property could remain uncertain and precarious for approximately 979 years and the impact on the property's marketability could be severe. In addition, as the adverse possessor is not considered to be a tenant, he does not benefit from the many statutory protections available to tenants in Ireland, including the right to buy the fee simple in appropriate circumstances under the Landlord and Tenant (Ground Rents) Act 1967–1978.[143] **[14–51]**

The Law Reform Commission has recommended the re-introduction of the parliamentary conveyance in the context of the adverse possession of leasehold land.[144] Such a development would result in a much more secure title for the adverse possessor, who would become the holder of a leasehold estate. The Commission also recommended that adverse possessors who are aware of the fact that they have become vested with a leasehold estate ought to be entitled to a copy of the lease in order to establish their rights and obligations in relation to the landlord.[145] The transfer of obligations under the lease to the adverse possessor could then occur and the normal rules requiring the landlord's consent to an assignment would not apply.[146] This would certainly cut a **[14–52]**

---

[139] [1965] Ch 426.

[140] See generally Chapter 15.

[141] See *O'Connor v Foley* [196] 1 IR 20.

[142] Such leases are commonly used in the purchase of apartments in modern developments and are therefore exceptionally common, particularly in urban areas.

[143] This is considered in Chapter 15.

[144] LRC, *Report on the Acquisition of Title by Adverse Possession* (2002), p 10.

[145] *ibid.*, pp 19–20.

[146] *ibid.*, p 27. On the rules governing liability for leasehold covenants and the assignment of leases, see Chapter 15.

reasonable path through the difficulties that currently exist, allowing for the vesting of a leasehold estate in the successful adverse possessor and the true extinguishment of the leasehold estate of the dispossessed tenant. In spite of the sensible nature of the proposal it was not introduced in the Land and Conveyancing Law Reform Act 2009. The uncertainty therefore persists.

VIII. Adverse Possession in Particular Situations

[14–53] The law of adverse possession operates in slightly different ways in relation to a number of ownership relationships. In all of these scenarios the complex ownership relations and, in particular, the multiple rights in existence over the relevant lands necessitate some additional attention from the perspective of the law of adverse possession.

1. Future Interests

[14–54] Where there are future interests over the property the limitation period does not run against the future interest-holders until they become entitled to the possession of the property.[147] If the previous owner has been dispossessed, however, the future interest-holder must sue within 12 years of the dispossession or within six years of his own interest becoming vested in possession, whichever is the longer.[148] Where the future interest is held by the State, the respective periods are 30 years from the dispossession or 12 years from the interest becoming vested in possessed, whichever is the longer.[149] By means of an exception, a remainderman or reversioner after a fee tail must sue within 12 years of the attempted barring of the entail.[150] Of course, as the fee tail now exists in only extremely limited situations,[151] that is of very limited remaining relevance.

2. Co-ownership

[14–55] Both joint tenants and tenants in common have an entitlement to possession of all of the co-owned land.[152] Where a co-owner is excluded from possession of co-owned land, the possessing co-owners are said to be in adverse possession against the excluded co-owner.[153]

3. Estates of Deceased Persons

[14–56] Adverse possession of the estates of deceased persons is a hugely significant phenomenon in Ireland. In cases of intestacy it appears to be quite common for the surviving spouses and, in some cases, children of a deceased to remain living in the house without any letters of administration being taken out on the estate. In such cases the rights of these possessors and, indeed, of any persons who may be entitled to a share of the estate may only be determinable by reference to adverse possession.

[147] s 15(1), Statute of Limitations 1957, s 15(1).
[148] s 15(2)(a), *ibid.*, s 15(2)(a).
[149] s 15(2)(b), *ibid.*, s 15(2)(b).
[150] s 15(3), *ibid.*
[151] s 13, Land and Conveyancing Law Reform Act 2009; see also the discussion in Chapter 4.
[152] See generally Chapter 8.
[153] s 21, Statute of Limitations 1957; *Bull v Bull* [1955] 1 QB 234.

Section 45(1) of the Statute of Limitations 1957, as amended by s 126 of the Succession Act 1965, provides that the limitation period in respect of claims for a share of the deceased's estate under a will, on intestacy or under s 111 of the Succession Act 1965[154] is "from the date when the right to receive the share or interest accrued". While this provision makes it clear that the general limitation period for claims against the estate of the deceased is six years, there is a considerable amount of controversy in relation to the limitation period for claims by the personal representative against the estate of the deceased. In general, the courts have interpreted s 45 of the Statute of Limitations as amended as being applicable only to claims *against* the personal representative, and considered the limitation period for claims *by* personal representatives to be 12 years.[155] The Law Reform Commission summarised the difficulty presented by this situation thus:

> ... the persons whom the section was designed to favour are not in fact safe from claims after six years because it remains open to other beneficiaries out of possession to take out a grant of administration, or to take action to compel an executor or administrator to take action on their behalf, between six and twelve years after the deceased's death.[156]

These difficulties are exacerbated by the fact that a person who wishes to protect his interest in the property cannot take advantage of this provision by taking out a grant of representation and acting as a personal representative because the provisions of s 71 provide that a personal representative who fails to discharge the duties of his office cannot take advantage of s 45 as amended to retain property for his own benefit. The Law Reform Commission has recommended that a personal representative ought to be able to acquire property by means of adverse possession in the ordinary way, although a failure by a personal representative to act in accordance with his responsibilities and duties may affect his capacity to avail of the Statute of Limitations through the operation of equitable principles.[157] The Commission also recommended that the limitation periods ought to be the same for claims either by or against personal representatives and that there ought to be a stopgap of 12 years, commencing at the time of death.[158]

4. Mortgaged Land

Although, as we have seen, it is common practice for a mortgagor to remain in possession of the mortgaged land, it is possible for the mortgagee to take possession.[159] **[14–57]** Where a mortgagee goes into possession of mortgaged lands, there is an exception to the requirement of "adverse" possession and possession alone will result in the

[154] This provides for the Legal Right Share of the surviving spouse and is considered in Chapter 16.
[155] *Drohan v Drohan* [1984] IR 311; *Gleeson v Feehan* [1993] 2 IR 113 (High Court) and [1997] 1 ILRM 522 (Supreme Court).
[156] *Report on Land Law and Conveyancing Law (7): Positive Covenants over Freehold Land and Other Proposals* (2003), p 63.
[157] *ibid.*, pp 69–75. See further the equitable maxims at paras 3–56 to 3–78.
[158] *Report on Land Law and Conveyancing Law (7): Positive Covenants over Freehold Land and Other Proposals* (2003), p 75.
[159] See generally Chapter 13.

limitation period running against the mortgagor. Twelve years' possession by the mortgagee without acknowledgment of the mortgagor's title will result in adverse possession *if* the mortgagee has not received payment or part-payment on account for the principal monies and interest arising.[160] It is entirely possible for a third party to go into adverse possession of mortgaged property. In such cases the limitation period will run against the mortgagee from the date of the last mortgage payment[161] and against the mortgagor from the date of possession.[162] As a matter of practicality, this means that the limitation period will always begin to run against the mortgagor from the time of possession, but it may well be some time before the limitation period begins to run against the mortgagee (if ever). Take, for example, a fairly typical case in which someone has a holiday home "down the country" that was purchased with the aid of a mortgage over the property. In those cases it is likely that the mortgage payments are made on a consistent monthly basis, even though the mortgagor may not be in constant occupation thereof. In such cases an adverse possessor might take possession a number of months before the mortgagor would become aware of this and during the period of this possession the mortgage payments are satisfactorily made. In such a scenario the "squatter" would be in adverse possession against the mortgagor, but not against the mortgagee.

[14–58] Where there is someone in adverse possession at the date of the creation of the mortgage, the limitation period can be said to begin to run at the same time against both the mortgagor and the mortgagee and expiration of the limitation period will result in the title of both the mortgagor and the mortgagee being extinguished.[163] Under the Law Reform Commission's proposals, an adverse possessor of mortgaged land would acquire the equity of redemption.[164] The mortgagor would continue to be liable for the payment of the mortgage debt, although the adverse possessor would be entitled to make payments in order to perpetuate the mortgage.[165] This is of benefit to the adverse possessor because repayment of the mortgage debt entitles the holder of the equity of redemption to discharge of the charge (in the case of registered land) or the re-conveyance of the security.[166]

5. Trusts

[14–59] As a general rule the same limitation period is applied to equitable interests as to legal interests.[167] In the context of trusts, however, the splitting of ownership between the trustee (who holds legal ownership) and the beneficiaries (who hold equitable ownership) can give rise to some complexity. A third party in adverse possession of land held under a trust will not bar the trustees' title until the beneficiaries' title has been barred.[168] Because of their fiduciary role, it is generally accepted that trustees

---

[160] ss 33–34, Statute of Limitations 1957.

[161] s 62, Statute of Limitations 1957.

[162] *Ludbrook v Ludbrook* [1901] 2 KB 96.

[163] *Thornton v France* [1897] 2 QB 143; *Munster and Leinster Bank v Croker* [1940] IR 185.

[164] LRC, *Report on the Acquisition of Title by Adverse Possession* (2002), pp 34–5. The equity of redemption is considered in full throughout Chapter 13.

[165] s 62, Statute of Limitations 1957.

[166] See generally Chapter 13.

[167] s 25(1), Statute of Limitations 1957.

[168] s 25(2), *ibid.*

cannot adversely possess against the beneficiaries of the trust if the land is held on a trust for sale or is under a settlement, although there will be only a six-year limitation period for the recovery of trust property or breach of trust in the absence of any other provision on that matter.[169] As trusts for sale and strict settlements now fall under the rubric of Part 4 trusts in the Land and Conveyancing Law Reform Act 2009, the same principle seems applicable there. If a trustee has engaged in a fraud against the beneficiaries or in the conversion of trust property to his own ends, then the trustee can never adversely possess against the beneficiaries.[170] In the normal course of events beneficiaries can never adversely possess against trustees of the trust or other beneficiaries,[171] however it appears that where a beneficiary is in possession and is the sole person entitled to the land, then the limitation period will be 12 years, as normal.

IX. Human Rights Implications of Adverse Possession

Questions have arisen—and have now largely been definitively addressed—about whether not the existence of adverse possession and the way in which the doctrine operates constitutes a breach of the right to possessions as contained in Art 1, Protocol One to the European Convention on Human Rights, which provides: **[14–60]**

> Every natural or legal person is entitled to the peaceful enjoyment of his possessions. No one shall be deprived of his possessions except in the public interest and subject to the conditions provided for by law and by the general principles of international law.
>
> The preceding provisions shall not, however, in any way impair the right of a State to enforce such laws as it deems necessary to control the use of property in accordance with the general interest or to secure the payment of taxes or other contributions or penalties.

Although Art 1 of Protocol One provides for a right to possessions (which includes property), it also allows, in the second paragraph, for the limitation of this right on the basis of, *inter alia*, "the general interest". There can be no doubt that adverse possession in and of itself is a breach of the first clause of this Article (i.e. the right to the peaceful enjoyment of possessions): the material question is whether this is an *allowable* breach within the meaning of the second clause. In other words, does adverse possession advance the general interest by means of a proportionate infringement of individual property rights? The compatibility of adverse possession with the European Convention on Human Rights arose in *JA Pye (Oxford) Ltd v Graham*,[172] which was taken to the European Court of Human Rights in a suit entitled *JA Pye (Oxford) Ltd v United Kingdom*.[173]

[169] s 43, *ibid.*
[170] s 44, *ibid.*
[171] s 25(4), *ibid.*
[172] [2000] Ch 676 (High Court); [2001] Ch 804 (Court of Appeals); [2002] 3 All ER 865 (House of Lords).
[173] *JA Pye (Oxford) Ltd v United Kingdom* (2006) 43 EHRR 43, reversed by the Grand Chamber in (2007) 46 EHRR 1083.

[14–61] The defendants in this case owned land adjoining that of JA Pye (Oxford) and had occupied the plaintiff's land under a grazing agreement until December 1983. At that stage the plaintiff refused to renew the agreement and requested that the Grahams vacate the land. The Grahams continued in occupation, but no further request was made to vacate the land or to pay for the grazing. In 1997 the Grahams claimed that they acquired title by means of adverse possession, which claim was disputed by the plaintiffs. In February 2000 the High Court held in favour of the plaintiff[174] but that decision was subsequently reversed by the Court of Appeal, which found that the Grahams did have the required *animus possidendi* to establish adverse possession because they had intended to posses the land until they were removed.[175] The Grahams succeeded on their appeal to the House of Lords, which approved of Slade J's judgment in *Powell v McFarlane*[176] and held that *animus possidendi* requires "the intention, in one's own name and on one's own behalf, to exclude the world at large, including the owner with the paper title if he be not himself the possessor, so far as is reasonably practicable and so far as the processes of the law will allow".[177] Under this interpretation the Grahams had successfully squatted over the land.[178] JA Pye (Oxford) Ltd submitted a complaint to the European Court of Human Rights, claiming that the operation of adverse possession in English law violated the right to possessions. Under the law then in place, adverse possession of unregistered land would result in extinguishment of the owner's title and adverse possession of registered land would result in the owner holding the land of trust for the adverse possessor.[179] Although this was originally found to be a violation of the Convention European Court of Human Rights[180] the Grand Chamber subsequently found that it was a proportionate, and therefore allowable, interference[181] thereby putting the question of compatibility with the Convention beyond doubt.[182]

[174] [2000] Ch 676.
[175] [2001] Ch 804.
[176] (1977) 38 P & CR 452.
[177] *ibid.*, pp 471–472.
[178] [2003] 1 AC 419.
[179] Limitation Act 1980 (UK); Land Registration Act 1925 (replaced by Land Registration Act 2002).
[180] *JA Pye (Oxford) Ltd v United Kingdom* (2006) 43 EHRR 43.
[181] *JA Pye (Oxford) Ltd v United Kingdom* (2007) 46 EHRR 1083.
[182] It is possible that the Grand Chamber would subsequently revise this finding, as there is no strict doctrine of *stare decisis* under the Convention, but this seems unlikely and for now this can be considered a definitive statement.

Chapter 15
Landlord and Tenant Law

[15–01] Leases have always been a popular way to grant rights over land and indeed during the "boom years", leasing became the only affordable way to secure a home for many people. Of course, leases are not only residential; commercial leases are also common. Throughout this chapter we will see that in some areas landlord-and-tenant law is far more protective of residential tenants than it is of commercial tenants, connected largely to our understanding of the "home" as a distinctive kind of property.[1] Landlord-and-tenant law is a particularly technical area, governed by a complex matrix of legislation that itself presents numerous anomalies and difficulties, which are addressed throughout this chapter.

[15–02] The focus in this chapter is to outline landlord-and-tenant law, especially the ongoing tension that underlines this entire area: the tension between the rights of landlords as superior title holders to control the land and its use, and the rights of tenants and leasehold owners to exercise autonomy over the land to the extent possible. We will see that, to a large extent, the law of landlord and tenant has developed in a manner that is focused on the "balancing out" of this relationship and even "rebalancing" the power away from the landlord and into a more even distribution between the two.

I. The Nature of a Lease

[15–03] Leases are landholding arrangements in which the tenant receives a proprietary interest in the property and the exclusive possession of it. If the tenant's rights are infringed by the landlord or by a third party, the tenant may sue to assert his leasehold title either in court or, in some cases, through an alternative dispute mechanism. Alternative dispute mechanisms are available for all private residential tenancies by means of the Private Residential Tenancies Board, which was established by the Residential Tenancies Act 2004.[2] In other leases, alternative dispute mechanisms such as arbitration may be allowed for by the terms of the lease itself, and this is particularly common in cases of commercial leases. While there are various types of leasehold relationship, all leases share a common character. We originally expressed this character in s 3 of the Landlord and Tenant Law Amendment (Ireland) Act 1860, commonly known as Deasy's Act. Section 3 provided:

> The relation of landlord and tenant shall be deemed to be founded on the express or implied contract of the parties, and not upon tenure or service, and a reversion shall not be necessary to such relation, which shall be deemed to subsist in all cases in which there shall be an agreement by one party to hold land from or under another in consideration of any rent.

[15–04] While the meaning of s 3 has resulted in some contention,[3] it is now widely accepted that although leases are contracts, they are not subjected in their entirety to contract law and continue to be governed primarily by the terms of property law as it applies to the landlord-and-tenant relationship. Importantly, however, s 3 expressly defines the lease as a contractual and not a feudal relationship. All leases are contracts,

[1] See generally Chapter 9.

[2] See Part 6 of the Residential Tenancies Act 2004.

[3] On the history of the Act and the controversy around s 3 in particular see Dowling, "The Genesis of Deasy's Act" (1989) 40 NILQ 53.

therefore the parties to the lease must have an intention to create legal relations of the nature of the landlord-and-tenant relationship. Importantly, however, the terms of this contract will not be the only matters to be taken into account when assessing the entitlements and obligations of the parties. The "contract" might say that the relationship between the parties is a licence, but a court can override and disregard that description if it believes that the relationship is more accurately described as a lease[4]: in addition, the conditions within the leasehold contract can be overridden by the terms of statute.

While it is usually the case that the landlord will hold a reversion (i.e. will lease the tenant rights for a lesser period of time than the estate held by the landlord), s 3 expressly provides that this is not required. For this reason it is possible in Ireland for a lease to be created "forever". Section 3 also mentions rental payment, although it does not state clearly whether rent is a requirement of a lease or merely a common characteristic of it. What is clear, however, is that any payment between parties who have the character of landlord and tenant can be said to be rent notwithstanding how it is described in the agreement itself.[5] Significantly, s 3 combined with s 1 of Deasy's Act also allows for the creation of leases over lesser interests, such as sporting rights and easements, because "land" is expressly said to include both corporeal and incorporeal rights. **[15–05]**

The Law Reform Commission has proposed the introduction of a new act to clarify a number of issues in landlord-and-tenant law, including the matter of defining the landlord–tenant relationship. In its *Report on the Law of Landlord and Tenant*,[6] the Commission included a draft Landlord and Tenant Bill 2007. Section 10 of the proposed bill as drafted provided: **[15–06]**

> (1) The relationship of landlord and tenant continues in all cases to be based on the express or implied agreement of the parties, and not upon tenure or service.
>
> (2) A reversion is not necessary to the relationship.
>
> (3) An obligation to pay rent is necessary in all cases to the creation of the relationship.

The clear intention here is to ensure that the basic principles of s 3 of Deasy's Act (contractual basis for the relationship and possibility of a lease without a reversion) would be maintained, but that uncertainties around rent, for example, would be excised from the law. It may well be the case that, as Wylie has noted, the uncertainties around the exact requirements of s 3 of Deasy's Act have been "of academic significance only",[7] but nevertheless it is surely more desirable to have clear and uncontroversial provisions in law than unclear provisions even if, in fact, we have conjured up practices and understandings in relation to same.

---

4 See the discussion on the identification of a lease in paras 15–11 to 15–33 below.
5 See, for example, *Irish Shell & BP Ltd v Costello (No. 2)* [1984] IR 511.
6 (2007).
7 Wylie, *Land Law in Ireland* (4th ed, 2010, West Sussex, Bloomsbury Professional), p 969.

[15–07] Section 11(3) of the Land and Conveyancing Law Reform Act 2009 provides a definition of leasehold estate as follows:

> the estate which arises when a tenancy is created for any period of time or any recurring period and irrespective of whether or not the estate—
> (a) takes effect in immediate possession or in future, or
> (b) is subject to another legal estate or interest, or
> (c) is for a term which is uncertain or liable to termination by notice, re-entry or operation of law or by virtue of a provision for cessor on redemption or for any other reason

In addition, the 2009 Act makes it clear that tenancies at will[8] and tenancies at sufferance[9] are no longer considered to be leasehold estates. Thus, the various kinds of leasehold estates with which we are concerned are periodic tenancies and fixed-term leases, both of which could be reversionary or present.

1. Periodic Tenancy

[15–08] A periodic tenancy will last for a defined period of time. Once that period of time expires, it will renew itself automatically. Thus a weekly periodic tenancy will last for an initial week, after which another week will begin to run, after which another week will begin to run and so on. Periodic tenancies are determined or brought to an end by means of notice, i.e. one party informing the other that they want to bring the landlord-and-tenant relationship to an end. The operation and amount of notice required to terminate a tenancy is considered in full below.[10]

2. Lease for a Term Certain

[15–09] Leases for a term certain are relatively common and quite straightforward. In these cases the duration of the lease is determined *ab initio*, and once the time has expired the lease is terminated automatically. Despite the automatic termination of leases for a term certain, there is no prohibition on inserting a clause into the lease that allows for its termination through a particular notice period: this does not rid the estate of its "term certain" character. A renewal clause will equally not change the estate from a term certain lease to some other genus of leasehold estate. In order to qualify as a lease for a term certain, the duration must actually be certain; duration cannot be said to correspond to some indeterminable or uncertain event, such as the end of a war, or the date at which the landlord decides to sell the property. In essence, the court will examine the terms of the agreement and from that determine the nature of the lease in operation.

3. Reversionary Lease

[15–10] Although almost all leases are followed by a reversion in favour of the landlord, there is no reason why a landlord could not a grant a lease that is to begin once the current lease terminates and the landlord is entitled to possession again by means of the

---

[8] s 11(3), Land and Conveyancing Law Reform Act 2009. See also para 4–86.
[9] *ibid.* See also para 4–87.
[10] See paras 15–56 to 15–65.

reversion. Indeed, s 11(3)(a) of the Land and Conveyancing Law Reform Act 2009 expressly provides for leases that will take effect in the future. A lease that is designed to first become effective in the landlord's reversion is known as a reversionary lease.

II. Identification of a Lease

Leases are particular kinds of legal agreements that result in a tenant receiving a right to exclusively possess land and a proprietary interest in it. In addition, leases attract a variety of different legal protections and enforcement mechanisms for both the landlord and the tenant. In this way, the lease is a very different kind of legal arrangement from other landholding arrangements, such as licences, franchises, caretaker agreements and so on. Because of the implications of a lease for the landlord—in particular, the legal entitlements of tenants to rights to a new tenancy and enfranchisement and tax implications of a lease,[11] for example—many landowners will be tempted to exploit their land by creating agreements through which a rental income can be generated, while at the same time trying to avoid landlord-and-tenant law. Such landowners will frequently describe the agreement as a licence; a merely permissive right not attracting proprietary entitlements and not affected by landlord-and-tenant law.[12] **[15–11]**

Contractual licences and leases look rather similar on the face of things: they are both based on contract and both allow one party to hold the land of another, usually subject to some kind of periodical payment. Conscious of this similarity, courts will be vigilant in respect of what the true nature of any particular landholding arrangement is. Courts have long asserted their right to disregard the "label" of lease or licence that the parties have placed on their relationship. In Ireland this task is generally undertaken by consideration of the relationship under four different headings: (1) construction of the agreement; (2) intention of the parties as inferred from their words and conduct; (3) exclusive possession on the part of the tenant; and (4) the payment of rent. **[15–12]**

1. Construction of the Agreement

As a result of the courts' commitment to discerning the true nature of the relationship between the parties, the decision as to whether or not a lease exists will essentially be a matter of construction and a court is empowered to treat that which is called a licence as a lease (and vice versa) where appropriate.[13] If a written agreement exists between the parties the court will attempt to construct its terms, but the label placed on the agreement will not be determinative; in other words, the fact that the parties expressly describe their relationship as a "licence" will not automatically result in the court finding that it is, in fact, a licence. In the same vein, the fact that the parties call a relationship a "lease" does not preclude the court finding that it is in fact a "licence".[14] Rather, a label placed on the agreement will merely be *prima facie* evidence of the intention of the parties, which can be overridden by the true operation of their **[15–13]**

---

[11] See further Ryall, "Lease or Licence? The Contemporary Significance of the Distinction" (2001) 6(3) CPLJ 56.

[12] See generally Chapter 10.

[13] *Whipp v Mackey* [1927] IR 372; *Irish Shell & BP Ltd v Costello Ltd* [1981] ILRM 66; *Governors of the National Maternity Hospital v McGouran* [1994] 1 ILRM 521; *Smith v Irish Rail* [2002] IEHC 103; *Ó Siodhachain v O'Mahony* [2002] 4 IR 147.

[14] *Ó Siodhachain v O'Mahony* [2002] 4 IR 147.

landholding agreement. Where there is no written agreement between the parties, the court will engage in construction of their words and conduct.[15]

2. Intention of the Parties

[15–14] All contractual relationships are contingent on the parties' intention to create legal relationships, but in the context of trying to assess whether a contract that constitutes a lease has been formed, the courts are concerned not only with an intention to create legal relations generally but with an intention to create *a particular type* of legal relation (i.e. a landlord–tenant relationship). The parties' intention is generally inferred from the conditions under which the land is held and from the words and conduct of the parties. The courts will try to assess whether, in its everyday operation, the relationship between the parties is more akin to a lease than to a licence. It is the courts' approach to assessing intention based on the actual operation of the agreement that has resulted in the label the parties place on the agreement being of relatively little significance; if the label does not match the actual operation of the agreement then it is liable to be disregarded by the courts. This position was substantively introduced into Irish law in *Whipp v Mackey*.[16]

[15–15] The right to discard the label placed on the agreement was reiterated by the Supreme Court in *Gatien Motor Company v Contintental Oil Company of Ireland Ltd*.[17] Continental Oil rented a garage premises to Gatien for a period of three years from February 1970. Before the full three-year term had expired, Gatien approached the landlords and expressed an interest in negotiating a renewal of the lease. The landlord was unwilling to grant a renewal unless Gatien vacated the premises for a week. This was because the legislation in force at the time provided business tenants with certain entitlements if they occupied premises for three years and three months, and the landlord wanted to ensure a break in Gatien's occupation so that he would not meet the three-years-and-three-months time limit. Gatien was unwilling to vacate the premises because he believed that it would have a detrimental effect on his business and, after a period of negotiation, it was agreed that he would remain in possession as a caretaker and for no rental payment for a period of one week, following which a new three-year tenancy would be issued. Gatien was fully aware that this caretaker week was expressly designed to evade the tenant's rights for such week, entered into the caretaker agreement and subsequently entered into the new three-year lease, which lasted until 1976. On the expiration of the new lease in 1976, Gatien claimed tenant's rights on the basis of leasehold occupation since 1970 and claimed that the "caretaker agreement" did not break his occupation because it was properly described as a lease. While the Supreme Court held that it was entitled to discard the label placed on an agreement in appropriate circumstances, there was no need to do so in this case. Although Gatien was said to be "in possession" of the lands for the caretaker period, he paid no rent and he was fully cognisant of the purpose and effect of the caretaker agreement when he entered into it. There were therefore no grounds for discarding the label and finding a tenancy.

[15] *Bellew v Bellew* [1982] IR 447; *Irish Shell & BP Ltd v Costello Ltd (No. 2)* [1984] IR 511.
[16] [1927] IR 372.
[17] [1979] IR 406.

The label was discarded in *Irish Shell & BP Ltd v Costello Ltd*.[18] The plaintiffs in this case had built a petrol station on a site owned by them and hired the equipment on the site (pumps, gas tanks etc.) to Costello from year to year from 1967 to 1974. Costello was described by these agreements as having a licence to use the premises in order to use the equipment. Over time some terms characteristic of a licence were removed from the agreements, as a result of which the defendant was no longer precluded from claiming exclusive possession of the premises and was no longer required not to interfere with the plaintiff's possession and use of the premises. Costello also had the only set of keys to the petrol pumps. A dispute arose as to the nature of his rights in relation to the land: did he have a licence (as the agreement stated), or were his rights more akin to a lease? **[15–16]**

Considering whether or not the agreement between the parties could be considered a lease, Griffin J endorsed the standard adopted by Lord Denning in *Shell-Mex v Manchester Garages*[19]: **[15–17]**

> [Whether the transaction is a licence or a lease] does not depend on the label which is put on it. It depends on the nature of the transaction itself... Broadly speaking, we have to see whether it is a personal privilege given to a person (in which case it is a licence), or whether it grants an interest in land (in which case it is a tenancy).[20]

Applying the *Shell-Mex* test and, as a result, considering the agreement as a whole and in light of its practical operation, Griffin J concluded that the parties were, in fact, in a landlord-and-tenant relationship. The *Shell-Mex* test goes right to the heart of the matter by making it clear that whether or not the arrangement will be a lease or a licence depends on whether it gives a proprietary or personal right to the landholding party. If the former, it will be a lease as a lease is a proprietary interest. If the latter it will be a licence as a licence is a personal and permissive interest. The test as applied in both *Shell-Mex* and *Costello* appears to require an assessment of the intentions of the parties based on the operation of the realistic agreement as a whole and not merely on the formal terms concluded between the parties. Whether or not this is always appropriate—especially in the context of a commercial agreement—is further considered below. **[15–18]**

3. Exclusive Possession

One of the most important indicators of the parties' intentions in relation to the landholding relationship is whether or not the holder of the land has been given exclusive possession of the property. Exclusive possession is essential to the existence of a lease, but is not determinative of a lease. In other words, there can be no lease without exclusive possession, but the existence of exclusive possession does not preclude a licence agreement between the parties.[21] Although "possession" refers to the use and enjoyment of land, a leasehold relationship implicates a more substantial kind of possession; one that not only gives the tenant the capacity to use and enjoy the land **[15–19]**

[18] [1981] ILRM 66.
[19] [1971] 1 WLR 612.
[20] *ibid.* at p 615.
[21] *Gatien Motor Company v Continental Oil Company of Ireland Ltd* [1979] IR 406.

but also gives him the capacity to exclude the world at large, including the landlord, and to exercise some kind of dominion over the property. The exercise of dominion (or "control") is entirely compatible with the proprietary nature of a lease.

[15–20] The English case of *Street v Mountford*[22] is an important starting point here. In *Street* the House of Lords held that, apart from in exceptional circumstances, where residential accommodation "is offered and accepted with exclusive possession for a term at a rent, the result is a tenancy", thus placing exclusive possession at the heart of the assessment in that jurisdiction. While *Street* was decided in the context of residential accommodation, it was later extended to commercial properties in *London & Associated Investment Trust Plc v Calow*[23] and, given its application in *Smith v Irish Rail*[24] (concerning a commercial lease), now appears to be of general application in Ireland.

[15–21] The exceptional circumstances in which the presumption of a lease will not arise under the *Street* doctrine are threefold: (a) where there is no intention to enter into a lease; (b) where the landowner does not have the legal capacity to grant a lease; and (c) where the exclusive possession enjoyed is referable to some other legal relationship. In general, the third of these requirements is the only one that gives rise to any difficulty because it can involve the courts in assessing whether or not any particular legal relationship (such as a licence,[25] service occupancy,[26] caretakers agreement, etc.) is valid. The inclusion of "lack of intention to enter into a lease" as an exceptional circumstance in *Street* may rebut an interpretation of *Street* as holding that exclusive possession is determinative, particularly in Ireland where the intention of the parties is so significant in the court's assessment. In other words, *Street* properly means that exclusive possession gives rise to a presumption of lease, but that presumption can be rebutted where there is a contrary *inter partes* intention.

[15–22] Since the introduction of the doctrine in *Street* some landowners have attempted to include clauses in landholding agreements that suggest that the landholder does not enjoy exclusive possession. While there is no prohibition on designing an agreement in which there is no exclusive possession, the courts do not appear to be willing to accept "sham" or "pretence" clauses that are inserted purely for the purposes of evading landlord-and-tenant law and are therefore *male fides*. Where such a sham or pretence clause is detected, the court can strike it out and construct the remainder of the agreement without it. Indeed, Lord Templeman himself did this in *Street*, holding that the Court ought to be vigilant "to detect and frustrate sham devices and artificial transactions whose only object is to disguise the grant of a tenancy and to evade the Rent Acts".[27] This is well demonstrated by the decision in *Antoniades v Villiers.*[28] In

[22] [1985] AC 809.
[23] (1986) 280 EG 1252.
[24] [2002] IEHC 103.
[25] See Chapter 10.
[26] A service occupancy arises where a person has exclusive possession over some property of their employer, but this exclusive possession is inherent in the nature of the employment and does not, therefore, result in a lease.
[27] [1985] AC 809, at p 825.
[28] [1990] AC 417.

this case a landlord entered into separate agreements with two members of a couple in relation to a one-bedroom flat owned by him. These agreements were labelled "licences". Both documents included the same terms and both were entered into simultaneously by the couple. The agreements stated that "the licensor is not willing to grant... exclusive possession" and that the use of the rooms concerned was "in common with the licensor and such other licensees or invitees as [he] may permit from time to time to use the said rooms". In other words, this clause suggested that the landowner could move whomever he wished into the premises at any stage, although this term was never exercised. When the couple attempted to assert tenants' rights the landlord claimed that they had no entitlements because they were mere licensees, but the Court held that the agreement was described accurately as a lease: this term had been inserted in order to give the appearance that the parties had no exclusive possession and was a sham that could be ignored.

Where a property is shared between a number of possessors, the occupants will not be deemed to be tenants in the collective sense unless they can prove that they have been granted a joint tenancy over the property[29] (within the meaning of the law of co-ownership).[30] **[15–23]**

4. Payment of Rent

Section 3 of Deasy's Act mentions rental payments as a characteristic of a lease, but does not make clear whether rent is a requirement of a lease or merely a particularly strong indication that such a landholding relationship exists. There is certainly authority on both sides of the Irish Sea that a gratuitous lease is acceptable,[31] although it is almost always the case that rent is reserved in practice. The Irish courts have consistently indicated that the existence or otherwise of a rental payment is an important consideration in their assessment of the true nature of a landholding relationship. Thus in *Gatien*[32] the fact that the caretaker week was "rent free" was significant and in *Costello*[33] a "hire purchase charge" paid ostensibly for the use of the petrol pumps was interpreted by the Supreme Court as a rent. Furthermore Kenny J, dissenting in *Costello*, held that rent is "essential for the creation of the relationship of landlord and tenant".[34] **[15–24]**

5. The Lease–Licence Distinction since *Irish Shell & BP Ltd v Costello Ltd*

The four indicia of a lease outlined above, and particularly the "on the ground" holistic approach endorsed in *Irish Shell & BP Ltd v Costello Ltd* raises two important questions. The first is what relative weight ought to be given to the various different indicia, especially in cases where there seems to be exclusive possession in practice but the terms of the agreement itself suggest that there is no exclusive possession. The second question relates to whether it is appropriate to disregard the label in the case of **[15–25]**

29 *AG Securities Ltd v Vaughan* [1990] 1 AC 417.

30 See Chapter 8.

31 *Corrigan v Woods* (1867) IR 1 CL 73 offers Irish authority for this proposition; *Ashburn Anstalt v Arnold* [1989] Ch 1 offers English authority.

32 *Gatien Motor Company v Continental Oil Company of Ireland Ltd* [1979] IR 406.

33 [1981] ILRM 66.

34 *ibid.*, p 72.

commercial leases, as opposed to residential ones. Ought we not to say that commercial actors have (or should be assumed to have) access to legal advisors and operate at arm's length in a business environment, meaning that they should be forced to stick by their original agreement even if that original agreement seems a harsh or difficult one? These two questions underline the decisions in an important series of three cases that followed *Irish Shell*. These are the cases of *Governors of the National Maternity Hospital v McGouran*,[35] *Kenny Homes Ltd v Leonard*[36] and *Smith v Irish Rail*.[37]

[15–26] The parties in *Governors of the National Maternity Hospital v McGouran* entered negotiations in May 1986 regarding McG opening a shop within the hospital. Throughout these negotiations the parties referred to the proposed agreement as a "tenancy" or "lease" that would include the payment of a "rent" and draft leases were drawn up. These leases were not signed, however, and in June 1986 McG entered a caretaker agreement in relation to the shop. In 1988 she entered into a franchise with the hospital in relation to the coffee shop within the hospital. The negotiations for this franchise again involved discussions of a "lease" between the parties. At this stage the shop, which McG ran, was moved to another location in the hospital. When new management was appointment in the hospital a meeting was held to clarify McG's status and the hospital clarified that it was prepared to offer her a licence, but not a lease, in relation to the shop and coffee shop. Following legal advice, on 9 August 1989 McG signed one-year licence agreements for both the shop and the coffee shop. Both agreements defined the term "licensee" as including "successors and assigns", and contained covenants prohibiting assignment and obliging the licensee to insure against public liability, effect repairs and pay rates. The agreements expressly stated that they constituted licences only and not leases, that the hospital retained possession subject to the rights granted by the agreement, and that the hospital reserved the right at any time while the agreement was in force, and on giving reasonable notice, to substitute for the premises any other premises within the hospital that were reasonably equivalent. After these agreements came into operation the hospital required the defendant to provide a price list for customers of the coffee shop, to fit safety catches to the windows and to add fans to the smoke-extractor unit that had been installed by the defendant. The defendant did not sign further licence agreements that were sent to her, but continued to run the shop and coffee shop while paying the increased amounts mentioned in the licences sent to her. In March 1993 the hospital informed McG that the franchise over the coffee shop was being put out to open tender, following which McG claimed that she was a tenant and had tenant's rights under the Landlord and Tenant (Amendment) Act 1980. The hospital denied her alleged status as tenant and required her to vacate the premises.

[15–27] The Court held that the agreements between the parties constituted licences only. This conclusion was substantively based on the terms within the licence agreements that gave the hospital substantial control over the properties, including the right to move their location within the hospital, and therefore denied McG exclusive possession. This

---

[35] [1994] 1 ILRM 521.
[36] [1997] IEHC 230.
[37] [2002] IEHC 103.

was so notwithstanding the fact that, in practice, McG had operated as if she had exclusive possession of the properties. According to Morris J, these terms constituted an acknowledgment by the defendant that the plaintiffs had the right to use the premises and that whether these rights were actually exercised or not was entirely irrelevant. The plaintiffs' actions in requiring price lists and effecting improvements demonstrated that they continued to exercise dominion over the premises, but even if they had not required this information the Court's conclusion would have been the same. As a result, the hospital was entitled to revoke the licence and require McG to vacate the premises. She had only a licence; the terms of the agreement trumped the practice of exclusive (or near exclusive) possession.

Much the same conclusion was reached in *Kenny Homes v Leonard*,[38] which concerned agreements between the parties in which it was clearly stated that there was no landlord-and-tenant relationship between the parties and that Leonard was not entitled to exclusive possession. Any sums payable under these agreements were expressly referred to as "licence fees" (as opposed to "rent"). The defendants occupied the property for an appreciable period of time under these agreements and claimed that they were properly described as tenants and entitled to protections and rights under landlord-and-tenant law. The High Court held that the terms of the agreements between the parties were abundantly clear and did not give the defendants any exclusive possession over the property. In spite of the fact that, in practice, the defendants enjoyed possession that was effectively exclusive, the clear and unambiguous terms of the agreement would override and the defendants were merely licensees. **[15–28]**

Quite a different result was reached by Peart J in *Smith v Irish Rail*.[39] This case concerned a shop at Tara Street Dart Station in Dublin, which Smith operated under the terms of a "licence" agreement entered into by the parties following a course of negotiations and the taking of legal advice, during the course of which the parties referred to the potential agreement as a licence. The agreement itself contained the following terms in Clause 10: **[15–29]**

> Nothing in this licence shall be construed as giving the licencee any tenancy in or right to possession of or any right or easement over or with respect to any part of the property of the Board or the property of the Company. In particular and without prejudice to the generality of the foregoing it is hereby declared that it is not the intention of either the board or the company on the one part or the licencee on the other part in relation to the premises or the said Railway arch or any part thereof to create between them the relationship of landlord and tenant or to confer such rights upon the licencee as would amount in law to a tenancy (including a tenancy at will) or to create any estate or proprietary interest for the licencee therein.

Peart J accepted that the clear and unequivocal intention of the parties at the time that the agreement was entered into was to create a licence between them, but went on to consider how that agreement actually operated in practice. Peart J interpreted *Street v Mountford* as introducing a position by which the reality of exclusive possession could **[15–30]**

[38] Unreported, High Court, 11 December 1997.

[39] [2002] IEHC 103.

result in the label of "licence" being discarded notwithstanding the intentions of the parties at the time the agreement was entered into. In addition, he held that Clause 10 and analogous clauses that expressly stated that the agreement was a licence were not determinative of the matter; rather, the agreement and how it operated in practice would have to be considered as a whole. In this context, Peart J held that the description of the monthly payment as a "licence fee" did not preclude the Court holding that it was, in fact, a rent. In addition, he placed a great deal of emphasis on the fact that the agreement at no stage expressly provided that Smith did not enjoy exclusive possession of the property (and, in this sense, the case could be distinguished from *McGouran*). Peart J accepted the following as a summary of how the agreement actually operated in practice:

> [Smith]... was left alone by C.I.E. apart from the occasions when he was called upon to desist from leaving rubbish on the station concourse and in relation to the parking of cars. No cleaning or other services were provided by C.I.E., C.I.E. never came in to the premises to inspect or carry out repairs, neither did they have a key to the premises. The applicant's stock for his shop was stored at all times within the premises. In all respects this was a self-contained business, save that the applicant and his staff were able to avail of toilet facilities within the station complex.
>
> ... in 1991 the applicant invested heavily in this business venture. He paid £75,000 by way of premium to the Respondent. He expended, according to his evidence, approximately £25,000 on fitting out the premises, and committed himself to a substantial annual sum (to use a neutral term). There is also no doubt, however, that while he clearly would have preferred a lease of the premises, he accepted what was on offer from C.I.E., namely the licence agreement. He was a clearly an energetic and motivated young man who was prepared to take a risk that at the end of ten years he might have to vacate the premises and close the business.

Peart J applied the *Shell-Mex* test adopted by the Supreme Court in *Costello* to these arrangements and found that Smith acquired far more than a "personal privilege". In light of the *ratio* in *Street v Mountford* that a prima facie licence can be recognised as a lease on the basis of exclusive possession, Peart J held that the actual exclusive possession enjoyed by Smith overrode Clause 10 of the agreement and, as a result, that Smith ought to be recognised as a tenant.[40]

[15–31] One could argue that *Smith* strongly reasserts the courts' capacity to give effect to the true nature of a landholding agreement between the parties based on how it operates in practice quite apart from what is clearly written and intended in the agreement.[41] However, it must also be acknowledged that one of the bases upon which the presumption of a lease can be rebutted under *Street* is lack of intention to enter into a lease and, in the case of *Smith*, it seems clear that there was no such intention on the part of either party. Given that lack of intention, one could argue that *Smith* somewhat

[40] This conclusion is also supported by the earlier case of *Whyte v Sheehan* [1943] IR Jur Rep 38.

[41] This was my position in de Londras, *Principles of Irish Property Law* (1st ed, 2007, Dublin, Clarus Press), p 413.

misapplies *Street*. One might also, of course, question the appropriateness of applying such an incredibly paternalistic approach to commercial arrangements even if, *as a general matter*, one were supportive of the proposition that the lack of intention ought not to necessarily always preclude the court in finding a lease in fact. This goes to the very heart of the reason why courts assert the capacity to disregard the label in the first place: the need to ensure enjoyment of tenant's rights even if, at the time of striking the bargain, one is not in a position to insist upon a clear designation as a tenant. This is likely to happen where particularly vulnerable people are in need of a place to reside and prospective landlords insist on describing the arrangement as a licence: students, people on rent allowance, older people, and people for whom English is not their first language are arguably all at risk of manipulation by landlords and of being incapable of insisting upon a "lease" designation at the time of striking the bargain. It is right and proper that courts would step in to protect these kinds of tenants and recognise them as such where the agreement does not align in its terms to the reality of the arrangement on the ground. Furthermore, in residential tenancies what we are concerned with is someone's home; a far more fundamental, and more protected, type of property than a commercial premises.

Businesses or other commercial actors are, however, in a somewhat different position. **[15–32]** They are not as inherently vulnerable as individuals are. Certainly commercial entities can experience commercial vulnerability, especially at a time of general economic disturbance, but company law has mechanisms in place to deal with that: winding down, receivership, etc. Apart from those kinds of situations we *generally* consider that commercial actors should be strictly bound to their contracts, even if those contracts are hard ones. We have already seen that in the case of mortgages, for example, courts will be far slower to "save" commercial entities from the hard bargains they have agreed to than to save individuals. Ought this not also to be the case in the context of the lease/licence distinction?

The implication in the Court of Appeal decision of *Clear Channel UK v Manchester City Council*[42] is certainly that less paternalistic approaches ought to be taken in **[15–33]** commercial contexts. This case concerned a company that was engaged in the construction and maintenance of advertising hoardings and displays. In the instant case they had been contracted to erect a permanent display of M-shaped constructions, which were to be placed in various locations around Manchester. By an agreement between the parties, which was expressly termed a "licence", the plaintiffs had "permission to erect and maintain" these displays but had no other rights over the properties concerned. The agreement was for a fixed period of time and was subject to a "rent". When the defendant attempted to terminate the agreement in accordance with its terms, the plaintiff claimed that the agreement between them was properly described as a lease and that, as a result, it was entitled to statutory protections against the proposed termination. The Court of Appeal accepted that the label placed on the agreement was not determinative of the true nature of their relationship, but that the substantive operation of the agreement and intention of the parties would be the bases upon which the existence of a lease or a licence would be determined. Applying this approach and, in particular, being cognisant of the equal bargaining power of

[42] [2005] EWCA Civ 1304.

commercial entities entering into an agreement of this nature with independent legal advice, Parker LJ held that there was no need to redact the chosen label in the agreement; it was rightly described as a licence. The Court of Appeal paid particular attention to the fact that this agreement was entered into by parties with equal bargaining power, who had contracted following independent legal advice.

[15–34] In its draft Landlord and Tenant Bill, appended to the *Report on the Law of Landlord and Tenant*,[43] the Law Reform Commission furthered the view it had expressed in an earlier consultation paper that the courts ought not to rewrite commercial agreements and should instead give effect to the terms of the agreement itself.[44] Section 11 of the proposed bill—which has not been enacted—provides:

> (1) Subject to *section 10*, in determining whether a tenancy has been created the court shall—
>
> (a) give effect to any express provision relating to the matter;
>
> (b) presume that each of the parties had received independent legal advice by the time of the creation of the tenancy.
>
> (2) Where it is established that any of the parties had not received such advice, it is open to the court to disregard any such express provision where it is satisfied, on all the evidence, that to give effect to it would not reflect the true intention of that party and would prejudice that party.

This draft provision seems to encapsulate a perfectly balanced approach to this area, allowing for intervention where it is required on the basis of the intentions of the parties *and* the detriment that can be caused by cynical manipulations of the label "licence" but at the same time making it clear that we will start from the position of giving effect to the parties' bargain, especially where (as is frequently the case in commercial contexts) legal advice has been acquired. It is a matter of some regret that this proposal has not yet been enacted in law.

III. Formation of a Lease

[15–35] Section 4 of Deasy's Act 1860 lays down the general conditions for the formation of a lease in law. In addition to compliance with s 4, however, landlord and tenant relationships can be created in law by means of assignment, sub-lease and implication. Like other proprietary interests, leases can also be created in equity either by means of estoppel or by specific performance of a contract for a lease under the Rule in *Walsh v Lonsdale*.[45]

1. Section 4, Deasy's Act 1860

[15–36] The formalities for the creation of a lease are laid down in s 4 of Deasy's Act, which provides that:

> Every lease or contract with respect to lands whereby the relation of landlord and tenant is intended to be created for any freehold estate or interest, or for any definite period of

43 (2007).

44 LRC, *Consultation Paper on the General Law of Landlord and Tenant* (2003).

45 (1882) 21 Ch D 9.

> time not being from year to year or any lesser period, shall be by deed executed, or in writing signed by the landlord or his agent thereunto authorised in writing.

As a preliminary point it must be noted that Irish law has never applied s 4 to contracts for the creation of a lease; as a result, this provision can be said to apply to leases alone.[46] The Law Reform Commission's recommendation that the words "or contract" be removed from s 4 is surely to be welcomed as practice has clearly rejected the application of s 4 to contracts for a lease.[47] Where s 4 does apply, however, it requires that leases would be created by deed or by some other kind of writing signed by the landlord or his lawfully authorised agent. Section 62 of the Land and Conveyancing Law Reform Act 2009 provides that legal estates (which include leasehold estates under s 11) are only to be created by deed with limited exceptions, including "a grant or assignment of a tenancy not required to be by deed".[48] Thus it seems to still be possible to create a lease under s 4 by some kind of writing that falls short of a formal conveyance, but where a formal conveyance is used it must be in the form of a deed.

Section 4 requires that all leases for a fixed term of more than one year must be made in writing, whereas practically all[49] periodic tenancies and leases for a fixed term of less than one year can be created orally. Whether or not a lease for a fixed term of one year certain must be made in writing has traditionally been a point of some contention, notwithstanding the fact that one year appears quite clearly to be a shorter period than "from year to year" (i.e. "for at least one year"). The uncertainty in this relation arises from *Wright v Tracey*,[50] in which it was held that a lease for a year was of longer duration than a yearly period tenancy (which last at least a year). The reasoning in *Wright v Tracey* has been widely discredited[51] and it now appears clear that leases for a year certain can be created orally. In the interests of certainty the Law Reform Commission's recommendations in relation to this controversy appear to be sensible and commendable. The Commission has recommended that the terms of s 4 ought to be clarified to show, without ambiguity, that all leases are to be created by writing except periodic tenancies and tenancies for a fixed period of under one year, apart from tenancies that contain renewal clauses (and can therefore extend for one year or more and ought, therefore, to be created in writing).[52] **[15–37]**

2. Assignment

Assignment is the out-and-out transfer of an interest in a lease (either the tenant's leasehold estate or, where applicable, the landlord's reversion). Where an assignment takes place the assignor is completely extricated from the leasehold arrangement and the **[15–38]**

---

[46] See, for example, Sheridan, "*Walsh v Lonsdale* in Ireland" (1952) 9 NILQ 190.

[47] LRC, *Consultation Paper on the General Law of Landlord and Tenant* (2003), pp 38–9.

[48] s 63(d), Land and Conveyancing Law Reform Act 2009.

[49] Periodic tenancies can be created for periods that are greater than one year, but this practice is exceptionally rare.

[50] (1874) IR 8 CL 478.

[51] *Lord Arran v Wills* and *Ryan v Chadwick* (reported together) (1883) 14 LR Ir 200; *Jameson v Squire* [1948] IR 153; *McGrath v Travers* [1948] IR 122.

[52] LRC, *Consultation Paper on the General Law of Landlord and Tenant* (2003), p 41.

assignee replaces the assignor within the pre-existing landlord-and-tenant relationship, and subject to the same rights and liabilities. [53] The means by which an assignment can be carried out is governed by s 9 of Deasy's Act, which provides that an assignment can take place by means of a deed or instrument in writing signed by the assignor or his agent lawfully authorised in writing, or on death, or by act or operation of law. Whether or not the leasehold interest being assigned is based on a written instrument is irrelevant to the application of the s 9 requirements.[54] While the provision for assignment by "act or operation of law" may allow for assignment to be recognised by means of the application of equitable principles, such as estoppel, this is by no means a required reading of s 9, which has led to the Law Reform Commission's recommendation that this provision ought to state clearly that courts retain the capacity to apply equitable principles when considering whether an assignment has taken place.[55]

[15–39] Landlords will occasionally want to restrict their tenants' freedom to assign the lease, but although ss 10 and 16 of Deasy's Act allowed for some limitation thereto, s 66 of the Landlord and Tenant (Amendment) Act 1980 has reversed this situation and now governs all attempts to try to restrict the alienation (i.e. assignment, sub-lease and mortgage) of tenants' leasehold interests. According to s 66(1), any term in a lease that attempts to restrict or prohibit alienation by the tenant will in fact have the effect of prohibiting alienation without the prior licence or consent of the landlord. An identical term is inserted in s 67 of the Landlord and Tenant (Amendment) Act 1980 in relation to covenants prohibiting change of user. Where the 1980 Act applies the landlord does not, therefore, appear to be capable of absolutely prohibiting alienation, although the consent requirement of course gives landlords an opportunity to prevent alienation by refusing to grant consent.

[15–40] In order to ensure that tenants' capacity to alienate property is not unduly restricted, s 66(2) provides that in most cases the landlord will not be entitled to unreasonably withhold his consent to a request for alienation.[56] This proviso applies to leases containing covenants not to alienate without the landlord's consent, leases containing absolute prohibitions on alienation, and leases or agreements for leases made between 1 June 1826 and 1 May 1832 for less than 99 years and containing no reference to subletting.

[15–41] The prohibition on "unreasonable" withholding of consent raises a clear and important question in this context: How is unreasonableness assessed? This question has given rise to a great deal of litigation on requests for consent to both alienation and change of user in Ireland, from which certain principles can be deduced. In *Rice v Dublin Corporation*[57] the Supreme Court held that the tenant has the burden of proving that consent was withheld unreasonably and, furthermore, that the landlord

[53] This is subject to the common law rules concerning the enforceability of covenants against original parties, considered below.
[54] See *Foley v Gavin* [1932] IR 339.
[55] LRC, *Consultation Paper on the General Law of Landlord and Tenant* (2003), p 52.
[56] s 66 (2)(a), Landlord and Tenant (Amendment) Act 1980.
[57] [1947] IR 425.

need not provide a reason for the refusal of consent until such time as the hearing is in motion.

In *White v Carlisle Trust*[58] the Court considered whether a landlord was obliged to take his own financial situation into account when considering whether or not to refuse consent. White, a tenant of Carlisle Trust, had applied to the landlord for its consent to a change of user of the rented premises from a tailoring business to that of a confectioner. Consent was refused on the ground that other tenants of the respondent, in adjoining premises, had objected that their businesses, which were of a similar nature, would be adversely affected. The appellant applied to the Circuit Court for an order dispensing with the respondent's consent, on the ground that it had been withheld unreasonably. He was unsuccessful in his application, but succeeded on appeal. McWilliam J held that a landlord may reasonably base a refusal of consent upon grounds of general policy relating to the management of his estate, but that in this case the landlord's refusal of consent was arbitrary and unreasonable as there was no threat or expectation of loss to the landlord himself. **[15–42]**

There then followed a duo of cases concerning Green Properties, in which the Irish courts built on the first principle from *White* to create a situation where landlords appear to have particularly broad discretion in terms of giving or refusing consent on the basis of "estate management". The first of these cases was *Green Properties Company Ltd v Shalaine Modes Ltd.*[59] Shalaine Modes Ltd rented two units from Green Properties in a shopping centre in Dublin. The lease contained a covenant that required the premises to be used as a general hardware store (i.e. a covenant relating to user). After some time the defendants began to use the units to sell toys, without obtaining written consent for the change of user. Shalaine Modes Ltd claimed that consent to the change of user was given verbally or by implication by the manager of the shopping centre, because they had for two years previously failed to act against subleases and changes of user that had been engaged in without written consent. In addition, they argued that the plaintiff did not act quickly enough once the matter came to their attention they were trying to resolve the dispute in negotiations with the other traders in the shopping centre, who were unhappy at the change in user). McWilliam J did not accept that there was an undue delay in making complaints to the defendants as to the change in the user; nor were they estopped from refusing consent now on the basis that they had failed to object in previous situations. The landlord did not act unreasonably in refusing his consent to the proposed change of user as he had the other renters within the shopping centre to take account of and, in addition, had a personal stake in ensuring the good estate management of the shopping centre. **[15–43]**

The second of this duo of cases was *OHS v Green Properties Company Ltd,*[60] which concerned s 67 of the Landlord and Tenant (Amendment) Act 1980 and applications for consent to a proposed change of user. OHS were leasing a retail unit subject to a **[15–44]**

[58] [1976–1977] ILRM 311.
[59] [1978] ILRM 222.
[60] [1986] IR 39.

covenant that the unit was to be used only "for the purposes of businesses of victualler, fruit, fish and vegetable merchants". The unit was originally used as a fruit and vegetable store, however, the tenants were finding it difficult to generate sufficient income from this user once a supermarket opened nearby. They subsequently received an offer for the premises from a building society, subject to the plaintiff obtaining the landlord's consent to a change of user to that of a building society. The landlord refused consent on the grounds that such a change of user would be contrary to good estate management in that there were already a large number of financial institutions in the shopping centre and the landlord did not want any more premises with "dead frontages". The plaintiff sought a declaration in the Circuit Court that the landlord had unreasonably withheld its consent. Lynch J held that in the circumstances of this case there was no unreasonableness on the part of the landlord as his decision was based on the grounds of "good estate management"—a valid and non-arbitrary reason for refusing consent.

[15–45] While it was originally the case that a landlord could more or less always be said to be acting reasonably if he refused to grant consent on the basis of a projected detriment to his own financial position,[61] landlords may now be required to act reasonably in terms of their decision-making process and, in so doing, to take into account the impact of their decisions on the tenants. This is suggested by the decision of the UK Court of Appeal in *International Drilling Fluids Ltd v Louisville Investments (Uxbridge) Ltd.*[62] In that case the tenants' predecessors entered into a 30-year lease in 1971, which included a clause not to assign the premises without the landlord's consent and providing that the landlord's consent would not be unreasonably withheld. The tenants sought consent to assignment in 1984, but the landlords refused consent on the grounds that the proposed use of the premises as serviced offices would be detrimental to the investment value of their reversion and would create a parking problem. At first instance it was held that the evidence did not justify refusal of consent on either of the two grounds advanced and, accordingly, that the landlord's refusal of consent was unreasonable. In the course of his judgment in the Court of Appeal, Balcombe LJ outlined seven principles relating to covenants that restrict alienation:

- the purpose of acquiring the landlord's consent to an assignment is to ensure that the leasehold premises is not used or held in an undesirable manner or by an undesirable assignee;
- as a result, the landlord is not entitled to refuse his consent on the basis of considerations that are unrelated to the landlord and tenant relationship;
- the onus of proving the unreasonableness of the refusal to consent lies on the party alleging it;

[61] *Burns v Morelli* [1953–54] IR Jur Rep 50; *Curragh Bloodstock Agency v Warner* [1959] IR Jur Rep 73; *W & L Crowe Ltd v Dublin Port & Docks Ltd* [1962] IR 194; *White v Carlisle Trust* [1976–77] ILRM 311.

[62] [1986] Ch 513. See also *Norwich Union Life Insurance Society v Shopmoor Ltd* [1999] 1 WLR 531; *Tollbench Ltd v Plymouth City Council* [1988] 1 EGLR 79; *Yorkshire Metropolitan Properties Ltd v Cooperative Retail Services Ltd* [2001] L & TR 26.

- it is not necessary for the landlord to prove that the conclusions which led him to refuse consent were justified, if they were conclusions which might be reached by a reasonable man in the circumstances;
- it may be reasonable for the landlord to refuse his consent to an assignment on the ground of the purpose for which the proposed assignee intends to use the premises, even though that purpose is not forbidden by the lease;
- while a landlord need usually only consider his own relevant interests, there may be cases in which there is such a disproportion between the benefit to the landlord and the detriment to the tenant if the landlord withholds his consent to an assignment, that it is unreasonable for the landlord to refuse consent;
- it is in each case a question of fact, depending upon all the circumstances, whether the landlord's consent to an assignment is being unreasonably withheld.

Louisville Investments therefore suggests that a landlord must take into account the [15–46] impact of his decision on both himself and the applicant tenant and then reach a proportionate conclusion. The question is whether or not this equitable and proportionate approach to reasonableness has been adopted by the Irish courts or whether the Irish jurisprudence continues to reflect a rather landlord-centric approach to this question. The recent High Court decision in *Irish Glass Bottle Ltd v Dublin Port*[63] suggests the latter. Carroll J outlined the law relating to consent as it currently stands in Ireland and did not identify proportionality as an important element of the test. Her summary of the law of reasonableness in Ireland is reproduced here in full as a result of its comprehensiveness:

> The principles of law to be applied derived from the various decided cases are as follows:
>
> 1. The onus is on the lessee to prove the premises are a tenement and that consent is unreasonably withheld (*see Rice v. Dublin Corporation*) [1947] I.R. 425.
> 2. The lessor must consider the application for the change of user on its merits. It cannot have a blanket policy of refusal (see *Rice v. Dublin Corporation*, [1947] I.R. 425, *O'Gorman v. Dublin Corporation* [1949] I.R. 40 and *White v. Carlisle Trust*) [1976-7] I.L.R.M. 311.
> 3. The lessor is entitled to consider its own interest in deciding whether or not to give consent (*W & L Crowe Limited v. Dublin Port & Docks Board* [1962] I.R. 294 and *Murphy v. O'Neill* [1948] I.R. 72).
> 4. The lessor is entitled to know precisely the nature of the proposed user and all details which might affect the question of whether to give consent or not (*Lloyd v. Earl of* Pembroke *& Anor* [1954] 89 I.L.T.R. 40).
> 5. This case also held that the tenant must intend to use the premises itself for the change of user. This question was reserved for further argument by the Supreme Court.
> 6. The reasonableness or not of the lessor's refusal of consent does not depend on the special circumstances of the tenant's case. The tenant's trading difficulties do not mean that the landlord must facilitate the tenant (*OHS v. Green Property* [1986] I.R. 39 and *Wanze Properties v. Mastertron Ltd.* [1992] I.L.R.M. 746).
> 7. The landlord may state the grounds for refusal to the court even if no reason had previously been given (*Rice v. Dublin Corporation* [1947] I.R. 425).
> 8. The landlord is prohibited from charging a fine or increasing the rent before giving consent to a change of user (s. 67(2) of the 1980 Act)...

---

[63] [2005] IEHC 89.

[15–47] *Irish Glass Bottles* would suggest that the proportionality element of the test of reasonableness considered in *Louisville Investments* has not been incorporated into Irish law and that the principles as outlined in the cases above continue to apply. Blacombe LJ's conclusion in *Louisville Investments* relating to the landlord's responsibility to take into account the proportionality of the impact of his decision on the tenant is an important development, and it could have a substantial impact in the context of Irish case law, which allows for landlords to reasonably refuse consent on the basis of "good estate management grounds". This concept was developed in Irish law through the decisions in *Green Property Company Ltd v Shalaine Modes Ltd*[64] and *OHS v Green Property Company Ltd*,[65] considered above. In essence, "good estate management grounds" will take into account the impact of the proposed assignment on the overall property portfolio of the landlord, particularly where the landlord has other, connected interests, such as in a shopping centre (the context involved in both of these cases). The concept itself, however, is certainly wide and nebulous enough to give landlords a great deal of latitude in their decision-making processes—the insertion of a requirement of "assessment of proportionality" could have the impact of reining in discretion to further equalise the relationship between landlord and tenant in this context. The case of *Meagher v Healy Pharmacy Ltd*,[66] also decided in 2005, does not disrupt the principles as they apply in Irish law, but simply reiterates that the landlord's reasons for refusing consent ought to be connected to the relationship of landlord and tenant. In that case Murphy J also reiterated the principle in *Kelly v Cussen*[67] that a tenant may be entitled to damages where he suffers a detriment as the result of an unreasonable withholding of consent.

3. Sub-Lease

[15–48] A sub-lease arises where a tenant creates a lease of part of his reversion to a third party. The creation of sub-leases is subject to the same requirements and doctrines as the creation of leases. A sub-lease does not disturb the landlord-and-tenant relationship between the original parties: it merely creates a subsidiary landlord-and-tenant relationship. If, for example, Patrick has leased a property from John for a period of 50 years and decides to sublet the property to Mary for 25 of those years, then Patrick is both the tenant of John *and* the landlord of Mary, *but* there is no landlord-and-tenant relationship between John and Mary. Any conditions that attempt to restrict or prohibit the sub-leasing of leasehold property are equally subject to the provisions of s 66 of the Landlord and Tenant (Amendment) Act 1980, considered above.

4. Tenancy by Implication

[15–49] Both the common law and Deasy's Act allow for a tenancy to be recognised by implication from the circumstances. As we have already seen, periodic tenancies will frequently arise by virtue of implication. However, s 5 of Deasy's Act introduced the concept that, where a tenant over holds on termination of a lease, this may result in an implied yearly tenancy at the liberty of the landlord. Unlike the common law

64 [1978] ILRM 222.
65 [1986] ILRM 481.
66 [2005] IEHC 120.
67 (1954) 88 ILTR 97.

presumption of a tenancy, the operation of s 5 is strictly limited to particular circumstances and can arise only where a tenant under a written lease remains in possession of the property on termination of the lease for at least one month following the landlord's demand for possession (provided the former tenant is not retaining possession under an alternative statutory provision[68]). In these circumstances the landlord is at liberty to imply a yearly tenancy from this over holding, although the landlord is not *required* to do so and may still take an action to assert his title against the over-holding former tenant.[69] If the landlord decides to imply a yearly tenancy, then this will be subject to the same terms and conditions as the prior written lease,[70] apart from those conditions that are incompatible with a periodic tenancy.[71]

Section 5 appears to be a provision without cause at this stage. The common law allows for the presumption of a tenancy in appropriate circumstances, such as in cases where a person has exclusive possession of property and pays a periodic sum to the reversioner. In these circumstances the common law can imply a periodic tenancy. As a result of the common law's capacity to imply a tenancy and the ongoing ambiguity about the relationship between this common law presumption and the implication of a tenancy under s 5, the Law Reform Commission's proposal for the repeal of s 5 ought surely to be implemented.[72] **[15–50]**

5. Rule in *Walsh v Lonsdale*

Where parties have entered into a contract to create a lease, but the lease itself has not actually been created between them, equity might intervene and specifically enforce that contract by recognising a lease in equity. In order for this to happen, a number of conditions must be fulfilled. First of all the court must be satisfied that there was a contract for a lease between the parties. In some cases a purported contract for a lease will be interpreted as a grant of a lease itself, in which case equitable intervention of this nature will not be required. In most cases, however, the existence of the contract will be proved by means of either compliance with s 2 of the Statute of Frauds (Ireland) 1695/s 51 of the Land and Conveyancing Law Reform Act 2009 or by application of the equitable doctrine of part performance. **[15–51]**

As leases are proprietary and therefore comprise conveyances of land, contracts for the creation of a lease were governed by the Statute of Frauds (Ireland) 1695 until the commencement of the Land and Conveyancing Law Reform Act 2009 on 1 December 2009. The Statute of Frauds required that all contracts for the sale of land (including contracts for a lease) would be evidenced by a note or memorandum in writing,[73] which would include the vital details of the proposed transaction (i.e. property, parties, **[15–52]**

---

[68] For example, where a tenant remains in possession as a result of a notice of intention to claim under the Landlord and Tenant (Amendment) Act 1980.

[69] Depending on the circumstances the landlord may be estopped from implying the tenancy—see *Eamonn Andrews Production Ltd v Gaiety Theatre (Dublin) Ltd*, unreported, High Court, 31 May 1976.

[70] See *Morrash v Alleyne* (1873) IR 7 Eq 487; *Earl of Meath v Megan* [1897] 2 IR 477; *Jameson v Squire* [1948] IR 153.

[71] See *Jameson v Squire* [1948] IR 153.

[72] LRC, *Consultation Paper on the General Law of Landlord and Tenant* (2003), pp 45–6.

[73] s 2, Statute of Frauds (Ireland) 1695.

price and particulars),[74] and be signed by the lessor or his lawfully authorised agent in writing. This note or memorandum made the original oral contract enforceable and acted as evidence of the existence and contents of that original oral contract. Thus, where there is a note or memorandum of a contract to create a lease and the lease itself has not been formally created, equity can exercise its discretionary jurisdiction to enforce that contract by means of a lease in equity. Section 51 of the Land and Conveyancing Law Reform Act 2009 makes some very minor changes when compared to s 2 of the Statute of Frauds. Section 51 provides:

> no action shall be brought to enforce any contract for the sale or other disposition of land unless the agreement on which such action is brought, or some memorandum or note of it, is in writing and signed by the person against whom the action is brought or that person's authorised agent.

It is clear that s 51 retains the same model as the Statute of Frauds by requiring the agreement to be in writing or for there to be a written note or memorandum of it but refers to this being "signed by the person against whom the action is brought or that person's authorised agent" rather than the reference in the Statute of Frauds to "the party to be charged [with the contract], or some other person thereunto by him lawfully authorised". Apart from this change the two sections are essentially the same.

[15–53] In some cases the contract for the creation of a lease will not have been evidenced by a note or memorandum in writing in compliance with the Statute of Frauds/Land and Conveyancing Law Reform Act 2009, but will have been acted upon by one of the parties. In cases of part performance of the alleged oral contract, the court can accept the part performance as evidence of the existence and contents of that original oral contract and enforce that contract as a mortgage in equity.[75] The acts that are alleged to comprise the part performance must be explicable by reference to the alleged contract[76] and must be such that non-enforcement of the contract would result in a fraud on the actor.[77]

[15–54] Thus, where there is a contract for a lease and the lease has not been formally created but where the contract is evidenced by *either* a note or memorandum further to the requirements of the Statute of Frauds (Ireland) 1695/Land and Conveyancing Law Reform Act 2009 *or* an act of part performance by either party, the law of equity may exercise its discretionary jurisdiction to enforce the lease in equity *on the basis* that "equity sees as done that which ought to have been done". The application of this maxim in the context of landlord-and-tenant law is known as the Rule in *Walsh v Lonsdale.*[78] Importantly, however, the Rule in *Walsh v Lonsdale* will be applicable only where the ordinary requirements of specific performance are fulfilled. Thus the court

[74] *Carrigy v Brock* (1871) IR 5 CL 501, *per* Palles CB at p 505; *Crane v Naughton* [1912] 2 IR 318; *Law v Roberts & Co.* [1964] IR 292; *Smith v Jones* [1952] 2 All ER 907; *Barrett v Costelloe* (1973) 107 ILTSJ 239.

[75] *Hope v Lord Cloncurry* (1874) IR 8 Eq 555; s 51(2), Land and Conveyancing Law Reform Act 2009.

[76] *Lowry v Reid* [1927] NI 142; *Steadman v Steadman* [1973] 3 WLR 56.

[77] *Clinan v Cooke* (1802) I Sch & Lef 22.

[78] (1882) 21 Ch D 9; *McCausland v Murphy* (1881) 9 LR Ir 9.

must be satisfied that the applicant has acted equitably and in compliance with the maxims of equity *and* that common law damages are insufficient[79] *and* that specific performance would not be futile because the defendant cannot comply with it[80] *and* that specific enforcement would not place the defendant in breach of a covenant in a head lease[81] *and* that the defendant has the legal capacity to grant a lease.[82] The courts will not apply the Rule in *Walsh v Lonsdale*, however, unless they are satisfied that the indicia of a tenancy are present within the landholding agreement and, in particular, that the parties had the required intention to create a landlord-and-tenant relationship.[83]

The fact that the courts can enforce an agreement for a lease as a lease in equity tempts the reader to think that a contract for a lease is as good as a lease, after all the application of specific performance is intended to place the applicant in the same position as he would have been in had the lease actually been created between the parties. Such a view, however, ought not to be taken as accurate. For one thing specific performance is an equitable remedy and, as a result, is dependent on the discretion of equity. Secondly, because there is no privity of contract or legal privity of estate between the parties, there may be some difficulties with the enforcement of leasehold covenants in relation to the landholding arrangement. Finally, the leasehold interest of a successful applicant will be equitable and therefore may be defeated by a legal interest in a competition of priorities, particularly where the land involved is unregistered.[84] **[15–55]**

IV. Termination of a Lease

While leases for a term certain will come to an end when the specified term expires, there are numerous scenarios in which either the landlord or the tenant will want to bring the lease to an end before that time and, of course, in the context of periodic tenancies there is no natural expiry: the period refreshes automatically until terminated. For the majority of leasehold relationships, the mechanism of terminating the lease will be dictated by either the terms of the lease itself or by statute. There are various mechanisms for the premature termination of a leasehold relationship, the most common of which are dealt with here. **[15–56]**

1. Notice to Quit

A notice to quit is used to terminate leases where the tenant has over held, in periodic tenancies and in all residential tenancies.[85] Notice to quit can generally be served for any reason and a breach is not required, however once a residential tenant has **[15–57]**

[79] *Davis v Hone* (1805) 2 Sch & Lef 341; *Harnett v Yielding* (1805) 2 Sch & Lef 549; *Sheridan v Higgins* [1971] IR 291.

[80] *Costigan v Hastler* (1804) 2 Sch & Lef 160; *Harnett v Yielding* (1805) 2 Sch & Lef 549; *Bayly v Tyrell* (1813) 2 Ba & B 358.

[81] *Mulholland v Belfast Corporation* (1859) Dru *temp* Nap 539; *Browne v Marquis of Sligo* (1859) 10 IR Ch R 1; *Carton v Bury* (1860) 10 IR Ch R 387.

[82] *Harnett v Yielding* (1805) 2 Sch & Lef 549; *Ellard v Lord Llandaff* (1810) 1 Ba & B 241; *O'Rourke v Percival* (1811) 2 Ba & B 58; *Power v Barrett* (1887) 19 LR Ir 450.

[83] See also *Ó Siodhachain v O'Mahony* [2002] 4 IR 147.

[84] For more on priorities in unregistered land, see Chapter 7.

[85] Residential Tenancies Act 2004, s 58.

completed six months' possession under the lease, a landlord may only terminate the tenancy for specified reasons during the next three-and-a-half years.[86] The operation of the doctrine of notice within the context of residential tenancies is considered in greater detail below.[87]

[15–58] A notice to quit can be served by either party to the lease and by any person who has been specifically authorised to serve such a notice (although implied authorisation will arise only in limited situations). In the case of agricultural land, "houses",[88] and property held under a residential tenancy,[89] the notice must be in writing, although it is common practice for notices to quit to be provided in writing notwithstanding the character of the premises involved. In relation to "houses" the requirement that the notice to quit should be in writing does not apply to service occupancies,[90] temporary convenience lettings,[91] holiday leases[92] or other leases defined as "excepted" by the Minister for Justice.[93]

[15–59] The common law prescribed that, in general, a periodic tenant was to receive notice equivalent to one period of the tenancy. Thus a weekly periodic tenant was entitled to one week's notice and a monthly periodic tenant to one month's notice. A yearly periodic tenancy could be terminated by service of a half-a-year's notice (i.e. 183 days, *not* six months), which should expire on the anniversary of the yearly tenancy. Notice to quit must normally expire on what is known as a gale day, i.e. the day on which a period of the tenancy expires. Section 16(3) of the Housing (Miscellaneous Provisions) Act 1992 appears to have introduced a statutory minimum notice period for the first time in Irish law and provides that at least four weeks' written notice must be provided to the tenant of a "house" that is held on a weekly tenancy, although the Residential Tenancies Act 2004 now introduces new statutory notice periods for all residential leases.[94]

[15–60] In general terms, a notice to quit ought to be served, by hand, on the tenant or any person present in the premises who could be said to be under a duty to deliver the notice to the tenant (e.g. the tenant's spouse). Whether or not someone has a duty to deliver the notice to the tenant will be a matter of fact that will be determined by the court, but if a court finds that the person on whom the notice was served did have a duty to deliver it, the fact that this notice did not in fact reach the tenant will be irrelevant. If the tenant has died the notice to quit ought to be served on the personal representatives or, where there are none, on the President of the High Court. If, however, a third party is in occupation of the leasehold premises, the service of notice to quit on the occupant will be sufficient.

---

86 *ibid.*, s 28.
87 See paras 15–61 to 15–65.
88 As defined by the Housing (Miscellaneous Provisions) Act 1992.
89 As defined by the Residential Tenancies Act 2004.
90 s 16(2)(a), Housing (Miscellaneous Provisions) Act 1992.
91 s 16(2)(b), *ibid.*
92 s 16(2)(c), *ibid.*
93 s 16(2)(d), *ibid.*
94 See paras 15–61 to 15–65.

The service of a notice to quit is not an irrevocable action; rather, this notice might be waived by the landlord, resulting in the continuation of the tenancy.[95] A notice to quit can be waived by the service of a fresh notice to quit (which then becomes the effective notice to quit); *or* by a demand for rent that has become due after the expiry of the notice period, if that demand is accompanied by an intention to waive the notice to quit; *or* the acceptance of rent that has become due after the expiry of the notice period, provided that acceptance is accompanied by an intention to waive the notice to quit. **[15–61]**

Parts 5 and 6 of the Residential Tenancies Act 2004 provide for the termination of private residential tenancies.[96] Notice of termination (as it is called in the Act) is now the only means by which a residential tenancy can be terminated.[97] Within the first six months both the landlord and the tenant can terminate the residential tenancy without cause on the service of at least 28 days' notice.[98] After the first six months, however, the tenant becomes entitled to three-and-a-half years of security of tenure (known as a "Part 4 Tenancy"), during which the landlord can only terminate the tenancy on particular grounds.[99] Once the initial six months has expired, a landlord may only terminate a residential tenancy for the following reasons[100]: **[15–62]**

(1) where the tenant has not complied with his obligations, the tenant has been notified of the breach and has not righted it; *or*
(2) where the dwelling is no longer suitable to the needs of the tenant; *or*
(3) where the landlord is selling the property, provided the landlord is in a position to enter into "an enforceable agreement for the transfer to another, for full consideration, of the whole of his or her interest in the dwelling" within three months of the termination of the Part 4 tenancy; or
(4) where the landlord requires the dwelling for his own occupation or for a member of his family to occupy. If the dwelling is required for a member of the landlord's family, the notice of termination must state the identity of the intended occupant, his relationship to the landlord and the expected duration of his occupation. The notice must also include a statement that the landlord will offer the tenant a fresh tenancy if the family member quits the property within six months; or
(5) where the landlord intends to substantially refurbish or renovate the dwelling and planning permission, if necessary, has been obtained, provided the notice of termination specifies the nature of the intended refurbishment/renovation works and requires the landlord to offer the property for rent to the tenant if it becomes available for re-letting; or
(6) where the landlord intends to change the use of the dwelling and planning permission, if necessary, has been obtained provided the notice of termination

[95] *Curoe v Gordon* (1892) 26 ILTR 95.
[96] For an excellent consideration of the termination of residential tenancies, see Cannon, "Termination of Tenancies under the Residential Tenancies Act 2004: The New System" (2005) 10(4) CPLJ 85.
[97] ss 58 and 59, Residential Tenancies Act 2004.
[98] ss 66 and 69, *ibid.*
[99] s 33, *ibid.*
[100] s 34, *ibid.*

specifies the nature of the intended change of use and requires the landlord to offer the property for rent to the tenant if it becomes available for re-letting.

[15–63] The tenant is entitled to terminate the lease for any reason upon service of the appropriate period of notice. The only exception is where a tenant attempts to serve a notice in order to cut short a fixed-term lease and there has been no breach on the part of the landlord.[101] There are certain situations in which the tenant can terminate the tenancy on the service of a shorter period of notice. If the landlord has engaged in behaviour that poses an imminent danger of death or serious injury, or imminent danger to the fabric of the dwelling or the property containing the dwelling, the tenant may terminate on seven days' notice.[102] If the landlord is in breach of his obligations under the lease, has been notified of the breach by the tenant and has failed to remedy the breach within a reasonable time, the tenant may terminate on the service of 28 days' notice.[103]

[15–64] Any attempt on the part of landlords to terminate a residential tenancy for a reason not specified in the Act will be invalid.[104] If the tenant has engaged in anti-social behaviour[105] or conduct "threatening to the fabric of the dwelling or the property containing the dwelling",[106] the notice period will be seven days;[107] if the tenant has breached a covenant of the lease, the landlord need serve only 28 days' notice,[108] except in the case of breach for non-payment of rent, in which case the landlord must notify the tenant in writing that the rent is in arrears and give the tenant 14 days to pay the rent prior to serving 28 days' notice of termination.[109] Section 17(1) defines anti-social behaviour as:

(1) behaviour that constitutes the commission of an offence, being an offence the commission of which is reasonably likely to affect directly the well-being or welfare of others; or
(2) behaviour that causes or could cause fear, danger, injury, damage or loss to any person living, working or otherwise lawfully in the dwelling concerned or its vicinity and, without prejudice to the generality of the foregoing, includes violence, intimidation, coercion, harassment or obstruction of, or threats to, any such person; or
(3) behaviour that prevents or interferes with the peaceful occupation of another occupant of the relevant dwelling, any person residing in any other dwelling contained in the property containing the dwelling concerned, or any neighbouring dwelling.

---

[101] s 58(2), *ibid.*
[102] s 68, *ibid.*
[103] *ibid.*
[104] See the decisions of the Private Residential Tenancies Board, available at www.prtb.ie, and the analysis of some decisions in Ryall, "Residential Tenancies Act 2004: Review and Assessment" (2006) 6(1) JSIJ 60.
[105] For the definition of anti-social behaviour see s 17, Residential Tenancies Act 2004.
[106] s 67(2)(a), *ibid.*
[107] s 67(2)(a), *ibid.*
[108] s 67(2)(b), *ibid.*
[109] s 67(3), *ibid.*

If a landlord is terminating a Part 4 tenancy on the basis of breach of covenant, the tenant must be informed of the basis for the termination and given an opportunity to remedy the breach.[110] The relative notice periods for both the landlord and the tenant are:[111]

Duration of Tenancy	Notice by Landlord	Notice by Tenant
Less than 6 months	28 days	28 days
Greater than 6 months, but less than 1 year	35 days	35 days
1 year or more, but less than 2 years	42 days	42 days
2 years or more, but less than 3 years	56 days	56 days
3 years or more, but less than 4 years	84 days	56 days
Greater than 4 years	112 days	56 days

If the 2004 Act requires a shorter period of notice than that provided for in the lease itself, the terms of the lease will govern the duration of the notice to quit,[112] subject to the proviso that the maximum period of notice in the case of a tenancy that has lasted less than six months is set at 70 days.[113] A valid notice of termination must be in writing and signed by the party terminating the tenancy and must specify the date of actual service,[114] be in the "prescribed form"[115] and include the date on which the tenancy will come to an end.[116] Finally, all notices of termination must state that any disputes as to the validity of the notice must be referred to the Private Residential Tenancies Board (PRTB) within 28 days of receipt. **[15–65]**

Although the rules introduced by the 2004 Act for the termination of a residential tenancy are to be commended for their sympathy towards both the tenancy and the various circumstances in which a residential tenancy may be terminated, it is difficult to find any fault with Ruth Cannon's conclusion that the rules "are perhaps unnecessarily tortuous and convoluted" and in need of some simplification.[117] **[15–66]**

2. Forfeiture

Forfeiture comprises the retaking of possession by the landlord, thereby ending the tenant's exclusive possession and, consequently, his leasehold rights. Forfeiture is appropriate only in those situations where the lease is still running and the landlord wishes to bring it to an end, but it is not available in the context of private residential tenancies.[118] Forfeiture is limited to particular situations and a landlord is required to **[15–67]**

[110] s 34, Table, Ground 1, *ibid.*
[111] ss 66–68, *ibid.*
[112] s 60, *ibid.*
[113] s 65(4), *ibid.*
[114] ss 62 and 64, *ibid.*
[115] s 62, *ibid.*
[116] *ibid.*
[117] Cannon, "Termination of Tenancies under the Residential Tenancies Act 2004: The New System" (2005) 10(4) CPLJ 85.
[118] s 58, Residential Tenancies Act 2004.

comply with certain statutory requirements in order to carry out a valid forfeiture.[119] Because this is essentially an equitable action, a landlord will also be aware of the importance of acting equitably while forfeiting the lease, and the tenant will be in a position to apply for equitable relief, where appropriate. Forfeiture is available in three situations: (a) disclaimer of the landlord's title; (b) breach of condition in the lease; and (c) breach of covenant in the lease *provided* the covenant allows for forfeiture as a result of breach.

[15–68] Under the doctrine of estoppel a tenant is not entitled to act in a manner that denies the superior title of his landlord. If a tenant engages in positive action that constitutes a disclaimer or disputation of the landlord's title, the landlord becomes entitled to enter the premises and forfeit the lease.

[15–69] Conditions in a lease are also subject to forfeiture for breach, even if they do not expressly allow for it. As a result of the availability of forfeiture for breach of a condition, it is essential that a condition in a lease can be identified. In essence—and resulting from the contractual nature of the leasehold relationship—a condition might be said to be a fundamental term of a lease, whereas covenants could be said to be lesser terms. The classification of any leasehold term will be a matter for determination of the court; the label placed on a term by the leasehold agreement will not be determinative, although it will be highly indicative of the nature of the term.

[15–70] The breach of leasehold covenants does not normally result in a right to forfeit on the part of the landlord. The agreement itself may specify forfeiture as a remedy for the breach of any particular covenant and, where such a "proviso for re-entry and forfeiture" is included, its terms will govern the availability of forfeiture. In many cases—particularly cases of commercial tenancies—it is now common practice to include a general forfeiture and re-entry clause in relatively wide terms, which would allow for forfeiture for breach of any express (and in some cases implied) terms.[120]

[15–71] In most cases of forfeiture the landlord is required to serve the tenant with what is known as a "Section 14 Notice" required by s 14 of the Conveyancing Act 1881. There are only a limited number of situations in which no Section 14 Notice is to be served,[121] the most prominent of which relates to forfeiture for non-payment of rent.[122] Because of the equitable nature of forfeiture and the resultant significance attached to the conduct of the parties, most landlords will serve a notice in relation to forfeiture for non-payment of rent in an attempt to prevent equitable relief for the tenant.

[15–72] Because the purpose of the Section 14 Notice is to give the tenant an opportunity to consider whether or not he wants to maintain the lease and, to avoid forfeiture, to make good on the breach,[123] it is essential that the notice would include sufficient information to enable the tenant to make these decisions. This is reflected in the

[119] s 14, Conveyancing Act 1881.
[120] See, for example, *Doe d Rains v Kneller* (1829) 4 C & P 3.
[121] s 14(6), Conveyancing Act 1881 *as amended by* s 2(2), Conveyancing Act 1882.
[122] s 14(8), Conveyancing Act 1881.
[123] See *Horsey Estate v Steiger* [1899] 2 QB 79 *per* Russell LJ at p 91.

requirements of s 14, which do not require any particular form of notice but do require that the following information is included:

(1) the basis (or multiple bases) of the forfeiture and, if applicable,[124] a requirement to remedy the breach,[125] although the form of the remedy is not specified and is a matter for the tenant[126]; and
(2) a demand for reasonable compensation; and
(3) a notice of termination by forfeiture for failure to remedy the breach and provide reasonable compensation within a reasonable time of the service of the Section 14 Notice. The reasonableness of the prescribed time period will be entirely dependent on the circumstances.[127]

If the breach is not remedied and the compensation is not paid *or* if the forfeiture is for non-payment of rent, the landlord is entitled to re-enter the premises, thereby forfeiting the lease. The re-entry can be either physical or legal, but the service of the notice without re-entry is not sufficient to actually forfeit the lease.[128] It does not appear that any court order is required to effect this re-entry once the Section 14 Notice requirements have been complied with.[129] Under both the common law[130] and criminal law,[131] a landlord who chooses physical re-entry is not entitled to use force. The landlord is not required to carry out a physical re-entry of the land and may instead choose to engage in legal re-entry, which can be achieved by means of issuing possession proceedings. This is primarily achieved by the issue of an Ejectment Civil Bill on Title or a plenary summons.[132]

Tenants can apply for relief from forfeiture. This relief could be granted under either s 14 of the Conveyancing Act 1881 or by means of an equitable remedy, such as an injunction. If physical re-entry has taken place, this relief can be applied for in its own right (provided the re-entry was not pursuant to a court order[133]), or it can form part of a defence to possession proceedings where they are taken. **[15–73]**

Section 14(2) of the Conveyancing Act 1881 provides that the High Court may grant relief from a forfeiture following the service of a Section 14 Notice "having regard to **[15–74]**

[124] If the breach is said to be "irremediable", there will be no requirement that the tenant remedy it, although the courts will be exceptionally reluctant to find that a breach is irremediable. See *Rugby School Governors v Tannahill* [1935] 1 KB 87; *Troop v Gibson* [1986] 1 EGLR 1; *Capital and Counties Property Co v Forbes* [1974] QB 575.

[125] If a landlord has remedied the breach himself under a power to re-enter the property, then this breach can not be the basis of a forfeiture—*SEDAC Investments v Tanner* [1982] 1 WLR 1342.

[126] *Fox v Jolly* [1916] 1 AC 1.

[127] See *Campus and Stadium Development Ltd v Dublin Waterworld Ltd* [2006] IEHC 200; *Walsh v Wightman* [1927] NI 1.

[128] *Bank of Ireland v Lady Lisa Ireland Ltd* [1993] ILRM 235.

[129] *Sweeney Ltd v Powerscourt Shopping Centre Ltd* [1984] IR 501.

[130] *ibid.*, seemingly varying the "reasonable force" position adopted in *Kavanagh v Grudge* (1844) 7 Man & G 316. See also Cannon, "Forfeiture for Breach of Covenant by a Tenant—the Need for Reform" (2007) 12(1) CPLJ 5.

[131] Prohibition on Forcible Entry and Occupation Act 1971, s 2.

[132] See Cannon, *art. cit.*

[133] *West v Rogers* (1884) 4 TLR 229.

the proceedings and conduct of the parties under the foregoing provisions of this section, and on such terms, if any, as to costs, expenses, damages, compensation, penalty, or otherwise, including the granting of an injunction, as it sees fit". When assessing whether or not to grant relief the courts will consider whether the alleged breach was deliberate or inadvertent,[134] any delay on the part of the landlord, and the impact of the forfeiture on the tenant in terms of any hardship that may be caused.

[15–75] In terms of equitable remedies, a tenant can seek an injunction against forfeiture on the basis of a defence even after the re-entry has taken place. In these cases the tenant might be permitted to go back into possession until the application for relief has been decided upon or, if the application is successful but the tenant has not been given possession pending decision on the claim, the landlord may be required to reduce the sum owed to him as a result of the possession he enjoyed, but which—because of the tenant's successful application—it transpires he was not entitled to.[135] A tenant can also apply for a general equitable relief against forfeiture, which may be particularly relevant if a landlord is threatening forfeiture in order to secure payment (as opposed to what you might call a bona fide forfeiture).[136] In the case of commercial leases, however, it appears that courts may be reluctant to grant relief just because the forfeiture concerned non-payment of rent. In *Cue Club Ltd v Navaro Ltd*[137] the Supreme Court noted that the commercial viability of rented premises (in this case a premises within a shopping centre) may well depend on the prompt payment of rent and charges. A commercial tenant may then need to satsify a somewhat higher standard before equitable relief from forfeiture will be granted.

3. Merger

[15–76] The general rule that one cannot be landlord and tenant of the same piece of land means that if a tenant becomes the owner of the landlord's estate, a merger will usually occur. As this is an equitable principle it will be applied only where it appears from the circumstances that a merger was the intention of the parties, and such a presumption will generally not arise where the merger would not be to the benefit of the receiving party. The operation of this equitable principle results in the termination of the lease and the receiving party enjoying the merged leasehold and reversion estates. This will only happen, however, where the landlord or tenant receives the other's estate in their capacity as landlord and tenant and not, for example, as mortgagee,[138] and where there is no intervening interest. A legal lease cannot merge with an equitable fee simple.

4. Surrender

[15–77] Surrender is the immediate transfer of the tenant's interest to the landlord and results in the termination of the lease. Surrender can occur by means of a deed[139] or by act or

[134] *Billson v Residential Apartments Ltd (No. 1)* [1992] 1 AC 494; *Campus and Stadium Development v Dublin Waterworld* [2006] IEHC 200.
[135] *Monument Creameries v Carysfort Estates* [1967] IR 462.
[136] *Shiloh Spinners v Harding* [1973] AC 691; *Whipp v Mackey* [1927] IR 372.
[137] Unreported, Supreme Court, 23 October 1996; *Cf Campus and Stadium Development v Dublin Waterworld* [2006] IEHC 200.
[138] See *Farrelly v Doughty* (1881) 15 ILTR 100.
[139] s 7, Deasy's Act 1860.

operation of law. Surrender by operation of law generally takes the form of the physical handover of property, keys and title documents (usually the lease) and needs to be accompanied by a statutory declaration of surrender of a competent independent person who was present at the surrender. The capacity to surrender a lease is dependent on the terms of the lease itself.

5. Ejectment

Where a lease has been terminated by one of the methods considered above, the landlord may continue to experience some difficulty in securing vacant possession of the land. The tenant may refuse to vacate the premises for various reasons—a belief of statutory entitlements or a hope that a court might provide relief from the termination of the lease, for example—but where the lease has been terminated the landlord will almost always want to take possession of the premises. This can be achieved through ejectment, which can arise in a variety of cases, three of which continue to occur on a relatively frequent basis.[140] **[15–78]**

Where a landlord has forfeited the lease, but has been unable to take possession peaceably, an ejectment civil bill on title will be the appropriate mechanism to retake possession. If rent is one year or more in arrears, an ejectment for non-payment of rent may be appropriate. Section 52 of Deasy's Act limits this form of ejectment to cases of at least one year's arrears of rent and requires that the tenant be not actually ejected until six months have passed from the making of the ejectment order. If payment is made within the six-month period the ejectment order will lapse. Over-holding is the third primary scenario in which ejectment might be used by a landlord. In such a scenario the tenant will have continued in possession following the service and expiration of a notice to quit *or* following the natural expiration of the lease.[141] **[15–79]**

V. Leasehold Covenants

Leases are ongoing relationships and, in many cases, will be completed after the landlord has engaged in a relatively diligent search for what he considers to be appropriate tenants. Because of the ongoing nature of the landlord-and-tenant relationship, leases will normally feature a large number of covenants on the part of both the landlord and the tenant. While the landlord and tenant are theoretically free to negotiate and include any covenants they wish, these must comply with the general rules of the law of contract and in some cases covenants (or "obligations" in the context of residential tenancies) will be implied by law. **[15–80]**

1. Express Covenants

The parties to a lease are entitled to negotiate express covenants, although those covenants must comply with the ordinary doctrines of contract law. In the case of private residential tenancies, these express covenants will be overridden by the terms of the Residential Tenancies Act 2004 and, particularly, the obligations of landlords and **[15–81]**

---

[140] Ejectment is also possible in a number of other scenarios (ejectment for deserted premises and against cottier tenants, servants, herdsmen and caretakers), but its usage in such cases is now practically obsolete.

[141] s 72, Deasy's Act 1860.

tenants provided in ss 12 and 16 where they are inconsistent with the terms of the Act. The application of the restraint of trade doctrine to leasehold covenants is of particular interest, especially in the context of commercial leases where such clauses are most likely to appear.

[15–82] The restraint of trade doctrine emanates from contract law and provides that conditions restraining trade are, prima facie, unenforceable and can become enforceable only if they are reasonable, having regard to the interests of the parties concerned and to the public interest. The question to consider at this juncture is whether the doctrine of restraint of trade can be employed in order to have a covenant in a lease struck out. This was considered in the Irish case of *Irish Shell v Elm Motors.*[142] The defendants in this case carried on a garage and petrol service business and the plaintiffs, an oil company, sold petroleum products. In 1969 Elm Motors bought a six-acre plot beside a public road and adjoining an acre plot that belonged to Irish Shell. Irish Shell had acquired planning permission for the development of their plot as a petrol and service station. The defendants' application for a similar permission for their plot was refused, and they decided not to appeal the decision once they agreed with Irish Shell that they would lease that plot of land from them. They then acquired planning permission to develop the combined plots as a petrol station. The lease between the parties included a covenant to buy all petroleum products required by the defendants for sale or use on the combined plots exclusively from the plaintiffs, to exhibit on the combined plots the plaintiffs' signs and advertising matter and to decorate the combined plots in the plaintiff's standard colours. This agreement was enforced for a while, but in March 1982 Elm Motors ceased buying their supplies from Irish Shell and removed all signs and advertising for Irish Shell from the property. The landlord sued, but Elm Motors counterclaimed that the covenant was unenforceable for restraint of trade. Costello J granted the relief sought by Irish Shell and held, *inter alia*, that where a tenant first takes possession of premises under a lease, a negative covenant by him in the lease restricting the businesses or trades which he may conduct on the demised premises is not rendered void by the common law doctrine of restraint of trade. The decision was appealed to the Supreme Court on the matter of how the doctrine operated in the case and on the matter of costs, but the Supreme Court decision did not reconsider Costello J's holding that the restraint of trade doctrine applied in leaseholds only where the tenant had freedom to trade in the first place, which was not the case here.

[15–83] Covenants for repair are one of the most common types of express covenant in leases but have the potential to be exceptionally onerous in particular situations. If, for example, the property is badly damaged by a storm, ought the tenant's repair covenant oblige him to repair it? Essentially, questions of this nature are left to the terms of the lease and all of the doctrines of contract law—such as unconscionable bargain and undue influence—are available to a tenant who may feel aggrieved. Where there is a repair covenant that is not fulfilled, the tenant will be obliged to pay damages to the landlord. Section 65 of Deasy's Act treats this issue and provides that the damages ought not to exceed the reduction in the value of the landlord's reversion by reason of the failure to repair. In addition, s 65 provides for certain situations in which no

[142] [1984] IR 200. See also *Bayzane Ltd v Galligan* [1987] IR 238; *Ferris v Ward* [1998] 2 IR 94.

damages ought to be payable, even where the property is returned in a bad state of repair:

(1) Where the age and condition of the premises make repair physically impossible.
(2) Where the repair would require expenditure that is disproportionate to the value of the leasehold property, having regard to the property's age, condition, location and character.
(3) Where the leased property could not profitably be used without a rebuild, reconstruction or considerable structural alteration (the character and situation of the leasehold property are taken into account).

It also appears to be settled law that a tenant subject to a covenant for repair is not obliged to repair the premises to a better condition than that in which they were at the time of the creation of the lease.[143] **[15–84]**

It is quite common for leases to include rent-review clauses, which are essentially covenants for the payment of rent at the agreed rate *and* at a rate that may change based on a review done according to the terms agreed. In commercial leases a practice had developed of including what became known as "upward-only rent-review" clauses, i.e. clauses providing that when a rent review is done it would result in the rent remaining stable or going up but could *never* result in the rent reducing. In fact, some rent-review clauses even went so far as to provide that rent would inevitably go up. While these kinds of review clauses raised relatively few eyebrows during the years of economic prosperity and, as a result, rents reached astronomical levels (particularly in very commercially active areas of Dublin city), the economic crisis brought the problematic nature of such clauses into sharp relief. Although in some cases individual landlords and tenants negotiated rent terms outside of the strict rent-review clauses in their leases, there can be no doubt but that some commercial tenants have suffered significantly from the operation of what are now economically inappropriate upward-only rent-review clauses. Attempts have been made in the Master's court to interpret what appear to be upward-only rent-review clauses in a manner that allows for rent to remain stable or even to be reduced on the basis of a public policy commitment to "fair rents",[144] but this does seem to fly in the face of the express terms of the lease, especially bearing in mind the commercial nature of the lease and the fact that tenants entered into such clauses with their eyes open to the risks they entailed. Section 132 of the Land and Conveyancing Law Reform Act 2009 attempts to prevent the creation of any such clauses in the future. Section 132(3) provides: **[15–85]**

> A provision in a lease to which this section applies which provides for the review of the rent payable under the lease shall be construed as providing that the rent payable following such review may be fixed at an amount which is less than, greater than or the same as the amount of rent payable immediately prior to the date on which the rent falls to be reviewed.

---

[143] See, for example, *Lister v Lane and Nesham* [1893] 2 QB 212; *Norah Whelan and Others v Patrick Madigan* [1978] ILRM 136; *Sotheby v Grundy* [1947] 2 All ER 761; *Údarás Na Gaeltachta v Uisce Gleann Teoranta* [2007] IEHC 95.

[144] *Kidney v Charlton* [2009] MR 1.

[15–86] This provision essentially provides that, no matter how worded, any rent-review clause in a lease is to be interpreted as allowing the rent to go down or up or to remain the same. Thus, any attempt to provide that rent can only be reviewed upwards will now be unsuccessful. Section 132 is limited to commercial leases[145] and has no retrospective effect.[146] While calls for retrospective abolition of upwards only rent-review clauses can be understood, especially in a difficult economic climate, there is some significant weight to be attached to the dual arguments that commercial parties should be bound by their pact no matter how hard because they were negotiated in a commercial context *and* that abolishing such clauses retrospectively would reduce the moral hazard for commercial entities in entering into property-related contracts in the future. In addition, abolishing such clauses retrospectively may have a serious impact on the commercial viability of the landlord, which ought not to be dismissed out of hand.[147]

2. Implied Covenants

[15–87] Even where the lease does not include express covenants, a number of covenants will be implied by both statute and the common law. In most cases the implied covenants are fall-back provisions inasmuch as they can be overridden by the terms of the lease itself. In the context of private residential tenancies, however, the obligations provided for by the Residential Tenancies Act 2004 override the terms of the lease and cannot be contracted out of.

(i) Implied Covenants/Obligations of the Landlord

[15–88] Section 41 of Deasy's Act implies a number of covenants on the part of the landlord. First, it implies that the landlord has good title to grant the lease. Secondly, it implies a covenant for the quiet and peaceable enjoyment of the land in the following terms:

> The tenant shall have quiet and peaceable enjoyment of the said lands or tenements without the interruption of the landlord or any person whomsoever during the term contracted for, so long as the tenant shall pay the rent and perform the agreements contained in the lease to be observed on the part of the tenant.

As is clear from the terms of s 41, this implied covenant places an exceptionally broad liability on the landlord: not only does he guarantee against interference by him or his agents but also by "any person whomsoever". As a result of this it is common practice for this implied covenant to be overridden by an express covenant for quiet and peaceable enjoyment, in which the landlord guarantees against interference by himself and his agents but not by third parties.

[15–89] The common law also implies a covenant relating to the condition of the rented premises. This position is a relatively recent one as the common law traditionally held that a landlord had no liability for harm resulting from the condition of the premises

[145] s 132(1), Land and Conveyancing Law Reform Act 2009.

[146] s 132(2), *ibid.*

[147] Hession, "Upward Only Rent Review (UORR) in Commercial Leases" (2005) 10(2) CPLJ 34; Canny, "Upwards Only Rent Reviews in a Declining Property Market, and Recent Case Law on Repudiating Leases in an Examinership" (2010) 17(2) CPLJ 19.

unless the condition of the premises was fraudulently concealed.[148] The development of the tortious "neighbour principle" in *Donohue v Stevenson*[149] resulted in a significant change to this position. The principle was stated by Lord Atkins thus:

> There must be, and is, some general conception of relations giving rise to a duty of care, of which the particular cases found in the books are but instances... The rule that you are to love your neighbour becomes in law you must not injure your neighbour; and the lawyer's question: Who is my neighbour? receives a restricted reply. You must take reasonable care to avoid acts or omissions which you can reasonably foresee would be likely to injure your neighbour. Who, then, in law, is my neighbour? The answer seems to be—persons who are so closely and directly affected by my act that I ought reasonably to have them in contemplation as being so affected when I am directing my mind to the acts or omissions that are called in question.[150]

The implications of this principle for housing authority landlords' liability relating to the condition of rented premises was considered in some detail in the case of *Siney v Dublin Corporation*.[151] Pursuant to its powers under the Housing Act 1966, Dublin Corporation made a first letting to the plaintiff of a flat in a block of flats that it had constructed. This was a weekly tenancy at a rent in excess of £130 per annum and upon terms which required the plaintiff to reside in the flat during the tenancy. Within two months water appeared under the floor, covering the bedroom of the flat, and a fungus spread over the walls. The condition deteriorated to the extent that Siney and his family were compelled to leave the flat and were provided with alternative accommodation by the defendant. Siney sued for damages, which resulted in some questions as to the liability of landlords for the condition of premises. On a case stated appeal to the Supreme Court, the Court, relying on *Donohue v Stevenson,* held, *inter alia*, that the defendant owed the plaintiff a duty to take reasonable care to ensure that the flat was fit for human habitation at the date of the letting. Reflecting on landlords' common law immunity from liability for the condition of the premises, O'Higgins J held that: **[15–90]**

> It is not easy to see the basis in logic for the existence of such an immunity, particularly where the defect which causes the damage was known or could have been known to the lessor, were it not for his carelessness, and was not known and could not have been known to the tenant or to those whom he brought into the building or house pursuant to the letting.

Following *Siney,* it is now well established that statutory authorities no longer enjoy this common law immunity.[152] In July 2011 a Circuit Court judge found Dublin City Council to be in breach of its obligations in relation to a flat in which raw sewage had

---

[148] *Robbins v Jones* (1863) 15 CB (NS) 221.
[149] [1932] AC 562.
[150] *ibid.* at p 580.
[151] [1980] IR 400.
[152] See, for example, *Burke (A Minor) v Dublin Corporation* [1991] 1 IR 341; *Howard v Dublin Corporation* [1996] 2 IR 235; *Ward v McMaster* [1985] IR 29; *Beatty v Rent Tribunal* [2006] 2 IR 191.

been a problem for years and never been properly addressed in spite of many complaints.[153]

[15–91] It should also be noted that local authorities are organs of the State under s 3 of the European Convention on Human Rights Act 2003 and would arguably have liability under that Act should someone be housed by the local authority in conditions that interfered with their Convention rights.[154] Although the European Convention on Human Rights does not include a right to an adequate standard of housing, it is conceivable that conditions of housing could be so bad as to violate the right to respect for one's home under Art 8 and the right to be free from degrading treatment under Art 3. If a particular group was assigned to especially bad housing by a local authority they could also claim that their right to respect for the home was being discriminatorily infringed under Art 14 in conjunction with Art 3. Whether such arguments would be successful is certainly doubtful, but they might nevertheless be made.

[15–92] Landlords of private residential dwellings are subject to liability for the condition of premises, which liability arises on a statutory basis. The Housing (Standards for Rented Houses) Regulations 1993[155] provide that rented houses must meet a certain minimum standard of structural soundness and amenity provision. The basic obligation is to maintain the premises in a proper state of structural repair, defined by Art 5(2) of the Regulations as:

> Essentially sound, with roof, floors, ceilings, walls and stairs in good repair and not subject to serious dampness or liable to collapse because they are rotted or otherwise defective.

The Regulations go on to specify particular requirements in relation to matters such as water supply, electricity, stairways and so on. Section 12(1) of the Residential Tenancies Act expressly refers to these Regulations and incorporates them into the Act. It is not possible for a landlord to contract out of these minimum standards requirements, which will override any conflicting clause in a lease or tenancy agreement. Section 18 of the Housing (Miscellaneous Provisions) Act 1992 provides for the enforcement of these standards—an authorised representative of the local authority can enter and inspect premises at any reasonable time.[156] In the normal course of events the local authority will have been aware of a breach and served a notice requiring rectification. If this notice has not been complied with in the opinion of the inspector, then the local authority is empowered to take a variety of measures, including carrying out any necessary work on the property, although the landlord is

---

[153] Managh, "Damages for Disabled Man over Sewage in Council Flat Shower", *The Irish Times*, 8 July 2011.

[154] On s 3 see generally de Londras & Kelly, *European Convention on Human Rights Act 2003: Operation, Impact and Analysis* (2010, Dublin, Round Hall), Chapter 5.

[155] SI No 147/1993, introduced pursuant to the Housing (Miscellaneous Provisions) Act 1992. These Regulations do not apply to bona fide temporary convenience lettings, holiday lettings and certain categories of dwellings let by health boards or approved bodies for communal use—Art 4(1).

[156] s 18(2), Housing (Miscellaneous Provisions) Act 1992.

entitled to stay these repairs by appealing the decision in the District Court.[157] If the work proceeds, then reasonable expenses can be recouped by the local authority against the landlord.[158] That said, the evidence suggests that in fact requirements and standards relating to the condition of housing are not consistently or fully enforced.[159]

In the context of private residential tenancies, the Residential Tenancies Act 2004 implies certain "obligations" on the part of the landlord. Unlike the implied covenants in Deasy's Act, these obligations apply regardless of the terms of the leasehold agreement and cannot be contracted out of.[160] It ought to be noted that there is no prohibition on the insertion of additional "special letting provisions" in relation to matters not covered by the 2004 Act, but any such conditions must be consistent with the Act.[161] Under the 2004 Act the landlord is required to[162]: **[15–93]**

(1) allow the tenant to enjoy peaceful and exclusive occupation;
(2) carry out repairs;
(3) insure the dwelling;
(4) provide a point of contact;
(5) refund deposits unless rent is owing or there is damage beyond normal wear and tear[163];
(6) reimburse tenants for expenditure on repairs that were appropriate to the landlord;
(7) enforce tenant obligations to "each person who could be potentially affected"[164];
(8) not penalise tenants for making complaints or taking action to enforce their rights;[165]
(9) provide for appropriate receptacles for rubbish outside of the rented property unless this is beyond the landlord's capacity for reasons outside of his control.[166]

(ii) Implied Covenants/Obligations of the Tenant

In keeping with the characterisation of Deasy's Act as a "landlord's charter", s 42 of the Act implies a great number of covenants on the part of tenants. Section 42 of Deasy's Act implies a covenant to pay rent. This, in itself, is not at all contentious. **[15–94]**

157 s 18(6), *ibid.*
158 ss 18(3) and (5), *ibid.*
159 See, for example, Ryall, "Great Expectations: Standards for Rented Housing" (2010) 15 CPLJ 15.
160 s 18(1), Residential Tenancies Act 2004.
161 s 18(3), *ibid.*
162 s 12, *ibid.*
163 For a critical analysis of the Act's treatment of rental deposits, see Ryall, "Landlords, Tenants and Rental Deposits—Is there a better way to deal with disputes?" (2006) 11(3) CPLJ 57.
164 s 15, Residential Tenancies Act 2004.
165 s 14, *ibid.*
166 s 12, Residential Tenancies Act 2004 *as amended by* s 100(3), Housing (Miscellaneous Provisions) Act 2009.

However, the question of whether or not tenants can make deductions from rent to cover expenses such as repairs was unsettled for some time. The original common law position was that deductions were never permitted, however the courts have shown a willingness to make exceptions to this in situations where deductions have become customary between the parties.[167] This issue is now controlled by s 87 of the Landlord and Tenant (Amendment) Act 1980, subsection 1 of which provides:

> Where a landlord refuses or fails to execute repairs to a tenement which he is bound by covenant or otherwise by law to execute and has been called upon by the tenant to execute, and the tenant executes the repairs at his own expense, the tenant may set off the expenditure against any subsequent gale or gales of rent until it is recouped.

[15–95] Section 42 of Deasy's Act also requires tenants to give up possession of the property on the expiration of the lease, leaving the property in a state of substantial repair (subject to wear and tear and to the right to remove certain fixtures). The fixtures that may be removed from the leasehold property can be determined by application of two principles: *superficies solo credit* and "tenant's fixtures" under s 17 of Deasy's Act. As considered in Chapter 1, *superficies solo credit* is the principle that those things attached to the land with a sufficient level of security and intended to be more than merely ornamental become part of the land and cannot, therefore, be removed at the expiration of the lease. Anything that does not fall within the test can be taken with the tenant; anything that does fall within the test can be removed only if this removal is permitted by s 17. Section 17 mostly codifies the previous law and allows the removal of trade, ornamental, domestic and agricultural fixtures and fittings from the land, provided they are removed at the termination of the lease or within a reasonable time period thereafter.

[15–96] Sections 25 and 26 of Deasy's Act deal with waste. Waste is "any action that has an effect on land"—usually negative. The common law made all tenants liable to voluntary, permissive and equitable waste. Section 25, however, provides that fee farm grantees and those who hold perpetually renewable leases are liable only for equitable waste. Under s 26, these tenants can also open mines and quarries. This reflects the autonomy due to them as individuals who have essentially perpetual ownership rights. The final implied covenant comes from s 40 of Deasy's Act 1860, which allows a tenant to surrender his lease where the property has been destroyed through no fault of the tenant. This provision is usually overridden by an express covenant in a written lease whereby tenants renounce their s 40 right to surrender.

[15–97] In the context of private residential tenancies, the Residential Tenancies Act 2004 implies certain "obligations" on the part of the tenant. Unlike the implied covenants in Deasy's Act, these obligations apply regardless of the terms of the leasehold agreement and cannot be contracted out of.[168] It ought to be noted that there is no prohibition on the insertion of additional "special letting provisions" in relation to matters not

---

[167] See, for example, *Shipsey v McGrath* (1879) 31 ILTR 77.

[168] s 18(1), Residential Tenancies Act 2004.

covered by the 2004 Act, but any such conditions must be consistent with the Act.[169] Under the 2004 Act the tenant is required to[170]:

(1) pay the rent and any other specified charges;
(2) avoid causing (or, if caused, make good) any damage beyond normal wear and tear;
(3) notify the landlord of any repair requirements;
(4) allow access for repairs to be carried out and by appointment for routine inspections;
(5) keep the landlord informed of the identity of the occupants;
(6) not engage in or allow anti-social behaviour;
(7) not act in a way that would invalidate the landlord's insurance;
(8) not cause the landlord to be in breach of statutory obligations;
(9) not alter, improve, assign, sublet or change the use of the dwelling without written consent.

3. Enforcement of Covenants

Original parties to the lease can enforce the covenants as against each other because of their privity of contract. The situation becomes more difficult, however, in cases of assignment or subletting. The common law position is that the covenants remain binding between the original parties to the lease, even where there has been an assignment or sub-lease, because the original parties are the only ones that have privity of contract in relation to them. As a result of the obvious practical difficulties to which this situation gives rise, assignors would create indemnity covenants with assignees, whereby the assignee would promise to indemnify the assignor against any damages that might result from a breach of covenant. This common law position remains firm today and will apply in all cases in which an assignment has not been carried out in accordance with s 66 of the Landlord and Tenant (Amendment) Act 1980, which in turn engages s 16 of Deasy's Act. **[15–98]**

The common law would allow for the enforcement of leasehold covenants as between assignees if two conditions were met: (1) the parties had privity of estate; (2) the covenant in question touched and concerned the land. The concept of privity of estate simply requires that there would be a relationship of landlord and tenant between the parties that the common law could recognise. The concept of "touching and concerning the land" simply requires that the covenant would not be a purely personal promise that is logically unenforceable between anyone other than the original parties. **[15–99]**

Section 16 of Deasy's Act provided that an original tenant could escape liability for the leasehold covenants if he assigned his interest with the consent of the landlord. This is an exceptionally important provision from a practical perspective. In order to try to ensure that landlords would not abuse their position in relation to s 16, the Act also **[15–100]**

[169] s 18(3), *ibid.*
[170] s 12, *ibid.*

provided that acts of the landlord do not constitute a waiver; rather, consent is to be provided in writing[171] and the landlord may not charge for his consent.[172] Deasy's Act also clarified that assignees of the landlord can enforce covenants against the tenant and his assignees and that assignees of the tenant can enforce covenants against the landlord and his assignees.[173]

[15–101] Although s 16 of Deasy's Act was an important development, it did contain one serious flaw: the landlord could simply refuse consent and was not required to act reasonably. Thus the Landlord and Tenant (Amendment) Act 1980 interjected in an attempt to further equalise the positions between the landlord and the tenant. In provisions dealing with both assignment and changes of user, the Act requires reasonable behaviour on the part of the landlord. As considered earlier,[174] s 66(1) provides that any covenant attempting to restrict alienation simply forbids alienation in the absence of consent from the landlord. Therefore it is no longer possible to insert a covenant that absolutely prohibits a tenant from alienating his leasehold interest. In addition, s 66(2) requires that the landlord cannot unreasonably withhold his consent to an application for permission to alienate the leasehold rights. If, in the circumstances, the landlord could not have reasonably refused consent, then consent will be deemed to have been provided, whether or not it was expressly obtained.

[15–102] The provisions relating to change of user are more or less the same. Section 67 of the Act provides that any covenant attempting to restrict changes of user simply forbids change of user in the absence of consent from the landlord. Therefore it is no longer possible to insert a covenant that absolutely prohibits a tenant from changing the user of the property. In common with s 66, the landlord may not unreasonably refuse consent to an application for change of user.

4. Remedies for Breach of Covenant

[15–103] Where one or both parties breach covenants in the lease, there are a number of potential enforcement mechanisms available:

(1) The aggrieved party might sue for breach of contract.
(2) If the rental covenant has been breached, the landlord might sue for arrears of rent or exercise the right to distress under a combination of s 5 Distress for Rent Act 1741 and s 51 Deasy's Act. This is permissible only where the rent is less than one year in arrears and constitutes entering the property and seizing personal property in lieu of rental payment. This is now forbidden in residential tenancies and is soon to be abolished due to concerns about its constitutionality.
(3) Forfeiture or ejectment may be engaged, depending on the circumstances. Both of these options are considered in full below in the context of "termination of the leasehold relationship".

---

171 ss 18 and 43, Deasy's Act 1860.
172 s 3, *ibid.*
173 ss 12 and 13, *ibid.*
174 paras 15–39 to 15–46.

VI. Statutory Rights under the Landlord and Tenant (Amendment) Act 1980

The primary purpose of the Landlord and Tenant (Amendment) Act 1980 was to amend and replace the law relating to the right to new tenancies, reversionary leases and compensation for disturbance and improvements, which were previously provided for in the Landlord and Tenant Act 1931 and in the Landlord and Tenant (Reversionary Leases) Act 1958. For a number of years following the introduction of the 1980 Act it was important to assess accurately whether a claim fell under the 1980 Act or an earlier provision because the 1980 Act did not have retrospective application.[175] More than 30 years later, however, the transition period between the two legislative schemes has effectively passed and it is unlikely that many cases would arise in which the pre-1980 regime is relevant. **[15–104]**

The Landlord and Tenant (Amendment) Act 1980 is of particular interest to business tenants, although the Act will apply only to "tenements"[176] as defined by s 5 where the landlord is not the State or a State authority.[177] In order to qualify as a tenement, a property must comprise of land[178] wholly or partially covered by buildings[179] and held under a lease or contract for a lease.[180] In this context it is particularly important to note that there is no exacting definition of "building", rather whether or not a structure (which need not be permanent[181]) is a building will very much depend on the circumstances of the case.[182] **[15–105]**

The definition of "tenement" in s 5 also requires any land uncovered by buildings to be subsidiary and ancillary to those buildings. This is a somewhat complex concept, but essentially requires that the purpose of the buildings be assessed, following which we can assess whether the uncovered land has a purpose that is ancillary to (or serves) the purpose of the buildings. This, too, is a question of fact, dependent on the circumstances, and to be decided by the court.[183] The case of *Kenny Homes Company Ltd v Leonard*[184] offers a good example of the operation of this requirement. *Kenny Homes* concerned a site in Cork City that was purchased by the plaintiffs from Irish **[15–106]**

---

175 See *Caulfield v Bourke & Son Ltd* [1989] ILRM 223.

176 s 13, Landlord and Tenant (Amendment) Act 1980.

177 s 4, *ibid.*; see also *Shanley v Commissioners of Public Works* [1992] 2 IR 477.

178 In this context land does not appear to include incorporeal hereditaments—see, e.g., *Brittan Fly-Fishing Club Ltd v Aimsitheoir Deantoreacht Teoranta*, unreported, High Court, 20 March 1993.

179 s 5, Landlord and Tenant (Amendment) Act 1980.

180 s 2, *ibid.*

181 See, for example, *Michael Terry v Edward J Stakes* [1993] 1 IR 204, in which it was held that sheds without foundations or planning permission could be said to be buildings as the Act did not require permanence; see *Dursely v Watters and Castleblaney Plant Hire Ltd* [1993] 1 IR 224, in which pre-fabricated and partially pre-fabricated structures were accepted as "buildings"; *Terry v Stokes* [1993] 1 IR 204, in which a "ramshackle" house was said to be a building; *O'Reilly v Kevans* (1935) 69 ILTR 1, in which a run-down shed with a corrugated-iron roof was said to be a building.

182 *Mason v Leavy* [1952] IR 40.

183 *ibid.*

184 Unreported, High Court, 11 December 1997.

Shell Ltd in 1996. That purchase was expressly subject to a hiring and licence agreement in favour of Leonard, who had occupied the property in question under a series of agreements over approximately a 20-year period. Leonard carried on a service-station business on about one-third of the site, and a car-park business occupied the remainder. When the agreement expired and the plaintiffs wanted to develop the property, Leonard claimed that he was entitled to a new tenancy under the Landlord and Tenant (Amendment) Act 1980. The plaintiff claimed that the property concerned was not a tenement because, *inter alia*, it did not comprise land wholly or partially covered by buildings where the uncovered land was ancillary and subsidiary to the buildings. The physical layout of the property was described in the High Court thus:

> There are presently, as one enters from Grand Parade, 4 petrol pumps under a canopy, then two petrol pumps under a canopy. There are two small offices between the first set of pumps. There is a small car park office which is used to receive payment and keys from users of the car park. There is a three storey building over the entrance arch on Grand Parade, which for a time was used for storage but now it is derelict. There are four large motor fuel tanks underground. These are built under the area now used as a car park. There is a garage and compressor house beyond the pumps as well as two garages which are derelict and boarded up. A low wall divides the filling station area from the car park area.

The High Court and Supreme Court concluded that the property in question was not a tenement—the majority of it was uncovered by buildings and, in fact, the part covered by buildings was actually ancillary and subsidiary to the uncovered part because it served the car park itself. As a result, Leonard could not claim a right to a new tenancy under the 1980 Act.

[15–107] Most of the rights provided by the 1980 Act can be applied for by means of a notice of intention to claim relief, which is issued either at the time of the termination of the lease or within a reasonable period of time thereafter. The tenant is entitled to stay in possession of the property under s 28 until a claim of rights under the 1980 Act has been determined, although it ought to be noted that s 28 provides for a merely personal right to remain in possession. The right to remain in occupation while a claim is being determined under s 28 does not, therefore, provide an absolute defence to claims of possession by the landlord; rather, the court can terminate such occupation "where there appears a risk of serious injustice to the landlord if the tenant is permitted to remain in occupation whilst continuing to act in breach of the terms of the tenancy".[185] The right to a new tenancy can be applied for as soon as it arises,[186] although it is usual practice to wait until the tenancy has been terminated to make such an application.

[15–108] Tenants may be disqualified from enjoying rights provided for in the Landlord and Tenant (Amendment) Act 1980 under the terms of s 17. According to s 17(1) any tenant whose lease has been terminated for non-payment of rent or for breach of a

[185] *Crofter Properties v Genport Ltd* [2007] IEHC 80 *per* Finlay-Geoghegan J.

[186] s 13(1), Landlord and Tenant (Amendment) Act 1980.

covenant will be disqualified from the rights provided, as will a tenant who has terminated the lease himself by means of surrender or other means. Section 17(1)(1)(a)(iv) also disqualifies from the right to a new tenancy those tenants whose tenancy has been "terminated by notice to quit given by the landlord for good and sufficient reason". Good and sufficient reason is defined as:

> a reason which emanates from or is the result of or is traceable to some action or conduct of the tenant and which, having regard to all the circumstances of the case, is in the opinion of the Court a good and sufficient reason for terminating or refusing to renew... the tenancy.[187]

Section 17(2) provides for a number of scenarios in which the tenant may be disqualified under the Act as a result of circumstances beyond his control. As we will see below, business tenants who lose the right to a new tenancy under s 17(2) are entitled to compensation for disturbance. The bases for disqualification under s 17(2) are: **[15–109]**

(1) the landlord intends or has agreed to pull down and rebuild or to reconstruct the buildings or any part of the buildings included in the tenement and has planning permission for the work; *or*
(2) the landlord requires vacant possession for the purpose of carrying out a scheme of development of property which includes the tenement and has planning permission for the scheme; *or*
(3) the landlord is a planning authority and the tenement or any part thereof is situated in an area in respect of which the development plan indicates objectives for its development or renewal as being an obsolete area; *or*
(4) the landlord is a local authority and will require possession, within a period of five years after the termination of the existing tenancy, for any purpose for which the local authority is entitled to acquire property compulsorily; *or*
(5) the creation of a new tenancy would not be consistent with good estate management.

1. Right to a New Tenancy

Part II of the Landlord and Tenant (Amendment) Act 1980 provides for a right to a new tenancy on the termination of an earlier one, provided the claimant satisfied the requirements of either the "business equity", "long occupation equity" or "improvements equity" and is not disqualified from the right under the provisions of s 17 of the Act. **[15–110]**

2. Business Equity

The "business equity" is provided for in s 13(1)(a) of the Act and entitles someone who has occupied a tenement as a *bona fide* business tenant "wholly or partly for the purpose of carrying on a business" for five years or more to a new tenancy.[188] The **[15–111]**

[187] s 17(1)(b), *ibid.*

[188] The time period was originally three years, but was changed to five years by s 3(1), Landlord and Tenant (Amendment) Act 1994. The right to new tenancy does not apply to business tenancies of financial services companies in the Custom House Docks area—Landlord and Tenant (Amendment) Act 1989.

five-year occupation must have been continuous and must run right up to the time of service of the notice of intention to claim relief, although the courts are entitled to disregard a temporary break in user (*not* in occupation) of the tenement, where appropriate.[189] The business tenant is entitled to take a period of occupation by a predecessor-in-title into account, provided the predecessor-in-title held "under the same tenancy". "Business use" has a particularly broad meaning in this context. Section 3 of the 1980 Act defines business as:

> any trade, profession or business, whether or not it is carried on for gain or reward, any activity for providing cultural, charitable, educational, social or sporting services, and also the public service and the carrying out by an authority being the council of a county, the corporation of a county or other borough, the council of an urban district, the commissioners of a town, a health board under the Health Act, 1970, or a harbour authority under the Harbours Act, 1946, of any of their functions.

The Act does not require business to have been the only use of the property concerned and, indeed, the courts have held that the business itself need not have been conducted in the premises as long as the premises were used for the business.[190] The business user must, however, be bona fide. It is clear that this excludes those who use a tenement for business purposes in clear and knowing breach of an express covenant prohibiting business user.[191]

[15–112] It was previously the case under s 85 that any provision effectively contracting out of the right to a new tenancy (either directly or indirectly[192]) was void. The inability to contract out of the right to a new tenancy in a business context was somewhat problematic from a principled perspective: in most contexts property law treats commercial entities in a manner that recognises their commercial sense and acumen and tries to take account of commercial realities. Any application of this approach to the matter of the right to a new tenancy would suggest that business tenants ought to be able to contract out of the right to a new tenancy. Section 4 of the Landlord and Tenant (Amendment) Act 1994 allowed a tenant of office premises to contract out of their right to a new tenancy before the commencement of the tenancy and after obtaining independent legal advice but only applied where the tenancy provides for the use of the premises wholly and exclusively as an office. Sections 47 and 48 of the Civil Law (Miscellaneous Provisions) Act 2008 now allow for business tenants to contract out of the right to a new tenancy under the 1980 Act, provided the right is freely renounced either before or after entering into the lease and following independent legal advice.[193]

---

[189] See, for example, *Farrell v Wine & Anor* [1973] ILT 107.

[190] *Plant v Oakes* [1991] 1 IR 185.

[191] See *M50 Motors v Byrne* [2002] 4 IR 161.

[192] *Bank of Ireland v Fitzmaurice* [1989] ILRM 452.

[193] See further Cannon, "Section 47 of the Civil Law (Miscellaneous Provisions) Act 2008 and ss 191 and 192 of the Residential Tenancies Act 2004: New Developments in Relation to Contracting Out under the Landlord and Tenant (Amendment) Act 1980" (2008) 13(3) CPLJ 68.

3. Long Occupation Equity

Residential tenants with long occupation were previously entitled to a new tenancy under s 13(1)(b) of the Landlord and Tenant (Amendment) Act 1980. Section 191(2) of the Residential Tenancies Act 2004 allowed for the renunciation of that right following independent legal advice, and the long occupation equity ceased operation on 1 September 2009. [15–113]

4. Improvements Equity

Where a tenant has carried out improvements for which he is entitled to compensation under Part IV of the Landlord and Tenant (Amendment) Act 1980 and those improvements account for not less than one-half of the letting value of the tenement, the tenant is entitled to a right to a new tenancy.[194] [15–114]

5. Right to a Reversionary Lease

Section 30 of the Landlord and Tenant (Amendment) Act 1980 provides that tenants who are entitled to acquire the fee simple under the Landlord and Tenant (Ground Rents) (No 2) Act 1978 are entitled to a reversionary lease. In the absence of agreement between the parties, the rent and other terms of the reversionary lease will be set by the court in accordance with the provisions of s 34 of the Act, which provides: [15–115]

> (1) Where the terms of a reversionary lease are settled by the Court the subsequent provisions of this section shall have effect.
> (2) The lease shall be for a term expiring ninety-nine years after the expiration of the lease to which it is reversionary.
> (3) Subject to subsection (5), the rent reserved by the reversionary lease shall be not less than the rent reserved by the previous lease or than the rent reserved by any superior lease the lessor under which is required to join in the grant of the reversionary lease.
> (4) Where the land to be comprised in a reversionary lease is part only of the land comprised in the previous lease or of the land comprised in any superior lease the lessor under which is required to join in the grant of the reversionary lease, such proportion of the rent reserved by any such lease as is fairly apportionable to the land to be comprised in the reversionary lease shall, for the purpose of subsection (3), be deemed to be the rent reserved by that lease in respect of the land to be comprised in the reversionary lease.
> (5) If any new covenant restricting the lessee's rights is included in the reversionary lease, the Court may, if it so thinks proper, fix a lower rent.
> (6) If the Court fixes the covenants of the lease, the lessee shall be made liable to pay all rates and taxes in respect of the land and to insure against fire and keep the premises in repair.

In *Gilsenan v Foundary House Investments Ltd*[195] the Supreme Court found the system outlined in s 34 to be unworkable because it was impossible to estimate inflation over a period of 99 years. As a result, s 3 of the Landlord and Tenant (Amendment) Act 1984 [15–116]

---

194 s 13(1)(c), Landlord and Tenant (Amendment) Act 1980.
195 [1980] ILRM 273.

introduced five-year rent reviews in cases where the court decides on the term of the reversionary lease. Under this provision there is no right to a reversionary lease where (a) the landlord's reversion is freehold or for less than 15 years and where he intends or has agreed to pull down and rebuild or to reconstruct the whole or a substantial portion of the buildings on the land and has planning permission for the work, or (b) where he requires vacant possession of the land for the purpose of carrying out a scheme of development of property, which includes the land, and has planning permission for the scheme, or (c) where the grant of a reversionary lease would not be compatible with good estate management. The right to a reversionary lease will also be excluded where a local authority has an involvement in the lease and can show that the property is in an obsolete area, or if the premises is used for five years and will need to be acquired by a local authority within five years. If the tenant would otherwise be entitled to a reversionary lease but is excluded under the terms of s 33, that tenant will be entitled to compensation for disturbance.

6. Right to Compensation for Improvements

[15–117] Part IV of the Landlord and Tenant (Amendment) Act 1980 provides for a right to compensation for improvements to the property provided the property concerns meets the requirements of "tenement" as laid down in s 5 and considered above.[196] This right can be described as "a method by which a tenant may recoup his expenditure on the demised property, which expenditure has enhanced its value for the landlord but in respect of which the tenant no longer enjoys occupation".[197] Section 46 provides for these rights, which accrue when a tenant leaves a tenement following termination of the lease, provided the tenant himself did not terminate the landlord-and-tenant relationship and the reason for termination was not the non-payment of rent.[198] The right to compensation for improvements[199] applies to improvements carried out by the tenant or his predecessors-in-title, provided those improvements increase the rental value of the property and have been carried out in accordance with the conditions laid down in the Act itself. Section 45 of the Act defines an improvement as:

> any addition to or alteration of the buildings comprised in the tenement and includes any structure erected on the tenement which is ancillary or subsidiary to those buildings and also includes the installation in the tenement of conduits for the supply of water, gas or electricity but does not include work consisting only of repairing, painting and decorating, or any of them.

[15–118] In order to claim compensation on this basis, the tenant or his predecessor-in-title must have complied with the provisions of s 48 of the Act. Section 48 requires that the tenant would serve an improvements notice on the landlord, detailing the improvements proposed and laying out costings and details of any planning permission acquired (where necessary). The failure to provide the landlord with a notice of the intended

---

[196] paras 15–105 to 15–106.

[197] *Harrisrange Limited v Michael Duncan*, unreported, High Court, 25 January 2002 *per* McKechnie J.

[198] s 46(1)(b), Landlord and Tenant (Amendment) Act 1980.

[199] See generally de Blácam, "The Compensation Provisions of the Landlord and Tenant Act" (1988) 6 ILT 252.

improvements will disqualify the tenant from the right to compensation if the landlord can satisfy the court that the failure to serve a notice prejudiced the landlord, or that the improvements were a violation of a covenant of the lease, or that the improvement injured the amenity of the property or the neighbourhood.[200] On receipt of this notice the landlord has three options[201] and must act within one month. Failure to act within a time limit of one month entitles the tenant to carry out the proposed improvements within a year.[202] The landlord's options on receipt of the notice are to:

(1) consent to the improvements as proposed; *or*
(2) undertake to carry out the improvements himself, in which case the improvements must be carried out within six months[203] and the landlord will be entitled to charge a higher rate of rent specified in the "improvements undertaking" and based on the improvements made[204];
(3) refuse consent to the improvements, although this can be done only if the tenant holds the property on the basis of an agreement that has less than five years left to run and the tenant is disqualified under the terms of s 17(2) of the Act. If a refusal is issued, the tenant is entitled to apply to the court for relief[205] and, provided there is at least five years to run and s 17(2) is not engaged, the court is empowered to authorise the tenant to make the improvement in accordance with his notice, either without modifications or with such modifications as it thinks proper.[206]

As a result of the provisions in the Landlord and Tenant (Amendment) Act 1980 for compensation for improvements, it may be logical to assume that many landlords would attempt to insert a covenant in the lease absolutely prohibiting any improvements. Such covenants, however, no longer absolutely prohibit improvements, but rather prohibit improvements without the consent or licence of the landlord.[207] **[15–119]**

A notice of intention to claim relief must be served by the tenant who wishes to exercise the right to compensation for improvements[208] If a claim is made, the landlord is at liberty to offer the tenant a new tenancy on terms specified in the notice or settled by the Circuit Court,[209] but if the tenant declines this offer the claim for compensation can proceed. It should be noted, however, that the court is entitled to order the tenant to accept the new tenancy (or a tenancy under such terms as the court provides),[210] in which case the claim for compensation is spent.[211] If a tenant establishes his **[15–120]**

[200] s 54(2), Landlord and Tenant (Amendment) Act 1980.
[201] s 48(2), *ibid.*
[202] s 50, *ibid.*
[203] s 51(2), Landlord and Tenant (Amendment) Act 1980.
[204] When an "improvements undertaking" is issued the tenant is entitled to object to the proposed increase in rent (s 51(7), *ibid.*).
[205] s 52(4), *ibid.*
[206] s 52(3), *ibid.*
[207] s 68, *ibid.*
[208] s 56(1), *ibid.*
[209] s 22(1), *ibid.*
[210] s 22(2), *ibid.*
[211] s 22(4), *ibid.*

entitlement to compensation for improvements, the amount of the compensation will be agreed between the parties or, if they cannot agree, by the Circuit Court pursuant to the calculation mechanism included in s 47 of the Act. This requires the court to take into account the capital appreciation to the property by virtue of the improvements, but also to make appropriate deductions in respect of benefits that the tenant may already have enjoyed as a result of having carried out the improvements (such as a decreased rate of rent).

7. Right to Compensation for Disturbance

[15–121] Compensation for disturbance[212] is payable where a tenant qualified for a new tenancy under the business equity, but is disqualified under the terms of s 17(2) of the 1980 Act. The payment made is intended to compensate for the loss, damage or expense suffered or which will be suffered as a result of having to leave the premises and engage in business elsewhere.[213] Compensation for disturbance is also payable where a person would, but for ss 33(1), 33(2) or 33(3) of the 1980 Act, be entitled to a reversionary lease under Part III.[214] In this case the payment ought to compensate for the "pecuniary loss, damage or expense which will, in the opinion of the Court, be suffered by the disentitled person as a direct consequence of the disentitled person having been declared not to be entitled to a lease".[215] Lastly, compensation for disturbance is payable where a court has ordered the termination of a tenancy on account of the building being obsolete or being situated in an obsolete area.[216] In a circumstance of this nature the payment ought to compensate for "the pecuniary loss, damage or expense which the tenant sustains or incurs or will sustain or incur by reason of his quitting the tenement and which is the direct consequence of such quitting".[217]

VII. Enlargement of Leases

[15–122] It has long been the practice for the owners of undeveloped land to grant leases over that land to prospective developers—usually building developers—who would pay a fine and a relatively small annual fee. The annual fee—or rent—would be in respect of the undeveloped land alone and would therefore be known as "ground rent", however the developer would normally proceed with the acquisition of planning permission and build on those lands. Once the development was completed, the newly constructed buildings would be sold (i.e. assigned or sublet by the developer), but once the original lease came to an end the landowner (i.e. the original landlord) was entitled to retake possession of the land and the buildings thereon (because they fell into the maxim, *superficies solo credit*). This situation was clearly problematic: the developer had invested money in the construction project and the purchasers had "acquired" the units as constructed.

[15–123] In order to try to ameliorate these difficulties the law now provides for a system by which the tenant can achieve enfranchisement—or the enlargement of his leasehold

[212] s 58, *ibid.*
[213] s 58(2), *ibid.*
[214] s 59, *ibid.*
[215] s 59(3), *ibid.*
[216] s 60, *ibid.*
[217] s 60, *ibid.*

interest to a freehold fee simple interest. This area of law is governed by no fewer than six pieces of legislation: the Landlord and Tenant (Ground Rents) Act 1967; the Landlord and Tenant (Ground Rents) (No 2) Act 1978; the Landlord and Tenant (Amendment) Act 1980; the Landlord and Tenant (Amendment) Act 1984; the Landlord and Tenant (Ground Rents) (Amendment) Act 1987; and the Landlord and Tenant (Ground Rents) Act 2005. The Oireachtas also attempted to prevent the creation of leases subject to a ground rent. Section 2(1) of the 1978 Act provides that a lease of land will be void if the tenant would have a statutory right to enfranchisement and the permanent buildings constructed on the land are constructed to be used wholly or primarily as dwellings. Where such a void lease is purported to be made for consideration, the "tenant" will be entitled to the fee simple at the expense of the "landlord", who is obliged to pay the costs of the acquisition and is not entitled to a purchase price for the fee simple.[218]

In order to be entitled to acquire the fee simple in the property, the tenant must satisfy **[15–124]** the three conditions outlined in s 9(1) of the 1978 Act and any one of the conditions outlined in s 10.[219] The three conditions of s 9 are: (1) that there would be permanent buildings on the land and that any uncovered land is ancillary and subsidiary to those permanent buildings; (2) that the buildings are not an improvement under the terms of s 9(2) of the Act, i.e. they are not an "addition to or alteration to the buildings... [including] any structure which is ancillary or subsidiary to those buildings, but [not including] any alteration or reconstruction of the building so that they lose their original identity"; and (3) that the permanent buildings were not erected in contravention of a covenant of the lease. Having fulfilled the three conditions of s 9, the tenant must then fulfil one of the seven conditions of s 10:

- the permanent buildings were erected by the person who at the time of their erection was entitled to the lessee's interest under the lease *or* were erected pursuant to an agreement for the grant of a lease once they had been built; *or*
- the lease was for a term of at least 50 years *and* the yearly rent or the greatest rent reserved is less than the rateable valuation of the property *and* the permanent buildings were not erected by the lessor or his superior lessor or their predecessor-in-title; *or*
- the lease was granted by a lessor to the nominee of a builder to whom land had been demised for the purpose of erecting buildings in pursuance of an agreement between the lessor and the builder that the builder, having contracted to sell the buildings, would surrender his lease in consideration of the lessor granting new leases to the builder's nominees; *or*
- the lease was granted by a lessor to the nominee of a builder in pursuance of an agreement between the lessor and the builder that the lessor, upon the erection of the buildings by the builder, would grant leases to the builders nominees; *or*
- the lease was granted, either on the expiration or surrender of a previous lease or subsequent to such expiration or surrender, at a rent less than the rateable valuation of the property at the date of the grant of the lease, or to the person entitled to the lessee's interest under the previous lease; *or*

---

[218] s 2(4), Landlord and Tenant (Ground Rents) (No 2) Act 1978.

[219] As amended by ss 71 and 72, Landlord and Tenant (Amendment) Act 1980.

- the lease is a reversionary lease granted on or after 31 March 1931 to a person entitled to it under Part V of the Landlord and Tenant Act 1931 or the Landlord and Tenant (Reversionary Leases) Act 1958; *or*
- the lease is for a term of not less than 50 years and was made partly in consideration of the payment of a sum of money (other than rent) by the lessee to the lessor at or immediately before the grant of the lease *or* partly in consideration of the expenditure (otherwise than on decoration) of a sum of money by the lessee on the premises *or* partly in consideration of both such payment and such expenditure. The sum of money paid or expended under such terms must be not less than 15 times the yearly amount of the rent or the greatest rent reserved by the lease, whichever is less.

[15–125] Section 15 of the 1978 Act also provides for a right to acquire the fee simple where a yearly tenant (or his predecessors-in-title) has held the land for not less than 25 years, where the land is wholly or partially covered by permanent buildings with the uncovered land being subsidiary and ancillary to the covered land, and where the yearly rent is less than the rateable valuation or the buildings were erected by the tenant or a predecessor-in-title (although in any case the buildings must not have been erected by the landlord or his predecessors-in-title).

[15–126] Section 16 of the 1978 Act outlines the disqualification provisions relating to this right. Where it has been declared that the tenant has no right to a reversionary lease, the tenant is not entitled to acquisition of the fee simple. Equally, a tenant has no entitlement to the fee simple if the property is used for business purposes and the lease includes a clause enabling the alteration of rent within 26 years of the lease. There will also be no entitlement to the fee simple where the lease applies to property, including a building divided into four or more flats, and includes a clause enabling the alteration of rent within 26 years of the lease. There will be no entitlement if the lease was granted prior to 1 March 1967, relates to land used for business and contains a provision requiring the property to be used for business purposes, but restricting that business by requiring the lessee to deal in commodities produced or supplied by the landlord. There will be no right to acquire the fee simple if the lease contains a covenant requiring the erection of buildings or the carrying out of a development and the covenant has not been substantially complied with. Finally, there will be no right to acquire the fee simple as against a Government Minister, the Commissioners of Public Works, the Industrial Development Agency (IDA), the Shannon Free Airport Development Company or Údarás na Gaelteachta.[220]

[15–127] The legislation provides for two mechanisms by which the fee simple can be acquired. The first, provided by s 4 of the 1967 Act, involves the service by the claiming tenant for a notice of intention to acquire on all those who have an interest in the property. In order to ensure that all interest-holders are identified successfully, s 7 of the 1967 Act allows the tenant to serve a notice on his landlord requiring details of his interest, all encumbrances affecting it and the identity of the person (if any) from whom he holds the land. Any superior title-holders can then be served with the same notice, and so on, until all interests in the property have been identified. Where any "dispute, question or

[220] s 2, Landlord and Tenant (Ground Rents) Act 2005.

difficulty" arises, an application can be made to the county registrar to have the matter determined by his arbitration.[221] The second process, which is provided for by the 1978 Act, applies to the acquisition of the fee simple in dwelling-houses only and empowers the Registrar of Titles to issue a "vesting certificate" conveying the fee simple and any intermediate interests to the tenant free from encumbrances.[222] This vesting certificate can be acquired by consent (where all of the interested parties consent to the acquisition) or, if this is not possible, notice must be served on the claiming tenant's landlord and the application is determined by the Registrar through a process of arbitration.[223] Before issuing any vesting certificate, the Registrar must be satisfied that the purchase price has been paid or deposited with him, that the prescribed fees have been discharged and that the rent (other than statute-barred arrears) has been paid up-to-date.[224]

VIII. Residential Tenancies

As considered previously, the "home" is an important concept in property law.[225] This is no less the case when one's home is held in leasehold. In order to give further effect to the importance of the home in the leasehold context, the Residential Tenancies Act 2004 was introduced.[226] We have already seen that the Act introduces new "obligations" for both the landlord and the tenant and provides that residential tenancies can be terminated only by means of a notice of termination. The Act, however, also introduces broad-ranging provisions relating to residential tenancies generally. The Act is expressly retrospective and therefore applies to all residential tenancies, regardless of their date of commencement,[227] and the Act can override the terms of written residential leases. **[15–128]**

The Residential Tenancies Act 2004 has a limited scope. It does not apply to dwellings that could qualify under the "business equity" provisions of the Landlord and Tenant (Amendment) Act 1980, any dwelling governed by the Housing (Private Rented Dwellings) Act 1982,[228] any dwelling let by or to a public authority, any dwelling in relation to which a tenant is entitled to acquire the fee simple under the Landlord and Tenant (Ground Rents) (No 2) Act 1978, any dwelling occupied under a shared ownership lease, service occupancies, holiday lettings, dwellings in which the landlord is also resident, dwelling in which the spouse, parent or child of the landlord resides and no lease or tenancy agreement in writing has been entered into by any person resident in the dwelling, or a dwelling over which a lease has been granted or is being claimed under the Landlord and Tenant (Amendment) Act 1980.[229] **[15–129]**

---

221 s 17, Landlord and Tenant (Ground Rents) Act 1967.

222 s 22, Landlord and Tenant (Ground Rents) (No 2) Act 1978.

223 s 21(3), *ibid.*

224 s 22(2), *ibid.*

225 See Chapter 9.

226 On the Act generally, see Ryall, "Residential Tenancies Act 2004" (2005) 10(1) CPLJ 10; Ryall, "Residential Tenancies Act 2004: Update and Review" (2006) 11(1) CPLJ 4; Ryall, "Residential Tenancies Act 2004: Review and Assessment" (2006) 6(1) JSIJ 60.

227 s 3(1), Residential Tenancies Act 2004.

228 This Act applies to premises that could be defined as "controlled dwellings" within the meaning of the Rent Restrictions Acts 1960–1981.

229 s 3, Residential Tenancies Act 2004.

[15–130] The Act establishes the Private Residential Tenancies Board (PRTB),[230] with which all new residential tenancies falling within the scope of the Act have to be registered. The PRTB has a number of distinct functions, as outlined in s 151 of the 2004 Act, including a dispute-resolution function outlined in Part 6 of the Act.[231] Section 78 of the Act provides a non-exhaustive list of the matters in relation to which the PRTB can adjudicate, which can be summarised as follows:

- retention of deposits by a landlord[232];
- rental obligations and rent review;
- compliance with the obligations by both landlords and tenants;
- disputes as to termination of the residential tenancy;
- alleged failures by tenants to vacate the premises following termination of the residential tenancy;
- claims for recovery of costs or damages relating to breaches of obligations;
- disputes as to compliance with determinations by the PRTB.

[15–131] All residential tenants are entitled to a rent book as a result of the Housing (Rent Books) Regulations 1993, which were introduced on foot of the Housing (Miscellaneous Provisions) Act 1992. The "book" (which need not take the form of an actual book) must contain information on the parties, the address of the premises, the rent reserved, any other payments made, rent paid in advance, deposit and particulars of furniture and appliances provided by the landlord. Article 7 of the Regulations requires that a note be made when rent is paid to the landlord or his agent, and that if the rent is paid otherwise than by cash (standing order, bank transfer etc.), then a receipt should be provided within three months of payment. The situation relating to rent books has not been altered substantially by the Residential Tenancies Act 2004, although penalties for non-compliance have increased.[233]

[15–132] As considered above, a Part 4 tenancy introduces security of tenure in four-year cycles: following six months' occupation of the property under the residential tenancy, the tenant becomes entitled to a further 3.55 years of tenure, during which the landlord may only terminate the lease for limited reasons. Where two or more people are in occupation of leased premises, but only one person is the named lessee, the protections of the law of landlord and tenant will be extended to the other resident either automatically or by application under the provisions of Chapter 5 of Part 4 of the 2004 Act. A spouse, civil partner, cohabitant,[234] or child of the tenant who has been in occupation for a continuous period of six months will be automatically granted a Part 4 tenancy. Other multiple occupants who have been in occupation for six months may apply for a Part 4 tenancy.

---

[230] Part 8, Residential Tenancies Act 2004.

[231] Determinations of the Board are available at www.prtb.ie.

[232] See Ryall, "Landlords, Tenants and Rental Deposits—Is There a Better Way to Deal with Disputes?" (2006) 11(3) CPLJ 57.

[233] s 17(3)(b), Residential Tenancies Act 2004.

[234] As defined by s 172, Civil Partnership and Certain Rights and Obligations of Cohabitants Act 2010. Section 39 amended to reflect the 2010 Act by s 203, Civil Partnership and Certain Rights and Obligations of Cohabitants Act 2010.

Chapter 16
Succession

The law of succession governs what happens to a deceased's property at the time of his death and is substantively contained in the Succession Act 1965. Upon someone's death, the question with which property law is primarily concerned is who receives what from the deceased's estate. The obvious difficulty for the law is, of course, that we cannot ask the deceased whom she wants to receive what elements of her estate **[16–01]** (by which, in this context, we mean all of the real and personal property to which the deceased is entitled at the time of her death[1]). In order to ameliorate this difficulty people will often use a will: a document by which the disposition of their estates upon death is laid out—this is known as a situation of testacy. The law governing wills—their effect, their validity, what they mean, etc.—is contained within the law of succession and considered in this chapter. In some situations people die either without having made any will at all, or without having any valid will: in other words they die intestate. In such situations the deceased has foregone the capacity to dictate the destination of the estate, and instead the law does it for him or her. Again, the law of intestacy is part of the law of succession and given consideration in this chapter. It is not uncommon for someone to die with a valid will, but where some parts of one's estate are not in fact disposed of by that will. This is known as a situation of partial intestacy, where some of the estate is disposed of by the will and the remainder by the law of intestacy. In such situation the rules relating to both testacy and intestacy must be applied.

I. Personal Representatives

[16–02] Whenever someone dies leaving an estate (i.e. property to which he is entitled on death and where that entitlement does not cease on his death) personal representatives take on a particularly important role. In the case of testacy, the personal representative is an executor or, if she is a woman, an executrix. In the case of intestacy the personal representative is an administrator. The personal representative carries out important functions in terms of the calling-in of monies owed to the estate, the payment of debts and the administration of the estate, either according to the terms of the will or in accordance with the rules of intestate distribution. Before a personal representative can act, however, he must be given a grant of representation, made on behalf of the High Court.[2] In the context of testacy—where the executor is named in the will—this is known as a grant of probate; in the context of intestacy—where the administrator is appointed by the High Court—this is known as a grant of letters of administration. This grant then authorises the personal representatives to proceed. Importantly, death does not result in any gap of ownership: rather the personal representative will become the owner of the deceased's estate for the purposes of administration and distribution.[3] In the case of intestacy, the President of the High Court will be the owner of the estate until the administrator has been appointed.[4]

[16–03] Once representation has been granted, the personal representatives will gather all of the assets of the deceased, including all relevant deeds and other documents, and will then proceed to discharge any debts or liabilities. In order to ensure the timely and efficient distribution of the estate, all creditors can be invited to make claims against the estate within a defined time limit by means of newspaper notices.[5] The personal representatives also have various powers of disposition and acquisition and may be trustees of certain properties.[6] Where real property is left to someone in a will, it is

[1] s 14, Succession Act 1965.
[2] ss 26 and 27, *ibid.*
[3] s 10, *ibid.*
[4] s 13, *ibid.*
[5] s 49, *ibid.*
[6] See, generally, Keating, *Equitable Succession Rights* (2005, Dublin, Round Hall), chapters 6–9.

transferred by the executor to the beneficiary by means of an assent.[7] As is clear, then, the personal representatives have particularly onerous responsibilities and it is vital, for the sake of beneficiaries and creditors alike, that they carry out their duties in an objective, timely and responsible manner. The High Court has jurisdiction to remove executors or administrators by means of revocation of the grant of probate or the grant of letters of administration, as appropriate.[8] The Court is, however, exceptionally reluctant to exercise this jurisdiction and will not remove a personal representative merely because someone feels "put out" by their actions: serious misconduct or a serious conflict of interest would have to be shown.[9]

II. Requirements for a Valid Will

As mentioned above, the law of testacy applies where someone dies with a valid will. A will, although a common concept, is an important legal document, the formation of which is subject to strict legal rules. Wills are said to be ambulatory and revocable, thus they are conditional and can be revoked or amended by the testator at any time up until death.[10] Sections 77 and 78 of the Succession Act 1965 lay down the requirements for a valid will, which can be neatly divided into requirements as to capacity and requirements as to formalities. **[16–04]**

1. Requirements as to Capacity

The first capacity-related requirement is that of age. In order to make a valid will a testator must *generally* be 18 years or over,[11] although a person who is under 18 but married can make a valid will.[12] The second capacity-related requirement is that one would be of sound disposing mind.[13] The concept of sound disposing mind is distinct from that of sound mind; the focus in succession is on whether or not the testator was capable of understanding the nature of what he was doing and who would benefit from his actions. In other words, the focus in succession is substantively on the testator's state of mind *in relation to* the alleged will. **[16–05]**

The test for soundness of disposing mind was originally laid down in *Banks v Goodfellow.*[14] This case concerned a will that was challenged on the basis of, *inter alia*, the alleged unsoundness of disposing mind of the testator, who had been convinced for some time that he was being harassed by a man who had been dead for quite a long while and that he was being pursued by visible evil spirits. Although the parties all agreed that there were some times during which the deceased was incapable of making a will, it was claimed that when he actually did make his will he appreciated what he **[16–06]**

---

[7] ss 52–4, Succession Act 1965.

[8] ss 26–7, *ibid.*

[9] *Dunne v Heffernan* [1997] 3 IR 431; *Re Flood: Flood v Flood* [1999] 2 IR 234; *Gunning v Gunning Hameed* [2003] IEHC 123.

[10] It should be noted that a revocation or amendment may be ineffective if the testator has entered into a contract not to revoke or amend, completed a mutual will with a clause not to amend or revoke, or if someone successfully claims estoppel against the estate.

[11] s 77(1)(a), Succession Act 1965.

[12] *ibid.*

[13] s 77(1)(b), Succession Act 1965.

[14] (1870) LR 5 QB 549.

was doing, had clear intentions and was not influenced by others, was not delusional, was rational, and managed his business and financial affairs well. When considering the direction to be put to a jury assessing the soundness of disposing mind of a testator, Cockburn LJ laid down the following test:

> It is essential that a testator shall understand the nature of the act and its effect; shall understand the extent of the property of which he is disposing, and shall be able to comprehend and appreciate the claims to which he ought to give effect, and with a view to the latter object, that no disorder of the mind shall poison his affections; pervert his sense of right; or prevent the exercise of his natural faculties; that no insane delusions shall influence his will in disposing of his property and bring about a disposal of it which, if the mind had been sound, would not have been made.

[16–07] This test was adopted into Irish law in the case of *O'Donnell v O'Donnell*.[15] The deceased in this case was a paranoid schizophrenic who had lived most of his life independently and in full management of his finances and business interests and had required hospitalisation on only three occasions, having suffered breakdowns in 1949, 1966 and 1991. The deceased was treated with anti-psychotic drugs and reacted well to them. In his will the deceased left the bulk of the estate on trust for his younger brother, who suffered from a more severe diagnosis of paranoid schizophrenia, with the monies being intended to pay for his medical treatment and other needs. Kelly J applied the test from *Banks v Goodfellow* and, based on the fact that the deceased's condition was well managed and that there were no manifestations of paranoid schizophrenia at the time the will was made, as well as the fact that the deceased had been conscientious and thoughtful in the distribution of his estate, concluded that the testator was of sound disposing mind.

[16–08] Questions as to capacity can often arise where the deceased executed his or her will after a particularly severe medical event, such as a stroke, which raise *prima facie* concerns about soundness of disposing mind but where the instructions for the will (i.e. the actual description of the disposition of the estate) were given prior to this medical event taking place. In such cases, the court will concern itself with: (a) whether the medical event constitutes an intervening act between the point at which instructions were given and the point at which the will was executed and, if so, (b) whether there was capacity at the time of instructions being given and, if so, (c) whether there is anything to show a "thread" of continuing capacity from the moment of giving instructions to the moment of executing the will.[16] This position is clearly illustrated by the case of *Re Glynn*.[17]

[16–09] The deceased here had given instructions for the making of his will following independent discussions with two (non-legal) advisors. In his will he made a bequest of £20,000 to his sister, the plaintiff; a charitable bequest of £1,000; and the residue of his estate, consisting of his farm and various monies, was left to his second cousin, the

[15] Unreported, High Court, 24 March 1999.

[16] *Parker v Felgate* (1883) 8 PD 171.

[17] [1990] 2 IR 326; conclusion reiterated in *O'Donnell v O'Donnell*, unreported, High Court, 24 March 1999.

defendant. After giving these instructions, but before executing his will, the deceased suffered a massive stroke as a result of which he was disorientated and unable to communicate in either written or verbal form. Some two weeks after the stroke two independent persons visited the deceased in hospital and read out his will to him, following which he nodded his assent and placed an "X" by means of signature on the document, which was then attested by two witnesses. The plaintiff claimed that the will was invalid and that the deceased was not of sound disposing mind at the time the will was executed, which, she claimed, was the material time. In the High Court, Hamilton P held that the onus of proof normally lies on the person challenging a will, but that where the deceased has suffered a stroke or any other condition that might affect his capacity, a heavy onus shifts to the person propounding the will to show that the deceased had capacity and understood the extent of his property and the nature of claims against that property. In this case the independent persons who had gone to the hospital had no interest in the estate of the deceased and therefore no ulterior motives in testifying that, as far as they were concerned, the deceased understood what he was doing. In addition, the document executed and attested actually reflected the true wishes of the deceased and his bounty had been distributed as he desired. On the basis of this, Hamilton P upheld the will and found that the testator was of sound disposing mind. The plaintiff appealed to the Supreme Court, where the appeal was dismissed, with the Court holding that at the time the independent persons visited the hospital and the testator executed the will, he was merely confirming instructions already given for his will and understood that these instructions were reflected in the document that he executed. The Supreme Court concluded that the testator had indicated his satisfaction that the document read out to him reflected his wishes (by nodding and placing his "X" on the page after the will was read out to him) and that nothing less than firm medical proof of incapacity would discharge the onus of proving that the testator was of sound disposing mind.

It is a necessary part of making a valid will that the testator would intend to make that will. The intention to make a valid will is known as *animus testandi* and can be found to have been absent where the testator made his will as a result of undue influence. While the law of undue influence can be said to encompass actual undue influence and presumed undue influence[18] (arising in cases where the donor regards the donee as an advisor, or as someone whose guidance ought to be trusted), the law does not appear to apply the doctrine of presumed undue influence to wills.[19] The doctrine of undue influence essentially attempts to prevent people from working upon the "weaknesses" of others or exercising dominion over others in order to give rise to an "agreement" or "will" that was not, in fact, freely made; in essence, it attempts to prevent the victimisation of one party by another.[20] The 1617 decision of *Joy v Bannister*[21] offers an interesting, although sad, example of this. In this case Mr Lydiatt, an 80-year-old **[16–10]**

[18] See, for example, *Carroll v Carroll* [1999] 4 IR 241.

[19] *Healy v Lyons*, unreported, High Court, 1978.

[20] *Allcard v Skinner* [1887] 36 Ch D 145; *National Westminster Bank Plc v Morgan* [1985] 1 All ER 821.

[21] (1617) BR 33.

gentleman, was befriended by the rather unfortunately named Mrs Death, who formed a close association with him until he made his will, by which he left a sizeable amount of property to her. Once the will had been made, Mrs Death apparently neglected her association with Mr Lydiatt, but treated him so cruelly that he was afraid to revoke the will. Upon his death it was claimed that the legacy to her resulted from her undue influence over the aged Mr Lydiatt. The Vice Chancellor, Lord Bacon, found undue influence and wrote of Mrs Death's association with the deceased in the following dramatically strong terms:

> [Lydiatt was] an old man about the age of eighty years and being weak of body and understanding and having a great estate of goods and lands... was drawn by the practices and indirect means of... [Mrs Death] to give his house here in London and to come to sojourn with her at her house in the country... [although she was married to Mr Death], and that she having him there did so work upon his simplicity and weakness and by her dalliance and pretence of love unto him and of intention after the death of her then husband to marry him, and by sundry adulterous courses with him and by sorcery and by drawing of his affections from... his kindred, telling him sometimes that they would poison him and sometimes that they would rob him.[22]
>
> After she had obtained control of his estate and property, Mrs. Death neglected such attendance of him as she had used before and used him in a most cruel manner reviling him and causing him to be whipped and suffered him to lie loathsomely and uncleanly in bed until three o'clock in the afternoon without anybody to help him so as all the skin of his loins went off, he being not able to help himself by reason he was troubled with a dead palsy and other diseases, and when at any time she did come to help him up she would pinch him and revile him and by such cruel and terrible courses kept him so in awe as that he durst not revoke what before he had done, neither would she suffer his nieces to come unto him lest he should make his moan unto them, for she said if they came there she would scald them out of her house."[23]

2. Requirements as to Formalities

[16–11] Section 78 of the Succession Act 1965 provides that for a will to be valid it must be in writing, signed and attested. As a result of the lack of express requirements, it can be assumed that the writing can take any form, including handwriting. It is also clear that the writing that constitutes a will need not be restricted to just one document[24]: rather, a number of documents together can be said to be a will (although in some cases a later document may revoke an earlier document[25]).

[16–12] The will must be signed by the testator, or by a third party acting on his direction and in his presence. In this sense the concept of signature is important. It is far from our concept of signature in everyday proceedings as a "signature" in this sense will be any mark intended to execute the will. Thus in *In bonis Ball*[26] the Court held that "your

[22] *ibid.* at p 34.

[23] *ibid.* at pp 34–5.

[24] *Douglas-Menzies v Umphelby* [1908] AC 224; *In b Wafer* [1960] IR Jur Rep 19.

[25] See paras 16–18 to 16–24 below.

[26] (1890) 25 LR Ir 556.

loving mother" was sufficient to constitute a signature where the intention of the testatrix was clear and she was identifiable by name from the will itself. Equally an "X" or other mark,[27] initials,[28] assumed name,[29] or stamp[30] will be perfectly acceptable, although a seal alone will not be enough.[31] Although the testator may also ask a third party to sign the will on his behalf, this signature will be acceptable only if it was done in the presence of the testator and under his direction.

The signature must be placed at the foot, or end, of the will in order to ensure that **[16–13]**
there is as little "white space" as possible between the end of the will and the signature and, as a result, there is a reduced capacity for a third party to "write in" a new clause without the knowledge of the testator. It should be noted, however, that this requirement is subject to a fairly relaxed application by the courts. This is reflected in the terms of Rule 3 in s 78 of the Succession Act, which provides that:

> it is sufficient if the signature is so placed at or after, or following, or under, or beside, or opposite to the end of the will that it is apparent on the face of the will that the testator intended to give effect by the signature to the writing signed as his will.

If the document can be read in such a way as to make the signature appear at the end of the disposition portion, then the court will endeavour to do this as courts generally favour the reading that makes a will valid.[32]

The signature of the testator, or the person signing on his behalf and in his presence, **[16–14]**
must be attested by two or more witnesses, who must all be present at the time of the signature (or acknowledgement of signature) and all be capable of seeing the act of signing.[33] The witnesses may place their signature anywhere on the document, although it is normal practice for the signatures of witnesses to be placed beneath the signature of the testator. The signature can take any form, provided the mark made was intended to act as an attestation of the testator's signature[34] and, because the witnesses are attesting the signature (and not the document), they do not need to know that what they are signing is a will.[35] The witnesses must actually sign the will in the presence of the testator: it will not be sufficient for a witness to acknowledge his signature in the testator's presence.[36] If the testator has signed the document outside of the presence of the witnesses, he can acknowledge the signature in front of the witnesses who are present together and, provided all witnesses have the opportunity to

---

27 *In bonis Kieran* [1933] IR 222.

28 *In bonis Emerson* (1882) 9 LR Ir 443.

29 *In bonis Glover* (1847) 11 Jur 1022.

30 *Jenkins v Gaisford & Thring* (1863) 3 Sw & Tr 93.

31 *In bonis Emerson* (1882) 9 LR Ir 443.

32 *In re the Goods of Hornby* [1946] P 171.

33 Thus a blind person or a person who was otherwise unable to see at the time of the signature cannot be a witness.

34 *In bonis Strealey* [1891] P 172; *In bonis Amiss* (1849) 2 Rob Ecc 116; *Re Bullock* [1968] NI 96.

35 *Re Devlin* [1939] IR Jur Rep 85.

36 *Wyatt v Berry* [1893] P 5.

see the signature, this will be sufficient.[37] There are no particular statutory qualifications to act as witness, although acting as the witness to a will may disqualify someone to benefit from that will,[38] as we will see below.[39]

[16–15] These formalities are all of the nature of things that we can see easily and quickly by simply looking at a document: we can see that it is written, signed and attested (or at least that it appears as it if has been signed and attested). The courts will normally apply the maxim *omnia praesumuntur rite esse acta*, meaning that we presume everything to have been properly and validly executed. Thus, our starting presumption—once we can see writing, signature and attesting signatures—is that they comply with the requirements of s 78 of the Succession Act 1965. The impact of that presumption is that a document that *prima facie* is written, signed and attested is presumed valid and the onus is on the party claiming failure to comply with the formalities to rebut that presumption. That can be particularly efficient as a matter of evidence where the alleged witnesses are not available to testify or make an affidavit as to the validity of the will because of death or incapacity, but it does not mean that witnesses to the will can never be called to testify to its validity (or lack thereof). Rather, in *Clery v Barry*, the Court held that the presumption should enjoy its full force only where the witnesses cannot give evidence (death or incapacity[40]) or where the evidence of the witnesses cannot be accepted because the witnesses themselves are deemed unreliable.[41]

III. Amendment of Wills

[16–16] Wills can be amended right up to the time of death, but facial amendments to wills (i.e. changes made on the face of the will itself) can present some practical difficulties: how is one to tell whether or not the "amendment" is genuine and was done by the testator, or whether it is an alteration made illegitimately by a third party? Amendments or alterations that take place before the execution of the will are valid without any additional formalities being fulfilled, although it ought to be noted that questions of proof can become quite difficult in such scenarios. Any alterations are subject to a presumption that they are made after execution, and therefore must comply with the terms of s 86 of the Succession Act 1965, which provides:

> An obliteration, interlineation, or other alteration made in a will after execution shall not be valid or have any effect, unless such alteration is executed as is required for the execution of the will; but the will, with such alteration as part thereof, shall be deemed to be duly executed if the signature of the testator and the signature of each witness is made in the margin or on some other part of the will opposite or near to such alteration, or at

[37] *Cooke v Henry* [1932] IR 574; *Kavanagh v Fegan* [1932] IR 566.

[38] s 82, Succession Act 1965.

[39] para 16–27.

[40] s 81 of the Succession Act 1965 expressly provides that one's incompetence to be admitted as a witness to the validity of the will does not cause that will to be invalid, i.e. it does not mean that the attestation by that witness is not effective.

[41] *Clery v Barry* (1889) 21 LR Ir 152; see also *Rolleston v Sinclair* [1924] 2 IR 157.

> the foot or end of or opposite to a memorandum referring to such alteration, and written at the end of some other part of the will.

Section 86 therefore requires that the alteration or amendment would be signed and attested in the same way as a will must be signed and attested. Where the signature and attesting signatures are absent, the presumption that the alterations were made after execution (and therefore ineffective in the absence of such formalities) will apply. This is well demonstrated by *Re Myles Deceased*.[42] In this case the will was handwritten and homemade. A number of paragraphs of the will had been "crossed out" and some notes had been written into the margin and signed, but not witnessed. The attesting witness to the will could not recall whether the paragraphs had been crossed out before execution or when the marginal notes had been made. Lardner J held that because these changes were not signed and attested in accordance with s 86, they could not be given effect as part of the will.

It should be noted at this point that unattested documents can be incorporated into a will provided they are complete at the time the will is made and are expressly referenced in the will itself.[43] The requirement that the unattested document would be fully formed by the time the will is made ensures that the incorporation of documents by reference does not infringe the "attestation" requirements of ss 78 and 86. **[16–17]**

IV. Revocation of Wills

By their very nature wills are revocable up to the time of death. This general principle is subject to cases in which a testator, by his own conduct, had stripped himself of the capacity to effectively revoke his will. This will arise where there is a case of mutual wills including a clause not to revoke or amend, where the testator has entered into a binding contract not to revoke the will, or where the testator is estopped from revoking his will. Apart from these circumstances, the testator can revoke all or part of his will at his pleasure.[44] The revocation of wills is governed by s 85 of the Succession Act 1965 as amended by s 79 of the Civil Partnership and Certain Rights and Obligations of Cohabitants Act 2010. This provides: **[16–18]**

> (1) A will shall be revoked by the subsequent marriage or entry into a civil partnership of the testator, except a will made in contemplation of that marriage or entry into a civil partnership, whether so expressed in the will or not.
>
> (2) Subject to subsection (1), no will, or any part thereof, shall be revoked except by another will or codicil duly executed, or by some writing declaring an intention to revoke it and executed in the manner in which a will is required to be executed, or by the burning, tearing, or destruction of it by the testator, or by some person in his presence and by his direction, with the intention of revoking it.

Thus, there are three means of revocation: marriage or civil partnership, formal writing, and destruction.

---

42 [1993] ILRM 34.

43 *Re O'Connor* [1937] IR Jur Rep 67; *In b Conwell* (1896) 30 ILTR 23.

44 *Forse and Hembling's Case* (1588) 4 Co Rep 61b.

[16–19] In the normal course of events wills include a clause that revokes all previous wills and testamentary dispositions.[45] Such clauses are almost uniformly successful in revoking earlier wills and the courts will require particularly probative evidence of a contrary intention to find that such a clause has not revoked previous wills.[46] A revocation clause of this nature is not required, however, to revoke a previous will by formal writing; rather, any writing that is signed and attested in the same way as a will and that is inconsistent with earlier formal writing may result in revocation of the earlier (and now inconsistent) writing.[47] It is important to bear in mind, however, that a subsequent "will" does not necessarily revoke an earlier "will" in its entirety, because wills can comprise a number of documents. Thus, subsequent documents that do not include a revocation clause and are not inconsistent with earlier dispositions may simply be "added to" and "read with" the earlier documents, so that together they constitute a will.

[16–20] Previous wills are revoked automatically by the marriage or civil partnership of the testator unless the will was made in contemplation of the subsequent marriage or civil partnership.[48] This reflects the fact that we conceive of our obligations to a spouse or civil partner as qualitatively different to our obligations to others. For those reasons, as considered later, we restrict testamentary freedom to protect spouses and civil partners[49] *and* we revoke previous wills in order to "nudge" newly wedded and civilly partnered individuals to consider the needs of their spouses and civil partners in their wills.

[16–21] A will can also be revoked by means of destruction[50] provided that the destruction is accompanied by an intention to revoke the will.[51] This intention is implied from the means of destruction, thus "burning [or] tearing"[52] a will is sufficient to show an intention to revoke, whereas crumpling up a will and throwing it in the wastepaper-basket would normally not be sufficient. A will can be revoked by destruction where that destruction is carried out by another, provided the testator was present at the time of the destruction and it was done under his direction.[53] Some of the difficulties with effective revocation can be seen in the well-known case of *Cheese v Lovejoy.*[54] In this case the testator drew a line through his will and wrote "this is revoked" on the back of it, but failed to sign this declaration or to have it attested. He then placed the will on a pile of waste papers for disposal. Upon seeing it there, a servant took the will and placed it in the kitchen, where it was found some years later upon the testator's death.

---

45 s 85(2), Succession Act 1965.
46 See, for example, *In b McCullagh* [1949] IR Jur Rep 49; *In b Keenan* (1946) 50 ILTR 1.
47 *Caldbeck v Stafford* [1930] IR 196; *In b Martin* [1968] IR 1.
48 s 85(1), Succession Act 1965.
49 paras 16–57 to 16–68.
50 s 85(2), Succession Act 1965.
51 *In b Walsh* [1947] IR Jur Rep 44; *In b Coster*, unreported, Supreme Court, 19 January 1978.
52 s 85(2), Succession Act 1965.
53 *Gill v Gill* [1909] P 157.
54 [1877] 2 PD 251.

As the writing was not accompanied by formalities and the document was not actually destroyed, it continued to operate as a valid will.

If someone attempts to revoke a will, but does not comply with the requirements of s 85, the will continues to be operative and, as a result, will be read in conjunction with any other "wills" or "parts of wills" that may be subsequently created and which do not revoke that earlier will under the rules of formal writing considered above.[55] If the document has been destroyed but has not been revoked (because of a lack of intention to revoke) the contents of the will can be proved through secondary evidence, such as drafts and photocopies of wills and so on.[56] [16–22]

Some revocations may be made subject to a particular condition and, in such cases, the will is not revoked until such time as the condition is fulfilled.[57] It is quite common for someone to revoke a will on the condition that he will make a subsequent and valid will. This doctrine—known as the "doctrine of dependent relative revocation"—provides that if a subsequent will is never made or is invalid, the previous will is operative and has not been revoked.[58] The doctrine can be traced back to *Onions v Tyrer*[59] in which a testator had created a valid will and, four years later, made a subsequent will expressly revoking the first. The testator then directed his wife to tear up the first will. The Court held that the second will was not valid because it had not been executed properly and, as a result, it could not be said to have revoked the previous will. The testator, the Court held, intended to revoke the first will by the second will and *not* by the act of tearing it up; thus, because the second will was invalid, the first will had not been revoked. The Lord Chancellor held that the tearing of the first will might be a good revocation at law, but equity ought to step in and make good the testator's mistake by finding that the first will was not effectively revoked. [16–23]

Where a will has been revoked, it may be possible for it to be made operative once again. This can normally be done by means of re-execution in compliance with the formalities laid down in s 78, or by means of a codicil that is duly executed (i.e. in compliance with s 78) and makes express reference to the will. [16–24]

V. Lost Wills

It is sometimes the case that we know someone made a will, but cannot find it after that person's death. In the cases of lost wills, the law presumes that the will was revoked by means of destruction. This presumption can be rebutted, however, by evidence to the contrary. Thus, if my will were held in a safe in my solicitor's office and it could be shown that the safe was stolen, a court would be unlikely to proceed as though I had revoked my will by means of destruction. If the court is satisfied that a will is lost and not revoked, some mechanism must be employed to establish the contents of the will. In this context secondary evidence, such as photocopies of the will, instructions on file [16–25]

---

[55] para 16–19.

[56] See, for example, *In b Cullinan* (1951) 85 ILTR; *In b Regan* [1964] IR Jur Rep 56.

[57] *Re Plunkett* [1964] IR 259.

[58] *In b Cullinan* (1951) 85 ILTR 180; *In b McCullagh* [1949] IR Jur Rep 49; see also Warren, "Dependent Relative Revocation" (1920) 33 Harv LR 337.

[59] (1716) 23 ER 1085.

with a solicitor, or, as is increasingly more common, a soft copy of the will that is stored on a client's electronic file by his solicitor, might be accepted as evidence of the contents of the lost will. Of course, the probative value of these various sources of information will dictate the extent to which the court concludes that they accurately reflect the contents of the lost will. Importantly, hearsay evidence can also be adduced in this context.[60]

VI. Failure of Gifts in a Will

[16–26] Even if a will is valid it may be the case that some of the dispositions in the will cannot be given effect and must fail. Thus, although the will is valid some of the gifts in that will cannot and will not go to the persons named therein. In such cases the gifts in question will either fall into the residual clause in the will (where there is one and where it is worded in a way that "captures" the gift in question) *or* be incapable of disposal by the will and therefore be disposed of by the rules of intestacy (meaning that there will be a case of partial intestacy). Even if a gift is valid, the beneficiary is entitled to disclaim it, which will either be done by conduct or more formally by means of a deed.[61]

1. Gifts to Witnesses and their Spouses or Civil Partners

[16–27] Section 82 of the Succession Act 1965, as amended by s 77 of the Civil Partnership and Certain Rights and Obligations of Cohabitants Act 2010, provides that, as a general matter, gifts to witnesses or the spouses or civil partners of witnesses have no effect. A gift to a spouse or civil partner of a witness to the will is not deemed invalid if the marriage or civil partnership was not in existence at the time of the will being made.[62] Similarly, if the gift is one whereby the witness or her spouse or civil partner is a trustee of the property, s 82 will not invalidate it. The rule can invalidate gifts where someone signs as an "additional" witness,[63] but not where someone has signed in a capacity other than as a witness.[64] The Succession Act 1965 requires "two or more" witnesses to the will,[65] therefore where there are additional signatures it is possible that these could also be construed as witness signatures and any gifts to those individuals could be struck out. For this reason it is advisable to ensure that all "additional" signatures are clearly shown not to be witness signatures. In *Re the Goods of Shaw*[66] the will, which was signed and attested by two witnesses, included an additional signature of one Hugh Wilson. Wilson's signature followed those of the witnesses and was preceded by a handwritten note saying, "Above signatures witnessed by Hugh Wilson". Wilson was a beneficiary under the will, and the Court held that his signature had not been added to the document with any intention of attesting the signature of the testator. As a result, Wilson was not a witness to the will and could, therefore, enjoy his gift under it.

---

[60] *Sugden v Lord St Leonards* (1876) 1 PD 154.
[61] *Towson v Tickell* (1819) 3 B & Ald 31; *Re Clout and Frewer's Contract* [1924] 2 Ch 230.
[62] *Thorpe v Bestwick* (1881) 6 QBD 311.
[63] *Re Bravda* [1968] 1 WLR 479; but see also s 1, Wills Act 1968 (UK), reversing this position.
[64] *In re the Goods of Shaw* [1944] IR Jur Rep 77.
[65] s 78, Succession Act 1965.
[66] [1944] IR Jur Rep 77.

2. Lapse

If a beneficiary predeceases the testator her gift will normally fail by means of lapse.[67] There are a number of exceptions to this general principle. The first relates to cases where someone was bequeathed a fee tail in a will, but had predeceased the testator; in such a case the gift of the fee tail would stand unless the will reveals a contrary intention on the part of the testator.[68] Importantly, the Land and Conveyancing Law Reform Act 2009 provides that the fee tail can longer be created either *inter vivos* or in a will[69]: rather any attempt to create a fee tail results in the creation of a fee simple[70] and, as a result, this exception to lapse is now defunct. The second exception relates to gifts to charities where the charity has been dissolved prior to the death of the testator. In such cases the doctrine of *cy prés* might be applied in order to allow the transfer of the gift to a charity that is very similar in object and structure to the charity named in the will. **[16–28]**

A gift of something more than a life estate to issue of the testator who predeceases the testator but dies leaving living issue will not lapse and will instead go into the estate of the deceased issue, unless the will reveals a contrary intention on the part of the testator.[71] In this context "issue" can be taken to mean children born outside of marriage as well as within marriage,[72] and unborn but conceived children *en ventre sa mere* (i.e. in the womb).[73] In *Re Stamp, Deceased,* however, it was held that this exception to lapse does not apply to adopted children.[74] This decision is in direct contrast with the Adoption Act 1952,[75] which provides that adopted children are to be treated the same as "natural" children, and on that basis the decision in *Stamp* appears to be wrongly decided. **[16–29]**

3. Causing the Death of the Testator

Section 120 of the Succession Act 1965 prevents a person who has killed the testator from taking any gift under the deceased's will unless that will was made after the time at which the act causing the death occurred. The terms of s 120 in this context are worthy of reproduction in full: **[16–30]**

> A sane person who has been guilty of the murder, attempted murder or manslaughter of another shall be precluded from taking any share in the estate of that other, except a share arising under a will made after the act constituting the offence, and shall not be entitled to make an application under section 117.

---

67 s 91, Succession Act 1965.
68 s 97, *ibid.*
69 s 13(1), Land and Conveyancing Law Reform Act 2009. See further Chapter 4.
70 s 13(2), *ibid.*
71 s 98, Succession Act 1965.
72 s 29, Status of Children Act 1987.
73 s 3(2), Succession Act 1965.
74 *In re Stamp Deceased* [1993] ILRM 383.
75 See also s 27(4)(b), Status of Children Act 1987 with which *In re Stamp Deceased* [1993] ILRM 383 seems also to be in conflict.

It is quite clear from the terms of s 120 that it operates to defeat gifts to anyone who has caused the death of the testator regardless of the circumstances, although one must be convicted of such: a mere suspicion or charge is not enough.[76] Thus, someone who caused death through vehicular manslaughter is treated in the same way as someone who cold-bloodedly tortures the testator to death. In addition, someone who kills as a result of provocation or self-defence—as may sometimes be the case in the context of violent attacks and domestic violence—is not given any relief under this provision. The only person who can enjoy a gift under the will notwithstanding having caused the death of the testator is someone who receives the gift under "a will made after the act constituting the offence". There is no requirement in s 120 that the testator would have known that this person actually killed him before making his will (criminal liability attaches to the act that causes death, even if there is a gap in time between that act and the death during which a will might be validly made), although where the deceased was not so aware it seems likely that equity would intervene and prevent the statute from being used as an instrument of fraud.

4. Uncertainty

[16–31] If a gift in the will is expressed with such uncertainty that it is not possible to tell what is to be bequeathed or upon whom it is to be bequeathed, even after the admission of extrinsic evidence, then the gift will fail.[77]

5. Simultaneous Death

[16–32] If two or more people die in circumstances that make it impossible to tell who died first, s 5 of the Succession Act 1965 provides that they are to be considered as having died simultaneously. This may result in the failure of a gift in the will of one of the deceased where a devise is made conditional on the devisee surviving the deceased for a certain period of time.

VII. Modification of Gifts by the Application of Equity

[16–33] In addition to the circumstances in which gifts in a will might fail on legal grounds, there are certain cases in which equitable doctrines may be applied, resulting in the devise in the will being modified. The main doctrines employed in this context are satisfaction, ademption, performance and election.

1. Satisfaction

[16–34] The doctrine of satisfaction is based on two equitable maxims: "equity imputes an intention to fulfil an obligation" and "equity leans against double portions". In essence, satisfaction applies to alter the nature of, or to cancel the effect of, a gift in a will where: (a) the beneficiary is also a debtor of the deceased (debts by legacies); *or* (b) where the beneficiary is a child of the deceased who is owed a portion (portions by legacies); *or* (c) where there is a duplication of provision in the will (legacies by legacies).

---

[76] *Re Nevin's Estate* [1997] IEHC 209.

[77] On the construction of wills generally, see paras 16–42 to 16–56, below.

Where a deceased bequeaths personal property[78] to someone to whom a debt is owed, this gift may be presumed to be satisfaction of the debt owed. This will arise only where the debt was in existence at the time the will was made,[79] and where the gift in the will is of equal or greater value than the debt owed[80] (although interest on either the debt or the legacy will not be taken into account[81]). The doctrine of satisfaction of debts by legacies is not applied to residual gifts or gifts that are uncertain or contingent.[82] **[16–35]**

If a father (not a mother) or a person standing *in loco parentis* agrees to gift his child a portion of money on marriage or aid in setting up in a business or profession but does not advance that sum, a legacy to the child will be presumed to be in satisfaction of the promised "portion".[83] This presumption will apply only where the legacy is substantial enough to be considered in the nature of a permanent provision,[84] and the presumption can be rebutted by a contrary intention in the will.[85] If the presumption of satisfaction of portions by legacies is applied, then the child can choose to take either the gift in the will or the portion, but may not take both.[86] **[16–36]**

Where the same amount of a legacy is given to the same person on multiple occasions in the same will, equity will presume that there was an accidental duplication and that the legacies are not cumulative. If the legacies are in different amounts[87] or in different wills[88] (although not necessary in a will and a separate codicil[89]) the presumption is likely to be rebutted, although the onus of proving that the legacies are cumulative lies on the party attempting to prevent the application of the presumption.[90] **[16–37]**

2. Ademption

Ademption can arise in one of two situations: the first is where the property devised no longer exists within the estate of the deceased at the time of death (ademption by failure of property), and the second is where the legacy can be deemed to have been satisfied by a later *inter vivos* portion (ademption of legacies by portions). **[16–38]**

In the case of ademption by failure of property, a specific legacy (i.e. one that specifically names a particular piece of property) will be adeemed if the testator is no longer entitled to it at the time of death, unless there is a corresponding item in his estate. For example, if my will includes a provision stating, "I leave my diamond watch to Mary," and by the time I die the diamond watch I owned at the time of making the will has been sold but I **[16–39]**

78 Realty is excluded from the doctrine in its application to debts by legacies—*Richardson v Elphinstone* 2 Ves Jun 463.
79 *Horlock v Wiggans* (1888) 39 Ch D 142.
80 *Coates v Coates* [1898] 1 IR 258.
81 *Re Rattenberry* [1906] 1 Ch 667.
82 *R Van de Burgh WT* [1948] 1 All ER 935.
83 See *Blundell v Blundell* [1906] 2 Ch 222.
84 See *Re Hayward* [1957] Ch 528.
85 Keating, *Equitable Succession Rights* (2005, Dublin, Round Hall), p 71.
86 *ibid.*
87 *Yockney v Hansard* (1844) 3 Hare 620.
88 *Foy v Foy* 1 Cox Eq Cas 163.
89 *Bell v Park* [1914] 1 IR 158.
90 *Quin v Armstrong* IR 11 Eq 161.

have replaced it with another diamond watch, then the gift will not be adeemed. If, however, I have sold the diamond watch and replaced it with a gold bracelet, the gift will be adeemed. Where there is a general legacy, however, ademption will not occur as long as the estate contains some property that can fall into the legacy. Thus if my will stated, "I leave all my jewellery to Mary," and, at the time of making my will, I had an extensive collection of diamond and sapphire jewellery, but, at the time of my death, had only one brass bangle in my estate, the legacy would not be adeemed.

[16–40] In a case of ademption of legacies by portions, a portion left to a child by a parent or by a person who is in *loco parentis* can be adeemed if, subsequent to making her will, she transferred a portion to the child on his marriage.[91] Unlike in a case of satisfaction of portions by legacies, in this scenario the child must take the *inter vivos* portion and cannot choose to accept the gift in the will in its stead. It appears that ademption of legacies by portions can take place between a testator and a stranger, but this will only happen where both the legacy and the later portion were given for the same specific purpose.[92]

3. Election

[16–41] If, in his will, a testator intends to dispose of property that does not belong to him and, in the same will, to make a gift to the proper owner, the doctrine of election applies.[93] This requires the owner of the property either to accept his gift under the will and give up any rights to his property, or to disclaim the gift in the will and take back his property (in which case the intended beneficiary is compensated). In order for an election to be valid the court must be satisfied that the elector knew the values of the properties, knew of his right to elect, and intended to make an election.[94]

VIII. Construction of Wills

[16–42] On occasion a disposition in a will may be ambiguous or unclear. In order to discern what was intended by the testator—which is the main objective of the court in such cases—various rules of construction will be applied. The court's primary role in constructing wills is to ascertain and give effect to the intention of the testator from the words on the page, although a court may not rewrite a will.[95] This does not mean that the court will necessarily give a will its literal meaning; rather, the court may "do violence" to the will if a literal meaning would clearly undermine or frustrate the testator's intention.[96] That said, in general the words as written within the "four corners" of the will form the basis of the court's interpretation.[97] To this end the court will give ordinary words their ordinary meaning and technical words their technical

[91] *Curtin v Evans* (1872) IR 9 Eq 553; *Barry v Harding* (1845) 7 IR Eq R 317.

[92] *Griffith v Bourke* (1887) 21 LR Ir 92.

[93] See, for example, *Re Edwards* [1958] Ch 168.

[94] *Sweetman v Sweetman* IR 2 Eq 141.

[95] *Oliver v Menton* [1945] IR 6; *Re Moore* [1947] IR 205; *Robinson v Moore* [1962–63] IR Jur Rep 29; *Re Curtin* [1991] 2 IR 562.

[96] See *Re Patterson, Dunlop v Greer* [1899] 1 IR 324.

[97] See, for example, *Re Rowland* [1963] Ch 1.

meaning, unless a contrary intention is shown[98] (although a testator who wants ordinary words to be taken as having a particular meaning must provide a lexicon[99]). This "ordinary meaning" rule reflects the court's mission in giving effect to the "expressed intentions" of the testator.[100]

Because the court focuses on the words as written in the will there will sometimes be occasions where conflicting words arise. In such circumstances the court may apply the *falsa demonstratio* rule or the *non accipi debent* rule, depending on the circumstances. If neither of these rules is suitable or results in a clear meaning, then it may be possible to apply extrinsic evidence.[101] The *falsa demonstratio* rule applies to descriptions of parties or property where the description is made up of a true part and a false part. In such cases the rule allows for the false part to be disregarded and the true part to stand and be given effect. This rule essentially allows for words that run contrary to the testator's intent to be excluded.[102] In some cases the *non accipi debent* rule may be more appropriate. This rule provides that where there is some ambiguity as to whether words cast a doubt on the intention of the testator or whether they are intended to restrict the general statement that preceded them, the court will conclude that they were intended to restrict the general statement; these words "will be construed... as words limiting or restricting the effect of a gift to those parts which are true".[103] **[16–43]**

The common law has long applied a presumption against intestacy, which is reflected in s 99 of the Succession Act 1965. Section 99 provides: **[16–44]**

> If the purport of a devise or bequest admits of more than one interpretation, then, in case of doubt, the interpretation according to which the devise or bequest will be operative shall be preferred.

Thus, by application of s 99 the court is empowered to construct an ambiguous clause in a manner that makes it effective, rather than in a manner that results in its invalidity. Such a rule is entirely sensible: after all, the court is obliged to ascertain and give effect to the intention of the testator and it must be reasonably assumed that a testator who has gone to the trouble of complying with the formalities for the creation of a will intended that will to be effective and not to die intestate.[104]

---

[98] See, for example, *Re Doran* [2000] 4 IR 551 *per* Herbert J: "Words used in a will are deemed to have been used in their ordinary grammatical meaning unless there is something in the text of the will read as a whole to indicate that they were used in some restricted sense or that some special meaning was intended".

[99] *Re Cook* [1948] 1 All ER 231.

[100] *Perrin v Morgan* [1943] 1 All ER 187 *per* Viscount Simons LC.

[101] The rules governing extrinsic evidence are considered in paras 16–42 to 16–56, below.

[102] For a detailed treatment see Keating, *Equitable Succession Rights* (2005, Dublin, Round Hall); Keating, *Construction of Wills* (2001, Dublin, Round Hall); Keating, "The Use of the *Falsa Demonstratio* Rule in the Construction of Wills" (2004) 9(4) CPLJ 78.

[103] Keating, *Construction of Wills* (2001, Dublin, Round Hall), p 226.

[104] See also Anderson, "Statutory Aids in the Construction of Wills: Sections 90 and 99 of the Succession Act 1965" (2002) 5(3) IJFL 2; *Re Harrison* (1885) 30 Ch D 390; *Mulhern v Brennan* [1999] 3 IR 528.

[16–45] The final general rule of construction of significance is found in s 89 of the Succession Act 1965, which provides:

> Every will shall, with reference to all estate comprised in the will and every devise or bequest contained in it, be construed to speak and take effect as if it had been executed immediately before the death of the testator, unless a contrary intention appears from the will.

Section 89 essentially provides that a will is to be read as though it were written immediately before death, and therefore references to people or property will be construed as at the time of death. It is open to a testator to specify an alternative time from which a gift is to be interpreted if he so wishes: thus a testator is entitled to provide that "all the houses owned by me at present" are bequeathed to "all my children now alive in equal shares" and, as a result, the houses owned by the testator at the time the will was written would be inherited by all of his children who were alive at the time that the will was written.[105]

1. Admission of Extrinsic Evidence

[16–46] In some cases, however, the general rules of construction will not be sufficient to give rise to a clear and unambiguous construction of provisions in the will. In such circumstances the court may be permitted to adduce extrinsic evidence, i.e. evidence from outside of the will. As the guiding principle in relation to construction is that the intention of the testator is to be ascertained from the terms of the will itself (i.e. from within the "four corners" of the document), extrinsic evidence may be adduced only in limited situations. When extrinsic evidence is adduced and applied its effect, as with all evidence, is dependent on its relevance and probative value.

[16–47] At common law, extrinsic evidence could be admitted only in limited situations where there was a mistake or ambiguity on the face of the will. Thus, the common law would allow for the admission of extrinsic evidence in cases of latent ambiguity (i.e. where a clause in the will could be said to accurately describe two or more people or things and the ambiguity was not clarified by the terms of the will itself[106]) or contradiction (e.g. where the description of a person did not match the name given).[107] In such circumstances the terms of the will could be afforded further clarity by reading them in the context of the knowledge, circumstances and habits of the testator, and as a result extrinsic evidence could be admitted and applied by means of the "armchair principle". This simply meant that the court would read the will as if it were in the "armchair" of the testator, i.e. with his knowledge, associations and habits in mind.[108] The common law did not, however, allow for extrinsic evidence to be adduced where there was a dissonance between the terms of the will and the known intentions of the testator but there was no ambiguity or contradiction. In such cases the terms of the will would govern the disposition of the deceased's estate *even though* knowledge outside of

---

[105] See *Re Willis* [1911] 2 Ch 563; *Re Champion* [1893] 1 Ch 101; *Re Horton* [1920] 2 Ch 1.

[106] *Healy v Healy* (1875) 9 IR 418; *Re Jackson* [1933] 1 Ch 237.

[107] *In the Goods of Twohill* (1879) 3 LR Ir 21; *Charter v Charter* (1874) LR 7 HL 315; *In re Plunkett's Estate* (1861) 11 IR Ch R 361; *Re Callaghan* [1937] IR 84.

[108] *Boyes v Cook* (1880) 14 Ch D 53; *McInerney v Liddy* [1945] IR 100; *Thorn v Dickens* [1906] WN 54; *Flood v Flood* [1902] 1 IR 538; *Re Moore* [1947] IR 205.

the document itself made it clear that the will did not reflect the testator's intentions and instead contained some kind of mistake. This difficulty came to the fore in the well-known case of *Re Julian*.[109]

This case concerned a bequest in the will of Mrs Julian of a sum of money to "The Seaman's Institute, Sir John Rogerson's Quay, Dublin". When the will was being administered, it became clear that there were two Seaman's Institutes in Dublin: The Dublin Seaman's Institute, Eden Quay, Dublin, and the Catholic Seaman's Institute, Sir John Rogerson's Quay, Dublin. The executrix of the will claimed that Mrs Julian intended to bequeath the monies to the Dublin Seaman's Institute and attempted to have extrinsic evidence of the deceased's religion and institutional affiliation with the Dublin Seaman's Institute admitted into evidence, as well as evidence from the solicitor who prepared the will that he had made an error in the description and address of the institute named in the will. The material question was whether or not this extrinsic evidence could actually be admitted. Although there was a minor mistake on the face of the will—i.e. the absence of the word "Catholic" in the description of the Institute as named—the Court held that this was not a sufficient misdescription to allow for the extrinsic evidence to be adduced: "The words used in the will are descriptive of the Catholic Seamen's Institute. It is clear that if there were no other seamen's institute in Dublin the description used in the will would be sufficient to indicate the beneficiary". Kingsmill-Moore J held that there was insufficient ambiguity or mistake on the face of the will to allow for the admission of extrinsic evidence and, accordingly, the monies were to be paid to the Catholic Seaman's Institute located at Sir John Rogerson's Quay, in Dublin. This was notwithstanding the fact that, from knowledge outside of the will, it was quite clear that Mrs Julian intended and wanted the monies to go to the other institute. **[16–48]**

In giving his judgment in this case, Kingsmill-Moore J was keen to point out his conviction that the deceased's intentions were, in fact, that the monies would be bequeathed to the Dublin Seaman's Institute, and he lamented the restrictive rules on the admission of extrinsic evidence in no uncertain way: **[16–49]**

> This is by no means the first—and, equally certainly, will not be the last—case in which a judge has been forced by the rules of law to give a decision on the construction of a will which he believed to be contrary to the intentions of the testator. The law reports are loud with the comments of judges who found themselves in similar plight; but I consider the law to be well established and conclusive that I must reject [the extrinsic] evidence and, in the absence of such evidence, I must hold that the Catholic Seamen's Institute is entitled to the bequest.

Taking this critique to heart, the Oireachtas included what was thought to be a radical and new approach to the admission of extrinsic evidence in the form of s 90 of the Succession Act 1965, which provides:

> Extrinsic evidence shall be admissible to show the intention of the testator and to assist in the construction of, or to explain any contradiction in, a will.

[109] [1950] IR 57; for similar scenarios in Scotland and Northern Ireland, see *National Society for the Prevention of Cruelty to Children v Scottish National Society for the Prevention of Cruelty to Children* [1915] AC 207 and *Re Carlisle* [1950] NI 105.

[16–50] The material question in relation to s 90 is whether it did, in fact, introduce a new rule of extrinsic evidence whereby such evidence could be admitted where there is a dissonance between the known intentions of the testator and the terms of the will itself, even in the absence of the common law prerequisites of latent ambiguity, mistake or contradiction. There seems to be little doubt that it was the Oireachtas' intention that this would, in fact, be the impact of s 90: however case law considering this provision has rejected such a proposition and found that s 90 has not displaced the common law prerequisites for the admission of such evidence. Before we consider this case law it is worth noting that the grammatical construction of s 90 suggests the same conclusion. Section 90 provides:

> Extrinsic evidence shall be admissible to show the intention of the testator and to assist in the construction of, or to explain any contradiction in, a will.

[16–51] Taking the clauses apart according to their grammatical construction, s 90 could also be expressed as follows:

> Extrinsic evidence shall be admissible to show the intention of the testator and to assist in the construction of a will.
>
> Extrinsic evidence shall be admissible to show the intention of the testator and to explain any contradiction in a will.

There is nothing in the grammatical construction of s 90 that in fact makes any kind of radical change from the common law position. Rather, on a literal legislative reading, s 90 provides that extrinsic evidence shall be admissible where it goes to intention (a basic relevant requirement) and *either* assists in the construction of the will *or* explains a contradiction. There are no plain words that displace the common law position that assistance in construction is required only where the will itself is not clear, i.e. only where there is some ambiguity or contradiction that the court needs to construct.

[16–52] This question of the meaning of s 90 came to the fore in the case of *Rowe v Law.*[110] This case concerned a will made in 1967 by which the deceased had bequeathed all of her property on trust, with the trustees being directed, *inter alia,* to set aside £1,000 for the purchase and furnishing of a cottage for the use of two of the defendants for life, and "any balance then remaining" was to be invested with the income being paid to these two defendants. A dispute arose as to whether the term "any balance then remaining" was a reference to a balance from the £1,000 that was to be set aside for the cottage, or a reference to the balance of her entire estate once all of the directions to the trustees had been carried out. Extrinsic evidence supporting both of these interpretations was available, but the Court did not allow for this extrinsic evidence to be admitted.

[16–53] According to Henchy J for the majority in the Supreme Court, the words in the will were not ambiguous and rather showed a clear intention to give the two defendants

---

[110] [1978] IR 55.

the balance from the £1,000 that had been set aside. Where there was no ambiguity, mistake or contradiction on the face of the will, extrinsic evidence was not admissible notwithstanding the terms of s 90 of the Succession Act 1965. Rather, he held, the effect of s 90 was to introduce a dual requirement for the admission of extrinsic evidence: (a) the evidence must go to the actual intention of the deceased; *and* (b) it must help in the construction of, or explain, a contradiction in the will. Section 90, he held, did not allow for the admission of extrinsic evidence in every case where it helped in the construction of the will: rather, it allowed for its admission where it was needed in order to construct the will. In the absence of ambiguity or mistake—neither of which was present here—extrinsic evidence is simply not required: the testator has complied with the formal requirements for making a will, the terms of the will are clear and unambiguous and, therefore, the intention of the testator is gleaned from these clear and unambiguous provisions. This portion of Henchy J's judgment is expressed with such certainty and force of logic that it is worth quoting in full:

> I read s 90 as allowing extrinsic evidence to be received if it meets the double requirement of (a) showing the intention of a testator *and* (b) assisting in the construction of, or explaining any contradiction in, a will. The alternative reading would treat the section as making extrinsic evidence admissible if it meets the requirement of either (a) or (b). That, however, would produce unreasonable and illogical consequences which the legislature could not have intended. If the section made extrinsic evidence admissible merely because it satisfies requirement (a), then in any case the court could go outside the will and receive and act on extrinsic evidence as to the intention of the testator. The grant of probate would no longer provide an exclusive and conclusive version of the testamentary intention as embodied in a will. However, it would be unreasonable and contradictory for the legislature, on the one hand to lay down in s 78 the formal requirements for the disposition of one's property by will, and on the other to allow by s 90 (without qualification or limitation as to purpose or circumstances or time) extrinsic evidence of the intention of the testator to be admitted. Such a sweeping and disruptive change, fraught with possibilities for fraud, mistake, unfairness and uncertainty, should not be read into the section if another and reasonable interpretation is open.
>
> Section 90 is no less tainted with repugnancy if it is treated as making extrinsic evidence admissible merely because it satisfies requirement (b), that is to say, if it assists in the construction of, or if it explains a contradiction in, a will. Since the function of a court in construing a will or in finding an explanation of a contradiction in it necessarily involves a search for the intention of the testator, it would have been unnecessary for the section to include requirement (b) if requirement (a) on its own were sufficient to allow the admission of extrinsic evidence.
>
> The plain fact is that the grant of an unlimited and undefined jurisdiction to admit extrinsic evidence to show the testator's intention would be so large in its scope and so untoward in its potential consequences that it would exceed the spirit and purpose of the Act. The necessary delimitation of the jurisdiction to admit such evidence is effected by the second limb of the section: "*and* to assist in the construction of, *or* to explain any contradiction in, a will." The conjunctive and cumulative "and" is to be contrasted with the disjunctive and alternative "or." It connotes a duality of purpose as a condition for the admission under the section of extrinsic evidence. The necessary conditions are: to show the intention of the testator *and* to assist in the construction of, or to explain a contradiction in, the will. If either condition is not satisfied, the section does not allow the evidence to be admitted.

[16–54] The dissent of O'Higgins CJ (as he then was) is no less worthy of sustained consideration. Although the then Chief Justice agreed that the will in question did not contain an ambiguity or uncertainty, he held that the effect of s 90 was far broader than that suggested by Henchy J. In his view the judgment of the majority essentially held that s 90 was to have no further impact than to codify and restate the law on extrinsic evidence as it stood prior to the promulgation of the Succession Act 1965, even though the circumstances surrounding s 90—and particularly Kingsmill-Moore J's comments in *Re Julian*—clearly indicated otherwise. Rather than this restrictive view of the impact of s 90, O'Higgins J held that the provision had the "clear purpose" of "giving primacy to the actual intention of the testator and to construe the will in accordance with that intention". On this interpretation s 90 would allow for the admission of extrinsic evidence that went to the intention of the deceased, even in the absence of an ambiguity, mistake or contradiction on the face of the will. To this end he held:

> Obviously, the ideal construction of any will or document is the one which reflects accurately and exactly the intention of the person who made it. In the absence of evidence to the contrary, it must be taken that a document made by a person reflects his intentions. The important statutory change brought about by s. 90 of the Act of 1965 was to ensure that this could be tested. The section made it mandatory to admit evidence *to show* the intention of the testator when it came to a question of construing a will. If the section had only intended to do little more than put in statutory form the common law as it existed prior to the section, it would have been worded very differently. It is to be particularly noted that the section makes special mention of the contradictions in the will itself which, as the punctuation indicates, is something quite different from the portion of the section preceding that provision.
>
> ...
>
> It appears to me clear that s. 90 of the Act of 1965 was drafted to provide for two contingencies: the first where there is a contradiction in the will itself and the second where there is a contradiction between the actual intention of the testator and what was said in the will, given its pre-1965 construction. This latter category would, of course, cover and include situations in which an error had been made by a solicitor or other person writing down the will.

Although the argument propounded by O'Higgins CJ is difficult to fault, the judgment of the majority also boasts an impenetrable logic. In essence, the difficulty appears to boil down to a legislative failure to express the intended consequence of s 90 in terms that are firm enough. As Jack Anderson has noted, "interpretations of section 90 have been bedevilled by the wording of the section itself".[111]

[111] Anderson, "Statutory Aids in the Construction of Wills: Sections 90 and 99 of the Succession Act 1965" (2002) IJFL 2.

There can now be no doubt but that the decision of the majority in *Rowe* as to the meaning and effect of s 90 is the law. In *Re Collins*[112] the Supreme Court unanimously adopted the view that s 90 comprised a dual test for the admission of extrinsic evidence as held in *Rowe*. In that case Keane J held that the alternative interpretation of s 90 would allow for extrinsic evidence to be admitted in all cases and would allow evidence of oral statements made before the execution of the will to supplement, vary or contradict the terms of the formally executed and attested document. Such a position would clearly be untenable. The *Rowe* interpretation of s 90 was reiterated by the High Court in *Crawford v Lawless*[113] and in *Butler v Butler*.[114] The fact that a will is ill-conceived or badly thought out will not be a basis for the admission of extrinsic evidence; the dual test outlined in s 90 and exposed in *Rowe* will apply as normal.[115] **[16–55]**

2. Construction Methodology

Where there is some difficulty with the meaning of a provision in a will the Irish courts will apply the construction methodology laid down originally in *Heron v Ulster Bank Ltd*[116] and subsequently approved of in Irish law in both *Re Howell*[117] and *Bank of Ireland v Gaynor*.[118] As originally stated by Lowry LCJ in *Heron*, this approach takes the following form: **[16–56]**

> [H]aving first read the whole will, one may with advantage adopt the following procedure:
>
> 1. Read the immediately relevant portion of the will as a piece of English and decide, if possible, what it means.
> 2. Look at the other material parts of the will and see whether they tend to confirm the apparently plain meaning of the immediately relevant portion or whether they suggest the need for modification in order to make harmonious sense of the whole or, alternatively, whether an ambiguity in the immediately relevant portion can be resolved.
> 3. If ambiguity persists, have regard to the scheme of the will and consider what the testator was trying to do.
> 4. One may at this stage have resort to rules of construction, where applicable, and aids, such as the presumption of early vesting and the presumptions against intestacy and in favour of equality.
> 5. Then see whether any rule of law prevents a particular interpretation from being adopted.
> 6. Finally, and, I suggest, not until the disputed passage has been exhaustively studied, one may get help from the opinions of other courts and judges on similar words, rarely as binding precedents, since it has been well said that "No will has a twin brother" (per Werner J. in Matter of King 200 N.Y. 189, 192 (1910)), but more often as examples (sometimes of the highest authority) of how judicial minds nurtured in the same discipline have interpreted words in similar contexts.

112 [1998] 2 IR 596.
113 [2002] 4 IR 416.
114 [2006] IEHC 104.
115 *In re Curtin, Deceased* [1991] 2 IR 562.
116 [1974] NI 44.
117 [1992] IR 290.
118 Unreported, High Court, 29 June 1999.

IX. Rights of Surviving Spouses and Civil Partners

[16–57] Although the introduction of wills was accompanied by a deep attachment to the concept of testamentary freedom (i.e. the concept that one ought to be free to leave one's property in whatever way one wishes and to whomever one chooses), the Succession Act 1965 introduced a number of restrictions on testamentary freedom in relation to both surviving spouses and children. With the introduction of the Civil Partnership and Certain Rights and Obligations of Cohabitants Act 2010 and civil partnerships for same-sex couples, the protections afforded to spouses under the Succession Act 1965 were extended to civil partners.

[16–58] There were a number of reasons why, when introducing the Succession Act 1965, it was sensible to introduce some limitations to testamentary freedom in order to protect spouses. In the first place, there was a clear moral case in favour of such provisions: when one marries, one enters into a lifetime commitment of partnership with another person and with this commitment comes a moral obligation to provide for your spouse's needs to the extent possible. It could be argued that this moral obligation is of such magnitude that one ought to be compelled to fulfil it by means of legislation if one has neglected to do so by means of choice. In addition to the moral argument, however, is a welfare argument: if one's spouse is not provided for adequately on death and is, for some reason, not in a position to provide for himself, then the burden of welfare is likely to fall on the State. Statutory restrictions on testamentary freedom in favour of one's spouse can therefore be said to privatise this welfare obligation[119]: to place it back inside the family so that the State's welfare obligation is only as extensive as is required when the capabilities of the family have been exhausted. Upon the introduction of civil partnership in 2010, it was logical to put the same kinds of restrictions in place for the protection of civil partners.[120]

1. The Legal Right Share

[16–59] The legal right share provided for in s 111 of the Succession Act 1965 as amended by s 81 of the Civil Partnership and Certain Rights and Obligations of Cohabitants Act 2010 applies only to lawful spouses and civil partners where the deceased spouse or civil partner died with a valid will. The legal right share takes priority over gifts, bequests and shares on intestacy[121] and, as a result, takes precedence over any gifts that have been created by means of the will.[122]

---

[119] See also Wills, "Reforming Inheritance Law—Providing for the Non-Marital Family" (2002) 7(3) CPLJ 58: "Inheritance law serves not only to facilitate donative intention but also to minimise society's social welfare burdens and to alleviate hardship".

[120] See generally Part 8, Civil Partnership and Certain Rights and Obligations of Cohabitants Act 2010.

[121] s 112, Succession Act 1965; *H v O* [1978] IR 194.

[122] *Dwyer v Keegan* [1997] 2 ILRM 401.

In the case of a surviving spouse, s 111(1) provides that where a testator dies leaving a spouse and no children, the surviving spouse is entitled to one half of the estate, whereas s 111(2) provides that where a testator dies leaving a spouse and children, the spouse is entitled to one-third of the estate. Section 111A lays down analogous provisions for civil partners. Section 111A(1) provides that if a testator leaves a civil partner and no children, the surviving civil partner's legal right share is one-half of the estate and s 111A(b) provides that if a testator leaves a civil partner and children, the surviving civil partner's legal right share is one-half of the estate. In this respect it is important to note that there is no provision in Irish law for the non-biological parent in a same-sex partnership to formalise his or her relationship with the biological child of the other partner; nor can a same-sex couple in a civil partnership adopt a child as co-parents. Thus, imagine a situation where two women—Alison and Barbara—enter into a civil partnership and, subsequent to that, they decide to have a child who is the biological child of Barbara. If Alison should die first, she is considered by law to be childless and, as a result, Barbara will have a legal right share of one-half of the estate. There would have been no way in law for Alison's social status as the parent of the child to be recognised. **[16–60]**

The legal right share will vest automatically in a surviving spouse or civil partner where she has not been left anything in the will.[123] Where a gift in the will is expressly said to be in addition to the legal right share, the surviving spouse or civil partner will be entitled to both the gift in the will and the legal right share.[124] Where, on the other hand, the gift in the will is not said to be additional to the legal right share, the Succession Act 1965 provides that the gift is "deemed to have been intended by the testator to be in satisfaction of the share as a legal right of the spouse or civil partner".[125] In such scenarios the surviving spouse or civil partner is entitled to elect (or choose) either the gift under the will or the legal right share.[126] In the absence of any election the surviving spouse or civil partner will take the gift under the will,[127] regardless of how insignificant in value that gift might be.[128] The executor has a statutory obligation to provide the spouse or civil partner with written notice of the right to elect, and the election must then be done within six months of receiving this notice or within a year of taking out representation on the estate, whichever is the later.[129] It ought to be noted, however, that it seems likely that the running of time would be postponed where the executor has failed to notify the surviving spouse or civil partner of his entitlements, depending on the circumstances of the case.[130] **[16–61]**

A spouse or civil partner is entitled to renounce the legal right share by means of an agreement in writing[131] made either before or after the marriage or civil partnership **[16–62]**

[123] *ibid.*

[124] s 114(1), Succession Act 1965.

[125] s 114(2), *ibid.*

[126] s 115(1)(a), *ibid.*

[127] s 115(1)(b), *ibid.*

[128] *Re Urquhart* [1974] IR 197.

[129] s 115(4), Succession Act 1965.

[130] *Gunning v Gunning Hameed* [2003] IEHC 123.

[131] On the writing requirements, see *In the Goods of Good*, unreported, High Court, 14 July 1986.

but during the life of the testator.[132] The courts will set an agreement renouncing the legal right share aside if they are satisfied that it breaches any of the rules for a valid contract, or that the agreement was obtained by means or "force, fear or fraud", or that the renouncing spouse or civil partner did not have the capacity to understand the nature of that to which he was agreeing.[133] Although the Succession Act 1965 allows for agreements to be made renouncing the legal right share prior to the marriage, the courts appear to be reluctant to enforce such agreements.[134] This may well be connected to the particular constitutional status of marriage in Irish law and whether or not such reluctance will show itself in relation to civil partnership remains to be seen.

2. Appropriation of the Home

[16–63] Personal representatives have a general right of appropriation under s 55 of the Succession Act 1965. Section 56 of the Succession Act allows a surviving spouse or civil partner to compel the personal representatives to exercise this right of appropriation in respect of the dwelling contained within the deceased's estate and in which the surviving spouse or civil partner was ordinarily resident at the time of his death,[135] together with the chattels contained therein.[136] Section 56 applies regardless of whether the deceased died testate, intestate, or partially intestate. In this context:

> dwelling [is defined as] an estate or interest in a building occupied as a separate dwelling or a part, so occupied, of any building and... includes any garden or portion of ground attached to and usually occupied with the dwelling or otherwise required for the amenity or convenience of the dwelling.[137]

[16–64] The dwelling is appropriated by means of satisfaction of the legal right share *or* share by testacy *or* intestate entitlement. If the legal right share is equal in value to the dwelling, then the procedure is very straightforward. Where, however, the legal right share is of lesser value than the dwelling, a number of options are available. Either the surviving spouse can raise the balance and pay it into the estate,[138] or the shares of any infant for whom the surviving spouse is a trustee under s 57 can be applied to pay the balance[139] (in which case, of course, the child acquires ownership of the property).[140]

[16–65] Personal representatives are under a statutory obligation to inform the surviving spouse or civil partner of the potential for appropriation,[141] and the surviving spouse or civil

[132] s 113, Succession Act 1965 *as amended by* s 83, Civil Partnership and Certain Rights and Obligations of Cohabitants Act 2010.
[133] *JH v WJH*, unreported, High Court, 20 December 1979.
[134] See Crowley, "Pre-Nuptial Agreements—Have They Any Place in Irish Law?" (2002) 5(1) IJFL 3.
[135] s 56(1), Succession Act 1965.
[136] s 56(2), *ibid.*
[137] s 56(14), *ibid.*
[138] s 56(9), *ibid.*
[139] s 56(3), *ibid.*
[140] For the difficulties surrounding valuations in the exercise of the right, see McDonald, "Appropriation as a Means of Satisfying the Legal Right Share?" (1999) 4(3) CPLJ 62.
[141] s 56(4), Succession Act 1965.

partner must make an appropriation direction (if at all) within six months of having received the notification or within a year from the date of the grant of representation, whichever is the later.[142] However, the failure of a personal representative to inform the surviving spouse or civil partner of s 56 rights will delay the commencement of the time period. This is clear from the case of *Gunning v Gunning Hameed*,[143] in which a deceased left his wife one half of the estate, with the other half being left to his two daughters, one of whom was the executrix of his will. Following his death his widow—who was the plaintiff in this case—continued to live in the house for some five years, at which stage the executrix moved in with her. The relationship between the parties deteriorated to the extent that the plaintiff left the house and went to reside with her other daughter, the executrix having made it clear that she would not leave the premises. The executrix had never informed her mother of her s 56 rights, and the court held that, as a result, the time limit specified in s 56 had not begun to run against the plaintiff. According to the judgment of Smyth J:

> ... the rights of the surviving spouse do not cease by mere effluction of time (i.e. the twelve month period) from the date of the grant, because the duty still remains on the personal representative to give notice in writing to the surviving spouse. The failure to give such notice in writing to the surviving spouse after the extraction of the grant of probate (in the instant case) means that such surviving spouse['s] rights remain until the notice is served and more than six months have elapsed form the receipt of such notice.

There are a number of scenarios in which the right under s 56 cannot be exercised without the consent of the court because the appropriation of the dwelling-house may result in the remainder of the deceased's assets becoming more difficult to administer or suffering a reduction in value as a result of the appropriation.[144] The court's consent to the appropriation will be required: (a) where the dwelling forms part of a building, and an estate or interest in the whole building forms part of the estate; (b) where the dwelling is held with agricultural land, an estate or interest in which forms part of the estate; (c) where the whole or a part of the dwelling was, at the time of the death, used as a hotel, guesthouse or boarding house; and (d) where a part of the dwelling was, at the time of the death, used for purposes other than domestic purposes.[145] The case of *H v H*[146] makes it clear that the court will not consent to appropriation in such circumstances unless the surviving spouse can prove both that such appropriation would not result in making the administration of the remainder of the estate more difficult and that it would not result in the reduction in value of the remaining assets within the estate. **[16–66]**

3. Disqualification of Spouses and Civil Partners under the Succession Act 1965

There are a number of scenarios in which a surviving spouse or civil partner will not be entitled to exercise spousal rights under the Succession Act 1965. The first is where the **[16–67]**

142 s 56(5)(a), *ibid.*
143 [2003] IEHC 123.
144 s 56(5)(b), Succession Act 1965.
145 s 56(6), *ibid.*
146 [1978] IR 138.

spouse or civil partner has renounced these rights by means of an agreement to that effect made before or after the marriage or civil partnership but during the lifetime of the testator.[147] A spouse or civil partner can also become disentitled by means of s 120 of the Succession Act 1965, or by desertion for at least two years up to the point of death of the deceased spouse.[148] While s 120(1) bars the succession rights of spouses who cause the death of the deceased, s 120(4) goes further than this, providing that any person (including a surviving spouse or civil partner) who has been convicted of an offence against the deceased or against a child or spouse or civil partner of the deceased will lose his rights to the deceased's estate, provided the offence committed is punishable by at least two years' imprisonment.

[16–68] If a married couple has divorced or a civil partnership has been dissolved, spousal and civil partner rights under the Succession Act 1965 will no longer apply because there is no longer any marriage or civil partnership to which they can be applied. This is not the case where the couple has separated. In such circumstances the marriage or civil partnership continues in law and therefore the rights under the Succession Act 1965 continue to operate unless these rights have been renounced in an enforceable separation agreement.[149] In the case of judicial separation of marriage a court can make an order to this effect under s 14 of the Family Law Act 1995, although courts will not make such an order where to do so would cause hardship to the surviving spouse.[150] In the context of divorce or separation, however, a (former) spouse who has not remarried and whose Succession Act rights have been extinguished may make an application for provision from the deceased's estate.[151] In such cases the court may make such orders as it considers appropriate, having regard to the rights of any other interest-holders.[152] Where such an order is made, however, the provision made cannot exceed that which would have been available if the surviving (former) spouse's rights had not been extinguished.[153] This procedure is not available to a spouse who has renounced Succession Act rights in a separation agreement, unless a decree of divorce has subsequently been granted.[154] Section 127 of the Civil Partnership and Certain Rights and Obligations of Cohabitants Act 2010 introduces the analogous system for former civil partners in the case of dissolution of a civil partnership.

X. Rights of Surviving Children

[16–69] The Succession Act 1965 does not provide for a set percentage share of the estate of the deceased in favour of his children: rather, s 117 allows a child of any age to make an application to the Court for adjustment of their parent's estate on the basis that the deceased parent has failed in his moral duty to make proper provision for the

[147] s 113, Succession Act 1965 *as amended by* s 83, Civil Partnership and Certain Rights and Obligations of Cohabitants Act 2010.

[148] s 120(2) and (2A), Succession Act 1965 *as amended by* s 87, Civil Partnership and Certain Rights and Obligations of Cohabitants Act 2010.

[149] See *Moorhead v Tiilikainen* [1999] 2 ILRM 471.

[150] *PS v PS*, unreported, High Court, 10 July 1996.

[151] s 15A, Family Law Act 1995 *as inserted by* s 52(g), Family Law (Divorce) Act 1996; s 18, Family Law (Divorce) Act 1996.

[152] s 15(A)(1), Family Law Act 1995; s 18(1), Family Law Divorce Act 1996.

[153] s 15(A)(4), Family Law Act 1995; s 18(4), Family Law (Divorce) Act 1996.

[154] s 18, Family Law (Divorce) Act 1996.

applicant child either during his lifetime or on his death. The terms of s 117 provide, in relevant part:

> (1) Where, on application by or on behalf of a child of a testator, the court is of opinion that the testator has failed in his moral duty to make proper provision for the child in accordance with his means, whether by his will or otherwise, the court may order that such provision shall be made for the child out of the estate as the court thinks just.
>
> (2) The court shall consider the application from the point of view of a prudent and just parent, taking into account the position of each of the children of the testator and any other circumstances which the court may consider of assistance in arriving at a decision that will be as fair as possible to the child to whom the application relates and to the other children.
>
> (3) An order under this section shall not affect the legal right of a surviving spouse or, if the surviving spouse is the mother or father of the child, any devise or bequest to the spouse or any share to which the spouse is entitled on intestacy.

Section 117 has a clear social purpose, which Kearns J considered in *Re the estate of ABC.*[155] Kearns J concluded:

> The social policy underlying s 117 is primarily directed to protecting those children who are still of an age and situation in life where they might reasonably expect support from their parents, against the failure of parents who are unmindful of their duties in that area.[156]

Where such an application is made, the court assesses whether or not the parent has fulfilled his moral duty to provide for his children to the extent possible having regard to the circumstances of the family involved. This duty is considered to subsist from the birth of the child to the death of the parent. In this context the assessment is an objective one,[157] with the court taking the viewpoint of a prudent and fair parent,[158] but within the particular circumstances of the family involved.[159] Section 117(3) makes it clear that the court will not readjust the estate in favour of the applicant child if all of the deceased's estate has been left to a surviving spouse who is also a parent of the applicant child. A new s 117(3A) has now been inserted by s 86 of the Civil Partnership and Certain Rights and Obligations of Cohabitants Act 2010, which provides that an order under s 117 is not to affect the legal right share of a civil partner *unless* the court is of the view that it would be unjust to not make this order taking into account all of the circumstances, including the means of the testator and her obligations to the surviving civil partner. This means that, unlike in the case of a child of a married couple, a s 117 order for the child of a civil partner can reduce the legal right share of a **[16–70]**

155 [2003] 2 IR 250.
156 *ibid.* at pp 262–3.
157 *Re IAC Deceased* [1989] ILRM 815; *CW v LW* [2005] IEHC 325.
158 s 117(2), Succession Act 1965.
159 *Re McDonald: McDonald v Norris* [2000] 1 ILRM 710.[2000] 1 ILRM 710.

surviving civil partner. A claim under s 117 must be taken within six months of the taking out of representation on the deceased's estate.[160] This time limit is a strict one that, it appears, the court may not extend, even where the strict application of the limitation period may result in an injustice.[161] Unlike in the case of surviving spouses, the personal representatives are not under any obligation to inform the surviving children of the provisions of s 117.[162]

[16–71] Section 117 of the Succession Act 1965 appears to be directed towards ensuring that the perceived moral duty of parent to child is fulfilled. This moral duty is said to apply between parents and all of their children notwithstanding the age of the children,[163] irrespective of whether they are "natural" or adopted children,[164] irrespective of whether they are children born within marriage or born in an extra-marital relationship,[165] and regardless of the state of the relationship between the parties.[166] That said, a child without any biological or legal relationship with the deceased does not appear to be in a position to make a s 117 application. This is of particular relevance to the non-biological children of a deceased civil partner who have no legally recognised relationship with their deceased parent (for lack of biological link and because second-parent adoption is not permitted in civil partnerships) and do not, therefore, seem to be in a position to make a s 117 application.

[16–72] Section 117 does not create an obligation to make provision for a child in a will. "Proper provision", to which s 117 refers, can be provided in its entirety during the lifetime of the deceased.[167] Barron J has expressed this purpose thus:

> The section recognises a moral obligation on the part of a parent towards a child. The section deals with whether or not that moral obligation still existed at the date of death of the parent. Nevertheless, it is an obligation which exists from the relationship between the parties and is one which is continuous from the date of birth of the child until the date of death of the parent unless in the meantime it has been satisfied or extinguished.[168]

It should be noted that if the fulfilment of an automatic moral duty arising on parenthood is the purpose of s 117, then there is the potential for unknown children to make s 117 applications. Thus, if someone had a child of whom he was not aware, there would not appear to be any reason why that child could not take a s 117 application (provided parentage could be established). This becomes even more controversial when one considers the position of sperm and egg donors: does the biological link between the donor and the child on its own create parenthood and the associated moral

---

[160] s 117(6), Succession Act 1965.

[161] *MPD v MD* [1981] ILRM 179.

[162] See also *Rojack v Taylor and Buchalter*, unreported, High Court, 10 February 2005.

[163] See, for example, *In the Estate of LB: EB v SS* [1999] 2 ILRM 141.

[164] s 110, Succession Act 1965; Adoption Act 1952.

[165] Status of Children Act 1987.

[166] *In Re the Goods of JH* [1984] IR 599.

[167] *FM v TAM* (1972) 106 ILTR 82; *In Re the Goods of JH* [1984] IR 599; *Re LB* [1998] 2 ILRM 141.

[168] *Re McDonald: McDonald v Norris* [2000] 1 ILRM 710.

obligation that can be tested by means of a s 117 application? The answer to this is unclear. On the one hand, a person might argue that the donation of sperm or eggs for the purposes of aiding the fertility of others does not constitute an act of parentage: that the intention of the donor is (generally) not to create any parental relationship, but rather to facilitate the parenthood of others. Where, however, someone has a sexual relationship, it could be argued that any act of intercourse brings with it an implied knowledge of the potential for, if not necessarily an intention to create, parenthood and that may engage the moral obligation the fulfilment of which is assessed by a s 117 application. This matter remains untested by the courts, but it certainly throws into sharp relief the implications of the perceived and apparent purpose of s 117. The fact that a child with a biological link to the deceased—but who had no real relationship to the deceased—seems capable of making a s 117 application, while a child who may have had a lifelong relationship of parenthood and fidelity with a deceased civil partner who was not the child's biological or legal parent cannot make such a link, seems clearly inequitable but is, nevertheless, the legislative position as it stands.

The extent to which the moral duty can be found to exist and can be said to have been fulfilled will be assessed by reference to a number of factors. The fact that the court's consideration is an objective one does not mean that it disregards the means or other moral obligations of the testator: rather, it engages in an objective consideration in the context of the relevant circumstances of the parties involved. The importance of contextual consideration of s 117 applications was outlined in the early decision of *FM v TAM*,[169] in which Kenny J outlined principles of assessment of s 117 applications that continue to be applied in such cases. *FM v TAM* concerned a deceased man who, with his wife, had adopted the applicant but had never treated him as his own son. The evidence showed that the deceased had adopted the applicant in order to make his wife happy, and that the wife had provided for the son by means of education, clothing etc. The deceased made no provision for the applicant in his will or during his lifetime and the applicant, who was by now a married man with a wife and children of his own, claimed that the deceased had failed in his moral duty towards him. Kenny J found in favour of the applicant and outlined principles of s 117 that he subsequently echoed in *Re George Moore Deceased*[170] and in *MacNaughton v Walker*[171]: **[16–73]**

> The existence of a moral duty to make proper provision by will for a child must be judged by the facts existing at the date of death and must depend upon (a) the amount left to the surviving spouse or the value of the legal right if the survivor elects to take this; (b) the number of the testator's children, their ages and their positions in life at the date of the testator's death; (c) the means of the testator; (d) the age of the child whose case is being considered and his or her financial position and prospects in life; (e) whether the testator has already in his lifetime made proper provision for the child.

These principles have been sophisticated to some extent since their original enunciation. In *Re IAC Deceased*,[172] for example, Finlay CJ (as he then was) held that the **[16–74]**

---

[169] (1972) 106 ILTR 82.
[170] Unreported, High Court, 2 March 1970.
[171] [1976–7] ILRM 106.
[172] [1989] ILRM 815.

child must prove, not that they were disappointed by the parent's failure to provide for them to a greater extent, but that there had been a positive failure of moral duty on the part of the parent. In that case the Court also held that although the s 117 procedure was available to all children of the deceased, the adult child would have a more arduous standard to meet than the infant child. In *Re ABC Deceased*,[173] Kearns J summarised the principles governing s 117 applications in commendably succinct form:

(i) The social policy underlying s 117 is primarily directed to protecting those children who are still of an age and situation in life where they might reasonably expect support from their parents, against the failure of parents who are unmindful of their duties in that area.
(ii) What has to be determined is whether the testator, at the time of his death, owes any moral obligation to the children and if so, whether he has failed in that obligation.
(iii) There is a high onus of proof placed on an applicant for relief under s 117, which requires the establishment of a positive failure in moral duty.
(iv) Before a court can interfere, there must be clear circumstances and a positive failure in moral duty must be established.
(v) The duty created by s 117 is not absolute.
(vi) The relationship of parent and child does not, itself and without regard to other circumstances, create a moral duty to leave anything by will to the child.
(vii) Section 117 does not create an obligation to leave something to each child.
(viii) The provision of an expensive education for a child may discharge the moral duty as may other gifts or settlements made during the lifetime of the testator.
(ix) Financing a good education so as to give a child the best start in life possible and providing money, which, if properly managed, should afford a degree of financial security for the rest of one's life, does amount to making "proper provision".
(x) The duty under s 117 is not to make adequate provision but to provide proper provision in accordance with the testator's means.
(xi) A just parent must take into account not just his moral obligations to his children and to his wife, but all his moral obligations, *e.g.* to aged and infirm parents.
(xii) In dealing with a s 117 application, the position of an applicant child is not to be taken in isolation. The court's duty is to consider the entirety of the testator's affairs and to decide upon the application in the overall context. In other words, while the moral claim of a child may require a testator to make a particular provision for him, the moral claims of others may require such provision to be reduced or omitted altogether.
(xiii) Special circumstances giving rise to a moral duty may arise if a child is induced to believe that by, for example, working on a farm, he will ultimately become the owner of it, thereby causing him to shape his upbringing, training and life accordingly.
(xiv) Another example of special circumstances might be a child who had a long illness or an exceptional talent which it would be morally wrong not to foster.

[173] [2003] 2 IR 250 at pp 262–4.

(xv) Special needs would also include physical or mental disability.

(xvi) Although the court has very wide powers both as to when to make provision for an applicant child and as to the nature of such provision, such powers must not be construed as giving the court a power to make a new will for the testator.

(xvii) The test to be applied is not which of the alternative courses open to the testator the court itself would have adopted if confronted with the same situation but, rather, whether the decision of the testator to opt for the course he did, of itself and without more, constituted a breach of moral duty to the plaintiff.

(xviii) The court must not disregard the fact that parents must be presumed to know their children better than anyone else.

ABC Deceased concerned a father who, by his will, had created a discretionary trust by which the defendants were trustees and both the plaintiffs and defendants were beneficiaries. By his letter of wishes the defendant had requested that certain sums of money be paid from the trust immediately to the first and second defendants, being his wife (who was wholly dependent on him) and his brother (who was also his business partner). The plaintiffs were his children, each of which had been provided for to an extent during the lifetime of the deceased by means of education, purchase of cars and guarantee of loans. The first plaintiff was unmarried, lived in rented accommodation and had been involved in a number of failed business ideas over the years, resulting in financial difficulties in respect of which he had received financial assistance from the deceased. At the time of his father's death he was in good health, running a video and print business and was 37 years of age. During the lifetime of his father, the son was provided with private primary and secondary school, sent to university, which he chose to leave after one year, trained in the family business, given the deposit on his first house, employed in the family business, had loans guaranteed by his father and in total was given advances agreed in the s 117 application to be of the value of £33,000. Both of the second and third plaintiffs were married and their husbands were in full-time employment: they both lived in their own houses at the time of their father's death. In respect of the second plaintiff—the deceased's older daughter—her father had paid for her private primary and secondary education, a one-year secretarial course, university education in London and Washington, a car, part of the deposit for a house, and part of her wedding costs. He had also arranged various mortgages and loans for her. She and her husband were property-developers and had made significant amounts of money from this endeavour. In respect of the third plaintiff—the younger daughter—the deceased paid for private primary and secondary education, a secretarial course, a car, a computer, some financial assistance in times of debt, a contribution to the deposit on a house and a contribution to her wedding. Her husband was a stockbroker and they enjoyed a very substantial income at the time of her father's death. All three children agreed that their father had been a fair and prudent man, who had taken a keen interest in their educations and the development of their careers, however they claimed that by establishing a discretionary trust he had failed to make proper provision for them. As a result they made s 117 applications for readjustment of their father's estate in their favour. [16–75]

Kearns J outlined the principles of s 117, as considered above, and held that when assessing the deceased's moral duty to the plaintiffs he must also bear in mind the [16–76] moral duties of the deceased to his wife and his elderly mother. Taking that into account he went on to consider the various circumstances of the three plaintiffs and found that the deceased did owe an ongoing moral duty to his son (the first plaintiff), who had shown himself to be unable to manage his business affairs. The deceased was deemed to have knowledge of this inability and the resultant unlikelihood that the plaintiff would succeed in business at the time of his death. This ongoing moral duty was satisfied by the establishment of the discretionary trust, as directed. The plaintiffs' case was based on an assumption that the trustees (the deceased's wife and brother) would act malevolently and in breach of their duty when there was no evidence to that effect whatsoever (particularly since they had both offered to resign as trustees). In addition, Kearns J took into account the fact that the discretionary trust was a prudent mechanism from the perspective of tax liability and in order to ensure that rental properties retained by the deceased could be managed effectively, which would in turn result in greater assets for the plaintiffs. All this taken into account, the plaintiffs could not succeed in their s 117 application. Importantly, Kearns J held that a discretionary trust would not always satisfy the moral duty of a deceased parent: it simply did so in the circumstances of this case.

1. Provision

[16–77] It is quite clear that the parent has a basic obligation to provide food, shelter and clothing for children; the provision envisaged by s 117 is something additional to the fulfilment of this basic concept. In *MPD v MD*[174] Carroll J outlined her concept of proper provision in the following terms:

> I would consider the proper provision for the children of the deceased according to his means should include provision not only to house, clothe, maintain, feed and educate them and ensure that medical, dental and chemists' bills are provided for until they finish their education and are launched into the world but should also include some provision by way of advancement for them for life.

[16–78] The idea of proper provision as extending beyond mere subsistence was reiterated in *Re McDonald: McDonald v Norris*,[175] in which Barron J in the Supreme Court concluded that an account in the cornershop paid for by his father, board and keep, and the right to farm an acre of land for his own purposes did not constitute proper provision within the context of s 117. He held that provision satisfying s 117 should be advancements that "relate either to an education which enables the child to make his way in life or else advancements of money which would enable the child to establish himself by their use".

2. Measuring the Moral Duty

[16–79] Every parent is said to owe a moral duty to his or her child: the function of the court in a s 117 application is to assess whether or not that moral duty has been fulfilled. In the course of making such an assessment, the court must consider a number of factors, some of which have received sustained judicial consideration.

---

174 [1981] ILRM 179.

175 [1999] 1 ILRM 270 (High Court); [2000] 1 ILRM 382 (Supreme Court).

(i) Moral Duty at Time of Death

The moral duty to be measured is that which existed between the parent and the child at the time of the parent's death. The deceased will be said to have knowledge not only of the child's needs at the time of their death but also of other circumstances that might be said to have an impact on any provision made for the child, such as taxation. Thus, in *Re NSM Deceased*[176] the three younger children of the deceased's four children claimed that their father had failed to make proper provision for them. In his will the deceased father had left nothing to his three applicant daughters, choosing instead to leave the entire residue of his estate to his son. The Court held that the father had not only failed to make proper provision for the children to whom he left nothing but also to his son because, following estate duty and the costs of litigation, the residue was worth nothing. Kenny J held: **[16–80]**

> It is not an answer to say that the testator tried to make provision for (the son) and that this failed because of the large amount of estate duty and legal costs which will be payable. The court must attribute to the testator on the day before his death, knowledge of the amount of estate duty which will be payable on his estate and a remarkable capacity to anticipate the costs of the litigation which will follow his death. I realise that this is unreal, that the amount of estate duty payable is usually mercifully hidden from most testators and that it is impossible to anticipate what litigation will follow on death. I am convinced, however, that s 117 must be interpreted in this way.

This interpretation of s 117 has been adopted by the Supreme Court in *Re IAC Deceased*[177] and results from the objective nature of the s 117 test. As Sullivan J held in *W(C) v W(L)*[178]: **[16–81]**

> [this is a] remarkable passage! The interpretation of the section is *unreal*. It is *impossible* to anticipate the litigation. Yet this is the way the Act has to be read... the test is an objective, not a subjective one. If the test were a subjective one it could well be said in the present case that the testator well knew that his wife would never claim her legal right share and would accept his will. Objectively, however, he must in my view of the authorities be credited with ... foreknowledge...

W(C) v W(L) concerned a father who had offered £190,000 to each of his three daughters before death, the money said to be in satisfaction of their entitlements under his will. Two of the three daughters refused to accept this money, claiming their father was trying to trick them into accepting his will. When he died, the father owned a farm that was valued at €3.5 million for the purposes of probate, but was worth €10 million at the time of this application. This farm was left on trust for his wife for life and thereafter to his son in fee simple. When she died, the applicants' mother left her estate in three equal shares between her daughters, with nothing to her son. There was a question mark over the validity of the mother's will, but it was agreed that if the will

---

176 [1973] 107 ILTR 1.
177 [1989] ILRM 815.
178 [2005] 4 IR 439.

was valid and she died testate, the applicant would have €1.2 million, but if she died intestate then the applicant would receive €900,000 from her mother's estate.

[16–82] The question that the Court had to consider was whether or not the deceased father was to be treated as having foreknowledge of his wife's will when he made his own. If so, then it might be said that they knew the wife would divide her estate in this manner and therefore thought it unnecessary to make additional provision for his daughters beyond the €190,000 left to each of them in his will. The Court held that even though conceiving of testators as if they had foreknowledge of what would happen on their death resulted in an "unreal" assessment of a parent's fulfilment of moral duty, the objective test employed requires such an approach. As a result, the father was said to have knowledge of the terms of the mother's will.[179]

(ii) Lifetime Provision

[16–83] As a result of the fact that s 117 treats of a moral obligation that subsists between parent and child from birth to death, the court must take into account the provision made by the parent for the child during his lifetime. Thus a child who had been left nothing in his parent's will, but who had been provided for adequately during the parent's lifetime, would be unlikely to have a successful application under s 117. Indeed, a child who had no provision whatsoever made for him during the parent's lifetime may well be unable to make out a successful s 117 application where the parent can be said to have fulfilled his moral duty based on the circumstances at the date of death.

(iii) Other Moral Obligations

[16–84] It has long been clear that the provision made by the deceased for his child is not to be viewed in a vacuum. Rather, the needs of other children are to be taken into account as are any other moral obligations that the deceased might be said to have. The recent case of *C(K) v F(C)*[180] demonstrates the Court's concern for the needs of other children of the testator. In this case the deceased died leaving 11 surviving children: she left all of her property to two of her sons as joint tenants. At the time of the hearing, one of those sons had died, therefore the surviving son—MC—was the sole owner of her entire estate. MC claimed that he had agreed with his mother that he was to have her house and that he had made a solemn promise to her to divide the residue of the estate between her 11 surviving children.

[16–85] The applicants were both daughters of the deceased. The first applicant—KC—was 36 years old and was the only one of the deceased's children who was unmarried. She had been educated up to the age of 12 and had been unemployed from that point onwards. She lived with her mother and nursed her until her death and she received no gifts from her mother during her lifetime, apart from a £10,000 distribution from her deceased father's intestate estate (this sum was given to all the children who were unmarried at the time). She claimed that she had continued to live in the house she

[179] It appears that this would have been the conclusion even if the solicitor who prepared the will had not claimed that the deceased had asked whether he could talk to his wife about the terms of her will when they were preparing them together.

[180] [2003] IEHC 109.

shared with her mother for six months after her death, at which point MC's wife "put her out". She then moved from sibling to sibling and at the time of the application was living with her brother and his family in a halting site that she claimed was infested with rats. The second applicant—BCF—was 43 years old and married. She had been educated up to Intermediate Certificate level and since then had been unemployed. Her husband, whom she married in 1979, was also unemployed as a result of an injury that prevented him from working. She had received no distribution from her father's intestate estate (because she was married) and claimed that she had received no gifts on her wedding, whereas her brothers' weddings had been paid for by their mother and they had also received either a caravan or other vehicle from her at that time.

Considering whether or not proper provision had been made for the applicants, Carroll J held that it had not and rejected MC's suggestion that the deceased had created a secret trust. Carroll J was satisfied that the applicants were without means and ought to have been provided for by their mother. In considering whether or not she ought to take the needs of the other children into account when considering what could be said to be "proper" provision, Carroll J cited the following *dictum* of Barron J from *MFH v WBH*[181]: **[16–86]**

> In this context, the expression "other children" means any other child who is also an applicant or who is a beneficiary under the will and whose benefit thereunder may be affected by the exercise of the court's powers. The court should not be required to take into account provision or lack of provision made for children not in either of these categories. The provision made for such children cannot be affected by its order. It must strike a balance where necessary between children before the court on the basis of what is just, having regard as well as to the other matters it has to take into account, to the means of the testator passing by his will.

As Carroll J noted, this suggests that in the normal course of events the court may take into account only the rights of children who have benefited from the will *or* who have taken a s 117 application. By this interpretation children who have neither taken an application nor been mentioned in the will would be outside of the scope of the court's consideration, which in this case would mean that all eight other children of the testatrix would have to be ignored by the court. Carroll J rejected this concept, claiming that where there are extraordinary or special circumstances, then the court could take into account the needs of children who fell outside of the will and were not s 117 applicants. She held:

> I think there are special circumstances which must be taken into account in this case. I do not think I can ignore those other children completely. M.C. has sworn an affidavit that he holds the money residue on a solemn trust for his brothers and sisters each to get 1/11th. Therefore, if he does follow through on this solemn trust which he has imposed upon himself (omitting K.C. and B.C.F.), the other brothers and sisters, while not beneficiaries under the will, will be affected by the exercise of the Court's powers. These

[181] [1984] IR 599.

> are circumstances which I believe I must take into account and I cannot deal with the matter as if there were only K.C., B.C.F. and M.C. to consider.

[16–87] The testator will also be required to take into account his other moral obligations, such as to dependent parents or siblings. Perhaps the clearest statement of this policy is that of Costello J in *ML & AW v ML*[182]:

> A parent in acting prudently and justly must weigh up carefully all his moral obligations. In doing so, he may be required to make greater provision for one of his children than for others. For example, one may have a long illness for which provision must be made; or he may have an exceptional talent which it would be morally wrong not to foster. But a just parent in considering what provision he should make for each of his children during his lifetime and by his will must take into account not just his moral obligations to his children and his wife, but all his moral obligations. The father of a family may have many moral obligations. Again to given an example, a father may have aged and infirm parents who are dependent on him and to whom he clearly owes a moral duty... Therefore, it follows that, if a child of the testator claims after his death that insufficient provision was made for such child, the Court, when considering whether this was so or not, must bear in mind all the moral duties which the testator may have had and all the claims on his resources thereby arising. In considering the validity of the judgments which the testator made during his lifetime and by his will and how he fulfilled his moral obligations it is obviously not relevant to consider only those obligations which could be enforced under the Act of 1965.

The "others" to whom a testator might be said to have moral obligations that can be taken into account included children of another relationship, even before "illegitimate" children were given the same status in law as children born within a marriage by the Status of Children Act 1987.[183]

(iv) Special Needs of Children

[16–88] It is quite clear that medical or other conditions that may result in a lesser ability to provide for one's self or a greater need for care and support are to be taken into account. In cases of this kind the parent is said to know of the medical condition and supports available to a child at the time of the parent's death. This is clear from the case of *S(D) v M(K) & Anor.*[184] In this case the deceased had two children: the applicant, DS, who suffered from diabetes, and the respondent, D, who suffered from schizo affective disorder. On his death the father left a 40-acre farm and house to his son, approximately one acre of building land to his son, but with his daughter to take a site from that acre, one-and-a-half bank accounts to his son D and a half bank account to his daughter DS, and the residue equally between the two. As it transpired, there was no residue following the payment of funeral expenses. DS claimed that her father had failed to make proper provision for her. During her lifetime she had received £3,000 for

182 [1978] IR 288.
183 *L v L* [1978] IR 288.
184 [2003] IEHC 120.

her wedding and approximately one half of the cost of her house in Scotland. She had suffered from diabetes for some 21 years and her condition had in fact deteriorated quite rapidly since her father's death. She worked as a child-minder and part-time bar worker and she had never been engaged in particularly lucrative employment. Although her medical condition was quite bad, DS was forced to continue working in order to support herself financially. The deceased's son, D, suffered from schizo affective disorder from the age of 14 and, although he had been hospitalised on a few occasions, his condition was medically managed and he was in receipt of long-term disability allowance. In addition, he farmed some ewes on his father's land. DS claimed that her father had failed to take into account her particular needs and, furthermore, that the site that she was to take under his will was essentially worthless. Carroll J held in favour of DS, finding firstly that although the deceased was aware of his children's medical needs and wanted to provide for them, he had to be seen to have known of the greater degree of need experienced by his daughter and of the fact that his son was in receipt of long-term disability allowance. In addition, the site was, in fact, worthless because it was to be taken from an area of only *c.* 1 acre and was traversed by various waterways. As a result of her finding that the deceased had failed to make proper provision for his applicant daughter, Carroll J held that the building site of *c.* 1 acre was to be given to the daughter absolutely, with the remainder of the estate being administered *per* the will.

Where one of the children of the testate has a physical or mental disability and, as a result, requires particular support, and the remainder are well-established in their lives and professions, then the testator may be said to have made proper provision if he left everything to the child with the disability and nothing to the remaining children, even if they were badly treated by the testator and not enabled to acquire further education when they were younger. This was the conclusion reached by McCracken J in *McC (M) v M.*[185] In this case the testator had 10 children, one of whom—A—had Down Syndrome. The applicants, who were both daughters of the deceased, claimed that their father had failed to make proper provision for them. The first applicant had left school after her Leaving Certificate and had been refused permission by her father to continue into third-level education. She then funded a secretarial course for herself and, at the time of her father's death, enjoyed a managerial position in a large firm. She and her husband owned two properties and had a combined annual income in the region of £68,000. The second applicant left school at 16 without her Leaving Certificate and, on her own initiative, trained as a children's nurse in Dublin and then went on to train and work in London and in the USA. Her husband—a member of the US Navy—was prevented from working by the effects of an accident and was in receipt of a US Naval pension. Their combined income was in the region of £50,000. While the Court acknowledged that the applicants may have had cause to complain about their father's treatment of them when they were younger, it was important to note, firstly, that their father had 10 children, only one of whom was facilitated in acquiring third-level education, and, secondly, that the relevant standard was "not whether the testator failed in some way in his moral obligation to the applicants thirty years before his death, but whether, at the time of his death, he owed any moral obligation to the applicants, and if so whether he failed in that obligation". Notwithstanding the lack of **[16–89]**

[185] [2001] IEHC 152.

such provision during his lifetime, the testator had not failed in his moral duty at the time of death, and therefore the application failed.

(v) Equality

[16–90] Section 117 does not require a parent to treat all children equally. In fact, such a requirement would fly in the face of the objective consideration of the case in its own particular circumstances. If, for example, a parent has two children, one of whom is a professional on a good salary who lives in his own house, and the other of whom is an unemployed person who lives in a rented house and is dependent on social welfare, then equal treatment by the parent may simply perpetuate inequalities between the children and might not be said to constitute "proper provision" for the less-well-off child. Thus, while a court will respect a parent's wish to treat their children equally, it will not necessarily find that proper provision has been made just because the children were treated equally.[186]

(vi) The Parent–Child Relationship

[16–91] The nature of the relationship between the parent and the child will be significant in the consideration of s 117 applications. First, a good and caring relationship will result in the court being relatively reluctant to interfere—as opposed to cases of tumultuous relationships where a parent may not have acted "fairly and prudently". Secondly, the behaviour of each party may have an impact on the extent of the moral duty in existence at the time of the parent's death.

[16–92] The fact that a parent feels somewhat put out or neglected by his children does not vitiate his moral duty towards them. This was confirmed in the early case of *JH & CH v Allied Irish Bank*.[187] The plaintiffs in this case were the only children of the testator, who was married to their mother in 1953. The marriage began to deteriorate in or around 1961/62, and in 1971 the testator left the family home and went to live alone in a flat, where he remained until his death. From 1971 to his death the testator had only formal communication with his family, and the relationship between him and his children suffered. There was some dispute as to who was responsible for the breakdown of the marriage, but the children remained in residence with their mother and had very little to do with their father. On his death the testator made only scant provision for both of the applicant children, and McWilliam J had to consider, *inter alia*, whether the children's neglect of their relationship with their father vitiated his moral duty towards them. On this point the Court held as follows:

> The first issue which I have to decide is whether the testator did or did not have a moral duty to make provision for his children in accordance with his means. In considering this I have no duty to decide any question of responsibility for the estrangement between the testator and his wife. Nor have I any duty to decide any question of responsibility for the subsequent lack of communication between the testator and the plaintiffs. In my opinion, there can only be one answer on this issue. The testator did have such a moral duty, however neglected, thwarted or aggrieved he may have felt.

[186] *In the Estate of LB: EB v SS* [1999] 2 ILRM 141.
[187] [1978] ILRM 203.

In some cases, however, the relationship between parent and child deteriorates to the point of outright hostility. What impact does this have on the parent's moral duty to his child? This question was considered in the case of *Re McDonald: McDonald v Norris*.[188] The testator had two children—the plaintiff and a younger son. Upon his death the testator left all of his property on trust for the daughter of a neighbouring family, with whom he had lived and who had taken care of him. This was subject to £5,000 left to the plaintiff "in discharge of any moral obligations" which the testator might have towards him. Since 1968 the plaintiff had run the farm on a constant basis and without remuneration apart from an account in the family farm and the right to take the income from tillage of a number of acres. Relations between the plaintiff and his father broke down in 1980 because of the plaintiff's marriage choice, and by 1982 the plaintiff was in occupation of the lands for his own benefit and had opened a quarry. The testator, who was in ill health, had moved in with the neighbouring family. Relations between the father and son became violent, resulting in the gardaí becoming involved and the testator seeking possession of the lands from his son. The plaintiff counter-sued for compensation for the work done, as a result of which the plaintiff was ordered to leave the land and the father was ordered to pay him £11,000. The plaintiff paid £2,000 to his father in order to remain on the land until 1985, but he stayed there for some time once the agreement had expired. As a result, the plaintiff was imprisoned for 11 months, during which time his wife and son ran the quarry. In October 1986 the testator regained possession and transferred the lands to the plaintiff's brother. From then on the plaintiff engaged in great hostility against his father and the family with whom his father lived, including threatening them and causing damage to their property. In May 1988 the plaintiff was bound over to keep the peace for two years following charges before the District Court involving verbal abuse and threatening behaviour. Following his father's death, the plaintiff made a s 117 application claiming that his father had failed in his moral duty towards him by leaving him only £5,000. **[16–93]**

The application was unsuccessful in the High Court, where McCracken J held that the son and his wife may not have been responsible for the hostility directed towards the deceased and the family with whom he resided, but they were aware of it and had done nothing to stop it. The Court found that the plaintiff had behaved appallingly towards his father from 1984 onwards, and had permitted and encouraged the intimidation and bullying of the testator when he was more than 70 years of age. The Court concluded that the testator, at the time of his death, was entitled to consider that he had given considerable benefits to the plaintiff while he was alive, and that his moral duty towards his son was affected by the plaintiff's conduct. According to McCracken J, the scheme of the Succession Act 1965 implied that the behaviour of a child towards his parent was something that the Court could take into account when assessing moral duty and, in the circumstances, any remaining moral duty (taking this behaviour into account) had been properly provided for by the deceased. **[16–94]**

On appeal in the Supreme Court, Barron J reversed the decision of the High Court. He held that the High Court had been correct in taking into account the behaviour of the applicant child, which could have the effect of extinguishing or reducing the moral duty of the parent. However, the behaviour had to be seen in its context. The reasons **[16–95]**

[188] [2000] 1 ILRM 382 (Supreme Court).

behind the son's behaviour, i.e. the father's disapproval of his marriage choice and attempt to have him removed from the land that he had farmed since being taken from school to do so in 1968, were relevant factors. Thus, while the applicant's behaviour did diminish the moral duty owed to him by his father, it did not extinguish it and the proper provision had not been made.

(vii) The Needs of Grandchildren

[16–96] The case of *EB v SS*[189] concerned a s 117 application stated to be for the benefit of the grandchildren of the testatrix. The applicant was the son of the testatrix, who had received many benefits from her and his father, including a house bought for himself and his sister by his father, in which the applicant resided with his wife and children, education, employment and a substantial sum of money. The applicant had previously had an alcohol and drug addiction and although his mother was aware of this, she did not make any further provision for him in her will. Rather, she considered that she had treated all her children equally by giving them equal shares from the proceeds of sale of shares in her late husband's company following his death, and that she was not obliged to provide further for her son. Her son, who had, as already mentioned, enjoyed sizeable provision from both of his parents during their lives, claimed that his mother had a moral duty to provide for his needs, one of which was his need to provide for his own children. As she was aware that, at the time of her death, he and his wife resided with their children and were dependent on social welfare and because she had a large estate, she ought to have made provision for him in her will. Her failure to do so, he claimed, constituted a positive failure in moral duty on her part. The son's application failed in both the High Court and the Supreme Court. While conceding that the deceased in this case might have had some obligation to help her son to provide for his own children, this was not a matter that could be taken into account by the Court in assessing whether or not she had fulfilled her moral obligation as provided for and required by s 117. Rather, to interpret s 117 as requiring a testator to take into account the needs of her grandchildren would stretch the bounds of s 117 beyond what was contemplated and intended by the Oireachtas and, as a result, the Court could not do so.

XI. Transactions Intended to Disinherit Spouses and Children

[16–97] Section 121 of the Succession Act 1965 gives the court the discretion to deal with dispositions of property (including by *donatio mortis causa*) made within three years of the death of the deceased that, the court is satisfied, were intended to defeat or substantially reduce the shares of a surviving spouse in testacy or intestacy *or* to defeat or substantially reduce the shares of a surviving child in intestacy *or* to leave any of the deceased's children insufficiently provided for. Under this provision the court is empowered to treat all or part of the property the subject of this disposition as a gift in a will,[190] resulting in the property being subject to the Legal Right Share of the surviving spouse, or a s 117 application by a child of the deceased. The court may also make any further orders on the matter that it considers to be "just and equitable having

[189] [1998] 4 IR 527.
[190] s 121(2), Succession Act 1965.

regard to the provisions and the spirit"[191] of the Succession Act. If the property has been sold on, then the claim relates to the consideration offered for the property.[192]

While s 121 appears to offer a relatively iron-clad defence against near-death transactions intended to disinherit spouses and children to whom the deceased has a moral obligation, s 121(7) provides for a potentially problematic exception to this power. Section 121(7) provides: **[16–98]**

> (7) An order shall not be made under this section affecting a disposition made in favour of any child of the disponer, if—
> (a) the spouse of the disponer was dead when the disposition was made, or
> (b) the spouse was alive when the disposition was made but was a person who, if the disponer had then died, would have been precluded under any of the provisions of section 120 from taking a share in his estate, or
> (c) the spouse was alive when the disposition was made and consented in writing to it.

The exception built into s 121(7) appears clearly intended to respect parental decisions in relation to transactions with children, but it also appears to accept the potential for a parent to disinherit one child by making lifetime provision to another child *provided* the deceased's spouse was either dead at the time the transaction was made, or was disentitled under s 120 of the Act, or had consented in writing to the transaction. There are a number of difficulties with this. First of all, it appears to conceive of s 121 as being primarily concerned with preventing the disinheriting of spouses and only marginally concerned with the welfare of children. Secondly, and most problematically, it appears (in s 121(7)(c)) to allow for parents (or a parent and spouse) to "gang up" together to disinherit a child by means of the non-transacting spouse simply consenting to the disinheriting transaction. This is particularly problematic because the exception in s 121(7) appears to apply even where the transaction was actually intended to disinherit a child.

Section 121(7)(c) does not appear to have been tested in the courts, but it seems that the literal interpretation of this provision should not be given effect in light of the object and spirit of the Succession Act, which is, *inter alia*, the recognition and enforcement of the moral obligations owed to children by their parents. It could well be that equitable maxims may be employed to undercut the apparent effect of s 121(7)(c); particularly the maxim that equity will not allow a statute to be used as an instrument of fraud. If this maxim were applied, it would, perhaps, be possible for equity to claim that the child to whom the contested property was transferred holds the property on constructive trust for the benefit of the disinherited or detrimentally effected child, or for the benefit of the estate, in which case it could then be distributed according to the terms of the will or by means of intestacy, whichever applies. Such an approach, it is submitted, is to be preferred to a literal interpretation of this provision. **[16–99]**

[191] s 121(4), *ibid.*
[192] s 121(8), *ibid.*

XII. Protection of Cohabitants

[16–100] The Civil Partnership and Certain Rights and Obligations of Cohabitants Act 2010 does not provide for a legal right share for cohabitants, but it does provide that certain cohabitants may make an application for provision from the estate of a deceased cohabitant under s 194. Only a qualified cohabitant[193] who is economically dependent[194] on the deceased and who is not married or civilly partnered[195] can make such an application. A qualified cohabitant is defined in s 172(5) as:

> an adult who was in a relationship of cohabitation with another adult and who, immediately before the time that that relationship ended, whether through death or otherwise, was living with the other adult as a couple for a period—
> (a) of 2 years or more, in the case where they are the parents of one or more dependent children, and
> (b) of 5 years or more, in any other case.

This definition is subject to an exception in s 172(6), which provides that where one or both adult is "or was, at any time during the relationship concerned" married to someone other than the other cohabitant *and* has not lived apart from his spouse for a period of at least four of the previous five years at the time that the relationship ends. A sub-category of qualified cohabitant—the qualified economically dependent cohabitant—has further rights in relation to property. A qualified economically dependent cohabitant must establish that she is financially dependent on the other cohabitant *and* that the financial dependence arises from the relationship or the ending of the relationship. Only such cohabitants can make an application under s 194.

[16–101] Not all qualified economically dependent cohabitants are entitled to make an application under s 194. Section 194(2) provides that where the relationship in question ended two years or more before the death of the cohabitant, the qualified economically dependent cohabitant may not make a s 194 application unless:

- The qualified economically dependent cohabitant was in receipt of periodical payments under a cohabitants' agreement[196] or under a compensatory maintenance payment order[197];
- The qualified economically dependent cohabitant had made an application for a property adjustment order,[198] compensatory maintenance order[199] or pension adjustment order[200] within two years of the termination of the relationship and

[193] s 194(1), Civil Partnership and Certain Rights and Obligations of Cohabitants Act 2010.
[194] s 194(5), *ibid.*
[195] s 194(5), *ibid.*; this includes someone who is in a relationship from another jurisdiction that is recognised as a civil partnership under s 5, *ibid.*
[196] s 194(2)(a), *ibid.* Section 202 of the Civil Partnership and Certain Rights and Obligations of Cohabitants Act 2010 allows for cohabitation agreements that can enjoy the force of law.
[197] s 194(2), *ibid.*; compensatory maintenance orders are governed by s 175, *ibid.*
[198] These are provided for by s 174, *ibid.*
[199] These are provided for by s 175, *ibid.*
[200] These are provided for by s 187, *ibid.*

the proceedings in question were pending at the time of death[201] *or* such an order had been made but had not yet been executed[202];

- The qualified economically dependent cohabitant had made an application for a property adjustment order,[203] compensatory maintenance order[204] or pension adjustment order[205] within two years of the termination of the relationship, an application for the variation, suspension or revival of such an order was subsequently made under s 173(6) and, either, that subsequent application was pending at the time of death[206] *or* an order under s 173(6) had been made but not yet executed.[207]

An application under s 194 must be made within six months of the representation being granted under the Succession Act 1965[208] and the applying cohabitant must give notice of the application to the personal representative of the deceased, any spouse or civil partner of the deceased or "any other persons that the court may direct".[209] All of these people can then make representations to the court, which will be taken into account when determining whether or not to grant an order under s 194,[210] and failure to serve such notice means that the estate can be distributed under the will (in a case of testacy) or intestacy without the personal representative being liable to the cohabitant.[211] **[16–102]**

When deciding whether or not to make an order pursuant to a s 194 application, a court is obliged to take a number of matters into account: **[16–103]**

- Any compensatory maintenance order, property adjustment order, pensions adjustment order and order varying, discharging or reviving such orders already made in favour of the applicant[212];
- Any provision made for the applicant in the deceased's will[213];
- The interests of the beneficiaries of the estate[214];
- The financial circumstances, needs and obligations of each qualified cohabitant existing as at the date of the application or which are likely to arise in the future[215];
- The rights and entitlements of any spouse or former spouse,[216] bearing in mind that no order will be made that "would affect any right of any person to whom

201 s 194(2)(b)(i), *ibid.*
202 s 194(2)(b)(ii), *ibid.*
203 These are provided for by s 174, *ibid.*
204 These are provided for by s 175, *ibid.*
205 These are provided for by s 187, *ibid.*
206 s 194(2)(c)(i), *ibid.*
207 s 194(2)(c)(ii), *ibid.*
208 s 194(1), *ibid.*
209 s 194(6), *ibid.*
210 s 194(6), *ibid.*
211 s 194(8), *ibid.*
212 s 194(4)(a), *ibid.*
213 s 194(4)(b), *ibid.*
214 s 194(4)(c), *ibid.*
215 s 194(4)(d) *referring to* s 173(3)(a), *ibid.*
216 s 194(4)(d) *referring to* s 173(3)(b), *ibid.*

the other cohabitant is or was married"[217] and that no order made under s 194 may affect the legal right of a surviving spouse[218] (although, curiously, the legal right of a civil partner is not mentioned here);

- The rights and entitlements of any civil partner or former civil partner[219];
- The rights and entitlements of any dependent child or of any child of a previous relationship of either cohabitant[220];
- The duration of the parties' relationship, the basis on which the parties entered into the relationship and the degree of commitment of the parties to one another[221];
- The contributions that each of the cohabitants made to the welfare of the cohabitants or either of them, including any contribution made by each of them to the income, earning capacity or property and financial resources of the other[222];
- Any contributions made by either cohabitant in looking after the home[223];
- The effect on the earning capacity of each of the cohabitants of the responsibilities assumed by each of them during the period they lived together as a couple and the degree to which the future earning capacity of a qualified cohabitant is impaired by reason of that qualified cohabitant having relinquished or foregone the opportunity of remunerative activity in order to look after the home[224];
- Any physical or mental disability of the qualified cohabitant[225];
- The conduct of each of the cohabitants, if the conduct is such that, in the opinion of the court, it would be unjust to disregard it[226];
- The rights of any other person having an interest in the matter[227];
- The representations of any party to whom notice has been given under s 194(6).

[16–104] Having taken all of these factors into account, the court must determine whether, in its view, "proper provision in the circumstances was not made for the applicant during the lifetime of the deceased for any reason other than conduct by the applicant that, in the opinion of the court, it would in all the circumstances be unjust to disregard".[228] Any order made can be made only out of the "net estate", which is defined in s 194(11) as being that which remains in the estate of the deceased following the satisfaction of all other liabilities[229] and the rights of any spouse[230] or civil partner[231] under the

217 s 194(4)(d) *referring to* s 173(5), *ibid.*
218 s 194(10), *ibid.*
219 s 194(4)(d) *referring to* s 173(3)(c), *ibid.*
220 s 194(4)(d) *referring to* s 173(3)(d), *ibid.*
221 s 194(4)(d) *referring to* s 173(3)(e), *ibid.*
222 s 194(4)(d) *referring to* s 173(3)(f), *ibid.*
223 s 194(4)(d) *referring to* s 173(3)(g), *ibid.*
224 s 194(4)(d) *referring to* s 173(3)(h), *ibid.*
225 s 194(4)(d) *referring to* s 173(3)(i), *ibid.*
226 s 194(4)(d) *referring to* s 173(3)(j), *ibid.*
227 s 194(3), *ibid.*
228 s 194(3), *ibid.*
229 s 194(11)(a), *ibid.*
230 s 194(11)(b), *ibid.*
231 s 194(11)(c), *ibid.*

Succession Act 1965. Furthermore, any order made under s 194 cannot make provision for the surviving qualified economically dependent cohabitant that exceeds what that individual would have acquired as a surviving spouse or civil partner.[232]

XIII. The Law of Intestacy

Intestacy relates to situations in which someone dies without a valid will. Partial intestacy relates to situations in which someone dies with a valid will, but only part of their property is disposed of by means of the will. In such cases, the remainder will be disposed of by the rules of intestacy. The main focus in relation to intestacy is in determining who gets what, in other words: What are the rules of distribution? As already considered, the first matter will be the appointment of an administrator and the issuing of the grant of letters of administration. Upon such appointment all of the real and personal property of the deceased is devolved to the personal representative, who holds the estate on trust for those legally entitled under either the will or the rules of intestate distribution.[233] Where there is a case of intestacy the administrator will ensure that all debts, funeral and testamentary expenses are paid and then begin distributing assets.[234] In cases of partial intestacy the administrator will ensure that the debts etc. are paid, the dispositions of the will have been completed, and then he will proceed with the distribution of the remaining assets. **[16–105]**

Where the deceased has a surviving spouse and no issue, the surviving spouse will be entitled to the entire estate.[235] Similarly, if someone dies leaving a surviving civil partner and no issue the surviving civil partner will take the whole estate.[236] Where there is a spouse and issue, the spouse will take two-thirds of the assets and the remaining third is distributed among the issue.[237] If someone dies leaving a surviving civil partner and issue, the civil partner will take two-thirds of the estate and the issue the remaining third.[238] This is subject to one exception applicable only to surviving civil partners. Section 67A(3) permits issue of the deceased to make an application for further provision from the intestate share of the surviving civil partner within six months of the representation being taken out on the deceased's estate.[239] In deciding such applications the court will take account of the provision made to the child during the deceased's lifetime, the age and reasonable financial requirements of the child, the financial situation of the deceased and the obligations of the deceased to the surviving civil partner.[240] Should such an application be successful, s 67A(4) of the Succession Act 1965 provides that the child cannot be granted an amount that is less than what **[16–106]**

[232] s 194(7), *ibid.*

[233] s 10, Succession Act 1965.

[234] s 66, *ibid.*

[235] s 67 (1), *ibid.*

[236] s 67A(1), *ibid. as inserted by* s 73, Civil Partnership and Certain Rights and Obligations of Cohabitants Act 2010.

[237] s 67(2), Succession Act 1965.

[238] s 67A(2), Succession Act 1965 *as inserted by* s 73, Civil Partnership and Certain Rights and Obligations of Cohabitants Act 2010.

[239] s 67A(7), Succession Act 1965 *as inserted by* s 73, Civil Partnership and Certain Rights and Obligations of Cohabitants Act 2010.

[240] s 67A(3), Succession Act 1965 *as inserted by* s 73, Civil Partnership and Certain Rights and Obligations of Cohabitants Act 2010.

she would have been entitled to had no such order been granted.[241] Nor can she be granted more than she would have been entitled to had the intestate died leaving neither a spouse nor a civil partner.[242]

[16–107] Where there is no surviving spouse or civil partner, the issue become entitled.[243] In terms of children, all children—adopted, marital and non-marital—are treated the same in this relation, although there must be some legally recognised relationship between the deceased and the child in question. Thus, where the intestate is not the biological parent of the child in a civil partnership, in which there is no legal provision for second-parent adoption, the child does not seem entitled to anything from the deceased's estate. If the issue are in an equal degree of relationship to the deceased they each receive the estate in what is known as a *per capita* distribution, i.e. in equal shares.[244] Thus, if the deceased has four children, all of whom are alive at the time of his death, and no surviving spouse or civil partner, the children will receive one quarter of the estate each. If, however, one's child has predeceased one, then the next generation will take. This will be a *per stirpes* distribution. Thus, if Paddy dies and is survived by three children—Dan, Evan and Fionn—and Fionn predeceased him, there can not be a *per capita* distribution as one of the children is dead. If, however, Fionn leaves children—Mike and Nóra—then they will take from his share. Thus, Dan and Evan will take one-third each (because there were originally three children), and Mike and Nóra will each take half of their father's one-third share, i.e. one-sixth each.

[16–108] Where someone dies intestate without a surviving spouse, surviving civil partner or surviving issue, the intestate's parents will inherit distributed with the parents taking in equal shares if both survive. If there is only one living parent she will take the entire estate.[245] If there are no living parents, then s 69(1) of the Succession Act 1965 provides that:

> his estate shall be distributed between his brothers and sisters in equal shares, and, if any brother or sister does not survive the intestate, the surviving children of the deceased brother or sister shall, where any other brother or sister of the deceased survives him, take in equal shares the share that their parent would have taken if he or she had survived the intestate.

If an intestate dies without a surviving spouse, civil partner, issue, parent or siblings, s 69(2) provides the estate is distributed in equal shares among his nieces and nephews.

---

[241] s 67A(4)(a), Succession Act 1965 *as inserted by* s 73, Civil Partnership and Certain Rights and Obligations of Cohabitants Act 2010.

[242] s 67A(4)(b), Succession Act 1965 *as inserted by* s 73, Civil Partnership and Certain Rights and Obligations of Cohabitants Act 2010.

[243] s 67(3), Succession Act 1965; s 67B(1), Succession Act 1965 *as inserted by* s 73, Civil Partnership and Certain Rights and Obligations of Cohabitants Act 2010.

[244] s 67(4), Succession Act 1965; s 67B(2), Succession Act 1965 *as inserted by* s 73, Civil Partnership and Certain Rights and Obligations of Cohabitants Act 2010.

[245] s 68, Succession Act 1965.

If there is no surviving spouse, issue, parent, siblings etc. then we must identify the next-of-kin. In simple terms, the next-of-kin is the person in the closest degree of relationship to the deceased. If there are numerous relatives in equal degrees, they will share in the assets, however a relative who is, for example, four degrees separated laterally will take precedence over a relative who is four degrees separated vertically because in real terms the latter will have been closer to the deceased. In order to assess next-of-kin, one counts back to the closest common ancestor and then down to the current relative. Section 71(2) provides: **[16–109]**

> Degrees of blood relationship of a direct lineal ancestor shall be computed by counting upwards from the intestate to that ancestor, and degrees of blood relationship of any other relative shall be ascertained by counting upwards from the intestate to the nearest ancestor common to the intestate and that relative, and then downward from that ancestor to the relative; but, where a direct lineal ancestor and any other relative are so ascertained to be within the same degree of blood relationship to the intestate, the other relative shall be preferred to the exclusion of the direct lineal ancestor.

In the absence of a next-of-kin, s 73 of the Succession Act 1965 provides that the State is the ultimate intestate successor.

Hotchpot

Importantly, all intestate shares are subject to the doctrine of hotchpot. This doctrine provides that advancements and portions made during the deceased's lifetime are to be seen as advancements on inheritance and taken into account in the distribution of assets. If, for example, Adam dies intestate with €60,000, no surviving spouse and two surviving children, the preliminary position is to say that the children each get €30,000. However, one of the children was given €40,000 as the deposit on a house during Adam's lifetime. We see this sum as an advancement on inheritance and factor it in. Thus we now conceive of Adam as having died with €100,000, leaving €50,000 to each child. One child simply received part of his share already and, therefore, now receives the remaining €10,000. Where the share advanced during lifetime is less than the share on intestacy, then the difference will be paid from the estate. Where the share advanced during lifetime is greater than the share on intestacy, the child is not required to make any repayments to the estate. **[16–110]**

XIV. Equitable Distribution of Property on Death

In certain cases property can be transferred outside of the formal requirements of a will or the rules of distribution in intestacy. The two primary instances of this arising on the death of a property owner are the *donatio mortis causa* and the doctrine of estoppel. **[16–111]**

1. *Donatio Mortis Causa*

If the court is satisfied that the deceased made a donation of property to a claimant in contemplation of death and that he intended the gift to first become effective on the event of his death, then the court might find that a valid *donatio mortis causa* had occurred. This can have the effect of overriding the provisions of the will and, as a result, the claimant will be under a heavy onus of proving that the donation actually took place. In order for a valid *donatio mortis causa* to occur, a number of requirements **[16–112]** must be fulfilled: (i) the donor must contemplate death; (ii) the donor must intend the gift to only become effective on his death; (iii) the donor must part with dominion; (iv) the subject-matter must be capable of being passed by means of a *donatio mortis causa*; (v) the donor must not revoke the *donatio mortis causa*.

(i) Contemplation of Death

[16–113] In order for a valid *donatio mortis causa* to occur, the donor must contemplate death, which must encompass something more than a morbid fear (such as a fear of flying[246]) or an intimation of one's own mortality.[247] Where a donor contemplates death from one cause and actually dies from another the *donatio mortis causa* will not be invalidated. This is well demonstrated by the case of *Mills v Shields and Kelly*.[248] The deceased, who was seriously ill at the time, had given cash and some share certificates to Kelly before travelling to Dublin for an operation and had said, "If anything happens to me while I am away, will you give this to my brother?" The deceased did not travel all the way to Dublin, but instead left the train and committed suicide. The fact that the cause of his death was not the same as the cause of death contemplated when the donation was made meant that the *donatio mortis causa* remained intact. Importantly, *Mills* was not a case of contemplated suicide—in other words, the deceased had not contemplated death by suicide at the time that the donation was made. Where the deceased contemplates death by means of suicide it appears that no *donatio mortis causa* can be made. This conclusion flows from the case of *Agnew v The Belfast Banking Company*,[249] although it may no longer be the case given the fact that suicide is not a criminal offence anymore and our understanding of the medical factors contributing to suicide has grown in the interim period.

(ii) Gift to First Become Effective on Death

[16–114] *Donatione mortis causa* are conditional (and therefore revocable) up to the death of the donor.

(iii) Donor Delivers Subject-Matter

[16–115] In order for the *donatio mortis causa* to take place, the subject-matter must have been delivered to the donee. The means by which this can be done will of course depend to an extent on the kind of property that forms the subject-matter of the donation. The donor need not deliver the subject-matter himself; it will be sufficient if this is done by his agent[250] or if it is constructively delivered. In the context of real property, it appears that this requirement translates to the "parting with dominion" by means of handing over the vital indicia of title. Thus, in *Sen v Headley*, the donor handed over the only key to a steel box in which the only deeds to the property were located—this was held to be sufficient parting with dominion within the context of the *donatio mortis causa*.[251]

---

246 *Thompson v Mechan* [1958] OR 357.
247 *Re Craven's Estate* [1937] Ch 423.
248 [1948] IR 367.
249 [1896] 2 IR 204.
250 *Re Thompson* [1928] IR 606.
251 *Sen v Headley* [1991] Ch 425; see also *Re Craven's Estate* [1937] Ch 423.

(iv) Subject-Matter is Capable of Passing in this Manner

The subject-matter of the donation must be capable of physical delivery. It has long been recognised that personal property can be transferred by means of *donatio mortis causa*, but the same principle has only recently been enunciated in respect of real property by the Court of Appeal in *Sen v Headley*.[252] In this case the deceased and the plaintiff had lived together as husband and wife until 1964, after which they remained close and in regular contact. While he was ill in hospital and shortly preceding his death, the deceased slipped keys into her handbag and said, "The house is yours, Margaret. You have the keys. They are in your bag. The deeds are in the steel box." The keys he had put into her handbag were keys to the house and also the only set of keys to a steel box in which the deeds were kept. Three days later the deceased died intestate and the defendant—who was his nephew—was appointed the administrator of his estate. The plaintiff claimed that she was entitled to the ownership of the house as a result of the alleged *donatio mortis causa*, but the defendants claimed that real property could not be the subject of such a transfer. Although this case concerned the technical requirements of the Wills Act 1837 and the Law of Property Act 1925, the principles laid down in the Court of Appeal by which the Court concluded that real property was not excluded from the ambit of the *donatio mortis causa* are relevant in Ireland. The Court of Appeal held that it was anomalous to allow the transfer of personal but not real property by means of the *donatio mortis causa* when the distinction between the two was now effectively meaningless. The law had developed to allow the transfer of property by informal means, such as the constructive trust, and therefore it could no longer be said that real property rights can only be transferred in compliance with written formalities. On this basis a gift of land by delivery of title deeds ought not to be excluded from the category of *donatio mortis causa*, and the plaintiff was entitled to ownership of the house. **[16–116]**

(v) The **Donatio Mortis Causa** *Has Not Been Revoked*

As the *donatio mortis causa* is intended to first become effective on the death of the donor, it is revocable up to that point. The *donatio* will be revoked automatically by the recovery of the donor from the condition that caused him to contemplate death, or if the donee predeceases him. The *donatio* might also be revoked by subsequent dealing with the property that constitutes a reassertion of dominion, although there will be no revocation where the reassertion of dominion has the purpose of preserving the subject-matter for the donee.[253] **[16–117]**

2. Estoppel

Where someone can satisfy the court that the deceased led them to believe that they would receive an interest in his estate, and the claimant acted to his detriment in reliance on this representation, then the beneficiaries of a deceased's estate might be said to hold that property on trust for the successful claimant. In this context the normal rules of estoppel will apply. **[16–118]**

---

252 [1991] Ch 425.

253 *Re Hawkins* [1924] 2 Ch 47; *Re Mulroy* [1924] 1 IR 98.

INDEX